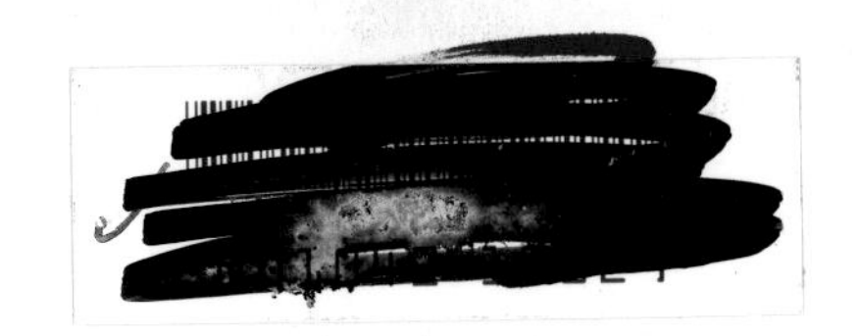

THE FIGHTING IRISH FOOTBALL ENCYCLOPEDIA

by

Michael R. Steele

SAGAMORE PUBLISHING

CHAMPAIGN, IL

Production supervision and book design: Susan M. Williams and Brian J. Moore
Cover and photo insert design: Michelle R. Dressen
Cover illustration: Ted Watts
Contributing editor: Jethrow Kyles
Editor: Jana Waite
Proofreader: Phyllis L. Bannon

10 9 8 7 6 5 4 3 2 1

Library of Congress Catalog Card Number:92-60838
ISBN: 0-915611-54-6

Photo credits:
Bagby Photo Co.: p.21 top, p. 34, p. 47, p. 49 top, p. 52, p. 57, p. 58 top and bottom, p 59 top, p. 62 bottom, p. 64 top, p. 64 bottom, p. 65 left, p. 70 bottom, p. 72 top, p. 76 bottom, p. 85 bottom, p. 86 top and bottom, p. 97 bottom, p. 105, p. 107 bottom, p. 115 bottom, p. 116, p. 118 bottom, p. 120, p. 130 top, p. 134, p. 138, p. 142, p. 144 top, p. 145, p. 146, p. 147top, p.148 bottom, p. 150 top, p. 153, p. 155 top, p. 161 bottom, p. 164 top, p. 173 bottom, p. 181 bottom, p. 182 top, p. 185, p. 200, p. 219 top. Union Pacific Railroad Photo, p. 123; Wolter Photo Service, p. 137; SC Photo, p. 141; J. B Clay, p. 149 top; Redwood Studio, p. 171 top. Credit also goes to the Notre Dame archives and the Sports Information Department for assistance in obtaining photos. Every effort was made to trace ownership of copyrighted photos. If we have failed to give adequate credit, we will be pleased to make changes in future printings.

Printed in the United States of America.

For my family

and

for all those who have ever wanted to play football for Notre Dame.

CONTENTS

Acknowledgments vi
Introduction vii
Foreword viii
Preface ix

1 The Place 1

2 Why Football? 3

3. Academics and the Student-Athlete 5

4 Fighting Irish Trivia 7

5 All-time Fighting Irish Teams 11

6 Season Reviews 17

The Early Years: 1887 to 1899 17
1900 - 1909 25
1910 - 1919 35
1920 - 1929 49
1930 - 1939 71
1940 - 1949 98
1950 - 1959 128
1960 - 1969 163
1970 - 1979 200
1980 - 1989 232
1990 - 1991 267

7 Fighting Irish Player Roster 277

8 Fighting Irish Statistics 341

9 Fighting Irish Records 413

ACKNOWLEDGMENTS

The gestation period for this book was more than eight years in duration. It would have been impossible without the generous, selfless help of people such as John Heisler and Herb Juliano of Notre Dame, especially in the early stages; and Alex Toth, who labored in the Pacific Library throughout the process. The entire staff of the Notre Dame Sports Information Department must be mentioned, with special thanks to Pam Carnes. Others at Pacific University helped considerably with statistics and viewpoints, particularly Chris Carley and Jon Stine. Numerous student assistants at Pacific have had a hand in this as well. A thank-you to all of them.

Within the Notre Dame football family, special thanks go to former Irish Head Coach Gerry Faust, his secretary, Jan Blazi, as well as Former Athletic Director Gene Corrigan, Assistant AD Brian Boulac, Special Assistant Joe Yonto, and Director of Counseling, Mike DeCicco. Moose Krause, as usual, was always available to help. A special thanks goes to Joe Bannon, Jr. and Susan Williams and everyone at Sagamore Publishing for all of their efforts in creating this book.

Those are the people personally known to be involved. There are many others. On a December night in 1979, I worked late at the Notre Dame library—with the personal help of Chet Grant, George Gipp's quarterback on the 1920 team. Grant had me going through the paces of the famous Notre Dame shift—I was the fullback, and two library chairs represented the halfbacks. In retrospect, Gipp must have been there watching the proceedings as the spry, nimble-witted Grant brought to life a style of football not seen for half a century. So, thanks also to the memory of George Gipp, who represents all of Notre Dame's players since 1887 (though few bear much resemblance to Gipp).

Finally,very special thanks go to Jim Peterson, whose act of faith in this book brought it back from the afterlife.

—M.S.

INTRODUCTION

When I became Head Football Coach at Notre Dame, I quickly realized that it was more than just a midwestern university. I had coached in the Big 10 for eight years, and I assumed that the transition would be a simple one. I realized after sitting in the Head Coach's chair a very short period, that interest in Notre Dame was not just regional or even national; it commanded international interest and attention.

Much of this respect came from the university's ability to blend the academic and athletic programs without compromising either. The principle reason for enrollment was an education and a goal of developing the whole person. Within those objectives were opportunities in other activities. In spite of its great athletic success, the academic program was never overshadowed by athletics, and both continued to prosper.

The *Fighting Irish Football Encyclopedia* is a beautiful reconstruction of Notre Dame history. It took nine years to complete and is a wonderful source of information on the 951 games, with 308 player profiles. In addition, one can digest statistics and photos to relive many historical moments. This allows all ages to reminisce and relive every Notre Dame game from the beginning. I do not know of any other book that covers the entire history of Notre Dame football with the completeness and accuracy you'll find here.

I'm sure you will enjoy this encyclopedia as much as I have.

—Ara Parseghian, 1992

FOREWORD

In my sixty-two years of involvement with the University of Notre Dame, I have been privileged to know and work with some of the greatest men in the pantheon of collegiate football—from Rockne to Layden, Leahy, Parseghian, Devine, and Holtz, as well as their tremendously gifted players. I have also come to know and appreciate the many young men who are not football heroes on a Saturday afternoon in the fall, but who worked diligently to play the game to the best of their abilities while also succeeding in the difficult world of academics.

From Knute Rockne I learned important lessons about teamwork, cooperation, accepting adversity, winning properly, practicing self-discipline, and loyalty. These lessons are still emphasized at the University of Notre Dame today, along with the same emphasis dedicated to academic success that Rockne preached. These have been constants at Notre Dame ever since I began my association with the University.

The brilliant story of Notre Dame football encompasses all of these lessons, the coaches, and the players. It also represents the struggles and successes of all the coaches and the young men who have played college football. There are so many valuable, important stories to be told regarding collegiate football, tales that help us better understand ourselves and the unfolding drama of athletics and sports in America.

Many, many books have been written about Notre Dame football. This encyclopedia is a compendium of those 951 games, the people, and the events that have gone into 103 seasons of football under the Golden Dome. Notre Dame has been blessed to have its many worthy opponents on football fields across America; this book will thrill not only the fans of Irish football but also the many millions who cheer Notre Dame's opponents. We would not have the opportunity for these wonderful athletic contests without our honored opponents.

Follow Notre Dame football game by game and season by season in this encyclopedia. Watch the development of individual stars through their years. . . and feel the drama of those whose careers became great struggles with adversity. Feel the uplifting triumphs and grieve the sad losses. But all the time recognize the blessings we all share as they are detailed in Michael Steele's *Fighting Irish Football Encyclopedia.*

—Ed "Moose" Krause
Emeritus Athletic Director
University of Notre Dame

PREFACE

All Fighting Irish fans have their favorite memories—those moments suspended in time when an athlete in his youthful prime performs a miraculous feat. Such memories have been fostered by 102 seasons of heroics, painful losses, great comebacks, and excellence in pursuit of a good life as the football playing sons of Notre Dame.

Notre Dame students rub shoulders with these young men for four years. They see them in their normal dimensions—in the dorms, the cafeteria, around campus, and in classes. And they seem not much larger than life, except they are gone in the fall in the late afternoons and much of the weekends.

Yet something happens when these student-athletes near the stadium. They *do* seem larger, as if the monolithic stadium imparts ruggedness to their frames, their shoulders, their chests. Some pause near the blue door of the team's locker room to sign a child's game program, to speak to hometown friends, or to meet someone's aunt who has made her first trip to this football shrine.

They enter the locker room and perform their rituals away from the public eye. They go on the field and do some stretching in a nearly empty stadium. They return to the locker room for full pads. Specialty teams warm up and then the whole team by units. Back to the locker room for final words, thoughts, and prayers. They go down the narrow steps to the tunnel under the north stands, their cleats clacking on the pavement, and touch the sign about champions above the steps for good luck.

The brilliant light of an Indiana autumn reflects off their newly painted gold helmets. They mass near the edge of the concrete and the field, then jog forward into full view of 59,075 people, and bear to their right—to the west, the Fighting Irish side of the field. And most of the 59,075 go slightly crazy. Some variation of this ritual has taken place hundreds of times since the dedication of the stadium in 1930, and similar rites met the needs of players and fans before that.

After all this, for some three hours, a game is played—a football game—on the field that Rockne built. And it is here that we properly find the subject of this Encyclopedia—in the game.

But how can all those glorious moments become mere fodder for statistics in a book? Let's not fool ourselves. This book is not Fighting Irish football; it is about it. Yet this book can still serve to fix in words and pictures some of the memories Fighting Irish fans love to ponder.

So, let's try to see Red Salmon slam into a turn-of-the-century pile up—and emerge angrily to go dashing toward his football destiny. . .

See the little guy, the balding one with the broken nose, limping—no, he's behind Army's deep backs, running into history . . .

There is Gipp, a shy Huck Finn grown-up, drop-kicking a 62-yard field goal, even though he was told to punt—he grins, he has a toothpick . . .

The Horsemen, four magicians synchronized to absolute perfection—the Notre Dame shift, the other team jumps, and the ball is snapped to a Horseman who has just the slightest advantage; he breaks it outside and is down the sideline . . .

The 1929-30 team of Carideo, Brill, Schwartz, and Metzger, tough but smooth. Fancy football on splendid fall afternoons—double laterals and a forward pass, or old "51" (Rock's favorite).

Leahy's powerhouses, big, mobile, world-wise war vets. The passing of Bertelli, the confidence of Lujak, or gigantic Leon Hart madly loose on an end around, careening through, and caroming off defenders, running into . . .

Hornung—a golden moment in a dim era—a throwback to the old triple threats that Walter Camp so admired. He has a bit of the Gipp insouciance. There, see the little smile . . .

Ara, intense, brooding, impatient, and demanding. "I don't know how many games they will win, but they will be in condition in the fourth quarter, I promise that." They were, too. See Ara, in agony at USC in 1964? And overjoyed at Alabama in 1973 and 1975? Ara . . .

Eric Penick, first play of the second half, 1973 USC game, takes the ball and swings wide left, cuts it up and turns it on, nobody touches him for 85 yards—so much speed . . .

Over there—not Huck Finn, but Tom Sawyer—call him Joe Montana. Smooth, quick release, a la Namath. Surrounded by such great players—Vagas and Big Mac. Joe's got his arms raised, imitating the umpire's touchdown call . . .

Or Bob Crable introducing himself to Charles White, "You might beat this team, but not *me*." White gingerly picks himself up, but takes a count or two on the ground longer than usual. Crable looms over him, then jogs back . . .

Rocket Ismail—who changed forever the way teams handle the kicking game. Holtz said he was the only person he ever saw play tennis with himself...

Or Jerome Bettis—slamming through defenses for 23 touchdowns in his sophomore campaign. With so much promise for the future . . .

It's magic. We know these moments, these faces. They are etched into our lives. Let this book complete the process—and keep them forever young.

Chapter 1

The Place

Many generations of young people have made the trek to north-central Indiana to begin their college studies. If they were lucky, they caught a glimpse of the Golden Dome soaring majestically above the flat, fertile Indiana landscape. After seeing the Dome from afar, their cars are slowly drawn to that central location. You cannot help but stare the first time in wonderment at the Dome as it moves in and out of view.

There are certain places in this country where a visitor feels a special relationship to a locale—the Lincoln Memorial, the Statue of Liberty, Mt. Rushmore and Arlington National Cemetery come to mind as such places where the individual meets the past, and feels a tangible quality that permeates the air.

Notre Dame is also such a place. It is calm there. In a world of senseless violence, confused values, seemingly irreparable breaks with the past, and with little hope for the future, you can find a measure of peace at Notre Dame, a sense of values not frustrated by contemporary confusions, a sense of the past and its traditions. You feel there. It's indisputable. Many writers and commentators have attempted to articulate this special sense, but you must visit to fully comprehend it. Go to the place.

But there is more. On five or six Saturdays each fall, in the midst of the serenity, the classical quietude of the academy, and its tree-lined cloisters, there is another activity—the noisiest, most raucous, most volatile student-body support for intercollegiate football that can be found in this land. They are not the "Fighting Irish" for nothing.

Paradoxically, Americans like both underdogs and winners. Notre Dame's history embraces both, which perhaps is part of the secret of its enduring success. Founded in 1842 by a visionary French priest, Father Edward Sorin, the school attracted upwardly mobile young Catholics. And they took up the game of football with abandon and flair that caught the fancy of fans. The school imparted discipline and demanded excellence—both in the classroom and on the playing field. Early on, the institution decided that the whole individual would be molded—body and mind, spirit and flesh. The active life of the mind would not be estranged from the active life of the body. Add to this a crusading spirit, and the framework for the unfolding history of Notre Dame football is complete. To understand what makes Fighting Irish football what it is, we must speak in the abstractions above, before going on to the concrete necessities of excellence in recruiting, rigorous training, perfection in teamwork, dedicated and brilliant coaching, and the sheer athleticism so often displayed in Notre Dame games.

The place, like the dancer and the dance, cannot be separated from what goes on there or from the intangible Notre Dame spirit. Countless commentators have remarked about the spirit of the place.

Thousands of visiting players have felt it. The saying is that you can cut it with a knife as you walk around the campus.

Spirit is many things. As a noun, spirit is an animating or vital principle, a supernatural being, disposition of mind, a special attitude or frame of mind, a brisk quality, a firm disposition. And as a verb, it means to infuse or animate. All of these are involved in the unique spirit that is Notre Dame. It is a sense that this place throbs and pulses quietly, confidently, with concern for the higher things of human life. It is also composed of memories—so many young men and women have dreamed great dreams, have lived intense lives, have burned with the deepest thoughts, and have rejoiced in the beauties of youth and the vigor of their games. These tens of thousands of lives, many already finished, have left tangible vestiges of their intensity amid the tree-lined walks of the campus, to reside in the halls of learning, and to remain by the playing fields.

Ultimately, spirit (from the Latin spirare, to breathe) is just that—a breath of life, hope, and determination to excel. Here we have it: Notre Dame, dedicated to Our Lady, has its purpose firmly dedicated to the best to which mankind can aspire. And this is the finest aspect of the spirit that characterizes Notre Dame football. In the game, you find humanity's dualities—flesh and spirit—united in an effort to do one's best.

Chapter 2

Why Football?

There is really no telling why certain sports appeal to people, or why different cultures appreciate a particular sport, even to the exclusion of other-widely accepted sports.

Our nation is barely more than 200 years old, and football has been with us for more than half of that period. It has been the dominant sport in this century, not so much because of spectators or the numbers who play the game, but for what it says about who and what we are.

There is an aesthetics in football. Well-edited film clips, played in slow motion, reveal a ballet-like quality to the motions of the players. The acrobatic catches of a well-executed pass route, or the gliding power of a halfback cutting through a crack in the defense is a wonder of human mechanics. Irish fans still marvel over the synchronized, hypnotic, musical quality of Rockne's carefully planned and executed shift plays. Even the ponderous agility of the defensive and offensive linemen have an artistic quality. All these athletic movements are choreographed in precise ways just as in a dance—or like a stage production. The players follow a "script," also known as a game plan, often like a Greek drama with agonistic conflict. But once performed, the movements and delivery of lines cannot be exactly recreated. Yet people like to remember those vivid moments when something truly heroic happened—the pass that won one for the Gipper, Shakespeare's heroics in overcoming Ohio State, the "perfect plays" from Leahy's tenure, Hunter's run that helped beat Alabama, Clements' pass to Weber that saved the game, Penick's long run to beat USC, the defensive gallantry against Campbell's Texas team in the Cotton Bowl, or the intensity of the rivalry with Miami. These become etched in the collective consciousness of Fighting Irish fans and are passed on from one generation to the next.

Then there is the sheer physical courage that football, properly played, requires—the courage to match one's physical gifts against those of another similarly gifted athlete before millions of witnesses. Humans like to test themselves in this fashion, a confrontation of egos and intellects. And there is a vicarious sense of identification on the part of the spectator.

People like to be associated with excellence. And from any viewpoint, Notre Dame football is the finest example of excellence in college football—and has been for most of this century. Many seek it out, wish to become close to it, or become a part of it. The emotional identification between the Fighting Irish fan and the team should not be underestimated. When the team triumphs, it is shared with its legions of fans. The fan can taste victory and empathize with defeat, wishing for those moments that might have turned the game around. The fan can enjoy the sense that he or she knows how it should have been. Thus, even after the game has been played, there is another "game" played alone with the raw data of the game, rearranging facts, and creating a mythical re-enactment. The game lives on in the minds of the beholders.

And Notre Dame's Fighting Irish have probably provided more such memories than any other college team in the country.

Chapter 3

Academics and the Student-Athlete

Notre Dame takes justifiable pride in its outstanding record of recruiting the highest quality student-athletes for its many varsity teams. The university also recognizes that it has an obligation to these student-athletes in that, having granted them scholarships for varsity athletics, these students will have far greater demands made of them than those students not involved in intercollegiate athletics. Accordingly, some twenty years ago, Notre Dame set up its own office of Academic Services for Student Athletes. This office was originally headed by Professor Mike DeCicco, a professor of mechanical engineering who also coached the Irish fencing team to numerous undefeated seasons and three national championships. The Academic Services office is now directed by Dr. Kate Halischak, who continues the enviable tradition of dedication to the academic success of Irish athletes established under Professor DeCicco. Their fine work has resulted in Notre Dame's being recognized on many occasions with the Academic Achievement Award of the CFA. Ample evidence of the program's worthiness is found in the fact that of the 548 student-athletes who matriculated between 1980 and 1986 (that is, those who would have graduated by 1991), 484 did indeed graduate by 1991—88.3% who entered Notre Dame. When those athletes who transferred elsewhere are factored out of the total, the adjusted graduation rate is 96%. Of Notre Dame's football players over this period, 92% graduated by 1991. Few schools in the country can boast of such sterling achievements.

Dr. Halischak leads a staff of four counselors who personally review the grades of student-athletes and other professionals who direct special projects such as orientations and study skill enhancement programs. Working directly with the full-time professional staff are from 40 to 60 tutors in the various subject disciplines. A staff supervisor coordinates study sessions for all freshman athletes that operate five nights each week of the school year (Sundays through Thursdays from 8 to 10 p.m.). The staff counselors also review the progress of all student-athletes, communicate with professors, and interview each student-athlete on both a regularly scheduled basis and as needs require. Dr. Halischak and her staff also coordinate all of the academic information services at Notre Dame insofar as they relate to NCAA and CFA requirements.

Three times each semester the progress of each student-athlete is surveyed by the counselors and discussed with the athletes. If additional tutorial assistance is required, adjustments are made immediately for the person involved. As the student-athlete makes appropriate progress toward a degree, these review sessions also involve advice about graduation requirements. More frequent monitoring and counseling activities are the norm for those identified as marginal students. Special attention is devoted in these cases to enhancing time management, writing, and study skills. Student-athletes who have been injured also receive special attention to guarantee "academic recovery" as they recuperate and rehabilitate. In their final years on the campus, student-athletes have available a series of seminars dealing with career goals, career planning, and placement.

Freshman football players may expect to devote as much time to academic orientation in the month of August as they will to football practice. The players are introduced to the university's library and computer facilities, and receive detailed guidance on academic and classroom protocols. This will not have been the first time that these players have met representatives of Academic Services—all football recruits have a scheduled stop on their campus tour so that the university's academic expectations and support services are made absolutely clear to the prospective player. During this campus tour, the football recruit will have already learned that there are no residence halls devoted exclusively to athletes; the players are fully expected to become integral members of campus residence life. Recruits will also learn that academics take precedence over team practices—Irish QB Tony Rice demonstrated this principle at work in the '88 championship season as he first attended to afternoon labs in his major, psychology, before suiting up for football practices.

With these academic services and expectations, Notre Dame stands virtually alone in the country in view of the quality of both the academic and athletic attainments reached by its students. The university and its programs stand as living proof that educational institutions need not compromise their ideals and purposes while striving for elusive, fleeting championships. No university in the country does a better job of educating the whole person.

Mike DeCicco, first head of the academic counseling program for Irish athletes.

Chapter 4

Fighting Irish Trivia

One of my fond hopes for this book is that it helps to resolve friendly discussions about Notre Dame football —that fans will have access to a complete source of information. To this end, this Irish trivia quiz will test how much you really know about the subject.

1. Who is the only player to win five monograms for playing football at Notre Dame? What years?
2. When was the first night game? Who was the opponent?
3. Of the time when team photos were regularly taken, which Notre Dame team was not recorded in a team picture?
4. There have been several two-time captains for the Fighting Irish. Who was the only three-time captain? When?
5. Who holds the record for the most consecutive carries running the ball? When? Against which team?
6. Who was the first African-American player to win a football monogram with the Fighting Irish? When?
7. Who scored the first official touchdown for Notre Dame? When?
8. Only one opposing quarterback has ever been privileged to beat the Fighting Irish in three consecutive years. Who was he? What team did he play for? What years?
9. Who was the last drop-kick artist for the Fighting Irish?
10. Who recorded the first Fighting Irish interception of a forward pass? When? What opponent?
11. Give the last two years when the Fighting Irish faced a team coached by the immortal Amos Alonzo Stagg.
12. Who holds the all-time Notre Dame punting average for a career?
13. Name the two principals who won the 1928 "Gipper" game with Army (Hint: a passer and a receiver).
14. What Fighting Irish squad was not scored on for an entire season?
15. What player was also a practicing Methodist minister during his Fighting Irish career?
16. Any Fighting Irish fan can name the Four Horsemen. Name the Seven Mules.
17. Who caught the first pass for a touchdown for Notre Dame? When? What opponent?
18. Who kicked the longest field goal for the Fighting Irish? When? What opponent?
19. How many seemingly miraculous comeback wins did Joe Montana engineer? Name the victims.
20. Who holds the probable (but unbelievable)

record for rushing yardage compiled in one game? When? What opponent?

21. Who replaced the injured Nick Eddy in the final game of the 1966 season, the 51-0 hammering of the University of Southern California?

22. Who was Notre Dame's first 1,000-yard rusher for a season? When?

23. Who was probably the youngest player for the Fighting Irish? When?

24. Name the reserve lineman who scored two touchdowns on interceptions in different seasons. When?

25. Who holds the career field goal accuracy record?

26. Name the player who had his face on television thousands of times in a men's toiletry ad.

27. Name the players who were involved directly in producing the winning touchdown in the 1935 game with Ohio State University.

28. Name the touchdown-producing Fighting Irish battery in the 10-10 tie with Michigan State University in 1966.

29. Everyone knows that Allen Pinkett was a great running back. Name five of his Notre Dame records.

30. Frank Varrichione faked an injury at the end of the first half in a 1953 game against the University of Iowa to buy the Fighting Irish some time. What happened on the next play?

Answers

1. Randy Harrison, 1974-1978. An injury cut short one season, which was good enough for a monogram award but not enough to cost him eligibility.

2. 1951 against Detroit. Notre Dame won 40-6.

3. 1974. Ara kept postponing the date, then never got around to it. It was his last, hectic season.

4. Jack Mullen, 1897-1899.

5. Red Salmon, 15 consecutive carries in the 1902 23-0 loss to the University of Michigan (he gained about 80 yards).

6. Wayne Edmonds, tackle, 1953.

7. Harry Jewett, in a 26-6 loss to the University of Michigan on April 20, 1888. Frank Springer, a guard, beat him to the end zone for a touchdown, but a penalty nullified his effort.

8. Mike Phipps, Purdue University, 1967-1969.

9. Stan Krivik, 1945, kicked 23 of 29 points after touchdowns for the year.

10. Paul McDonald, left halfback, in the 8-4 win over Wabash College in 1908.

11. An amazing fact: 1899, when he coached Chicago and then again in 1940, when he coached the University of the Pacific.

12. Craig Hentrich, 1989-1991, with a 44.2-yard average.

13. John Niemiec, left halfback, fired the winning touchdown pass to Johnny "One-Play" O'Brien.

14. The 1903 team scored 292 points to 0, won eight games, and tied Northwestern 0-0.

15. The Rev. Marv Russell, linebacker, 1973-1975.

16. Left end Chuck Collins, left tackle Joe Bach, left guard John Weibel, center Adam Walsh (he reportedly came up with the name), right guard Noble Kizer, right tackle Rip Miller, and right end Ed Hunsinger.

17. Fay Wood, a 40-yard touchdown pass in a 64-0 rout of Franklin in 1908.

18. Dave Reeve, a 53-yard field goal in 31-10 loss to Pitt in 1976.

19. Six games: North Carolina and Air Force in 1975, Purdue and Clemson in 1977, Pitt in 1978, and Houston in the 1979 Cotton Bowl.

20. John Farley, left end, ran for a total of 464 yards in 62-0 "drilling" of Chicago Dental in 1897.

21. Dan Harshman. The Irish were hurting for running backs after the MSU game; he filled in admirably.

22. Al Hunter, 1976, 1,058 yards on 233 carries.

23. Al Fortin was 16 years old when he started for the Fighting Irish at right tackle in 1898 against the University of Illinois, Michigan Agricultural College (now MSU), and the University of Michigan. He later captained the 1901 squad at the age of 19.

24. Al Zmijewski, against USC in 1947, with an intercepted lateral pass followed by a 30-yard touchdown effort, then in 1948 when he grabbed a Purdue pass and found the end zone only seven yards away. Al knew what to do and Notre Dame won a thriller, 28-27.

25. John Carney, 17 of 19 (.895) in 1984.

26. John Lium, reserve center, class of 1967 appeared on the other side of an open medicine cabinet in a series of toiletry ads in the early 1970s. John is now a lawyer.

27. Henry Pojman (playing with the second string line) snapped the ball to Shakespeare (replacing the injured Pilney) who then threw it to Millner for the win.

28. Tim Monty (replacing the injured Goeddeke) snapped the ball to Coley O'Brien (replacing the injured Hanratty), who then fired a 46-yard touchdown strike to Bob Gladieux (replacing the injured Nick Eddy).

29. Most rushing attempts in a game, 40, vs. LSU in 1984 (shared with Phil Carter). Most rushing yards per game for a career, 96.1. Most games rushing for 100 yards or more in a season, 9. Most consecutive 100-yard games, 5, at the expense of Colorado, South Carolina, Army, USC, and Navy, all in 1983. Most points scored in a career, 320.

30. After Varrichione swooned, Guglielmi threw a 14-yard touchdown pass to Shannon with 2 seconds left on the clock. Actually, Shannon did it again at the end of the game, with 6 seconds on the clock, with another touchdown pass from Guglielmi to salvage a tie.

Chapter 5

All-time Fighting Irish Teams

There is a certain unfairness about any all-star team. In a team sport, the other players have as much to say about an individual's performance as does the individual. Many players have had weaknesses buttressed by the strength of the men next to them. And memories fog when we try to recreate performances of stars from the past. Much of the brilliance of the great stars of the past is not recorded on film; we have only written accounts until well into the mid-1930s when film became a standard coaching tool. Still, there is a desire to want to define the best.

There are many variables to consider in selecting an all-star team. Size is one of the most important. Modern training methods guarantee that today's players are stronger, faster, and bigger. Tackles from the first quarter of this century might only be big enough today to play as defensive backs. For example, it would be hard imagining 149-pound Bert Metzger doing very well against Mike McCoy, almost twice his weight, or Metzger stopping the pass rush or punt blocking charge of a player like Chris Zorich.

To do away with part of the bias that creeps into the selection of all-time teams, here is a sample of the best of the smallest and the largest players in the annals of the Fighting Irish.

The Best "Small" Offensive Players (under six feet)

LE	Knute Rockne	5' 8", 165	1910-13
LT	Joe Bach	5' 11", 181	1923-24
LG	Clipper Smith	5' 9", 164	1925-27
C	Al Feeney	5' 11", 180	1910-13
RG	Bert Metzger	5' 9", 149	1928-30
RT	Sam Dolan	5' 11", 210	1906-09
RE	Eddie Anderson	5' 10", 163	1918-21
QB	Harry Stuhldreyer	5' 7", 151	1922-24
HB	Allan Pinkett	5' 9", 184	1982-83
FB	Jerome Bettis	5' 11", 247	1990-91
FL	Rocket Ismail	5' 9", 175	1988-90

*Note: The entire backfield could have come from the Horsemen.

Most of these men either played with or for Rockne, except for Dolan, Pinkett, Bettis, and Ismail. Rock liked the "small" players, since he was one himself, and he preferred their speed, quickness, and agility over what he called "the bovine."

The Best "Big" Offensive Players (six feet and taller)

LE	Ken MacAfee	6' 4", 249	1974-77
LT	Larry Williams	6' 6", 284	1981-83

LG	Tim Grunhard	6' 3", 292	1986-89
C	Dave Huffman	6' 5", 245	1975-78
RG	Ernie Hughes	6' 3", 253	1974-77
RT	George Kunz	6' 5", 240	1966-68
RE	Leon Hart	6' 4", 245	1946-49
QB	Joe Montana	6' 2", 191	1975-78
LH	George Gipp	6' 0", 180	1917-20
RH	Vagas Ferguson	6' 1", 194	1976-79
FB	Wayne Bullock	6' 1", 221	1972-74
K	George Gipp		

This group averages 6' 3" and almost 236 pounds. They are five inches taller than the best of the small men and outweigh them by 60 pounds. The two offensive lines look like this: the small men average 5' 10", 173 pounds, while the big men average 6' 4," 248 pounds, for a 6-inch height differential and 75 pounds in weight. The backfields are closer in size, probably because sheer speed has an outside limit as far as size goes. The small backfield averages 5' 9 1/4" and 187 pounds, whereas the larger backfield is 6' 1", 196 1/2 pounds.

The Best "Small" Defensive Players

LE	Knute Rockne	5' 8", 165	1910-13
LT	Hunk Anderson	5' 11", 170	1918-21
RT	Dick Arrington	5' 11", 227	1963-65
RE	Eddie Anderson	5' 10", 163	1918-21
LLB	Jack Alessandrini	5' 11", 197	1950-52
MLB	Nick Buoniconti	5' 11", 210	1959-61
RLB	Al Ecuyer	5' 10", 190	1956-58
LCB	Reggie Barnett	5' 11", 180	1972-74
RCB	George Sefcik	5' 8," 170	1959-61
SS	Mike Crotty	5' 9," 180	1969-71
FS	Tom Schoen	5' 11", 178	1965-67

This is an interesting group, cutting across several eras; good, small defensive players can expect to play some football. A very interesting game would be played between this group and the small offensive team. This defensive group is about the same height as their offensive counterparts, but weigh a bit more. As much as we would want to see a good game between this group and the large offensive team, it would probably be a mismatch.

The Best "Big" Defensive Players

LE	Ross Browner	6' 3", 248	1973-77
LT	Chris Zorich	6' 1", 266	1988-90
RT	Kevin Hardy	6' 5", 270	1964-67
RE	Alan Page	6' 5", 238	1964-66
LLB	Jim Lynch	6' 1", 225	1964-66
MLB	Bob Golic	6' 3", 244	1975-78
RLB	Bob Crable	6' 3", 225	1978-81
LCB	Luther Bradley	6' 3", 202	1973-77
RCB	Stacy Toran	6' 4", 195	1980-83
SS	Jim Browner	6' 3", 214	1975-78
FS	Mike Townsend	6' 3", 183	1971-73

Like the big offensive team, this group is not representative of the sweep of Fighting Irish football. It is composed exclusively of men who played for or after Ara Parseghian. The linemen average 6' 3 1/2" and 254 pounds; linebackers are 6' 2 1/2" and 231 1/3 pounds; and backs are 6' 3", 198 1/2 pounds. Make no mistake, there is speed in this group. Browner caught Tony Dorsett from behind on a long run once, and Page outran a Purdue halfback for a touchdown with a blocked punt, not to mention Bradley's record-setting return of a Purdue pass. The interior linemen, Hardy and Zorich, had it all—but especially lateral mobility and quickness to go with their great strength. The linebackers are a superb group, with plenty of speed on the flanks behind the quick ends, and even more speed behind them among the backs. Sad to say, this group would crunch the small offensive team, but what a game could be played between this team and the large offense! The lines match up well, with the offense coming in at 6' 4", 258 pounds and the defense slightly smaller.

All-time Notre Dame Players by Era

The following players have been selected from among their Notre Dame peers as the best of their respective eras.

1887-1910:

LE	John Farley	5' 9", 160
LT	Pat Beacom	6' 2", 220
LG	George Philbrook	6' 3", 225
C	John Eggeman	6' 4", 256
RG	Rosy Dolan	5' 11", 210
RT	Ralph Dimmick	6' 0", 225
RE	Frank Lonergan	5' 10", 168
QB	Nate Silver	5' 8", 150
LHB	Red Miller	6' 0", 175
RHB	Dom Callicrate	5' 11", 160
FB	Red Salmon	5' 10", 175
K	Red Salmon	

1911-1930:

LE	Knute Rockne	5' 8", 165
LT	Frank Coughlin	6' 3", 215
LG	Hunk Anderson	5' 11", 170
C	Adam Walsh	6' 0", 187
RG	Clipper Smith	5' 10", 160
RT	Buck Shaw	6' 0", 185
RE	Eddie Anderson	5' 10", 163
QB	Harry Stuhldreher	5' 7", 151
LHB	George Gipp	6' 0", 180
RHB	Don Miller	5' 11", 160
FB	Ray Eichenlaub	6' 0", 210
K	George Gipp	

1931-1940:

LE	Wayne Millner	6' 0", 184
LT	Moose Krause	6' 3", 217
LG	John Lautar	6' 1", 184
C	Jack Robinson	6' 3", 200
RG	Joe Kuharich	6' 0", 193
RT	Joe Kurth	6' 2", 204
RE	Johnny Kelly	6' 2", 190
QB	Wally Fromhart	5' 11", 180
LHB	Marchy Schwartz	5' 11", 167
RHB	Ray Brancheau	5' 11", 190
FB	George Melinkovich	6' 0", 180
K	Marchy Schwartz	

1941-1950:

LE	Jim Martin	6' 2", 205
LT	George Connor	6' 3", 225
LG	Bill Fischer	6' 2", 230
C	Bill Walsh	6' 3", 205
RG	Marty Wendell	5' 11", 198
RT	Ziggy Czarobski	6' 0", 213
RE	Leon Hart	6' 4", 245
QB	Johnny Lujack	6' 0", 180
LHB	Terry Brennan	6' 0", 175
RHB	Creighton Miller	6' 0", 185
FB	Emil Sitko	5' 8", 180
K	John Lujack	

1951-1960:

LE	Monty Stickles	6' 4", 225
LT	Frank Varrichione	6' 1", 205
LG	Ray Lemek	6' 1", 207
C	Art Hunter	6' 3", 226
RG	Al Ecuyer	5' 10", 205
RT	Bob Toneff	6' 1", 230
RE	Bob Wetoska	6' 3", 225
QB	Paul Hornung	6' 2", 205
LHB	Joe Heap	5' 11", 180
RHB	Johnny Lattner	6' 1", 190
FB	Neil Worden	5' 11", 185
K	Paul Hornung	

1961-1970:

Offense:

LE	Jim Seymour	6' 4", 205
LT	Jim Reilly	6' 2", 230
LG	Larry DiNardo	6' 1", 235
C	George Goeddeke	6' 3", 228
RG	Dick Arrington	5' 11", 232
RT	George Kunz	6' 5", 240
TE	Jim Winegardner	6' 4", 225
QB	Joe Theismann	6' 0", 170
LHB	Nick Eddy	6' 0", 195
RHB	Rocky Bleier	5' 11", 195
FB	Bill Barz	6' 2", 216
K	Scott Hempel	6' 0", 235
P	Kevin Hardy	6' 5", 270

Defense:

LE	Walt Patulski	6' 6", 260
LT	Mike McCoy	6' 5", 274
RT	Kevin Hardy	6' 5", 270
RE	Alan Page	6' 5", 238
OLB	Jim Lynch	6' 1", 225
ILB	Nick Buoniconti	5' 11", 210
ILB	Jim Carroll	6' 1", 225
OLB	Mike McGill	6' 2", 225
LCB	Clarence Ellis	6' 0", 178
RCB	Tony Carey	6' 0", 190
S	Nick Rassas	6' 0", 185

1971-1980:

Offense:

SE	Kris Haines	6' 0", 181
LT	Rob Martinovich	6' 5", 260
LG	Frank Pomarico	6' 1", 250
C	Dave Huffman	6' 5", 245
RG	Ernie Hughes	6' 3", 253
RT	Tim Foley	6' 5", 265
TE	Ken MacAfee	6' 4", 249
QB	Joe Montana	6' 2", 191
HB	Vagas Ferguson	6' 1", 194
FB	Jerome Heavens	6' 0", 204
FL	Pete Holohan	6' 5", 228

K	Dave Reeve	6' 3", 198
P	Joe Restic	6' 2", 192

Defense:

LE	Ross Browner	6' 3", 248
LT	Steve Niehaus	6' 5", 260
RT	Mike Fanning	6' 6", 250
RE	Willie Fry	6' 3", 237
OLB	Bob Crable	6' 3", 225
ILB	Bob Golic	6' 3", 240
ILB	Steve Heimkreiter	6' 2", 224
LCB	Luther Bradley	6' 2", 202
RCB	Dave Waymer	6' 3", 182
SS	Jim Browner	6' 3", 204
FS	Joe Restic	6' 2", 192

1981-1991:

Offense:

SE	Tim Brown	6' 0", 195
LT	Mike Perrino	6' 5", 278
LG	Tim Grunhard	6' 3", 292
C	Mike Heldt	6' 4", 267
RG	Tom Thayer	6' 5", 268
RT	Larry Williams	6' 6", 284
TE	Derek Brown	6' 6", 252
QB	Steve Beuerlein	6' 3", 201
HB	Allen Pinkett	5' 9", 183
FB	Jerome Bettis	5' 11", 247
FL	Raghib Ismail	5' 10", 175
K	John Carney	5' 10", 170
P	Craig Hentrich	6' 1", 197

Defense:

LE	Jeff Alm	6' 7", 248
NT	Chris Zorich	6' 1", 266
RT	Mike Gann	6' 5", 256
OLB	Frank Stams	6' 4", 237
ILB	Michael Stonebreaker	6' 1", 228
ILB	Demetrius DuBose	6' 2", 234
OLB	Cedric Figaro	6' 3", 232
LCB	Stacy Toran	6' 4", 206
RCB	Todd Lyght	6' 1", 181
SS	George Streeter	6' 2", 212
FS	Dave Duerson	6' 3", 202

All-time Notre Dame Players by Position

Pre-1942:

The following players were selected as the best at their positions and whose careers were over before Leahy introduced the T-formation in 1942. Invariably, they were one-platoon players.

LE	John Farley
LT	Moose Krause
LG	Hunk Anderson
C	John Eggeman
RG	Clipper Smith
RT	Ralph Dimmick
RE	Eddie Anderson
QB	Harry Stuhldreher
LHB	George Gipp
RHB	Don Miller
FB	Ray Eichenlaub
K	George Gipp

Post-1942:

The following players have been selected from among those whose careers took place after 1942, the year that modern football began at Notre Dame.

LE	Jim Seymour
LT	George Connor
LG	Tim Grunhard
C	Dave Huffman
RG	Tom Thayer
RT	George Kunz
RE	Ken MacAfee
QB	Joe Montana
HB	Allen Pinkett
FB	Jerome Bettis
FL	Raghib Ismail
K	John Carney
P	Craig Hentrich

Best All-time Teams

The following players represent the best two offensive and defensive units from the history of Notre Dame football. These players would have excelled in any era, under any coach, under any conditions, and against all opponents. There are probably some surprises—the center and fullback, for instance. Two players make both offense and defense—George Gipp and Leon Hart.

All-time Offense:		Second Team:
LE	Jim Seymour	Wayne Millner
LT	George Connor	Moose Krause
LG	Tim Grunhard	Larry DiNardo
C	John Eggeman	Dave Huffman

RG	Tom Thayer	Dick Arrington
RT	George Kunz	Larry Williams
TE	Ken MacAfee	Leon Hart
QB	Joe Montana	Johnny Lujack
HB	George Gipp	Allen Pinkett
FB	Jerome Bettis	Ray Eichenlaub
FL	Raghib Ismail	Tim Brown
K	George Gipp	Craig Hentrich

All-time Defense:		**Second Team:**
LE	Ross Browner	Walt Patulski
LT	Chris Zorich	Kevin Hardy
RT	Steve Niehaus	Mike Fanning
RE	Alan Page	Leon Hart
OLB	Bob Crable	Frank Stams
MLB	Bob Golic	Jim Carroll
OLB	Jim Lynch	Steve Heimkreiter
LCB	Todd Lyght	Luther Bradley
RCB	Stacy Toran	Tony Carey
SS	Jim Browner	Nick Rassas
FS	George Gipp	Dave Duerson

Chapter 6

Season Reviews

The Early Years: 1887 to 1899

1887

Notre Dame football had an inauspicious beginning. The young men who wanted to start a team found that the University did not own a football. They also had no playing field, no uniforms, and no opponents.

In March, Henry Luhn, a student, called a meeting in Brownson Hall and 15 students showed up. Brother Joachim was charged at that meeting with buying a football; in two weeks the first football arrived in South Bend from Chicago. The campus literary society took over fund-raising and acquired clean, white cotton uniforms—but only 11 of them.

A field of sorts came into being near Sorin Hall, about 100 yards south of the Golden Dome; the sidelines were marked by two rocks and the goals by two trees. Soon two old poles were put up for goal kicks. Practices were organized for the original 15 enthusiasts and bystanders were cajoled into the fray as well. Experience was not a high priority, but eventually 11 players were selected—because that was the number of uniforms they had.

The Founding Fathers of Notre Dame football. Standing: Hepburn, Houck, Sawkins, Fehr, Nelson, Melady, Springer. Sitting: Jewett, Cusack, Luhn, and Prudhomme.

An inauspicious beginning: the 1887 Fighting Irish.

The first trial "game" was with the South Bend Shamrock Athletic Club in April. The Club team threatened to make this a memorable affair, and Notre Dame students responded in kind. Intimidated officials hired for the game failed to show up, so a "cheerleader" for the A.C. team became the referee, and John Burke, a janitor from Brownson Hall, served as umpire. Notre Dame won 8-4, with touchdowns being scored by Joe Cusack and Luhn for the home team. In this period, touchdowns were valued at 4 points, field goals at 5 points, and point after kicks at 2 points. Several players were knocked senseless during the melee; Notre Dame finished the game with only nine players.

Emboldened by their modest success, Luhn's team arranged for a game with the University of Michigan. On November 23, the Michigan team took the train to South Bend and were warmly greeted with a sightseeing tour. Then they played a demonstration match of rugby, with mixed teams. The groups reorganized into their original teams, and the football game commenced.

Playing conditions were horrible—the field was a quagmire—and the game ended after a partial "inning" (what we now call a quarter). Michigan shut out Notre Dame 8-0. It would be six more years before Notre Dame's record would indicate more wins than losses, but the enterprise was begun. The student newspaper commented on the enthusiasm displayed, and stated its hope that "...coming years will witness a series of these contests."

Record to date: 0-1-0 (.000)

1888

Undaunted, Notre Dame invited the University of Michigan back to help celebrate their first anniversary of football. Michigan players stayed at the Sheridan House in South Bend and were met by a group from Notre Dame on April 20. The game was played off campus at Green Stocking Ball Park. Festivities began with a 100-yard race, with Michigan's James Duffy nipping Notre Dame's Harry Jewett in the elapsed time of 11 seconds. The football game began at 3:00 pm, and the first half was marred by arguments with the referee, who was from Ann Arbor and would play against Notre Dame the next day. Michigan's experience earned them a 24-0 lead, before Notre Dame's Frank Springer wrestled the ball away for an apparent touchdown; the referee disallowed the score. Jewett thus gained football immortality when his subsequent score became the first official Notre Dame touchdown. Ed Prudhomme made the conversion, and the Fighting Irish lost 24-6. But they were on the right path.

The boys were learning fast and almost upset Michigan the next day. Sprague, the referee from the day before, switched with Babcock. The game was played on campus, and Notre Dame jumped out to a quick 4-0 lead on two safeties—Michigan's center, W.W. Harless, was tackled with the ball behind his goal, as was Duffy. Yet another rules argument started, and Michigan's Sprague took off with the ball and scored an unmolested, but not uncontested, touchdown. The ball was not in play, the Fighting Irish claimed, and besides, he had stepped out of bounds. Babcock ignored them. Michigan scored again. Jewett responded with a touchdown, but Babcock disallowed it. Notre Dame lost 10-4. It would be 21 years before a Michigan team would lose to Notre Dame.

The young team practiced hard. There were some new faces for the Irish, and Jewett and Cusack switched positions. Their next game was in early December with Harvard School of Illinois, who deemed themselves champions of that state. Notre Dame won 20-0, and declared themselves champs of both states.

1888 record: 1-2-0 (.333)
Record to date: 1-3-0 (.250)

1889

Perhaps sensing something good, the team scheduled an away game with Northwestern University. They prepared diligently with early morning runs around the campus lake. The Fighting Irish turned in a 9-0 shutout in their first road game. Play was ragged—one opponent's dash to the goal was stopped when a Notre Dame player simply sat on the runner. Notre Dame's first field goal was drop-kicked by Dezera Cartier, who distinguished himself later in the game, according to the accounts of the time, when he "dribbled" the ball for a 25-yard gain, the best on record to that point. The Fighting Irish showed ingenuity in scoring, when quarterback Ed Coady hid the ball, making it appear that end Steve Fleming had it. As Northwestern chased Fleming, Coady ambled into the end zone with a touchdown and the first recorded Fighting Irish fake.

The win wrapped up Notre Dame's first undefeated season—and also marked the end of football at Notre Dame for more than two years. Football ended because it was only a club sport, and the students were unable to maintain its momentum.

1889 record: 1-0-0 (1.000)
Record to date: 2-3-0 (.400)

1892

The team had to start over by recruiting personnel. Only Pat Coady, the new captain, had any connection with the previous teams, since his brothers had been quarterbacks in 1888 and 1889. Fred Schillo, at left tackle, would be a fixture until 1897, and several other players were in for the duration. This continuity was a crucial factor in reviving the program.

The schedule was not very ambitious. In playing South Bend High School, Notre Dame established a trend of playing some rag-tag outfits well into the new century. The ambitious high schoolers suffered a 56-0 loss as Notre Dame's Ed Brown became the school's first game-breaker with five touchdowns. The next game with Hillsdale College was a well-played, hard-hitting affair ending in a 10-10 tie. It was the first time Notre Dame rallied from a halftime deficit (6-4) to avert a loss. Football was back.

1892 record: 1-0-1 (.750)
Record to date: 3-3-1 (.500)

The 1892 team revived the game after a lapse of two years. Captain Pat Coady with the ball.

The 1893 Fighting Irish, with almost double the number of players from 1892.

1893

In 1893 there was an attempt to schedule serious major opponents. (Earlier encounters with Michigan were the result of mutual friendships, with Michigan helping out the new kid). The most important addition to the season was scheduling the University of Chicago for the final game, a school that was challenging the smug eastern football powers for recognition.

Kalamazoo folded easily 34-0 in the opener. Albion lost 8-6, thanks to a safety made by Ernest DuBrul. Schillo impressed people with his running from the dreaded "tackles back" formation. DeLasalle collapsed 28-0 in a blinding snowstorm; Fighting Irish tackle, Charles Roby, scored with a "turtle crawl"—on all fours, with three DeLasalle players smothering his body. Roby capped his day's work by carrying Schillo, who carried the ball, for a 5-yard gain. Such was football in 1893. Another snowstorm hit a week later, but the game with Hillsdale went on. Notre Dame's 22-10 win featured a 50-yard run by John Barrett. For New Year's, the team went to Chicago, but the University of Chicago won 8-0. In spite of that loss, the 1893 season showed that Notre Dame could play with established teams and pummel lesser ones.

1893 record: 4-1-0 (.800)
Record to date: 7-4-1 (.625)

1894

Notre Dame took a significant step toward respectability, prominence, and stability when they hired a part-time coach, bearded James L. Morison. Morison had once played tackle for the University of Michigan. He stressed conditioning, speed, and an abundance of end runs. Such tactics led to an opening 14-0 win over Hillsdale. Next came Albion, fresh from a 26-12 loss to Michigan, who proved to be tough. The game ended in a 6-6 tie, when substitute fullback John Studebaker fell on a fumble for the only Fighting Irish touchdown. Next, Wabash was dispatched easily, 30-0; the score might have been higher, but Wabash left the field with 18 minutes to go in the game. Notre Dame then whipped Rush Medical 18-6 in a workman-like game, serenaded by a band led by Professor Prescott. The season finale was a 19-12 loss to Albion in a return match, although Notre Dame felt the game was stolen from them when it was called due to darkness.

1894 record: 3-1-1 (.700)
Record to date: 10-5-2 (.647)

The 1894 Notre Dame Football Team.

1895

The new season brought a new coach, H.G. Hadden, who emphasized creating depth behind the starters. In fact, he was the substitute for portly Rosy Rosenthal at center, a fairly common practice in those days.

The Fighting Irish won their opener 20-0 over Northwestern. Next, Notre Dame tallied an 18-2 win over the Illinois Cycling Club due to better tackling. The winning streak ended against Indianapolis Artillery, however, a team that boasted a former All-American player named Osgood. Somerville, the referee, apparently did not detect an offside penalty when it took place, maybe because his brother played for the Artillery squad. The Fighting Irish also lost two costly fumbles on a slick field. Coach Hadden, however, did his best to help his team win: game accounts tell of him playing left tackle, returning kick offs, recovering a fumble, running the ball four times, and making tackles, although he was unable to stop the referee's brother from dashing 90 yards for a touchdown. A Renaissance figure on the field, Hadden next served as a referee as his scrubs, an early version of junior varsity, romped 46-0 over LaPorte High School. Less than a week after that, more medical students from Chicago came to the campus, only to lose 32-0. Notre Dame's backfield duo of Bob Brown and Lucian Wheeler rushed for more than 150 and 116 yards, respectively, the first time Notre Dame had two players break the century mark in one game.

1895 record: 3-1-0 (.750)
Record to date: 13-6-2 (.666)

The 1895 Team—Jack Mullen, far left second row, became the only three-time captain for Notre Dame.

1896

This was a pivotal season. Notre Dame was led by its first full-time coach, Frank Hering from Bucknell—a football nomad (he played for the University of Chicago in 1893 and 1894, and was the Maroon quarterback in Notre Dame's 8-0 loss in 1893), a bit of a dreamer (he was responsible for campaigning to put Mother's Day on the national calendar), a heady tactician, and a believer in positive reinforcement. He came to Notre Dame in the triple capacity of coach, quarterback, and captain.

He coached an advanced form of the game imported from the east, especially involving line play, and he arranged an expanded schedule of seven home games. His team lost its first game 4-0 to Physicians and Surgeons, partly because they left the field to protest a bad possession call. Then Hering's former Chicago teammates shut out Notre Dame 18-0, based on strong line play and weak Irish tackling. Two weeks later, Hering's coaching paid off in a 46-0 rout of South Bend Commercial Athletic Club. Notre Dame's Bob Brown had a big day with 50- and 65-yard touchdown runs and Jack Mullen scampered 90 yards for another. Hering, who had earlier berated the student body for heckling players at practice, had the playing field enclosed with a fence. Next Albion fell 24-0 as the Fighting Irish tuned up for the state championship game with Purdue. In that game, Notre Dame's offense clicked, but the defense faltered in a 28-22 loss. Three muffed conversion kicks sealed the team's fate.

That loss spurred the team on to a 82-0 win over Highland Views. Only three starters for the Fighting Irish did *not* score in the blitz of 15 touchdowns. Mike Daly booted 11 conversion kicks, and Brown ran for three touchdowns, each over 60 yards. A highly-touted Beloit team arrived next, fresh from tying undefeated Wisconsin and Northwestern. Notre Dame slogged to an 8-0 win on a wretched field. Hering had put together a very solid team in his first campaign.

1896 record: 4-3-0 (.571)
Record to date: 17-9-2 (.642)

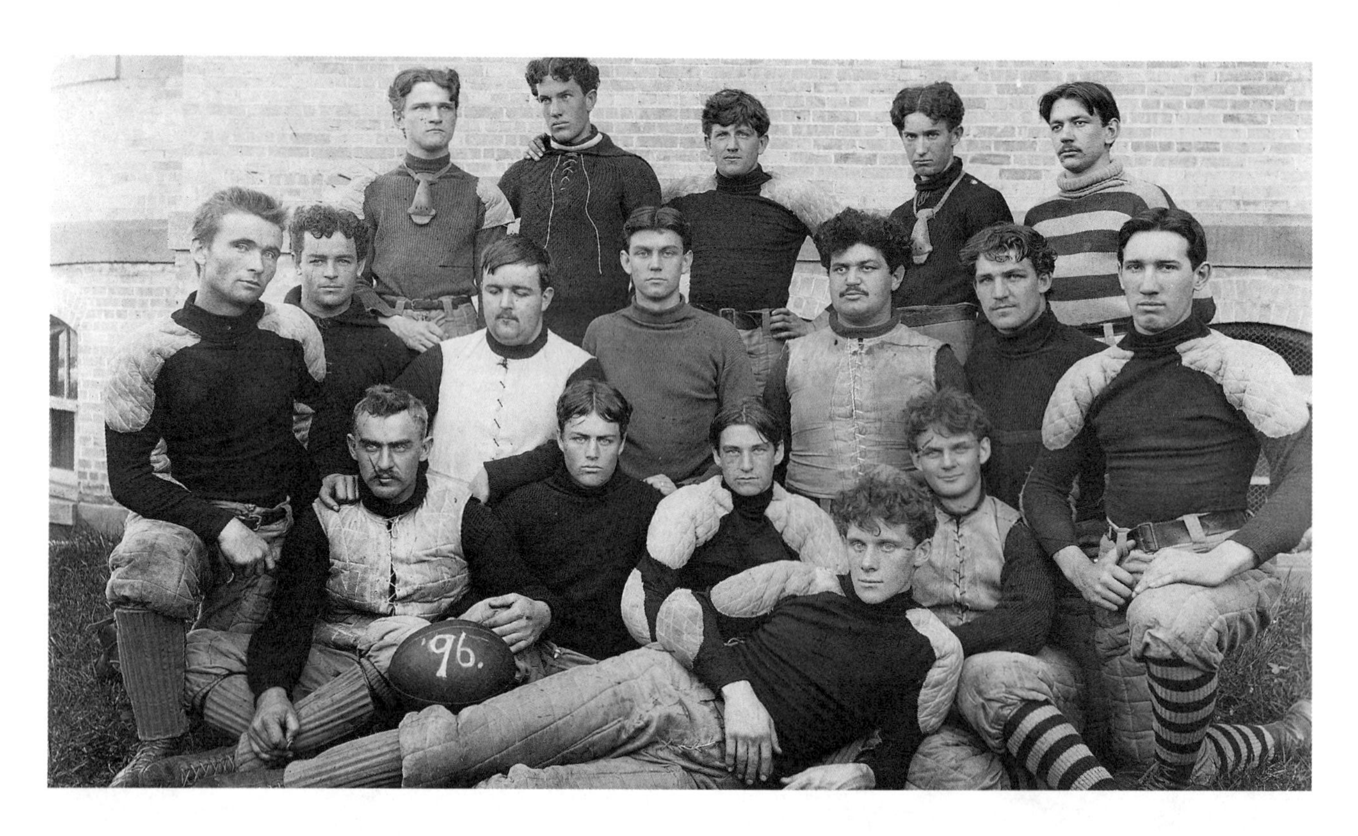

The 1896 squad: front: Frank Hering; second row: Charles Moritz, Robert Emmett Brown, Michael Daly, William Kegler; third row: John Mullen, Frank Hanley, Thomas Cavanaugh, Frank Lyons, Jake Rosenthal, Fred Schillo, John Murphy; top row: Sidney Corby, Angus McDonald, Houser (trainer), Thomas O'Hara, William Fagan.

1897

Hering returned for his second year as coach, and the Western Conference was created (now the Big 10). Notre Dame applied for membership, but was told, more or less, to grow up some more. Two new players must be mentioned—John Farley at left end (he would later become a priest and spend his life under the Dome) and massive John Eggeman (6-4, 256 pounds) became an instant fixture at center for Hering's sophisticated brand of football. Farley would be the best player for the Fighting Irish until Red Salmon matriculated a few years later. He personally demolished Chicago Dental Surgeons in his third game by rushing for 464 yards.

The season started with another shutout—a 0-0 tie with Rush Medical. Farley and Eggeman played well, and the big center used his bulk to push fullback Bill Kegler "into the line like a battering ram." Similar tactics helped the Fighting Irish win 4-0 over DePauw (TDs were worth 4 points in 1897), with Kegler registering the lone score. The next game was Farley's big day of 464 yards against the dentists—more than twice the yardage of any Fighting Irish back of any era. He scored four touchdowns, one on a short run and others on runs of 25, 50, and 45 yards. The last time anyone saw him he was scooting 85 yards with a backwards pass on the last play of the game.

The euphoria of this 62-0 win lasted two weeks, until Chicago dumped Notre Dame with a bruising 34-5 win. The scoring machine found new life a week later, however, when St. Viator was demolished 60-0. The season ended on a 34-5 victory over Michigan Agricultural College, the nascent Michigan State University. Kegler and George Lins led the way with two touchdowns each. This was probably the best of Hering's three teams as head coach.

1897 record: 4-1-1 (.750)
Record to date: 21-10-3 (.661)

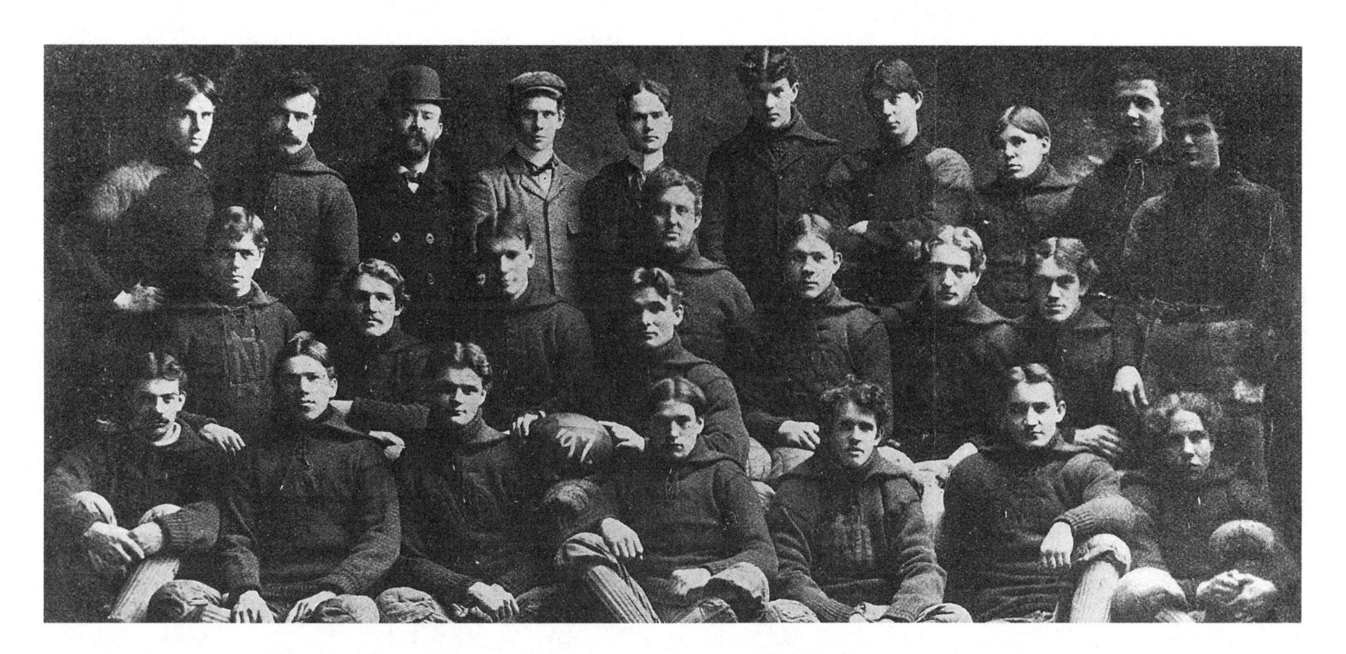

The 1897 team: first row: Bauwens, Kearney, Kegler, Captain Mullen, Daly, Fennessey, Monohan, McNaughton; middle row: Healey, Schillo, Swonk, Eggemen, Lins, Niezer, Farley; top row: Powers, Dr. Berteling, Coach Hering, O'Malley (manager), McDonald, Murray, Waters, Bouza, Williams.

1898

Facing a rugged schedule, Hering had the team go to a resort hotel at Hudson Lake for pre-season training. Seventeen hopefuls made the trip and the week-long stay helped them avoid the slow starts of the previous seasons. Hering also noted that touchdowns were now valued at 5 points, the same as a field goal, and conversion kicks were worth only one point. They were bold enough to open on the road, at the University of Illinois in Champaign, winning 5-0, thanks to a late field goal by Charles Fleming and Eggeman's block of an Illini field goal try. A desperate Fighting Irish defense stopped the Illini on the last play of the game with the ball on the 6-yard line.

The Aggies of Michigan Agricultural College were next, fresh from being whipped 39-0 by the University of Michigan. Notre Dame was still trying to measure itself by the Michigan standard and piled up an impressive 53-0 rout. Farley, now oddly known as "Tiger Lily," made 11 runs for 225 yards and three touchdowns, including scoring bursts of 38 and 45 yards.

The Irish travelled to Ann Arbor to try their luck, but Michigan prevailed 23-0. The field was a mud bath, and Michigan players had long cleats, which the Irish lacked. Michigan triple-teamed Eggeman and nullified the rest for the win.

Six days later, Notre Dame rebounded with a 32-0 rout of DePauw. Then downstate rival Indiana pinned them with an 11-5 loss. Farley tallied the only Fighting Irish touchdown on a 14-yard sweep around left end. Unable to claim the state championship, they vented their frustrations on Albion, winning 60-0 to close the season. Angus McDonald streaked 95 yards for a touchdown on the opening kickoff, and scored twice more. Eggeman also racked up a touchdown on a 15-yard run.

It was a frustrating season, perhaps blighted by overconfidence after the good start. The Fighting Irish were still not ready to defeat a major power.

1898 record: 4-2-0 (.666)
Record to date: 25-12-3 (.662)

1899

Frank Hering would coach the team through only five games before turning it over to rough, abrasive James McWeeney, who would prove to be a problem in later years as an assistant coach under Pat O'Dea. Hering launched the team on a 10-game schedule, a first for Notre Dame, although most of the opponents were nearby.

The first game was with Englewood High School, who put up a good fight before losing 29-5. Then Michigan Agricultural College was defeated 40-0. The opportunistic Irish blocked two late field goal attempts to save the shutout.

Riding this modest crest, the Fighting Irish met up with the great Amos Alonzo Stagg's Chicago team, but were disappointed in a 23-6 loss. Farley scored the only Fighting Irish touchdown, dashing 15 yards with a recovered fumble. But his effort was eclipsed by Chicago's Hamill who ran 105 and 100 yards for touchdowns, the latter coming on a blocked field goal try.

Ten days later, only 325 spectators watched Notre Dame blank Lake Forest 38-0, with Angus McDonald using the new-fangled "Princeton kick" (using a holder rather than the drop kick) for a field goal. Then Michigan again and another loss, 12-0. For

The 1899 Fighting Irish: front row: Monohan, Kuppler, Fleming, Daly, Duncan, MacDonald, Hayes, Glynn, Winters; second row: Schneider, Hanley, McNulty, Eggeman, O'Malley, Wagner, Fortin; third row: Pÿm, Smith, Coleman, Captain Mullen, Lennon, Hayes, McWeeney, Farley, Engledrum (trainer); top: Coach Hering, Crumley (manager).

some unrecorded reason, Eggeman kept the time for the game. The Michigan team kept Farley in check, although he dropped a Wolverine runner who seemed destined for a long touchdown run.

The Fighting Irish rebounded by beating Indiana 17-0 to make a partial claim on the state championship. The student body helped out with a cheering contest and asked the referee—former coach and player Hadden—to give a speech. Farley racked up two punt returns of 45 yards each, other runs of 40 and 35 yards, and a stop on an opposing player who threatened the shutout. Four days later, Notre Dame blanked Northwestern 12-0, again blocking field goals to save the shutout. Eggeman and others missed that game and the 17-0 whitewash of Rush.

Injuries mounted, and new players were thrust into unfamiliar positions as Notre Dame went to Purdue to claim the rest of the state crown; the game ended in a 10-10 tie, with McDonald salvaging that with a field goal from the 40-yard line.

A crowd of 2,000 showed up for the finale with Chicago Physicians and Surgeons, a mature, experienced bunch good enough to use a former All-Western player only as a substitute. Eggeman had quit, and his replacement had only three days to prepare. The overmatched Fighting Irish played a good game, bowing 5-0, and used McDonald's punts of 68 and 82 yards to keep the other team bottled up.

Notre Dame's student paper pointed out that Indiana and Purdue had each lost an in-state game, whereas they had not, so a modest claim for the state title was made.

1899 record: 6-3-1 (.650)
Record to date: 31-15-4 (.660)

1900 to 1909

1900

Pat O'Dea and James McWeeney were the coaches for the year. O'Dea had been an All-American fullback and kicker for Wisconsin, and McWeeney established rapport with those who liked a rough game. Chet Grant recalled McWeeney's advice to runners: "double your fist when you run into the line and they'll get the message." This probably missed the point, since their line needed good replacements. Farley moved from left end to fullback, an interesting change since his backup was named Red Salmon. Other moves were made to shore up the depleted squad.

The changes looked pretty good when Notre Dame demolished Goshen College 55-0. Farley and Fortin had four touchdowns between them; five others were spread around. Englewood High School, who had just held Stagg's Chicago team to 27 points, lost to the Fighting Irish 68-0. Farley's score on a 75-yard run was the play of the game. South Bend Howard Park lost 64-0, with George Kuppler and Jim Faragher scoring three touchdowns each and Farley and Fortin two each. The momentum continued through a 58-0 demolition of Cincinnati, with Kuppler scoring three times and Farley twice. One of Farley's scores came on a "fake kick," which he converted for a score on a 90-yard run.

Having scored 245 points to 0 in four games, there was reason to expect the Fighting Irish to be a power in the state, but Indiana shocked them 6-0. Then Beloit College added to the skid with a 6-6 tie, although Fighting Irish honor was upheld with a valiant four-play stand at their 1-foot line. The downward slide was completed a week later when Notre Dame lost to the University of Wisconsin 54-0, their worst defeat on record to that point. Farley was injured early in the game to make it worse.

With ample reasons to be depressed, the Fighting Irish faced a tough Michigan team. But the team pulled together, played solid defense, matched Michigan punt for punt, and even drove to the Michigan 3-

The 1900 edition of Notre Dame Varsity Football.

yard line, but could not score. A recovered fumble led to a touchdown for Michigan, and Salmon was caught for a safety, resulting in a 7-0 win for the Wolverines. It was Notre Dame's best game against a powerhouse team and showed promise for the future.

Rush Medical then came to Notre Dame, where a drenching rain turned the field into a lake. Farley blocked a kick and ran 35 and 70 yards to help Notre Dame win 5-0. Salmon scored the only touchdown in his first game starting at fullback. The season ended with another 5-0 win over Physicians and Surgeons, with Frank Winters kicking a 40-yard field goal into a stiff wind.

1900 record: 6-3-1 (.650)
Record to date: 37-18-5 (.658)

1901

The1901 season did not start well. A replacement team had to be found for the scheduled opener; South Bend Commercial Athletic Club gladly filled in for Milwaukee Medical, too gladly as it turned out. They held the Fighting Irish to a scoreless tie. Captain Al Fortin, only 19 years old but in his fourth season with Notre Dame, saved the day when he blocked a field goal try. Then the Fighting Irish took a long road trip to Columbus, to play Ohio Medical University. They were glad to escape with a 6-0 win, with Fortin scoring the only touchdown. Irish fumbles made the game tighter than it should have been. Travelling in the opposite direction the next week, they went to Northwestern, only to find the mud there four inches deep. Salmon could not operate in the wet condition, and a bad snap on a punt from his end zone resulted in a safety and a 2-0 Northwestern win. Notre Dame then played Chicago Medical College at home and won handily, 32-0. With the defense playing well, a tough Beloit squad fell 5-0; their offense was stymied by Salmon's booming 70-yard punts. Yet another shutout, the fifth in six games, took Lake Forest to defeat, 16-0. Salmon scored a touchdown and booted a field goal.

Coach O'Dea planned on a first-half schedule of easier opponents to prepare his team for the challenges in the state, an early version of Fighting Irish scheduling that was practiced for many years. His plan worked as Purdue came to Notre Dame, only to run into an aroused student body that had even written special songs for the occasion. O'Dea's offense was designed around Salmon's vicious line bucks followed by ponderous tackle back plays, a crunching combination that earned a 12-6 win. A week later, the in-state sweep became a reality, as Notre Dame whipped Indiana 18-5. Salmon scored twice on short runs and also had a 55-yard kickoff return. Physicians and Surgeons were dispatched 34-0; running backs switched positions with linemen to allow them scor-

The 1901 Notre Dame University Football Team.

ing chances. Both guards and the center scored, and another center who took over at fullback also scored a touchdown.

The finale was a rematch with the South Bend Commercial Athletic Club (with O'Dea as its kicker). The Fighting Irish won 22-6 as Salmon outkicked his coach, although O'Dea scored the club team's only touchdown.

Notre Dame thus concluded its most successful season yet. They claimed a state championship, with six shutouts in 10 games and only three touchdowns scored against them. The Fighting Irish were on the verge of reaching the prominence they had been seeking for a decade.

1901 record: 8-1-1 (.850)
Record to date: 45-19-6 (.685)

1902

O'Dea moved on to coach at Missouri; the Cornell coach who was supposed to replace him never showed up, so Salmon took the job. His first chore was to find a new interior line before playing Michigan Agricultural College. His backs looked good, scoring two touchdowns in the first moments, and Notre Dame kept the pressure on for a 33-0 blitz. Lake Forest fell next, 28-0, led by Salmon's two touchdowns.

The Fighting Irish had played Michigan both at home and in Ann Arbor, so they tried them in Toledo for a change. Michigan won 23-0, although Salmon's spirited play and leadership caught their attention, especially in the first half when Notre Dame was behind only 5-0. Before it was over, Salmon was knocked out four times—and showed it.

Although disappointed once again in that big test, Notre Dame bested Indiana 11-5. A recovered Salmon broke loose for two touchdown runs (40 yards and a short plunge). His line smashes set up a nice 55-yard ramble by Jim Doar on a fake when the Hoosiers went after Salmon. After this win, Notre Dame went to Columbus, Ohio, winning 6-5. A booming Salmon punt of 65 yards was misplayed into Notre Dame's only score. The team moved on to Rock Island, Illinois, for a game with Knox College, losing 12-5, although Salmon left the 3,000 spectators agog with an 85-yard punt. He also plunged for Notre Dame's only touchdown near the end of the game.

The road trip behind them, the Fighting Irish met American Medical, winning 92-0. The longest touchdown run, by Frank Lonergan, was 106 yards. Fighting Irish ball carriers racked up no less than 940 yards on 12 long-distance scores, and seven players joined the century mark for the day! The 92 points were scored in just 32 minutes of play, with American Medical leaving the field early. The season's fourth shutout was handed to DePauw, 22-0. Salmon did his usual—a touchdown on a fierce run, a 75-yard punt, and a field goal.

The in-state rivalry ended sourly in Lafayette with a 6-6 tie with Purdue. Salmon was Notre Dame's only scorer. He played on a badly sprained ankle, which spoiled his last-minute drop kick effort to win the game. Purdue used 35 players in the second half to wear out the 12 Fighting Irish who suited up. The tie left the state championship to be shared.

1902 record: 6-2-1 (.766)
Record to date: 51-21-7 (.689)

1903

This was the year for which the Fighting Irish had long waited. Salmon, as head coach and a senior in college, led the team to an undefeated, unscored-upon season.

Michigan Agricultural College fell first, 12-0. Newcomer lineman Pat Beacom, 220 pounds of mean on the line, hit the Aggies all day. Salmon tinkered with his line assignments before the next game, and an improved squad downed Lake Forest 28-0, with Salmon scoring three times in the second half.

It rained for the DePauw game, both precipitation and points, as Notre Dame prevailed 56-0. American Medical showed some improvement from the previous year, but lost 52-0. Frank Lonergan scored three touchdowns. The Missouri Osteopaths were the next losers, 28-0. Salmon led the way, and Nate Silver saved the shutout when he tackled a Missouri player on the 4-yard line after an 80-yard run.

The Fighting Irish played Northwestern in the American League baseball park of the day, a sign of the game's growing popularity; the game ended in a 0-0 tie. Lonergan scored a touchdown on a 45-yard burst, but Salmon was called for illegal use of the hands on the block. The Fighting Irish stunned the spectators with their defense when consecutive punts from their end zone went awry, at their 2- and 5- yard lines, but the Wildcats could not score in six tries. The team travelled to Toledo again to play Ohio Medical, winning 35-0. Four Notre Dame players scored two touchdowns each, including Salmon. He closed the scoring with a 20-yard burst with three opponents dangling from his shoulders. Notre Dame finished its season with a 35-0 romp over Wabash (who had beaten Indiana) and made some noises about the state crown.

For his illustrious efforts, Salmon made Walter Camp's All-America third team.

1903 record: 8-0-1 (.944)
Record to date: 59-21-8 (.715)

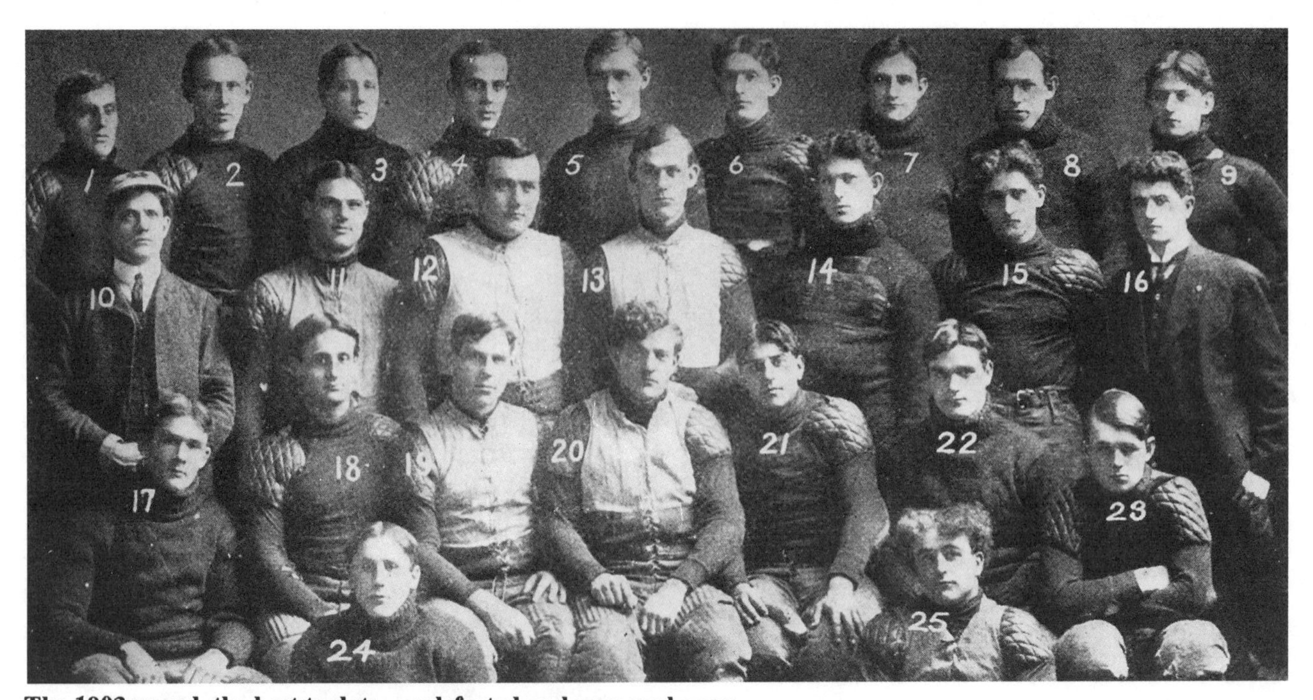

The 1903 squad, the best to date, undefeated and unscored upon.

The 1904 Irish: first row: Sudheimer, Silver, Coad; second row: Holland, McInerney, Shaughnessy, Guthrie, Daley, Coach Salmon; third row: Funk, Donovan, Beacom, Fansler, Sheehan, Murphy, Bracken; top row: O'Neill, O'Keefe, Draper, Church, Healy, Waldorf.

1904

Salmon coached a third season, since he had to finish his engineering studies; his team was strong in desire, but weak in talent and experience. Injuries would make matters worse. Salmon purchased a "charging machine," similar to the one used at Northwestern, to train the linemen "to charge fast and low and together." The rulesmakers had tinkered with the scoring vlaues again: touchdowns were still 5 points, but field goals were reduced to 4 points.

Armed with the latest technology, the Fighting Irish charged against Wabash in an unimpressive 12-4 win. Frank Shaughnessy looked good on some long runs and a 30-yard sprint on a fumble he recovered in mid-air. Pat Beacom thrilled the fans when he charged through the Little Giants on a punt play and forced the punter into surrendering the ball. American Medical was next, losing 44-0. Newcomer Bob Bracken ran for three touchdowns, and Shaughnessy followed up a blocked kick with a 101-yard touchdown dash.

After that, the deluge. The Fighting Irish took 25 men to Wisconsin (with 60 on its squad). Notre Dame played stoutly for 14 scoreless minutes, then a series of injuries decimated its players. Wisconsin won 58-0. Beacom was the only ray of light in an otherwise gloomy picture.

With injured players at many positions, quarterback Silver tried to compensate against Ohio Medical by exchanging backs with linemen. Left guard Beacom scored twice, as Notre Dame struggled to a 17-5 win. Shaughnessy dislocated his collar bone to keep the bad luck going. Similar emergency plans allowed for a 6-0 win over Toledo, but disaster struck in practice the next week when fullback Bill Draper sprained an ankle. Shaughnessy at least had his shoulder sling removed.

Taking plenty of liniments and plasters, the Fighting Irish made their longest road trip, to the University of Kansas in Lawrence. They played as well as they could with four starters out, but fell 24-6. Captain Shaughnessy could not bear to just watch and inserted himself over the roaring protests of Salmon; he promptly ran 100 yards for the only Irish touchdown. Bad luck went on the trip too—even the substitutes were hurting when Keefe and O'Neil saw action for two plays and were kicked unconscious. It would be 30 years before Notre Dame played Kansas again.

A two-week breather helped the Irish prepare for DePauw and Purdue. They needed it. DePauw played tough but lost 10-0; Draper broke his collar bone after booming a 75-yard punt. Notre Dame limped on to Lafayette, but it was no contest, with Purdue winning 36-0. The team played like madmen, though; Salmon had to take Shaughnessy out of the game when he was so weak no one could hear his signals. Beacom was a pillar of strength, but it was not enough.

1904 record: 5-3-0 (.625)
Record to date: 64-24-8 (.708)

1905

Salmon moved back east to pursue his career in civil engineering, and former quarterback Henry McGlew advanced to become head coach. Having helped Salmon late in the 1904 season, he knew the players well, and there were some good ones. But the season started on a sour note when unfounded charges in the press of favoritism regarding starting positions and personnel eroded team morale following the opener with North Division High School. Nate Silver, a North Division grad, played well, but three North Division recruits on the Notre Dame bench abruptly quit the team following the 44-0 rout; they were apparently lured to Wisconsin. In the game, Beacom scored twice, and Bill Downs scored three times. A brouhaha welled up a few days after the game; it was the last time Notre Dame played a high school team.

Michigan Agricultural College tried again, but lost 28-0; six players scored touchdowns, all on short runs. The Fighting Irish could not sweep MAC's ends, so they went up the middle. On to Wisconsin, a tough assignment in view of the controversy regarding the pre-season charges, plus the defection of players from Notre Dame to Wisconsin. Notre Dame lost 21-0, but not before serving notice that they could play with the Badgers. Some clear scoring chances were lost while Beacom unceremoniously stuffed the tentative plays sent in his direction. The Fighting Irish were good enough to earn accolades from Alonzo Stagg: they "looked every bit as good as Chicago, and in several particulars seem to have the better of the argument." The Notre Dame student paper called it a "glorious defeat."

Glorious it might have been, but the students ran out of words in the 5-0 loss to Wabash. Although statistically they had twice the yardage of Wabash, they could not score from the 1-foot line and they fumbled on the Wabash 10. Two consecutive shutout losses, one to tiny Wabash.

It was too bad for American Medical that Wabash beat Notre Dame. The student paper told the story:

"NOTRE DAME 142; AMERICAN COLLEGE OF MEDICINE AND SURGERY, 0."

" That looks good anyway. Rather relieves the feeling after the Wabash game."

Every starter scored, 142 points in 33 minutes. There were 27 touchdowns (with 21 mercifully missed conversion kicks—a pattern for many Fighting Irish blowouts in later years); interior linemen scored 11 of them. The longest drive was five plays; most were only two. (Remember, in those days, the team that scored received the following kickoff.) Ten scores came in 8 minutes. Four players scored three times each, six scored twice, and newcomer Dom Callicrate wandered into the end zone once.

DePauw lost by a 71-0 score. Bill Draper scored six touchdowns. Indiana, however, was not impressed, and beat Notre Dame 22-5. The lackluster loss was followed by a modest 22-0 win over Bennett Medical College. Then Purdue finished the season in rude fashion with a 32-0 win over the Fighting Irish. Henry McGlew had seen enough of coaching.

1905 record: 5-4-0 (.555)
Record to date: 69-28-8 (.695)

The 1905 Notre Dame team.

1906

With McGlew gone, Notre Dame looked eastward again and came up with Thomas Barry, one of Camp's All-American choices for 1902. Barry had coached at Brown and Bowdoin and played minor league baseball in Buffalo and Montreal between stints at Harvard Law School. He inherited a good talent pool and newcomers who would soon make their marks. One of these was Harry "Red" Miller, the first of the Miller clan to attend Notre Dame (they would keep coming right into World War II). John Eggeman's "little" brother showed up, all 220 pounds of him, to line up next to Beacom for a powerful left side.

The rules had changed, too, but Notre Dame would not take advantage of them for awhile. There would be less "mass play," and the forward pass could be thrown—cautiously, carefully, and conservatively.

Barry did not favor ridiculous scoring and told his players to take it easy on Franklin College. The opening kickoff turned into a Fighting Irish touchdown. Beacom strode in for a touchdown four plays later, then again moments later. Barry in the second half unloaded the bench. The game was marred by more than 100 yards of penalties because the exuberant Irish who could not break their habit, now illegal, of hurdling the line. Notre Dame won 26-0. Hillsdale was next, losing 17-0. The first half was a restrained 0-0 tie—too much for Beacom to take. He scored twice soon after the half.

Physicians and Surgeons fell 28-0. Barry was scouting Purdue's game with Chicago and let captain Bracken handle the game. Beacom scored three touchdowns.

Barry's professionalism emerged after his scouting trip when he ordered lights for the field house for three night practices before the Purdue game. But first, Michigan Agricultural College, aware of the new rules, came to Cartier Field ready to play flashy football. They had improved, but lost their sixth straight shutout to Notre Dame 5-0; the lone score came on a blocked kick.

Next up was Purdue. Two straight shutouts at their hands rankled, so the Fighting Irish returned the favor, 2-0, thanks to a bad snap on a punt that earned a safety. The game was marred by fumbles and penalties.

Next was Indiana for the state crown. But it was not to be. The Hoosier punter kept the Fighting Irish bottled up with 18 punts, the big Notre Dame linemen tired, and Indiana prevailed 12-0. Notre Dame ended the season on a high note with a 29-0 victory over Beloit, the sixth shutout of the year.

1906 record: 6-1-0 (.857)
Record to date: 75-29-8 (.705)

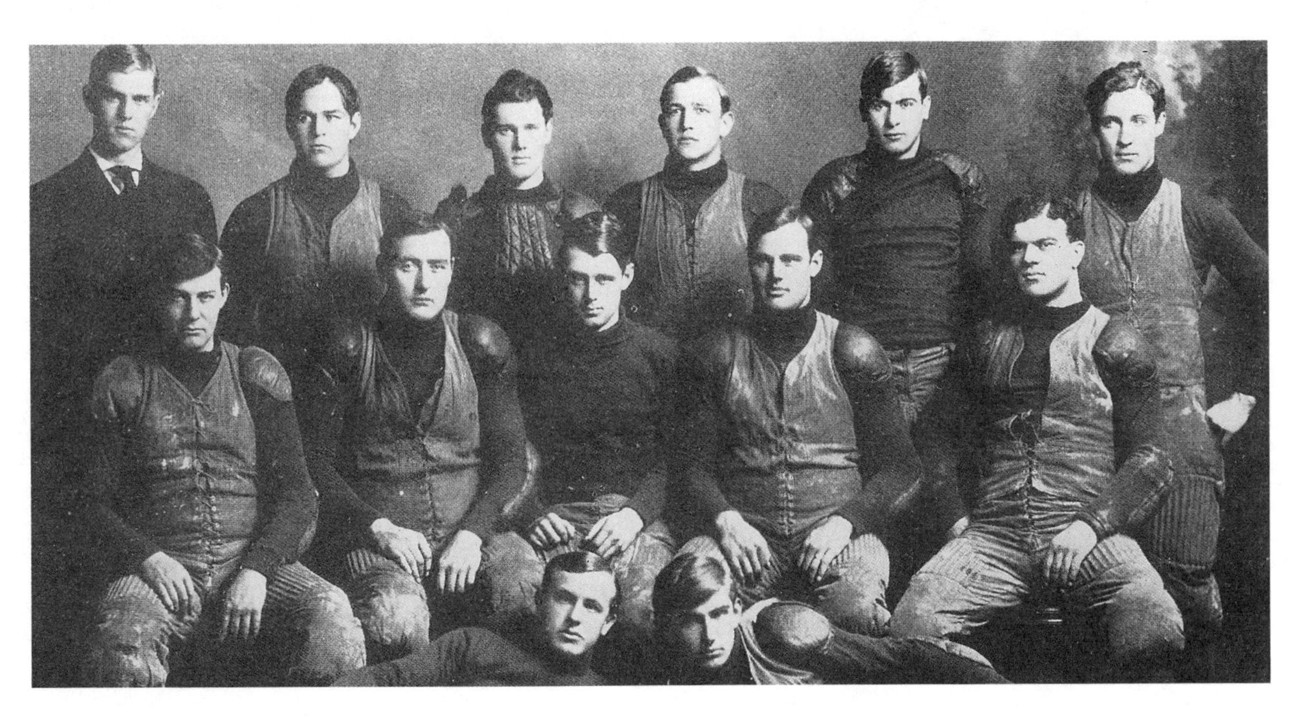

The 1906 Notre Dame varsity.

1907

Barry wanted to practice law, but stayed for one more year. Hopes were high that the elusive state crown would be won. The schedule was not very demanding, except for Purdue and Indiana. Barry was a master of defense—six shutouts in 1906 and four more would be added in 1907.

Physicians and Surgeons opened the season, and the Irish held them to one first down in a 32-0 rout. There were many long runs for touchdowns, although some were called back for infractions. Franklin tried again but lost 23-0. For some reason, Red Miller was at center, although he still scored two touchdowns. Tiny Olivet was next; they had beaten Michigan Agricultural College in 1906 and also earned respect in a 22-4 Fighting Irish win. They had good speed and used it in a variety of trick plays, onside kicks, and forward passes. Callicrate broke it open, with a touchdown plunge from the 5-yard line, followed by a touchdown run of 100 yards. Olivet at one point used a play with five forward passes.

Indiana was a different story. They were tough. The game ended up in a 0-0 tie, which was marred by fumbles, lost possessions on incomplete passes (a rule then), and stalled drives. Miller seemed to be everywhere to stymie Hoosier plans.

Knox lost 17-0 even though Barry rested his starting backfield for Purdue. The Knox quarterback weighed only 117 pounds and spent most of his day trying to avoid the Notre Dame linemen. The Fighting Irish met Purdue without Miller, who was suffering from an abscess on his leg, and won 17-0. Callicrate successfully made up for the absent Miller. The season ended with a poorly played 21-12 win over St. Vincent's. Oddly enough, for a reward, Miller made the All-State team as a center.

1907 record: 6-0-1 (.928)
Record to date: 81-29-9 (.718)

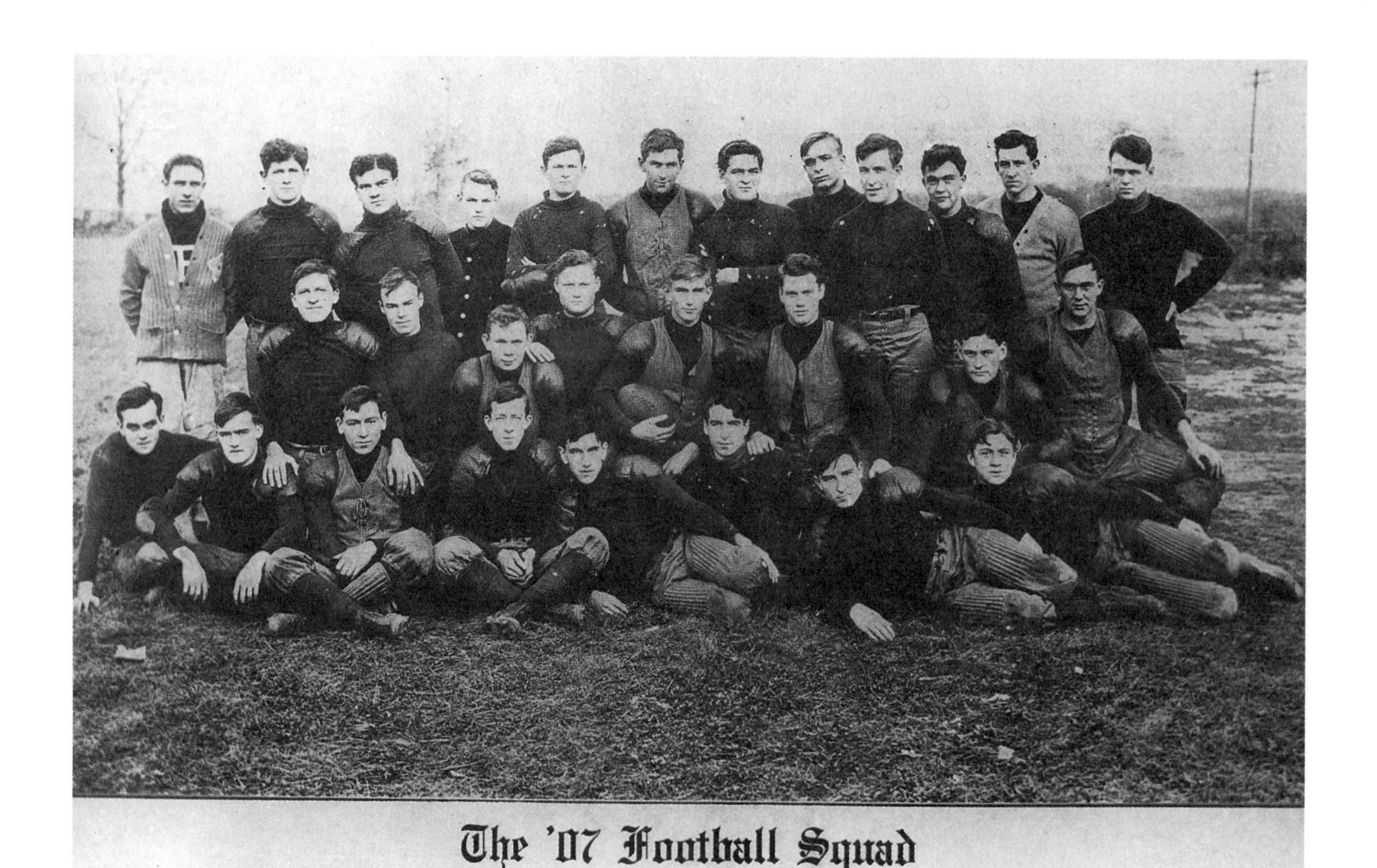

The 1907 Notre Dame football team.

1908

Barry left to coach at Wisconsin. Notre Dame continued its practice of hiring easterners when Victor Place, an All-America from Dartmouth, was hired. He specialized in power football, a throwback to the pre-1906 rules. Place came to be known for gruelling practices and constant scrimmaging. Red Miller spoke of his two-a-days running for two hours in the morning and three to four hours in the afternoon. Scrimmages would last up to two hours. All this tended to make the players overtrained.

In the opener against Hillsdale, the Fighting Irish scored within the first three minutes, got 23 points before the half, and held Hillsdale to one first down. Paul McDonald had the play of the day, a 65-yard touchdown sprint. Pete Vaughan scored twice, once on a 35-yard line buck intended for short yardage. His methods seemingly vindicated by the 39-0 score, Place continued to work his charges hard. Mismatched Franklin was pounded 64-0 and never earned a first down. The Irish were conducting a sprinter's clinic with several long touchdown runs when history was made as quarterback Don Hamilton tossed a forward pass to second-string left end Fay Wood, who turned the play into a score—Notre Dame's first recorded touchdown through the air. There were more passes after that, but McDonald racked up three touchdowns on the ground in the second half to attract most of the attention.

Miller had been rested in that game to be ready for Michigan. UM's coach and athletic director Fielding Yost's team was a bit past its "point-a-minute" express featuring Willie Heston, but they were a national power nevertheless. Michigan won again, 12-6, but the Fighting Irish scored the only touchdown, when Pete Vaughan dashed 50 yards on a double pass play. Michigan's Allerdice scored three field goals. Perhaps the game was lost on a mistaken out of bounds call that nullified McDonald's 85-yard touchdown run. In the loss, however, Notre Dame sacked the Wolverines six times and stopped their ground game all day.

Physicians and Surgeons watched an amazing performance by a bevy of Fighting Irish runners, losing 88-0 in 40 minutes of play. Notre Dame accumulated 1,316 yards rushing (to minus 15 yards for the opponents). Miller scored three times while Ulric Ruell and McDonald tallied twice each. Eight other players scored touchdowns. They also kicked a field goal and scored a safety just to make sure.

Ohio Northern University fell next 58-4. Ruell had a touchdown on a run of 85 yards within the first 40 seconds of the game. Miller and McDonald scored three times each and four others scored once. ONU managed a 40-yard field goal to keep the Fighting Irish record intact of not having an opposing player cross the goal with the ball.

Having established that they could play stifling defense, Notre Dame went to Indianapolis to meet Indiana. The Hoosiers managed to reach the Notre Dame's 20-yard line, but that was all, as the Fighting Irish won 11-0. Left tackles Kelly and Edwards scored twice and Miller piled up 175 yards rushing, with 150 yards of that in five end runs.

Wabash was outmanned but tough, because of their coach Jesse Harper. It was a defensive game with all the scoring coming on field goals in an 8-4 Irish win. Vaughan intercepted two passes to ice the game. St. Viator was defeated in a 46-0 rout, and a tough Marquette squad lost 6-0. (Marquette had tied Illinois and lost a close 9-6 game with Wisconsin.) The first half was scoreless, and Place opted to put in his speedsters, McDonald and Schmitt. Their outside speed resulted in the lone touchdown by McDonald, after his long passes to Rosey Dolan and Joe Collins. Marquette had a chance when it pinned Notre Dame on its 1-yard line, but Vaughan sidestepped a charging tackler and broke a 35-yard gainer. The Milwaukee paper praised Irish tackling as "brief and to the point," so that "the play stopped right there." This was the key to the season in which no opposing team scored a touchdown, as the Fighting Irish racked up 326 points to 20. In the last 24 games, only two touchdowns had been scored against them while they registered 16 shutouts. The Fighting Irish had reached an important threshold—they were ready to beat a major power.

1908 record: 8-1-0 (.888)
Record to date: 89-30-9 (.730)

1909

Place was replaced by Frank "Shorty" Longman, a former fullback for Yost at Michigan from 1903 to 1905. He had coached at Arkansas and Wooster; at Wooster he had beaten Ohio State, the first time in 18 tries for the small school. In picking Longman, Notre Dame signalled the end of the domination of eastern personnel and methods.

The 1909 squad—names are incorrect in three places: "Schmitt" should be Vaughan, "Maloney" should be Schmitt, and "Vaughan" is Maloney.

The Fighting Irish had some good players—especially Miller and Vaughan in the backfield and linemen Ralph Dimmick and George Philbrook. The school also now had its own song, the "Notre Dame Victory March." The scene was set for a good year of football. It should also be noted that this was the first season in which the field goal scored the 3 points known in modern football.

Olivet opened the season, losing 58-0. The Fighting Irish had a big lead at the half but still used an onside kick. Longman also showed a preference for "smash-mouth" football, as his big linemen scored five touchdowns.

Rose Poly befell a similar fate, 60-11. Longman showed that he could combine power with passing by turning loose the towering Philbrook as a receiver. He promptly scored on a 50-yard touchdown pass. Dimmick also scored, but on the ground. Miller scored four times and Vaughan three. Rose Poly did score a touchdown when a Fighting Irish onside kick went astray, and a Rose Poly player snatched it just in time to see Philbrook steaming after him. Notre Dame blocked a field goal try that ended up in a second touchdown for Rose Poly.

A still-improving Michigan Agricultural College lost 17-0 in a well -played game. Dimmick ran in a touchdown from the 20-yard line, and Vaughan scored twice. Then Notre Dame went east to begin a series with Pitt and escaped with a 6-0 win; the issue was settled with the first game-winning touchdown pass in Fighting Irish history—a 35-yarder from Don Hamilton to Lee Mathews. The referees were so objectionable that Pete Dwyer, substitute QB (second team), protested too much, was ejected, and then tried to hit a referee. They invented a 45-yard penalty to end the argument.

After that, Ann Arbor must have seemed peaceful. But the 5,000 Michigan fans were stunned by a thrilling 11-3 Fighting Irish win. Walter Camp was there, too. Longman had been showcasing a long passing attack, but changed to a patient, short game. He still liked the onside kick, but it backfired when Allerdice recovered the first one and scored a field goal. Vaughan replied with the first Irish touchdown, shocking the fans when at the end of his run, he ran into and demolished the goal posts. Michigan fought back; but a blocked field goal try was recovered by Notre Dame on the Michigan 35-yard line, setting up Billy Ryan's touchdown. A dejected Yost said afterwards, "Those are the worst kind of games to lose. They leave a worm in a man's heart to gnaw and gnaw." Longman introduced Miller to Yost the next day, who (Yost) promptly complained that Miller had called for fair catches too late three times, earning cheap penalties. A week later, Yost changed his tune completely: "...we went into the game caring little whether we won or lost." He would eventually define it as a "practice game"—even though 5,000 fans came to the proceedings on November 6, and Camp just happened to drop by.

The Fighting Irish high lasted through a 46-0 win over Ohio Northern. Longman turned his tackles loose on tackle-around plays, and Philbrook and Dolan garnered two touchdowns each. Wabash was dispatched 38-0. Harper liked what he saw and chose seven Fighting Irish players for his 11-man All-State squad.

Mounting injuries contributed to a scoreless tie with Marquette to end the season. Vaughan was out; Dolan broke his collarbone early in the game, although he continued to play. The field was a sticky mess, and the referees called a tight game. Still, the team thought Marquette was the best they'd seen all year. Dimmick, Dolan, and Vaughan made All-Western; Dimmick earned honorable mention All-American. Walter Camp praised Miller.

1909. Let it stand with the other great years and other great teams. After waiting 22 years, Notre Dame had finally reached the point that it considered commensurate with its destiny. Although there would be genuine national championships ahead, this was a year to cherish for its special accomplishments.

1909 record: 7-0-1 (.937)
Record to date: 96-30-10 (.742)

1910 to 1919

1910

The team lost a number of excellent players. Gone were Miller, Dolan, Vaughan, Ryan, Hamilton, and other stalwarts. The 1910 team would be hard pressed to do well.

Dimmick and Philbrook were back, and Dorais was an early lock at quarterback. Olivet was scheduled for the opener, and Longman used it to check out his new players. College football was beginning the process of sorting out the large schools from the small schools; Olivet had been able to compete earlier, but not anymore. Notre Dame won 48-0. Longman used every player, including a small, balding fellow with a broken nose and a funny name as third-string fullback. "Rochne," the papers reported—Knute Rockne, new to college after several years with the U.S. Post Office. Longman thought maybe he could eventually contribute something.

The coach of Buchtel (Akron) erred in judgment when he said that Notre Dame's colors contained a shade of yellow. His team was highly ranked in Ohio circles. Fifty-one Fighting Irish points later, he probably regretted the remark. Philbrook started the touchdowns, and Captain Dimmick took the honors with three scores. Philbrook made the play of the day when he started around end, fumbled, recov-

The 1910 Fighting Irish—Knute Rockne, far left, second row.

ered, blasted through three converging would-be tacklers, and ran 75 yards for his second touchdown.

But Michigan Agricultural College turned the tables, winning 17-0. Notre Dame suffered a general breakdown—fumbles, miscues, muffed punts, weak running, and poor blocking.

The night before the Michigan game, University of Michigan Coach Yost cancelled the scheduled game between Notre Dame and Michigan, claiming that Philbrook and Dimmick had used all their eligibility in the Pacific Northwest before coming to Notre Dame. Yost's point was probably worth considering, but his tactics were not. There was the lingering suspicion that he did not want to run the risk of consecutive losses to the upstart Fighting Irish. Wabash coach, Jesse Harper, also had to cancel Wabash's game because of the death of a player. Rose Poly substituted for them, only to lose in a 41-3 rout. Dimmick scored three touchdowns; Dorais hit three conversions and a field goal.

Ohio Northern became the 100th victim of the Fighting Irish football program. Ryan sprinted 95 yards to score, Mathews ran 75 for another, and Dorais went cross country for a third to go with seven conversion kicks.

Marquette spoiled the finale with a 5-5 tie. Joe Brennan, Notre Dame's backup center in 1909 (and father of Terry Brennan, a later star under Leahy, and head coach, 1954-58), scored for Marquette on a 1-yard plunge. Bill Martin recovered a fumble for Notre Dame's score. Although this had not been a particularly good year, there were some impressive players working their way to the starting lineup—men who would launch Notre Dame from a regional powerhouse into the national spotlight.

1910 record: 4-1-1 (.750)
Record to date: 100-31-11 (.742)

1911

Jack Marks from Dartmouth replaced Longman; he was assisted by Philbrook for the line and Hamilton for the backs. Losing Dimmick and Philbrook left yawning holes in the line, but speed was the order of the day. There was not a 200-pounder on the 1911 line. Only fullback Ray Eichenlaub, a rock-hard, 205-pounder, had any size.

Ohio Northern started the second 100 wins for Notre Dame with a 32-6 loss to a team with only four monogram winners in starting positions. A new brand of football was unveiled for Notre Dame—speed turned loose on end runs and long passes, but also a shift formation, the predecessor of the Notre Dame shift used later by Harper and Rockne. Scoring was distributed among the players, and the starters rested for a quarter before they went back in to score three touchdowns in the last 6 minutes. Eichenlaub set up one of those scores with a 20-yard pass to Dorais. The ONU score came on an official's error when a blocked pass hit the ground but was not called incomplete; a surprised halfback named Stump scooped up the ball and scored what was to become the only touchdown against the Fighting Irish for the year.

The Irish dismantled St. Viator 43-0 in the next game. Dorais kicked an early field goal and paced a second quarter five-touchdown scoring burst with a touchdown pass to Dutch Bergman and a quarterback sneak for another.

A reputedly strong Butler team looked good through much of the game, down only 6-0 at halftime. The Fighting Irish were killing themselves with fumbles, so Marks sent his second team in for the third quarter, then blitzed a tiring Butler with his starters to end the game. The final score was 27-0. Eichenlaub scored twice, the second with most of the Butler team along for the ride. Bergman returned a 65-yard punt for a score that was the play of the day.

In the next game, Loyola of Chicago was immolated 80-0 in only 54 minutes of play. Dutch Bergman returned a kick off for 105 yards, but missed a touchdown by 5, due to the longer field in use then—a record that may never be broken. Marks used his substitutes liberally against Loyola; back-up halfback Art Smith racked up seven touchdowns, the last one a 75-yard effort. Bergman pitched in with three.

The Fighting Irish headed for the University of Pittsburgh with 20 good players and Marks' caution was accurate; the Panthers fought to a tough 0-0 tie. Notre Dame stopped Pitt twice near the goal, once from the 2-yard line, and Rockne lost a 40-yard touchdown dash on a recovered kick (the referee said the whistle never blew). Pitt lost a touchdown on an offside call and Dorais narrowly missed a late field goal. It was a game of lost opportunities for both teams.

Marks rested his starters against St. Bonaventure,and the reserves won 34-0. Joe Pliska scored three touchdowns, Heine Berger added two more, and Bill Kelleher one. Wabash was next, and Wabash coach Harper had his team ready, duelling the Fighting Irish to a stirring 6-3 Notre Dame win. Wabash took the early lead with a drop kick and then made it last until the fourth quarter. Facing defeat, the Fighting Irish marched the length of the field, and Berger scored from the Wabash 2 for the win. In those days, a pass could not exceed 20 yards.Modern rules would have declared Wabash the winner, since their touchdown pass was disallowed for going more than 20 yards.

Marquette tied Notre Dame for the third straight year, in yet another scoreless affair. Notre Dame did manage a drive to the Marquette 2, but a holding penalty killed the chance for a score. Dorais flubbed two field goal tries. Eichenlaub played well, and Charlie Crowley intercepted a pass to end a Marquette scoring threat.

The 1911 season marked a gradual shift into a brand of football similar to the modern game. All the early signs were there to indicate what would eventually happen at West Point in 1913.

1911 record: 6-0-2 (.875)
Record to date: 106-31-13 (.750)

1912

Marks continued his quiet ways, emphasizing team speed. After he filled holes and tinkered with personnel, he had what he wanted—a very fast squad, mostly of small men, with Eichenlaub for the hammer. Rockne and Crowley were great ends and Gus Dorais was a gutsy quarterback. This was the first season for college ball in which the scoring values were virtually the same as today, except for the 2-point conversion, instituted in 1958.

St. Viator had the misfortune to field a team that was both smaller and slower, losing 116-7. Sheer speed accounted for 19 Fighting Irish touchdowns, with Berger garnering five, sub Curly Nowers four, and Eichenlaub and Eddie Duggan three each; the rest were sprinkled among the masses. The tradition of botching conversion kicks in routs continued; Notre Dame made only seven of 19.

Marks opted to slug it out with Adrian College, a much larger, more physical team, in a display of old-

The 1912 football team. First row: Harvat, Finegan, Gushurst; second row: Jones, Pliska, Rockne, Dorais (Capt.), Crowley, Lathrop, Feeney; top row; Fitzgerald, Yund, Banbar (manager), Cotter (manager), Coach Marks, Berger, Eichenlaub.

fashioned straight football. The Irish enjoyed the anachronism, winning 74-7. Berger and Pliska got four touchdowns each; Dorais booted eight conversions and consistently put the Fighting Irish in excellent field position with brilliant punt returns.

Morris Harvey, from West Virginia, put up a good fight before bowing 39-0. Eichenlaub stunned them with a 50-yard touchdown sprint in the first minute, but they played well for a long time after that. All the Notre Dame backs scored, but not in bunches.

Wabash was next; they had pulverized a good DePauw team where Indiana and Purdue had not, so Fighting Irish fans were buzzing about the implications. It ended in a 41-6 Notre Dame win and indicated the end of mythical intrastate championships. Still, Wabash played well until the third quarter. Notre Dame's Freeman Fitzgerald broke it open when he grabbed a risky Wabash pass and scored. Eichenlaub scored twice to lead the Irish, and a long pass earned the final Irish touchdown.

If Notre Dame was to be a national force, it needed to beat Pitt on the road. It did, but only on Dorais' fourth quarter field goal for a 3-0 final score. A similar Pitt kick just missed. Rockne helped the cause with a 33-yard pass play from Dorais.

St. Louis fell easily 47-7. (Ironically, St. Louis, under coach Eddie Cochems, had showcased the passing game for easy wins in 1906.) It couldn't stop Eichenlaub's runs, and Berger executed a perfect stiff arm on a defensive back on his way to an 85-yard score. Pliska chipped in three touchdowns, and Dorais hit five conversions and two field goals.

Tired of ties with Marquette, the Fighting Irish exploded for 69 unanswered points to end the season. Dorais set the tone early when he smashed his 145 pounds into, through, and over seven potential tacklers during an 80-yard touchdown run. Eichenlaub dragged four opponents for the better part of 70 yards before the mud slid him to a stop, but he scored four touchdowns for the day anyway.

The rout completed Notre Dame's first unblemished season since the one-game 1889 season and showed that the Fighting Irish could play good teams outside the midwest and beat them.

Marks compiled an impressive two-year record of 13 wins and two ties as the Fighting Irish piled up 611 points to 36. The average score under Marks was almost 41 to 2. He can be credited with initiating the trademark Notre Dame blend of speed, quickness, and passing that would come to full fruition under Harper and Rockne.

1912 record: 7-0-0 (1.000)
Record to date: 113-31-13 (.761)

1913

Any Fighting Irish fan knows about this year—it is the stuff of legends. Jesse Harper, the former

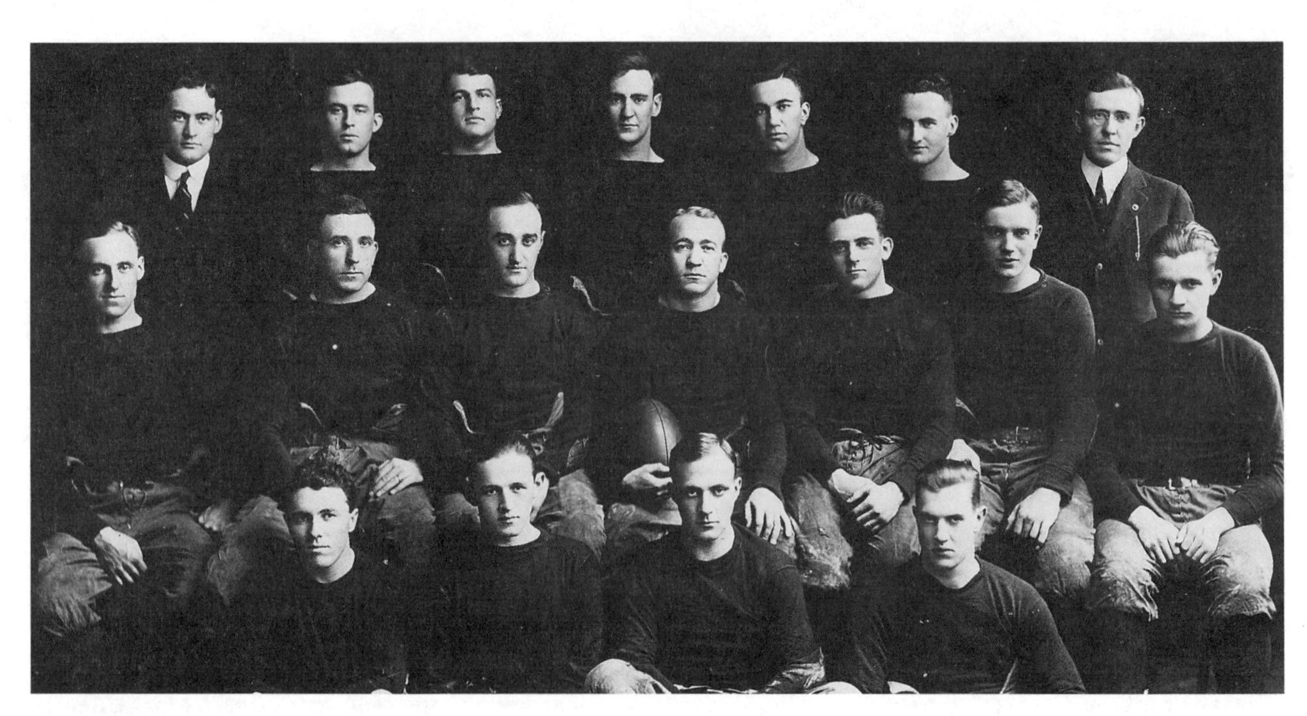

The 1913 team: conquerors of Army.

Wabash coach, was a son of the midwest, from Pawpaw, Illinois. He played for Stagg at Chicago in 1902 and 1905, subbing at quarterback for Rockne's boyhood hero, Walter Eckersall. He also played for Stagg's baseball team. He first coached at Alma, losing only three football games in 4 years. His 1907 baseball team won the state championship, beating Michigan to do it. His best year at Wabash was 1910, when he was undefeated with four shutouts before a player died in the St. Louis game. He beat Purdue three times in four tries. Notre Dame wanted him for his obvious coaching skills but also for his keen business acumen since the Fighting Irish were launching themselves on the national scene with Penn State and Texas. Army was substituted for a cancelled opponent. This was the beginning of the national scheduling that Rockne would insist on a decade later.

Ohio Northern came up short again, 87-0. Eichenlaub scored four touchdowns and Pliska three more. Rockne tore rib cartilage and was out early. Then a scrappy South Dakota team showed up, bold enough to score within the first minute. They played a tight, containing defense, but were vulnerable to Dorais' passing, which made them spread out a little, which then made them easy prey for Eichenlaub's smashes—in other words, modern football. The later win over Army got all the credit for ushering in the era of "modern football," but Notre Dame beat South Dakota 20-7 with an integrated passing and running attack that befuddled the defense. Eichenlaub responded to the South Dakota score, then Dorais hit two field goals before throwing a pass to Curly Nowers for a 40-yard touchdown to end the scoring.

Alma fell next, 62-0, on good, fundamental, patient drives, killing time as much as gaining ground. Rockne, who had missed the previous game, was back to make a nuisance of himself—good defense, solid blocking, an occasional run, and his patented pass receptions caught on a dead run. Al Feeney somehow intercepted three passes from the center (nose guard) position. Pliska scored three times, Eichenlaub twice, and Dorais returned a punt 65 yards to score.

On Thursday, October 30, the team left on a train for its first trip to the eastern seaboard, to West Point. The Cadets were spurned by other eastern teams because some of their players had already graduated elsewhere. While the Army was willing to play the Fighting Irish, they were not overwhelmed by the prospect. No top-notch sports writers were assigned to the game. One New York paper had Notre Dame coming from South Bend, Illinois. Just another game.

But cadet Omar Bradley saw something strange the evening before the game—the Notre Dame play-

The completion of one of the startling "Dorais to Rockne" passes which beat the Army in 1913 and modified the entire game of football. Here's Knute making a touchdown.

The completion of one of the startling "Dorais to Rockne" touchdown passes that beat Army in 1913 and modified the entire game of football.

ers were doing some sort of running with and juggling of the football; it was hard to tell. He failed to report the intelligence, however, unless he mentioned it privately to injured Army punter Dwight Eisenhower. What he had seen was the Fighting Irish practicing their passing game.

Army went into the game undefeated, having beaten Stevens 34-0, Colgate 7-6, and Tufts 2-0. Myth has it that Army simply thought it had the game won by showing up, but respect was closer to what they felt; they still did not know a great deal about Notre Dame.

The first Fighting Irish score came on an 85-yard drive, keyed by passes from Dorais to Pliska for 30 yards, Dorais to Rockne for 35 yards, to Rockne for 10 yards, and capped by Pliska's 5-yard touchdown run. Army scored twice in the second quarter using "straight" football tactics. Dorais fired a 25-yarder to Rockne for a score. The last play of the first half found Dorais and his center on one side of the field with all the others on the opposite side. Dorais threw long to Rockne, but it was intercepted. Notre Dame led 14-13 at halftime. In the third quarter, Dorais missed a 45-yard field goal try, and the Cadets threatened with a drive to the Notre Dame 2. Rockne got under the runner, flipped him to a stop, and then assisted with a sack on the next play to set up a Dorais interception of an Army pass for a touchback. The Irish steamed back into a drive ended by an Eichenlaub touchdown burst. Army stalled. Then it was Pliska's turn—a 30-yard run to their 5-yard line, and a pass from Dorais for the score. Thoroughly baffled, the Cadet defense surrendered an insurance touchdown to Eichenlaub to end the game: Notre Dame 35, Army 13. Midwest football had arrived in the east with a vengeance; the same day Michigan blasted Syracuse 43-7. And Colgate beat Yale 16-6 (remember, Army had already beaten Colgate). Dorais hit 14 of 17 throws for 243 yards and two touchdowns, one to Rockne and one to Pliska.

The Irish then faced a Penn State team that had not lost at home since 1894. Notre Dame pulled off another "upset" by a 14-7 margin. Penn State threatened first with a field goal after recovering a fumble, but it was blocked. Dorais set to work: a 40-yard strike to Pliska, a quarterback keeper for 35 yards, and a short touchdown pass to Rockne to conclude the three-play drive. Harper killed the third quarter using Eichenlaub for three-fourths of the ground game before his touchdown put the game out of reach.

The Irish headed towards Texas but stopped for a courtesy game with Christian Brothers in St. Louis. Harper used his substitutes. The field was wet; the Brothers took a 7-0 lead. Send in the regulars, Harper said, but they weren't in synch either. Finally, Eichenlaub scored; Dorais dashed 65 yards to score on a punt return and again on a 40-yard end run for a 20-7 win.

More rain awaited the Fighting Irish in Texas, but they won 30-7. Dorais called a beautiful game, directing the runners to 248 yards gained on 77 time-consuming carries, while booting three field goals. He connected on 10 of 21 passes for 200 yards (Texas hit two of six). The first score confused Texas when Dorais faked a pass and ran 15 yards for a touchdown. Eichenlaub shrugged off some Texans from their 2-yard line for a touchdown, and Rupe Mills intercepted a terrible Texas pass and dashed to the end zone.

Surely, this season surpassed Harper's fondest hopes. Eichenlaub and Dorais made All-American teams and Rockne got Camp's attention as a third-team All-American.

1913 record: 7-0-0 (1.000)
Record to date: 120-31-13 (.771)

1914

The 1913 season was a hard act to follow. Notre Dame had not tasted defeat since 1910. The class that played with Rockne and Dorais had a marvelous career: 24 wins, one loss, and three ties (a .910 winning percentage). The Fighting Irish had grown from a state and regional power to a position of modest national prominence. Notre Dame consciously tried to schedule eastern teams—Army, Syracuse, and Yale—for 1914.

The season started with the expected rout of Alma, 56-0. Harper kept out Eichenlaub and played straight football, using only two passes, one for a touchdown. Pliska racked up three touchdowns: 50 yards up the middle, another 50 around end, and a punt return for 65 yards. Kelleher snagged a touchdown pass, and Cofall added two more.

More conservative football smashed Rose Poly 103-0. It was a blocking clinic; Irish ball carriers literally had nobody to run over, by, or around. The starters played briefly, and the second unit gave the Fighting Irish a second-half cushion of 75 points. Cofall scored four touchdowns, Kelleher three, and Bergman, Finegan, Duggan, and John Miller two each.

Harper worked the team hard the week of the Yale game; Tuesday's practice ran six hours. He took

Stan Cofall, the first of a long series of All-American left halfbacks for the Fighting Irish.

23 players to New Haven, but the game did not live up to its advance notices. Too much may have been expected of the Fighting Irish, and Yale was splendidly prepared. The Elis used a new weapon—lateral passes—and Notre Dame had not expected that twist. They started well with five first-quarter first downs to none for Yale, but both teams muffed the ball too much. Then Yale opened up with a triple pass for a 13-yard gain. Yale's first score came on a backward pass and a circle route around Notre Dame's left end. Eichenlaub started to punish the Elis, but Notre Dame had not scored when the half ended, although they reached the Yale 3. The field was getting soggy; Yale scored on a 32-yard run with Fighting Irish tacklers slipping and missing. Harper opened up the passing game but Yale intercepted. In the fourth quarter, Bergman drove the Irish to the Yale 2, but an illegal substitution killed the drive. Yale won 28-0. The Irish had 16 first downs to Yale's 15, completed six passes (Dorais was missed), and struck deep into Yale territory often enough to have kept the pressure on Yale. Eichenlaub had two 40-yard runs, and Bergman was a one-man drive with 55 yards on two carries. The glum Irish returned to the campus to be met by their mates—classes had been cancelled to welcome them back, thus starting the tradition of cheering the team after a tough loss.

Feisty South Dakota was next, holding the Fighting Irish scoreless for the first half. The team finally pulled out of the doldrums, scoring 33 unanswered points. Cofall scored the first touchdown on a run and passed to Harry Baujan for another. Bergman scored twice and Pliska once.

A tough Haskell squad from Nebraska fought hard before losing 20-7. Their star halfback, Richards, carried 11 consecutive times for 75 yards on a desperate second half drive. Although they did not score, they earned a great measure of respect. Bergman used a double pass for Notre Dame's first touchdown, then sped 85 and 80 yards with punts in the second half to end the scoring. Although Notre Dame won, observers thought that the line play had slipped since the Alma game, and Army was up next.

Against Army, the Irish developed "fumbleitis"—on Army's first punt. Bergman booted it, and Army recovered on the Notre Dame 15-yard line to lead to an easy touchdown. In the third quarter, Cofall and Pliska teamed up on a drive that ended with Cofall's 1-yard plunge for their only score. Army won 20-7 and was bidding for another score at the end when the Fighting Irish stopped them at the 1.

Eichenlaub came back against Carlisle in Chicago's Comiskey Park after missing a month of play probably due to injury, and Notre Dame rolled 48-6. There were some stunning plays: Bergman sprinted 50 yards after a fumbled punt; Cofall punted for 90 yards; a triple pass set up a 30-yard touchdown run by Bunny Larkin. Pliska scored twice on long runs.

The Fighting Irish downed the Syracuse Orangemen 20-0. Syracuse had beaten Michigan; it was a huge team by 1914 standards—210 pounds across the line—but they wilted rapidly under Eichenlaub's insistent hammering. Cofall, Bergman, and Finegan were the scorers.

The year's two losses in the east rankled, but they weren't blowouts. Perhaps too much was expected too soon.

1914 record: 6-2-0 (.750)
Record to date: 126-33-13 (.770)

1915

Harper had a good core to work with for the new campaign. The line would be the largest since Dimmick and Philbrook were there. Younger brothers Bergman and Miller (Arthur and Walter) arrived. Bergman

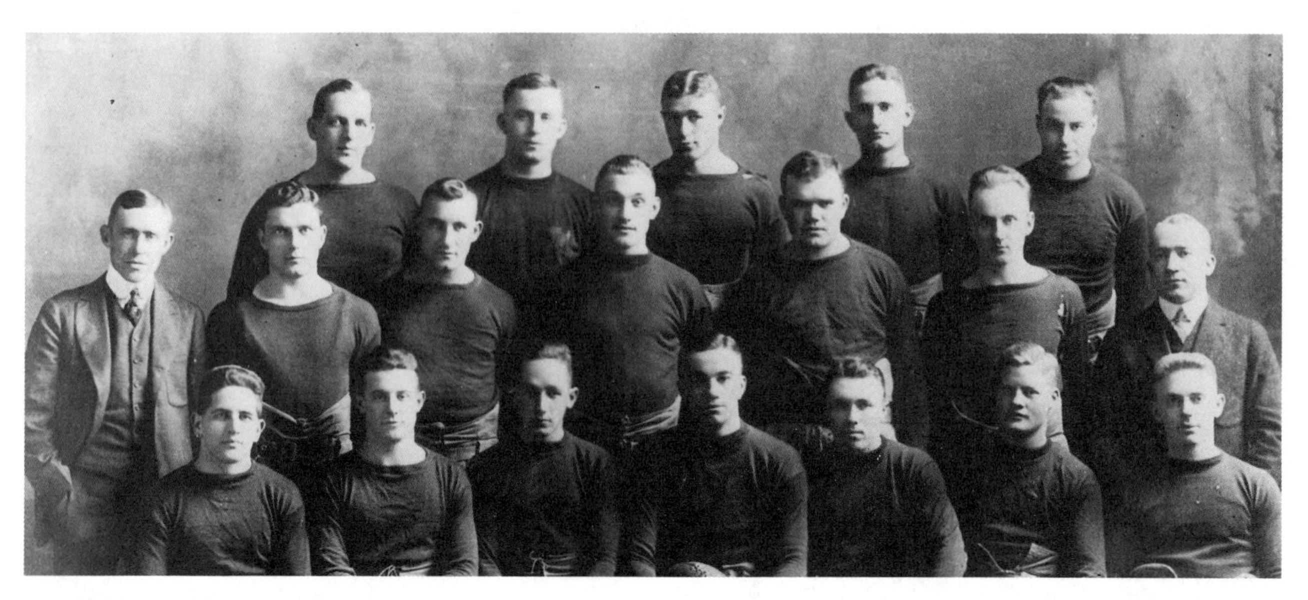

The 1915 Notre Dame monogram winners.

took over the important left halfback position (which would be the key position for the Irish offense for the next quarter century). Cartier Field, in use until about 1930, was improved by adding practice fields for the freshman and varsity, saving the main field from overuse.

Alma was the opener and made its best showing in South Bend in a 32-0 loss. The halftime score was a surprising 13-0, and the third quarter yielded only one Fighting Irish touchdown on a tough drive. Harper sent in his reserves in the fourth quarter; they scored two quick touchdowns.

Everyone remembered Haskell from the year before. Harper moved Jim Phelan to starting quarterback, and Rockne worked the line hard after a mediocre showing against Alma. On the first drive, Phelan ran the kickoff to the 40, Cofall zipped around right end for 20, Bergman went left for 10, Bachman punched through the middle for 10, and then Cofall turned right end for the score. Haskell soon had to punt, and Bachman sped 60 yards with the kick for another quick touchdown, breaking six tackles. Cofall added another touchdown later, and Bergman roared for a 50-yard touchdown on a punt. Reserves held on for a 34-0 shutout.

The Irish went to Nebraska to meet the powerful Cornhuskers, undefeated for three seasons. Notre Dame lost 20-19 in a great game with a big Nebraska team using a modest passing game (five completions in eight attempts), as an instrumental part of three touchdown drives. Notre Dame had several good drives finished off by penalties. Baujan scored what would have been the winning touchdown after chasing a loose ball on a punt, but one official "did not see" the play, and another claimed the whistle stopped play when the receiver touched the ball. A missed conversion after Notre Dame's first score also hurt badly. Cofall scored the first two touchdowns and Bergman the third, but that conversion was missed as well.

The loss lingered as a factor in the next game, a 6-0 Fighting Irish win over perennially tough South Dakota. The Coyotes played dead even with Notre Dame in the first half. In the second half, Bergman scored the only touchdown on a criss-cross play.

Army was next, and they were not having a good year. Notre Dame barely sneaked out of town with a Hudson River cliffhanger, 7-0. The score came on a 50-yard pass from Cofall to Bergman in the final moments. Army almost scored with a field goal try, but it hit the crossbar and fell back on the field. The Irish missed three field goals and had just two completed passes in seven attempts for 73 yards and the touchdown. The running game was strong with 261 yards to Army's 75.

Red Miller was now coaching at Creighton, but his team was no match for Notre Dame, losing 41-0. Cofall scored twice, once with a lateral pass from Bachman. Phelan also scored twice, and Bergman and Bachman each scored. Notre Dame racked up 25 first downs to eight, and nine backs tromped 468 yards to 174 for Creighton.

After seeing the Illinois-Chicago game on their off day, the Irish went to Texas for two games. The Longhorns lost four fumbles on the way to a 36-7 loss. Their lone score came when someone fell on a loose ball in the end zone. Bergman took scoring honors for

Notre Dame with two touchdowns, one from 75 yards out. Cofall, Bachman, and Malone each scored. The Fighting Irish hammered the middle of the Texas line on 14 plunges for 147 yards. But the real story was in 42 trips around the ends for 315 yards.

Two days later, Notre Dame dismantled the Rice Owls 55-2. The deluge came in the second half after Rice played respectably to a 14-2 halftime disadvantage. But in the second half, Cofall returned a kickoff 90 yards for a touchdown; on the next series, he capped it with a 30-yard scoring jaunt. Bergman scored on his favorite play, a double pass from 20 yards out. Cofall got his third score of the quarter scooting around end for 7 yards. Bachman and Keefe also scored, the latter when he started a Fighting Irish drive with a recovered fumble and finished when he recovered a fumble for a touchdown.

Only two missed conversions and a disputed touchdown kept Notre Dame from enjoying its third undefeated season in four years. Nebraska joined Army as a major rival.

1915 record: 7-1-0 (.875)
Record to date: 133-34-13 (.775)

George Gipp—the best of the best.

1916

A Notre Dame baseball player, Dolly Gray, enters the picture now. During the summer of 1916 in upstate Michigan, he gave a good sales talk about the university to a friend by the name of George Gipp from Laurium. Gipp borrowed the money for the train ride to South Bend, but he seemed to be having some trouble coming to terms with his new environment. He would start something and quit—interhall football, basketball, baseball (Notre Dame had a full team for each of its dorms). He was 20 years old, but still liked to play games, perhaps to break up the monotony of the classes he had never excelled in as a teenager. He'd grab an acquaintance (few were close enough to be his friend) and go out to one of the open spaces to kick the ball around.

Like 1913, this is the stuff of legends. As the story goes, Rockne was on his way to practice when he saw a guy dropkick a ball for 70 or 80 yards at a time. Rockne introduced himself, and a diffident Gipp was not impressed. Yet Gipp took up Rockne's challenge and played a little ball for Notre Dame. In so doing, Gipp's short life, little more than a thousand days under the Dome, would enter American culture and sports immortality. In his freshman year, he would stun his coaches and fellow players. In a freshman game against Western Normal (now Western Michigan), on his own 45 and with instructions to punt, he drop-kicked a 62-yard field goal instead. This was typical of the man—a player who loved the challenges found on the gridiron, willing to take almost any legal route to victory, but who was also utterly uncaring about the whole deal. More about Gipp later.

Harper had a team with several legitimate All-American candidates. Even his substitutes were talented and would fill starting positions soon. In Gipp's class was another older fellow, Chet Grant, a speedster at quarterback who would be involved with Notre Dame for nearly three-quarters of a century. The schedule was not very demanding, especially since Western Conference teams (now Big 10) were not scheduling games with the Irish. None of them had met Notre Dame since 1909—the year Yost's Michigan team lost.

Case Tech was pummeled 48-0. Grant, nervous in his first game, made the mistake of fielding a punt on his 5-yard line and then having to look for help—a zig here, a zig there—find some blockers, up this sideline, one guy to beat (Baujan got him), and a 95-

Jesse Harper as athletic director.

yard touchdown for the record books. Western Reserve met an identical fate, 48-0. But these blowouts were costly in terms of injuries: Miller, Grover Malone, Bergman, and Cofall.

Haskell was up next. The Native Americans playing for their college fought brilliantly, but sheer talent overwhelmed them 26-0. Then Wabash, who a few seasons earlier had been in the picture with the bigger schools of the state, was obliterated by Notre Dame. Rockne's pre-game pep talk, as it was recalled, urged the team to "go out there and kill 'em, crucify 'em." Fortunately for Wabash, they stopped short of that, 60-0. Nine touchdowns came on end runs and tackle smashes. Cofall got a touchdown from his 40-yard line on the first play. Harper pulled his starters in the second quarter, but put them back in when it looked like Wabash would hold on for a 39-0 loss. At the half, three former Irish greats (Dorais, Art Bergman, and Pliska) toured the field in a car driven by the senior class president, Royal Bosshard. Three more touchdowns ended the affair. The referee for the game was Guernsey Van Riper, who would later write *Knute Rockne: Young Athlete.*

Notre Dame now faced Army. The Cadets featured Elmer Oliphant, the former Purdue star, who was big, fast, daring, and a fine passer. The Irish played well in the first half, down only 6-3, but then the sky fell. Oliphant passed for three touchdowns and kicked two field goals for a 30-10 triumph. Bergman got Notre Dame's lone touchdown. Reporters thought the Fighting Irish the better team in all phases, except passing.

Notre Dame blanked South Dakota 21-0. Then they went to East Lansing to meet Michigan Agricultural College, who had not been on their schedule for six years. The Fighting Irish won 14-0, with Cofall scoring twice to avenge the 1910 loss. (MAC was not in the Western Conference then.) Alma lost 46-0; the Fighting Irish were tuning up for the grudge match with Nebraska.

In Lincoln, Notre Dame got the 20 points it so badly wanted in 1915, and left the Huskers scoreless. Bergman got the first score on a 55-yard run that saw him break into the secondary with no less than four blockers still with him. In the second quarter, Baujan emerged from a pileup on a busted punt to score from the 22. John Miller wrapped it up with a 55-yard touchdown strike to Bergman. The Fighting Irish defense broke up nine of Nebraska's 10 passes, the other fell incomplete. Notre Dame garnered 11 first downs to Nebraska's four. The Huskers ran for 89 yards to Notre Dame's 324. The Fighting Irish held the Huskers to only 7 yards running in the second quarter and to only 6 in the fourth. This was the eighth Irish shutout in nine games this year.

Cofall, Bachman, and Slip Madigan, a reserve, made All-American honors. Arnold McInerney and Frank Rydzewski achieved All-Western accolades. And the best player on the team had not even played for the varsity. He would, though, in 1917 . . . George Gipp.

1916 record: 8-1-0 (.888)
Record to date: 141-35-13 (.780)

1917

This would be Harper's last season at Notre Dame. The war was making inroads into the team's personnel, and Harper would be hard pressed to match the stunning 1916 results. Talented sophomores would have some impact: the gangly, indifferent Gipp and Pete Bahan would replace departed starters in the backfield. Dave Philbin filled the spot vacated by Arnold McInerney, who had joined the Army (and would later be killed in France). A brace of smallish guards, Madigan and Clyde Zoia, averaging 159 pounds, showed Rockne's emerging influence on line play.

Kalamazoo was first on the Notre Dame schedule, losing 55-0, Notre Dame's fifth straight shutout. Bahan ran 75 yards for a touchdown on the season's first play from scrimmage. When the dust settled, Phelan and Bahan led the rout with three touchdowns each.

After defeating Kalamazoo, the Irish travelled to Wisconsin. (The Irish were now both wanted and unwanted by the Western Conference—wanted as opponents, unwanted as a member due to philosophical differences-i.e. Notre Dame was not academically oriented, too interested in sports). The game ended in a 0-0 tie, the sixth straight shutout for Notre Dame. The Badgers missed four field goals. Phelan's try hit the left upright and fell the wrong way. It was a tight game.

Then a rematch with Nebraska, who enjoyed a 15-pound advantage per man on the line, and had eight returning starters to Notre Dame's two. They won 7-0, although the Irish almost scored on a drive to their 10-yard line. Quarterback Phelan played the whole game knowing he belonged to the Army an hour after the game, yet observers said it was his best game ever directing the attack, and he played demonic defense. Gipp made his first appearance for the Fighting Irish, carrying 15 times for 31 yards but returning five punts for 69 yards.

Harper rested his starting interior linemen in a 40-0 blitz of South Dakota. Gipp flew 40 yards on the first play to set up the first score, then Walter Miller dashed 40 for the tally. Tom Spalding received a double pass—quarterback Tex Allison to Gipp to Spalding—for a touchdown. Three more touchdowns ended the show. Gipp's second game for Notre Dame was his first over the 100-yard mark—24 carries for 110 yards.

Notre Dame and Army had split four games previously; this one would be for bragging rights. Army practiced diligently to stop the expected aerial game. Harper gave them off-tackle plays instead, mixed with short passes to keep them off balance. Joe Brandy scored the game's only touchdown on a 7-yard run to end a drive he had started on his 23 with an interception. Gipp set up his score with a 13-yard run from the 20. Army was held to eight first downs, five in a furious fourth quarter. Brandy and Philbin recovered late fumbles to save the win. The 11 Irish starters never saw a substitute the entire game. Gipp punted 11 times, a sign of the game's defensive intensity.

Gipp broke his left leg against Morningside the next week after a 35-yard gain; a tired, crippled Notre Dame squad escaped with a 13-0 win. Rydzewski speared an interception and ran 40 yards for a touchdown to go with one earned later via passing. But the Fighting Irish were hurting.

Against Michigan Agricultural College, Notre Dame suffered more injuries—right guard Basil Stanley broke a leg, and quarterback Allison strained his back. Irish numbers were thinning quickly. When Allison went down, the passing game stopped too. Clipper Smith moved from right half to fullback and scored a touchdown on a 10-yard bolt up the middle; Bahan and Barry both scored 50-yard touchdowns to lead Notre Dame to a 23-0 win. Rydzewski, upon returning to South Bend, received a silver loving cup from proud Polish fathers.

An exhausted squad went east to play Washington and Jefferson. Brandy's 45-yard field goal ended the scoring for a 3-0 win.

Massive injuries and military call ups made this season a difficult one to coach. But Harper got his men to produce four more shutouts (17 in his last 25 games). They were only a handful of points from another undefeated season.

1917 record: 6-1-1 (.812)
Record to date: 147-36-14 (.781)

1918

The death of a relative forced Harper to take over the family ranch near Sitka, Kansas. He made sure that his choice for the vacated position would get the job—Knute Rockne. He had taken a team poised for success beyond its wildest dreams, and he left it in extremely capable hands.

Harper's fate was inextricably bound up with Rockne's, both as the man he coached to modest stardom in his senior year, as his coaching mentor for four years, and as the man who would be asked to fill the athletic director's job following Rockne's death on March 31, 1931. It was perhaps fitting that his 30,000-acre ranch was less than 100 miles from the isolated hilltop near Bazaar, Kansas, where Rockne died in an airplane crash. Of Fighting Irish coaches with more than five seasons on the job, Harper's .863 winning percentage places him second only to Rockne, ahead of Leahy's .855 and Parseghian's .836. In 40 games, he won 34, and shutout the opponents 25 times.

Knute Rockne—there is no greater name in Fighting Irish football. The man's background is as

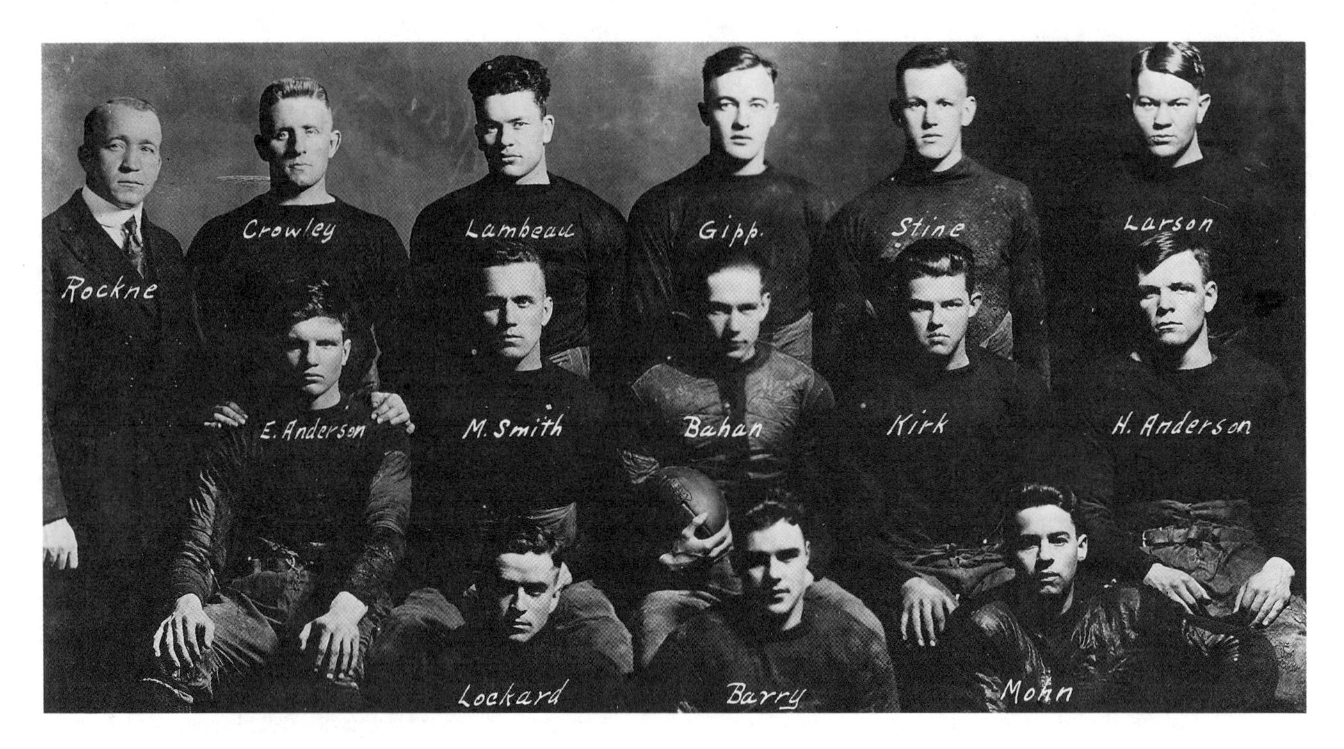

The 1918 Notre Dame war-depleted team.

unbelievable as his coaching record was impressive: a Norwegian immigrant...grew up in a tough Chicago neighborhood...learned his new culture mostly through street and sandlot games...never graduated from high school because he was caught skipping school to practice track...worked for the U.S. Post Office for five years to save money for college...passed an entrance exam for Notre Dame and threw himself into the strange life of an overage undergraduate...sports (football, track)...campus theater, music...life of a hustler (pool, boxing) to make ends meet...brilliant student in chemistry and pharmacology...All-American football player...learned lots about good and bad coaching...magna cum laude graduate 1914...matriculated in medical school in St. Louis in 1914, but they would not let him work to cover expenses...returned to Notre Dame, now married, and a flip of the coin sent Dorais to Iowa and kept Rockne under the Dome...taught chemistry, coached football and track...learned how to temper himself under the calming influence of Harper. Horatio Alger could not have created a more interesting fictional life. He loved Notre Dame. He never left the place...to this day.

The Fighting Irish of 1918 had almost nothing to fight with or against. The war had taken scores of the best athletes. The schedule was curtailed to six games. But there were some impressive players on hand: Gipp, freshman guard Heartley "Hunk" Anderson (Grantland Rice later called him "the toughest man, pound for pound, I have ever known"), Clipper Smith, Eddie Anderson, Bahan, Lambeau from Green Bay, and Norm Barry.

The Fighting Irish opened away from home for the first time in 20 years, at Case Tech. Notre Dame was down 6-0 in the early going, so Rockne sent in Bahan and Gipp to spark matters. They did, and Curly Lambeau scored the first touchdown of the Rockne era at Notre Dame. Rockne probably gave them an earful at the half, because in the second half, Gipp shifted into high gear to score two touchdowns, gained 88 yards on the ground, and hit five of 12 passes for another 101 yards for a 26-6 win.

October went by without a game. Rock tried to schedule a game with Municipal Pier, but it was cancelled by medical authorities because of the influenza epidemic that was killing tens of thousands of people across the country. Practices were cancelled. Then a game with Camp Custer was cancelled. Rockne scrimmaged the varsity against the freshmen, loaning the freshman team Gipp, Bahan, and himself, and they tied it 7-7 with a Gipp fumble.

The Fighting Irish mangled Wabash 67-7. It was a spur-of-the-moment game; no one knew until Friday night that there would be a Saturday game. The team left at 4:00 am Saturday. Bahan, Lambeau, and Gipp each scored two touchdowns and the subs did the rest. Gipp racked up his second game with century-mark running, 119 yards on 16 rushes. With government permission, the team stayed overnight in Crawfordsville.

Refamiliarized with winning, they faced a formidable Great Lakes Naval squad loaded with good players—Paddy O'Driscoll, George Halas, and Notre Dame's erstwhile Bachman. The papers made it out to be a hopeless case for the college boys, but Rockne willed a 7-7 tie. The touchdown was scored by Bill Mohn after some great running by the other backs. Gipp missed a 40-yard field goal, carried 15 times for 69 yards, hit two of seven passes, and punted eight times.

A truly sloppy field and injuries to Bahan and Gipp took away whatever advantages Notre Dame might have had over Michigan Agricultural College; the Aggies won 13-7. This was followed by another road trip (only one home game all year) to Purdue. The Fighting Irish were banged up, tired, sick, and coming off an upset defeat. The broken blood vessel from the MAC game in Gipp's face had healed enough for him to play; he led the team with 137 yards on 19 carries for two touchdowns, and he kicked a point after with his bad leg. He sped up a drive at the end with two runs covering 37 yards for his first score, then later passed for 22 yards twice, the second for a score to Bernie Kirk, and capped his day with racking up almost all of the yardage from the Notre Dame 20 for a score. Mohn returned a 73-yard punt for a touchdown. Gipp led the way, though, and he played the game hurt.

The season was wrapped up at Nebraska, also on a sloppy field. Notre Dame garnered 12 first downs to 0. Nebraska also scored no points. Unfortunately, neither did the Irish. The Fighting Irish had a score disallowed by a referee who claimed Lambeau helped Barry with his belt, then a whistle stopped a pass play at the Husker 8. Gipp played heroically with 15 carries for 76 yards, four completions in nine throws for 65 yards, a kickoff return of 40 yards, and 12 punts.

Rockne's first season was not overtly the stuff of legends, but it was an incredible coaching job in the face of nearly insurmountable problems—the war, the flu epidemic, injuries, horrible weather, and all-star teams.

1918 record: 3-1-2 (.571)
Record to date: 150-37-16 (.778)

1919

After the trials of 1918, Rockne must have been pleased to see the return of his war vets: Walter Miller, Dutch Bergman, Grover Malone, Slip Madigan, Frank Coughlin, and Cy DeGree. Their return duplicated

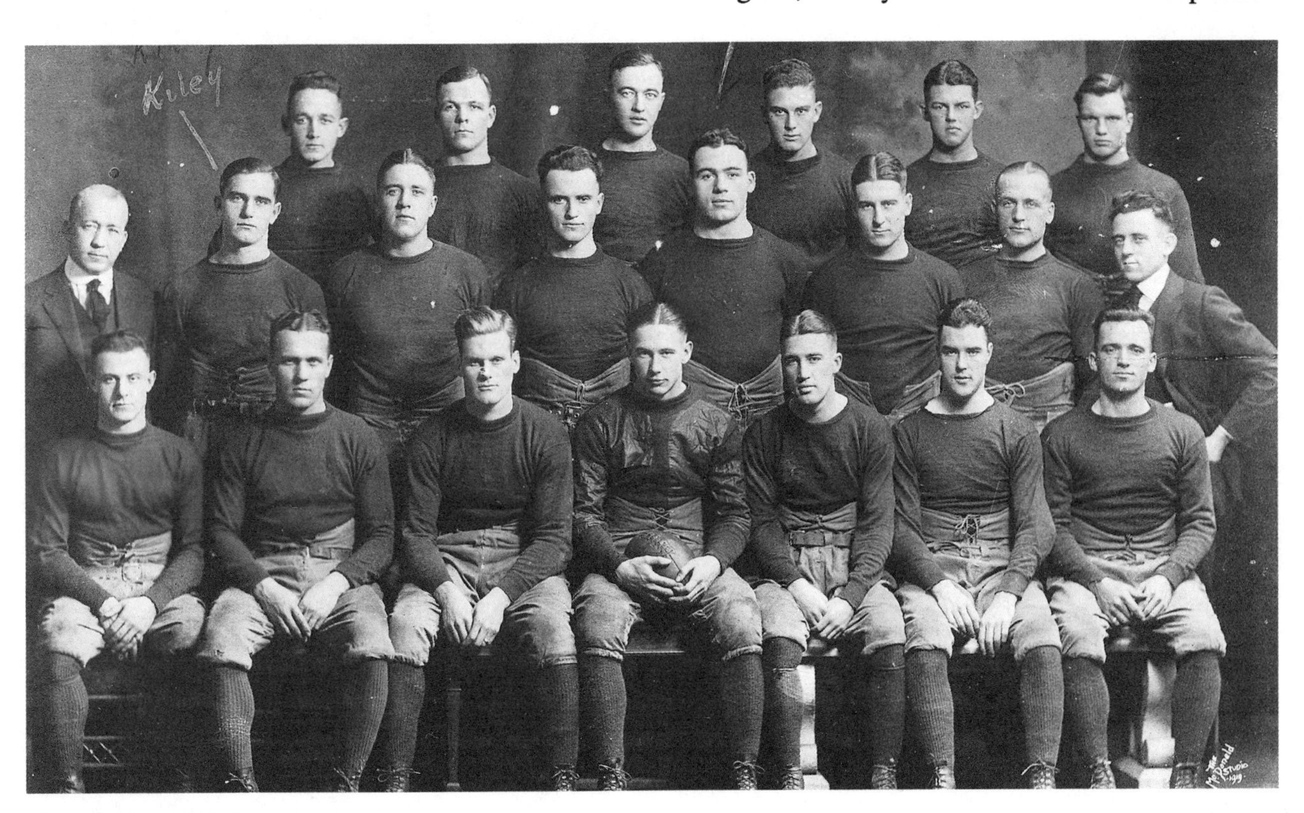

The undefeated 1919 team.

what the great post-war Leahy teams enjoyed—a sudden infusion of mature talent from previous squads. The end result would be two consecutive undefeated teams. In essence, Rockne had the heart of the great 1916 team again. Add them to the 1918 starters—Gipp, Hunk Anderson, Eddie Anderson, and Pete Bahan—and there was the making of an awesome football team that would lose only one game in the next 28.

Half of the 1919 schedule was composed of major or emerging powers (Nebraska, Army, Purdue, Indiana, and Michigan Agricultural College), and the rest were pretty good teams. Kalamazoo fell first 14-0. Gipp lost touchdown runs of 80 and 68 yards because of tight calls by the referees. (After his second futile run, he told the referees to give him two whistles as a sign to keep running, one whistle to stop.) He still managed to rush for 148 yards. Bergman scored on a 55-yarder.

The defending champs of Ohio, Mt. Union, played the Fighting Irish to a 7-7 first-quarter tie. Then Gipp ran for two touchdowns on identical runs of 30 yards, threw two passes for 49 yards, added another 63 yards in incidental rushing, and raced 56 yards on two kickoff returns. All ambulatory backs scored: Bergman, Fritz Slackford, Phelan, Malone, John Mohardt, Cy Kasper, and Earl Walsh, as Notre Dame won 60-7.

Nebraska knew all about Gipp's running, and prepared for it, but they had not counted on his other talents. Bergman had the play of the day in the first Fighting Irish series with a 90-yard touchdown run on a lateral pass. Guess who tossed the lateral? Gipp also completed five of eight passes, good for 124 yards, all on a wet field. The Huskers tied it, so Gipp took charge with his passing in the third quarter: he hit Bergman with a 33-yard gain, then Kirk for 20 more to the 16-yard line, then he ran for 5, passed to Kirk for 10 more, but the drive stopped there. Nebraska punted out of trouble, and Gipp started again. He passed to Bergman who ran 45 yards, Miller ran for 4 on a criss-cross, and Gipp passed for 5 yards to Bergman to set up Bahan's 1-yard dive for the winning touchdown. Near the end of the game, a Husker drop-kicked a field goal for a 14-9 Irish win.

The Irish then beat Western Normal, recent winners over Michigan Agricultural College, 53-0. Malone scored first, and Gipp twice in the first quarter, then Brandy and Barry shook loose in the second quarter. It was all subs after that, although Rockne put the starters in for a while, and Bergman went long distance for the final touchdown.

Indiana and Notre Dame met in Indianapolis in rain and mud. Rockne wanted to save the starters for Army, so most of them didn't play. Gipp played some—82 yards on 18 carries, 57 yards on three of seven passes, and a drop-kicked field goal. Bergman scored the touchdowns for a 16-3 win, but he hurt his knee and didn't go east to Army.

Gipp had to pick up the slack; he rushed for 70 yards and hit seven passes for 115 yards as Notre Dame beat Army 12-9. The Fighting Irish stopped Army several times inside their 5.

Michigan Agricultural College was next—physically a much bigger team—and they even brought a 50-piece marching band with them. The Fighting Irish sent them home with a 13-0 loss, but it was probably too close for Rock's liking. Gipp passed well, ran at will around their ends, and had two interceptions; but Rockne had to come up with a tackle eligible play for Notre Dame's clinching score.

The following week, the Fighting Irish played even with Purdue, in that they beat Purdue by the 20-point margin of 1918, this time 33-13. Purdue scored first, but it was all Notre Dame after that. Gipp completed 11 of 15 passes for 217 yards and two touchdowns to go with those scored on interceptions by Anderson and Trafton.

Gipp had been hurt in the 1918 Morningside game, and it looked bad when they trapped him on the Notre Dame 11 on a busted punt play. Morningside scored, and with Miller and Bahan out it looked gloomy. Gipp took over in the second quarter, orchestrating a long drive that he capped with a 3-yard touchdown burst. In the third quarter, a bad punt gave Notre Dame the ball at Morningside's 10. Gipp probed the left end for a yard, then went back for the rest on the next play. Later he added a 25-yard run and iced the game with an interception. With the win, Notre Dame commanded the west, and only Harvard, at 9-0-1, made noises about the national crown being theirs.

1919 record: 9-0-0 (1.000)
Record to date: 159-37-16 (.787)

1920 to 1929

1920

The 1919 effort showed what a Rockne team could do with a full complement of players; many of those stars returned in 1920. The schedule had a mix of easy marks with traditional tough challenges. Kalamazoo opened and hoped to give the Fighting Irish a second rough go, but Notre Dame was ready. Chet Wynne earned the first score, then Gipp got in the saddle on the third possession, scampering for 30 yards to set up two short runs for a touchdown. In the third quarter he rambled for 30 again, and hit Kiley with a 28-yard pass to set up Norm Barry's touchdown. Paul Castner intercepted a pass to set up Joe Brandy for a touchdown. Reserve Cy Kasper grabbed

The undefeated 1920 national champs.

a fumble and ran 35 yards to set up his own touchdown a little later. The other reserves punched over another score for the 39-0 win. It was Gipp's best game as a runner—183 yards on 16 carries.

Another Michigan team, Western Normal, met a similar fate, 42-0, even though three touchdowns were called back. Gipp mangled their defense for 123 yards, two touchdowns, and three point-after kicks. Mohardt ran for two touchdowns; Phelan had the best touchdown run, a 55-yarder; Castner powered in from 35 yards out; and Brandy returned a punt for a touchdown.

The Fighting Irish moved west for the game with Nebraska. Husker coach Schulte had rested his starters in the Colorado game the week before, barely winning 7-0. At first, the game was a punting duel, until Notre Dame put together a drive to the Husker 2, where it stalled. Following common practice for those days, the Huskers immediately went into a punt

Chet Wynne, two-time starter at fullback in 1920 and 1921.

Action from the 1920 game against Nebraska. Quarterback Brandy has just spun and pitched the ball to Gipp; Castner is getting ready to block in front of Gipp.

formation to kick out of trouble. Buck Shaw blocked the kick out of the end zone for a safety. In the next quarter, two more Fighting Irish drives fizzled. Gipp took command after that, hitting Eddie Anderson with two passes for 60 yards to set up Brandy's 1-yard plunge for the touchdown. Late in the game, Gipp hit Anderson again with a 28-yard pass to set up his own 7-yard touchdown run. Notre Dame won 16-7, but statistically the Huskers dominated: 13 first downs to 6; 550 total yards to 174; 425 yards rushing to 135; 10 of 28 passes for 125 yards to four of 18 for 39 yards. Gipp owned 218 yards of Notre Dame's total offense for the day.

Against in-state foe Valparaiso, Rockne unveiled another pet project: starting the second unit as "shock troops." This let his starters build motivation while assessing the other team's strengths and weaknesses. Rockne liked the inherent suspense. His only requirement was that the subs have a good punter to keep them out of the hole. He'd send in his starters after the first quarter to save the day. Valparaiso took advantage of the move and drove for a field goal and the lead. Castner took his cue and started booming towering punts to avoid trouble. The subs tired, and Rockne sent in the cavalry. Gipp hit Kiley with a 38-yard pass, but his next one was intercepted. In the third quarter, a quick drive ended with a Wynne touchdown, and Gipp scored shortly thereafter. Rock tried a tackle eligible play, on which Gipp hit Coughlin for 32 yards, but the drive failed. Mohardt and Gipp led a two-play drive, with Gipp going in from 25 yards out. Mohardt ended the scoring with a crashing run from the 5-yard line for the 28-3 final score.

Army waited, undefeated. It would be Gipp's finest hour, even though trained observers might have noticed the early stages of the debilitating illnesses that would claim his life in a matter of weeks. (He'd ignored his physician's advice that summer to have his infected tonsils removed; he just wanted to play ball.)

Army recovered an early fumble by Wynne to register the first touchdown, but its two first downs on the drive would be half its total for the game. Notre Dame drove to midfield, but a penalty threatened its momentum. Gipp fired a pass to Kiley, Gipp slanted off tackle, and then he swept end, and Mohardt tied the game. Army punted and the Fighting Irish struck with a 35-yard touchdown pass to Kiley. But Army ran back a Gipp punt 60 yards for a touchdown and used a bad kick for an easy field goal to lead at halftime 17-14. Notre Dame's center, Ojay Larson, had been playing with a dislocated hip and had to leave the game. In the second half, Rockne tried everything, but they still could not buy another score. Finally, in the fourth quarter, Gipp set up a Mohardt touchdown; then he dashed for 50 yards and threw short passes to set up Wynne's 20-yard sideline sprint for a touchdown and a final score of 27-17. Gipp rushed for 150 yards, returned kicks for 207 yards, and passed for 123 more, for a total of 480 yards.

Cover of the program and menu for the dinner honoring the 1920 team.

Cadets who saw him in the showers after the game recalled later that he looked a bit emaciated.

On November 6, Notre Dame enjoyed its first Homecoming against Purdue. Red Salmon was there as an honored guest, and he saw Notre Dame win 28-0. Shock troops (the subs used to start a game until Rock sent in his starters) started and scored when Grant ran 50 yards with a pass. Rock tried to rest a tired Gipp and let him play only briefly, but that was all he needed: he careened through Purdue's team for a 35-yard touchdown, fired passes good for 128 yards to Anderson and Kiley, rushed for 129 yards, and kicked three conversions. Buck Shaw recovered a Barry fumble for a touchdown; and Mohardt stopped a drive late with an interception to preserve the 28-0 shutout. With this win, the Fighting Irish had defeated all intrastate rivals since 1906.

With Notre Dame behind 10-0, the Indiana Hoosiers almost broke that streak. Gipp piled into the Hoosier line for the first Notre Dame score—even though he had a separated shoulder. Later, the Hoosiers stacked their defense at the end of an Irish drive to stop Gipp, only to see Joe Brandy run in the winning touchdown in a 13-10 nail-biter. The wear and tear was showing; Hunk Anderson played the whole game with cracked ribs.

Notre Dame travelled to Chicago for a game with Northwestern, billed by alumni as "George Gipp Day." The day was bitterly cold and Rockne did not want to play his sick star, but the fans chanted for their man. As it turned out, all Notre Dame scoring resulted from the passing game, perhaps a first. Coughlin recovered a fumble deep in Northwestern territory to set up a 5-yard touchdown pass from Brandy to Eddie Anderson. Mohardt, in for Gipp, grabbed a Wildcat pass to set up a Barry touchdown. Danny Coughlin grabbed a fumble, and later intercepted a pass which set up a pass from Mohardt to Anderson for the third score. The crowd got its hero in the fourth quarter. In two plays he threw a long pass to Kiley for a touchdown, and another to Barry for a 25-yard touchdown. In addition to completing five of six passes for 157 yards, Gipp also tried to run back a punt, but his strength was failing him. The papers noted that the respectful Wildcat tacklers brought him down as gently as possible. With that poignant moment, Gipp had played his last game. The Irish won 33-7 before 20,000 people. Gipp stayed in a frigid Chicago an extra day to help an old friend with a punting clinic.

In mid-week, at the team banquet, Gipp left early and checked into a South Bend hospital, where he died three weeks later. There was much mourning following Gipp's passing, including a lights-out memorial on the campus. The team later went to East Lansing for the finale with Michigan Agricultural College. The subs got things rolling as the Fighting Irish won easily 25-0. Danny Coughlin flashed 95 yards with the opening kickoff to score and served notice that Notre Dame meant to finish undefeated. In the third quarter, Paul Castner racked up two touchdowns. And Anderson strolled 25 yards to pay dirt with a blocked punt.

The win assured Notre Dame of its first undisputed National Championship, its first consensus All-American player in Gipp, and the nation its first truly great college football immortal when Gipp died December 14 at the age of 25. Kiley also earned All-American accolades. Rockne, at 32, was on the verge of becoming a national phenomenon.

1920 record: 9-0-0 (1.000)
Record to date: 168-37-16 (.796)

1921

Rockne enjoyed another strong year. His seniors had suffered only one loss in their careers. This was the first attempt at what came to be known as a "suicide schedule"—two easy games followed by nine strong challenges.

The 1921 team— only a field goal away from being Rock's third consecutive undefeated team.

Kalamazoo capitulated 56-0. Chet Wynne won the game on the opening kick with an 80-yard touchdown run. Frank Thomas scored two touchdowns, Wynne another one on a dive play, Mohardt ran for touchdowns on plays covering 39 and 40 yards, Frank Desch—the fastest man for the Irish—tallied a 15-yard touchdown run, and fifth-string quarterback Frank Reese scored twice but one was negated by a penalty. Kalamazoo completed its first pass in the third quarter—for a loss. Fighting Irish defenders caught more of their passes than they did.

DePauw was obliterated 57-10 to complete the tune-up portion of the year. Wynne and Mohardt shared four touchdowns and solos went in the books for Desch, Thomas, Kiley, and Frank Seyfrit.

But Iowa beat them in the next game, 10-7. Statistics are for losers, its said, and this case appears to prove it: 456 total yards for Notre Dame to Iowa's 216; 239 yards on the ground against 206 for Iowa; 227 yards passing to Iowa's 10; and 22 first downs to Iowa's 14. Fighting Irish penalties aided Iowa's touchdown scoring drive in the first quarter and they ended their scoring with a field goal on their second drive. Notre Dame never caught up, though Mohardt hit Kiley for a 50-yard touchdown in the second quarter. Castner was a force, blasting a punt 70 yards and just missing a 50-yard field goal.

The Fighting Irish were not accustomed to coming off a loss. As in 1918, they faced Purdue after a loss, winning this time, 33-0. Notre Dame was invincible in the first half—scoring 30 points and holding Purdue to no first downs. Hunk Anderson scored two touchdowns within three minutes, incredible for a guard in modern football. Anderson's feat came when Eddie Anderson blocked a punt his way, and moments later when Castner's punt was mishandled just as Hunk arrived in the vicinity, and took it 25 yards for the score. Mohardt garnered two more on short runs. Castner hit a late field goal as Rockne used the second half to improve the kicking game, and Seyfrit saved the shutout with his nose while blocking a Purdue field goal try.

Nebraska wanted this game; they had not beaten Notre Dame since 1917. They were frustrated again, 7-0. A poor Husker kick gave the Irish good field position, and Mohardt took it in. In the fourth quarter, Nebraska used an impressive air attack, but the Fighting Irish backs played great defense.

Eddie Anderson, three-year starter at RE from 1919-1921, on two national championship squads, All-American in 1921.

Indiana went down 28-7. After the subs mixed it up early, Rockne sent in the starters, and Coughlin quickly scored from the 3-yard line. An Irish fumble led to a short drive for the Hoosiers and their only score. Mohardt clicked on a series of medium-length passes, and Wynne scored. Coughlin tallied his second touchdown on a 10-yard end run in the fourth quarter. Castner grabbed a Mohardt pass for an 11-yard touchdown. Castner stopped an aroused Hoosier team in the final moments with three interceptions. Such defense had allowed the last three opponents a total of 10 first downs.

Rockne scheduled four games in 14 days, starting with Army. The Fighting Irish passing game was too much for the Cadets in a 28-0 rout. Mohardt fired to Kiley, who ran it in from 47 yards out. Then Mohardt threw a 40-yarder to Wynne. The Cadets backed off a bit to accommodate Notre Dame's speed. So Mohardt threw under them and Kiley scored again. In the last quarter, Mohardt used his own 45-yard kick return to start a drive that he finished with a 15-yard sprint to the end zone. The Cadets lost an interception to Castner, and the Andersons grabbed fumbles. Notre Dame had 16 first downs to Army's two. So went Saturday, November 5.

The following Tuesday, it was Rutgers' turn. Castner appeared well rested, since he took the opening handoff and sped 55 yards for a touchdown. Rutgers punted; Notre Dame probed twice, then Wynne struck for a 35-yard score. Castner drop-kicked two field goals to end the first half. Mohardt passed to Kiley for an 8-yard score in the third quarter, and Castner added a touchdown from the Rutgers' 1-yard line. Frank Thomas swiped a pass, and Desch slipped around end for a 6-yard touchdown. The final score was 48-0. Notre Dame scored 76 points in two games played within three days.

On Saturday, November 12, Notre Dame obliterated Haskell 42-7. Castner ran for three scores, one from 50 yards out. Earl Walsh, third-string left halfback, added two more, and Desch added one. The starters played a total of four minutes. Rockne didn't bother to attend the game; he scouted Marquette.

Marquette did not fold easily. They scored first after they stuffed a Castner punt. Mohardt scored a 48-yard touchdown on the next possession, with Wynne blocking. Then he fired a pass to Eddie Anderson for a 45-yard score and the lead. His 35-yard jaunt later in the game set up Wynne's closing score for a 21-7 victory.

The following week Notre Dame bested Michigan Agricultural College 48-0 in a home game. MAC gained no first downs. Harry Mehre, Notre Dame's center, intercepted a pass and lumbered for the first touchdown. Mohardt, who was playing with a broken nose, passed for more than 100 yards and scored a touchdown to go along with those he set up for others. Desch's speed got a touchdown, and Joe Bergman closed the scoring for the season.

Six players received All-American honors: Kiley, Eddie and Hunk Anderson, Mohardt, Castner, and Shaw. The Fighting Irish were tantalizingly close to a third consecutive undefeated season.They were also now wanted for post-season bowl play. The Rose Bowl showed interest, but some players got caught playing semi-pro ball, and Rockne did not push the matter.

1921 record: 10-1-0 (.909)
Record to date: 178-38-16 (.801)

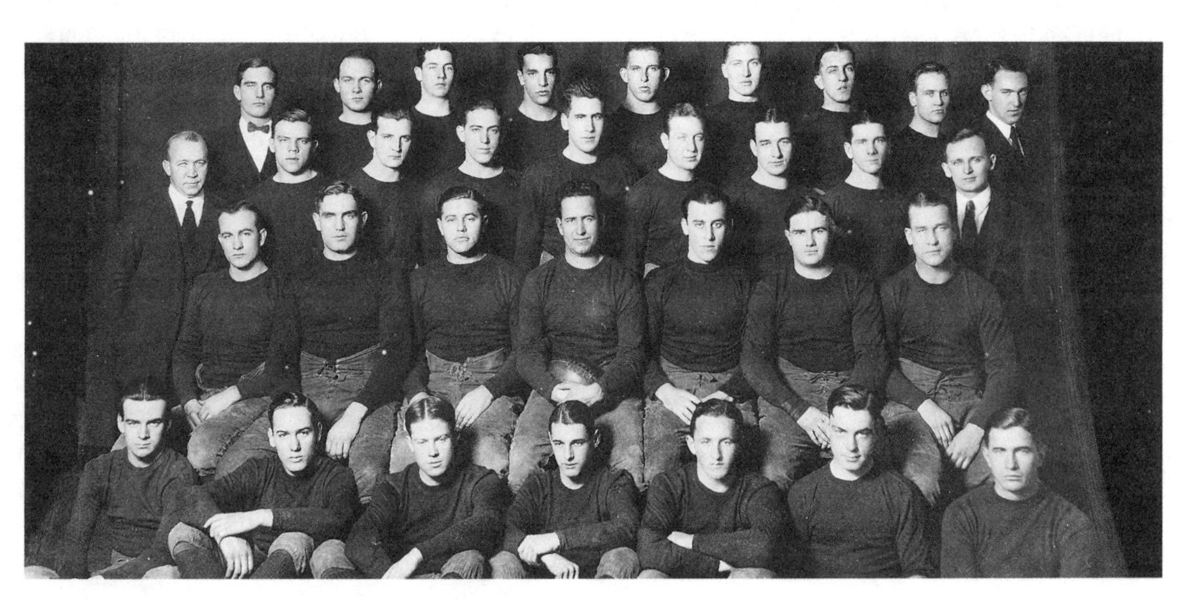

The 1922 team, with the Horsemen as sophomores.

1922

The new season appeared problematic. Some excellent players were gone, most notably Hunk Anderson. The seniors had played with Gipp and would serve as transitional figures to the Four Horsemen, who were sophomores in 1922. The basic problem was to mold a backfield unit out of the young raw material. Rockne had seen leadership quality in a 1921 freshman, Harry Stuhldreher. There was fine speed in sophomores Elmer Layden and Don Miller. Paul Castner would start at fullback.

Kalamazoo lost to Notre Dame, 46-0. Rockne used three different backfields. He liked what he saw as they ran all over, but something was missing that he couldn't quite define. St Louis was up next. They played well, but succumbed 26-0; fewer backfield combinations were tried. The defense was solid enough to allow the young backs to learn the intricacies of the Notre Dame shift.

The Irish next met Purdue, coached by Notre Dame alumnus Jimmy Phelan. The Boilermakers tried hard but couldn't score. The Fighting Irish scored three touchdowns for a 20-0 win, but lost tackle Tom Lieb with a broken leg. DePauw broke the shutout string the following week, but lost 34-7. Rockne could see that the kids were learning.

Just in time, too, for Georgia Tech. Rockne had the team work out with terrible noise around them so that the infamous Rebel Yell wouldn't fluster the youngsters. Tech outplayed the shock troops for a 3-0 lead when Rockne, who had seen enough, sent in his starters. This added pressure caused Tech's Red Barron to muff a punt at the Tech 42, which Notre Dame recovered. They took their time on a careful drive; Stuhldreher fired a short pass to Castner off a line fake for the touchdown. The game settled into a defensive stalemate in the middle quarters, with Castner's booming punts keeping Tech at bay. Good Irish defense caused fumbles to kill Tech drives, but the Irish couldn't capitalize. In the fourth quarter, however, two Tech lapses in the secondary allowed Stuhldreher to complete some medium range passes, followed by a run to their 1-yard line. He sneaked it in to clinch a 13-3 win.

Homecoming against Indiana belonged to Castner. He did virtually all the scoring and played great defense in a 27-0 win. Castner drop-kicked two field goals of 45 and 35 yards, scored touchdowns from the 20 and 22, intercepted a Hoosier pass on their 35 to zip in for a touchdown, and kicked three conversions in a performance to rival Gipp's 1920 Army marvel. A crushing Fighting Irish ground game reduced their need to pass; only four were attempted. Indiana tried five, and the Fighting Irish snagged three.

Paul Castner, a 1922 All-American, played with both Gipp and the eventual Four Horsemen.

Castner should have saved some for the Army game, which ended in a 0-0 tie after both teams did what they could to lose it. The Cadets drove to the Notre Dame 12, but could not score. Layden stopped another deep threat with a pass interception, but nothing eventuated. In the fourth quarter, the Fighting Irish put together a drive, mixing delayed passes and off-tackle slants, to reach the Army 4-yard line. But Castner fumbled on a line plunge. On Notre Dame's next possession, with a broken nose and a sprained ankle, Castner tried a 55-yard drop kick that missed.

Rockne nursed his big fullback all week hoping he would recover for Butler. He did, but was lost for the season in an early pileup. At first they thought he had a dislocated hip and manipulated it back into place, but it was really broken. The Fighting Irish won the game handily, 31-3, but Rockne had to replace his All-American fullback within a week. He asked Layden to try moving from left halfback, the glamor

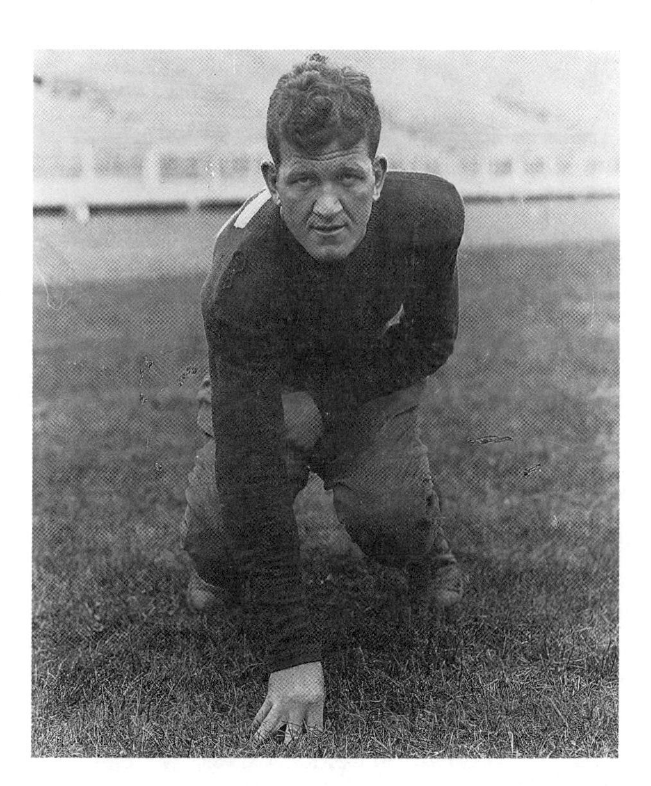

Glen Carberry, left end and captain of the 1922 team.

spot then, to fullback, and Crowley moved up to fill the halfback position. It worked—and Rockne had four sophomores for his backfield. He had also just created the Four Horsemen. Rockne recognized that this backfield unit now had what had been missing—perfect timing for the shift, a blend of speed, power, rhythm, and headiness for this deceptive offensive tactic.

In the next game, Carnegie Tech opened the game with old-fashioned mass plays, vintage 1905, to rumble for two quick first downs. The Notre Dame defense clamped down, stopped them, got the ball back, and showed Carnegie modern football—Bergman zipped for 27 yards; then from the 10 Layden did the shake-and-bake, but lost the ball; however, Stuhldreher recovered it for the score. Don Miller later scored on a 10-yard burst. In the fourth quarter, good passing finished off the Scots as Crowley scooted for 25 yards to set up a 10-yard touchdown pass from Stuhldreher to Layden. The 19-0 win was the sixth shutout of the season.

They all knew that Nebraska wouldn't be as easy. Another week of intense practice gave the young backfield a better grasp of the offense, but it wasn't enough to beat a loaded Husker squad in a game attended by WWI hero General Pershing. The Huskers ran for two quick touchdowns in the second quarter, on a 2-yard plunge and a 38-yarder. The Fighting Irish passing game was not clicking, although Layden hit Miller in the flat for a score. It wasn't enough, and Notre Dame lost 14-6.

Those few (Castner, Thomas, and Carberry) who would graduate after 1922 could say they had played with the immortal Gipp—and with the Four Horsemen. It had been a transitional year from 1921, when the Irish should have won it all, to the great 1923-1924 years. The 1922 team played with distinction. And Rockne knew he had a good thing in his backfield, but perhaps even he did not fully know just how good they would prove to be.

1922 record: 8-1-1 (.850)

Record to date: 186-39-17 (.803)

1923

Starting his sixth year, Rockne had the longest tenure of any Fighting Irish head football coach. The backfield was set, and no opponent knew how good they'd be. The new center, Adam Walsh, was talented enough to be called the best Irish center long after he was gone. Joe Bach and Noble Kizer would become excellent linemen. The whole team had great speed, and the line had the quickness this backfield needed.

Kalamazoo was demolished 74-0. Red Maher took the kickoff 90 yards on a touchdown run that saw all 11 opponents flattened. His next carry was for 53 yards; then he scored from the 7 (and this was a sub—shock troops started the game). Miller tallied from 59 yards; Rex Enright from the 25; Crowley from the 68; Bernie Livergood, Bergman, and Max Houser all scored, before the substitutes got three final touchdowns. Kalamazoo never earned a first down. The two teams never met again.

Lombard tried next. Rockne played it very tight in a 14-0 win with basic football—Army was scouting. Rockne usually prepared no more than 12 plays for a whole season, so when he hid the offense, the scouts learned very little.

The Army-Notre Dame game was now being played at Ebbets Field in New York City. The Cadets, with their usual supply of fifth- and sixth-year college students, were much bigger than Notre Dame, but lacked speed. The Cadets came out wearing bright yellow jerseys rather than the usual blue. The Fighting Irish shock troops sparred with Army for the opening quarter, then the regulars came in: Stuhldreher

The beginning of a perfect play in the 1923 Princeton game.

hit Miller for a 35-yard gain to the Cadet 21; Layden ran to the 6-yard line, and a pass resulted in a touchdown. Notre Dame's defense throttled the slow Army attack; Crowley intercepted a pass and ran it 37 yards to their 24. He went around end for 15; Miller started in the same direction, then he reversed field and scored untouched. Army's size was humiliated: two first downs to Notre Dame's 13, 0 completions in 11 tries (and three interceptions), and 49 yards rushing to Notre Dame's 165. Army was beaten 13-0.

A week later, Notre Dame completed its conquest of eastern football with a 25-2 blitz of Princeton, who had been undefeated since 1921. Notre Dame's superior talent showed: 27 first downs to five; 465 yards of total offense to 101; 241 yards rushing to 54. Miller scored first with a burst around end in the first quarter; Stuhldreher sneaked in from the 1-yard line in the next quarter; and a Layden-to-Stuhldreher pass set up Red Maher's 21-yard run for the third tally. Late in the game, Layden picked off a Princeton pass and sped 40 yards to score. The east had fallen.

The south was next. Georgia Tech found Irish speed too much, losing 35-7. Miller ran 59 and 23 yards for touchdowns, and lost an 88-yarder on a penalty. Tech relaxed when Maher replaced Miller near the end, but Red dashed 46 yards for a touchdown on a cut back. Joe Bach blocked two punts, the second going to Gene Mayl for a score.

Purdue was again the Homecoming opponent. Miller starred, with at least four runs over 25 yards each, to go with 50 yards receiving and two touchdowns; Enright and Maher both scored. Notre Dame had 22 first downs to Purdue's five. The final score was Notre Dame over Purdue, 34-7.

Next, Nebraska defeated Notre Dame on the strength of two Dave Noble scores, 14-7. The Huskers mounted a fine pass defense that stymied the Fighting Irish most of the day. Rockne tried to energize matters in the third quarter with substitutes, and Bill Cerney scored on a 20-yard toss from Stuhldreher, but the rally fell short.

Butler went down easy, losing 34-7. As in 1922, however, Butler knocked out a star. It had been Castner the year before; this time it was Don Miller, with a broken rib. He had scored early in the game, and was seemingly on his way again with a 38-yard dash when the play ended in injury. Layden scored twice, both on short runs. Stuhldreher ran 65 yards for a score on a punt return. Ward Connell registered the final score as the subs took over. Butler scored on a blocked punt; otherwise they had five first downs to Notre Dame's 22.

The Irish played Carnegie Tech at Forbes Field in Pittsburgh. The Fighting Irish scored in each quarter for a 26-0 victory. Layden scored first with a short dive to end an 86-yard march. Connell looked like he should be a starter when he ran 41 yards around end to score in the second quarter. He also scored in the third quarter on a short run to end a meticulous, time-killing drive. More subs came in, and Red Maher, who probably would have been a three-year starter anywhere else, got the final score.

The season finale was with St. Louis at Sportsman's Park, with three inches of mud on the field. Notre Dame won 13-0 and survived a scare when a big lineman, Kalkman, blocked a Layden punt and recovered it on the 18, but he was apparently unused to carrying the ball, especially in a mudbath. A mud puddle felled him, ending the threat. Most of the day was spent slithering, sliding and mucking in the mud. It was a good play when someone actually managed to maintain balance.

The year could be summed up in one distasteful word—Nebraska. The Irish wanted Nebraska.

1923 record: 9-1-0 (.900)
Record to date: 195-40-17 (.807)

1924

This season should be displayed as a monument to excellence. Notre Dame football was at the pinnacle of the collegiate game, replacing the fading eastern triumvirate. Rockne had it all: a devastating backfield and a powerful, quick line. His shift was operated by men with an appreciation for its subtleties. A late-season trip to the Rose Bowl would give Rockne the expertise needed to begin the series with the University of Southern California in 1926, creating the first coast-to-coast agenda in college football.

Kalamazoo, outscored 284-0 in six games against the Irish, was dropped from the schedule. Lombard took its place, losing 40-0. Miller scored the first touchdown of the year, then the subs scored on runs of 50 and 57 yards. Crowley, Bill Cerney, and Miller again scored. Cerney literally somersaulted into the end zone for his touchdown after being hit. Quarterback Stuhldreher did not play due to a minor injury.

Wabash closed its series with the Fighting Irish with a well-played 34-0 loss. Rockne played mostly substitutes, watching them carefully, and kept the regulars ready for Army. Crowley scored on one of his classic end runs and Ward Connell had a long gainer with five Wabash players in tow. Still, the Irish seemed preoccupied with thoughts of Army.

This game with Army completed the transition of Notre Dame from a state power to a regional power to a national power. Rockne personified all that was deemed admirable in college football. His backfield would be immortalized as media heroes in ways unknown before Grantland Rice wrote his famous story of the game. For the rest of his career, Rockne and the Fighting Irish would play the game as if on a plateau removed from mortal teams.

Elmer Layden, All-American fullback in 1923 and 1924, made the switch in 1922 from left halfback to fullback after Castner was hurt—and Rock had his Four Horsemen.

Both teams were undefeated and star-laden. The crowd at the old Polo Grounds reached 55,000, almost twice the gate of any previous Notre Dame game. And Rice would write his famous sports story. Heroic feats would happen: Irish captain and center, Adam Walsh, would play most of the game with two broken hands and still manage to intercept an Army pass and return it 20 yards.

The first quarter was spent reconnoitering and punting. Notre Dame opened up in the second, from its 15. Crowley burst for 20 around end, then Miller for 11 yards. Stuhldreher fired a pass to Crowley for 12 more, and Miller went outside for 20 more. After two thrusts, Layden took it in. In the third quarter, Layden intercepted a Cadet pass to start another march, capped by Crowley's 20-yard flanking end run for the touchdown. Army tried; Wood ran for 45 yards once, but the drive died. Poor punting led to an Army score, but Notre Dame prevailed 13-7. The game was played nearly 70 years ago, so words cannot relay the speed, power, and grace of the shift, nor fully capture a swarming defense that stifled a fine Army team. The team was welcomed back to South Bend the next day with a huge crowd, speeches, and

The 1924 National Champions: line: Hunsinger, Rip Miller, Kizer, Captain Walsh, Weibel, Bach, Collins; backs: Stuhldreher, Miller, Layden, Crowley.

an impromptu parade.

When the excitement subsided, there was a week to prepare for Princeton, one of the old lions of the east. The Fighting Irish dominated them, although the 12-0 final score did not reflect that. Crowley scored both touchdowns and ran 250 yards, virtually uncontested. Notre Dame racked up 20 first downs to Princeton's four and never let them get beyond the Notre Dame 30-yard line. Rockne let the shock troops have the whole first quarter; they held Princeton to 1½ yards on 20 runs. When the regulars came in, a five-play drive of 50 yards ended in a Crowley touchdown. In the fourth quarter, Crowley scored on a run in which he was hit four times and spun away from each. When Princeton kicked off in the second half, Rock intentionally used a flying wedge formation to return the kick. Don Miller almost topped this with a 35-yard run dodging three tacklers while running backwards, after being spun around on the play.

The next week, Notre Dame spotted Georgia Tech a field goal, then roared back for a 34-3 win. Stuhldreher was hurt; Red Edwards started, and the Fighting Irish didn't skip a beat. The first score came on a fourth down play when Crowley hit Miller for an

The Horsemen, somewhat baffled by their new-found identity. From the left, Miller, Layden, Crowley, and Stuhldreher.

11-yard touchdown; the drive started with Miller's 35-yard run. Layden soon ran for another; John Roach sparked a drive with a 45-yard scamper, capped by his 3-yard touchdown plunge. The same pass play that worked for Crowley and Miller also worked for Eddie Scharer and Roach in the fourth quarter. Bernie Livergood, who owned the right side of the line with his dashes, scored the final touchdown. The fans enjoyed seeing the surviving members of the 1887 team honored at the game. It was, appropriately enough, the 200th career win for Notre Dame.

Wisconsin held the subs to a 3-3 standoff before Rockne sent in the starters, who rocked the Badgers for four touchdowns before the subs went back in. Miller and Layden scored one each, and Crowley twice, one on a pass from Stuhldreher. Roach scored after Joe Harmon intercepted a Badger pass. Notre Dame won 38-3.

The close losses to Nebraska in 1922 and 1923 rankled. Rockne, determined to break the streak, did so, winning 34-6. The Huskers scored first following an Irish fumble, then the sky fell. Stuhldreher and Miller scored quickly in the second quarter. Miller scored again in the third quarter, and Crowley steamed 65 yards with a pass from Layden, who had thrown it from a prone position, which was then allowed. After that, Notre Dame just pounded the middle, and Layden scored the last touchdown. Notre Dame had 24 first downs to Nebraska's three; 566 yards total offense to 76; eight of 11 passes for 101 yards to one of seven for 20; and 465 yards rushing to 56.

Northwestern turned tough at Grand Park Stadium in Chicago. Two early Wildcat field goals made Rockne send in the regulars. The passing game turned the tide. Stuhldreher threw a long one to Crowley, who ran it to the Northwestern 9; two plays later, a quarterback keeper tied the game. And in two more plays, Stuhldreher snagged a pass and ran it back 40 yards for the winning touchdown in a 13-6 cliffhanger.

Carnegie Tech ended the regular season, losing 40-19, although the game was closer than the score shows. At the half, the Scots had fought to a 13-13 stalemate. When it was over, their three touchdowns were the most scored by anyone since 1916. It took a great Fighting Irish passing game to earn the win; at one point Notre Dame completed 12 consecutive passes. Miller scored first with a 40-yarder from Crowley, and Cerney bolted in from the 3 to tie the game. Stuhldreher fired two touchdown strikes in the third quarter, one to Livergood and one to Crowley. Livergood and Stuhldreher wrapped it up with short runs for scores. It was a fierce game. Adam Walsh was knocked out six times before leaving the field.

Harry Stuhldreher, slick quarterback for the Four Horsemen.

Three weeks later, 33 Irish players took a train to the Rose Bowl. After many stops, practices, and festivities, they arrived in Pasadena, each man about eight pounds lighter. The game against Stanford highlighted two different approaches, the Rockne System vs. the Warner System. Stanford used a wingback offense designed to move the ball in long, time-consuming drives, led by all-time great fullback Ernie Nevers. Rockne's system was designed for the lightning-quick strike (the "perfect play") executed from anywhere on the field; theoretically, if all 11 players executed as designed, the play should score. Opposing defenses faced this possibility on each play. Under Warner, a defense was nibbled to death, while Rockne went for the jugular.

Stanford opened the scoring with a 27-yard field goal, and the Fighting Irish shock troops stalled. With the starters in, Layden capped a 46-yard drive with a 3-yard plunge. As the Notre Dame defense set up, Rockne made a subtle shift in Layden's alignment, a few inches from his regular spot, so he could read Stanford's passing game better. (Years later, Bert Metzger would say that Rockne coached "in inches.") Five minutes into a meticulous Stanford drive, Layden saw what he wanted—a handoff to

Nevers, who floated a bit wider than usual, opening up an area just behind the linebackers. Nevers fired the ball in the direction of an end, but Layden intercepted it for a 78-yard touchdown, helped by right end Ed Hunsinger's blocking. Both men were involved in the next score when Stanford's Solomon couldn't handle one of Layden's punts; Hunsinger recovered and ran 20 yards for the score. Four minutes later, Stanford scored on a 7-yard pass. But they kept misfiring—missing three field goals, Solomon in the open field with a long pass dragged down by a speedy Horseman, and so on.Then Layden saw it again—the handoff to Nevers, who swings a bit wide, the soft spot just behind the linebackers, and the pass. And just as before, he had it all the way, tipped it to himself, and ran 70 yards for the touchdown.

It wasn't easy. Stuhldreher played most of the game with a broken ankle, and Bach went against much bigger Stanford linemen with two cracked ribs. Stanford won the statistics, but Notre Dame won the game, 27-10. Warner's offense could move the ball; Rockne's could score at any moment. The game also showed that football is not a game of territory, but of opportunity. Stanford amassed 316 yards to Notre Dame's 186, 17 first downs to 7, and 138 yards passing to 56. But Rockne's scouting and coaching led to eight turnovers as the opportunistic Irish intercepted five passes and recovered three fumbles. Stanford simply made too many mistakes, and the Fighting Irish capitalized on them. Notre Dame was crowned the national champion.

Four players won first team All-American awards: Layden, Stuhldreher, Crowley, and Walsh. Rockne was 58-4-3 (.915) after seven seasons, with three undefeated teams and the others with only one loss.

1924 record: 10-0-0 (1.000)
Record to date: 205-40-17 (.814)

1925

The basic challenge for the 1925 season was to replace the entire starting unit. All 11 men had graduated. Rockne's shock troop theory fortunately provided a large number of players with game experience. There were some dependable, if not particularly flashy, players available: Red Edwards for quarterback, Clem Crowe, and Joe Boland on the left flank, and Rex Enright at fullback. A lanky Texan, Christy Flanagan, showed promise.

Bucky Dahman, Christy Flanagan's running mate from 1925 to 1927 from his right halfback position.

Baylor, defending two-time Southwest Conference champion, was first. Rockne tried eight different backs in the game. The passing game worked well enough, eight completions in 11 tries (while Baylor showed how not to pass—0 for 15). Tom Hearden scored first from the 11 after Edwards got them there passing. More passing, especially from Eddie Scharer to Joe Prelli, followed by persistent smashes by guard/fullback Dick Hanousek, led to Flanagan's first touchdown, an end run from the 6-yard line. Prelli scored the third touchdown by sweeping Baylor's left end. In the third quarter, Fighting Irish speed kept Baylor in trouble; Harry O'Boyle broke six poor tackles to score from the 18. Baylor's right side allowed Hearden to score the next one, and Bucky Dahman made a leaping catch of a pass from Charlie Riley to conclude a 41-0 rout.

Lombard was blitzed by the Irish, 69-0. Lombard used a huddle, something that had not been seen before at Cartier Field. It looked like they were trying to kill time (players in those days got up, aligned themselves, and waited for the signals). The Irish rampaged for 10 touchdowns. O'Boyle and Prelli capped good drives in the first quarter; in the second, John Roach had a long-distance score on his first run; then Lew Cody was a one-man drive on three runs. Before it was over, Hanousek scored three, and

O'Boyle, Dahman, and Flanagan were the other scorers. The winning streak was 15, half of them shutouts.

The next week, the Fighting Irish had a rude awakening when Beloit scored first with a field goal and then used something new—a screen pass. The defensive subs took a while to adjust to this. But in the second quarter with the veterans in, O'Boyle scored on a short run. Later, Prelli slashed off tackle for a 67-yard scoring burst. Lew Cody intercepted a Viking pass and ran 47 yards to the end zone for the 19-3 Irish win.

Army, with only one tie in the previous seven encounters with Notre Dame, ruined the season with a 27-0 win, exposing all of Notre Dame's weaknesses in the process. The line play was deficient in blocking and on defense. Army rolled at will. They scored twice in the second quarter and twice in the fourth. The Irish played fairly well in the third quarter; they blocked an Army punt, but the threat ended when a Cadet blocked the ensuing Irish punt and scored a touchdown in the melee.

More than 5,500 students and fans went to Minnesota. Notre Dame did not play well through the third quarter, and the score was tied 7-7. Poor Minnesota punting let the Fighting Irish take the lead when Flanagan went 40 yards on two runs on a 28-yard touchdown drive (a penalty took place between the runs). On the next series, Red Smith grabbed a Gopher fumble at the 28. Flanagan ran for 24, and Enright took it in from the 4-yard line. Joe Boland recovered two fumbles, and Art Parisien recovered a fumble at the Notre Dame 2 and ran it back 80 yards.

Joe Boland, a tackle on the 1924 and 1925 squads, later a coach at Notre Dame, and still later the voice of the Irish on the national radio hookup.

Notre Dame went to the deep south to play Georgia Tech. Edwards intercepted a Tech pass and the Fighting Irish were in business at the Tech 25. Flanagan ran for 11 of that before he scored from in close. In the second quarter, Flanagan marched 51 yards with a 20-yard burst past left end and a 10-yard scoring run to the opposite side. A Ramblin' Wreck drive ended as Hearden intercepted a pass at the Fighting Irish 25 to seal the win, 13-0.

From there, the Fighting Irish travelled to Penn State. The Nittany Lions allowed the Irish backs to run around the field almost at will, but when they neared the end zone, Penn State shut them down. The field was so bad from heavy rain that Enright's field goal try from the 13 failed miserably. Captain Clem Crowe tore a back muscle and was lost for the year. The 0-0 tie pleased no one.

Back on campus for Homecoming, Notre Dame whipped Carnegie Tech 26-0. The Irish got off to a slow start with the subs being used through nearly two quarters; and then it took two drives before the regulars hit stride. From the Tech 35, Enright slammed into the middle, and Flanagan went wide for 24. Enright pounded the middle twice; Flanagan finished it off for the touchdown. Enright scored in the third quarter to end a drive, then scored again on a fumble recovery. The subs finished; Riley faked a pass and rolled in for a 20-yard score.

Northwestern visited Cartier Field and shocked everyone with a 10-0 halftime lead. The Wildcats had also held the Fighting Irish to no first downs. Rockne reminded the team at halftime that memory could not recall the last team to do what Northwestern was doing. The team got the point. Flanagan carried for 25 yards. A quick march, led by Flanagan and Enright, finished with an Enright touchdown from the 4-yard line. On the next drive, Flanagan ran for 29 yards to the Northwestern 17, then for 12 more; Enright ran for no-gain, and Flanagan raced in for the touchdown and a final score of 13-10.

Flanagan was injured, and Nebraska was next. The Huskers had not played the weekend before. Rockne started the subs again, but it backfired. A strong Nebraska team shredded them for two touchdowns in the first quarter to sink Fighting Irish hopes. They added a field goal in the third quarter. Notre

The 1926 Fighting Irish team.

Dame's passing game disappeared; they hit one of 12, with Nebraska intercepting three. The season ended on this sour 17-0 note, but Rockne had overcome the loss of his entire 1924 starting team to keep this young team in contention much of the season.

1925 record: 7-2-1 (.750)
Record to date: 212-42-18 (.812)

1926

Rockne had to deal with two key points: the schedule for 1926 was the most demanding ever, and a full second stop was now mandatory after the shift (in 1924, the Horsemen could all be in motion, as a unit, at the snap). He was not overly concerned on either score.

Beloit was the only breather in the nation's first coast-to-coast schedule, from Yankee Stadium to the Los Angeles Coliseum. Rockne had hired Tommy Mills, the Beloit coach who scared the Irish in 1925, so Beloit was hurting even before the Fighting Irish obliterated them 77-0. Of Notre Dame's 11 touchdowns (10 rushing), Flanagan's 95-yard kickoff return in the third quarter was the best. Vince McNally scored two touchdowns and Hearden, Dahman, John Niemiec, Jack Chevigny, Red Edwards, Fred Collins, and Joe Maxwell each scored.

Minnesota was much tougher, so much so that Joe Boland and Collins were lost for the year. Dahman opened up Notre Dame's scoring with a 65-yarder designed to be a short gainer. For two quarters, it was a defensive struggle. Then Flanagan broke the log jam with another 65-yard touchdown run. Hearden wrapped up the 20-7 win on a late drive with a 20-yard run and a 15-yard scoring burst.

Hugo Bedzek's Penn State team wanted to avenge the 0-0 tie, but Notre Dame was ready. Parisien, working with the subs, fired a 35-yard strike to Harry O'Boyle, who ran 15 yards for a touchdown.

The great Christy Flanagan, three-year starter at left halfback. Another in a long line of great red-headed Irish players.

Penn State stalled and punted. Parisien threw to O'Boyle, who was open again and turned it into a 53-yard touchdown. Penn State stiffened, stopping four Irish drives. Edwards finally shook loose for a 48-yard touchdown run in the second quarter. Jack Chevigny ended it in the fourth quarter when he crashed through seven Penn State tacklers for a 17-yard touchdown and a 28-0 win. Notre Dame gained 506 total yards to Penn State's 85.

Northwestern christened its new stadium against Notre Dame and played well for nearly four quarters. With only 5 minutes left, Rockne sent in Parisien. He promptly hit Chile Walsh with a pass play for 66 yards to the Northwestern 14. Then he hit Niemiec with a touchdown pass, but the point after was missed. Superb punting kept the Wildcats at bay, and Hearden later intercepted a threatening pass for a 6-0 win.

Georgia Tech came north and ran into John Roach: from the Tech 40, he gained 20 yards and slammed in for a short-yardage touchdown. After several punts, O'Boyle ran to the Tech 40 but left hurt. Niemiec passing set up a short run for Dahman and a 12-0 final score.

Indiana swooned 26-0. Parisien was hurt early. But Flanagan started to roll in the second quarter: a 20-yard gain and a short touchdown sprint; and later, a sideline-to-sideline touchdown ramble. Dahman took over the second half with two touchdowns for a 26-0 win. This was Notre Dame's fifth shutout in six games.

Army would be difficult with many players back from the 1925 win over Notre Dame. But Rockne had used the train ride home a year ago to challenge the team to make this game their top priority. The team won a thrilling 7-0 game; the score came on the old "51" play—the left halfback, Flanagan, off tackle with plenty of blocking to escort him for the 68-yard touchdown run.

Drake made their first visit to the Dome. The Bulldogs played even with the shock troops; in the second quarter, Drake drove to the 3-inch line before being stopped. Notre Dame took over on a 95-yard drive that ended when Edwards took it in from the 2-yard line on a quarterback sneak. Drake came back, but John Wallace intercepted a pass, turning it into a 30-yard touchdown. As the snow fell, Riley pitched a 21-yard touchdown strike to O'Boyle for a 21-0 win.

Six shutouts for the year so far. Only Minnesota had scored. The next game against Carnegie Tech would be a shutout, too. Confident of an Irish victory, Rockne went on to Chicago to scout a 1927 opponent, Navy, and saw a 21-21 tie game. The team went to Pittsburgh under Hunk Anderson to meet Carnegie Tech. In Chicago, Rockne got the news of the stunning upset—Tech had destroyed a championship year with a 19-0 win over Notre Dame. Two touchdowns on the ground and two field goals were scored against the Fighting Irish defense, who had trouble with the running game all day.

On to the University of Southern California. This game set the tone for the series, including the surprise ending that would be duplicated more times than either team would care to remember. Notre Dame scored first as Riley led a drive to USC's 20, then faked a plunge and broke outside for the touchdown. Notre Dame missed the point after kick. USC earned a touchdown following an interception, but also missed the conversion. In the fourth quarter, USC's Wheeler ran 44 yards on five carries for the go-ahead touchdown. USC missed another conversion, but led 12-6. The Fighting Irish struggled to get back into it but did little until Rockne sent in Parisien with 90 seconds left. He immediately fired passes to Niemiec, good for 50 yards and the winning touchdown; the final score was 13-12.

It had to be painful for Rockne to contemplate seven shutouts and sustained success in college football's first truly national schedule, almost gone for nought due to Carnegie Tech.

1926 record: 9-1-0 (.900)
Record to date: 221-43-18 (.815)

1927

Fighting Irish fans could expect only three games with genuinely good teams this year—Minnesota, Army, and USC. Notre Dame, though not great, was certainly good, led by Flanagan (second team All-American in 1926) and underrated Bucky Dahman, who had exceptional speed and good hands. The left side of the line was intact, and the right side was filled capably as good men moved up.

Rockne, as usual, played his hand close to his vest early in the season so that Navy's scouts (the third game scheduled) would learn little. Notre Dame toppled a scrappy Coe team, 28-7, and then Detroit, 20-7. The starting unit was quite capable, but the quality dropped off quickly after that.

The Irish took a train to Baltimore to meet Navy. Niemiec bobbled a punt early in the game to give Navy good field position and Navy's Spring ran

1927 Notre Dame starting team: In the line (l-r): Charlie Walsh, John Polisky, George Leppig, Tim Moynihan, John Smith, Fred Miller, and John Voedisch. In the backfield: Bucky Dahman, Charlie Riley (QB), Elmer Wynne, and Christy Flanagan.

for a 6-yard touchdown. Rockne pulled the subs out and tried to stay close. In the third quarter, Notre Dame twice blocked Navy punts; a penalty killed the first one; but John Frederick's block of the second punt was recovered by Chile Walsh for a touchdown. On the next drive, Flanagan ran 35 yards off tackle and 25 yards past right end, and Riley attacked the other side for a 12-yard touchdown run. Niemiec redeemed himself with sharp passing on a 44-yard drive, capped by his touchdown. The Fighting Irish escaped with a 19-6 win, but their passing game was not sharp throughout.

On to Bloomington—different town, different team, same score (19-6). It had the same start, too, when Indiana's Reinhardt streaked through the subs for a 45-yard touchdown. Niemiec tallied in the second quarter with a plunge from the 1. A quarter later, Dahman completed a five-play drive with a touchdown bolt. Flanagan completed the scoring.

The 1927 football squad.

Undefeated Georgia Tech came to South Bend. The shock troops did better, playing even for their quarter. The starters relieved them and began moving—Fred Collins started it with a 20-yard run and finished it with a 17-yard touchdown jaunt. In the third quarter, Tech fumbled and Collins dashed 25 yards for a score from scrimmage. In the fourth quarter, Chevigny sparked a score with a 25-yard run, capped by Billy Dew's 4-yard touchdown on a fullback dive. Tech lost 26-7.

Minnesota, with stars Bronko Nagurski at guard and Herb Joesting at fullback, came next. Early in the game, Clipper Smith grabbed a fumbled punt at Minnesota's 18, and Niemiec scored on the next play for a 7-0 lead. For almost three quarters after that the defenses dominated; neither Joesting nor Flanagan was able to shake loose. In the fourth quarter with 15 seconds remaining (or so they were told), Niemiec went into punt formation, but Riley called for a plunge to kill the time. Somebody missed the call because the ball was snapped into the middle of the backfield, and Nagurski fell on it at the Notre Dame 15. After three Joesting runs, Minnesota scored with a pass and tied the game as time expired. It was a superb defensive game, but Minnesota showed that the Fighting Irish could not run up the middle with impunity.

On to Yankee Stadium and Army, another star-laden team, led by Christian Keener Cagle at half-back. Army was a good, big team and handled Notre Dame with some ease, 18-0. Cagle scored twice on a run of 48 yards and with a pass of 32 yards; quarterback Billy Nave intercepted an Irish pass and sped 60 yards for the final score.

Clipper Smith, one of Rock's great "watch-charm guards" at 5' 9", 164 pounds. Started at left guard in 1926 and 1927, All-American in 1927.

Notre Dame took out its accumulated frustrations on Drake, 32-0. Rockne had the offense practice its off-tackle smashes and its passing game against the Bulldogs, and he rested the starters as much as possible, saving them for USC. Jack Elder, Rockne's fastest player, took an interception 86 yards for a score and also threw a short pass to John Colrick for another. Niemiec had opened the scoring, and Dahman and Prelli closed it, on a 14-yard touchdown catch and a 15-yard run, respectively. Flanagan was held in check, with 23 yards being his longest gain.

USC came to Soldier Field in Chicago. The records show 120,000 fans attended, but 135,000 is probably more accurate. Fans stood on top of the colonnade circling the upper deck; others were on ladders between the columns. It was, and still is, the largest crowd ever to see a college football game. The Fighting Irish thrilled these packed masses with a 7-6 win. Bucky Dahman was the most valuable player of the game: he caught a 25-yard touchdown pass from Riley after four Flanagan runs netted 28 yards; he kicked the winning point after; in the fourth quarter he kicked a 65-yard punt to the USC 2; and then he intercepted a Trojan pass on their 20 to ice the game. Notre Dame killed the clock, won the game, and concluded the season.

There were three All-Americans: Flanagan, Clipper Smith, and John Polisky at tackle, a second team choice. In retrospect, the 1927 team lacked a knockout punch. They had also been lucky in escaping injuries. They would not be so lucky in 1928.

1927 record: 7-1-1 (.833)
Record to date: 228-44-18 (.817)

1928

There are cycles in football. The 1928 Fighting Irish team was a transitional team, akin to the 1921 team sandwiched between the passing of Gipp and the arrival of the Horsemen. With Flanagan and key supporters gone, Rockne had to look for help from sophomores, and hope that the team could sustain the effort through a tough schedule. This team, like last year's, also lacked a knockout punch. Rockne moved some veterans so that the left side of the line was solid; other spots were filled with former reserves. The

The 1928 team, the group that "Won One for the Gipper."

running backs were good: Chevigny, Niemiec, and Elder as halfbacks and Collins and Moon Mullins at fullback. There were some bad knees here and there. Rock knew he'd have a difficult season.

The Wolf Pack of New Orleans' Loyola University provided the first test. Notre Dame's 12-6 victory was won in the final moments against a determined Loyola team. The Wolf Pack had a 6-0 lead through the first half, then Elder brought Notre Dame back with a 48-yard touchdown sprint. The teams traded punts and miscues until late in the game,

John Law, starter at RG in 1928 and 1929, captain in 1929.

when Rockne inserted new ends, Johnny O'Brien and Tom Murphy. Niemiec lofted a long pass to O'Brien, who took it to the Loyola 8. Niemiec hit him again at the 2, then took it in himself, going off left tackle—all in less than a minute.

Playing Wisconsin in Madison, the Fighting Irish simply did not look good. They lost key fumbles, seven in all, and scored only once (Chevigny from the 3). Elder was trapped for a safety, so the Irish clung to a 6-2 lead until the third quarter. They fumbled at their 20, recovered it, but lost 8 yards, then promptly fumbled again; Wisconsin recovered it on the Notre Dame 3-yard line. The Badgers took the lead for good on the next play, a touchdown sweep. In the fourth quarter, Wisconsin pitched a 65-yard pass and run to close it out 22-6. Notre Dame, although they moved the ball, could not sustain a drive.

Against Navy in Soldier Field, Rockne had to do something—so he suited them up in Kelly Green. The Fighting Irish moved the ball well, but scoring was another matter. Rockne played the regulars from the start. Notre Dame won the game in the fourth quarter with a slant-in pass from Niemiec to Colrick for the game's only touchdown. Other long drives fizzled. The 120,000+ spectators were treated to a stifling defense that allowed Navy only 93 total yards. The final score was Notre Dame 7, Navy 0.

The passing game failed against Georgia Tech, who held on to an early lead and waited. Father Lumpkin from Tech intercepted two Notre Dame passes, running the second one to the Irish 3-yard line

Fred Collins, starting fullback for the star-crossed 1928 team.

to set up the clincher. Georgia Tech won 13-0. Guard John Law was injured, and a glaring deficiency at fullback was exposed when insistent line smashes close to the Tech goal were stopped fairly easily.

Drake provided a breather. Notre Dame won handily, 32-6, and Rockne saw that moving Moon Mullins to the fullback spot improved things. Niemiec hit Colrick with a touchdown pass, then Chevigny scored. Carideo was next, crawling under a pile of Bulldogs. Sub Dinny Shay scored, and Joe Nash, a center, grabbed an errant pass and ran 50 yards to complete the scoring. Mullins did not score, but showed great doggedness in resisting tackles. Drake's score came on an 80-yard pass and run.

Notre Dame beat Penn State 9-0, but the score could easily have been higher. Carideo crawled in, literally, for a score. Colrick's speed netted a safety in the fourth quarter. Eddie Collins sacked a Penn State back for minus 20 yards, then recovered a fumble on the next play.

After six games, the Fighting Irish were 4-2, but Rockne knew that matters ahead looked grim. The team *had* to beat Army to prevent a losing season. He had a thought. He told Grantland Rice the night before the game that he might have to use the ghost of George Gipp to help the Irish play beyond capacity. The rest is, as they say, history.

Army was a loaded team built around Cagle. The Irish defense showed that it could play with the larger Cadets and neutralize Cagle. The first half ended in a 0-0 deadlock. At the half, Rockne played his ace—the now famous "Win One for the Gipper" ploy. They'd have to keep Cagle in check, an assignment they almost blew when play resumed. Cagle shook loose for a 20-yard gain, then fired a 41-yard pass to spark a Cadet touchdown and a 6-0 lead. He also stopped Irish backs that his mates let loose. Then Chevigny matched the touchdown, on a fourth down plunge, highlighted by his cry, "That's one for the Gipper!" A little later he was hurt recovering a fumble. Rock substituted; he sent in Johnny "One Play"

Action from the first quarter of the 1928 Army game; Niemiec with the ball setting up for a pass, which was incomplete. This is what the play looked like that went to O'Brien for the winning TD.

Jack Chevigny scored the first TD of great 1928 over Army, shouting "That's one for the Gipper!" as he crossed the goal.

Johnny "One-play" O'Brien won the 1928 Army game with a TD reception from Niemiec.

O'Brien to match his height against the diminutive Nave, the hero of the 1927 game. Niemiec got the ball and saw Cadets breaking through his front wall. He heaved a prayer in O'Brien's direction—who caught it and stumbled for the score, just out of Nave's desperate reach.

Cagle inspired a long drive deep into Notre Dame territory, but had to be removed, totally exhausted. With mere seconds left in the game, Army reached the 1-foot line, but lost possession on downs. The Irish line held, each man driven by the ghost of Gipp perhaps, and the game ended. Rockne had succeeded in pumping up a mediocre team to beat a superior foe. It is doubtful that Gipp said "Win one for the Gipper," as Rockne claimed, (both Castner and Grant have said that Gipp never called himself that), but it is the best example in Notre Dame's history of the use of motivational psychology.

Babe Ruth showing them how a southpaw does it, circa 1928.

The rest of the season was anticlimactic, although the Fighting Irish had to face even better teams—Carnegie Tech and USC. The Scots were led by a 230-pound fullback named Karcis, who was too much for the smallish linemen to handle. Tech won 27-7. Mullins earned the only Irish score on a 10-yard fumble recovery. It was the first defeat at Cartier Field in 23 years, and also the first time a Rockne team had lost three games.

Notre Dame moved on to the west coast for USC, the 300th game for the Fighting Irish. They lost 27-14, but played gamely. Chevigny scored on a 51-yard run, and Albert Gebert, a sub quarterback, tallied the other. The defense drilled USC four times while dug in at the Notre Dame 4-yard line.

Rockne's most painful season was at last behind him. Things could only get better.

1928 record: 5-4-0 (.555)
Record to date: 233-48-19 (.808)

1929

Rockne felt good about his prospects for 1929. The line was solid, and Carideo had matured. Elder's blazing speed was perfect for left halfback, and his backup was excellent—Marchmont Schwartz. Marty Brill, a transfer from Penn, was big, strong, and fast. Mullins was at fullback, with Joe Savoldi behind him.

This was a transitional backfield, since the days of the shift were severely numbered. Rockne knew he would need bigger players, especially as backs. The metamorphosis was complete by 1930, when the backfield would average 20 pounds more per man than the Horsemen.

It was a suicide schedule, with all games on the road. Cartier Field was a memory, dug up for a new stadium under Rockne's watchful eye. He was already aware of something called television, and intuitively knew the entertainment appeal of college football. He designed his teams with this in mind—the uniforms, play selection, shock troops, tiring road trips, and manipulation of the media. It was all there. Now he was constructing the perfect stadium.

Off to Indiana. The shock troops started and played even. Savoldi and Schwartz showed flashes of brilliance. Elder scored on a 20-yard streak, having set it up with a pass to Mullins. He ended the scoring with a 60-yard sprint that left the defense in the dust (he held the world sprint record for 75 yards). The Hoosiers did not threaten, and the Fighting Irish lost scoring chances with fumbles and other slips for a final score of 14-0.

The real news of the game happened on the sidelines; a pileup smashed into Rockne and bounced him around. It was almost fatal since phlebitis had then set in; he was confined to bed much of the season. Although he went to extraordinary lengths to stay active in coaching, it probably cost the team a little bit of edge. He would never again be the active, vigorous man of before.

The team that week went to Rockne's house to prepare for Navy; quarterbacks spent 14 hours there that week, enjoying Mrs. Rockne's cooking. Before

The 1929 National Champions.

The conclusion of Jack Elder's 95-yard interception and TD runback to beat Army in 1929.

the game, Rockne spoke to each starter on the phone, and fidgeted upon hearing that Navy scored first. Carideo brought Notre Dame back, hitting Elder with a touchdown pass thrown kneeling on one knee after absorbing a hit. Carideo broke Navy with an interception, running it back to their 32. The ensuing drive included runs of 7 and 17 by Brill, setting up Mullins' 1-yard TD plunge.

Rockne started attending practices in a specially arranged hearse from the McGann funeral home. The squad worked out well. At Soldier Field, Wisconsin went up 3-0, but Savoldi hit pay dirt twice, from 40 and 71 yards out, runs before and after Elder's 43-yard touchdown run. The Fighting Irish won 19-0.

Carnegie Tech's victory over the Irish in 1928 had smashed the home winning streak that started before most of the current players were born. Tech fielded a huge team, and Notre Dame knew it would be a rough game. As expected, it was a scoreless game in the third quarter; finally, Carideo returned a punt to mid-field, and Elder ran to the 17. Brill crashed to the 8. Savoldi came in against Tech's 230-pound Karcis. Savoldi ran up the middle three straight times, with grudging inches gained on each. On the fourth down, Savoldi went in for the winning touchdown. And in the midst of all this was Jack "Boom Boom" Cannon, the last lineman for Notre Dame to play *sans* helmet. The final score was 7-0.

The 1928 national champions, Georgia Tech, hosted the Fighting Irish next. Tech grabbed a Mullins' fumble on the Notre Dame 19 and took a 6-0 lead. The Irish came right back: Brill returned the kickoff to the 40, and Elder ran 53 untouched yards to finish the drive with the go-ahead touchdown. Cannon used his bare head to block a punt, allowing Mullins to score for a 13-6 halftime lead. After intermission, Carideo danced 75 yards with a punt return for a touchdown.

Jack "Boom Boom" Cannon, the last man with guts enough to play without a helmet. Captain of the 1929 National Champs and a consensus All-American pick.

In the fourth quarter, Schwartz gave Tech a glimpse of the Fighting Irish future with an 8-yard touchdown run for the 26-6 final score.

Fresh off the victory over Georgia Tech, the Irish were quickly brought back to earth as Drake grabbed a 7-0 lead. Rockne let the subs extricate themselves; Al Howard dashed 35 yards before going another 3 for a touchdown. Late in the third quarter, Elder zipped 17 yards to score and Mullins crunched the tiring Bulldogs for a 23-yard touchdown late in the game. Notre Dame won 19-7.

Against his doctor's order, Rockne went to Soldier Field for the USC game. It was a close game, almost decided by Bucky O'Connor's swollen black eye. With the eye freshly shut, he never saw the Trojan touchdown pass play coming his way that put USC ahead. Elder could throw, too, and he hit Tom Conley for a 54-yarder to tie it 6-6. Savoldi led a ground attack and scored the next Irish touchdown. USC ran the kickoff back 92 yards, but missed the conversion. Notre Dame escaped with a 13-12 victory.

Rockne stayed home for the Northwestern game and told the team to win for him—it would be his 100th victory. He was wrong (and knew it), but the Fighting Irish got his wish for him, 26-6. Three touchdowns were scored against Northwestern in the second quarter: it started with a Schwartz run of 40 yards to the Northwestern 40, and Savoldi ran it in. Next Schwartz passed to Brill for 25 yards, reaching the Wildcat 10; Schwartz slanted in standing up. Northwestern started passing and Carideo intercepted for an 85-yard touchdown. Late in the game, Savoldi careened for 32 yards and then plunged in to end the scoring.

The finale matched Army, and its star halfback Cagle in his last game against Notre Dame. Yankee Stadium, and a frozen field, was the locale for their 16th meeting. They sparred at first, until a Cadet rushing a punt knocked Elder into Carideo, the Notre Dame kicker, and Army was set up on the Notre Dame 13. Two runs and two yards later, Cagle threw a pass in the left corner to Carlmark and the massed Cadets cheered—but a blur cut in front of Carlmark and snatched the ball. Elder running, dodging three tacklers, sidestepping more Cadets, was gone—95 yards for the game's only touchdown. Carideo kicked the point after and the national championship turned on this one play. Notre Dame intercepted three more of Cagle's passes to ice the game.

The Irish won the Rissman Trophy—the equivalent of the national championship—based on comparative schedules. They never played a home game and did not have their coach for six games. Their statistical dominance was complete in all categories. No Fighting Irish team to date had faced more adversity and performed better.

1929 record: 9-0-0 (1.000)
Record to date: 242-48-19 (.813)

1930 to 1939

1930

If anyone was capable of performing an exciting encore, it was Rockne. The 1929 team had been great, but the 1930 edition was stupendous. The line produced three All-Americans (149-pound guard Bert Metzger, Al Culver, and Tom Conley) while the backfield could be favorably compared to any under the Dome. Carideo, Brill, Schwartz, and Savoldi posed a fearsome set of problems for defenses to solve. Rockne added "spinners" to the shift—the quarterback took the ball and spun around to lateral or hand off, or rolled out to pass—a concept close to the veer offense used by Parseghian 40 years later.

The stage was set for the defending national champions as they opened in South Bend at the new stadium against pass-happy Southern Methodist University, three-time defending Southwest Conference champs. Four plays into the game, SMU scored on a 48-yard catch and run play. Savoldi bobbled the ensuing kickoff slightly, then raced up the middle for a 98-yard touchdown. It was 7-7 after five plays. In the second quarter, Carideo returned a punt to the SMU 11, and Schwartz took it in two plays later off tackle. Three long SMU passes made the halftime score 14-14. It was a stand-off into the fourth quarter until a Schwartz pass to Ed Kosky, good for 48 yards, landed the ball at the SMU 27. Schwartz tried Conley but he was decked at the 4—pass interference.

The 1930 National champs, Rockne's last team. Line (l to r): Conley, Kurth, Metzger, Yarr, Kassis, Culver, Kosky. Backs (l to r): Carideo, Brill, Mullins, Schwartz.

Schwartz ran a cut back past left end for the touchdown. Tommy Yarr's three interceptions iced the game, 20-14.

The stadium was formally dedicated before the Navy game. Three previous games with Navy had been close, but the Fighting Irish won easily this time, 26-2. Mullins was hurt and Savoldi filled in, scoring three touchdowns while rushing 11 times for 123 yards. A third-string back, Clarence Kaplan, had 96 yards on six carries, enough to make Navy marvel at Notre Dame's depth. Navy played a modified wingback offense, like Warner's, but didn't have a Nevers to ram it home. Savoldi's first score came on a 23-yard lateral from Brill, repeated moments later for a 55-yard scoring play. In the third quarter, Savoldi muscled in from the 8, then retired to the bench exhausted. Kaplan owned the fourth quarter, setting up Fritz Staab's touchdown for the final score.

Carnegie Tech was next. Notre Dame won this one, 21-6. Carnegie Tech's score capped the only time they were in Notre Dame territory. Kurth and Culver dominated Tech's linemen. After a placid first quarter, Rockne unleashed a series of spinners, reverses, and laterals that dizzied defenders. Schwartz ended a scintillating drive with a 13-yard touchdown pass to Kosky. The teams exchanged interceptions; Notre Dame reached the Tech 2-yard line, and Schwartz piled in for the touchdown. A 72-yard run

Marchy Schwartz scores the winning TD against SMU in 1930.

Joe Kurth, two-time consensus All-American at right tackle, won his starting spot in the spring of 1930, and held it for three years.

for a score by Tech's Eyth brought them close in the third quarter, but Schwartz threw a 44-yard strike to Conley for the closer.

Notre Dame moved on to the University of Pittsburgh, also undefeated in 1929. Pitt's Jock Sutherland worked his charges hard to stop the expected aerial show, but Rockne told Carideo to keep it on the ground. The result was Notre Dame 35, Pitt 19. Pitt's plans evaporated on the first play from scrimmage when Schwartz had a 60-yard touchdown run. Notre Dame scored four more times before the half ended: Mullins in from the 1; Savoldi recovered a fumble to lead to his blast from the 1; Savoldi picked off a Pitt pass and ran 42 yards for a score; and Bucky O'Connor ran 32 and 45 yards before Mike Koken tallied from the 5-yard line. Pitt got two consolation touchdowns on drives and a third on a fumble recovery.

Against Indiana, Savoldi started things with a 33-yard scoring run, and Schwartz raced around right end 26 yards for a touchdown. Later, Schwartz set Brill up with a 79-yard kickoff return, and Brill scored on a 9-yard run; he scored again on a 23-yard jolt. Notre Dame's racehorses compiled 432 yards of offense to Indiana's 76 for the 27-0 win.

The Fighting Irish beat Penn back east, 60-20. Brill had been told that he was not good enough for Quaker football, so he had given the Fighting Irish a try. Running with the starters, Brill saw his work rout Penn 43-0 before the subs went in. On his first carry, Brill scored a 65-yard touchdown. He added two more on similar runs. Carideo, Schwartz, Savoldi, Mullins, and O'Connor also scored. Penn never moved the sticks against the starting unit.

Against Drake, Rockne unveiled yet another threat, Dan Hanley. As a sub, he scored on a 32-yard canter. (Savoldi, secretly married but already divorcing, had been expelled, so the fullback position needed the help Hanley provided.) Drake scored, but Schwartz ran the kickoff back to Drake's 13. The running game got them to the 3-yard line; Carideo faked a pass and handed off to Brill for the touchdown. Schwartz's

Schwartz throwing a pass in the 60-20 rout of Penn in 1930. Penn's Paul Riblett (#5) applies the pressure a bit late.

passing paved the way for a Mullins touchdown in the third quarter, and Schwartz wrapped it up with a 43-yard score. Notre Dame won 28-7.

Northwestern had played to a 0-0 tie with only 10 minutes left. They even reached the Fighting Irish 5-yard line twice in the first half, but came up empty. Finally, Schwartz scored from the Northwestern 18. Hanley secured the 14-0 win with a 1-yard touchdown plunge a bit later.

Then came the annual game with Army, also undefeated, but with one tie. Conditions were wretched at Soldier Field, but the Fighting Irish worked another perfect play, and Schwartz scored on a 54-yarder. Army scored on a blocked kick moments later, but Notre Dame blocked their conversion try. It was a bruising affair, won by the Irish 7-6.

Too bruising, in fact, since Mullins went down, leaving Hanley to face a monstrous USC team. USC was undefeated. They had beaten assorted opponents 389 points to 39. On the long trip west, Rockne orchestrated an elaborate ruse; Bucky O'Connor practiced in the guise of Hanley, purposely running slowly, fumbling a lot, and showing sophomore jitters. The ruse was designed to prepare USC for a slow fullback; in fact, O'Connor was almost as fast as Elder, two steps faster from scrimmage than the Trojans expected. Only Notre Dame alumnus and writer, Francis Wallace, knew of the trick. All the other reporters took it in hook, line, and fullback.

The Trojans literally never knew what hit them. Entering the game as 9-point favorites, they left defeated 27-0. O'Connor ran for an 80-yard touchdown in the second quarter, and later zipped in from the 7-yard line with a lateral (he also lost a 60-yard touchdown run due to a penalty). He averaged 11 yards per carry. Following a USC fumble, Schwartz fired a 19-yard pass to Carideo. USC back Marshall Duffield tried to avert a big loss on a fumble by kicking the ball out of the end zone—his end zone—for a safety. Hanley intercepted a USC pass, and Nick Lukats scored from the 11. The Trojan offense gained only 140 total yards while the Fighting Irish punched out 433.

With its perfect 10-0 record, Notre Dame thus officially became the first school to win consecutive national titles in football.

Bert Metzger, perhaps the smallest All-American for the Irish, started at RG for the 1930 National Champs, weighing all of 149 pounds.

Action in the 1930 ND-USC game. Schwartz makes a short gain.

The Depression was in full force. Rockne coached charity All-Star games against the New York Giants and a Northwestern team, with the proceeds going to the needy. He visited the Mayo clinic for his bad leg and spent the week in bed next to a Fighting Irish player who had missed his senior year with a back injury. He was from Winner, South Dakota. His name was Frank Leahy.

Rockne headed south for some Florida sun. He left his family in Miami while he went back to South Bend to organize spring practice and to tidy up some Studebaker business. Then he went to Chicago to celebrate his mother's birthday early. From there he moved on to Kansas City to see an old friend, Dr. D.M. Nigro. He was on his way to Los Angeles to sign a contract for a Lew Ayres movie about "The Spirit of Notre Dame." He waited an extra 20 minutes in Kansas City to see his two sons who attended boarding school there, but the flight couldn't wait any longer and he missed them by minutes.

The weather was miserable, but the plane took off anyway. They never reached their next stop in Wichita. Over Bazaar, Kansas the plane went into a violent spin, flinging Rockne from the cabin 650 feet above ground before crashing.

A terrible earthquake hit Managua, Nicaragua, that same day, March 31, 1931. Thousands were killed, but their deaths received about a quarter of the U.S. newspaper space that Rockne's did. At the funeral, his players served as pallbearers. He was knighted posthumously by King Olaf of Norway. They knew well what kind of man Knute Kenneth Rockne, 43 years old, had been.

1930 record: 10-0-0 (1.000)
Record to date: 252-48-19 (.819)

1931

An era had come to a terrible, abrupt end. But the pieces had to be picked up. Notre Dame's authorities, led by President Charles O'Donnell, appealed to Jesse Harper to assume the Athletic Director's posi-

The 1931 team, the first since 1918 without Rockne.

tion. Harper did so. Hunk Anderson became the head coach. Anderson had been a fine assistant coach, but he did not have the flair for the head coaching job. He would coach for three seasons, the last a total dud. It would be a decade before the team's fortunes would be placed in the hands of someone with Rockne's flair, intensity, and drive—Frank Leahy.

Anderson inherited a solid team. The line was good, but only Schwartz returned in the backfield (Hanley would miss two seasons because of injuries). How the players would conduct themselves in the absence of Rockne was anyone's guess.

Rockne seemed to be with them for the opener, a 25-0 shutout of Indiana. Three units played and all scored. Joe Sheeketski scored on a 70-yard effort capped by a fake. Reserve center Kitty Gorman intercepted a pass and returned it for a 35-yard touchdown. Sheeketski set up a Schwartz touchdown with a 32-yard pass to Kosky, Marchy tallying from the 11. The deep reserves constructed an 85-yard drive, with Carl Cronin running off tackle for a 35-yard touchdown.

Lake Michigan appeared to have encroached on Soldier Field when Notre Dame met Northwestern the following week. The teams sloshed and splashed to a 0-0 tie, marred by 17 fumbles, a battle Notre Dame won 9-8. The Fighting Irish recovered six fumbles, intercepted two passes, blocked one kick, and deflected another. Schwartz averaged 46 yards on his punts, a detail that might have saved a loss. Moose Krause blocked a kick and had several sacks.

The shutouts continued when Drake was annihilated 63-0. The Irish punted once; all other drives scored. Drake's best field position was the Notre Dame 46. Melinkovich scored two touchdowns, Koken three, and Bernie Leahy, Sheeketski, Jim Leonard, and Frank LaBorne one each. The best was Sheeketski's 45-yarder.

The shutout string ended against Pitt, but Notre Dame won 25-12. Jock Sutherland tried to stop Schwartz's running, so Marchy went to the air for two touchdowns. Melinkovich caught a pass for a 30-yard touchdown and also slammed in from the 1.

Anderson took 115 players to face Carnegie Tech's 29. Still, Tech played a great game in a 19-0 loss, exactly reversing the 1926 score when Anderson subbed for Rockne. Leahy scored twice, a 2-yard burst and a 13-yard run on a lateral. A fake spin play shook loose Schwartz for a 59-yard touchdown; he accumulated 188 of Notre Dame's 388 yards of offense.

The Fighting Irish next trampled Penn 49-0. The starters scored three quick touchdowns, then the subs had fun. Schwartz scored first, untouched from 16 yards out. Other backs noted the gaping hole—Sheeketski went through the same place for a 49-yard touchdown. Schwartz fired a long scoring pass to Chuck Jaskwhich. Sub scorers were Koken, Paul Host, Jim Leonard, and Carl Cronin.

Navy was coached by Notre Dame alumni Rip Miller, Christy Flanagan, and Johnny O'Brien. Notre Dame shut them out, 20-0, although the fullback position took a beating. Schwartz scored on a 17-yard run over the left side, escorted by six Irish players. Steve Banas, once the starting fullback, scored on a

Tommy Yarr, 1931 Captain, starter at center for two years.

plunge. Navy's punter, Chung Hooh, rushed a punt; and Koken subsequently threw a touchdown strike to Emmet Murphy from the 32.

Ten million fans heard the Notre Dame-USC game over the radio. Melinkovich and Koken were hurt, but Notre Dame seemed superior for most of the game. Banas scored on a short plunge. Schwartz crashed in from the 10 for a 14-0 lead at the half. The teams sparred for the third quarter. The Irish knocked out the Trojan quarterback with a broken nose; coach Howard Jones shifted some personnel, and two touchdowns and a field goal later, USC won 16-14. Jones took his team to Rockne's grave after the game.

Whatever snapped in that fourth quarter did not mend quickly. Army shutout the Fighting Irish 12-0. A tired Irish team played heroically, especially Nordy Hoffmann on torn knee ligaments. Army's Ray Stecker won the game on a catch after a fake punt, good for a long gain to set up a touchdown, then iced it with a 70-yard touchdown run.

Schwartz, Kurth, Tommy Yarr, and Hoffmann made All-American teams.

1931 record: 6-2-1 (.722)
Record to date: 258-50-20 (.817)

1932

The Fighting Irish could start this season relatively untraumatized and unburdened. National media attention had diminished, and there was no streak to defend. The line was in great shape, especially with Kurth and Krause, but it would not be easy to replace two-time All-American Marchy Schwartz. Having a healthy Steve Banas would help.

Banas led the Fighting Irish to a 73-0 opening season shutout of Haskell. His flashy running framed the win, with 54-yard and 74-yard touchdowns. In between he scored on a 10-yard run and with a 20-yard pass, while averaging 19 yards per carry for the game. Melinkovich scored three touchdowns, and Lowell Hagan scored one more to give the fullback position 8 of 11 touchdowns. Al McGruff and Red Tobin added scores as Notre Dame racked up 673 yards.

Drake was the next victim, being trampled 62-0. Anderson had the team work on its passing game: the first score came on a 44 -yard pass from Lukats to Ray Brancheau. Then Melinkovich ran 31 yards for a touchdown. Krause blocked a punt for a safety.

Carnegie Tech, in the early stages of what was

Mike Koken, a speedster who backed up Schwartz for two seasons, then started at left halfback in 1932.

to be a long football decline, lost 42-0, bringing the Irish score for the first three games of the year to an astounding 177-0. The 42-0 drubbing was the worst defeat for Carnegie Tech to that point. Mike Koken fumbled at Notre Dame's 10, but the Fighting Irish could not capitalize. Koken ran 58 yards for a touchdown on the next drive. He hit Norb Rascher with a 31-yard pass, and Laurie Vejar passed for the final 9 yards to Sheeketski. Melinkovich scored from a foot out and Jaskwhich ran 66 yards for another. In the third quarter, Krause grabbed a fumble that led to a Brancheau score around left end. Lukats hit three different receivers on medium range passes and a 21-yard finale to Host. Banas wrapped it up when he scored from the 1 late in the game. Irish dominance was total—466 yards to 79 for Tech.

Pitt stopped the Notre Dame string of victories with its own shutout, a 12-0 upset (they had already beaten Army and tied Ohio State). The Fighting Irish seemed to be in control for three periods, driving well but not scoring. Pitt needed little more than 1 minute to win the game. Following an interception late in the fourth quarter, Sebastian ran 55 yards for another Pitt touchdown; another interception was also run back for a touchdown. The running games were about even, but Notre Dame hit only 10 of 29 passes.

Notre Dame next went to Kansas and pounded the Jayhawks, 24-6. Kansas scored first through the air, which seemed to wake up the Fighting Irish. Lukats streaked 45 yards for a score, and the extra point conversion gave Notre Dame the lead. In the second period, Sheeketski ran 60 yards for another touchdown. Melinkovich scored on a 70-yarder in the third quarter. Koken wrapped it up with a 3-yard touchdown dive.

Against Northwestern, Melinkovich took the opening kickoff 98 yards for a touchdown, taking the heat off the Fighting Irish ground game that was staring at the Wildcat's unusual 4-3-1-2-1 defense. Northwestern's defense was vulnerable to passes, however, and Notre Dame took advantage of that route. Kurth trapped their punter for a big loss to set up Koken's touchdown pass to Dom Vairo. On the next Irish drive, at the Northwestern 6, Koken got the ball and did a double spinner before handing off to Kosky coming from around end. Kosky lateralled to Jaskwhich, who had drifted wide as the Wildcats converged on Kosky, and sauntered in for the touchdown. Notre Dame won 21-0.

At Navy, Rip Miller scrapped the midshipmen's wingback system and installed a Notre Dame offensive look. The Irish would be looking at a mirror image of themselves. Unfortunately, the game was played in a mudbath. Played in Sheeketski's hometown, Cleveland, he scored twice before the field turned to jello. He scored untouched from the 11 when he cut off a sweep to go inside. Navy's poor punting gave Notre Dame good field position and Emmett Murphy found Sheeketski alone in the right corner for a 9-yard touchdown pass. Later, Sheeketski intercepted a pass to stop a drive and cap his best day for the Fighting Irish.

Moose Krause, recruited by Rockne in 1930. Rockne knew that he would need larger players for the new style of the game.

The flu bug hit South Bend just before the game with Army in Yankee Stadium. The Cadets were favored, but had never beaten Notre Dame in consecutive outings. The Fighting Irish upended Army 21-0 in spite of the flu. The Irish defense stifled Army all day, while the offense twice drove to the Cadet 5 but stalled. The third time down, Koken faked a run and threw to Melinkovich for the touchdown. In the third quarter, Banas fired a 45-yard touchdown to Hugh Devore, who caught it with a broken hand. Guard Jim Harris scored on a busted punt snap to close the day. Devore continued his injured heroics with an interception and a fumble recovery.

USC was on a roll—18 straight wins. The Fighting Irish became number 19. Anderson had predicted a 13-0 USC win and that's what happened. Not since Nebraska in 1922 and 1923 had a team defeated Notre Dame in consecutive years. USC scored on a 31-yard pass play in the second quarter; in the third quarter Koken misplayed a USC quick kick to give USC great field position for a score seven plays later. Superior USC punting kept the Fighting Irish in the hole all day, and combined with good kick returns, the Trojans enjoyed a 200-yard advantage in that department alone. Otherwise, the teams were even.

Kurth, Krause, Melinkovich, and Kosky earned All-American honors.

1932 record: 7-2-0 (.777)
Record to date: 265-52-20 (.816)

1933

Not since 1888 had Notre Dame experienced a losing season. The success of Notre Dame football was breeding the difficult expectations that they would have a shot at the national title year in and year out. However, Anderson would steer the 1933 Irish to only three wins.

Following Rockne as he did, Hunk Anderson probably never had a chance and the 1933 season cinched it. The pool of Rockne's recruits was dwindling; his last group were seniors in 1933. Recruiting was not going well. On paper, it was a good group, comparable to the 1925-1928 years. Moose Krause was the best college lineman. Wayne Millner, a sophomore, looked fine at left end. Don Elser, at 6-3 and 215 pounds, was the largest Notre Dame fullback since

Bud Bonar, starting QB for the 1933 team, the worst offensive contingent in Irish history with only five TDs all season and 32 points.

Eichenlaub. Lukats was solid at left halfback. The quality slipped at quarterback; Bud Bonar lacked speed. Two 1932 starters, Robinson and Melinkovich, were lost for the year because of illness, and Hanley was still out with a knee injury. Anderson's teams always played great defense (11 shutouts in 18 games), but the offense was suspect. In the four games where total scoring would be a touchdown or less, the Fighting Irish would win one, lose two, and tie one.

The season started with a 0-0 tie against Kansas. Notre Dame struggled to the Kansas 14 on the first possession, but could not score. That was it for the offense, but the defense played well. Kansas had only two scoring chances, both field goals; Notre Dame blocked one. A blocked Elser punt at the Notre Dame 13 gave Kansas another field goal try; but it was hurried as the offense was backing up before a Notre Dame line rush.

At Indiana, Notre Dame pulled out a 12-2 victory. Lukats had a fine run of 53 yards for a score in the second quarter, and Elser followed up a blocked punt for an 11-yard touchdown romp. Notre Dame's defense stopped the Hoosier running game, holding them to 30 yards, while Notre Dame earned 223 yards. The Notre Dame passing game was invisible.

At Carnegie Tech, the Irish dug their own hole quickly when Red Tobin fumbled the opening kickoff at his 26. Tech scored on the next play, and the Irish never recovered. They reached the Tech 17 once, but misfired. Most of the game was spent in a punting duel. Notre Dame's passing was dismal: one completion in 10 tries for 12 yards. Tech won 7-0.

Things got worse. Pitt dominated Notre Dame for a 14-0 win. The Irish offense was throttled: seven first downs to Pitt's 18, 97 yards rushing to Pitt's 251; and 6 of 16 passing for 96 yards. A Pitt interception set up a 78-yard touchdown, and another set up a 14-yard touchdown run. Notre Dame lost Brancheau with two broken ribs.

The Irish now had a scoreless streak of 10 quarters going, and Navy extended it to 14 with a 7-0 win. The Fighting Irish manhandled Navy in all departments except the scoreboard. After the Navy score, Notre Dame put together an 85-yard march on two Banas passes, but an interception at the 15 ended the effort. The Fighting Irish held Navy to 9 yards rushing for the game and only 37 yards in the air for an offensive production of 306 yards to 46, yet Navy won. In the turnover column, Navy dropped the ball five times, but lost it only once; Notre Dame fumbled four times and lost three.

The scoreless streak reached 18 quarters, when Purdue swamped the Irish 19-0. An intercepted Lukats pass earned a Purdue touchdown, and Purdue's offense scored twice. Notre Dame reached the Purdue 2-yard line late in the game but could not score.

Northwestern was next. Someone remembered the basic objective of the game as Notre Dame won 7-

Kitty Gorman, starting center and co-captain for the 1933 team.

0. These points represented 20 percent of the scoring for the whole season. Krause blocked a Wildcat punt at their 13, Kitty Gorman recovered, and Andy Pilney took it in on two runs, the last an 11-yard reverse around the right end. The defense was merciless against Northwestern, allowing no pass completions and holding them to 46 yards on the ground.

USC beat Notre Dame 19-0 at South Bend. Cotton Warburton did most of the damage, gaining 95 yards on 18 carries for two short touchdowns early and late in the game. A short pass between his scores provided the final score. This was the first time since the Fighting Irish's humble beginnings against Michigan that a team had taken three in a row from Notre Dame.

Ten more scoreless quarters had passed before Notre Dame could score against Army. The Cadets were holding a 12-0 lead with 5 minutes to go; they were unbeaten and counting the votes for the national crown, when Moose Krause blocked an Army punt at the Notre Dame 48. Lukats ran to the 32-yard line, Millner picked up 13 yards on an end around; Millner gained the final 19 yards in four tries. Army had to punt again. Krause told Millner to stay put as he moved in tighter to the guard. Army read Krause as the "hot" man and left no one on Millner. Millner blocked the punt and scored a touchdown on the recovery. Red Tobin intercepted an Army pass to ice the 13-12 win. It was a magnificent win, but it was not enough to save Anderson's job. Officials announced that both Anderson and Harper resigned.

No one made an All-American team, but Krause should have.

1933 results: 3-5-1 (.388)
Record to date: 268-57-21 (.804)

1934

Elmer Layden, the "quiet one" of the Four Horsemen, was named head coach. He had played fullback at 160 pounds and helped beat Stanford with two long touchdown interceptions. He had coached at Columbia College in Iowa, and then Duquesne, where he compiled a 47-13-3 record in seven seasons. He also earned a law degree, but never used it.

At Notre Dame, he made some staff changes, keeping only Tom Conley and adding Joe Boland and Chet Grant. He stayed with the 1930's version of the shift. He also worked under a university-imposed limit on scholarships. He had a good mind for detail and a warm personality that wore well with the players. All in all, he was probably the right man for the job, even though Jimmy Crowley of Fordham, the jovial Horseman, also applied.

Layden had to rebuild the team's morale. At least he was not following a legend or coming on the heels of two undefeated seasons. There was less stridency for total Irish dominance. Layden was able to consolidate, much as Harper did in 1913.

USC's Cotton Warburton tries the Irish line in Trojan shutout of Irish in 1933. Wayne Millner (38) moves in.

His new team had more strengths than weaknesses, especially in the backfield. Fromhart looked good at quarterback, Elser was solid at fullback, Melinkovich was back at right halfback, and Bill Shakespeare was promising at left halfback. Moose Krause left a huge pair of shoes to fill. Millner was one of the best in the country at end. Overall, it was a larger team, with marginally better speed and good players in the pipeline.

Texas, coached by former Irish hero Jack Chevigny, came to the Dome and won a good game, 7-6. Layden wouldn't be burdened by ideas of instant success, and the team did not look that bad in the loss. Gusty winds were a factor in both scores: Texas recovered a fumbled kickoff by Melinkovich and scored four plays later. In the second quarter, the Texas quarterback fumbled a punt, kicked it backwards, and dropped it again for John Michuta to recover near the goal. Melinkovich scored the touchdown three plays later, but Millner missed the conversion. The teams played even after that in a well-played game.

Missed conversions were instrumental in a lot of games at this time, but it should be noted that the kicker for the PAT came from the 11 men on the field at the time of the score. There was no wholesale changing of personnel (no special teams).

Layden broke into the win column the next week with an 18-7 triumph over Purdue. Three Irish touchdowns within a 10-minute span of the second quarter ruined Purdue's day: Melinkovich ran for a 60-yard touchdown; Fred Carideo intercepted a pass and ran it 70 yards for a score; and Melinkovich caught a 35-yard pass from Mike Layden and hammered twice from the 3 for the touchdown.

Beating Carnegie Tech 13-0 was a measure of the team's improvement over 1933. Shakespeare scored on a 56-yard run past right end. Andy Pilney hit Vairo with a 32-yard pass near the end zone just as three Tech defenders tackled him. He held on somehow and staggered in for the score. Pilney later broke up a Tech pass on the goal line to kill the only Tech threat.

Freezing sleet marred weather expectations for the last home game, against Wisconsin, but the Fighting Irish managed a 19-0 victory. Carideo scored off left tackle from the 10. In the third quarter, Melinkovich ran 38 yards for a touchdown around left end, and then a 1-yard touchdown over left end again to end a drive. John Lautar preserved the shutout when he grabbed a Badger fumble at the Notre Dame 13.

Pittsburgh stopped the Irish momentum with a 19-0 win. Pitt's Nicksick scored twice, once on an interception return of 62 yards. Notre Dame's offense suffered a general breakdown—only 54 yards rushing and 34 yards passing. It was Pitt's third straight shutout of the Irish; they were closing in on Michigan's turn-of-the century record of four straight.

The Irish once again pushed Navy all over the field in a losing 10-6 effort. Navy only had two

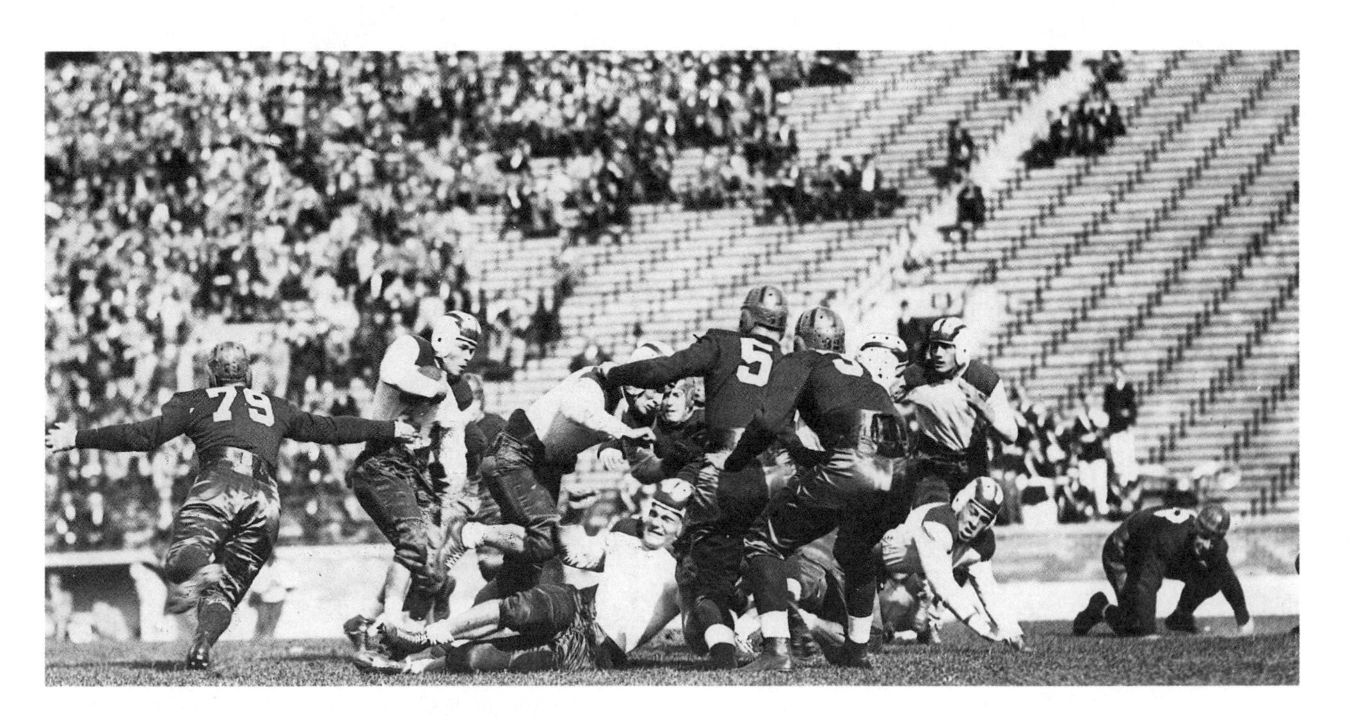

Texas's Hillard scores the winning TD of the 7-6 game in 1934.

The 1934 backfield: from left, RH George Melinkovich, QB Bud Bonar (but Fromhart would play most of the time), FB Don Elser (one of the largest Irish backs until the 1950s), and LH Andy Pilney.

scoring chances and made good on both, an early field goal and a pass for a 10-yard touchdown in the fourth quarter. To get the field goal, they blocked a Shakespeare punt. Their touchdown followed an interception and 35-yard return. Notre Dame moved at will between the 20 yard lines, but eight drives ended in Navy territory. They gained more than 300 yards total offense to Navy's 118 (with 47 on the ground). As Yogi Berra once said, more games are lost than won.

Northwestern was defeated 20-7. The Wildcats did well at first, although Notre Dame almost stopped them four times from the 1. However, on the fourth down, Northwestern was able to push the ball across the goal line for the first score of the day. That was it for Northwestern. In the third quarter, Shakespeare's

Dan Hanley played for three different Irish mentors—Rockne, Anderson, and Layden.

Jack Robinson, starting center in 1932 and 1934, played with severe eye problems, yet made All-American in 1934.

24-yard throw to Melinkovich reached the 18, and two Melinkovich runs set up a short touchdown burst. A 17-yard pass from Pilney to Millner was followed by a 14-yard Pilney sweep for the touchdown. Melinkovich shook loose for a 40-yard gain to the 4, and Shakespeare rammed four times from there to end the scoring.

The following week, Shakespeare helped script a thrilling 12-6 win over Army with his first-quarter pass to Vairo for a 52-yard score. Pilney hit Hanley (playing for his third head coach) with passes for 48 yards, the second a 15-yard touchdown. It was a defensive game for both teams, with Notre Dame getting six first downs and Army only four. Superior Fighting Irish passing was the difference.

Passing again saved the day when Notre Dame beat USC 14-0. Shakespeare hit Layden with a 51-yard touchdown in the first quarter. In the next quarter, a long pass deflected off Warburton to Millner at the USC 2, and Layden jammed it in. USC could not pass well, and that was the ball game.

It had been a quietly successful season, just what Notre Dame needed. Layden was building an effective operation rather than living off past merits. Jack Robinson returned from a missed year to earn All-American honors at center.

1934 record: 6-3-0 (.666)
Record to date: 274-60-21 (.801)

Joe Sullivan replaced graduated Moose Krause at left tackle in 1934, died of pneumonia in 1935.

1935

Stabilized, the Notre Dame football program continued to come together, and Layden relied on the natural drawing power of Notre Dame in his recruiting. He was beginning to put together future dividends. There was a terrible loss in the spring when tackle Joe Sullivan died of pneumonia. The other tackle, John Michuta, would suffer a career-ending head injury in the third game. Millner was back to lead a solid line. The backfield was deep with talent and experience, and Layden's calm leadership kept competing players happy. Ohio State was added to the schedule.

Notre Dame opened with Kansas and was determined to avoid the 0-0 mishap of 1933. Layden's defense gave the Jayhawks only 8 yards rushing and two pass completions in nine tries. Millner grabbed a fumble on Kansas' 26 and Carideo scored on a 15-yard sprint past a block by Millner. In the second period, Carideo had another 15-yard gain, followed by a 2-yard touchdown plunge. Millner caught a 46-yard touchdown throw from Shakespeare and Notre Dame wrapped it up late in the game when Vic Wojcihovski concluded a 60-yard drive with a 2-yard smash for the 28-7 final score.

Pitt Stadium had been the scene of Irish losses since 1931. The Fighting Irish let a Carnegie Tech 3-0 lead stand through the first half. Tech offered a tribute to Rockne at the half, and maybe that helped the Irish. Shakespeare soon tallied a 5-yard touchdown—the first Notre Dame score in Pittsburgh since 1931. In the fourth quarter, a 94-yard march of spinners, reverses, sweeps, and line smashes ended with a

John Michuta, starting RT in 1934 and 1935, was injured in the third game of 1935 to end his career.

Wayne Millner, three year starter at LE, 1935 consensus All-American.

9-yard score by Bob Wilke. Tech lost 14-3 and was held to 44 yards rushing and only 14 yards passing.

In Madison, Layden showed the Wisconsin Badgers an offense with as many tricks as possible (film was now a scouting tool). Passing earned the first two scores: Wojcihovski to Shakespeare for 19 and a touchdown, and in the second quarter, Pilney for 5 yards to Joe O'Neill. Then the Irish switched to a series of lateral passes before Carideo scored from the 1. Pilney later scored, sprung by a Frank Gaul block, on a 40-yard sprint to close the scoring at 27-0. Millner earlier had blocked a punt and recovered the loose ball to help lead a defense that stymied the Badgers all day, allowing only 49 yards rushing.

A tough Pitt team visited the Dome, losing in a close 9-6 game. In the second quarter, Pitt scored first, on a 2-yard plunge, but Millner showed them how to block a conversion try. Shortly after that, Shakespeare tied it up with a 4-yard touchdown run. Later he rocketed an 86-yard punt to keep Pitt penned in. The teams went back and forth through most of the second half. With three minutes left, basketball player Marty Peters made a 27-yard field goal. Fred Solari intercepted a Pitt pass in the final moments to end the game.

Pilney sunk Navy 14-0 with two second-quarter touchdown throws. He threw a long one to Frank Gaul, who had a convoy of Fighting Irish blockers, and later a 3-yarder to Mike Layden, younger brother of Coach Layden. The defense kept Navy in home port the rest of the way.

Ohio State loomed next (in 1969, the centennial year of college football, this would be voted the "game of the century" by the Associated Press). The 1935 Buckeyes were a razzle-dazzle team that used laterals almost indiscriminately—a very high risk offense. They were very big, very physical, and had a

Fred Carideo, cousin of Frank Carideo, started at FB in 1935.

Andy Pilney, hero of the fantastic resurgent win over Ohio State in 1935.

bevy of fine backs. They manhandled the Fighting Irish in the first half. Their first score came when Antenucci intercepted a Layden pass and lateralled to Boucher, who was trailing the play; Boucher ran 65 yards for the score. Another interception started a 50-yard drive that ended in the second quarter when their brilliant sophomore, "Jumpin' Joe" Williams, slammed over for the score from the 4.

Down 13-0 in front of 81,000 screaming Buckeyes, coach Layden quietly told his team to calm down, play steady ball, and announced that the second unit would start the second half. They were rested, determined, and experienced. He had faith in them.

Buckeye fans had spent the first half waving green hankies at the few Fighting Irish fans. But in the third quarter, Notre Dame's ends pinched down hard to the inside when they rushed, so as to make the Ohio State laterals more dangerous to execute. Ohio State could not move, and when the quarter ended, Notre Dame was sitting on the Buckeye 12. Pilney got them there with a 28-yard punt return. Then he passed to Frank Gaul to reach the 2, and Steve Miller took it in. But Notre Dame missed the point after for a 13-6 score. A later Fighting Irish drive ended when Miller lost a fumble. The Buckeyes eventually punted to the Notre Dame 20. There were three minutes to go.

Bill Shakespeare, two-time starter at LHB, 1935 All-American, best remembered as the man who threw the winning TD pass to Wayne Millner in the great 1935 win over Ohio State.

Layden sent in the veterans. Pilney hit Fromhart, who had been open all day (because scouts said he was a blocking back), with a 37-yard pass. Pilney caught a 9-yard pass from Layden. Then Pilney passed to Fromhart to the 15, and again for the touchdown. But Notre Dame missed another conversion.

The Fighting Irish tried an onside kick but Ohio State retained possession. The Buckeyes fed the ball to Dick Beltz, who was "belted" between Danbom and Pilney. The ball went skittering toward the sideline where Notre Dame's Henry Pojman, subbing at center, recovered it. On the second play after the fumble, Pilney ran through a gap over center for a 30-yard gain to the 19. But Pilney was writhing with torn knee cartilage. He tried to watch from his stretcher.

Shakespeare replaced him. They had to pass, and Beltz intercepted—but dropped it. There were 32 seconds left. Layden had a problem—he was out of subs, except for Jim McKenna (whom Layden had asked to pay his own way to the game). Layden sent him in with the play.

The ball was snapped to the fullback, who handed it off to Shakespeare on what appeared to be a reverse as the ends ran a crossing pattern. Then Shakespeare threw to Millner for the winning touchdown. Pilney missed it as they took him to the lockers. He heard the noise, though—81,000 gasps. True to form, the Fighting Irish missed the conversion, ending the game 18-13. The game was won on passing; Notre Dame hit 10 of 21 for 140 yards, while the Buckeyes managed only 2 of 4 for 7 yards. The incredulous fans just milled around the silenced stadium.

The team returned to South Bend and found that students had been dismissed early from classes to vent their joy—for three days. But the team had to go on with its season, and Northwestern was next. The expected letdown came, and the Fighting Irish dropped this game, the first to the Wildcats since 1901, and dashed their emerging hopes for a national championship. Notre Dame scored first when Elser boomed in from the 13, but a penalty negated it. Fromhart later scored from the 1-foot line. Northwestern, scoring in the second half, held on fiercely. Shakespeare shook loose on a 48-yard sprint to the 10, but holding brought it back. Fromhart lost a late fumble, and that cinched the 14-7 Irish loss.

The following week against Army, the Cadets scored first on a 40-yard pass to Grove, and then hung on until late in the fourth quarter. Monk Meyer grabbed a Fighting Irish fumble and ran 50 yards, but Notre Dame stiffened, and Army punted. From their

1935 Notre Dame varsity team.

own 15, Fromhart moved the Irish to the Army 29. Shakespeare threw to Millner, and an interference call put the ball on the Army 1. With 29 seconds left, Danbom powered over for the touchdown. Fromhart missed the point after to conclude a great 6-6 game.

Finally, USC. The Trojans scored first from the 6, after Elser fumbled the ball on his 18. The lead stayed that way through the half. The Irish opened up in the second half with Mike Layden throwing a 38-yard touchdown to Fromhart. Then Fromhart hit Millner with a 44-yard touchdown pass, caught on his fingertips. USC fired back with a 24-yard touchdown pass. Notre Dame was ahead 14-13. They exchanged possessions, then Fromhart iced the 20-13 win, when he returned an interception 72 yards to the USC 8. Shakespeare scored from there. Layden sent in the limping Pilney for one play.

The Irish were back, only one bad game and a conversion away from being undefeated. Millner, Pilney, and Shakespeare made All-American teams.

1935 record: 7-1-1 (.833)

Record to date: 281-61-22 (.802)

1936

Layden had a few problems to solve in 1936. Two All-American left halfbacks (Pilney and Shakespeare) were gone. Millner was gone—and also seven others. John Lautar would anchor the line. There were some fine replacements: Joe Kuharich, Andy Puplis, and Joe Zwers. But overall, the Fighting Irish were too green. Fortunately, the first half of the schedule would allow them some learning time before the heavyweights showed up.

Carnegie Tech lost 21-7, as did Washington University of St. Louis, 14-6. However, Notre Dame played an uninspired game against Washington University. Danbom hammered several times to score from the 4 and O'Neill caught a 12-yard touchdown

Joe Kuharich, two-year starter for the 1936 and 1937 teams at RG—later the head coach.

The 1936 coaches: Joe Boland, Bill Cerney, Johnny O'Brien, Chet Grant, Elmer Layden.

pass from Bob Wilke. Washington University managed one score near the end.

The game with Wisconsin the following week started slowly; a Notre Dame touchdown in the first half was the only action. Wilke earned it on a 17-yard scamper to end an 80-yard drive. In the third quarter, Fred Mundee blocked a Badger punt and Wojcihovski scored two plays later. Third-string halfback George Kovalcik threw a 52-yard pass to Len Skoglund, who reached the Wisconsin 4. Chuck Borowski, with the fourth string, banged in from there. The subs scored once more, and Ben Binkowski preserved the 27-0 shutout with an interception at the Notre Dame 10.

The Pitt Panthers demolished Notre Dame 26-0 in a game the Fighting Irish played poorly. They made their first first down with 15 seconds left in the third quarter. Pitt gained 310 rushing yards to Notre Dame's 58 rushing and 26 passing. Three Pitt drives were long, meticulous affairs led by Marshall Goldberg, a sophomore.

The Ohio State game started as a rerun of 1935, with the Buckeyes muscling Notre Dame all over the Fighting Irish home turf. They drove to the Irish 3, but Joe Gleason intercepted. Notre Dame stalled on the ensuing series, and its punt was blocked out of the end zone for a safety. The Fighting Irish didn't panic, but used up much of the second quarter on a drive that ended with a Bunny McCormick touchdown. The second half was played in torrential rain that ruined the field. The two teams have not met since. The Irish won this second meeting 7-2.

Notre Dame's offensive problems continued against Navy, where the Irish lost 3-0. The Irish reached the Navy 4, but fumbled three plays later. They reached the 12 but were intercepted. Navy played ball control and kicked well to win.

Andy Puplis, starting QB for the 1936 and 1937 Irish.

Layden needed a win over Army, or the season would look very bleak. The defense saved the day in a 20-6 win. Army marched right away, 73 yards to the Notre Dame 6, but Andy Puplis intercepted a pass. Army did the same a quarter later and reached the Notre Dame 5, but could not score. Wilke led a 57-yard march for the Irish, hitting Puplis for a 36-yard gain, before taking it in from the 2. After the half, Army came out with a combination of laterals and passes, but the Fighting Irish converted a fumble recovery and intercepted a pass for their last two scores. After Cronin fell on a fumble, Wilke scored on a fake reverse from the 15. Andy Puplis ran in from the

Art Cronin, starter at RT for the 1936 Irish.

Len Skoglund started at RE for the 1936 and 1937 Irish.

3 after Lautar grabbed a Cadet pass. Notre Dame's defense stopped Army's offense in the second half, allowing only 6 net yards (Army's Monk Meyer dashed 60 yards for their score on a punt return.)

Northwestern came in ranked number one, but self-destructed for a 26-6 Fighting Irish win. Three Wildcat errors ended up as scores for Notre Dame. Wilke made carbon-copy touchdown runs of 30 yards in the first two quarters, and Joe O'Neill grabbed the loose ball after an Irish quick kick was muffed. Danbom scored three plays later. A 6-yard shovel pass from McCarthy to Skoglund ended the Irish scoring in the fourth quarter. Notre Dame's defense did not allow Northwestern to complete a pass.

Notre Dame had a modest two-win streak going over USC; neither had won three straight since the series started. A 13-13 tie kept it that way. The Fighting Irish scored on a 78-yard, 12-play drive, with Wilke scoring off tackle from the 3. He had earlier hit McCormick with a 32-yard pass. USC scored on a

Joe O'Neill, starter at RE for the 1936 team.

Hard-charging, speedy Larry Danbom, starter for the 1936 Irish at FB.

busted play, a half lateral, half fumble that broke for 65 yards. The Fighting Irish drove right back to the USC 9. Puplis went for it all, but a USC reserve named Langley intercepted and took it 100 yards for a Trojan touchdown. In the third quarter, Notre Dame drove 88 yards in 12 plays, ending with Wilke's 15-yard touchdown pass to McCormick. Puplis missed a field goal a little later to ensure a tie. Notre Dame won the statistics: 18 first downs to 1; 223 yards rushing to 24; 138 yards passing to 23.

John Lautar was the only player to earn All-American honors.

1936 record: 6-2-1 (.722)

Record to date: 287-63-23 (.800)

1937

Many question marks arose as the new season approached. There were no obvious stars, but the team looked sound. There were no game-breaking backs that the Notre Dame system demanded. The backs were smallish; Bunny McCormick was the smallest to start in more than a decade. Puplis was stable at quarterback. His backup, Joe Ruetz, made a strange switch from quarterback to left guard. Alec Shellogg would develop into a great tackle.

Bunny McCormick, the 1937 team's starting RHB.

Jack McCarthy, starting LHB for the 1937 team.

Notre Dame opened the season against Drake. Layden used 53 players in a 21-0 exercise. Jack McCarthy lobbed a 5-yard touchdown pass to McCormick in the second quarter. In the third quarter, Kuharich intercepted a pass deep in Notre Dame territory. McCarthy then ran 85 yards for the touchdown. He intercepted a pass later to set up Mario Tonelli's closing touchdown.

Illinois' Bob Zuppke, a great coach, innovator, and amateur artist, was celebrating his silver anniversary as the Illini mentor. The University of Illinois fought the Fighting Irish to a 0-0 tie. Illinois missed a 14-yard field goal, and Notre Dame missed on three passes from the 12. Beyond that, it was a dull game. Lou Zontini, a third-string back, led all runners with 40 yards.

Next, Carnegie Tech upset Notre Dame 9-7. The defense played the typical hard-nosed football that Layden's teams specialized in, and the offense accumulated good yardage but only scored on a 34-yard pass from McCarthy to McCormick. The Fighting Irish lost the game when a Zontini pass was picked off to set up the winning field goal from the 16. Notre Dame fought to the Tech 1 in the fourth quarter, but for the fourth time in the young season failed to score. Tech gained only 7 yards on the ground and completed one pass, and still won. Carnegie Tech would drop football in only a few seasons.

The Fighting Irish offense continued to sputter against Navy, although they escaped with a 9-7 win. The game was played in snow; neither team threw any

Joe Zwers captained the 1937 Fighting Irish, but did not start.

passes. The Middies dominated for three quarters, scoring on an Irish fumble. McCarthy got the only Fighting Irish touchdown on a 31-yard run. Puplis ran back a Navy punt 54 yards to the Midshipmen's 8, but a fourth-down fumble lost the ball. Moments later Navy had to punt; the snap was low, and the kicker tried to run it out. Notre Dame's Chuck Sweeney engulfed him from his right end spot for a safety and the win.

Similar heroics led to a 7-6 win over heavily-favored Minnesota. Sweeney did it again, blocking a Gopher conversion attempt. The Fighting Irish scored early, and the defense had to hang on. Puplis scored on a 35-yard run to the Gopher 34 and then went in from the 2-yard line moments later. The Minnesota score came on a double lateral that turned into a pass for a touchdown. The Irish nullified the extra-point attempt to preserve the victory over Minnesota. It was not an artistic success, but the Fighting Irish defense was a force.

Jock Sutherland's powerhouse Pitt team crunched the Fighting Irish 21-6 for his 100th win, keeping them undefeated for the year. Notre Dame played well in the first half and held the lead into the fourth quarter on a touchdown pass from McCarthy to Puplis. But in the fourth quarter, Goldberg rifled a 51-yard pass to set up a plunge for Pitt's first touchdown. Then they intercepted a wayward Irish pass, leading to a 22-yard touchdown run on a fake reverse. Pitt picked up the pace in its passing game, and Notre Dame's defense never recovered. A third touchdown put the game away. Pitt runners gained 328 yards, with Goldberg claiming 110 yards. The Fighting Irish defense had not been battered that way all season.

Notre Dame beat Army 7-0, scoring only the lone touchdown, despite six Irish ventures into scoring territory. The Fighting Irish scored first and then weathered the storm. Ed Simonich scored after Ed Beinor recovered a fumble on a botched Statue of Liberty play at the Army 14. Simonich took it in from the 3-yard line. A penalty killed a drive to the Army 6 when the trainer was on the field without benefit of a timeout. They lost a sure touchdown when Thesing fumbled on a plunge from the Cadet 1. The defense held Army to 99 total yards, with only 27 on runs.

If anything, the offense looked worse the following week against Northwestern. Notre Dame did not score, and neither did Northwestern. Chuck Sweeney beat Northwestern, it seems, by himself: he

Alec Shellogg, starter at RT for the 1937 team, had a twin brother playing for the reserves.

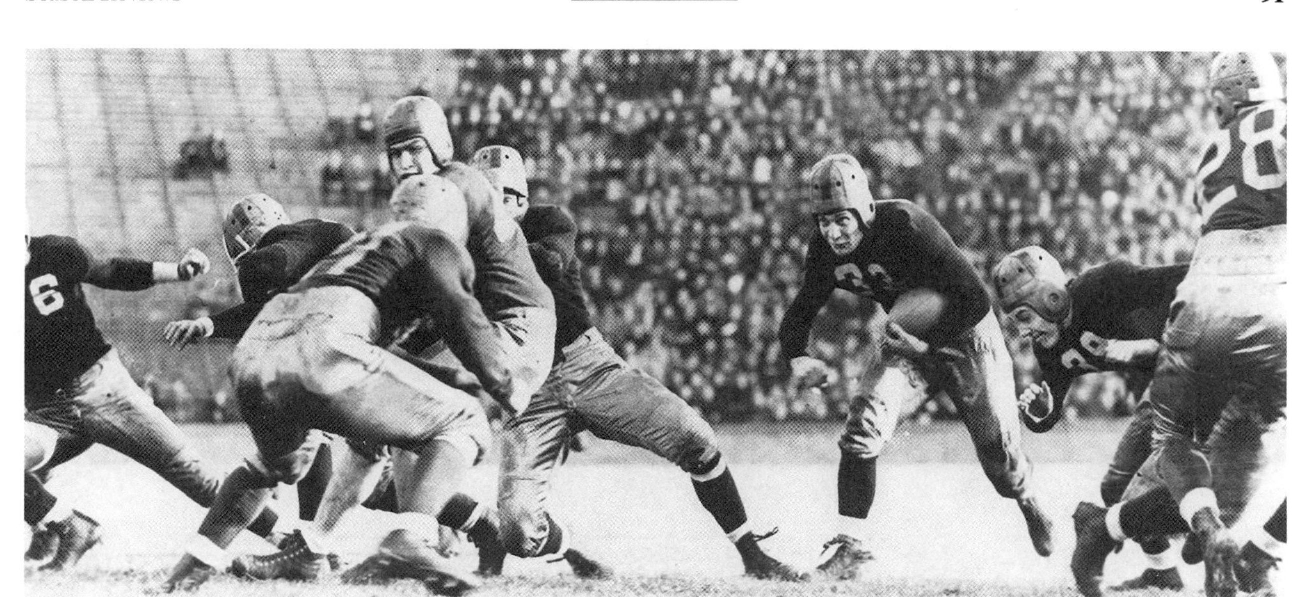

Fullback Joe Thesing finds a big hole in the 1937 USC game. Jack McCarthy (39) blocks to the right of the picture.

blocked a Wildcat punt and recovered it for the only score; he recovered a fumble; he intercepted a pass; he downed an Irish punt at the Northwestern 1-yard line; and he teamed with Alec Shellogg to recover another fumble. It was Notre Dame's fourth shutout of the year.

The Fighting Irish sneaked past USC 13-6 in the season finale. The Trojans dominated the first half, and led 6-0 after a touchdown pass. Puplis scored in the third quarter following a 58-yard run in which he started right, reversed his field to pick up blockers, and then steamed down the sidelines. Tonelli ran 70 yards to the USC 13, and two plays later took it in on an 8-yard scamper. For once, Notre Dame's offense clicked, doubling USC's yardage (301 to 155 yards), with 264 yards on the ground.

Layden must have been relieved when the season ended. Sweeney and Beinor earned All-American recognition.

1937 record: 6-2-1 (.722)
Record to date: 293-65-24 (.798)

1938

The 1928 Fighting Irish had been a low-scoring team (4.2 points per game) with a good defense, and national championships followed. The 1937 season mirrored that of 1928, and the results would be remarkably similar. In 1929, the Fighting Irish averaged 16.1 points; Layden's 1938 Fighting Irish would average 16.5 points—up from 4.3 the year before.

Layden had a solid core of veterans; Beinor anchored the line and was joined by future All-American Jim McGoldrick. Steve Sitko won the

Jim McGoldrick, captain of the 1938 team, and starting LG.

The 1938 Fighting Irish.

quarterback job. Lou Zontini and Harry Stevenson were halfbacks; the fullback position was stacked with Tonelli, Thesing, newcomer Milt Piepul, and dependable Ed Simonich.

Kansas, with future basketball coaching great Ralph Miller at the quarterback helm, opened the season. Notre Dame dismantled the Jayhawks 52-0 (this would be almost a third of Notre Dame's points for the year). Subs scored five touchdowns. Benny Sheridan scored twice, and Bob Saggau had the best run of the day, a 51-yard sprint for a touchdown. The defense intercepted five Kansas passes. Tonelli started the scoring with a 6-yard end run. In the second quarter, Sheridan sped 30 yards for a score, followed shortly by Simonich's 11-yard touchdown run. They kept up the pace in the third quarter: Zontini ran 25 yards for a touchdown; Earl Brown caught a 30-yard touchdown pass from Harry Stevenson; Sheridan went off tackle on a reverse from the 13. In the fourth, Saggau scored and Piepul went in from the 6. The ground game amassed 392 yards, the best in years.

The Fighting Irish went to Atlanta to meet a good Georgia Tech team and escaped with a 14-6 squeaker. Zontini's interception set up a 42-yard run and 9-yard touchdown by Tonelli. John Gubanich

Steve Sitko, starting QB for the Irish in 1938 and 1939.

Ed Beinor, two-year starter at LT, All-American in 1938 .

John Gubanich (66) blocks a Kansas player in the 1938 opener over Kansas.

blocked a Tech punt in the fourth quarter, before "We The" Piepul rammed in from the 1, and the Irish capitalized with runs of 17 and 10 by Sheridan. Both teams ran well but had difficulties with their passing game, but the Irish won 7-0.

Back home, the Irish met Zuppke's Illini and repeated the Tech score, 14-6, on good running and stern defense. Stevenson threw a 47-yard touchdown pass to Earl Brown for the first score, taking the lead into the third quarter. Then Sheridan intercepted an Illinois pass and streaked 68 yards for the score. The Illini blocked a punt and scored, but center Ed Longhi ended the Illini's hopes with an interception on the Irish 9. Notre Dame wasted three good drives on fumbles, but ran for 264 yards, while holding Illinois to 70 yards running, and only three completed passes.

Ed Longhi, starter at center for the 1938, 1939 Fighting Irish and an All-American.

Carnegie Tech's football program was not dead yet, dominating the Fighting Irish for three quarters before an official's error broke their momentum. With the ball on fourth down, the Tech quarterback asked about the down situation; the umpire said it was third down. Tech ran its play before the official recognized his mistake, he then had no choice but to give the ball to the Fighting Irish. Tech protested vigorously, but to no avail. The Irish had it at the Tech 36; Piepul ran to the 18. Sheridan ran for 10 more but fumbled; however, Bud Kerr recovered the ball for the Irish at the Tech 7. Kerr got the call for an end around and scored the game-winning touchdown. Both teams had played brilliant defense.

In the next game, Army tested Notre Dame's defense when it took the kickoff and executed a 73-yard drive, ending with a 5-yard touchdown pass. Piepul brought the ensuing kickoff back 43 yards, but the Irish drive stalled, and despite John Kelly's recovery of a Cadet fumble, Army's 7-0 lead held into the second half. In the third quarter, from short punt formation, Thesing took the ball up the middle for 34 yards. From the same formation, Saggau lofted a 46-

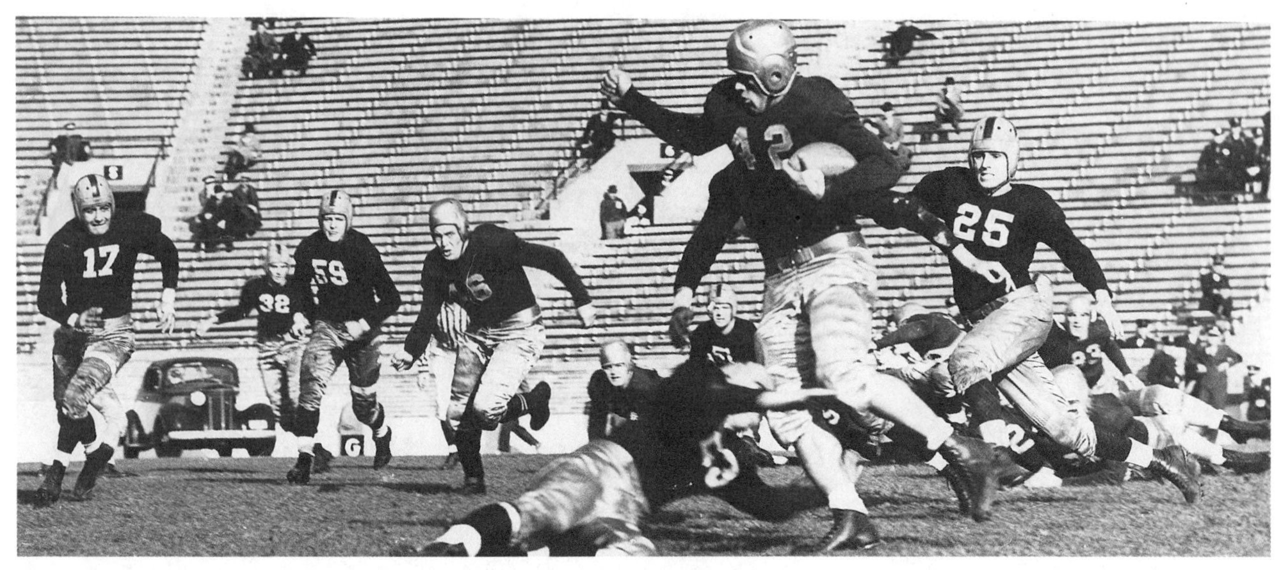

Carnegie Tech's Muha about to be finished off in 7-0 Irish win in 1938. Zontini makes the first contact as Bossu (17), Stevenson (32), McGoldrick (59), and Brown (25) close in to end the play.

yard touchdown pass to Brown, but Notre Dame missed the point after. Army stifled Notre Dame's next drive, but Saggau hit a 74-yard punt to keep Army on the defensive. In the fourth quarter, Bud Kerr blocked a punt, Bud Hofer recovered, and Sheridan slipped in from the half-yard mark for the second Irish score. Notre Dame wrapped it up with a Thesing touchdown of 48 yards. Good defense held Army to 49 yards to Notre Dame's 260 as the Irish prevailed 19-7.

The Fighting Irish defeated Navy next, 15-0. Saggau scored first, from the 7, to end an 80-yard drive on the ground. Johnny Kelly grabbed a Navy fumble in the third quarter, and Thesing converted it into an Irish touchdown. Subs tallied a safety in the fourth quarter for the final margin of victory.

Notre Dame's 300th win was against Minnesota, 19-0. Zontini started with an 84-yard run early in the first quarter. Minnesota never recovered. In the second period, Saggau found Brown open for a 48-yard scoring toss; and he hit Kelly with a 13-yarder in the final quarter. Notre Dame's pass defense allowed Minnesota only five completions in 18 tries for 1 yard.

Northwestern bowed 9-7. Bill Hofer ensured the Notre Dame win with a 65-yard touchdown return on an interception in the second quarter, and a 20-yard field goal in the third quarter. Northwestern ran well, but the Fighting Irish did not pass well, which accounted for the close game.

The eight-game Irish winning streak ended when USC shutout the Fighting Irish 13-0. Notre Dame's offense choked, losing two fumbles and three interceptions. USC scored on a pass from Day to Krueger in the second quarter, and Anderson took it in from the 3 after a Piepul fumble. Three interceptions late in the game spelled doom for the Fighting Irish. Their ground game never materialized. The loss cost them any hopes of an undisputed national title.

Beinor was a consensus All-American; Earl Brown and McGoldrick made honorable mention.

1938 record: 8-1-0 (.888)

Record to date: 301-66-24 (.800)

1939

The powerful Notre Dame backfield returned intact for the 1939 season. Thesing and Piepul powered the fullback operation while Sitko, Zontini, and Stevenson had good speed as a unit and plenty of experience. Three All-Americans were gone from the left side, so a strong running game was not likely.

Layden's fears were substantiated when Notre Dame hung on to beat Purdue 3-0 in the season opener. There was no passing game, and Notre Dame's running was modest. Third-string quarterback John Kelleher hit the winning field goal in the third quarter, but it was not a satisfying win.

Georgia Tech made the trip north the following week, and played tough football before bowing 17-14. Stevenson hit a field goal in the first quarter, the eventual winning margin, which served as a keynote for the year, as the kicking game would have to work

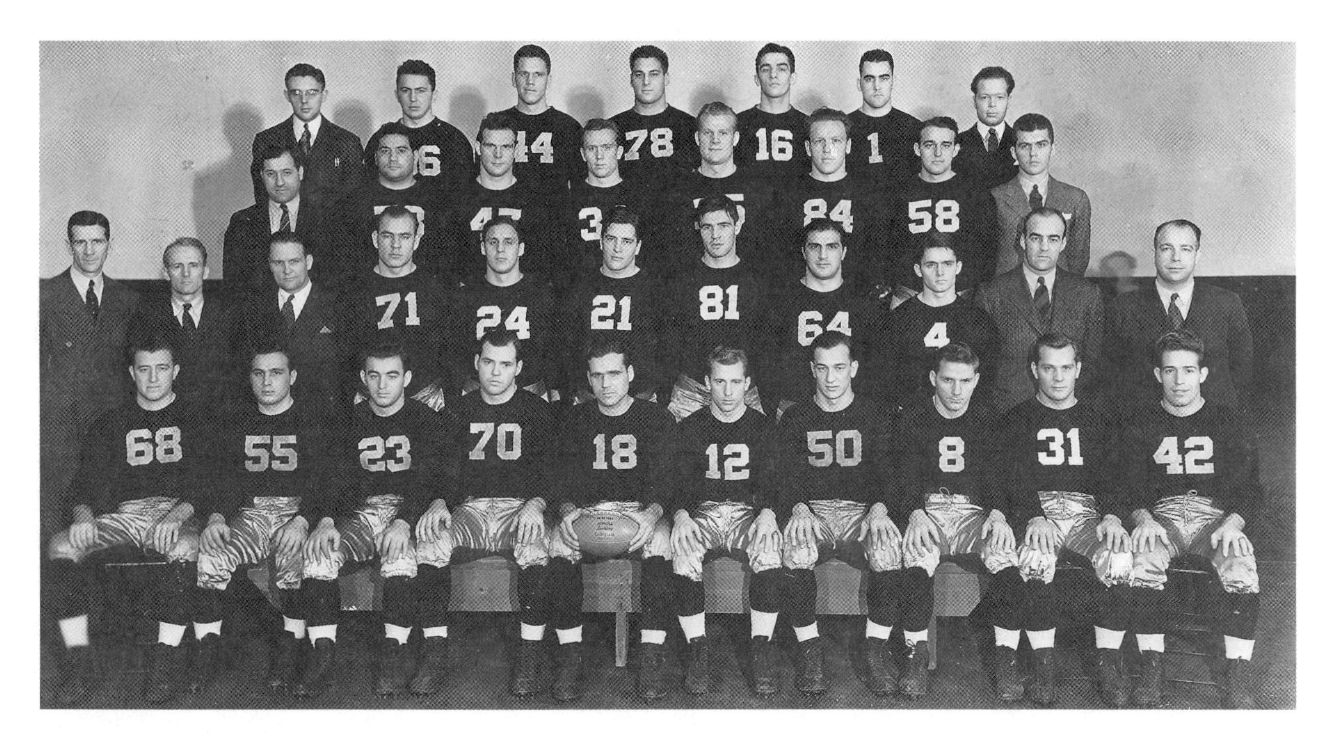

1939 Notre Dame Fighting Irish.

well for Notre Dame to win. Tech blocked a punt in the next quarter and earned a touchdown to go ahead 7-3. Notre Dame responded with two scores when Saggau slammed in from the 6-yard line and Thesing from the 4-yard line on consecutive drives. The third period was dull, but Tech was learning that Notre Dame was vulnerable to the pass. Tech scored again to pull within three, and then watched as a last-gasp pass went off the fingers of an open receiver. The Fighting Irish offense had 246 yards running, but only 5 yards in the air.

In the third game of the season, the Fighting Irish twice had to overhaul the SMU Mustangs to win 20-19. SMU jumped on a Thesing fumble in the first quarter and turned it into a touchdown. Notre Dame came back with two passes, one netting an interference call and the other a 21-yard touchdown from Stevenson to Zontini. In the second quarter, the Mustangs drove 69 yards for a go-ahead touchdown. Notre Dame then went 67 yards the other way in 13 plays, with Piepul carrying seven times; he finally scored from the 1-foot line. In the fourth quarter, Piepul ran 10 yards around right end to cap another drive. Kelleher kicked the important point after. With two minutes to go, SMU blocked a punt at the Notre Dame 2-yard line, and "Presto" Johnson scored, pull-

The 1939 starting backfield: RH Zontini, FB Thesing, QB Sitko, LH Saggau.

Saggau rips for a TD in the 17-14 win over Georgia Tech in 1939.

ing SMU within a point. But SMU missed its conversion and Notre Dame won its third straight game on the strength of its kicking play.

Notre Dame won a 14-7 game over Navy to go 4-0 for the season. Notre Dame backs ran for 419 yards to Navy's 33. Sheridan opened the second quarter with a 26-yard touchdown thrust. A 64-yard drive, highlighted by Piepul's 22-yard burst, ended when Piepul tumbled in from the half-yard mark.

Bud Kerr, starting LE for the 1939 squad.

Navy finally scored on a 64-yard pass late in the game. The Fighting Irish had another woeful passing day—one completion for 0 yards. Offensive consistency and balance were missing from the Notre Dame game.

Snow and Carnegie Tech in Pittsburgh were a tough combination. Notre Dame escaped 7-6, with the defense winning the game. A Tech runner was squeezed by a triple Irish hit, the ball went straight up, and an alert Bud Kerr picked it out of the air and scored from the 19. Zontini made the point after. In the fourth quarter, Tech was unstoppable on an 89-yard touchdown drive. But on the conversion kick, Notre Dame's center, John McIntyre, slammed through his blocker and took the ball in his chest to save the win.

Undefeated after five games, the Fighting Irish had outscored their opposition by a total of only 15 points. In their sixth game against Army, the Fighting Irish beat the Cadets 14-0, but the offense did not have that much to do with it. Both Notre Dame scores came from Cadet errors. A second quarter fumble on Army's 31 was recovered by Notre Dame's Jack Finneran; Stevenson scored from the 6-yard line on a sweep. In the fourth quarter, Steve Bagarus intercepted an Army pass and streaked down the sidelines for 45 yards and a touchdown, evading six Cadets.

Notre Dame next faced the University of Iowa, and Iowa standout Nile Kinnick, who was only weeks away from winning the Heisman. Kinnick scored on a 4-yard plunge, and drop-kicked the point after. Kinnick's score followed Sitko's interception, who

The Rockne Memorial just prior to its dedication in 1939.

Interior of the Rockne Memorial lobby.

then lost the ball to the Hawkeyes with an ill-advised lateral. Late in the third quarter, Piepul also tallied from the 4, but Zontini missed the point after to clinch a 7-6 Iowa win.

Notre Dame managed a 7-0 squeaker over Northwestern to raise its season record to 7-1. It was a dull affair, punctuated only by Sheridan's non-scoring 52-yard run in the second quarter. In the third quarter, Bob Hargrave returned a punt 50 yards, and with 3:30 remaining, Piepul went in for a 5-yard touchdown. The defense held on for the win.

USC won the season finale 20-12. Trojans Lansdell and Schindler accounted for USC's three touchdowns, the latter on a 40-yard run. Piepul bulled in from the 6, and Sheridan jetted 60 yards to account for Notre Dame's scoring. A last-second drive by the Irish reached the USC 7 but died there. The Fighting Irish almost sacked Trojan passers six times, but missed each time. Notre Dame had three fumbles and three interceptions, which was more than enough to offset 291 yards of offense to USC's 246. It was Notre Dame's 400th game.

Knowledgeable observers could see that change was needed to keep the Fighting Irish among the nation's elite teams. The old Notre Dame box and the shift could not operate as originally designed. The idea for the modern T was forming in Stanford's Clark Shaughnessey's head. It was only a matter of time before Irish football would have to make a clean break from the Rockne-influenced tactical past. Still, the 1939 season should be appreciated as a minor gem, with Layden the jeweller who knew how to make it shine more than it should have. Bud Kerr and Piepul won All-American honors to add to the luster.

1939 record: 7-2-0 (.777)

Record to date: 308-68-24 (.800)

1940 to 1949

1940

Administrative changes at Notre Dame may have portended the end of the "de-emphasis" of football under which Layden had worked. A new President, Fr. Hugh O'Donnell—the 1915 starting center—understood football as an insider. Still, the opinion about the Layden years was tending toward disillusionment. This "quiet one" of the Four Horsemen did not quite seem able to put the team over the top. But Layden still had a job to do.

He had to rebuild the line. Player turnover was high; he seemed to be getting only 1-2 years of starting time from them. Subs filled in the line's holes, except for sophomore flash Bob Dove at left end. The backfield had to be replaced, but the reserve backs had enjoyed more playing time, so the transition was easier. Piepul started at fullback, Saggau and Juzwik ran as halfbacks, and Bob Hargrave was quarterback.

The Irish first faced Amos Alonzo Stagg and his Pacific team. Stagg had coached four times against Notre Dame in the 1890s and never lost. He was in his 51st year of coaching. It was also "National Knute Rockne Week," a promotional device for the soon-to-be-released motion picture starring Pat O'Brien and Ronald Reagan.

Pacific scored right away, using a mix of passes and trick plays on a 60-yard march, ended by a 1-yard touchdown up the middle. But in the second period, Saggau threw to Juzwik for 40 yards to the Pacific 25. Piepul waited for an incompletion, then ran 18 yards to the 7. Juzwik faked a reverse and scored. Tied until the middle of the third quarter, Notre Dame blew it open with three touchdowns. Bernie Crimmins went in from the 16 with a run around end. Piepul ran 17 yards, starting right and then cutting back to the

Layden's last coaching staff, 1940: Bill Cerney, Chet Grant, Elmer Layden, Joe Benda, Joe Boland.

Milt Piepul on his way to a gain around left end in 1940 action with Georgia Tech. Tech's Sanders (8) leaps over Bassas (66), Gubanich (69) and Hargrave (3).

middle, to score. He then intercepted a pass on the Pacific 20, and Juzwik ran a cut back to score on the next play. Notre Dame had finally beaten Stagg, 25-7.

Georgia Tech, historically tough for the Irish, visited next. Notre Dame moved the ball well in the opening quarter but did not score. They scored in the second quarter on an 87-yard drive in seven plays, ending in a touchdown pass from Saggau to Hargrave. Two minutes later Saggau streaked off left tackle and ran 60 yards for another score. Saggau and Steve Bagarus traded passes to each other before Saggau scored from the 5-yard line. Tech's John Hancock returned a kickoff 90 yards for a touchdown. Bernie Crimmins blocked a Tech punt, and Jim Brutz collected it in the end zone for Notre Dame's fourth TD of the day. Tech scored twice more in the fourth quarter, but Notre Dame held them off for the 26-20 win.

Carnegie Tech was sent packing 61-0, the largest score of Layden's years. Tech was helpless, entering Fighting Irish territory only in the third quarter against the fourth-string defense. Notre Dame scored nine touchdowns. Bernie Crimmins led with three, Piepul and sub Al Lee had two each, and Johnny O'Brien and Juzwik had one each.

Following the victory over Carnegie Tech, the largest crowd in 11 seasons met the Irish in Champaign for the game with the University of Illinois. Layden's subs struck, with Dippy Evans passing to Bagarus from the 6 for the touchdown. Late in the opening quarter, with the starters in, Juzwik rammed for 17 yards and then Saggau threw to him for a 29-yard touchdown. In the next period, Saggau threw a 3-yard scoring pass to Crimmins. In the fourth quarter, Notre Dame wrapped it up with a 63-yard march crowned by Juzwik's 6-yard run past left end for the final score, 26-0. The Irish ran for 262 yards to 26 for Illinois.

Army played inspired football to hold the Fighting Irish to a pathetic three yards of total offense in the first half, but the Cadets also made some big errors. With the ball about 15 yards from the right sideline, the Army quarterback tried to pass across the field to the wide side. Juzwik picked it off cleanly and headed for the end zone, but the Cadet quarterback had the angle on him. Juzwik slowed a bit and the potential tackler overran the play. He then cut back to go 80 yards for the only score of the game. It was a replay of the Elder touchdown in 1929; even the sideline was the same. Army also missed a short field goal try, fumbled at the Notre Dame 14 (Dove recovering), and lost another interception in the third quarter to kill a drive. Army won the statistics as the Irish passing game earned 0 yards, but Notre Dame won the game 7-0.

Luck and good scouting beat Army; but it was Saggau who beat Navy the following week. In the first quarter, he passed to Dove for a 32-yard score and a 6-0 Notre Dame lead. Navy cruised to Notre Dame's 15 twice in the second quarter but could not score. The Midshipmen finally punched over a touchdown and took the lead on the extra point. This lead stood until

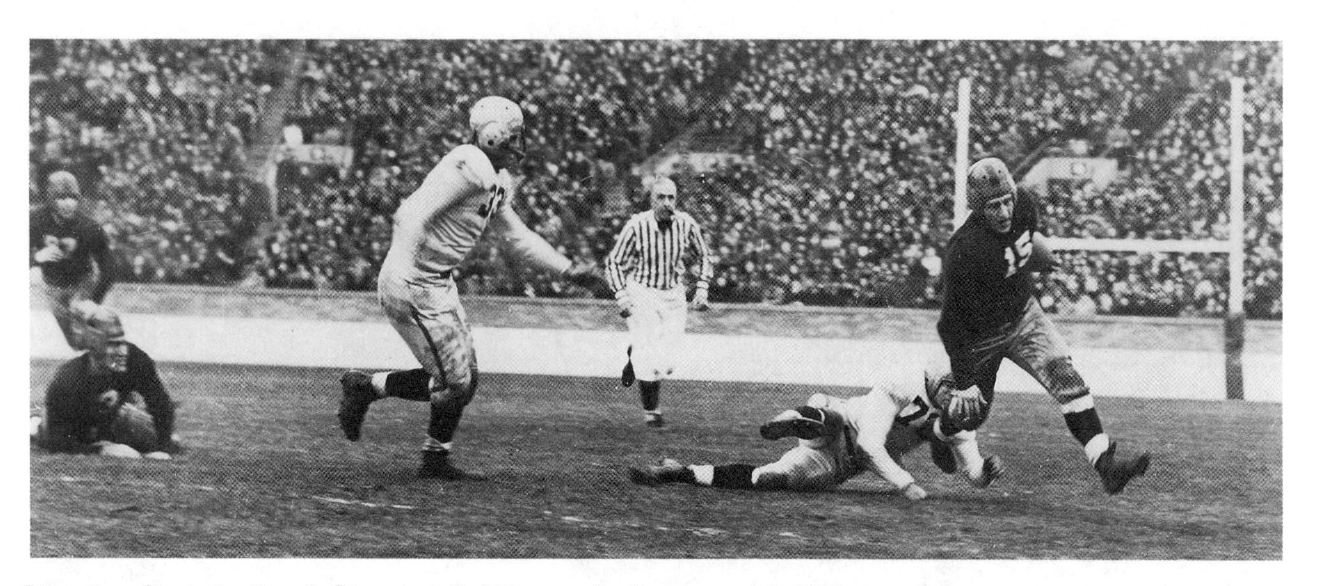

Steve Juzwik evades Iowa's Strauss as Enich moves in; Iowa won this 1940 game 7-0.

the fourth quarter, when Saggau scored from the 7 behind great blocking. The offense was atrocious; good defense with three interceptions saved the day in the 13-7 Irish win.

After two ugly offensive outings, something had to give against Iowa. It did; the offense failed to materialize, and Notre Dame lost its first game of the year, 7-0 to Iowa. The loss was considered a giant upset, since Iowa had lost four straight while Notre Dame had won six straight. The defenses dominated a scoreless affair into the fourth quarter. Then, Notre Dame muscled a drive to the Iowa 1 but couldn't score. After an Iowa punt, Notre Dame drove again to the 10. Piepul coughed up one of his two career fumbles. Iowa drove, punted, intercepted a Saggau pass, moved to the Irish 25—and missed a field goal. Notre Dame had the ball for only one play on the ensuing drive and fumbled. Two plays later Iowa scored. Notre Dame had self-destructed with four fumbles in the final five minutes.

The Fighting Irish troubles continued, as they were drubbed by Northwestern, 20-0. Bill De Correvont played a fine game for the Wildcats, throwing one touchdown pass and scoring from the 4 for another. Notre Dame had been shut out eight straight quarters.

Notre Dame would win the next close one, 10-6, over USC. The weather provided a broiling day; all the scoring was in the first half before everybody dehydrated. Sixteen USC players had been hospitalized with the flu the week of the game. Piepul made a first-quarter field goal. (Layden had four game-winning field goals kicked in his Notre Dame coaching career by four players who booted only once.) USC scored on a split back play that broke for a 54-yard touchdown. Juzwik saved a touchdown, tackling a Trojan who had gained 45 yards. Notre Dame's winning drive started with Dippy Evans at quarterback, who fired a 46-yard pass to Ray Ebli; Piepul ended the scoring and his career with a 3-yard touchdown moments later. Saggau intercepted a USC pass in the third quarter to save the win.

Two months later, Layden announced his resignation to become the NFL commissioner. He had won 47, lost 13, and tied three for a .770 percentage. He had also saved a deteriorating situation and consolidated matters under stringent Notre Dame rules.

Piepul earned All-American honors.

1940 record: 7-2-0 (.777)

Record to date: 315-70-24 (.799)

1941

When the 1941 season rolled around, times were tense, as world events gyrated out of control. As a result of WWII, life seemed to be lived with greater purpose in 1941. The decision to hire Frank Leahy to replace Layden (Buck Shaw withdrew) matched the intensity of the day.

Leahy was tough, shrewd, intense, and dedicated to a fault. A marginal player his first two years at Notre Dame, he started at tackle in 1929, and again in 1930, until injuries sidelined him. While with Rockne at the Mayo Clinic, he decided to go into coaching. He coached at Georgetown, Michigan State

The changing of the guard—Leahy's first coaching group: Ed McKeever, Frank Leahy, John Druze, and Joe McArdle.

(with Jimmy Crowley), Fordham (where he coached Vince Lombardi and with Bud Wilkinson), and Boston College in 1939 and 1940 where he was undefeated, including an upset win over Tennessee in the Cotton Bowl. Leahy paid attention to detail—any detail, anywhere, anytime. He later even kept a bed in his office at Notre Dame so he could collapse there rather than go home. He was almost as hard on his players as he was on himself, except that the players did not become physically sick, as he did, over missed assignments, busted plays, and—the worst of all—losses. They'd better come close to getting sick, though, or they didn't play for "The Man."

Leahy had the best and the worst of football in him. He could bend the rules in his favor and was blindly devoted to a game, seeing it as an end, letting it dominate his life and his players' lives for so long each year that their existence seemed one-dimensional. Yet, the players loved him for his drive, determination, dedication, and supreme willingness to encourage them to get the most out of themselves. He believed that one always strives for perfection, never slacks off, and never takes the easy way out. Rockne had preached the same message, but with humor that put things in a different perspective. Rockne enjoyed life—Leahy wrestled with it.

Leahy inherited a solid core. His best players were Bob Dove and Steve Juzwik; two fine sophomores were on hand in Angelo Bertelli and another of the Miller clan, Creighton. He moved Crimmins from fullback to guard and Dippy Evans from left half to fullback.

Three-year starter at LE, Bob Dove was an All-American in 1941 and 1942.

Bob Maddox, starter at LG for the 1941 squad.

The Leahy era opened at home against Arizona, and the football world waited to see if Leahy's magic would transfer from Boston to Notre Dame. Bertelli, an unknown at the start of the season, threw seven passes in the first quarter and completed six. His last throw hit Bob Dove for a 16-yard touchdown. More passing led to the second Notre Dame touchdown, with the subs in, when Jack Warner found Bill Earley for a 22-yard scoring strike. Arizona struck back with a 66-yard pass and run play for a 12-7 Irish lead at halftime. In the second half, Bertelli's passing got the ball to the Arizona 9-yard line, and Juzwik swept left end for the touchdown. Dippy Evans, on the next Irish possession, sliced past left guard, spun away from tacklers, and ran 78 yards for a touchdown. Sub Don Hogan scored a late touchdown and passed for another. Crimmins intercepted a pass to stop an Arizona drive as Notre Dame blasted Arizona 38-7. Four of six Notre Dame touchdowns came as the direct or indirect results of the passing game.

Notre Dame beat Indiana next, 19-6, with a balanced attack and a fine pass defense that allowed Indiana only two completions in 12 tries for 65 yards. Bertelli and Juzwik worked the ball to the Hoosier 4-yard line, and Evans went in from there. Evans' punting kept Indiana in a hole and opened up a short drive in the second quarter with Evans piling in from the 2. Evans earned all the yardage on a 48-yard drive in the third quarter, including his 7-yard run over right tackle for the final Notre Dame score. The lone Indiana touchdown came on a long pass and lateral.

The Fighting Irish went to Atlanta and beat Georgia Tech, 20-0, raising their season record to 3-0. Notre Dame's George Murphy blocked a Tech punt and later caught the resulting touchdown pass from Bertelli. For the next score, Evans got the snap and started to run towards Tech's left end, but he spun around and gave the ball to Juzwik, who stormed past the right end to score standing up 67 yards later. In the third quarter, Dove smothered a Tech fumble, and after seven plays Juzwik scored from the 4-yard line. The Irish ran for 221 yards and intercepted six of Tech's eight passes. After three games, the Fighting Irish also had 14 holding penalties called on them.

Carnegie Tech fell next, 16-0, in a rainstorm that almost prohibited the running game but did not slow down Bertelli's passing. He sparked a 74-yard march with passes and Juzwik ran in from the 7-yard line for the touchdown. The second unit drove 49 yards, and Creighton Miller earned his first touchdown for the Irish from the 1-yard line. Good defense and speed trapped a Tech back for a safety to end it.

The following week, Illinois bolted to an early lead after intercepting a Bertelli pass. This was answered by Juzwik's end sweep for a 12-yard touchdown at the end of the first quarter. The Fighting Irish scored twice in the next quarter: a Bertelli pass to Juzwik from the 13, and Evans ran in from the 6 for a 21-7 halftime lead. The Illini got back into it in the third quarter with a 65-yard scoring march, but a flagrant personal foul against Juzwik aroused the student body. The Fighting Irish slammed in four scores to turn it into a rout: Bertelli threw twice to Evans for touchdowns; Wally Ziemba intercepted a pass and Evans went in from the 3; and Miller raced 40 yards with a Dick Creevy pass to score. The final score was 49-14.

Army played the Irish to a 0-0 tie. The weather was atrocious, and Army punting kept Notre Dame in its backyard all day. On the last play of the game, Leahy called a triple wing back set for Harry Wright, Juzwik, and Bertelli as the ball was snapped to Evans. But the ball never reached him. It wobbled out of reach, and he chased it around with Cadets in hot pursuit until he literally slid out of bounds.

Undefeated Navy was next, and Bertelli beat them with three touchdown passes. Juzwik sparked the first score with an interception and a 49-yard run; Bertelli went for the jugular with a 42-yard pass to the 2-yard line, and Evans slashed in from there. Navy

1941 Notre Dame Monogram winners.

came right back with a score, but Notre Dame offset that score with a Bertelli to Juzwik pass for an 18-yard touchdown. In the third quarter, Bertelli was intercepted for a touchdown, pulling Navy to within a touchdown. Bertelli kept passing in the fourth period to reach the 8, and Evans did the rest for a 20-13 hard-earned win.

A tired Irish team eked out a 7-6 win over Northwestern. This was basically the same Otto Graham team that had smashed the Fighting Irish the year before. A Crimmins interception let Bertelli pass on a short drive, hitting Matt Bolger with the winning touchdown. Juzwik made the important point after. Northwestern marched right back with Graham scoring, but Ziemba blocked the conversion try. Good defense stymied Graham the rest of the way for the Irish win.

USC was next, and the Fighting Irish were in the hunt for an undefeated year. USC blocked a quick kick and soon scored on a pass, but Ziemba again blocked a point after kick. Poor punting led to a Juzwik run of 23 yards to the USC 6-yard line and from there Evans scored on a reverse. The Trojans fumbled on their next possession, and Bertelli fired three passes to Dove, good for 19, 10, and 16 yards to put the ball almost on the goal line. Juzwik rammed in from there, giving Notre Dame a 14-6 lead. USC scored, but John Kovatch blocked the conversion kick. In the third period, Bertelli flipped to Evans, who ran 18 yards for the last touchdown. USC scored again, but missed a pass for the conversion, giving Notre Dame a 20-18 victory.

Bertelli hit 13 of 21 passes for 156 yards and was 70 of 123 for 1,027 yards for the year—staggering statistics for those days. The Fighting Irish were ranked third behind Minnesota and Duke, and Crimmins and Dove earned All-American accolades. Notre Dame was back.

1941 record: 8-0-1 (.944)
Record to date: 323-70-25 (.802)

1942

Leahy knew that he had to change the obsolete Irish offense. The school's president gave him permission to scrap the time-honored Notre Dame box and what was left of the shift. Leahy tinkered with the pass blocking scheme in 1941 to help protect Bertelli. Next he proposed the T formation. He prepared diligently, interviewing the Bears' George Halas (who had just obliterated the Redskins 73-0 in the NFL title game using the T), Bears' quarterback Sid Luckman, and Clark Shaughnessy, architect of Stanford's great pre-war T-formation teams and the formation's major theoretician and proponent.

Bertelli may have been the slowest halfback ever fielded at Notre Dame. Putting him at quarter-

Leahy's 1942 coaching staff: Wayne Millner, Ed McKeever, Bob Snyder, Ed Krause, Frank Leahy.

back would open up a halfback spot where speed mattered. He had a great arm—the best ever at Notre Dame to that point and one of the best of all time. Leahy's planning was so good, the T would stay at Notre Dame well into the Fifties.

Football prior to the T was essentially a ground game, with an occasional pass to keep a defense honest, or thrown in desperation in a losing effort. But the T isolated the passing to the quarterback position, shifting it from the left halfback or even other backs, and left the quarterback to concentrate on the passing game.

Leahy's new backfield had Bertelli at quarterback, Miller at right halfback, Bob Livingstone at left halfback, and Cornie Clatt at fullback (after a preseason injury ended it for Evans). The offensive line was a big, fast, mobile unit—precisely what the T called for.

Everything was ready for the grand unveiling against Wisconsin. The Fighting Irish took a train to Madison—except Bertelli, who was on the wrong train. He figured it out, changed trains, and reached the stadium just in time for the game. He must have left his passing game on the train, however, as the Badgers tied the Irish 7-7. Wisconsin's all-time great, Elroy Hirsch, had a 35-yard touchdown run in the third quarter for the Badger's only score. Bertelli hit one of his four completions on the next drive, for 26 yards to Livingstone, and Jim Mello ran in from the 3-yard line for the tying touchdown. Bad ball handling demolished Fighting Irish drives at Wisconsin's 27, 13, 16, 12, and 23.

Passing won the next game—Georgia Tech's passing. The Rambling Wreck scored on a short run after a Fighting Irish fumble, then cranked an 8-yard touchdown pass in the third quarter for the winning

George Murphy, captain of the 1942 Irish and a two-year starter at RE.

margin. Tom Miller scored for Notre Dame from the 7-yard line in the fourth quarter. Bertelli had three passes intercepted to offset Notre Dame's total yardage superiority over Tech. Notre Dame lost 13-6.

The loss perhaps made Leahy sick; he did not coach the next few games (this was a pattern in Leahy's later years). Ed McKeever took his place for three weeks. During this time, the Fighting Irish went 3-0 against some tough foes. The first victory of the season was over Marchy Schwartz's Stanford team, 27-0, as Bertelli found the range: nine straight completed passes and all four touchdowns. In the second quarter, he connected with Dove for a 36-yard touchdown and later with Paul Limont for a 16-yarder. In the third quarter, Bertelli found George Murphy for a 26-yard score and Livingstone with a 15-yarder. He had 14 completions in 20 tries for 233 yards on the day.

Leahy was in the Mayo Clinic while the Fighting Irish whipped Iowa Pre-Flight 28-0, an upset since this was an all-star group. Bertelli threw to Livingstone for a 47-yard score, and 47 seconds later Cornie Clatt intercepted a pass and ran 37 yards to score. His backup, Gerry Cowhig, scored the other touchdowns on short runs.

Illinois was undefeated and was prepared to stop Bertelli, but three Notre Dame running scores downed the Illini, 21-14. Notre Dame trailed at the half and twice had to come from behind to win. Clatt followed up an Illini fumble to score from the 5-yard line for a 7-7 first quarter tie. In the third quarter, down 14-7, Pete Ashbaugh ran 40 yards with a punt to the 1-yard line, and Bertelli sneaked it in. Notre Dame won it in the fourth with a 77-yard march crowned by Cowhig's 1-yard touchdown blast. The teams ran equally well; Bertelli's passing was the difference.

With Leahy back on the sidelines, the Fighting Irish shut out Navy 9-0. Bertelli hit a crucial pass of nine yards to Dove on the game's only touchdown march, then scored the touchdown himself from in close. John Creevey made a 17-yard insurance field goal in the fourth quarter. Bertelli helped the cause with an interception in the Notre Dame end zone in the first quarter. Both offenses were sluggish.

A solid Army team played the Fighting Irish even for the first half, but Notre Dame's power wore them out. Ashbaugh recovered an Army fumble at the Cadet's 25 to set up Creevey's 15-yard touchdown run for the first score. Near the end, Bertelli threw a 17-yard touchdown pass to Murphy for the 13-0 win. Notre Dame's 265 yards on the ground made the difference; Army had only 79.

Creighton Miller, who could do just about anything he wanted to on a football field, started at LH in 1942 and 1943.

After a hiatus of three decades, Notre Dame played Michigan again. Leahy worked hard to schedule the Wolverines. He even invited the retired Yost to watch the game. Yost, who had complained to Red Miller about calling his fair catches too late, would be watching Red's son, Creighton, starting for the Irish. Michigan won 32-20, the first team to score five touchdowns on Notre Dame since Army in 1916, and the first to score 32 points since Purdue in 1905. Notre Dame actually led 14-13 at the half. Bertelli hit Dove with a 7-yard touchdown throw. Michigan responded with a drive ended by a 14-yard quarterback run for the touchdown. Fighting Irish errors in the second quarter let Michigan off the hook—a fumble that the Wolverines grabbed led to a 4-yard touchdown on a fake field goal play. But Michigan fumbled on its next possession, and Miller barged in from the 3 for a touchdown. The Wolverines owned the third quarter, scoring touchdowns on a 59-yard drive, a 25-yarder after Notre Dame fumbled the kickoff, and then an interception of a Bertelli pass led to a 1-yard touchdown run. Miller scored on a well executed Statue of Liberty play from the 14, but Irish mistakes were too much to overcome.

They redeemed themselves the following week against Otto Graham's Northwestern team, beating the quarterback of the decade, 27-20. The Wildcats had early leads. Clatt caught up with a 5-yard touchdown buck and a 1-yard scoring dive. Livingstone scored from the 14 on a drive in which Clatt netted 47 yards running. Clatt intercepted a Graham pass to set up a 31-yard touchdown strike from Bertelli to Miller. Graham won the quarterback duel, but the Fighting Irish ground game netted 295 yards to Northwestern's 95.

Leahy's team whipped USC for the third straight time, 13-0. The scores came from Bertelli's passing: a 48-yard pass and run play to Miller and an 80-yard march ended by a 9-yard touchdown pass to Livingstone. Again, Notre Dame's ground game dominated the offense, but the passes garnered the points.

Notre Dame played a "bowl" game against Great Lakes Naval Base at Soldier Field. The sailors had an all-star team and jumped out to a 13-0 lead on a strong running game. In the second half, Clatt ran 82 yards for a touchdown, and Miller had a 72-yard touchdown bolt. Great Lakes missed four field goals and Bertelli moved the Fighting Irish 62 yards in the last minute. But Creevey's field goal on the last play fell just short for a 13-13 tie.

The team matured nicely as they learned the T system, which could score from anywhere. Bertelli, Dove, and Harry Wright earned All-American honors.

1942 record: 7-2-2 (.727)
Record to date: 330-72-27 (.800)

1943

Once again a world war was impacting college football—and every other aspect of American life. Service call ups had countless players shifted from one campus to the next. Arbitrary assignments sent players to schools where the military training matched their service. Notre Dame was a Navy center. In the next three seasons, several Notre Dame players would be seen playing against the Fighting Irish. Likewise, Notre Dame picked up some good players, notably Julie Rykovich of Illinois and John Perko of Minnesota. Of the 1942 starters, only Pat Filley, Bertelli, and Miller returned. The line had to be rebuilt, but the backfield was in better shape with starters and good reserves. Bertelli's back up was a legend in waiting, Johnny Lujack.

Notre Dame 1943 National Champions.

The Springfield Rifle—Angelo Bertelli, the first T-formation QB for the Irish, winner of the 1943 Heisman Trophy.

Notre Dame opened the season against Pittsburgh and Coach Clark Shaughnessy, who had been lured from Maryland after leaving Stanford. This opening matchup pitted Leahy's T against the master's. They sparred evenly until Pitt fumbled on their own 35, and the Fighting Irish quickly drove to the 4-yard line. Miller ran in the first touchdown. For an encore, he sped past a Pitt defense on the next series for a 40-yard score. Bertelli scored an easy touchdown when he recovered a Pitt fumble and stepped across the goal line two yards away. Rykovich tallied two touchdowns and Bob Palladino one to make the final score 41-0.

Georgia Tech had picked up several stars from other Southeast Conference schools, but Notre Dame's running game couldn't be stopped, ending in a 55-13 win. This was Georgia Tech's worst defeat since 1929. Notre Dame's backs ran 451 mostly unopposed yards for 24 first downs and eight touchdowns. Bertelli threw touchdown passes to Rykovich, Miller, and Ray Kuffel, while Mello scored three touchdowns on the ground. Bob Hanlon and George Sullivan scored for the subs.

Next was Michigan at Ann Arbor. The already-strong Wolvreines were even better with the addition of Wisconsin's Elroy Hirsch. This game would pit the top-ranked teams in the country. The Fighting Irish struck in the first six minutes when Miller went over left guard and cut right for a 66-yard score. Michigan came right back with a Bill Daley touchdown, but missed the point after. Four plays later, Bertelli found Earley loose and hit him with a 20-yard pass that Earley converted into a 70-yard touchdown. Moments later, Miller took off again, 57 yards to the end zone, but a penalty negated the apparent score. The Fighting Irish kept coming, driving to the 9-yard line, but stalled. Michigan had to punt, and the Irish drove again; Jim Mello scored from the 4-yard line. In the second half, Rykovich returned a punt 40 yards, and Bertelli scored on a short plunge. Then he fired a touchdown pass for a 35-6 Fighting Irish lead. Michigan scored a consolation touchdown on the last play. Miller had 159 yards on 10 carries. Even the Fighting Irish subs stopped Michigan's All-American backs twice from the 1-yard line in a nice stand.

Notre Dame went to Wisconsin, who was coached by former Horseman Harry Stuhldreher. Wisconsin gained only five yards rushing all day and lost 50-0. Notre Dame scored within three minutes on a Rykovich run from in close. Then it was Mello's turn after a 52-yard drive, and then Miller continued the onslaught. The starters scored five touchdowns in the 22 plays they executed. Leahy emptied the bench, who scored three more touchdowns.

Leahy knew that his team, ranked number one, would soon be losing the services of Bertelli to the war effort. Illinois was next, and Leahy was looking for good spots to put in his future star, Lujack. Bertelli led the Irish in a 47-0 romp over the Illini. The opening touchdown was a 47-yard pass play from Bertelli to Rykovich. Other tallies went to Miller, Earley, and Lujack, among others.

John Yonakor, starting RE for the 1943 National Champs and a consensus All-American pick.

Jim White, starting LT for the 1943 National Champs.

Undefeated Navy was next. Notre Dame struck immediately—Bertelli to Rykovich for 50 yards and a touchdown. Then he tried a short pass to Miller, who ran 40 more yards for a touchdown. In the third quarter, Bertelli fired another touchdown pass, then Mello intercepted one of Navy's 38 passes and lumbered to the Midshipmen's 12. Miller scored from there. After stopping a Navy drive, Vic Kulbitski exploded for a 71-yard touchdown. Bertelli scored from the 8 for the 33-6 final, and his glorious career was over; he was called up by the Marines.

Having lost its star and eventual Heisman winner, Notre Dame faced another undefeated team—Army. Lujack, a sophomore, took Bertelli's place. The Fighting Irish opened the game with a drive to the Army 3, where penalties and a gritty defense stopped the Irish. Army promptly punted, and Notre Dame returned it to the Cadet's 31. Lujack struck, with a pass to John Yonakor for a touchdown. The Fighting Irish defense was playing well, too: Miller intercepted a Cadet pass, and Bob Kelly picked off two; Jim White stripped Glenn Davis to set up the second touchdown. Lujack plunged for the third touchdown, and Earley muscled in from the 3 for the final score, 26-0.

Northwestern played tough for a half, down only 6-0 on a Lujack to Kelly touchdown pass. Lujack and Kelly did it again in the third quarter, followed by scores from Miller and Rykovich. Northwestern's only score came when a lateral intended for Miller was intercepted to make it a 25-6 Irish win.

Yet another undefeated team—Iowa Pre-Flight, a team with several pro players—was next for Notre Dame. The Seahawks had a touchdown lead at the half, but Lujack had hit them hard, including a 59-yard pass to Yonakor. In the third period, good Fighting Irish running got to the 17; Lujack hit Kelly for 13, and then Kelly took it in from there. The Seahawks used a fumble recovery to get their second touchdown, but a botched extra point eventually provided the margin of victory for the Fighting Irish. A long Notre Dame march garnered Miller a 6-yard touchdown, and the successful extra point gave Notre Dame the win, 14-13.

The Great Lakes team was even better than Pre-Flight, but Lujack worked a long, patient drive and then scored on a sneak. The Bluejackets answered with two scores, the first one scored by Emil Sitko, playing against his old team. Dewey Proctor also scored for Great Lakes on a 50-yard run. The Fighting Irish responded with an 80-yard march in 18 plays; Mello picked up 54 of them. Miller threw the go-ahead touchdown with 1:05 to play. But Great Lakes came right back and scored again on a 5-yard pass for a 19-14 Irish defeat.

Leahy met Sitko after the game and said, "It's too bad we lost, Emil." Sitko, who had not forgotten his old school, replied, "Yes, coach, it is too bad that we lost, isn't it?" Nevertheless, the team was honored as National Champions, Bertelli won the Heisman, and five made All-American: Miller, Yonakor, White, Pat Filley, and Herb Coleman.

1943 record: 9-1-0 (.900)
Record to date: 339-73-27 (.802)

1944

On May 1, 1944, Frank Leahy joined the Navy as a commissioned officer. Bertelli was already in the Marines, and Lujack was also in the service. Creighton Miller had graduated. Without a coach, and with its team weakened by the war effort and graduation, Notre Dame appointed Ed McKeever as interim head coach. He had a pool of talent with good size in the line and a somewhat smaller backfield. Frank Dancewicz at quarterback had excellent speed. Behind him were halfbacks Chick Maggioli and Bob Kelly, with lanky Elmer Angsman at fullback. The tackles and ends were big by 1944 standards at 6-5 and 210 pounds. Notre Dame would need all the help it could muster since both service academies were loaded with talent.

1944 Notre Dame varsity squad.

The Fighting Irish conducted an offensive clinic in their season opener against Pitt, 58-0. In the first quarter Dancewicz passed to Kelly for a touchdown. Angsman started the second quarter with a fumble recovery on the Pitt 13; and Kelly caught his second touchdown pass. Moments later he scored from the 5 to end a drive started when Dancewicz intercepted a Pitt pass. Kelly, behind excellent downfield blocking, sprinted for an 85-yard touchdown. Two interceptions and two more fumbles led to more Pitt woes, with Zeke O'Connor, George Terlep, Joe Gasparella, and Mark Limont scoring. Kelly gained 137 yards on 11 runs and four touchdowns. The Fighting Irish offense produced 622 yards.

Against Tulane, the offensive barrage continued during a 26-0 Notre Dame win. After an even first quarter, Dancewicz fired to Kelly for a 6-0 lead. A second drive overcame penalties to have Angsman bang it in from the 4-yard line. In the third quarter, Maggioli caught a pass from Dancewicz for 45 yards to get the Fighting Irish away from their goal, then ended the march smashing in from the 3-yard line. Maggioli later shook loose on a sweep for 20 yards, followed by a 23-yard end run for the final score, 26-0. The Irish had 438 yards on offense for the day.

Kelly started the 64-0 rout of Dartmouth on the first play from scrimmage when he ran 52 yards past left end. Dancewicz scored on the next drive. Dartmouth showed occasional flashes of football savvy, but kept handing the ball to the Fighting Irish. Notre Dame's other scorers were Terlep with two (his second from 32 yards out), and Kelly, Gasparella, John Corbisiero, Nunzio Marino (from 54 yards), Steve Nemeth (from 59 yards), and Ed Clasby with one each. Notre Dame had almost 600 yards of total offense, with 440 on the ground. They missed five conversion kicks.

After the first three games of the season, Notre Dame not only stood undefeated, but had outscored its opposition by an incredible 148-0. The winning

Bob Kelly, starting RH for the 1944 squad.

Elmer Angsman, starter at FB for the 1944 Fighting Irish.

streak would continue against Wisconsin the following week, although the Badgers would manage to score some points.

Against Wisconsin, the Fighting Irish started early; Kelly scored on a 51-yard streak on the second play. The Badgers dropped the ball at their 10, and Kelly scored again, prompting McKeever to play the subs in the second quarter. In the opening play of the third quarter, the Badgers' kickoff return man, Thompson, apparently did not like what he saw coming his way after fielding the ball on the 2-yard line and calmly trotted into his end zone for a safety. Notre Dame received the ensuing kick, and Angsman scored on a 35-yard run. Gasparella later fired a 31-yard touchdown strike to Maggioli. Angsman lost a 75-yard touchdown run on a referee's mistake when the line judge saw Wisconsin offside and blew the play dead. The Badgers scored two meaningless touchdowns later, bringing the final score to 28-13.

Illinois won everything but the game, when Notre Dame escaped 13-7 with a sputtering offense. The Illini scored first and led until the fourth quarter. Fred Rovai helped the Irish with a fumble recovery on the Illini's 16; Kelly scored from the 2. The Irish won on a hook and ladder play: Dancewicz's short pass to Kelly was lateralled to Maggioli—and he scooted 71 yards to win it. The Illini lost two touchdowns on penalties. They pounded the Fighting Irish defense with 343 yards running. Maggioli was called up a few days later by the Marines.

A fine Navy team exacted retribution for seven straight losses with a 32-13 victory. Kelly scored first for Notre Dame, but it was in the third quarter, long after Navy had built a big lead. He also scored on a 3-yarder. The Fighting Irish watched former teammate Fred Earley kicking Middie conversions. Navy's blocking was superb and led to four touchdowns on the ground.

Army was next—it was the worst defeat ever for Notre Dame, 59-0. The Cadets had not won against Notre Dame since 1931. Army intercepted six Fighting Irish passes and ran at will. Glenn Davis scored three times and Doug Kenna ran for one, scored on an interception, and passed for one to lead the Cadets. An Army man named Travel intercepted a screen pass for another touchdown.

A week later, Notre Dame shut out Northwestern 21-0. Jim Brennan, future-coach Terry's older brother, scored two early touchdowns, one on a 41-yard scorcher, and the second a 29-yarder after a fumble recovery. Northwestern reached the Irish 2-yard line on penalties, but could not score. Marty

Chick Maggioli, starter at LH for the 1944 Irish, had his season interrupted by a service call.

Pat Filley, starter at LG, and captain of the 1944 team—an All-American pick.

Wendell ran 7 yards in the fourth quarter to finish the scoring.

Georgia Tech was waiting in Atlanta for the Fighting Irish—Tech had beaten Navy and now wanted the Fighting Irish. Notre Dame disappointed Tech 21-0. Brennan scored an 11-yard touchdown on a lateral in the first quarter. There was no more scoring until the third quarter when Dancewicz passed to Kelly for 40 yards and a touchdown. Brennan later scored from the 1 to wrap it up.

Great Lakes was the last game. Great Lakes had stars galore, including Notre Dame's Jim Mello. The Sailors pushed the Fighting Irish around in the first quarter, but didn't score. Dancewicz rifled a 15-yard pass to Kelly for the halftime lead. In the third quarter, John Mastrangelo sacked Great Lakes' quarterback, causing a fumble. The fumble was kicked into the end zone, and Doug Waybright hauled it in for a touchdown. In the fourth quarter, Kelly punched out runs of 18, 9, and 9 yards to reach the Sailors' 3. The Sailors set up their defense for another run but Dancewicz passed to Skoglund for the touchdown. Kelly intercepted a later pass, and Dancewicz got the final score on a 3-yard plunge for the 28-7 win.

The 8-2 record was a good one under the circumstances. The Fighting Irish showed resilience and courage after the academy routs. Pat Filley repeated as an All-American, and Kelly was also named to the honor.

1944 record: 8-2-0 (.800)
Record to date: 347-75-27 (.802)

1945

McKeever moved on to Cornell, although he had signed for another year with Notre Dame. Hugh Devore agreed to coach until Leahy returned from the service. Devore had begun his career as a coach at

Notre Dame 1945 varsity football squad.

Notre Dame, before starting the rounds: Fordham, Providence, and Holy Cross. Leahy brought him back to Notre Dame in 1943. Two decades later he would serve as interim coach again, the only man to do so.

Devore took over a depleted squad. Only eight monogram men returned, and two of them would be shipped to Great Lakes (Szymanski and Wendell.) He had some talent; the problem was sifting through it. Only Fred Rovai returned on the line. There were some fine quarterback prospects behind Dancewicz: Gasparella was reliable, and Frank Tripucka (Kelly's father) and George Ratterman showed promise. Angsman moved to right halfback to make way for 5-8, 200 pound Frank Ruggerio. Phil Colella was at left halfback.

Colella won the season opener, 7-0, over Illinois with a 78-yard touchdown run. In the next game, Georgia Tech made it tough for a while with an early 7-0 lead before Notre Dame unloaded 40 points on them. Colella caught a short touchdown pass from Dancewicz to tie it, then Angsman capped a short drive with a 19-yard touchdown run. Gasparella came in for Dancewicz; he spotted Bill Zehler in the clear and hit him with a 54-yard touchdown pass. After the half, Tech was driving, but Terry Brennan intercepted a pass and returned it 42 yards. Angsman scored shortly afterwards. John Agnone and Emil Slovak finished the Fighting Irish scoring. Notre Dame had 560 yards and Tech 440, for an even 1,000 yards of offense for the game. In spite of the yardage, Tech was wrecked by a 40-7 margin.

Dartmouth fell short by 34 points, keeping the Notre Dame record unblemished at 3-0. Colella caught a Dancewicz pass and jetted 50 yards for a score on the first play. Devore called off the passing game and made the Fighting Irish do it on the ground. But the Irish couldn't stop entirely and threw a 4-yard pass to Bob Skoglund and a score. In the second period, Zip Zehler had a 24-yard touchdown, and Notre Dame led 20-0 at halftime. Later, Stan Krivik ran in from the 3 for a touchdown and then drop-kicked the point after. Joe Yonto wrapped up the Irish 34-0 shutout with a plunge from the 2-yard line.

Pitt's football fortunes had been on the wane in recent years, and Notre Dame kept it that way, 39-9. Pitt fumbled early, and Colella scored from the 23. A penalty killed Colella's run, so Dancewicz passed to him to the 1. Ruggerio smashed over from there. Pitt tackled Brennan in the Notre Dame end zone for a safety. The game was pretty even until the last play of the half when Dancewicz threw a touchdown to Bill Leonard. Pitt tired in the second half: Angsman took

Frank Ruggerio, a tough starter at FB for the 1944 Irish.

a Dancewicz pass in the flat and scored from the 20; he also plunged for a touchdown in the fourth quarter. John Panelli went 19 yards up the middle for a touchdown and Ernie Virok picked off an errant Pitt pass to go 40 yards for the final Irish touchdown.

Iowa was next. Devore saw a mismatch early on, let the regulars throw one pass in 11 minutes, and then pulled them out. Notre Dame blew out Iowa 56-0. Ruggerio and Angsman scored on offense, and Colella picked off an Iowa pass to score. In the second quarter, subs Bill Gompers, John Agnone, and Emil Slovak scored. Agnone intercepted a pass to set up his own touchdown. It was 41-0 at the half. Joe Yonto scored from 30 yards out, and Leon Traney dashed 51 yards, then scored from the 19 to cap the scoring.

The Fighting Irish were eager for Navy. Both teams were undefeated and looked evenly matched on paper. In the morning papers the next day, they were still evenly matched, 6-6. Notre Dame looked strong on its first series, with a 43-yard pass—but no drive emerged. Later Ruggerio intercepted a Navy pass and took it to the Midshipmen's 34. Four plays later, Ruggerio slammed in for a 6-0 lead. The Fighting Irish continued to dominate, when Navy's "Smackover" Scott scored the Midshipmen's only touchdown on an interception. On Navy's last drive, Notre Dame stopped the opposition's passes four times. Devore sent in Ratterman, who was sacked for 12 yards. Then he fired a pass for a 54-yard advance. Dancewicz, now in, threw to Colella. With under a minute to go, Colella caught the ball and dove for the

Pete Berezney, starter at RT for the 1945 Irish.

end zone. A Navy back tackled him and threw him sideways. Colella's feet crossed the plane of the goal line, but the officials said the ball hadn't. No score, and the game ended in a 6-6 tie.

There were distinct levels of football by this time. There were all of the colleges at a certain level (with Georgia and UCLA at the top), then a large gap before Notre Dame, then at the next highest level the NFL, and finally, at the top was Army. They really were that good. It has been said that Notre Dame had an NFL franchise from 1946 to 1949, but Army beat them to it in 1944 and 1945. Army wanted its 16th straight win; they were four touchdown favorites over Notre Dame.

Frank Dancewicz, QB starter for the 1944 and 1945 teams, one of the fastest men on the squad.

The Fighting Irish were banged up going into the Army game. Ruggerio had 13 stitches in his chin; Angsman and Colella were hurting. Angsman fumbled to Army on the third play at the Notre Dame 30. Davis whipped through on the second play for a 27-yard touchdown. In the second quarter, Davis caught a long pass from Arnold Tucker for another touchdown. Blanchard busted in from the 1-yard line for a 21-0 halftime Army lead. Davis in the third quarter ran for a 21-yard touchdown. Blanchard intercepted a Ratterman pass and scored from the Notre Dame 36. Army's subs, who were good enough to have played in Canada's Gray Cup, scored after a 71-yard march. The last score came with 17 seconds left in the game—on a pass. The Fighting Irish would remember Red Blaik for that pass at the end of the 48-0 demolition.

Leahy was out of the service and watched the Fighting Irish play Northwestern from the press box. Northwestern played well at first but couldn't stop a 90-yard march by the Irish; Angsman ran for 50 yards and finished it off from the 1. A Wildcat fumble in the second quarter was converted into a touchdown. Floyd Simmons scored on a 4-yard run in the third quarter. Northwestern started passing carelessly; Gompers intercepted one and dashed 32 yards for a score. The Wildcats used a lateral for their only score, then Ratterman threw 42 yards to Gompers on the 10 who dragged a defender the rest of the way as Notre Dame won 34-7.

The Fighting Irish let Tulane score an early touchdown, but Mastrangelo blocked the conversion kick. The 6-0 score held until the third punt of the third quarter, when Brennan returned it for 30 yards, and made 52 yards and a touchdown on the next play. After a stalled drive, Angsman added another touchdown. Ratterman hit Brennan with a pass for the third touchdown. The Fighting Irish scored on an 84-yard drive, and on a Tripucka pass to Agnone for the 32-6 final score.

Great Lakes played its last game (because the war came to an end) against Notre Dame. They had former Irish quarterback George Terlep and a fullback better than Army's, Marion Motley. Living up to his reputation, Motley scored the first touchdown

Ed Mieszowski, starter at LT for the 1945 team.

from the Notre Dame 10 in three tries. Ruggerio responded, after recovering a fumble, from the 2-foot line. That would be it for the Fighting Irish. Terlep scored for a 13-7 halftime score. Notre Dame held Great Lakes scoreless until the fourth quarter. Then Aschenbrenner went wide for an 11-yard touchdown and Motley shrugged off five Irish tacklers as he ricocheted 44 yards for a score. The combination of Terlep to O'Connor scored again, and a late interception led to the last touchdown and a 39-7 win for Great Lakes.

It was a commendable season in view of wartime conditions and service academy manpower needs. Mastrangelo and Dancewicz earned All-American honors.

1945 record: 7-2-1 (.750)
Record to date: 354-77-28 (.801)

1946

Fighting Irish gridders from the good 1942 and the great 1943 teams were returning to campus after the war, eager to get on with their interrupted lives. There was a wealth of football talent surrounding Leahy. At quarterback, the Irish had Ratterman, Tripucka, and Lujack—the best trio at that position ever at the Dome. At left halfback were Terry Brennan, Cowhig, Livingstone, Coy McGee, Ernie Zalejski—all good enough to start anywhere. At right halfback were Emil Sitko, Mike Swistowicz, Gompers, Simmons, and at fullback, Mello, Clatt, and Panelli. Of the 15 backs, half were All-American material. The line had Jim Martin, George Connor, Ziggy Czarobski, and as a freshman sub, Leon Hart would *never* see Notre Dame lose a game in his four years. Mastrangelo was an All-American.

Notre Dame opened with Illinois, who was also loaded with talent. They played even for much of the first quarter until Lujack flipped a short lateral to Sitko, who went 83 yards before Rykovich stopped him. Livingstone scored from the 3-yard line. Just before the half, the Irish scored on a quick drive: Mello for 30 around left end; Sitko for 11 to the 14;

Cornie Clatt, starter at FB in 1942 and 1946—played as a backfield starter with both Bertelli and Lujack.

1946 Notre Dame National Champions.

and Mello for the touchdown. The third quarter was scoreless, but in the fourth quarter, a fumble recovery by the Irish gave Brennan a chance to tally from the 4-yard line. Swistowicz, who earlier had intercepted a 42-yard pass, intercepted another one, and Clatt scored for the 26-6 win.

The following week, Notre Dame slept through the first quarter against Pitt. Finally, Lujack passed to Jack Zilly and then to Livingston for a 24-yard touchdown. A George Strohmeyer interception led to a touchdown run by Brennan from the 7-yard line. Pitt fumbled in the third quarter, allowing Lujack to throw a touchdown pass to Mello for a 19-0 lead. Mello scored once more, and Brennan tacked on one for a 33-0 win. Notre Dame gained 468 yards in a lackluster day.

Purdue came out and played good football—until Livingstone was injured and carried off. This seemed to spark the Fighting Irish: Mello bulled 33 yards, Panelli gained 28 more on two runs, and Mello went in from the 1-yard line. After a wasted fumble recovery, Brennan ran three times for 42 yards to the Purdue 2-yard line; Clatt smashed in from there. The next drive was swift: Cowhig returned a punt 47 yards, Swistowicz for 5, and Lujack to Brennan for a 28-yard touchdown pass. The halftime score was 21-0 in favor of Notre Dame. In the third period, Martin engulfed a fumble on Purdue's 18 and Panelli scored on a reverse. Shortly thereafter, Panelli ran for 42

The irrepressible Ziggy Czarobski, starting RT for Notre Dame in 1946 and 1947, an All-American pick.

The all-time Irish QB, Johnny Lujack, started Bertelli's unfinished season at QB in 1943, repeated in 1946 and 1947, was the Heisman Trophy winner, and twice a consensus All-American.

yards and Lujack passed to Zilly for yet another Notre Dame touchdown. Purdue finally got on the scoreboard with a quarterback run of 52 yards. Notre Dame quickly responded with an intercepted pass for a touchdown, and Gompers ended the blowout with a 20-yard touchdown run with the subs.

Lujack struck quickly the next week against Iowa. In the third minute of the game, he found Brennan in the Hawkeye secondary for a 65-yard scoring pass. A fumble led to a Panelli score from the 1-yard line. Lujack lost the handle on the ball on the next series, but recovered and ran 47 yards for a touchdown. Sitko led a Notre Dame march on the ground and scored from the 3-yard line. Ashbaugh intercepted a pass, and Sitko scored from the 47 on three runs. Leahy sent in the subs. Gompers wrapped it up with a 20-yard scoring sprint for the 41-6 win.

Against Navy, Leahy wanted to keep it simple for Army's scouts. Playing a conservative offense, the Irish dominated 28-0. Cowhig scored first on a 31-yard end sweep. Floyd Simmons owned the next quarter, scoring two touchdowns. Gompers finished it with a 2-yard burst in the last quarter.

Army players—two-time defending national champions with 25 consecutive wins—had never scored against a Leahy-coached Notre Dame team. The game was a titanic struggle, ending in a 0-0 deadlock. The only long drive belonged to Notre Dame, an 85-yarder that fizzled at the Army 3-yard line. Both teams had runs of 21 yards, one by Brennan and one by Blanchard. It was Blanchard's run that decided the game's outcome; he was in the open and had a full head of steam, when Lujack made a picture-perfect tackle on the Notre Dame 36 to end the play and save the game. This was the only time in Blanchard's illustrious career that anyone had tackled him in the open field without help. The Fighting Irish survived the loss of two key fumbles, one by Sitko and the other by Brennan. Their finest moment followed a double fumble: Sitko intercepted, but fumbled on his 5-yard line, and Lujack recovered, only to have Cowhig do it again. The defense rose to the occasion and stopped Army's four plays. Notre Dame got the ball, punted it out of trouble, and Zilly sacked Army's quarterback, Tucker, who fumbled; Martin recovered. Neither team could move the ball after those defensive plays.

Northwestern seemed to always have the misfortune of playing Notre Dame following an upset or disappointment. True to form, Notre Dame dominated the game, 27-0. Sitko began the scoring, from in close, with a 34-yard run. Near the end of the game, Ratterman led marches of 43 and 59 yards for scores; Panelli tallied both. Tripucka led a drive that Slovak wrapped up with an 18-yard run past left end. Fighting Irish backs ran for 423 yards.

The Irish offense was in high gear against Tulane in New Orleans, 41-0. Mello and Zalejski both scored twice, and Brennan and McGee each once. A bruising defense made Tulane look all but inept.

Leahy's health failed him again, so assistant coach Moose Krause, soon to become Athletic Director, had the honor against USC in the finale. He was high-strung as the team prepared to go on the field; someone asked him who was starting. Moose replied in his booming voice, "Who are we gonna start? Why, we'll start everybody!" Notre Dame trampled USC 26-6. Coy McGee was the game's featured player: he opened with a touchdown on an 80-yard kickoff return, lost to a penalty; he scored on a 77-yard pass reception from Ratterman; and ran one in for 11 yards. In between, Ratterman threw a 22-yard touchdown pass to Leon Hart. Cowhig ran 15 yards through a cavernous hole to score the final touchdown. McGee, unknown to the press and the Trojans, gained 146 yards on only six runs.

Lujack, Connor, Mastrangelo, and Strohmeyer were honored as All-Americans. Navy beat Army to end the season and Notre Dame won the national title.

1946 record: 8-0-1 (.944)
Record to date: 362-77-29 (.804)

1947

Almost everyone returned from the 1946 defending national champions. Three positions lost graduates (right guard, right end, and fullback). Leahy had his pick from a wealth of players. Leon Hart took over at right end and would be a three-time All-American. At fullback were three players who could start anywhere in the country—Panelli, Simmons, and Clatt. Lujack, Connor, Martin, and Hart must be considered as All-time Notre Dame players, and perhaps also Sitko. Then there were the mere All-Americans: Fischer, Czarobski, and Strohmeyer (who was a reserve).

Notre Dame opened the season by clobbering Pitt 40-6, in spite of it being Pitt's second game, in spite of losing six fumbles, and in spite of gaining only 209 yards rushing. Brennan scored first, from the 3-yard line, after a Lujack pass to Martin gained 34 yards. Lujack sparked the second drive with an improvised 21-yard gain and a touchdown pass from the 9-yard line to Waybright. In the third quarter, Lujack threw a 65-yard touchdown to Martin. And in the fourth quarter, he threw a touchdown pass to Hart. McGee scored on a run, and Lancaster Smith rounded out the scoring by running for a 17-yard touchdown.

Purdue played a tough game, but lost 22-7. Lujack fired to Brennan for a 21-yard touchdown to start the scoring. Purdue scored soon after, a 9-yard touchdown pass by DeMoss. They made the point after, their first successful one against Notre Dame since 1945. After a fumble, Lujack threw to Larry Coutre, who took it to the Purdue 21. Lujack called a pass, saw it defensed well, and ran for the touchdown. Steve Oracko kicked the first Notre Dame field goal in 5 years, from the 18. McGee ran back a punt 43 yards with the reserves, and Simmons bulled in from the 3-yard line to complete the win.

Notre Dame 1947 National Champions.

Moose Krause shows how it should be done in a 1947 practice.

Fans had waited for the next game for 22 years—Nebraska. It was billed as a match of two great lines, but only one showed up—Notre Dame won 31-0. Panelli ended a 74-yard march with an 8-yard touchdown run. The Fighting Irish mixed runs and passes as Swistowicz hammered at their left tackle on a series of short runs for 22 yards; Tripucka threw to Brennan for 22 more. And Swistowicz ran three times from the 11 for the touchdown. McGee returned a punt 35 yards to the 50; Lujack fired to Swistowicz for a 36-yard gain. McGee scored from the 14 untouched. Waybright scored on a 14-yard pass from Tripucka, who later used a shovel pass to Sitko for a 10-yard score. The Irish gained 390 total yards to the Huskers' 153.

Iowa was next, coached by former Fighting Irish Eddie Anderson and Frank Carideo. Brennan scored the first Irish touchdown four plays after an Iowa fumble. On the next drive, McGee returned a punt to the 50, Sitko ran to the 18, and Brennan trampled four Hawkeyes for the score. Notre Dame's defense choked every Iowa possession except one, when Emlen Tunnell took a handoff, slipped between Connor and Martin and saw a hole—it was 65 yards before Lujack and Brennan could maneuver him out of bounds. The defense stopped the drive there. The last Notre Dame drive went for 98 time-killing yards; Coutre scored from the 1-yard line for a 21-0 win over Iowa.

Navy was swamped 27-0. Lujack started it with a 29-yard touchdown strike to Brennan. Later, Lujack, on a pass play, ran 72 yards but fumbled. Tripucka spelled him and found Hart open for a 31-yard touchdown pass. Brennan slammed in on a short yardage play and Livingstone finished it with an interception and a 42-yard touchdown. Hart also recovered two fumbles, Brennan's scores following each. Irish quarterbacks passed for 308 yards. Tripucka was nearly perfect, hitting 8 of 9 for 136 yards.

Army knew that its glory days would be hard to match now that the the talent pool was equalized. With that in mind, the Cadets sought to end the series with Notre Dame. Army scouts knew of the great Fighting Irish passing, but the Cadets lost the game on Notre Dame's 361 yards rushing. Brennan opened with a 95-yard kickoff return for a touchdown. Army failed with its possession; a few plays later Notre Dame scored again on a Brennan touchdown. In the third quarter, Army blew a kickoff to give Notre Dame a 47-yard drive, with Livingstone scoring from the 6-yard line. The Cadets scored, but Notre Dame came

George Connor, starting LT for the 1946 and 1947 Irish, twice a consensus All-American.

back with an 80-yard march; Coutre's 11-yarder finished the 27-7 win.

The Fighting Irish went flat the following game against Northwestern, winning a close one 26-19. Panelli scored first from the 9-yard line to end a quick, decisive drive. Northwestern fumbled on the ensuing kickoff return, and the Fighting Irish had the ball on their 8-yard line. Lujack passed to Brennan for a 3-yard touchdown. The Wildcats intercepted a Fighting Irish pass and got to the 15, then scored. Just before the half ended, Tripucka rifled a touchdown pass to Lancaster Smith, who made an acrobatic catch. In the third quarter, Northwestern scored on a pass play when Brennan slipped in the mud. Lujack put together a 62-yard drive, passing to Hart from the 6-yard line for the score. The Wildcats intercepted for another touchdown, and Leahy responded by sending the starters back in to finish things.

Perhaps the purist in Leahy found the narrow win frustrating, because he missed the next game. Moose Krause again took charge, and the Fighting Irish dismantled Tulane 59-6. The first quarter, which ended 32-0, was a blend of Tulane's incompetence and Notre Dame's talent. Tulane backs failed to field two kickoffs that led to quick Irish touchdowns—both in the first quarter. In the second quarter, Sitko scored twice, on a 5-yard run and a 20-yard pass from Lujack. Brennan also scored twice, on an 18-yard run and a 5-yard pass from Lujack. Gompers thrashed the Tulane defense for 37 yards and a score. Meanwhile, Fred Earley missed three conversion kicks. Tulane finally scored on an 83-yard drive. In the third quarter, Krause used everyone: Panelli, Livingstone, Clatt, and Jim Brennan (of the *fifth* backfield) all scored.

There had been no west coast games during wartime, so it was something new for many of the players to meet USC on the coast. With a perfect season in their grasp, the Fighting Irish beat USC 38-7. Earley kicked an 18-yard field goal after the USC quarterback lost the ball near his goal. In the second quarter, Sitko wrapped up an 87-yard march with a 1-yard smash. In the third quarter, Sitko ran 76 yards for a touchdown behind Connor's blocking. Lujack intercepted a pass, and Panelli scored from the 5-yard line. After USC reached the Notre Dame 8-yard line and fizzled, Livingstone ran 92 yards for the score. A fifth-string tackle, Al Zmijewski, intercepted a USC lateral and lumbered 30 yards for the final score.

The win ended Leahy's fifth season at Notre Dame and brought him his third national crown. His record under the Dome stood at 41-3-4, an .895 winning percentage. There were five All-American selections: Lujack (plus the Heisman), Connor (1946 Outland Trophy), Fischer (1948 Outland), Czarobski, and Hart (1949 Heisman). No other team in the history of the game has had that much talent on the field at one time. Leahy could have won the title with his second unit.

1947 record: 9-0-0 (1.000)
Record to date: 371-77-29 (.808)

1948

The Fighting Irish faced some big losses via graduation—Lujack, Connor, and Czarobski. The 1948 starters would be a good unit, but there was a drop-off in talent after that. The line was solid, and the backfield had Tripucka, Brennan, Sitko, and Panelli. Overall, Leahy had fewer options and more coaching challenges. It would be a while before another Notre Dame team could compare with that of 1947.

Bill Fischer, 1948 captain, three-year starter at LG, consensus All-American.

Four players enjoying themselves—Coy McGee, Emil Sitko, an unidentified player, and Frank Tripucka.

Two early touchdowns in the opener against Purdue bred some complacency as the Boilermakers came back strong only to lose 28-27. Sitko scored twice on short runs to cap short marches. Early on, the Fighting Irish seemed in complete control. Purdue fought back to a 12-7 halftime deficit, which they quickly turned into a 13-12 lead in the third quarter with a 70-yard touchdown drive. Jim Martin deflected a Purdue punt to Panelli, who scored the third Fighting Irish touchdown. Oracko missed his third point after, but kicked a 23-yard fourth-quarter field goal to give Notre Dame a 21-13 lead. Purdue's quarterback brought them back again with a 50-yard touchdown pass. With two minutes to go, Zmijewski grabbed an errant Purdue pass and scored from the 7-yard line for his second career touchdown. Purdue

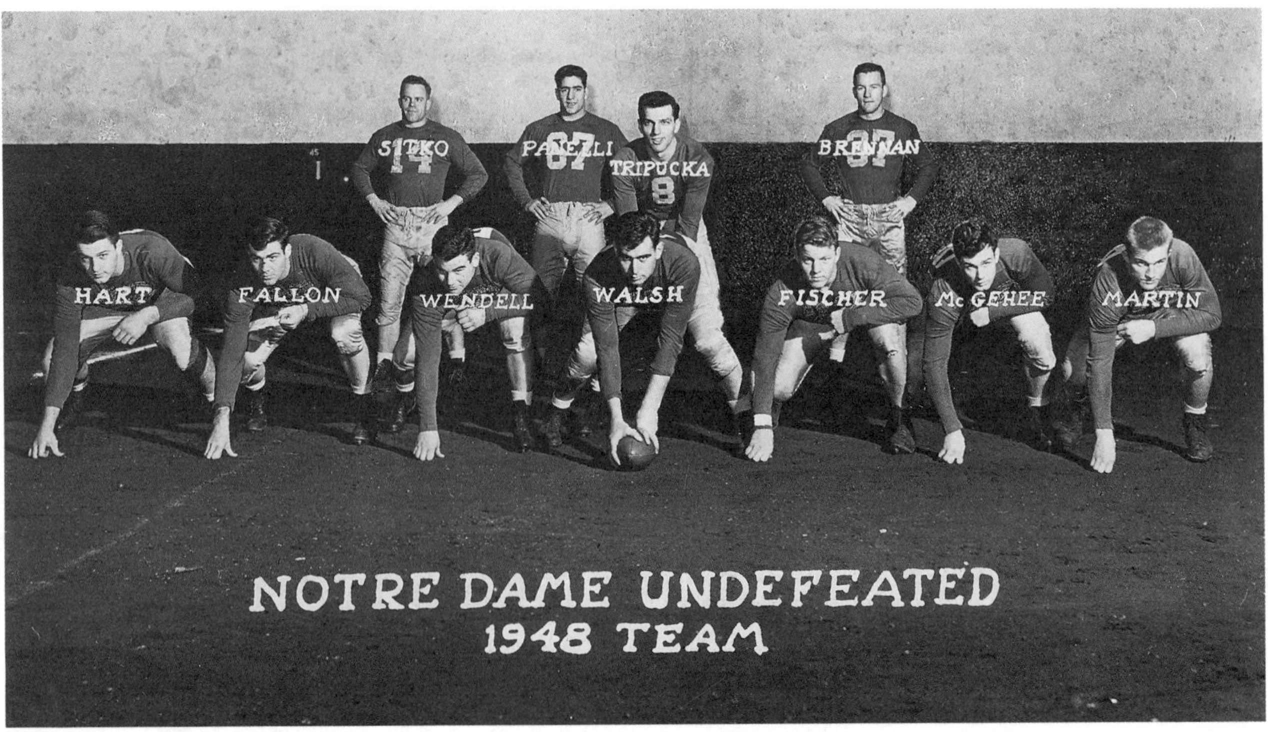

Notre Dame's 1948 undefeated team.

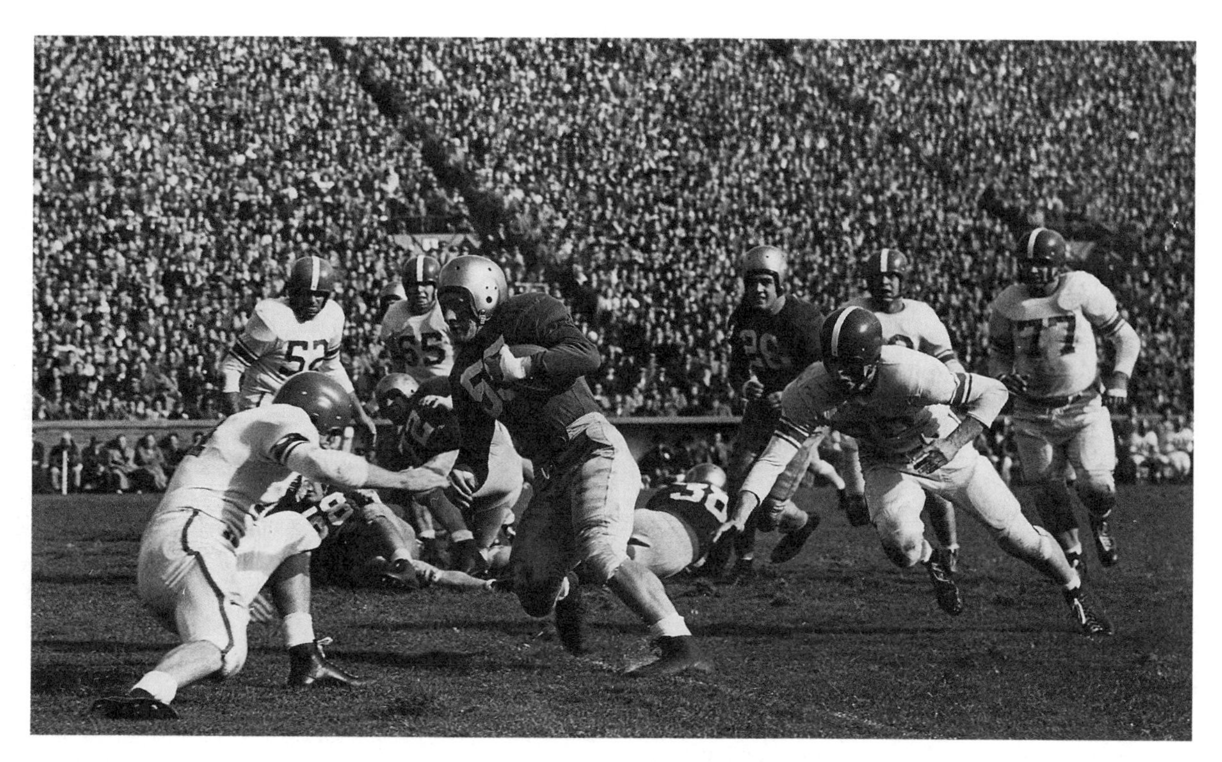

FB Mike Swistowicz cuts back in 26-7 win over Michigan State in 1948.

kept coming, scoring at the very end to close the final score to within a single point. Purdue's offense worked well; Notre Dame won on the strength of two great defensive plays.

Notre Dame buried Pitt, 40-0. The starters played only the first half and gave the subs a 28-0 lead. After a Frank Spaniel interception and 30-yard return, Tripucka hit Hart for a 10-yard touchdown. In the second quarter, Sitko wrapped up an 84-yard drive with a 2-yard smash. Bill Gay intercepted a Pitt pass, and Spaniel soon scored from the 1-yard line. Jack Landry scored from the 1-yard line for the 28-0 halftime lead. In the third period, Lancaster Smith returned a Pitt punt 85 yards for a touchdown. Leo McKillin ended the Notre Dame scoring with a 9-yard burst. Notre Dame seemed to be able to stop Pitt whenever the need arose.

After a 27-year hiatus, the Michigan State University Spartans (formerly the Michigan Agricultural College) showed up. They intercepted Notre Dame right away, and LeRoy Crane later scored for the Spartans. The Fighting Irish struck back with a grinding 94-yard march ended by a Tripucka touchdown pass to Hart. Much of the second quarter was consumed with another lengthy drive by Notre Dame, a 96-yard effort, capped by Swistowicz's 12-yard run for the go-ahead score. Brennan scored from the 1-yard line in the third quarter, as Notre Dame took the kickoff back on another meticulous series. In the fourth quarter, Gay intercepted a Spartan pass and returned it 35 yards to the Michigan State 11. Sitko rammed it in for the 26-7 win. The Irish running game chalked up 398 yards.

Six-yard Sitko—a fixture at RH in 1946, 1947, and 1948, and All-American in 1948.

The Fighting Irish moved west to Nebraska, winning 44-13. Sitko scored twice in the first half, on runs of 8 yards and 4 yards, while Panelli raced 74 yards past the Huskers for the second score in the opening period. Tripucka threw to Wightkin for a 28-yard touchdown. Right after that, Groom intercepted a pass, which led to Landry's 7-yard score. It was 31-7 at the half in favor of the Irish. Gay kept it rolling in the second half with a 67-yard punt return, and Martin caught a 13-yard touchdown pass. The Huskers fumbled the ensuing kickoff; Coutre recovered and later scored from the 14. Nebraska scored on the last play of the game to close the scoring at 44-13.

Forty-seven seconds into the Iowa game the Fighting Irish had the first score. Iowa fumbled the opening kickoff on their 34, and Tripucka used a "toss lateral" to Panelli for a quick touchdown. Fighting Irish runners would gain 372 yards on the day, but only one pass was completed for minus 7 yards. The Hawkeyes recovered quickly from their opening mistake, answering with a 74-yard drive in six plays for the touchdown. Sitko took the ensuing kickoff 69 yards to the 11. No score resulted, but Iowa was pinned deep in its own territory. Hart recovered a fumble on the Iowa 9-yard line a little later in the second quarter and Gay sprinted in from the 4-yard line for the touchdown. Tripucka and Panelli worked the toss lateral again for a 39-yard touchdown in the third quarter, and Coutre exploded in the fourth on a 35-yard touchdown run up the middle. Iowa scored off an interception for the 27-12 final. Panelli gained 154 yards on 12 runs and played a great game linebacking. A problem was emerging, though—missing the conversions.

Marty Wendell, two-year starter at RG in 1947 and 1948, an All-American in 1948.

Frank Tripucka, 1948 starter at QB.

Navy was routed 41-7, bringing the Irish season record to 6-0. Sitko led Notre Dame with 172 yards on 17 carries. He ran 55 yards to set up the first touchdown, which he scored from the 3-yard line. Navy fumbled, and Notre Dame scored in three quick plays: Tripucka passed to Hart, who lateralled to Sitko for 18; Sitko for 11 more; and Panelli for 18 and the touchdown. After trading fumbles, Gay scored from the 3-yard line. Navy fumbled again on its 25, and quarterback Bob Williams tossed a lateral to Lank Smith for a one-play touchdown drive. It was 28-0 at the half. Coutre intercepted Navy in the third quarter, and Spaniel scored with a 6-yard pass from Williams (after the referees killed two other touchdowns on the drive). Landry muscled in from the 1-yard line for the last Notre Dame score.

The Indiana Hoosiers played against the Notre Dame starters for five drives and five touchdowns before Leahy relented in a 42-7 rampage. Sitko opened with a 23-yard score. The Hoosiers returned the kickoff to the Notre Dame 7-yard line, but the defense moved them back to the Irish 30. Tripucka struck again with a pass to Gay to the Indiana 15, and Landry scored from the 3-yard line. In the next quarter, Panelli took a pitch out and followed a blocking clinic for a 51-yard touchdown. Tripucka opened up the passing game with touchdown strikes of 45 yards to Wightkin and 20 yards to Gay. The subs punched over a touchdown for the final Irish total, Landry going in from the 1-yard line. Indiana threw a touchdown pass near the end.

The missed conversion syndrome almost caught up with the Fighting Irish, when Northwestern played a fine game, losing 12-7. After a surprise Northwestern drive to the 9-yard line, Notre Dame came back; Brennan ran for 22 yards, and then 230-pound Hart smashed 13 yards on an end around to the Wildcat's 1-yard line. Panelli did the rest, but Notre Dame missed the conversion. The Wildcats kept driving, only to falter around the Irish 30 twice. Leahy unveiled yet another variation—both Tripucka and Williams in the backfield. The Wildcats made three interceptions in the second half to keep Notre Dame at half throttle. One interception was returned 90 yards for a Northwestern score and a 7-6 Wildcat lead. The Fighting Irish fumbled on the next series, but the defense got it back. Notre Dame worked carefully on a 63-yard drive, all on the ground, for the winning score by Gay. Four interceptions by the Wildcats almost ended the Irish winning streak.

Washington made the long trip from Seattle. The Fighting Irish decimated the Huskies 25-0 in the first quarter on the way to a 46-0 rout. The Huskies lost four fumbles close to their end zone. Panelli scored from the 12 after the first fumble, then Brennan on a 30-yard pass from Tripucka, Hart scored on an end around for a 19-yard touchdown, and again on a 41-yard touchdown pass from Tripucka. That was the first quarter; in the second quarter, Washington lost the ball on their 14, and Tripucka threw to Wightkin for 7 on the second play. In the third quarter, Gay was a one-man drive: he returned a punt 26 yards to the Washington 44; ran 38 yards to their 6, and scored on a 1-yard plunge. In the last quarter, a Husky punt of 10 yards allowed Landry to score on a 30-yarder.

The fumble contagion spread to Notre Dame the following game against USC; the Irish lost six miscues, and USC tied them 14-14. Hart opened the scoring with a 35-yard pass from Tripucka. USC reached the Notre Dame 1-yard line but was turned back. The Irish lost Tripucka as he tried to wedge the ball forward and was hurt in a pileup. Bob Williams replaced him. The half ended with Notre Dame leading 7-0. In the third quarter, Sitko fumbled on the USC 21, and Gay lost a punt return due to a clip. The mistakes were adding up, as Williams was intercepted at the end of the third quarter. USC went ahead 14-7 in the fourth quarter with two touchdowns by Martin.

The chapel car in use during the long trip to play USC in early December, 1948.

Gay returned the kickoff 87 yards, and a penalty moved the ball on the 1. Sitko scored with 35 seconds left, and Oracko converted the point after to tie the score. Notre Dame recovered an onside kick a few seconds later, but time ran out before the Irish could score again.

Fischer won the Outland Trophy while Hart, Sitko, and Wendell made All-American teams.

1948: 9-0-1 (.950)

Record to date: 380-77-30 (.811)

1949

If any team compared favorably to the great 1947 squad, it was the 1949 contingent. There were five Notre Dame All-Americans in 1947, and four in 1949. Both teams produced a Heisman winner. Both teams threw 154 passes and completed 86, but the 1949 team gained more yardage and scored more points. The 1949 Fighting Irish were more dominant over the opposition, but they did not have Lujack as that intangible element. The rules changed to permit a defensive unit by 1949 (and would revert at least once more),whereas the 1947 team was made up of two-way players unless mass substitutions gave them a break. The 1949 offensive line was big and tough, anchored by Hart and Martin, the latter moved to tackle. The backfield lost three starters but the depth of the 1948 squad filled out the new one with Williams at quarterback, Spaniel and Coutre as halfbacks, and Sitko at fullback. The defense also fea-

Leon Hart and Jim White let themselves hurdle Indiana in fall drills before the 1949 season.

The Four Horsemen circa 1949.

1949 Notre Dame National Champions.

tured Hart, a fine group of linemen for support, good linebackers, and excellent speed in Gay and Swistowicz.

Indiana fell first. After some initial resistance, Notre Dame pieced together a 52-yard drive, thanks to a fourth-down pass from Williams to Coutre to the Indiana 17; Sitko scored the first touchdown on a short/long run. In the second quarter, Bob Toneff blocked an Indiana punt for a Notre Dame safety. The Hoosiers responded briefly and marched in for their only score of the day. Notre Dame fired back with a Williams pass to Gay, who made a contortionist's catch for a 28-yard touchdown. By the third quarter, Notre Dame touchdowns rained: Sitko had a 6-yard touchdown, Gay's 50-yard punt return set up Coutre's 13-yard touchdown, Sitko scored on a 6-yarder, and Swistowicz went in from the 1-yard line in the fourth quarter. Quarterback John Mazur threw a 17-yard touchdown pass to Wightkin for the final tally in a 49-6 blowout.

The Fighting Irish returned Washington's visit and found themselves deadlocked 7-7 at the half. A Coutre fumble led to the Husky score. West coast officials, unfamiliar with the midwest's greater use of arms in blocking, made holding calls that stunted Irish progress. The Fighting Irish score came on a 21-yard pass from Williams to Hart. In the third quarter, Toneff again blocked a punt, and the Fighting Irish were on the Washington 14. Sitko rumbled for 6, then Hart scored an 8-yard touchdown on an end around, as assorted Huskies tried to get out of the way. Another Husky fumble resulted in a 36-yard touch-

Ralph McGehee, starting RT on the 1949 National Championship team.

Doug Waybright menaces a Purdue passer in the 35-12 Irish win in 1949.

down by Coutre. Hart separated a Husky from the ball at their 18 and took off on another end around for 12 yards. Landry wrapped it up with a short run for the 27-7 win.

Having defeated Indiana and Washington, Notre Dame met its old nemesis, Purdue. Sitko opened the scoring with a 41-yard touchdown early in the game. At the end of the first quarter, Coutre raced for a 48-yard score, giving the Irish an early 14-0 lead. In the next period, a recovered fumble started a Notre Dame drive from its own 33. On good running, the Fighting Irish reached the Purdue 9; Sitko hammered it in. Purdue tried more passing, but Gay intercepted and dashed 61 yards for a tally. In the third quarter, an interception by Notre Dame linebacker John Helwig led to Billy Barrett's 6-yard touchdown run. Two Purdue touchdowns made the final score 35-12 in favor of the Fighting Irish.

Tulane's Green Wave was highly touted in 1949, but Notre Dame crushed them 47-6 for its fourth straight victory of the 1949 campaign. This game was over early, as Notre Dame led at the end of the first quarter 27-0. Coutre scored three touchdowns within the first 10 minutes: a 14-yard dash, an 81-yarder on a pitch out, and a 2-yard burst after a long pass to Wightkin. Notre Dame also scored on a pass from Williams to Spaniel. In the second quarter, the Fighting Irish moved 83 yards quickly: Williams for 19 yards on a bootleg; a 44-yard pass to Wightkin; two runs to the 20; and a touchdown pass to Hart. Tulane scored its lone touchdown, but four plays later Notre Dame scored again on an 11-yard touchdown run by Spaniel. In the fourth quarter, Barrett ran 59 yards for the final score. The defense held Tulane to minus 23 yards rushing.

Walt Grothaus, starting center for the 1949 National Champs.

Notre Dame continued its onslaught with a 40-0 blowout over Navy. Quarterback Williams pleased hometown Baltimore when he threw to Zalejski for a 48-yard score to open. In the second quarter, Coutre outran the Middies for a 91-yard touchdown. Sitko ran 44 yards, followed by a 16-yard touchdown. Williams closed the first half's scoring with two passes to Zalejski for 46 yards and another touchdown. The Fighting Irish headed to the locker room with a 27-0 halftime lead over Navy. The subs played the second half: Landry racked up a 14-yard touchdown and Zalejski sped 76 yards for a touchdown. The win was Notre Dame's 33rd straight without a loss.

At East Lansing, the Michigan State game started as a punting seminar until Williams found Zalejski for Notre Dame's first score, a 19-yard touchdown. Moments later, Williams fumbled at his 5, and the Spartans scored. Notre Dame answered with an 89-yard march, highlighted by Wightkin's 21-yard, fourth-down catch; Coutre scored on a short run. Notre Dame led 14 to 7 at halftime. The Fighting Irish took the opening possession of the second half 79 yards in eight plays, with Williams running the last 40 yards after a fake lateral to Sitko on a later drive at the MSU 12. Sitko got the ball and faked MSU's Chandnois, an all-everything candidate, for the touchdown. Hart scored on a pass from Williams, giving the Irish 34 points. MSU kept trying, and made the final score 34-21.

After Army declined to play Notre Dame, the Fighting Irish looked for someone else willing to play them in New York. North Carolina answered, losing 42-6. The Tarheels scored first, after an Irish fumble, and then watched the Notre Dame parade: Spaniel tied it with a 78-yard punt return; Williams threw long to Hart, who lateralled to Barrett for the score; Hart tackled a Tarheel for a safety; Williams threw touchdown passes to Spaniel and Barrett; Swistowicz ran 85 yards for a score on an interception; and Mazur threw 18 yards to Barrett for the final score.

Iowa tried next, but lost 28-7. Williams lobbed a high pass to Spaniel from the 20 for the first Irish score. Iowa tied it after a fumble recovery in the second quarter, but Notre Dame came right back. Hart deflected a punt at their 22; Barrett scored from the 8 for a 14-7 halftime lead. The third quarter was scoreless. Notre Dame consumed a lot of time in the fourth quarter with a 14-play, 95-yard drive, sparked by a 54-yard pass from Williams to Spaniel, who scored later. Hart grabbed a touchdown pass in the last minute to end it. Williams passed Bertelli's single season passing marks.

Notre Dame had been waiting impatiently for over a year to face USC. The 32-0 rout by the Fighting Irish was certainly more pleasing than the 1948 tie. The Four Horsemen were honored guests on their silver anniversary. Leahy moved Hart midway through the game, (at 255 pounds) to fullback, a tactical enormity the Trojans hadn't expected; Hart started at end and caught a 40-yard touchdown pass from Williams. John Petitbon scored the second Irish touchdown with a 43-yard interception return. Up 14-0, Leahy made his move. After USC fumbled a punt, Barrett ran to the 11. Hart shifted to fullback, got the ball, and broadsided the USC line for 7 yards. He lined up again at fullback, but as a decoy; Sitko scored untouched on an end run. Hart helped later with a 60-yard drive, and Spaniel went in from the 2-yard line. In the fourth quarter, Williams threw a 32-yard pass to Barrett to set up the final touchdown. Hart drove to the 15, Zalejski went for 9, and Barrett rammed in from the 6-yard line. USC got only 17 yards rushing to the Fighting Irish's 312.

The game with Southern Methodist University, led by Kyle Rote (Doak Walker was hurt.) was a classic, with Notre Dame prevailing 27-20. Notre Dame had a quick 14-0 lead on two Williams passes, a 42-yarder to Wightkin and a deflected pass to Zalejski for 35 yards. SMU scored on four Rote runs from the 6-yard line. In the third period, a Zalejski fumble led to Rote running twice from the 3-yard line to score. Jim Mutscheller, a budding Fighting Irish star, intercepted a Mustang pass and Barrett tallied from the 3-yard line; Notre Dame was up 20-14. Rote tied the game after penalties and poor punting, but Groom blocked the point after try. Leahy moved Hart to fullback on the last drive to preoccupy a tiring SMU team. The strategy worked, and Barrett scored the winning touchdown from the 2. But SMU drove to the Notre Dame 5-yard line where a fourth-down Rote pass was intercepted by Groom and Bob Lally.

Leahy at Notre Dame had amassed 60 wins, three losses, and five ties, for a .919 winning percentage. Notre Dame was undefeated during the1946-1949 seasons, compiling an astounding 36-0-2 record. Hart won the Heisman, the only lineman ever to do so. Sitko, Hart, Williams, and Martin made All-American teams. Twenty-nine players from this team were drafted by the NFL. Leahy and Notre Dame were at the height of excellence.

1949 record: 10-0-0 (1.000)
Record to date: 390-77-30 (.814)

1950 to 1959

1950

Success does not always breed success. Leahy's talent pool was thinning. Two of the best Notre Dame players in its history were gone after the 1949 season—Hart and Martin. The rest of the offensive line were gone, too. Leahy brought up some good players, such as Bob Toneff and Jerry Groom, but overall it was not an overpowering bunch. The backfield was in better shape: Williams was back, with Petitbon and Barrett as halfbacks, and Landry replacing Sitko. Seven players on the starting offense had to go two ways as Leahy tried to get the most out of his personnel. The 1949 defensive line averaged 219 pounds; the 1950 group was 204. All Notre Dame linebackers returned, but they'd have their hands full.

North Carolina made its first visit to Notre Dame and fumbled the opening kickoff on its own 25; Notre Dame's Paul Burns recovered. Notre Dame was able to move on that series, and the Tarheels got the ball back only to fumble on the next play; Toneff recovered at the Tarheel 10. After three plays, Williams threw to Mutscheller from the 3-yard line for the touchdown. Later in the first half, Barrett ran 52 yards, but the drive died. The Fighting Irish took a 7-0 lead into the locker room. In the third quarter, the Tarheels tied the game. With only 2:40 left, Williams passed to Mutscheller for the winning touchdown, the 14-7 final score, and the 39th straight game without a Notre Dame loss.

Purdue shattered the streak with a 28-14 win. Notre Dame was never in the game, losing 21-0 at halftime. Purdue's defense held Williams to seven completions in 22 tries for 46 yards. Purdue's running and a tiring Notre Dame defense were too much to overcome, although Notre Dame tried in the second half: Williams hit Mutscheller for a 3-yard touchdown, and Petitbon dashed 10 yards for a score.

The Green Wave of Tulane gave the Fighting Irish all they wanted before losing 13-9 in the 500th game for Notre Dame. Tulane took the opening kick and drove 63 yards in five plays, exposing serious defensive flaws, scoring from the 4-yard line. Notre Dame responded with an 80-yard scoring drive,

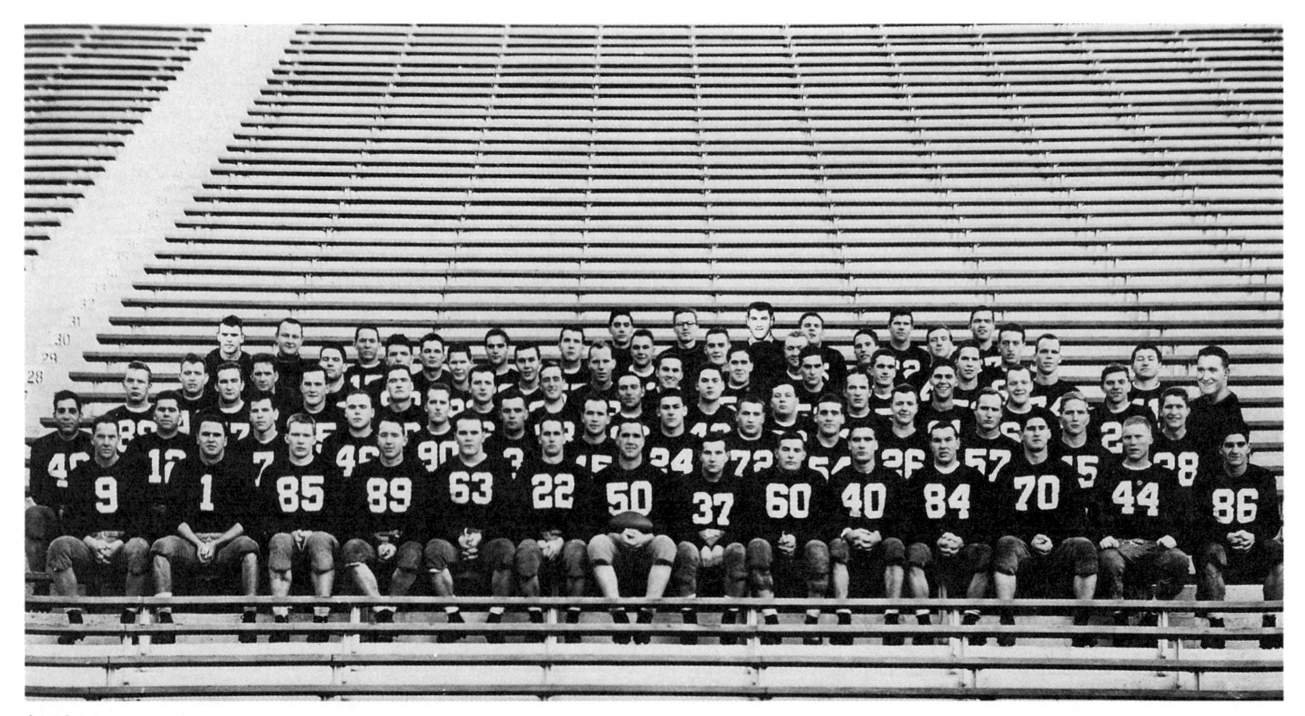

1950 Notre Dame Varsity Football squad.

Leahy's inauguration of the 1950 campaign. Groom does the honors.

which included passes to Mutscheller for 23 yards and to Petitbon for the 58-yard touchdown. Similar passing in the second quarter set up Del Gander's 10-yard touchdown. In the second half, Tulane fumbled, and the ball was recovered by Groom deep in Notre Dame territory. Tulane sacked Williams for a safety in the ensuing series, for the 13-9 score. The Notre Dame rushing attack gained only 34 yards to Tulane's 224. Bob Williams' passing won the game, with 16 completions for 225 yards.

Indiana beat the Fighting Irish the next week 20-7. Indiana scored first on a short pass, following a 51-yard punt return. Irish defenders were slow to react and the Hoosier quarterback had time to find the open receivers. Indiana went up by two touchdowns with another drive before halftime. As the second half opened, Robertson outran Fighting Irish defenders on an 83-yard streak on the second play from scrimmage in the third quarter. Del Gander got the only Irish score on an 8-yard run up the middle. Williams was hurt on the first play of that drive, and did not return for the rest of the game.

Michigan State, resurgent in the Big 10, won 36-33 at Notre Dame. The Fighting Irish scored first with a 19-yard pass from Mazur to Mutscheller. MSU roared into the lead with drives capped by a Pisano run of 15 yards and one by Grandelius for 7 yards. A blocked punt was recovered by MSU for another touchdown. Early in the second quarter, the Fighting Irish responded with an 85-yard march, finished by Petitbon's 5-yard touchdown plunge. Then the teams settled into a defensive draw, until MSU hit a 31-yard

The T-formation circa 1950.

Bob Williams-All American QB for Notre Dame in 1949 and 1950.

field goal in the third quarter. Notre Dame scored twice on touchdown throws from Williams to Mutscheller to go ahead 26-23 in the third quarter, but MSU fought back with touchdown runs by Grandelius and McAuliffe. Notre Dame came close at the end with a touchdown pass from Mazur to Gerry Marchand, but the Irish rally fell short. Petitbon gained 171 yards on 10 trips to pace the Irish's 526 yards.

Jerry Groom, 1950 captain, and an All-American at center, leader of a tough Irish defense as MLB.

Going into the Navy game, Notre Dame sported a sub .500 record (2-3) for the first time in a long time. The Navy game did not start well for the Irish, as Navy took a quick 7-0 lead on an interception. Notre Dame's Dave Flood returned the favor, and Landry sped 54 yards to the Midshipmen's 10; Williams passed to Gay for a 5-yard touchdown and the halftime tie. Navy drove for a field goal and the lead in the second half, but Notre Dame responded with a 6-yard touchdown pass from Williams to Ostrowski. Later, Groom blocked a punt, and Landry scored from the 5 for a 19-10 win.

Despite the Irish .500 record, Pitt still could not win a game from Notre Dame. The Fighting Irish scored first with a 15-yard pass from Williams to Mutscheller to conclude a 70-yard drive. Pitt fumbled the ensuing kickoff on its 38, and a half dozen plays later, Williams fired a 12-yard touchdown pass to Petitbon. The defense then stopped a Pitt drive that reached the 5-yard line; the Panthers came right back and scored on a 13-yard pass. The halftime score was 12-7. Notre Dame controlled much of the clock in the third and fourth quarters, and fashioned a touchdown drive boosted by Landry's 22-yard run, and his 3-yard touchdown plunge. The final score was 18-7. Williams hit 13 of 21 passes for 171 yards, surpassing Bertelli's 169 as a game high. Notre Dame was relieved to be back over .500 for the season.

Iowa tied Notre Dame 14-14 in the next game. The Hawkeyes threatened to win it with a 14-0 first quarter lead on interceptions and short marches. Mazur sparked a 63-yard, seven-play drive, featuring Landry's 43-yard run to the 20. Petitbon scored from the 11 on an end run. Before the half, Notre Dame used 20 plays on an 80-yard drive to tie the game. Williams went in from the 1-yard line. Vince Meschievitz's conversion kicks were both good.

Leahy was ill for the USC finale in California. The 9-7 USC win did not make him feel any better. Crimmins handled the team in his absence, but injuries decimated attempts to sustain the effort. Seven starters and two subs were knocked out of action. USC won with a 94-yard kickoff return by Jim Sears and a safety on a blocked punt. Williams scored on a 1-yard quarterback sneak. Notre Dame's defense held the Trojans to 70 yards on the ground and four in the air.

It was only the fourth time in 62 seasons that Notre Dame had lost four games. Williams and Groom earned All-American status.

1950 record: 4-4-1 (.500)

Record to date: 394-81-31 (.809)

1951 Notre Dame starting eleven.

1951

Leahy brought up some fine youngsters and good reserves to strengthen the team's weak areas: Ralph Guglielmi, Art Hunter, Neil Worden, Joe Heap, and John Lattner. Mazur took over at quarterback; Petitbon and Barrett were halfbacks, and Worden was the fullback. The defense would feature the hard hitting of Dan Shannon and the good linebacking of Dick Syzmanski, with fine defensive coverages from Lattner.

Indiana paid for its 1950 win over the Irish when Leahy's team pasted them 48-6. After conducting secret fall practices, Leahy showed an "I" formation with Petitbon, Barrett, and Worden lined up behind Mazur. The Hoosiers were confused, and Notre Dame moved 75 yards for the first score. Barrett logged the touchdown from the 6-yard line. In the second quarter, Worden set a school record with four touchdowns: from the 6-yard line, from the 1 after an Indiana turnover, from the 5 after a fumble, and from the 11 after Lattner's interception. Then Lattner scored from in close. Del Gander answered Indiana's only score when he scored in the fourth quarter.

Notre Dame's first night game ever was against the University of Detroit in Briggs Stadium. The offense pulverized the Titans 40-6. Petitbon set the tone for the blowout when he returned the opening kickoff 85 yards for a touchdown. He and Barrett then worked a criss-cross on a punt, with Petitbon scoring from 73 yards out. He tallied again from the Detroit 39 with a pitchout. The scoring for the half ended when Mazur threw a 30-yard touchdown to Mutscheller. Detroit finally scored in the third quarter, but Lattner matched that score by intercepting a pass and return-

A look at how things went for Indiana as they lost to the Irish 48-6 in 1951.

The 1951 defensive front: Bob O'Neil, Bob Ready, Jack Lee, Sam Palumbo, Fred Mangialardi.

ing it 32 yards for a Notre Dame touchdown. Guglielmi scored from the 1 after Walt Cabral fell on a Detroit fumble. Petitbon averaged 13 yards per carry to go with his long kick returns.

The Fighting Irish suffered the first loss of the season against Southern Methodist University, 27-20. SMU scored on a touchdown pass of 57 yards in the first quarter, but Paul Reynolds got it back on a crossbuck and cutback for a 33-yard touchdown run. SMU hit three quick passes for their next score, the last good for 37 yards. In the second quarter, SMU dropped a punt, and Lattner recovered on SMU's 24. Mazur threw a 19-yard touchdown pass to Chet Ostrowski to tie it, 13-13. SMU's Benners hit two more touchdown passes; SMU picked off Mazur twice, and Lattner scored from the 5 as time ran out.

Pitt had lost its best quarterback and receiver to early-season injuries before playing Notre Dame. Taking advantage of Pitt's misfortune, Notre Dame pounded the Panthers 33-0. Mazur started the scoring with a 10-yard pass to Barrett for a touchdown. In the second quarter, Mazur and Barrett repeated with a 28-yard score. Lattner, who started the second drive recovering a Pitt fumble, later grabbed an interception that led to a Mazur sneak from the 1. Mazur did the same in the third quarter to finish an 80-yard drive. Syzmanski got an interception and Tom Carey looked good at quarterback on a 71-yard touchdown drive. Seven turnovers and a blocked punt completed the 33-0 victory over Pitt.

The first quarter was a sparring match between Notre Dame and Purdue. In the next quarter, Mazur fashioned a 75-yard drive, wrapped up by a fake to Worden and the score by Reynolds. Purdue took the lead following Irish fumbles with a field goal and a quick touchdown. Minnie Mavraides put Notre Dame back in front with a 10-yard field goal. Dan Shannon intercepted a Purdue pass to set up a Lattner touchdown run of 40 yards. Barrett and Mutscheller scored the last two touchdowns—on a 1-yard slam and an 8-yard pass for a 30-9 Irish victory.

Joe Katchik at 6' 9", 255, and Billy Barrett at 5' 8", 180, at spring practice in 1951.

The Navy game was a punting duet, with 25 punts on a soggy day. The Middies kept it scoreless until well into the second quarter; Worden used a delay play to score on a 36-yard run. Shannon and Dave Flood grabbed a fumble and two plays later

Neil Worden, three-year starter at FB, scored four TDs in the second quarter of his first game, the 1951 mangling of Indiana.

Mazur used a "split T sweep" to score from the 21. Winless Navy gained only 3 yards in the first half. In the second half, Barrett returned a punt 76 yards for a touchdown, with Shannon blocking. Navy and the weather kept the Fighting Irish to 11 net rushing yards in the half, but the Irish managed to pull out a 19-0 win.

MSU routed Notre Dame 35-0, scoring the first touchdown with chicanery. With the ball on MSU's 12, the Spartans lined up but with the single wing backfield off to the right. A tackle looked left, over to an end, and said he wasn't lined up right. With that, the ball was snapped to the fullback, Dick Panin. The Irish never caught up with him on an 88-yard touchdown chase. Conventional football drilled Notre Dame after that: a 1-yard dive, two short touchdown passes, and a touchdown off an interception. The Spartans smashed Notre Dame's defense with 353 rushing yards.

The Irish rebounded from the MSU game with a 12-7 win over North Carolina. Reynolds scored the first Notre Dame touchdown in the second quarter on a short run, and Worden went in from the 4 in the third quarter. The Tarheels' only score came on a 37-yard pass. It was Notre Dame's 400th win in 514 games. Leahy did not use most of his starting backfield, choosing instead to build experience for good young players.

Notre Dame tied Iowa 20-20 the following week, bringing the Irish season record to 6-2-1. The Hawkeyes scored first on a 58-yard pass. Notre Dame fired back; Worden scored from the 9, but the Irish missed the point after. Iowa responded with a five-play drive that culminated in a 45-yard touchdown pass, giving the Hawkeyes the halftime lead. Iowa was using a spread formation during the first half that seemed to frustrate the Fighting Irish. Leahy made adjustments at the half to stop it; so the Hawkeyes used a straight T to move 62 yards, scoring from the 7 on an end run. Down 20-6 in the third quarter, Notre Dame started its rally with a 5-yard score by Lattner.

The set-up for publicity shots, circa 1951.

This touchdown was set up by Guglielmi's passes of 31 yards and 44 yards to Reynolds and Lattner. On the next drive, Lattner completed a 23-yard pass to Mutscheller on fourth down from punt formation. Later, interference put the ball on the 1, and Lattner scored. Sophomore Bob Joseph kicked the point after with 55 seconds left to avert a loss.

After his strong second half showing against Iowa, Leahy picked Guglielmi to start against USC, who boasted Frank Gifford and Leon Sellers. Gifford scored first from the 8. Notre Dame roared back with a 13-play, 78-yard drive that ended with Lattner scoring from the 1. An interception led to a USC score, but Gifford missed his second conversion try, leaving the USC lead at 12-7. Leahy chose to use the youngsters in the backfield; Worden ran 39 yards, untouched, for the go-ahead score. Petitbon scored an insurance touchdown later for the 19-12 win.

The 1951 season was a satisfying return from the oblivion of 1950; Notre Dame's offensive output increased about 25 percent, resulting in15 more touchdowns than the previous year. Toneff and Mutscheller were All-Americans.

1951 record: 7-2-1 (.750)
Record to date: 401-83-32 (.808)

1952

If the 1951 season represented a good comeback from 1950, the 1952 season earned back a strong measure of respect for the Fighting Irish. They were not quite a dominating team, but then few teams would ever dominate an era as the Irish had from 1946 through 1949. The 1951 season allowed talented youngsters to mature beyond their raw potential. The backfield was set with Guglielmi at quarterback, Heap and Lattner as the halfbacks, and Worden at fullback. This was a fast unit, with Lattner excelling in guile and instinct, and Worden in blocking. The line was adequate. Leahy shifted Art Hunter from center to left end. The defense was a bit undersized, although all three linebackers were back—Shannon, Syzmanski, and Jack Alessandrini. Lattner and Reynolds starred in the secondary (Lattner would play a substantial 422 minutes in the year.)

The opener with the University of Pennsylvania ended in a 7-7 tie. The Fighting Irish started with an 89-yard march in 15 plays. Lattner blasted runs of 21 and 22 yards, and from the 11 he hammered three times for the touchdown. Notre Dame scored again shortly thereafter on a 44-yard pass to Heap, but a

The 1952 Notre Dame Varsity.

The 1952 Fighting Irish starting eleven.

penalty killed the play, and eventually the win. Penalties killed another Notre Dame drive. In the third quarter, a secondary lapse let Penn score on a 65-yard pass for the tie. Notre Dame had one last chance if Guglielmi could move them 80 yards in 2 minutes. He almost did: he passed to Lattner for 21 yards, to Heap for 7, to Bob O'Neil for 15, and to Lattner near the Penn 25, but the ball came loose as he spun away from the tackler, and Penn recovered to preserve the tie.

The Notre Dame-Texas series, last played in 1934, was resumed in Austin for the 1952 season. Texas started strong, driving to the Notre Dame 2, but they fumbled and settled for a field goal. Their defense stifled Notre Dame's offense, allowing the Irish only 55 yards for the first half. In the third quarter, on the Texas 25, Guglielmi passed to Lattner in the flat. Lattner in turn threw to Heap for a gain to the 1-yard line. Lattner scored on the next play. A fourth-quarter Irish punt hit the Texas returner squarely in the chest, and Shannon recovered the ball at the Longhorn 2. Heap scored for a 14-3 win over Texas.

Notre Dame returned home and lost to Pitt 22-19. The Panthers struck first with a 79-yard touchdown on a pitchout to Billy Reynolds. Then quarterback Mattioli threw a 63-yard touchdown pass to end the first quarter, with Pitt leading the surprised Irish 13-0. Penalties and Pitt's gritty defense kept Notre Dame scoreless in the second quarter, giving Pitt a commanding 13-0 halftime lead. In the third quarter, Guglielmi put together a seven-play series of 78 yards; Worden scored from the 12. Several Irish penalties and a punt later, Mattioli scored from the Notre Dame 2. Guglielmi drove the Fighting Irish again, scoring himself from the 1-yard line. Then Heap returned a punt 92 yards for a score, drawing the Fighting Irish to within a point. However, they

Joe Heap latches on to a 10-yard pass from Guglielmi in the 1952 Pitt game.

One of the great Irish backfields: the 1952 quartet of Johnny Lattner, Neil Worden, Joe Heap, and Ralph Guglielmi.

missed the point after, their second. More penalties, a lost pitchout, and Guglielmi was caught for a safety—of such things are upsets made. Notre Dame lost 22-19.

As bad as the Pitt game was, the Irish looked even worse against Purdue in a fumbling derby (21 fumbles combined, 10 for Notre Dame). Nevertheless, the Fighting Irish won 26-14, largely because they recovered 15 of the fumbles. Notre Dame started quickly, scoring three plays after Purdue fumbled the opening kickoff. Even the Irish score involved a fumble, as tackle Joe Bush scored the touchdown when Lattner fumbled into the end zone. Purdue scored on a 27-yard pass, then Worden finished off a 68-yard drive by Notre Dame with a 1-yard smash. Guglielmi threw a 47-yard touchdown to Lattner on the last play of the first half, giving the Irish a 20-7 halftime lead. In the third quarter, an Irish fumble led to a Purdue score. Notre Dame put together a solid drive, sans fumbles, that ended with another Worden score. Art Hunter keyed that drive with a 41-yard catch from Carey. Leahy was so upset by the fumbling of the talented Lattner, that he had a football taped to the halfback's hand for the entire week following the Purdue game.

A brush with polio had kept the North Carolina team hospitalized for three weeks; the Fighting Irish won the contest 34-14. A Worden touchdown opened it, but a fumble let Carolina tie. A scrappy defense kept Notre Dame off balance until Leahy sent in Guglielmi. Guglielmi used two fourth-down gambles to keep moving, leading to a 10-yard touchdown to Hunter. After the half, Heap returned a kickoff 84 yards for a score. Sub Tom McHugh tallied twice, and the Tarheels scored once more for the final result.

Navy had lost six straight to Notre Dame—the 1952 game made it seven. The Irish scored first, settling for a field goal after losing a halfback touch-

The studious Ralph Guglielmi.

Joe Heap(42) wrapping up an 84-yard TD run against North Carolina to help Irish win 34-14 in 1952.

down pass on a penalty. Two other field goal kicks by Notre Dame were either blocked or goofed during the low-scoring first half. Worden ran for an 8-yard score, but the point after was missed, and the Irish headed to the locker room with a 9-0 lead at halftime. In the third quarter, another Notre Dame drive stalled; Bob O'Neil tackled Navy's quarterback for a safety. Later, Worden scored again, and Navy salvaged six points from Guglielmi errors for the 17-6 final.

Leahy was concerned; the Fighting Irish were staring at the fourth-ranked Sooners of Oklahoma, led by Billy Vessels. This was one of the earliest nationally televised games, and hc ran for 195 yards on 17 tries and scored three times. An early Irish drive stalled, and the Sooners' quick drive ended when Eddie Crowder threw a 20-yard touchdown pass to Vessels. Notre Dame fought back with a 59-yard drive capped by a 16-yard touchdown pass from Guglielmi to Heap. Two minutes later, Vessels made a 62-yard touchdown run. Oklahoma led at the half, 14-7. The opening moments of the second half thrilled the national television audience: Notre Dame drove from its own 20 to the Oklahoma 6, but fumbled. However, on Oklahoma's ensuing drive, Lattner intercepted a Crowder pass and returned it to the Sooner 7. Worden tried three times and scored, 14-14. Three plays later Vessels ran for a 47-yard touchdown. The Fighting Irish came back with a 79-yard drive, with a 36-yard halfback pass from Heap to Lattner reaching the 27. Worden ran seven straight times for the touchdown. Notre Dame kicked off to the 6 where Larry Grigg fielded it and ran to his 24; Dan Shannon met him going full speed, hitting him so hard that Grigg did a half loop in mid-air and lost the ball. Shannon lost consciousness. Al Kohanowich recovered for Notre Dame. Lattner ran it to the 7. Then the Irish shifted from the T into the Notre Dame box, and the Sooners went offside. Worden went to the 1-foot line, and Carey sneaked it in. A rejuvenated defense stopped Oklahoma over the final 13 minutes for the 27-21 win and an all-time great victory.

Next, the Fighting Irish faced Michigan State, ranked number 1. Notre Dame lost seven fumbles, and MSU beat them 21-3. The first two fumbles did not result in MSU scores, although they were deep in Notre Dame territory—the 34 and 15—but the Irish defense's efforts must have dipped far into their reserves of strength. The Irish grabbed the lead in the third quarter with a 14-yard field goal by Bob Arrix. Notre Dame's defense turned back the Spartans yet another time, but the offense fumbled. MSU's Willie Thrower kept firing the ball, Lattner intercepted on the Notre Dame 10, and Notre Dame promptly fumbled on its 13. A holding penalty moved it to the 1, and McAuliffe scored. One minute later, the Irish dropped the ball at their 21; and again they were called for holding—the ball was on the 1 again. McAuliffe scored. The Fighting Irish managed a drive, with Lattner slashing for 36 yards and Heap catching a Lattner option pass for 24 yards. But Guglielmi was intercepted and MSU drove for their third touchdown. Notre Dame out gained the Spartans across the board, but turnovers and penalties sealed the loss.

Leahy missed the next game against Iowa with the flu. Line coach Joe McArdle led them in a 27-0 win. Running from the right halfback slot, Worden led a 66-yard drive in 13 plays for the first score, going in from the 4. Lattner seemed left out of things as a new backfield started with Worden, Carey, Heap, and McHugh. Iowa punted, and Lattner returned it 84 yards for a touchdown. Officiating held Notre Dame scoreless in the third quarter. Then Worden scored from the 2. Guglielmi sparked the last score with a fake for a 12-yard touchdown pass to Heap.

USC was undefeated and ranked in the top three. The Trojans hurt themselves to lead to Notre Dame's only first-half score when the Trojans' Jim Sears tried to gain more yardage with a lateral on a punt return, but no one was there, and Mavraides grabbed the loose ball on the Trojan 19. Lattner scored a few plays later, and Arrix added a third-quarter field goal for the 9-0 final score. The Fighting Irish defense stymied USC, allowing only 64 yards rushing and five first downs, while grabbing five interceptions.

The Fighting Irish had averaged one lost fumble per quarter of football. To make matters worse, the fumbles were bunched in key games. The quarterbacks hit only 93 passes in 205 tries, an unimpressive .453 rate. The interception to touchdown ratio was 4:1, far too high for a great team. Nevertheless, Notre Dame managed to upend highly-ranked Oklahoma and USC, and finished with a very respectable season record of 7-2-2.

Lattner was a consensus All-American, and O'Neil made the second team.

1952 record: 7-2-1 (.750)

Record to date: 408-85-33 (.807)

1953

Rules changes now mandated that a player could not leave the game and return in the same quarter—back to "Iron Man Football." Only Lattner had much two-way experience. Leahy shuffled his linemen around, moving Hunter from end to right tackle and Shannon to left end. This was a good group, and some 1952 players found themselves backups. The backfield was set: Guglielmi, Heap, Lattner, and Worden, which was probably the best set of Notre Dame backs for the next decade.

Oklahoma was the opener in Norman. Lattner let the kickoff dribble out of his hands at the 4, but Notre Dame retained possession. Worden fumbled on the fourth play, at the Notre Dame 23. Larry Grigg scored for Oklahoma on the eighth grudging play. Heap fumbled on the Sooner 23. Notre Dame's defense asserted itself, and took the ball back at its 2. Guglielmi threw to Lattner who reached their 12. Four short runs later Heap scored. Tied 7-7, punts dominated much of the first half until a long Oklahoma pass got to the Notre Dame 18. They scored. Frank Varrichione smothered one of their quick kicks

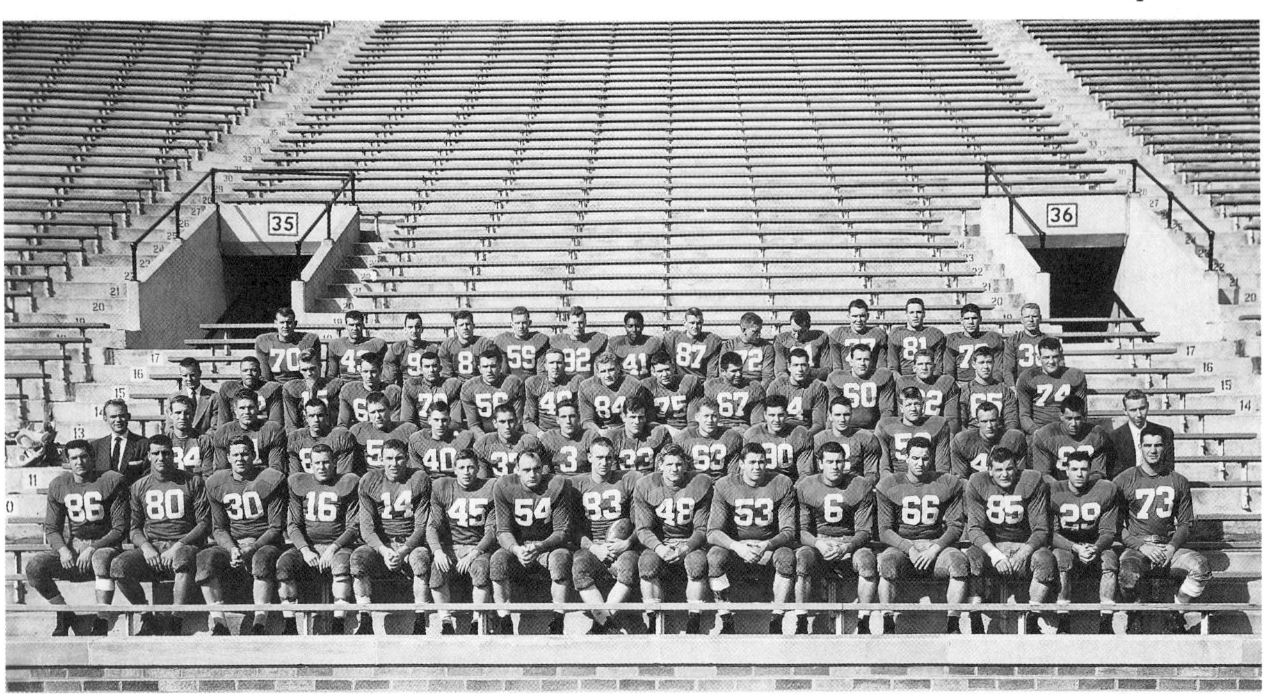

The undefeated 1953 Notre Dame football team.

Lean and lanky Johnny Lattner, 1953 Heisman Trophy winner.

Frank Varrichione held down the LT spot in 1952 and 1953, switched to RT in 1954, and made All-American.

on the 9, and three plays later Guglielmi tied the game, for a halftime score of 14-14. In the third quarter, Guglielmi intercepted a Sooner pass and then threw a touchdown to Heap. The Sooners fumbled on their 38 in the next series; Don Penza recovered, and Worden ran in from the 9 a few plays later. Oklahoma returned a Lattner punt 60 yards for a touchdown, but he later intercepted a pass to cinch the 28-21 win for Notre Dame.

Notre Dame met Purdue in Lafayette and swamped the Boilermakers 37-7. Guglielmi looked sharp, got it started, and then watched the results. Mavraides on the second possession kicked a 22-yard

The 1953 Notre Dame starting eleven.

Art Hunter, 1951 center (later a consensus All-American at RT in 1953), gets ready to snap to QB John Mazur.

field goal. Purdue dropped the ball two plays later on their 29. Worden slammed in from the 11 four plays later. The Fighting Irish stalled on two series and Purdue threw a 75-yard touchdown. Lattner returned a kickoff for an 86-yard score. Late in the first half, Dick Washington ran 32 yards for a touchdown and a 23-7 halftime lead. Purdue kept fumbling, and Guglielmi scored from the 5. Purdue punted to their own 17, and Worden scored from the 10 two plays later to cap the 37-7 win. Guglielmi completed seven of nine passes, and Irish backs ran for 302 yards.

Pittsburgh started with a 65-yard drive. The Fighting Irish came back on the next seven and put together a 67-yard march, with Worden scoring. Pitt intercepted and scored from the Notre Dame 4. Pitt's 14-7 lead lasted into the third quarter when Varrichione tallied a safety. A fumble deep in Pitt territory gave the Fighting Irish the lead when Guglielmi sneaked over for a touchdown. Guglielmi scored the final touchdown from the Pitt 9 in the fourth quarter for Notre Dame's 23-14 victory.

Georgia Tech, riding a 31-game winning streak, came to South Bend ranked number one. Notre Dame showed good concentration on the opening 80-yard drive, keyed by Heap's 33-yard run and Lattner's 21-yarder, that set up Worden's touchdown from the 7. Leahy sent in the subs after another long march, but they fumbled it away. The 7-0 score lasted into the third quarter, but Leahy didn't. An attack of gastroenteritis—an inflammation of the membrane lining the stomach and intestines—in the locker room sent him to the hospital. Tech tied the game after an interception. Heap started to take over, with a return to the 44 and a touchdown reception. Hunter scored by recovering a loose punt snap in the Tech end zone. Tech threw a 44-yard touchdown pass, but Lattner scored from the 1 for a 27-14 upset win over the nation's number-one team.

Leahy stayed home and watched Notre Dame dismantle Navy 38-7. The defense gave up only 8 yards in the first half to Navy, while the offense staggered the Middies with four second-quarter touchdowns: a Heap plunge from the 1, a long pass to Heap after a fumble recovery, a Guglielmi interception and 47-yard touchdown return, and a Tom McHugh dive. The regulars never returned to the game. Carey scored in the third quarter with a 27-yard keeper, and later threw a 3-yard scoring pass to Dick Keller. Navy scored later on a lateral for the 38-7 final.

Penn was reported to be stronger than the team that tied Notre Dame in 1952, and they looked stronger when they scored on their first possession, 61 yards in seven plays. Lattner took the ensuing kickoff 92 yards for a touchdown, breaking three tackles on the way. After an exchange of possession, Notre Dame, in a 68-yard drive, scored on a 3-yard run by Guglielmi. A Penn punt went to Heap, who handed off to Lattner for a 38-yard return. From the 3, sub quarterback Don Schaefer scored to open the second quarter. Trailing 21-7, Penn drove for a score to start the second half. Lattner returned their kickoff 56 yards and two plays later Guglielmi fired a 23-yard touchdown pass to Heap. Penn drove for another score, and threatened again, but Lattner intercepted in his end zone for a 28-20 victory.

The fullbacks took over against North Carolina, Worden and McHugh scored four touchdowns in a 34-14 win. Worden did most of the work for the first tally: Worden 14 yards to the Notre Dame 46; Worden 23 yards to the Carolina 31; and Heap's lateral to Worden for a touchdown. Schaefer scored for the subs to start the second period. Then McHugh finished a drive with a 2-yard touchdown slam. Carolina scored, the teams punted for a while, and Worden thundered for a 52-yard touchdown. In the fourth

USC's Des Koch finds the going tough in the 1953 48-14 loss to Notre Dame.

quarter, McHugh ended a drive with a 1-yard scoring dive. The Tarheels scored later as Notre Dame prevailed.

Iowa came east to play Notre Dame. Iowa intercepted a pass and pieced together a 71-yard drive capped by a 12-yard touchdown run late in the first quarter. The Irish looked sluggish, and Iowa looked sharp. A Fighting Irish drive to the goal line ended when a tipped pass went to a Hawkeye. Finally Lattner returned a punt to his 41; Heap caught a 22-yard pass to their 37; and Lattner ran for 5. Time was running out in the first half. Worden grabbed a pass and went to the Iowa 25. A pass to Heap reached the 14, but there were no time outs left. Two seconds left—and time stopped. Notre Dame's Frank Varrichione groaned and collapsed, gripping the small of his back. The officials called an injury timeout. Varrichione was taken from the game, and Shannon scored with a pass from Guglielmi, making the half-time score 7-7. After a scoreless third quarter, Iowa scored on a pitchout that turned into a touchdown pass. Only 2:06 remained, and the Irish still trailed 14-7. Worden returned the kick to the Notre Dame 42. Five plays later, the ball was on the Iowa 9 with 32 seconds left. Two incomplete passes wasted 26 seconds, and there were no more time outs. Suddenly, there were five Notre Dame linemen writhing on the ground, including a rehabilitated Varrichione, Penza, and Hunter. Guglielmi went to each and kicked them, telling them to get up. The referees called an injury timeout. On the last play, Guglielmi took the snap and faded left, then fired a pass across the field where Shannon caught it for the touchdown. Schaefer kicked the point after for the 14-14 tie, and the Fighting Irish were still undefeated. The NCAA authorities were not pleased by the Fainting Irish. The controversy raged all week—resulting in an end to faked injuries—and Leahy was sent to bed by his doctor.

Notre Dame went to Los Angeles to meet USC. Notre Dame annihilated USC 48-14. Lattner scored four touchdowns and gained 157 yards on 17 carries. Heap opened on a 94-yard touchdown kickoff return. Lattner scored from the 9 with a pitchout. USC scored. Fighting Irish sub Ray Lemek intercepted a Trojan pass, and the regulars came back in. Worden ran 54 yards to the 3, and tallied. In the third quarter, USC fumbled; Lattner took a pitchout wide left from the 5. USC scored again. Lattner finished a quick drive with a 1-yard touchdown. A Trojan back mishandled a handoff in his end zone, and Pat Bisceglia scored a touchdown on the fumble recovery. A USC fumble let Lattner run 50 yards up the middle for a touchdown. Later, disgruntled LA sportswriters complained that Notre Dame's jerseys tore off too easily.

SMU boasted one of the finest defenses in the country. Lattner and Worden combined for five touchdowns in their last game. Worden scored three to reach 29 for his career (Red Salmon had 36). Lattner threw a 55-yard pass to Shannon on the SMU 4. Worden scored from the 1. In the second quarter, Varrichione fell on a fumble for a touchdown. On the next Irish possession, Lattner scored on a 23-yard pass from Guglielmi. In the third period, he ran in from the 5 on a sweep. SMU finally scored with a pass. Guglielmi passed 42 yards to fellow quarterback Schaefer, to the 10. Worden hammered in from the 1 moments later. He scored again from the 3 after a Lemek interception. SMU scored once more to make it 40-14.

The Fighting Irish lost the national championship to Maryland. Lattner won the Heisman and the Maxwell trophies. Hunter and Penza earned All-American accolades.

Leahy was 45 years old with two years left on his contract. His teams had won 87 games, lost 11, and tied 9. The Fighting Irish had won national titles in 1943, 1946, 1947, 1949, and now almost in 1953. He had coached four Heisman winners. He had also missed six games due to illness over the years. His doctor advised him that the stress of coaching was killing him. Leahy's friends concurred. On January 31, 1954, his resignation was made official. And it was also announced that Terry Brennan, then 25 years old, would be the new head coach. Frank Leahy never coached another football game.

1953 season: 9-0-1 (.950)
Record to date: 417-85-34 (.809)

1954

Terence Patrick Brennan. His father, Joe, had been the backup center for the great 1909 Notre Dame team, but then transferred to Marquette. Terry had started at left halfback at the height of the glory years, 1946-1948. After graduating from Notre Dame, he coached Mt. Carmel High School to three straight Chicago city championships while earning his law degree at DePaul. He was the freshman coach for Notre Dame and worked the phones in the press box in 1953. President Hesburgh, who once had Brennan as a philosophy student, said that he'd been considered coaching material since his undergraduate days. He also advised Brennan to stick with older coaches since he had no experience as a head coach in college.

He inherited a great team. The entire line was made up of starters or former starters. Guglielmi and Carey were back, as was Heap. Jim Morse would try to fill Lattner's shoes and Don Schaefer moved from

Notre Dame's 1954 Fighting Irish Team.

The Irish coaches under Brennan: Bernie Witucki, Bill Fischer, Jack Zilly, Terry Brennan, Bill Walsh, Jim Finks, and Jack Landry.

reserve quarterback to fullback. Sophomore Paul Hornung subbed for him.

The Fighting Irish opened with a 21-0 shutdown of Texas. Varrichione saved the shutout on the fifth play of the game when he recovered a Longhorn fumble at his 7. Later, Guglielmi intercepted a Texas pass on his 19 and raced 42 yards to their 39. Shannon caught a 19-yard touchdown pass from Guglielmi early in the second quarter. In the third quarter, a 44-yard pass from Guglielmi to Heap keyed a 79-yard march. Guglielmi scored from the 3. Lemek killed a Texas drive with a fumble recovery at the Notre Dame 5, and Varrichione recovered his second to keep Texas frustrated. Guglielmi scored again from the 3 to wrap up the game.

Purdue ended the euphoria with a 27-14 win behind two sophomores—former NFL player and Hall of Famer Len Dawson and Lamar Lundy. Dawson passed for four touchdowns and intercepted a pass, and Lundy rumbled 73 yards with a pass for his touchdown. Paul Hornung looked good on a 59-yard return of a free kick after a safety. Nick Raich scored from the 1 on the next play. Schaefer bulled in from the 2 after Shannon caught a 41-yard pass. Fighting Irish fumbles and Dawson's brilliance accounted for the loss.

Brennan's Irish recovered to beat Pitt 33-0. Carey threw a 24-yard touchdown to Sherrill Sipes. In the second quarter, Shannon caused a fumble that Sam

Terry Brennan flanked by his 1954 co-captains, Paul Matz and Dan Shannon.

Palumbo recovered; Guglielmi threw deep for 34 to Heap, and scored a few plays later on a sneak. After another fumble, Dean Studer took a pitchout and ran 5 yards for a score. Late in the third quarter, Hornung subbed at quarterback for a couple of drives, the second finished by his touchdown run from the 11. Later he intercepted a Pitt pass in his end zone and ran it back 22 yards. Carey scored with three seconds to go on an 11-yard touchdown strike to Jim Munro.

The Fighting Irish spotted Michigan State a 13-point lead before taking charge to win 20-19. Clarence Peaks scored first for MSU, then Earl Morrall threw a touchdown pass. Heap crashed in from the 1 to break the ice. In the second half, MSU drove to the Notre Dame 11 but fumbled. By this time the field was a mess due to steady rain. The Irish put together a long drive through the muck; Heap went around right end from the 16 for a touchdown. Early in the fourth quarter on a fourth-down play, Schaefer ran 30 yards to the MSU 11. Paul Reynolds took a Guglielmi lateral from the 8 for the winning points. The Spartans drove for a score, but Bisceglia forced a bad conversion kick for the win.

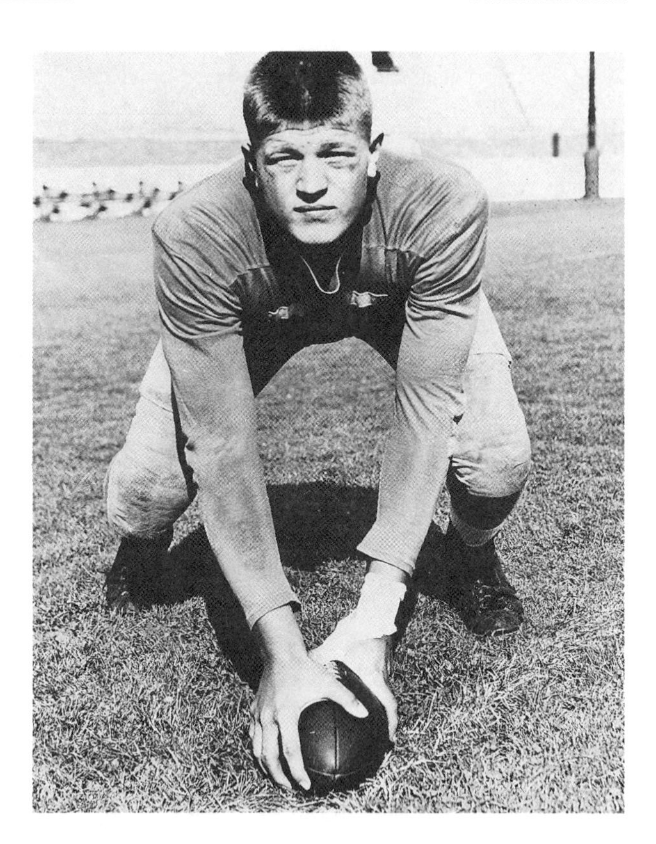

Dick Szymanski, outstanding Irish linebacker and starting center in 1954 before an injury ended his season.

Ralph Guglielmi, three-year starter as Irish QB, consensus All-American in 1954.

Notre Dame barely escaped against Navy 6-0. Notre Dame should have mauled them. The Fighting Irish looked great in the first quarter; Navy had the ball for six plays. In the next quarter, Guglielmi threw to a streaking Morse for a 46-yard touchdown. Schaefer missed the point after. Navy had trouble getting out of their territory, but in the third quarter, they moved to the Notre Dame 12, where a penalty killed the drive. They intercepted an Irish pass and were at the 15. The Fighting Irish stopped them twice, and caused a fumble that Guglielmi recovered in the end zone. Guglielmi later intercepted a pass, as did Hornung, to save the win.

Brennan faced his first Ivy League team, Penn. The Quakers moved well in the first quarter, but errors close to the end zone stopped them from scoring. Schaefer, from his 3, ran 70 yards. Guglielmi finished the drive with a sneak from the 4. Lemek intercepted a Quaker pass, and Guglielmi hit Shannon with a 22-yard touchdown. The halftime score was 14-0. Penn kicked off to start the second half, and Notre Dame drove 95 yards in seven plays. Shannon scored on an 18-yard pass from Guglielmi. Penn scored but the Irish marched right back for one. Heap intercepted a Penn pass and ran it back to their 22. Two plays later,

Carey found Studer open for a 20-yard score. Then Carey grabbed a fumble to set up Hornung's score from the 3 and the 42-7 final score.

Jim Morse opened the Irish blowout of the visiting Tarheels of North Carolina with a 77-yard kickoff return, and Heap scored six plays later. Heap also scored the second touchdown, ending a nine-play drive of 50 yards. Heap gained 42 yards on a reception in an 82-yard drive, and Morse scored. Carey threw a 47-yard pass to Studer and a touchdown pass to Jim Munro. Hornung's subs, Frank Pinn and Jack Witucki, scored twice. The Tarheels scored twice for a 42-13 final.

After last year's controversial game, Iowa had been waiting a year to play the Irish in Iowa. Evashevski's Hawkeyes were blasted 34-18. Notre Dame ran and passed at will, and the defense surrendered only 8 yards on seven plays in the first quarter. Heap ran 43 yards to the 6, and Morse scored on a dive from the 1-foot line. Heap scored on a dive. Iowa scored on a 47-yard pass in the second quarter, but a fumble at mid-field in the third quarter stopped their momentum. Notre Dame's passing got the ball in close, and Schaefer scored from the 3. The fourth Irish score came on a 9-yard pass from Guglielmi to right end Paul Matz. Carey threw from the Iowa 38 to Gene Kapish who scored. Iowa came back for a score on a rainbow pass.

Rain and mud met USC. The conditions also hurt the Fighting Irish, leading to nine fumbles and two interceptions; they still won 23-17. Morse "splashed" 179 yards on 19 rushes. A fumble on the fourth play of the game at Notre Dame's 14 let USC score early. The Fighting Irish looked bad on three more possessions, and they lost Lemek with a broken leg. Heap sprinted for 40 yards, took a pitchout, and fired a touchdown pass to Morse. USC drove for a field goal and a 10-7 lead. The Irish moved 80 yards in 20 plays, with Schaefer piling in from the 2 for the touchdown. The Trojans drove for another touchdown on a 21-yard pass. They led until the last 7 minutes of the game, when Morse took a pitchout and ran 72 yards down the sideline for the winning touchdown. A safety for Notre Dame lifted it to 23-17. The Irish rushed for 373 yards.

Similar running helped Notre Dame beat SMU, 26-14. Heap drove in from the 4 to end an opening 60-yard drive, but SMU answered. Guglielmi led a 12-play, 62-yard series, calling his own number from the 3. Bob Scannell blocked a Mustang punt and recovered it for a touchdown and the 19-7 halftime lead. Heap concluded his career with an 89-yard run down the sidelines for a score. SMU rallied for one more score, but that was it.

Brennan's first campaign ended with a number-four ranking, and his offense clicked for 6 yards per play. Guglielmi was a consensus choice for All-American, while Varrichione and Shannon shared several post-season honors.

1954 record: 9-1-0 (.900)
Record to date: 426-86-34 (.811)

1955

In his first year Brennan had produced outstanding results. However, the 9-1 record in 1954 would set a difficult standard to match. His most pressing concern was that six starting linemen had graduated, and the sole returner, Lemek, had missed spring practice with surgery. Brennan came up with a starting unit that was one of the smallest in recent memory—the center and guards averaged only 5-10 and 200 pounds. Hornung was a capable replacement for Guglielmi, a better runner, but a more questionable passer. Behind him were Jim Morse at right halfback, and tremendous speed in Dean Studer and

Ray Lemek, captain and RT on the 1955 team.

Notre Dame's Fighting Irish Team of 1955.

Aubrey Lewis at left halfback. Schaefer was at fullback. Lewis, with world class speed, and Dick Lynch were the best of the sophomores. Brennan had to hope for an injury-free season since this team had little depth.

The Fighting Irish started with SMU at home. Hornung led the rushing on the first drive, scoring a touchdown on an 11-yard keeper; he booted a 35-yard field goal later. The touchdown came on a third-and-10 in which his fake to Lewis fooled the Ponies. Lewis had two interceptions in the third period, the second leading to a 15-play touchdown drive. He also saved that drive on a fourth-and-16 play; he chose against the option pass, reversed his field, and ran to the SMU 19. Paul Reynolds scored on a fourth-and-long from the 14. The Fighting Irish defense played well: Larry Cooke grabbed a fumble and an interception near the end to save the shutout, and Dick Prendergast recovered a loose ball, as the Irish won 17-0.

The smallish Notre Dame team had played

Hornung intercepting a ball against Indiana in 1955.

The 1955 Notre Dame starting eleven.

well against SMU, but Indiana was a much larger group that would really test them, the critics said. Hornung opened the scoring with a fake pass and bootleg run around left end for a 33-yard touchdown. Indiana drove to the Notre Dame 15, but Hornung intercepted. The Hoosiers drove to the 6 in the second quarter but couldn't score, and Notre Dame led 6-0 at the half. In the third quarter, Bob Gaydos hauled in a Hoosier fumble on their 7; Morse scored on an off-tackle run. Lewis set up the final score with a pass interception; Hornung passed to Prendergast from the 7 for the 19-0 final score.

The Fighting Irish earned their third consecutive shutout win, 14-0, over Miami. Hornung threw two touchdown passes. On the first, two Irish receivers bracketed the Miami safety, forcing him to make a choice, and he chose the wrong one; Kapish caught an 11-yard touchdown pass. In the third quarter, looking at another fourth-and-long, Lewis zipped out of the backfield to catch Hornung's pass on the 5 to score and to complete a 32-yard play. Morse lost a 65-yard interception touchdown on a penalty. The Fighting Irish defense stopped Miami at the 13, 11, and 2 to save the shutout.

The euphoria ended in East Lansing against a powerful Michigan State squad. Clarence Peaks scored in the second quarter from the 1 to cap a long drive for MSU. (The Irish had played 196:48 minutes of shutout ball in the season to that point.) Notre Dame, meanwhile, ended three drives with fumbles. The only Fighting Irish score came on a 40-yard pass from Hornung to Morse; Hornung evaded three MSU pursuers to make the play. MSU scored on a short burst from the 2 and a sneak by Earl Morrall after an Irish fumble on their 16. The Irish outgained MSU's offense 374 yards to 367, but lost the game 21-7.

Wayne Edmonds, the first black letter winner at Notre Dame, started at LT in 1955.

Don Schaefer, starting FB for the 1954 and 1955 Irish.

Brennan came up with an unbalanced line set—shifting interior linemen to load up on one side—that befuddled Purdue for a 22-7 win. Purdue fumbled at the Notre Dame 39 on the first series. Morse picked up 23, and Studer gained 19. Schaefer scored from the 2. A missed Fighting Irish pitchout gave Len Dawson a chance for a 13-yard touchdown pass. On his next series, Bob Scannell and Prendergast crunched Dawson and caused a fumble on the Purdue 26. Five plays later,

Pat Bisceglia, starting LG for the 1955 Irish.

Studer slashed in from the 1 for the lead. Morse stopped Purdue with an interception, and Lewis sped in from the 10 for a 20-7 halftime lead. Hornung intercepted a pass in his end zone. Then, inspired defense on a later drive earned three straight sacks for minus 27 yards and a fourth-and-52. The Purdue center snapped a rainbow on the punt play for a safety and the 22-7 win. The line helped Fighting Irish runners gain 325 yards to Purdue's 75, but Irish passing gained only 8 yards.

Fumbles and punts took the better part of two scoreless quarters against Navy until Hornung led a 21-7 Irish victory. Hornung started the scoring by directing a 57-yard drive in 12 plays and his tally from the 1. Both defenses played well, or the offenses didn't, with more fumbles and interceptions. Finally, Hornung recovered a Schaefer fumble; Lewis scored on a 12-yard burst. Hornung intercepted yet another Navy pass and eventually threw to Kapish for a 14-yard touchdown. Navy scored later for the final 21-7 score.

Penn's Frank Riepl started the next game with a 100-yard kickoff return for a touchdown. In the hole, Fighting Irish fumbles stopped several drives. Finally, Morse went over from the 5 to complete an 80-yard drive at the end of the first quarter. Riepl fired an 8-yard touchdown pass in the second quarter. The Irish overcame some penalties on a 70-yard march; Kapish tallied with an 8-yard Hornung pass. Then Penn collapsed. Schaefer scored twice, from the 3 and the 24. Reserve Dick Fitzgerald bumped in from the 1. Dick Shulsen got a Penn fumble and Carl Hebert threw a 24-yard touchdown strike to George Wilson for the 46-14 final score. Schaefer and Morse teamed up for 114 and 113 yards rushing, respectively.

The Irish allowed another weaker team, North Carolina, to play even for the first half. Notre Dame scored first, led by a 38-yard Schaefer run to the 9 before Morse tallied from the 2. The Tarheels tied it in the second quarter on a 53-yard march. In the third period, Hornung patched together a 66-yard drive and scored from the 2 on a sneak. Sub Ed Sullivan took in a fumble on the North Carolina 27 and Lynch later scored from the 2. Reserve tackle Lou Loncaric finished the scoring with an interception and a 75-yard touchdown, one of the longest on record for a modern Notre Dame lineman, as Notre Dame won 27-7.

It would be hard for Notre Dame to continue its poor play and beat Iowa. Prendergast's second-quarter fumble recovery on the Hawkeye 44 led to a 1-yard

Hornung closes in on a Tarheel as the Irish whipped North Carolina 27-7 in 1955.

score by Studer. Iowa tied it in the third quarter after driving 54 yards. Then they came right back, reaching the Notre Dame 4; the Fighting Irish defense took over at the 1-foot line. A poor punt brought Iowa back, and they scored on a pass for a 14-7 lead. Ten minutes were left in the game. Hornung hit three passes for 47 yards on a 62-yard march, tying the game with a 16-yard touchdown pass to Morse and the conversion kick. Seven and a half minutes were left. Great kickoff coverage penned up Iowa at their 2; they punted, and Notre Dame took over at the Iowa 43. Morse made a leaping catch at the 9. Notre Dame wanted to try a field goal after Iowa held them at the 3. With 1:16 left to play, a kicking tee flew onto the field, and a referee flagged it for "coaching from the sidelines." Hornung kicked the winning field goal anyway—for 18 yards—to win 17-14.

Brennan had been doing all this basically with 16 players. Only four were truly ambulatory for the USC game. USC blitzed Notre Dame 42-20. Jon Arnett outscored the Fighting Irish with three touchdowns and five point-after conversions. Hornung scored from the 8, fired a 78-yard touchdown pass to Morse, and scored from the 1 on a plunge. USC won going away in the second half.

Brennan had taken a relatively weak team and made the most of it. The weak passing game was one of the worst on record: only 846 yards all season and a .421 completion rate. Hornung was the only Irish All-American selection.

1955 record: 8-2-0 (.800)
Record to date: 434-88-33 (.811)

1956

The 1955 team had been overachievers. Brennan would be glad to have the same numbers for wins and losses in 1956. And that's what happened—but in reverse. This season would go down in the record book with those of 1933 and 1888—the only two losing seasons on record.

For starters, Brennan had Hornung, who seemed to do everything in 1955: second in rushing, first in scoring, first in passing, second in kickoff returns, first in punting, and first in interceptions. He could run, kick, play defense, throw, and provide a form of leadership that some mistook for cockiness. He was physically strong, hard to tackle, and could improvise with the best of them—a throwback to Gipp. He also had Gipp's flair for the dramatic. He was also plain, old-fashioned tough, as he showed when he played a game with two dislocated thumbs. He would win the 1956 Heisman, edging out Johnny Majors.

Lewis returned, as did Jim Morse. The fullback position was weaker, although a future star was there in Nick Pietrosante. However, the entire 1955 line was gone, along with some good reserves. He had to

The 1956 Notre Dame starting eleven.

patch together five sophomores and gamble on their raw skills. Ranked third, the Fighting Irish prepared for SMU.

The Irish were upset by SMU 19-13, although they fought to the last second and had a chance to win. A 31-yard touchdown pass by SMU was the first score, but the Irish blocked the point after. SMU intercepted a Hornung pass but could not capitalize. They scored after getting a Hornung fumble, when nine plays took Charlie Arnold to a 1-foot touchdown sneak. In the third quarter, Morse caught a pass from Hornung for a 55-yard touchdown. Prendergast blocked a field goal try. To start the fourth quarter, Hornung ran from punt formation, faked to the trailing fullback, and dashed down the sideline for a 57-yard touchdown; the game was tied, 13-13. SMU twice gambled on fourth downs, earning a 14-yard touchdown; Prendergast blocked the point after. Al Ecuyer recovered a Mustang fumble on the Notre Dame 41 but only 28 seconds remained in the game. Lewis ran for 17 yards; Hornung sent everyone deep and heaved it. Morse caught it and was dragged down at the 7 on the game's last play.

The Fighting Irish recovered, beating Indiana 20-6. Hornung led a 73-yard march, sparked by Jim Just's 19-yard run and Hornung's own 25-yard keeper, before he slammed twice from the 5 for the touchdown. In the second quarter, Hornung fired a 12-yard touchdown pass to Lewis. Indiana scored next. In the

Paul Hornung, 1956 Heisman Trophy Winner for a 2-8 team.

Jim Morse, starting RH and captain of the 1956 Irish.

third quarter the Hoosiers were at the Irish 1. Notre Dame held and took over on downs; they drove 99 yards to put it away. Lewis ran 25 yards to move away from the goal line, and then ran 9 yards for the touchdown.

Purdue ran roughshod over the Fighting Irish 28-14. The Boilermakers' Mel Dillard rushed for 142 yards, scored twice, and had an interception to set up another Purdue touchdown. Purdue dominated with 27 first downs and ball control, running 86 plays to Notre Dame's 48. In spite of all that, it was tied 14-14 in the third quarter. Len Dawson and Erich Barnes powered Purdue on an 80-yard march, and Dawson passed for a 13-yard tally. Notre Dame fought back, lost a fourth-down gamble, and Purdue's Dillard scored from the 8, making it 14-0, Purdue. Hornung brought Notre Dame back on a 70-yard drive, in six plays, with 50 yards on passes and Dick Royer scored from the 7. In the third quarter, Notre Dame tied it 14-14, when Frank Reynolds raced in from the 11. Purdue marched 75 yards, ending with a 1-yard score. The final score was on a 28-yard pitchout from Dawson to Fletcher.

The long season got longer when Michigan State crunched Notre Dame 47-14. They intercepted a Hornung pass on the game's fourth play, but couldn't capitalize, allowing Notre Dame to score first, in the second quarter. MSU later showed it could score when it wanted. They scored on a long drive; then Peaks intercepted a pass meant for Morse at the MSU 5. The halftime score was 7-7. Dennis Mendyk ran 62 yards for a touchdown to open the third quarter. It was 27-7 before Sipes scored for Notre Dame from the 3.

Captain Tubbs, meet Captain Morse—ND versus Oklahoma, 1956.

The story of the 1956 campaign—Morse, wide open, grabs for an Irish pass, but the ball eludes his grasp. The Irish were crunched by the Sooners 40-0, and won only two games all year.

Then Mendyk struck again, from 67 yards, for a touchdown. Five plays later, an Irish pass was intercepted and returned 35 yards for a touchdown. MSU's Don Arend scored the fourth touchdown of the final quarter on a 65-yard run, then the Spartans intercepted another Irish pass to finish things.

The Oklahoma Sooners, under Bud Wilkinson, had won 35 straight. At the end of the game, it was 36, after a 40-0 rout of Notre Dame. This was to be the only Oklahoma win over Notre Dame in eight games. Oklahoma played superb football on both sides of the line of scrimmage, moving the ball at will and stopping Fighting Irish drives with ease. Clendon Thomas did the most damage, scoring from the 11 on a run, catching a pass for 49 yards on a scoring drive, and scoring with an interception and a 36-yard touchdown return. Sooners John Bell, Jay O'Neal, and Tommy McDonald also scored. It was the first shutout of Notre Dame since 1951.

Navy added to Irish woes with a 33-7 win. The Midshipmen held Notre Dame's runners to a total of 50 yards; Hornung got 10 yards on six carries. The field was muddy, negating Lewis' strengths. He was held to minus 6 yards. It was 0-0 until near the half, when a Fighting Irish fumble led to a short scoring drive by Navy. Lewis fumbled the first play of the new half, and Navy scored in four more plays. The Irish scored in two plays after that: a 38-yard pass from Hornung to Lewis, and Bob Ward ran 27 yards for Notre Dame's only tally. The Middies came back with a touchdown after a 65-yard march, and an interception led to yet another touchdown. After another Irish fumble, Navy put in the reserves who scored in 12 plays.

Pittsburgh kept the losing streak going when it toppled Notre Dame 26-13. The first quarter was close, then Pitt drove 72 yards for a touchdown. After some punts, another drive ended with a Joe Walton touchdown. Hornung scored on a 50-yard run to make it 13-6. Pitt widened the gap with a 91-yard touchdown drive in the third quarter. A Fighting Irish pass was intercepted and returned for another touchdown. Bob Ward ran 84 yards with the kickoff for the final Irish score. It was Notre Dame's fifth straight loss, the worst string in the school's history.

This was the last chance for people to see The Golden Boy play under the Golden Dome. A 21-14 win over North Carolina made it special. Notre Dame was in trouble early. Lewis stole a pass on the 11 to dodge a threat, and Hornung ran 32 yards on fourth down to break out of trouble again. He passed 45 yards to Morse, who reached the 7. Three plays later Hornung scored from the 1. Moments later, Lewis sprinted 78 yards to the North Carolina 15. Hornung scored on the third play. The Tarheels used the next drive to go 63 yards and score on a pass. In the third quarter, a Notre Dame fumble let the Tarheels tie it up, 14-14. On a scoreless Notre Dame drive, Hornung hurt a thumb and was replaced by Bob Williams. The new backfield could not score, so Hornung went back in to direct a 63-yard drive, score again, and win the game. With 1:16 left on the clock, he scored from the 1-foot line. He had scored all three touchdowns, rushed for 91 yards, made all three conversions, and completed four passes for 103 yards.

Iowa blasted Notre Dame, 48-8. Notre Dame's first drive netted minus 19 yards, and its second drive gained 1 yard. By that time, Iowa had the lead. The next Irish drive ended when Dick Klein intercepted a Bob Williams handoff and ran it back to the Iowa 37. The Fighting Irish got a safety and a touchdown on a pass from Cooke to Ward to avert the shutout. Iowa scored seven touchdowns with relative impunity. Hornung reinjured his thumb early in the game.

Hornung moved to left halfback for the USC game and played courageously. USC scored first after moving 66 yards. Notre Dame came back, using

Hornung here and there, such as a 9-yard pitchout he took (with two dislocated thumbs) to the 6; Williams scored. The Trojans marched right back, scoring with a 15-yard pass. Williams did the same, scoring with a throw to Bob Wetoska; USC led at halftime 14-13. The Trojans scored first in the second half on a 16-yard pass. On the subsequent kickoff, Hornung fielded it on his 5, and started up field, bulling through a wave of Trojans at the 25; he used his injured hands to ward off tacklers as he went 95 yards for the score. But USC scored again, on a 38-yard run, to win 28-20.

The Fighting Irish played with class and dignity in this 2-8 season. The opposition outscored Notre Dame 2:1. Notre Dame rushed for 1,000 fewer yards than last year; scored only 67 percent of the previous season's touchdowns. The air game, however, improved by 50 percent, largely because Hornung had to play catchup. Hornung accounted for 45 percent of the total offense, and led in rushing, passing, scoring, kickoff returns, punting, passes broken up, and was second in interceptions. And he did this for a third of the season with a dislocated thumb or two.

1956 record: 2-8-0 (.200)
Record to date: 436-96-33 (.800)

1957

Hope springs eternal. Hornung was gone, but Brennan was an optimist and decided to diversify the offense, rather than keying in on one man. His line now had good depth. Monty Stickles was a good addition at end, a prototype of future tight ends. Bob Williams was an adequate replacement for Hornung; George Izo was the backup. Frank Reynolds and Dick Lynch won the halfback jobs, and Nick Pietrosante would show flashes of brilliance at fullback. So, Brennan had an improved line and a more balanced attack.

A modest 12-0 win over Purdue opened the season. The game started slowly. The Irish unveiled a halfback option pass, Lynch to Lewis for 22 yards. Later, Lynch took a pitchout and ran 22 yards around left end for the first score. Lewis missed the point after, but later intercepted a Purdue pass. Most of the third quarter was spent fielding punts, until Williams heaved one to Wetoska at the Notre Dame 45, who ran to the Purdue 8. Reynolds scored. Pietrosante led all runners with 62 yards on 10 carries, as the Fighting Irish racked up 323 yards of total offense.

The 1957 Notre Dame starters.

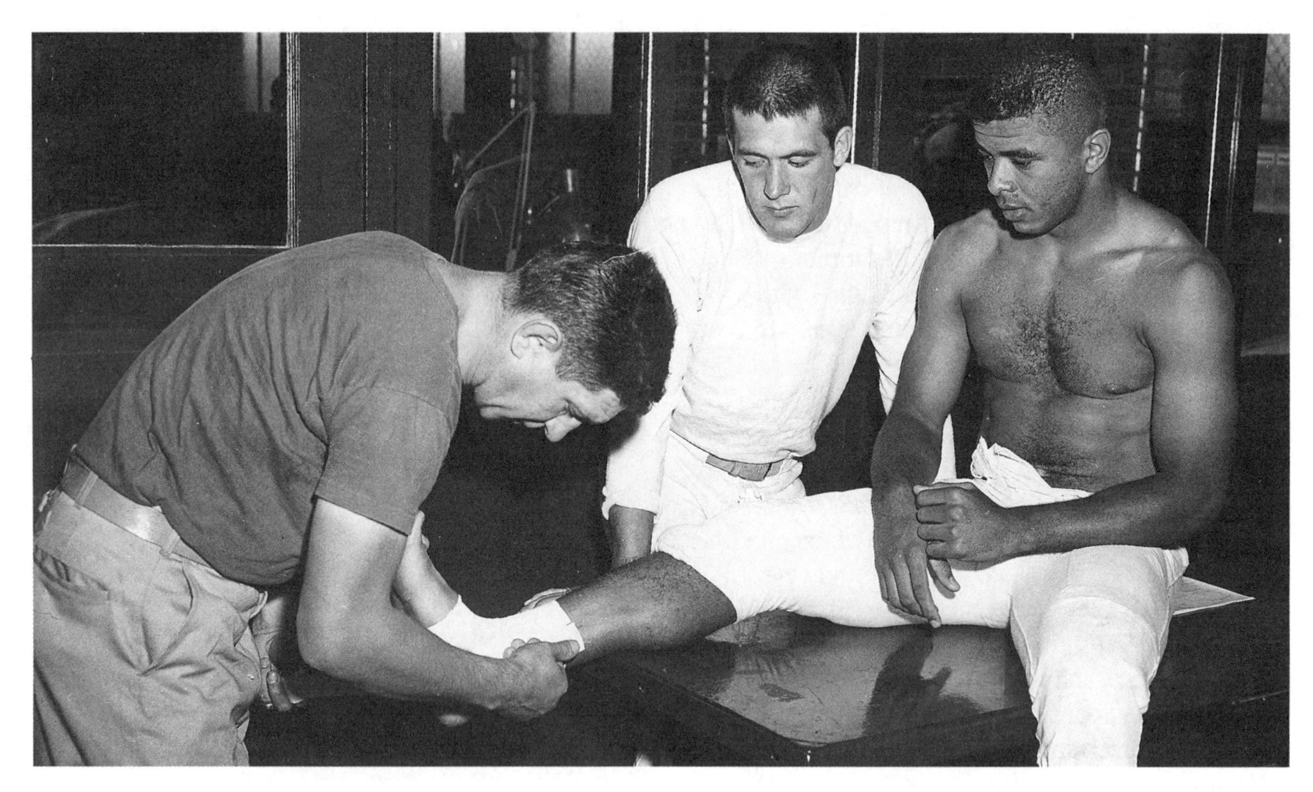

Longtime head trainer Gene Paszkiet tapes up the injured ankle of Aubrey Lewis as Ed Sullivan watches—just prior to the 1957 Indiana game.

Notre Dame also started slowly with Indiana. Notre Dame finally put together a 54-yard touchdown drive that took some tough running from the 7. Lynch crashed in from the 1. Indiana failed to move and a heavy rush made the punter shank the kick—Notre Dame's ball at the Indiana 27. Three running plays put the ball in the end zone: Chuck Lima for 5, Izo for 21, and Lima for 1 and the touchdown. Just before the half, Williams scored on a short sneak for the 19-0 halftime lead. Most of the third period was dull. In the last quarter, Izo intercepted a pass; Lynch ran for 17; Just finished it off with runs of 12, 14, and 7 yards and the touchdown. Notre Dame won 26-0.

Army was next, after a decade's hiatus. Cadet Bob Anderson ended the shutout string when he took off on an 81-yard touchdown sprint for a 7-0 Army lead. Then Williams patched together a sporadic drive, letting Pietrosante do much of it, and his fullback rammed it in from the 1 to tie the game at 7-7. In the third frame, Pete Dawkins and Anderson scored for Army using almost all of the quarter for a 21-7 Army lead. Pietrosante countered when he slammed over guard, brushed off two Cadets, and ran 65 yards for a score. Notre Dame stopped Army and got the ball on their 44. Lynch rolled for an 18-yard gain, then ran four times at the end before scoring from the 1. Stickles missed the point after as Notre Dame took a 20-14 lead. Army elected to start passing. Geremia deflected a pass and Pietrosante caught it from a prone position. On a fourth-and-6, Stickles had to go for a field goal, something he'd never done before. He made it for a 23-21 lead. Army was then stalled by good defense to ensure the win.

The excitement carried over to a 13-7 win over Pitt. The Fighting Irish were tight—Gary Myers rescued two fumbles by Reynolds and Lynch. The first score came on a short run by Reynolds. Pitt scored in the second quarter on a quarterback keeper from the 6. Late in the game, Williams and Lynch were ejected from the game when they disputed a punt call. Izo and Lewis replaced them. Moments later, Izo threw to the streaking Lewis, who won the game with a 74-yard touchdown. Pitt drove to the Irish 19 before losing the ball on downs.

Notre Dame jumped out to an early lead over Navy when Lynch intercepted a Middie pass and scored from the 46. Then Navy shut down the Fighting Irish to win 20-6. The Irish allowed a 79-yard touchdown run, a 1-foot touchdown plunge, and a 36-yard screen pass for a touchdown, all scored by Wellborn. Irish penalties and an inspired Navy defense were the difference.

Michigan State whomped the faltering Irish 34-6. MSU scored on an 11-yard run in the second quarter

Dick Lynch, starting RH in 1957, scored the winning TD in the great upset of Oklahoma that year.

for the halftime lead. The third quarter was the roughest, as the Spartans moved 57 yards in 17 plays to go up by two touchdowns. The officials made a bad pass interference call on Pietrosante to allow a MSU score, but it took them four plays to move the final 5 yards. Notre Dame drove back to the MSU 11, but a lost fumble started an 85-yard march highlighting Art Johnson's 50-yard touchdown run. Two more scores came on fumbles by Irish reserves. Al Ecuyer played a great game for Notre Dame—15 tackles, one pass broken up, and one intercepted. With the score 34-0, Williams tallied on a dive play.

The Fighting Irish rallied for one of their all-time classic wins, a 7-0 thriller over Bud Wilkinson's Sooners. Notre Dame went into the game as 19-point underdogs. Oklahoma had won 47 in a row (the Irish were the last to beat them, in 1953). Oklahoma reached the Irish 13 on their first drive, but that would be as far as they would get that day. In the second quarter, Notre Dame's pass rush made their quarterback drop the ball twice on one play, and Pietrosante recovered on their 49. Notre Dame drove to the 1 but lost it on downs, Oklahoma punted, and the Irish came back again. The Sooners intercepted a pass, and the game stalled until the middle of the third quarter. After several punt exchanges, Notre Dame had the ball on its 20, still 0-0, in the fourth quarter. Driving carefully, Notre Dame moved to the Sooner 25 in 11 plays. Reynolds ran for 1, Williams passed for 10 to Royer,

The starting tackles for the 1957 squad: RT Bronko Nagurski and LT Chuck Puntillo.

Bob Scholtz, starting center from 1957 to 1959.

Pietrosante rumbled for 7, Lynch ran to the 4, Williams fumbled back to the 8, and after three runs Notre Dame was on the Sooner 3. On fourth-and-3, Williams faked to Pietrosante up the middle, then pitched to Lynch, who swung wide around his right end for the only touchdown of the game. There was only 3:50 left. The Sooners, held to 98 yards rushing, started using their passing game, and moved to the Notre Dame 36, but Williams intercepted a pass in the end zone. Oklahoma had not been shutout in 123 games. Defensive coach Bernie Witucki was voted the game ball.

Iowa won the following week, 21-13. Pietrosante was hurt and missed the game, and it was frigid and windy. A Fighting Irish drive stalled at the Iowa 27, then an Iowa fullback scored on a powerful 36-yard run. They were ready to score again when Bob Scholtz recovered a fumble at the 13 (Notre Dame would stop them five times inside their 25). Iowa scored on a 24-yard interception return. Brennan put in Izo, who promptly found Stickles in the clear for a 55-yard touchdown. In the third quarter, Ron Toth grabbed a fumble caused by Royer, and scored from the 15. In the fourth period, Iowa ended a 51-yard drive with a 16-yard touchdown pass—tipped twice by Irish defenders.

Notre Dame recovered to blitz USC 40-12, again without Pietrosante. Brennan showcased Pat Doyle and Jim Crotty. Two quick touchdowns gave Notre Dame a 13-0 lead: Toth followed a Williams interception with a 3-yard score; Puntillo fell on a loose ball, and Stickles caught a 17-yard touchdown pass. A series of fumbles let USC get a touchdown, they kicked off, and Doyle blasted through for a 92-yard touchdown return. In the third quarter, Notre Dame drove 66 yards to score in 13 plays, and USC ended its scoring with a ground drive (the 25° weather hurt USC passing). Stickles, using the same play as earlier, caught a 7-yard touchdown pass. Izo threw an 8-yard touchdown to Prendergast for the final score. The loss closed USC's worst season at 1-9.

The Fighting Irish "stampeded" the SMU Mustangs 54-21. The Mustangs scored first on future Dallas Cowboy star Don Meredith's touchdown pass of 47 yards. The Fighting Irish banged, fumbled, and punted, but finally tallied on a Lima slam from the 2. Lynch intercepted a Meredith pass to lead to Williams' 4-yard quarterback option for a score. Williams grabbed an SMU pass, Toth ran, Stickles caught passes, and Williams scored on a 2-yard keeper. Prendergast hit Meredith; the ball came loose, and Nagurski recovered. Doyle shook loose for a 45-yard touchdown run on a pitchout for the fourth Irish score in 9 minutes. The Fighting Irish kept the pressure on in the second half: Doyle ran for an 18-yard touchdown; Crotty returned a kickoff 70 yards; Toth scored from the 3; and Norm Odyniec went in from the 1.

Five opponents ended up in the top 10, so the 7-3 season was respectable. The defense played well all year and led Notre Dame to a ranking of ninth. Ecuyer was selected as an All-American.

1957 record: 7-3-0 (.700)

Record to date: 443-99-33 (.799)

1958

The Fighting Irish looked set for the new season. The sophomores who were mangled in 1956 were now seniors—more experienced, bulkier. The line was a known quantity and Stickles and Wetoska were two of the best ends in the country. Williams and Izo were the quarterbacks, with Red Mack and Jim Crotty as halfbacks, and Pietrosante at fullback. There was excellent depth at all running spots.

Brennan's job had been on the line after the 2-8 season of 1956 when the Athletic Board wanted him replaced. Hesburgh overruled the move and Brennan got a one-year contract, then another after the resurgent 1957 year. The team would go 6-4 in 1958, and many would see it as a failure to get the best out of the talent on hand. Rumors abounded that a new de-emphasis on athletics was taking place, but, in fact, the school was in an early phase of much-needed academic, endowment, and physical plant improvements. Brennan must have known that disappointment was rife, and Leahy had been sniping from the sidelines. Conditions were not the best for the Fighting Irish football squad.

Red Mack, starting LH in 1958.

Monty Stickles and Nick Pietrosante, Irish All-Americans in 1958.

The Irish beat Indiana 18-0 in the opener, but the critics thought they lacked polish, a perception that stuck for the season. They also wasted 14 of 17 scoring opportunities. Indiana fumbled the kickoff at their 20 but Notre Dame did not score. Finally, on the fourth possession, the Fighting Irish tallied when Mack sprinted 11 yards. Dropped passes and fumbles plagued Notre Dame well into the third quarter. Williams managed to put it all together in a 71-yard drive, running it in from the 20. Near the end, Indiana handed over another fumble, to Stickles at the 7, who scored with a 4-yard flip from Williams. Pietrosante led all runners with 75 of Notre Dame's 238 rushing yards.

An improved Southern Methodist University team awaited Notre Dame in Dallas. In the second quarter, Williams used Pietrosante for six runs and 41 yards on an 18-play march. Sensitive to the damage from fullback, SMU bit on a fake to him and Mack scored an 11-yard touchdown. In the third quarter, a good drive ended without a score; Meredith used a pitchout to score from the SMU 46. The Fighting Irish moved back deep, but an interception stopped them. In the fourth quarter, Williams made a screen pass for

The 1958 Notre Dame starters.

23 yards to Odyniec to spark a scoring drive that he ended with a sneak from the 1 for the 14-6 Irish win.

A resurgent Army squad, ranked third and featuring Pete Dawkins, who would win the Heisman, and the "Lonesome End," Bill Carpenter, came to Notre Dame for a 14-2 win. There were numerous turnovers created by good defense. Army scored first on a 16-yard touchdown pass. Stickles later stuck their punter with a safety. Several Fighting Irish drives were stopped with fumbles, bobbled snaps, interceptions, and penalties. Dawkins scored a touchdown with 7 seconds left. Brennan's tenure at Notre Dame began to slip away with this game.

Against Duke, Notre Dame had nine penalties that nullified a touchdown and more than 200 yards of rushing, most on long gainers. Notre Dame squeaked through with a 9-7 win. Two potential touchdowns in the first three plays were lost on penalties. Eventually, Williams found Stickles for an 8-yard touchdown, but they missed a 2-point conversion. Duke scored on its next possession. After a number of penalties, Stickles made a 23-yard field goal for the win.

Co-captains Al Ecuyer and Chuck Puntillo psyching up for the Army game.

Jesse Harper accepts a Helms Hall of Fame award from Father Joyce at the halftime of the 1958 Army game.

The Fighting Irish started fast against Purdue—a Boilermaker fumble led to a 14-yard touchdown run by Williams. It was all Purdue after that, until late in the game. Purdue's Jarus scored three touchdowns: from the 1 after a bad punt from terrible field position, from the 1 after a fumble, and from the 5 after an interception. A 26-yard touchdown run iced it for Purdue. Izo tried to throw Notre Dame back into the game; he hit Stickles for two touchdowns, one for 43 yards. Pietrosante scored a safety, but Notre Dame lost 29-22.

For Navy, Izo started out of a winged T formation. It worked for a 40-20 win. Izo hit Mack with a 5-yard touchdown pass, then Joe Bellino ran with a hand off on the kickoff for a touchdown to tie. Notre Dame took control: Pietrosante hammered in from the 3; Izo threw to Royer for a touchdown; Notre Dame recovered an onside kick, and Izo threw to Doyle for a 38-yard touchdown; Mack returned a 65-yard punt return for a touchdown. Bellino scored again when the Irish were up 34-6. Williams ended Notre Dame's scoring with a soft pass to Myers that he broke loose for a 74-yard touchdown. Navy subs scored after that.

Izo continued his hot hand against Pitt, with 332 yards passing (the best total in college ball since 1954), two touchdown passes, and two rushing touchdowns. Still, the Fighting Irish lost five fumbles and the game, 29-26. Pitt started its first drive from the Notre Dame 2 after a fumble. Ninety-seven yards later, they scored from the 1. Three plays later, they intercepted Izo and scored for a 15-0 lead. The Irish fought back; Stickles scored from the 11 on an Izo pass. In the second quarter, they clicked for an 8-yard touchdown pass. Pitt led at the half, 15-14. Pietrosante caused a fumble in the third quarter, and Izo scored. Pitt drove for a score from the 11. Notre Dame came back, but a fumble killed the drive at the 8. Izo later threw to Mack in the flat who ran 72 yards to Pitt's 2. Izo sneaked it in for a 26-22 lead. Pitt turned Mike Ditka loose on a drive, and won the game on a quarterback roll out from the 5 with 11 seconds left. Izo used the last play to fire a 47-yard pass to Mack, who was tackled at the Pitt 15.

The Fighting Irish won a wild one back home in the mud against North Carolina, 34-24. North Carolina scored a touchdown after Notre Dame fumbled for an early lead. Izo intercepted them moments later and the drive ended on a Pietrosante run from the 2. A Tarheel fumble led to another Pietrosante touchdown from the same spot. A poor North Carolina punt earned Mack a 7-yard touchdown run and a 21-6 lead for the Irish. The Tarheels scored just before the half. Their momentum carried over to the first possession of the new half, a 65-yard drive and touchdown. Then

Nick Pietrosante, two-year starter at FB, 1958 All-American.

Al Ecuyer, 1958 co-captain, starting RG, and two-time All-American.

they intercepted a pass and scored again. Crotty ran well on the return drive, getting 51 yards on four tries before Mack went in from the 15. Notre Dame had to stop the 235-pound Tarheel fullback in a fourth-down situation, did so, and Izo scored from the 3 to end it.

Joe Scibelli works on the bag as captain Al Ecuyer watches in a 1958 practice.

Iowa, in beating the Fighting Irish 31-21, exposed all of their weaknesses. In the first quarter, there were numerous punts, but Iowa was starting to move. They scored from the 6 to open the second quarter. Fumbles and interceptions eventually got the Hawkeyes a 36-yard touchdown. Notre Dame fought back with a 69-yard Izo-to-Stickles pass, highlighted when Stickles stiff-armed a Hawkeye into an early trip to the locker room. Iowa led at the half, 13-7. In the third quarter, a Fighting Irish drive died, and Iowa moved 76 yards, capped by a 1-yard touchdown. Izo stepped up the passing game: to Odyniec for 16, to Myers for 9, and to Scarpitto for a 52-yard touchdown. Iowa came back with a 53-yard touchdown pass; they picked off a screen pass and slammed in from the 1. Izo finished the scoring with a 4-yard keeper.

Notre Dame earned a winning season with a 20-13 victory over USC in Los Angeles. Dave Hurd intercepted a pass and ran to their 43; Pietrosante scored from the 4. USC answered with a 42-yard touchdown pass. Three interceptions later the Trojans scored again, from the 1. Bob Williams led a 70-yard march, scoring from the 10. In the second half, Wetoska grabbed a 20-yard touchdown pass. Notre Dame's defense made a four-play stand at its 2-foot line to stop the last USC threat.

Turnovers killed the Irish in 1958—45 turnovers. Brennan had coached his last game. Stickles, Pietrosante, and Ecuyer made All-American teams.

1958 record: 6-4-0 (.600)

Record to date: 449-103-34 (.795)

1959

The public learned of Brennan's departure four days before Christmas 1958. It was not an easy decision. He was universally recognized as a fine man. The press supported him, but the student body had hung him in effigy three times in 1958. He was probably too young and inexperienced to be running such a demanding college football program.

His replacement, Joe Kuharich, was born in South Bend and attended Fighting Irish practices as a child, watching Rockne. He played under Layden and coached at all levels: high school, college (he coached Ollie Matson and Gino Marchetti at San Francisco), and the NFL. He was the Coach of the Year in the NFL in 1955 for the Redskins. He brought "pro" football with him to Notre Dame: he emphasized passing, passing, and more passing, from complicated sets, motions, and shifts. The Fighting Irish would be exciting to watch—if they could just learn it all in time. And therein was the rub; close observers noted that Kuharich did not have the knack of teaching the game to those who still needed to work on fundamentals. He was accustomed to having pro players who knew it all.

Head coach Joe Kuharich.

He inherited only 12 monogram winners. There was some quality in the line: Stickles, Pottios, Buoniconti, and Joe Carollo, but they weren't a unit yet, and injuries would hurt. Izo had a major league arm but was slow and tended to fumble. Both he and Mack suffered knee injuries early in fall practice. Don White, a steady, dependable type, would get the nod at quarterback. George Sefcik and Scarpitto were the halfbacks, backed up by Angelo Dabiero. Gerry Gray won the fullback's job, with Crotty behind him. This was not an overwhelming group, without a game-breaker.

Against North Carolina, the Fighting Irish came out in the rain in new jerseys—dark blue with gold shoulder stripes (the helmet shamrock would come later). The first break came at the end of the first quarter when Notre Dame's Pat Heenan splashed his way to a loose ball. White threw to Scarpitto for 22, and Scarpitto slashed in from the 2 for a touchdown. Crotty tallied in the next quarter with a 19-yard run around end and scored again just before the half on a 3-yard burst. In the third quarter, Stickles turned a Tarheel punt into a safety and moments later Ray Ratkowski intercepted a pass and ran 43 yards for a touchdown. North Carolina scored a late touchdown. Notre Dame won 28-8.

Purdue was a different case. Jarus scored to end Purdue's first drive, a 76-yarder, going in from the 5 (his fourth career touchdown against the Fighting Irish). Then they put together a 77-yard effort, in eight plays, ending with a 7-yard touchdown pass. Crotty fumbled the kickoff, and Jarus ran for his fifth touchdown. Purdue was up at the half, 21-0. Notre Dame scored on its first drive of the second half, pumped up by a 38-yard Stickles catch. Crotty ran twice from the 4 to score. Purdue's Jim Tiller raced 74 yards moments later for the 28-7 final.

Notre Dame beat California's Golden Bears in a costly 28-6 win. Pottios was lost for the year, and Crotty, Gray, and Roy would be out for a few weeks. Notre Dame's John Powers grabbed a lost pitchout on Cal's first play; Izo found Scarpitto on Notre Dame's second play for a 27-yard score. On the second touchdown drive, Gray ran up the middle for 17 yards, White passed to Henry Wilke for 18 more, and Dabiero got 15 on a trap. White tallied from the 1. A minute

Jim Crotty, starting RH for the 1959 squad.

later, Cal fumbled and Heenan grabbed it. Nine plays later, Gray went in from the 1-foot line. Cal had one good drive and scored, on a pass from the 5. Irish subs ended it with a 45-yard touchdown pass from George Haffner to Les Traver. There were 158 yards of penalties against Notre Dame, including one for 25 yards (15 for roughing the passer and 10 for interference against the receiver).

An up-down, on-off, win-loss pattern was emerging (and would hold true for the Kuharich years) as Michigan State blanked Notre Dame 19-0. In the first quarter, there were five fumbles and eight changes of possessions. Eventually the MSU quarterback, Dean Look, ran 41 yards and set up a touchdown from the 7. This score held into the third quarter, which was marred by five more fumbles (Herb Adderly now had four) and interceptions. MSU's Look threw a touchdown pass to Fred Arbanas (legally blind in one eye) for 52 yards. MSU reserves tacked on a third touchdown.

Northwestern, coached by Ara Parseghian, knocked off Notre Dame 30-24 in South Bend. Their first drive dismantled the Fighting Irish secondary, using a down-and-out pass pattern for 14, 14, and 18 yards for a touchdown. The Fighting Irish only made it to their own 7 before fumbling; Northwestern quickly scored for a 12-0 lead. Notre Dame drove to the 3 but lost it on downs, the Wildcats fumbled, and Scarpitto scored. Before the half, a fake into the line suckered the entire Irish secondary and Northwestern scored on a 54-yard pass. Northwestern led at the half, 18-7. Notre Dame closed it up in the third with an Izo-to-Sefcik touchdown pass, but Northwestern's John Talley fired a 78-yard bullet to Irv Cross for a score, then following a failed Irish drive, ran 61 yards for a touchdown when his man covered. White threw a deflected pass to Scarpitto for a late 52-yard touchdown. Stickles added a field goal to end it. It was a game Notre Dame could have won, except for their mistakes.

A week later, Navy quarterback, Jim Maxfield, sliced and diced Notre Dame's secondary with six straight completions on an 89-yard touchdown drive. Sefcik tied it up near the end of the first quarter with a 14-yard run. Scarpitto grabbed the ball when Bellino bobbled it on a pass and ran for a 52-yard touchdown, and Maxfield threw a 38-yard touchdown pass in response. The Fighting Irish fumbled, and Maxfield went right to work: two quick passes, the second for a touchdown with no one near the receiver. An interception earned Navy a field goal a few plays later. Notre Dame tied it up when Williams led a drive that Scarpitto finished from the Navy 2, then hit a 2-point conversion, White to Rutkowski. Navy was unable to move, and Notre Dame worked it down close. Bob McCuthan, Notre Dame's student manager, stepped on the field and threw out a tee. Flags went flying—"coaching from the bench." Stickles had to make a 33-yard field goal with 30 seconds left. It was good for a 25-22 win (Stickles' third game-winning field goal in his career), but Navy had shown how weak the secondary was.

The modest progress seen against Navy disappeared against Georgia Tech, where, once again, turnovers and penalties mangled Notre Dame's chances. Stickles made a 41-yard field goal in the first half; he caught a 43-yard touchdown pass from White and booted the point after for all of Notre Dame's scoring. But Tech scored two touchdowns to win—from the 1-foot line and from the 6, both by the reserve quarterback. Tech did not pass much, but Notre Dame gave them seven turnovers to lose 14-10.

On to Pitt and a complete mud bath. The Fighting Irish ground game stayed in South Bend, although Pitt ran 248 yards in a 28-13 win. Pitt scored first on a 64-yard punt return. Later, Fred Cox (who was a good kicker as a halfback) lurched for a 44-yard touchdown. In the third quarter, White's fake freed up

Angelo Dabiero, 1958 and 1959 starter at RH.

Scarpitto for a 58-yard touchdown pass. Other drives faltered until the fourth quarter when Notre Dame simply dropped the ball on its own 5. Two plays later, Pitt scored. Their last score came on a 72-yard drive, scored from the 3. Izo tried to fire back; Scarpitto scored on an 8-yard Izo pass, but it was too late.

Iowa's Evashevski tried to become the first coach to beat Notre Dame four straight times, but Izo foiled him. In a 20-19 upset win, Izo passed for 295 yards and three touchdowns as the Fighting Irish came from behind twice. Iowa had been rampaging for 400+ yards per game, but an alert Irish defense shut them down. Iowa scored after an interception, but used nine plays to go 22 yards. Six plays later, Izo hit Stickles with a touchdown pass. Iowa grabbed another pass to set up Bob Jeter's touchdown run. Notre Dame punted in the next series, and Iowa ran it back for a 19-7 lead. Izo used a third-and-one situation to suck in the Hawkeyes before throwing a pass to Heenan for a 55-yard touchdown. Iowa stopped a drive at their 4, but Izo later threw a 58-yard touchdown pass to Sefcik. Stickles made the winning point after, and Sefcik got an interception to wrap up Kuharich's biggest win of the year.

Kuharich avoided a losing season by beating USC 16-6. Stickles deflected a punt, and Gray overcame his own fumble to score from the 3. USC intercepted a pass. The Trojans' passing was suspect and they lost two good opportunities. Their running game wasn't working either. Notre Dame scored when Gray smashed in from the 10 after a Stickles reception. On the second half kickoff, USC's Angelo Coia ran it out to the 18, drifted backwards, and Gray tackled him in the end zone for a safety. Gray also scored Notre Dame's final touchdown for the 16-6 win.

The 1959 Fighting Irish were 5-5 in a season where their running game did not work well, they committed 40 turnovers, and their passing game disappeared. Stickles earned All-American honors.

1959 record: 5-5-0 (.500)
Record to date: 454-108-34 (.790)

1960 to 1969

1960

Kuharich had two problems to overcome—losses due to injuries and losses via graduation. The line was in fair shape, but the quarterback situation was clouded: the returners did not have much experience and sophomores were potential problems at the helm. Daryle Lamonica, blessed with a great arm, would take most of the snaps but would not be used much in the passing game. The halfbacks were Sefcik and Dabiero; the fullback was Mike Lind. Injuries to Mack and Gray basically kept them sidelined.

Notre Dame started with a 21-7 victory over California. Carollo recovered a fumble, and Scarpitto ran 8 yards for the touchdown. Cal tied it up with a 76-yard drive, using mainly passes. In the third quarter, Scarpitto returned the kickoff 44 yards, and a few plays later, saw a lane open up for a 33-yard touchdown run. Cal had earlier tried a quick kick; when

The 1960 Notre Dame starters.

Nick DePola saw the same formation, he split the blockers and literally took the ball off the foot of the kicker for a 15-yard touchdown.

The Fighting Irish suffered their worst home defeat in history when Purdue demolished them 51-19. The Irish fumbled too much, failed to tackle well, and played poor pass defense. Purdue's scores came in: a 44-yard touchdown pass, a 78-yard touchdown run that broke three tackles, another touchdown pass, a 34-yard field goal after a Notre Dame fumble, a touchdown run after an interception, a touchdown pass after a Notre Dame fumble, a 65-yard punt return for a touchdown, and then Purdue subs scored a touchdown. Scarpitto got the first Irish touchdown on a 64-yard run, Dabiero tallied with a George Haffner pass from the 24, and the subs got one. Ironically, each team had 358 yards of total offense.

Another setback awaited Notre Dame—North Carolina. The first quarter was a display of incompetent football—interceptions, fumbles, stalled drives, and penalties. The Tarheels had the first sustained drive, a 74-yard effort ended by a 47-yard touchdown pass. Then they intercepted a pass from Clay Schulz and took it 42 yards for their other touchdown. The Fighting Irish kept playing poorly in the second half. Scarpitto eventually scored from the 2, but the game was one of the worst displays of major college football to be seen as the Tarheels won 12-7.

Michigan State was Notre Dame's 600th game. Kuharich juggled his quarterbacks to find the right combination. Notre Dame kept the game scoreless for 23 minutes, until a Spartan deflected a pass and ran it back for a touchdown. The Fighting Irish defense put on a great pass rush next time out. However, MSU's coach, Duffy Daugherty, called for a screen pass, and the Spartans broke for a 52-yard touchdown. The Irish kept trying to come back but bobbles, interceptions, and incomplete passes ruined each effort. Herb Adderly

George Sefcik, three-year starter at LH, 1959 to 1961.

Kuharich and his 1960 QBs: Ed Rutkowski, George Haffner, and Daryle Lamonica.

scored the final MSU touchdown on a 22-yard reception for the 21-0 win.

The Irish offense solved its problems of killing its long drives against Northwestern—they did not have any to kill, as they failed to gain a first down for two quarters. The Wildcats got their only touchdown following a punt return to the Notre Dame 41; 10 plays later Elbert Kimbrough scored on a 3-yard run. The Irish improved in the second half by reducing their problems to one—penalties. The only Fighting Irish score came on a 25-yard pass from Haffner to Jim Sherlock. After that, penalties killed two promising drives. Notre Dame lost 7-6.

Notre Dame's next opponent, Navy, had the eventual Heisman winner in its lineup—Joe Bellino. Bellino dominated the opening drive, as he returned the kickoff to the 19, gained 43 yards around left end, gained 18 yards over left tackle to the 19, and scored from the 12. Meanwhile, two Fighting Irish drives ended with a fumble and a sack. Bellino also fumbled, leading to a Dabiero touchdown from the 3-yard line. Moments later, offensive pass interference in the end zone killed a drive for Notre Dame. The Fighting Irish kept plugging away, with a blocked Navy field goal try and a 69-yard pass to Scarpitto that reached Navy's 14. Good defense kept it there. Navy won, 14-7, when a Haffner pass was intercepted, and Bellino scored from the half-yard line. Irish drives had ended at Navy's 22, 14, and twice at the 5.

Pittsburgh kept the Irish losing streak alive by beating Notre Dame 20-13. Their second play from scrimmage went to Ditka, who was caught at the Irish 30, but just kept lumbering along with a struggling Dabiero hanging from his shoulder pads for 22 more

Myron Pottios, 1960 captain and an All-American at LG.

Joe Carollo, starting RT in 1960 and 1961.

yards. Notre Dame held for three plays, but they scored from the 1-foot line. For the first half, Notre Dame accumulated more yards in penalties, 55, than in total offense, 50. Haffner had completed one pass. Fred Cox, a good kicker for a halfback, intercepted the ball and ran to the Irish 2; he scored on the next play. Two Fighting Irish possessions went nowhere; Pitt sauntered 73 yards, mostly on end runs, for their third score. The Irish went down to defeat in a flurry of passes. It was the sixth consecutive defeat.

Number seven came against Miami, a 28-21 cliffhanger. Miami ran a draw play that gained 56 yards on the pass-conscious Irish, then scored from the 1 on a dive. Notre Dame fumbled on its first drive, but then put together an 80-yard effort in seven plays; Dabiero led the charge on a 43-yard run. Lind tallied from the 1. Miami answered with a 60-yard touchdown drive in the next quarter. Notre Dame moved well again and scored to end a 77-yard march when Kuharich's ninth fullback for the year, Bill Ahern, went in from the 5. A 2-point conversion pass by Lamonica made it 14-14 at the half. Miami took the lead in the third quarter using a long pass to Bill Miller, then two short runs for the touchdown. Lamonica teamed with Scarpitto on a 37-yard pass and a drive reached the 1; Lamonica took it in for a 21-21 deadlock. A Notre Dame drive was killed by a penalty, Perkowski missed a long field goal, and Miami went on to win. A quarterback keeper broke for a 49-yard advance, then they muscled it in from short range.

The Fighting Irish fumbled on their first play from scrimmage against Iowa. Iowa went 28 yards in six plays for a touchdown, winning eventually 28-0.

Coach Joe Kuharich with the 1960 Captain Myron Pottios and the Irish mascot of the day, Mike.

Iowa also scored on a 28-yard pass, a run from the Notre Dame 3, and a 2-yard run. Fighting Irish drives usually ended in interceptions. The losing streak now reached eight.

Notre Dame had the pleasure of giving USC's John McKay a losing season when they beat the Trojans 17-0 to end the season. Notre Dame dominated the whole game, driving well enough on its first series to salvage 3 points on Perkowski's kick from the 21. This was their first lead in a game since September 24 (this game was played on November 26). Lamonica intercepted a Bill Nelson pass and scored a few plays later from the 1. With 10 minutes to go in the second quarter, Scarpitto shrugged off several hits to score from the USC 9. Good defense kept the Trojans out of the end zone for the whole game, and the win kept this team from being the worst Notre Dame squad of this century.

The real story of the season was in hospital bills. Virtually every starter lost playing time—some most of the season, some all. The defense often played well, but the offense was wretched. The passing game gained 37 percent less yardage than in 1959. Pottios was the only All-American pick.

1960 record: 2-8-0 (.200)
Record to date: 456-116-34 (.780)

1961

Things had to get better this year, and they did, at least marginally. Kuharich had eight starters from 1960 and two from 1959. The backfield was the same, although Lamonica hoped not to be in a revolving door as the quarterback. There were some excellent sophomores in Bob Lehmann, Frank Budka, Jim Kelly, and two behemoth running backs, Paul Costa (6' 4", 230) and Jim Snowden (6' 4", 235). They indicated good recruiting skills for Kuharich, but Snowden and Costa would both play their NFL careers as offensive tackles, so perhaps there was a problem knowing where such talent should line up.

The Fighting Irish opened with Oklahoma. The Sooners moved well, but when they tried a field goal, Buoniconti blocked it so hard at the 22 that Dabiero recovered on the 41. Sefcik carried for 8; Dabiero broke loose for a 51-yard touchdown run—a 9-point swing in three plays. Oklahoma drove 72 yards for a 4-yard touchdown. Notre Dame's answering drive ended with a 23-yard touchdown for Mike Lind. The game was a 13-6 standoff until halfway into the fourth

Nick Buoniconti was an All-American in 1961.

quarter when Dabiero ran for 23 yards to the 2, and Lind punched in for the 19-6 final score. The Fighting Irish rushed for 367 yards, 176 of it from Dabiero.

The Fighting Irish avenged the previous year's blowout by Purdue with a 22-20 victory over the Boilermakers. Purdue scored first, using nine plays for 74 yards, ending with a quarterback sneak from the 1. The Irish fired back with a 73-yard drive; Dabiero gained 32 yards, and Lind scored from the 27. Purdue scored from the Notre Dame 4. A bad punt snap led to a Purdue field goal from the 26. An Irish field goal failed, but Lamonica soon had them back at the 2, where a Purdue linebacker tried to stop the 235-pound Snowden and didn't. Purdue led at the half, 20-13. A failed onside kick led to a Purdue field goal. Near the end of the third quarter, Snowden ran for 11 and 16 yards; a few plays later, Jim Kelly caught a Lamonica pass for a touchdown. A 2-point conversion failed. Kuharich sent in an all-sophomore backfield to pummel a tiring Purdue team. Costa ran 29 yards. Perkowski won the game with a 29-yard field goal. Two later Purdue drives failed.

USC was next; the weather was frigid, and the Trojans skated to a 30-0 loss. Fighting Irish backs ran for 322 yards to USC's minus 4, the first time such an indignity had happened to USC in 69 seasons. The Irish defense sacked quarterback Bill Nelson for minus 128 yards. The Irish scoring was: Lamonica

QB Lamonica handing off to FB Mike Lind on 1961 photo day.

around right end for a 12-yard touchdown; Lamonica to Kelly for a 17-yard touchdown; quarterback Ed Rutkowski around left end for a 6-yard touchdown; Lamonica on a 1-yard sneak; and Perkowski with a 49-yard field goal. Dabiero ran 43 yards to set up Rutkowski's touchdown, and Carollo recovered a fumble before Lamonica's sneak. It was the fifth straight win over USC and the second consecutive shutout. It was probably the high-water mark of the Kuharich years.

Another big rival was next, Michigan State. The Fighting Irish scored on a 68-yard drive, with Lamonica going 22 yards on a fourth-down play and then 2 yards for the touchdown, giving Notre Dame a 7-0 halftime lead. After being held scoreless until late into the third quarter, MSU exploded for 17 points in the final 18 minutes of the game. The scoring began when a Budka pass was intercepted at the MSU 8. Another interception followed. George Saimes scored from the 24 on a pitchout. The tide had turned. Another interception, and Saimes scored a 25-yard touchdown behind great blocking. A failed Irish drive led to an MSU field goal for the 17-7 victory. The Spartans became the only team to beat Notre Dame six straight times, but they had been held scoreless for 42 minutes.

Parseghian always had Northwestern ready for Notre Dame—he never lost to the Irish in four tries. The Fighting Irish stopped Northwestern, and then Lind scored from the 14. The 7-0 lead held into the second half, although three injured Irish starters were out (Hecomovich, Lind, and Kelly). Northwestern started getting some breaks—a whistle stopped a Notre Dame fumble recovery, a punt touched an Irish lineman, and the Wildcats recovered. They scored on a broken screen pass; the receiver darted around long enough for blocking to form and then ran 50 yards for the touchdown. Perkowski kicked a 36-yard field goal for a 10-6 Irish lead. Northwestern scored the go-ahead touchdown on a short pass play and then tried to stop the Irish with 8 minutes to go. Behind 12-10, Budka moved Notre Dame to the Northwestern 28, passed to Traver for a short gain, and handed off to Snowden to set up a good field goal angle to try to win the game. But Snowden lost the ball and the ball game with a fumble.

Navy added another loss, 13-10, even though the Fighting Irish seemed to have the better team. Perkowski scored first with a 45-yard field goal, then Navy came back with a 72-yard drive that scored on a 1-yard run and a later field goal. Dick Naab, another Kuharich fullback, tied the game at 10-10 from the 1 in the third quarter. In the fourth quarter, Lamonica tried to throw a long pass, but the ball slipped out of his hands, and Navy recovered at the Irish 10. They settled for a 22-yard field goal and the 13-10 lead. Two late Irish drives ended on downs and a fumble.

Kuharich went with Budka for the Pitt game, and Notre Dame won 26-20. The first touchdown came on a 59-yard touchdown pass from Budka to Traver. Fred Cox hit a field goal in the second quarter, giving Notre Dame a 7-3 halftime lead. Then Cox scored in the third quarter after a Naab fumble for a 10-7 lead. Budka intercepted a Panther pass and geared up a 72-yard march, keyed by his 40-yard pass to Traver to the 2. Naab scored. Marty Olosky fell on the Pitt fumble of the kickoff at their 12, and Sefcik scored around right end from the 8. Cox hit a 52-yard field goal. Reserve halfback Charlie O'Hara got the winning touchdown on a 53-yard run over tackle before Pitt made the last score of the game on a pass.

Sometimes, timeless games and incidents come out of nowhere, and that's what happened in this game with Syracuse, won by *the kick*. Everybody eventually was involved—the school's administration, the NCAA, and the media. But it started out like any other

Joe Perkowski, famous for his "overtime" kick that beat Syracuse in 1961.

game; it was a tight defensive match, until Budka sent out Dabiero into territory defended by Ernie Davis, soon to be the Heisman winner. Angelo put some moves on Davis that left him open; Budka threw to him for a 41-yard touchdown for a 7-0 Irish halftime

Tom McDonald, excellent defensive back for the Irish in the early 1960s.

lead. In the third quarter, a punt hit a Syracuse lineman, and Gene Viola recovered. Les Traver tallied a 25-yard touchdown on a Budka pass against Davis, pushing Notre Dame's lead to 14-0. Syracuse's John Mackey scored on a 57-yard pass, they got 2 points, and drove 53 yards, scoring on a pass from the 3, taking the lead, 15-14. Interceptions killed drives by both teams, until Notre Dame took over on downs at their 30, with 17 seconds left. Budka tried to pass, saw nothing, and ran 21 yards before going out of bounds. With 8 seconds left, Sefcik caught a pass for 10 yards and went out of bounds. Three seconds. Perkowski would have to try a 56-yard field goal, Sefcik held. Walt Sweeney rushed the play from his end position, crashed through his blocker and into Sefcik, annihilating the kick. Head linesman F.G. Skibble called a roughing the kicker penalty. They moved the ball 15 yards and Perkowski made a 41-yard field goal for an Irish win, 17-15.

Syracuse pointed to Rule 3, Section of the NCAA Football Rules Interpretations, which stated that a foul during the act of kicking does not call for another down or extension of time that may have expired. Notre Dame asserted that the infraction happened before time ran out and before the ball was dead. A strict construction of the rules would have allowed total mayhem on similar plays since no penalties could have been called or enforced. Some called for Notre Dame to forfeit. The Irish never did, and rightly so.

Continued fumbling doomed the Irish in a 42-21 loss to Iowa. Iowa got five scores in the first half as the partial results of three Irish fumbles and three interceptions: a 43-yard touchdown pass after an interception, a quarterback sneak for a touchdown after a penalty, a 1-yard touchdown sneak after a fumble, a 45-yard touchdown pass after Notre Dame's only drive failed, and a 104-yard touchdown runback of a kickoff. In the third quarter, Notre Dame drove deep, but Lind fumbled on the Iowa 1; the Fighting Irish came back to score on a drive, started with a 37-yard pass. Two Fighting Irish scores came on a 16-yard run by Sefcik and Dabiero's 42-yard interception return within the game's last minute. Notre Dame outgained Iowa 365 yards to 337.

Against Duke, Dabiero ran 54 yards down the sidelines for a touchdown on the first series. Duke came back with a quarterback sneak for a touchdown. In the second quarter, Duke intercepted a Budka pass on their 30 and scored on a 21-yard pass. The Fighting Irish came back: Costa to the 38, Lind for 15, Budka to Tom Goberville for 19, Budka to Sefcik for 20, and

Lind on a 1-yard touchdown plunge. Duke drove on a 43-yard pass and a 16-yard touchdown pass for a 20-13 halftime lead. In the second half, Duke added a field goal and two touchdowns. The Irish collapsed, and Duke won 37-13.

Turnovers and terrible pass defense ruined chances for a winning season. And the offense had its own miscues. This was not a season in which a few close calls would have changed much. There were growing doubts about the quality of the coaching. Buoniconti was the lone player who made All-American.

1961 record: 5-5-0 (.500)
Record to date: 461-121-34 (.775)

1962

This was Kuharich's last season. He left as the only Fighting Irish coach with a losing career record. The pro-style passing offense never fully materialized. He did not win the hearts of his players; there was too much shuffling of personnel at key positions. Two things stood out: an inordinate number of injuries, cause undetermined—bad luck or bad conditioning— and excellent recruiting. But with all this talent, why not win more? Could he have turned it around with the maturing of an excellent sophomore group? It's doubtful. The 1962 record of 5-5 would be the end of the Kuharich years.

Ron Bliey, starting LH in 1962.

There were holes to fill in the line, but good players moved up, especially Jim Carroll and Bob Lehmann. Lamonica would start most of the time. His halfbacks were Ron Bliey, one of the fastest men to play for Notre Dame, and Don Hogan, a runner with much promise. Lind never recovered from surgery, and Gray was not completely healthy. It was a big team and promised much in its offense.

The Fighting Irish opened the season in Oklahoma and they muscled two touchdowns over the smaller Sooners for a 13-7 win. Rutkowski scored on a drive he led with rushing, scoring from the 7 and kicking the point after. Oklahoma's Paul Lea ended a 58-yard drive with a 1-yard touchdown. The Irish wore out the Sooners with an 89-yard drive in the third quarter that took 11:35. After 18 plays, Ahern went in for an 8-yard touchdown. The Irish stopped the Sooners' last drive and were pleased to get out of Norman with a win.

Purdue came to South Bend and beat Notre Dame handily. The Fighting Irish had reverted to their old form—untimely penalties and fumbles. Purdue spent much of the first half in the vicinity of Notre Dame's goal. They finally capitalized with a 17-yard field goal after a short punt and run back. Notre Dame lost the ball on downs, and Purdue marched 63 yards, capped by a 25-yard touchdown pass by Ron DiGravio, with Purdue up at halftime, 10-0. In the third quarter, another Irish possession ended at Purdue's 42; Purdue's DiGravio put together a 58-yard drive, capped by his 1-yard sneak. Denny Murphy lost an interception and a 55-yard touchdown return on a penalty (and the Fighting Irish would lose another touchdown with a penalty). Kuharich put in Denis Szot for Lamonica. Szot fumbled the snap on his 20, and Purdue scored on the next play. Szot fired a 17-yard touchdown pass to Hogan, but it was too late. Purdue won easily 24-6.

At Wisconsin, Notre Dame ran into an emerging media darling, Ron VanderKelen, who would play a magnificent Rose Bowl game against USC. Vandy got the Badgers in range for an opening field goal and a 3-0 lead. Notre Dame could not move, punted, and Vandy threw a 20-yard touchdown pass

Notre Dame first team in 1961.

to Pat Richter. Wisconsin fumbled away its next two drives, but the Fighting Irish did nothing, ending the half at 10-0 in favor of Wisconsin. In the third quarter, the Irish dropped the ball on their 5, and Vandy took

Don Hogan, starting RH on the 1962 squad.

it in three plays later. Szot put together a touchdown drive in a lost cause, 68 yards in eight plays with Hogan scoring the touchdown. Jack Snow caught a 2-point conversion pass. The Badgers won 17-8.

Michigan State won easily 31-7; George Saimes rushed 153 yards for the Spartans, scored three times, and played great defense. Saimes sprinted 54 yards for his first touchdown on MSU's fifth play. Sherm Lewis ran 72 yards for a touchdown on their tenth play. Szot and Joe Farrell led the Fighting Irish back to score, with Farrell going in from the 2. Then Saimes took charge: he intercepted a Lamonica pass at the Notre Dame 22 and scored from the 16; and later he cruised 49 yards for a touchdown. In between, MSU scored on a pass play. It was Daugherty's seventh straight victory (still unequalled) over Notre Dame.

Northwestern's Tommy Myers was the next hero. The Fighting Irish fumbled on the first play. Eight plays later, Northwestern scored. After trading turnovers, Myers found Paul Flatley alone for a 23-yard scoring strike and a 14-0 Wildcat lead. They blocked an Irish punt and scored on the ground for a 21-0 halftime lead. Notre Dame turned the ball over again in the third quarter, and Myers found Flatley for 40 yards and a 7-yard touchdown. Lamonica threw for 39 yards to Sherlock, then to Kelly for 10 to set up Farrell's 3-yard touchdown. The Wildcats closed it out, 35-6, with a score from the 6. Notre Dame was 1-4.

George Bednar, starting RT in 1962.

Next was Navy and their new quarterback, Roger Staubach. Notre Dame won, 20-12. The first Notre Dame drive reached the Navy 13 where an interception killed it. Navy could not move, punted, and Hogan ran 16 yards to the 1; Lamonica scored. The 7-0 lead lasted through the half as Notre Dame stopped Navy's offense, allowing no first downs, no pass completions, and only 3 yards of total offense. The Middies switched to delayed traps and draws to hold off the Fighting Irish rush in the third quarter, and they scored a touchdown but missed a 2-point conversion. Staubach took advantage of a fumble to sneak in from the 1 for a 12-7 lead. The Middies' kicker topped the ball on the kickoff and a reserve Irish tackle ran to the Navy 45. Lamonica threw deep to Denny Phillips; it was tipped, but Phillips hauled it in for a 13-12 lead. On the next drive, Budka appeared at flanker and made a catch at the Navy 2. Lamonica used a jump pass to Kelly for the final score.

The Fighting Irish beat Pitt 43-22 with great performances from Lamonica and Kelly. They clicked on passes of 14 and 11 yards to set up Hogan's 6-yard touchdown for the first score. Pitt punted, and Lamonica used a jump pass to Kelly from the 5 for a touchdown. Pitt fumbled, and Bliey ran in from the 7 on an end sweep. Moments later, Tom Goberville blocked a punt, and Lamonica went to Kelly for another touchdown. Pitt then used a double reverse for a 56-yard touchdown. The halftime score was 21-6. After intermission, Lamonica hit Stephens for a 40-yard touchdown. Kelly caught another touchdown pass, a 13-yarder from Lamonica, before Pitt added a 93-yard kickoff return for a touchdown. Lamonica completed 11 passes to Kelly and tied Bertelli's record of four touchdowns.

The defense played well in the 21-7 win over North Carolina. The Tarheels scored first, helped by

Lamonica, long before he became known as a "bomber," gets set to throw long against Iowa in the 35-12 1962 win.

a tipped pass that Ken Willard caught at the Notre Dame 5. The Carolina defense kept the Fighting Irish bottled up throughout the first half, so good defensive play was needed. Tommy MacDonald helped with three interceptions, tying Bertelli's record of eight for a season. Farrell scored from the 1 after the second interception. Right after that, he grabbed his third and raced to their 8. Farrell went in from the 6 to take the lead. Gray then intercepted a Tarheel pass and returned it to the Notre Dame 28. Hogan capitalized with a 59-yard touchdown run to end the scoring. Notre Dame fought back to .500, 4-4.

Lamonica looked good as he led the Fighting Irish to a 35-12 win over Iowa. Hogan scored first with a 29-yard run. Notre Dame had a 7-0 halftime lead. Iowa scored in the third quarter, but it was all Irish after that: a six-play drive of 71 yards ended with Minik's 19-yard touchdown; a Lamonica touchdown on a fake pass and a 27-yard run; a Minik touchdown set up by a Lamonica run; an Ahern touchdown after a Budka interception. MacDonald also picked up his record-setting ninth interception. The win pushed Notre Dame's record over .500 for the first time since the season opener over Oklahoma.

Any chance for a winning season, however, seemed doomed by the final opponent—USC, who was trying to win a national title for McKay's third season at the school. The Fighting Irish did not play well against USC's backs, Ben Wilson and Willy Brown, and three quarterbacks, Pete Beathard, Bill Nelson, and Craig Fertig. The Trojans shut out Notre Dame 25-0. It was Kuharich's last game as Notre Dame's head coach.

The 1962 Fighting Irish never developed much of a running game; rushing yardage decreased 38 percent from 1961. They did stop the negative turnover ratio of previous seasons. The passing game was marginally better, with the statistics padded in the three games where Lamonica couldn't miss. They simply never put together all the parts of a successful season, which was true for all four years under Kuharich. He had been a superb recruiter and left behind a fine core of talent. Jim Kelly was the sole All-American selection.

1962 record: 5-5-0 (.500)
Record to date: 466-126-34 (.771)

1963

Kuharich left Notre Dame on March 13, 1963, to become the NFL's head of officials. The recruiting season was almost over. The administration felt it had insufficient time to do a proper search and decided to go with an interim coach. Hugh Devore was on hand,

1963 Notre Dame Fighting Irish.

1963 Notre Dame coaching staff: (l to r) kneeling: John Murphy, Dave Hurd, Gus Cifelli, Head Coach Hugh Devore, Lou Stephens, Bill Daddio; standing: Jerry Stoltz, Brad Lynn, and George Sefcik.

having made all the stops after his one interim season for Notre Dame in 1945. Devore recruited one of the best classes of football players ever at Notre Dame, a group that would have seven All-Americans. The team bequeathed to him was loaded with talent—seven more eventual All-Americans. He made several adjustments in the line, switching the positions for about half of the players. Budka was quarterback and Farrell moved to left halfback. Don Hogan was injured in an auto accident and would never play

Captain Bob Lehmann interrupts Badger Hal Brandt's plans for a completion. Tommy McDonald intercepted the throw in the 1963 opening 14-9 Irish loss.

football again. Devore used Jack Snow at right halfback and Joe Kantor at fullback. This was, on paper, a fine group of players.

Budka was still recovering from a leg broken in the 1962 USC game, so Szot started against Wisconsin. Snow scored on a pitchout that he took for a 24-yard touchdown. John Huarte kicked the point after. Goberville blocked a Badger punt for a safety and a 9-0 lead. In the second quarter, Wisconsin's Hal Brandt found Jimmy Jones for a 5-yard touchdown pass. Good defense stopped Badger drives in the third period, but the Fighting Irish were tiring. Wisconsin won 14-9 when Jones intercepted a pass and Ralph Kurek smashed over from the 1. It was only the third Irish loss in an opener in 75 tries.

Purdue was next. In the first quarter, Purdue tried a field goal that missed. Huarte came in and fired to Alan Loboy for 39 yards and to Kelly for a 15-yard touchdown. But Huarte injured an ankle on the play, tried a 2-point conversion pass, and missed. The ankle would be a large factor as the season progressed. Purdue came back for its only touchdown, in the fourth quarter, on a 7-yard pass from DiGravio to Bob Hadrick. Purdue made the point after, giving Purdue a 7-6 lead. Huarte limped out and cajoled the Fighting

Bill Pfeiffer, defensive specialist in 1963.

Irish to the Purdue 10, but a field goal try missed, preserving the Boilermaker's 7-6 victory.

Budka started against USC, the third quarterback in three games. MacDonald intercepted a Beathard pass in the first quarter and sped 62 yards to score. The Trojans immediately advanced 74 yards in nine plays, and Beathard scored from the 3. Sophomore Bill Wolski returned the kickoff to the 37, then ran twice for 39 yards, blocked on a Budka run, and ran 22 yards for the touchdown and a 14-7 lead. The Trojans showed their championship quality: Beathard to Bedsole for 43 yards; ditto for 13 more; and Beathard to Mike Garrett for a 24-yard touchdown. Good defense kept USC scoreless in the third quarter. Ken Ivan kicked a field goal from the 16 for a 17-14 Notre Dame lead with 6:30 left. The defense, led by Bill Pfeiffer, then hogtied the Trojans for the upset win. Pfeiffer made 17 tackles on the day.

Budka and Notre Dame whipped UCLA 27-12. He lofted a screen pass to Kantor from the 11 for the first touchdown to end a 72-yard drive. A shanked UCLA punt led to a 4-yard touchdown run by Wolski. A UCLA drive reached the Irish 2, but Pfeiffer caused a fumble. The Bruins scored using a tackle-eligible play, Larry Zeno to Mitch Johnson for 12 yards. In the third quarter, Notre Dame went 54 yards in six plays, with Kelly blasting through two deep backs for a 17-yard touchdown pass. Budka scored from the 4 after Charlie O'Hara set him up with a 33-yard run. UCLA scored later on a pass.

The Irish went to Stanford. Notre Dame scored first after a fumble, on a 1-yard Budka sneak. An interception set up a Stanford touchdown from the Irish 4; they hit a field goal later for a 10-7 lead. On the return drive, Budka threw a 10-yard touchdown pass to Dave Pivec. But that was it for the Fighting Irish. Stanford scored twice for a 24-14 victory. Notre Dame killed a good drive with penalties and was unable to stop Stanford on a consistent basis.

Roger Staubach was in his Heisman-winning year and led Navy to a 35-14 win that exposed some previously undetected problems. A bad punt snap gave Navy the ball at the Notre Dame 18; Staubach used four runs before using play action on a 3-yard touchdown pass. The Fighting Irish put in a behemoth backfield of Costa at 235 pounds, Pete Duranko at 220, and Kantor to jam the football for a Budka score from the 2. Staubach hit three passes for another touchdown and the lead. Navy scored from the 2 in the third quarter. Middie Gary Kellner intercepted a Notre Dame screen pass and scored, then Staubach outpaced a lunging defense to throw a last touchdown

Jim Kelly, starting RE in 1962 and LE in 1963, All-American in 1963.

pass. A Navy fumble let Kantor rumble in from the 10 to end it. Notre Dame's Bob Lehmann made 20 tackles.

Four Irish quarterbacks were not enough against Pitt, losing 27-7. A Tom Longo interception led to a Budka sneak from the 1, but Pitt ran away with it after that: a 92-yard touchdown kickoff return by Paul Martha; a 1-yard touchdown plunge; a touchdown run of 10 yards after an interception; and a penalty-assisted touchdown.

Michigan State continued its dominance over Notre Dame with a 12-7 win, its eighth victory over Notre Dame. The Fighting Irish got inside the MSU 30 four times, and inside the 15 twice, but failed to score. MSU completed one of eight passes for 0 yards; MacDonald intercepted his 14th career pass, a Notre Dame record at the time. Following a Spartan fumble, Denny Phillips went for a touchdown from the 11. The Fighting Irish could not move in spite of bad MSU punting and an interception. Spartan Sherm Lewis scored from the 3, but a 2-point try failed. In the fourth quarter, a bad punt gave Notre Dame the ball at the MSU 18—no score after three runs and a pass. Longo intercepted an MSU throw on their 11—no score after three runs and a pass. Lewis won the game for MSU with an 85-yard touchdown run.

The assassination of President Kennedy cancelled the Iowa game, and Notre Dame went a week later to Yankee Stadium to play Syracuse. The Irish took an early lead, and then faltered. Syracuse scored first on a 6-yard touchdown pass, but Dick Arrington blocked the kick. Lehmann blocked a field goal try. Sandy Bonvechio pitched out to Budka who then threw to MacDonald for a 20-yard touchdown. In the fourth quarter, MacDonald intercepted his 15th career pass, Pfeiffer got one, as did Lehmann. Notre Dame's Ken Maglicic grabbed a fumble. Finally, Syracuse scored on a 47-yard pass to win it 14-7.

There were not many signs of life in the Fighting Irish offense all season. They gained 1,980 yards of total offense all year (Vagas Ferguson would come within 500 yards of that by himself in 1979). There were only 54 completions all year for a scant 654 yards, the kind of statistics Joe Theismann would generate in two games. The defense played well and gave the offense numerous chances. Kelly and Lehmann made All-American teams.

1963 record: 2-7-0 (.222)
Record to date: 468-133-34 (.763)

1964

On December 3, 1963, Notre Dame officials announced that for the first time in half a century they would turn over the school's football fortunes to an outsider—Ara Parseghian of Northwestern. He immediately made a promise to the students, "Notre

Jack Snow, All-American end in 1964.

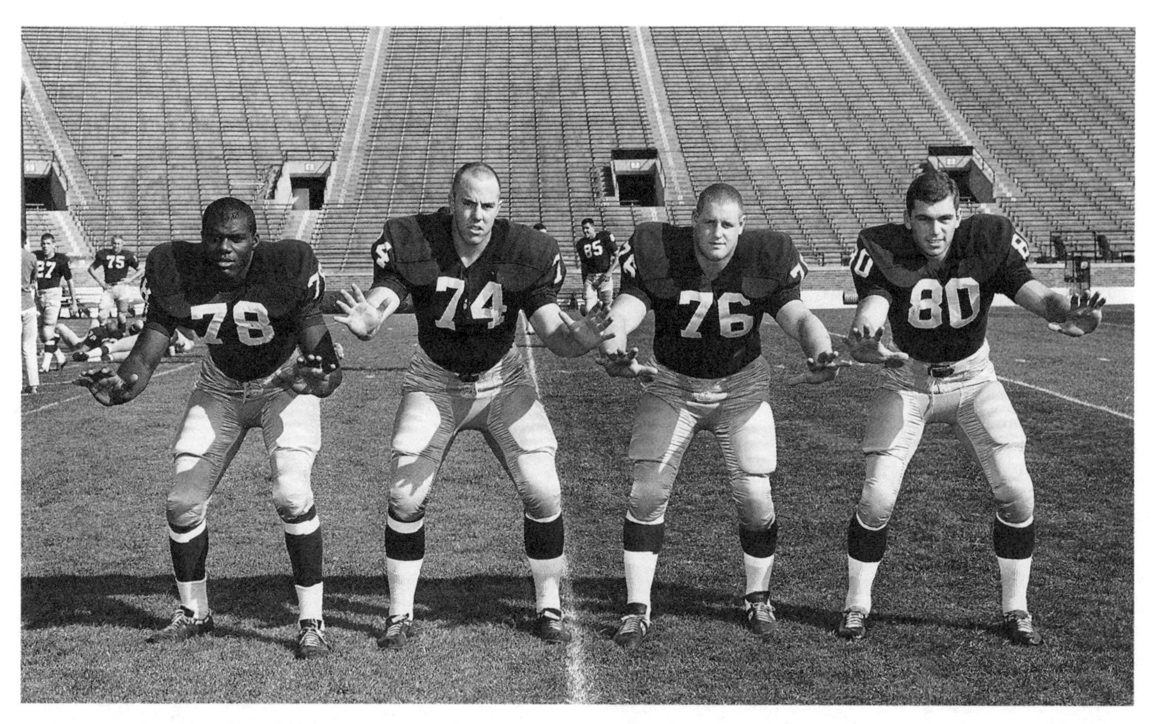

The great 1964 defensive front: Alan Page, Kevin Hardy, Tom Regner, and Don Gmitter—who helped the Irish register four shutouts and give up only 77 points in the season.

Dame's players will be in shape in the fourth quarter of their games." Parseghian had a firm sense of dedication, quiet dignity, and a burning desire for excellence. There were no short cuts. He was a brilliant football tactician who had Northwestern playing over its head for years.

His football mentors were Paul Brown, Sid Gilman, and Woody Hayes. He had been the head coach at Miami of Ohio and Northwestern. There he had beaten Notre Dame four times, using inferior football talent to do it. At Notre Dame he would have talent, but the task would be motivational. He found a marvelous group of players who had lost faith in themselves. It's often easier to take an average player and have him play beyond his capacity than it is to make a psychologically wounded star play to his potential. There are hidden obstacles and resistances; they've heard all the pep talks, but they still break down at crucial moments. Ironically, his 1964 seniors had met as a group earlier in their careers and promised that they would win a national crown. Most observers were hoping for a 6-4 season.

Two-platoon football was back as a result of an NCAA rule change; Ara could make instant use of the large talent pool and hone skills for specific jobs. He insisted on getting the country's best group of sophomores on the defense where they would have an immediate impact. Huarte was quarterback, hoping that complete rest would solve a shoulder problem instead of surgery—it worked. Huarte had an uncanny ability to make fakes, very quick feet, a calm confidence, and a good throwing arm with a peculiar three-quarter sidearm motion. The halfbacks were Bill Wolski and Nick Eddy, who had brilliant speed and fine hands. Joe Farrell won the fullback's job. Jack Snow was a wide receiver. The line was technically solid, with good tacticians, led by Dick Arrington. The defense was led by Jim Carroll at linebacker, Nick Rassas as a deep back, and Kevin Hardy and future NFL Hall of Famer Alan Page on the line. Page would prove to be an all-time player, both in college and as a pro. He had unbelievable quickness. This group was an unknown quantity as a team, with good size, excellent speed in the right places, good leadership, and talent.

Wisconsin was blown out 31-7. Huarte and Snow combined for 217 yards in passing (33 percent of the 1963 season total). Wisconsin's running game was held to minus 51 yards. Tom Carey intercepted a Wisconsin pass and Ken Ivan kicked a 31-yard field goal. The first touchdown came on a 61-yard bomb from Huarte to Snow. Another field goal stretched the lead to 13-0 at the half. Wisconsin scored on a 45-yard pass. Kantor went in from short yardage for a touchdown, Wolski banged in from the 2, and Snow ended the scoring with a 42-yard catch and run on a Huarte pass.

Jim Carroll, Parseghian's first captain, two-year starter at LG and RG in 1962 and 1963, then starting MLB in 1964, and an All-American for Ara's wonder team.

Bob Griese led Purdue to a score in 75 yards on 12 plays, capped by his sneak from the 1. A Fighting Irish drive misfired with a failed field goal, but Huarte charged back, throwing to Snow to set up Wolski's 3-yard touchdown burst. In the second quarter, Longo intercepted a Griese pass, and Notre Dame went 47 yards in seven plays, Snow scoring on a 2-yard touchdown reception. In the third quarter, Hardy blocked a Purdue punt to Page, who sprinted 57 yards for a touchdown, losing a Boilermaker running back in the foot race. Purdue could not drive, punted, and Notre Dame marched 76 yards; Pete Andreotti scored from the 23 with a pitchout. Snow later rocketed a 70-yard quick kick; it hit a Purdue player, and Phil Sheridan recovered at their 3. Huarte threw to Rassas for the touchdown. Purdue scored against the reserves to end it 34-15. Jim Carroll led the Irish with 21 tackles.

The Irish flew to Colorado to play Air Force; the Falcons scored when a Huarte pass was intercepted and returned for a 25-yard touchdown. Huarte led Notre Dame back with a ground game, and Eddy zipped outside for a 7-yard touchdown. The next score also came from a battering ground game; Huarte faked to Farrell; while the Falcons tackled him, Huarte went in for the touchdown. The Fighting Irish had to overcome penalties before Wolski caught a 19-yard pass for another score. A Carey interception led to Huarte's touchdown sneak in the third quarter; Rassas intercepted a Falcon aerial and returned it to the Air Force 7. Huarte faked to Wolski up the middle, then lobbed a pass to Snow for the touchdown. The Fighting Irish defense mangled the Falcon running game, holding them to 38 yards as they soared to a 34-7 win.

The Fighting Irish defense under coach John Ray was allowing less than one yard per carry and

Three All-Americans: Bob Lehmann, Roger Staubach, and Jim Kelly, before a 1964 basketball game.

Ara congratulating John Huarte after the Heisman Trophy award in 1964.

now faced the country's offense leader, UCLA's Larry Zeno and sophomore star Mel Farr. The result was Ara's first Notre Dame shutout win, 24-0. Wolski blasted in from the 1-foot line for the first touchdown. After a missed Notre Dame field goal, Zeno marched UCLA to the Irish 37 where Carey intercepted the ball. Huarte threw a 37-yard touchdown pass to Sheridan for a 12-0 halftime lead. In the second half, Zeno lost the football on his 16 after a crushing hit. Huarte threw a touchdown pass to Snow. Alan Page tackled Zeno, and Costa recovered another fumble. Farrell scored the final touchdown.

Stanford played good football for nearly two quarters before Ivan drilled a 28-yard field goal for the Irish. Stanford punted, and the onslaught began with a 54-yard touchdown strike from Huarte to Wolski. The Fighting Irish scored again in 53 seconds and seven plays after a Carey interception; Eddy went in from the 1 on a pitchout. In the first half, Stanford had 31 yards of total offense, failed to move the sticks, and failed to complete a pass. Wolski pounded in a touchdown from the 1-foot line in the second half. The Indians made a first down midway into the third quarter, but linebacker Ken Maglicic intercepted their next pass. Wolski scored on a 6-yard run, and Stanford scored against the subs for Notre Dame's 28-6 win. Huarte completed 21 of 37 passes, eight of them to Snow, who already had the season record for receiving yards in five games. Wolski tripled Stanford's total offense with 102 yards rushing and 60 yards receiving.

The 1963 Heisman winner, Staubach, met the 1964 winner to be in Huarte. The Fighting Irish demolished Navy 40-0. Notre Dame had 504 yards of total offense and scored in inventive ways: Eddy on a 74-yard touchdown screen pass; Snow with a 55-yard touchdown pass; 68 yards on three passes, and Wolski from the 1; Farrell on a 20-yard touchdown run; a 1-yard Huarte touchdown pass to Snow; and Denny Conway from the 2. Huarte had thrown 12 touchdown passes for the year; Snow had equalled Kelly's total catches, 41, in the 1962 season.

Pittsburgh lost 17-15 in the first real test for the Fighting Irish. Notre Dame scored on an 80-yard march with Farrell slashing in from the 2. On their next series, Huarte and Eddy hooked up for a 91-yard touchdown. But an Andreotti fumble led to a Pitt score and a 14-8 scoreboard. Joe Azzaro kicked a 30-yard field goal to make it 17-8 at the half. Pitt used up much of the third quarter on a series that scored in the fourth quarter, 17-15. The Panthers made their move late in the game, but Carroll and Tom Regner stopped a fourth-down run at the Notre Dame 16; some strategic punting by Snow and a fumble recovery by Tom Kostelnick wrapped it up.

Notre Dame had not beaten Michigan State since 1954; this year they came away with a 34-7 win. Ara had the offense line up in a double wingback set

Tom Regner prepares to tackle a Spartan back in the 34 - 7 1964 win.

and Eddy dashed 61 yards with the first play for a touchdown. Farrell scrapped for the next score: three runs for 15 yards, a 22-yard reception, and a 13-yard touchdown reception. MSU backed the Irish up to the 14, but Huarte calmly brought them out: a 20-yard pass to Snow, a 26-yard pass to Bob Merkle, some Eddy runs for 33 yards, and Eddy in a 5-yard touchdown burst for the 20-0 halftime lead. In the third quarter, Eddy lost a 78-yard touchdown run on a penalty; the Spartans scored on a 51-yard touchdown pass play by Gene Washington. Carey intercepted a Spartan pass; Huarte fired a 16-yard scoring pass to Snow, and Eddy caught a 2-point conversion pass. Carroll grabbed a fumble on their 15; Andreotti scored from the 2 to wrap it up. When it was over, Duffy said he wouldn't want to play a better team than Notre Dame.

Norm Nicola, starting center for the 1963 and 1964 teams.

A bitterly cold day slowed down the passing game against Iowa, but the ground game led to a 28-0 win. Wolski jammed it in from the 3 for the first score after Arunas Vasys recovered a fumble. Huarte found Snow open for a 66-yard touchdown. Iowa stayed cold in the third quarter, but Eddy scored on a sweep from the 7. Notre Dame scored in the game's final minute for their 9-0 record.

With the national championship within their grasp, the Fighting Irish headed to Los Angeles for the Thanksgiving day matchup with USC. Unfortunately, USC spoiled the Irish championship dreams with a 20-17 victory. Ken Ivan kicked a field goal from the 15 after Maglicic caused a Rod Sherman fumble. From the Notre Dame 26, Huarte passed to Snow for 23 yards, then to Sheridan for 13, and Snow ran 10 yards on a draw play to the USC 35. Huarte froze USC's defense with two fakes, followed by a 22-yard touchdown pass to Snow. Wolski scored from the 5 to end a 72-yard drive. In the second half,

Mike Garrett scored from the 1. Notre Dame's Joe Kantor scored from the half-foot line, but a holding penalty took the score away. Notre Dame was unable to score after that. This was a crucial turn of events; USC scored on a 23-yard pass from Fertig to Fred Hill. USC's defense held the Irish; the Trojans drove for the winning touchdown, a 15-yard pass to Sherman, with 1:34 left. The Fighting Irish managed two drives but couldn't score.

Ara had taken a doormat team to a possible national title. In 1963, total offense was 1,980 yards, but in 1964 it increased to 4,014—from 654 yards passing to 2,105, from 15 touchdowns to 41, from 159 opposition points to 77. Snow almost doubled the 1963 passing total with his 1,114 yards. Huarte won the Heisman. Ara was Coach of the Year. Huarte, Snow, Carroll, Hardy, and Carey were All-Americans.

1964 record: 9-1-0 (.900)
Record to date: 477-134-34 (.765)

Bill Zloch, starting QB for the 1965 Irish.

1965

Huarte's graduation stripped the Irish of their devastating passing game. They'd sink or swim with the run in 1965. Parseghian adjusted with a much larger offensive line, from the 1964 average of 217 pounds to 226, end to end, actually 233 from tackle to tackle. Regner switched from defense to left guard and Sheridan and Tom Talaga were essentially a

1965 Notre Dame Fighting Irish.

The 1965 starting offense and defense.

double tight end set. Bill Zloch, a dependable runner but not a great passer, was quarterback. Behind him were Wolski and Eddy, who had teamed for 1,629 yards of offense in 1964. Larry Conjar was fullback with fine blocking and excellent speed. The defensive line was solid with Harry Long, Duranko (whose fullback's quickness was an asset as a lineman), Arrington, and Page. Kevin Hardy's season was curtailed by an injury in the Purdue game. Jim Lynch led the linebackers and all three deep backs returned. This was a fair team, not outstanding at the skill positions, and thus without the quick-strike capability of the 1964 team.

The strengths and weaknesses were evident immediately in the 48-6 trampling of the University of California. Fighting Irish running gained 381 yards, but the passing game only gained 68. Notre Dame had control of the game from the outset: an 80-yard march

Parseghian and staff for 1965: kneeling—George Sefcik, Joe Yonto, Tom Pagna, Paul Shoults; standing—Brian Boulac, Doc Urich, Ara Parseghian, John Ray, and Dave Hurd.

The great defensive backfield of 1964 and 1965: Tony Carey, Nick Rassas, and Tom Longo.

for Ivan's 28-yard field goal; a Rassas interception followed by Zloch's 3-yard touchdown sneak; a Page fumble recovery to set up a Conjar touchdown; Rassas for a 65-yard touchdown punt return; a Cal score offset by Zloch's 11-yard keeper for a tally; a third quarter drive of 74 yards in six plays, Eddy scoring with a 24-yard pass; a Wolski touchdown run from the 6 after a Cal fumble; and a Dan Harshman touchdown scored with the reserves. Parseghian showed concern over linebacking errors and pass completions in the secondary.

Bob Griese and Purdue awaited the number-one ranked Irish. Griese completed 19 of 22 passes for 283 yards and three touchdowns in a 25-21 Purdue win. He also punted to keep the Fighting Irish penned deep. Notre Dame led 21-18 with only moments to go after Wolski ran 54 yards for a score and Ivan hit a field goal. Griese hit three passes on the game's concluding 70-yard march, and then used a fullback plunge for the winning tally. He did this in the face of a tremendous pass rush, throwing completions a half dozen times as Irish defenders clutched at his jersey. Many completions went into a vulnerable area just behind the linebackers. The defense lost a star when Hardy went down with a bad back.

Notre Dame recovered to beat Northwestern 38-7, although Northwestern had the halftime lead at 7-6. Wolski scored the first touchdown, then an interception of a Zloch pass went back for a 50-yard touchdown return. Eddy went out with an apparent concussion, and Wolski was bruised badly, so the defense would have to stop Northwestern. They created five turnovers in the second half. Rassas atoned for a fumbled punt when he took a pass away from Woody Campbell and ran 92 yards for the go-ahead score. He broke it open with a 72-yard punt return for another tally 7 minutes later. Two more fumbles and another interception let sophomores Paul May and Rocky Bleier score the final touchdowns.

Sophomore Tom Schoen started against Paul Dietzel's Army team in a night game at Shea Stadium. He threw a touchdown pass to Don Gmitter for starters. That score held into the third quarter when Tom Rhoads deflected a pass and recovered it to set up Eddy's end sweep for a tally. Larry Conjar, on a 12-play drive, ran 10 times, eight in a row, to get Ivan in field goal range for the 17-0 win.

It had been building since spring practices. The ruined Thanksgiving dinner, the lost perfect season, the game won until the last 94 seconds—each Notre Dame student and player knew to *remember*. That word was repeated at Notre Dame thousands of times in the weeks and days leading to the USC rematch. The student body had to wait two weeks after the win over Army; 3,000 students jammed the practice field two days before the game and chanted "*Remember!*" The avenging Fighting Irish held USC's Garrett to 7 yards in the first half on their way to a 28-7 win. Wolski and Conjar led a 45-yard scoring drive, with Conjar scoring the first of four touchdowns for the greatest day of his career. The Trojans were penalized on a roughing call and Conjar scored his second

The halfbacks for 1964 and 1965—Nick Eddy and Bill Wolski.

touchdown. He kept up the pace in the second quarter gaining most of the 67 yards on a drive for a 21-0 lead. When USC went back on the field after halftime, they were met by the Notre Dame student body who had made a tunnel for the Irish players. Conjar led a carbon copy 67-yard drive for the four-touchdown lead. USC scored, but spent the rest of the day in reverse. Conjar gained 116 yards for the day, 42 more than the USC team. Each starting Irish back had more yardage than Garrett.

Navy jammed the scrimmage line with nine defenders and kept two deep. They nursed a 3-0 lead into the last 14 seconds of the half, when Zloch lofted a swing pass to Eddy, who ran for a 55-yard touchdown. In the third quarter, Zloch and Conjar tallied to finish long drives. Rassas returned another punt, this one for 66 yards and a score for the 29-3 win.

Against Pittsburgh, Wolski scored five touchdowns to lead Notre Dame in a 69-13 rout. Eddy scored first on a 26-yard touchdown run. Other scores were: Conjar for 43 yards up the middle after a fumble; Eddy for 56 yards with a pass; Gmitter for 30 yards with a pass; and singles by reserves May, Bleier, and Conway. Wolski's five touchdowns came on only 54 yards rushing. Zloch completed six of seven passes for 184 yards.

North Carolina held Notre Dame scoreless until the fourth quarter. Ivan kicked a 38-yard field goal. Eddy sped 34 yards on a sweep past right end for a touchdown halfway into the quarter. Mike McGill intercepted a Tarheel pass, and Eddy capitalized with a 3-yard touchdown. It was a 17-0 win, but the Fighting Irish were not operating smoothly on offense.

Dick Arrington, starting LT in 1963, starting RG in 1964, starting RG in 1965 and consensus All-American in 1965.

The number-one Spartans boasted a tremendous defense with Bubba Smith, George Webster, and 320-pound nose guard Harold Lucas. Ivan hit a field goal early after a Michigan State fumble. Two other turnovers, however, were wasted by the Irish.

MSU's Dwight Lee and Clinton Jones scored touchdowns; MSU harassed Zloch with its defense to win 12-3.

The Fighting Irish played Miami to a 0-0 standoff. Miami used the Navy ploy of a stacked defense with nine men near the line of scrimmage. They pressured Zloch into six of 20 for 60 yards. Ivan missed two field goals. The Irish defense, however, stopped Miami's offense. Notre Dame finished its season 7-2-1.

There was a 59 percent drop in passing yardage in 1965 compared with 1964. Overall, the offensive output fell 25 percent, although scoring was about the same. They failed to capitalize on a couple of crucial turnovers. The big task was to do something about the passing game. Arrington, Regner, Rassas, and Lynch made All-American teams.

1965 record: 7-2-1 (.750)
Record to date: 484-136-35 (.765)

1966

At the end of the 1965 season, Parseghian had been watching film of the Pennsylvania Big 33 game, that state's annual high school all-star game, when a player caught his eye as a deep back. Ara told the assistant coaches to "Get him." Eventually, he showed up and blended in with hundreds of other aspirants.

Ara coached from a tower above the practice fields. Word filtered up to him during the 1965 season that he had a couple of fine prospects as freshman quarterbacks. One was a Coley O'Brien, and the other was the kid he'd seen on the film, Terry Hanratty. Every now and then Ara would catch a glimpse of hard-thrown, flat passes zinging out of the backfield—some by Hanratty, some by O'Brien. Then he'd see this tall, rangy kid with a middle distance runner's stride and Paul Warfield's hands—Jim Seymour.

He could turn them loose in 1966. There were other sophomores who could help, especially George Kunz, the most dominating tackle ever seen by Assistant Athletic Director Brian Boulac, and Bob Kuechenberg at the other tackle. Hanratty edged out

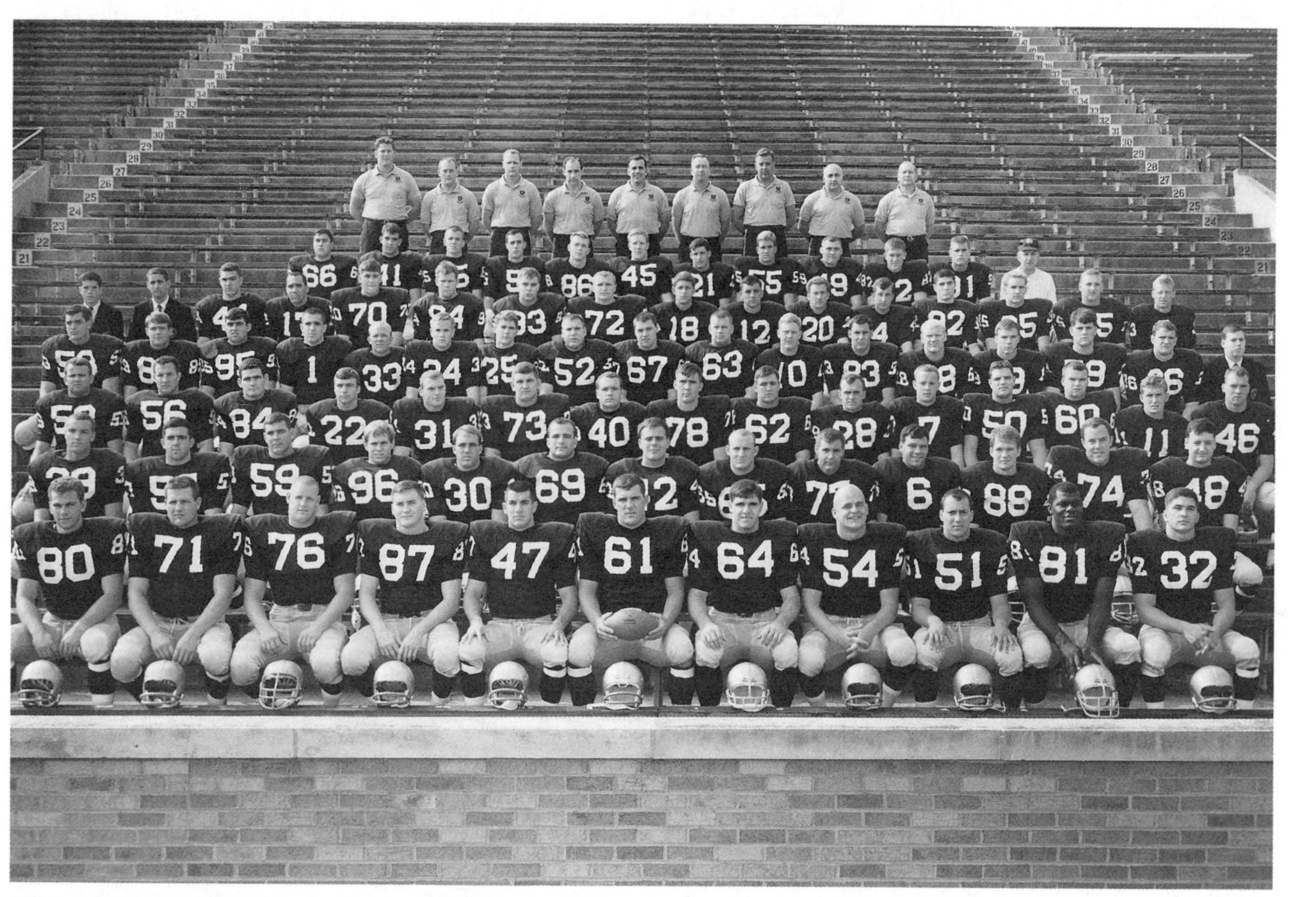

The great 1966 championship team.

The 1966 defensive front and linebackers. They helped the Irish record six shutouts in 1966, giving up a mere 38 points in the undefeated season.

O'Brien for the starting quarterback job. Eddy moved to left halfback and Bleier moved up. Conjar stayed at fullback. On defense, Tom Rhoads moved up to start with Duranko, Hardy, and Page. Lynch led a good group of young linebackers. Ara had to replace the entire secondary, so he switched Schoen to safety and made him a two-time All-American. Jim Smithberger and Tom O'Leary worked the corners. Overall, this was a young but talented team, with good depth in most places.

Jim Lynch had studied Purdue's offense until he knew it better than Griese. He kept a binder filled with flip cards of their sets on one side, and the appropriate Fighting Irish defense on the other. He memorized it. Griese set up for Purdue's first play, and Lynch hunched just across from him. The Purdue quarterback looked at the Irish defense, checked off, and called a new play. Lynch checked off; the Irish adjusted. Griese checked to a new play. Lynch checked off; the Irish adjusted. Frustrated, Griese stood up behind center and called time out. Griese knew then it would be a long day. And it was—26-14. Leroy Keyes speared a fumble in mid-air and jetted 95 yards for a Purdue touchdown. They kicked off. Eddy fielded it, hesitated, started to his right, got past the first wave, and cut right again. He was gone—97 yards to the end zone. There had been two plays and two touchdowns. On the next Fighting Irish series, Hanratty threw a 42-yard pass to the loping Seymour. On the next Notre Dame series, with third-and-14 at their own 16, Hanratty threw to Seymour for an 84-yard touchdown. In the second half they connected again for a 39-yard score. Purdue scored, but Notre Dame scored on a 7-yarder for the final score. Although Purdue would go to the Rose Bowl that year, Notre Dame's sophomores made 13 completions, 276 yards, and three scores.

The starting running backs for the 1966 National Champions: Bleier, Conjar, and Eddy.

Pete Duranko, starting LDT in 1965 and 1966, All-American in 1966.

Northwestern came up with the idea of crashing the ends in on Hanratty and double-teaming Seymour. It was marginally successful, but left other spots vulnerable; Notre Dame exploited them and won 35-7. Conjar plunged for the first touchdown. In the second quarter, the Fighting Irish survived a deep thrust, and Eddy shook loose on a long-distance score. Bleier scored, untouched, on a short run. Schoen scored twice, but lost the first to a penalty, and kept the second on an interception. Northwestern's tactics held Seymour to nine catches and 141 yards.

Army was next in a mismatch. Bleier ran from the 2 for the first score, set up by Seymour's 19-yard catch. Duranko fell on a fumble, and Hanratty showcased Seymour for a touchdown. Hanratty scored on a keeper, and Eddy tallied twice for a 35-0 halftime score. The starters gained 323 yards in the half; the subs played the rest. The score did not change.

North Carolina ran into problems when they found themselves using a fullback as quarterback within a span of four plays, because injuries had decimated their quarterback corps. Conjar capped marches of 73 and 55 yards with touchdowns from 1 yard out. Hardy engulfed a fumble; and Hanratty went to Seymour for a 56-yard touchdown play. In the third quarter, Eddy ran 52 yards for a touchdown. Bob Gladieux took an O'Brien pitchout 5 yards for a score to end a 67-yard drive by the reserves. Notre Dame kept its modest shutout string with a 32-0 win.

Undefeated Oklahoma was next; it was a typical Southern team for that era—light, quick, aggressive, and great at "pursuit." They were unprepared to meet men 50-70 pounds heavier who were just as fast. The Fighting Irish shut them out, 38-0. A great linebacker led the Sooners, Granville Liggins, but he was injured. Notre Dame scored 17 points in the second quarter: Eddy and Hanratty both had 2-yard end runs after drives, and a field goal followed an injury to Seymour. There were three more touchdowns in the third quarter: Eddy, Bleier, and O'Brien. When it was over, all of the Fighting Irish wide receivers were hurt.

With a crippled passing game, Notre Dame scuttled Navy 31-7 with a running attack. Linebacker John Pergine intercepted three Navy passes. The Navy defense scored on a blocked punt; their offense was 28 yards passing and 36 yards running. Hanratty scored twice, Conjar and Gladieux once each, and Azzaro kicked a 42-yard field goal. Jim Lynch tipped a pass, which went to Pergine, and then Lynch tackled *him* just to be sure. It was the last tackle of a Notre

Jim Lynch, an all-time great for Notre Dame as a three-year starter at LB. Captain and consensus All-American in 1966.

Conjar catches a "flare" pass against Duke in 1966.

Dame player by a member of the Lynch family (his brother, now the Naval Academy's Superintendent, had played for Navy in 1963).

Pitt folded 40-0, but held Notre Dame scoreless for the first 25 minutes. Hanratty scored from the 3. In the third period, Eddy zoomed 85 yards with the kickoff for a touchdown. Schoen returned a punt 63 yards to score. Eddy hurt a shoulder at the end of a 51-yard trip, so Ara started shuffling in strange combinations for the opposing scouts: Hanratty and O'Brien, or two fullbacks, May and Conjar. Conjar scored one, and May scored two.

Duke, another quick, small team, trailed 43-0 at the half and 64-0 at the end. Eddy on the second play ran for a 77-yard touchdown. John Horney intercepted a pass and tossed a lateral to O'Leary, who scored from the 25. Bleier scored twice, Conjar once, and a healed Seymour followed Hanratty's 50-yard

John Horney, diminutive starting LB in 1965 and 1966.

George Goeddeke, starting center in 1965 and 1966.

Jim Lynch and Kevin Hardy dressing for a 1966 game.

run with a 43-yard touchdown catch. Dave Haley, O'Brien, and Frank Criniti scored for the reserves. The defense had four interceptions, two fumble recoveries, and one touchdown. The defensive line from 1964—Gmitter, Hardy, Regner, and Page—went in for one nostalgic play and stuffed it to a standing ovation. Ara played 64 men, 29 of them seniors.

Michigan State—Number one Notre Dame against the number two Spartans—more marriages were broken by this one game than any other in the century. The networks still show it as they count the anniversaries of this classic contest. The mystique of this matchup began even before the teams took the playing fields, as Eddy reinjured his shoulder getting off the train in frozen East Lansing. The casualties continued: Bubba Smith wiped out Hanratty in the first quarter; center George Goeddeke sprained an ankle two plays later; and O'Brien, who had been recently diagnosed as diabetic was weakened as his insulin intake had not yet been regulated. Ara had a surprise—275-pound Kevin Hardy did the punting, seemingly putting it above the second deck of the stadium. The center-quarterback units stayed the same, O'Brien worked with Tim Monty after Goeddeke's injury. Gladieux had a good day in Eddy's spot. He had the lone Irish touchdown. MSU scored on a plunge by Regis Cavender, and a barefooted Dick Kenney kicked a field goal. O'Brien was chomping on candy bars to keep his blood sugar up. The Fighting Irish scored a touchdown on a 34-yard pass, O'Brien to Gladieux. It was 10-7 at the half. In the third quarter, a long drive got Notre Dame close, and Azzaro tied the game with a 28-yard field goal to begin the fourth period, 10-10. Moments later, Schoen intercepted a Michigan State pass and ran it to their 18. Two runs didn't work; O'Brien tried a pass to Seymour, but it missed. With 4:39 left in the game, Azzaro tried a 42-yard field goal into the frigid wind.

Alan Page, three-year starter as RDE from 1964 to 1966. Consensus All-American in 1966.

Hardy, Duranko, and mates dig in as USC tries to get something going in the 51-0 finale of the 1966 season.

It missed to the right by less than a foot. The Fighting Irish stopped the next MSU possession and got the ball back on their own 30 with less than 3 minutes to go. Ara saw that O'Brien was really tired; Schoen was the only other experienced quarterback, but he wasn't prepped. MSU was in a prevent defense. Notre Dame ran three plays for nine yards. The third was a draw play by Conjar. Now fourth-and-1, O'Brien took the snap and got 2. MSU called a time out, but for the Irish, time was not the issue. Still in their own territory, the Irish were most concerned with moving the ball without any turnovers. Ara tried an option play, but Bubba smeared it. There was time for one more play; but with O'Brien fatigued, and MSU in a prevent defense, Ara decided there was no percentage in trying a deep pass pattern. Instead, O'Brien ran into the line. Tie game. MSU had not crossed Notre Dame's 45 in the second half.

Over the past 25 years, many accounts of this game have reported that the Irish failed to go for the win in the closing moments against MSU. However, the game facts prove otherwise. It was Notre Dame's aggressive defense that created the Schoen interception, setting up Azzaro's missed field goal attempt with less than 5 minutes to play. With less than 2 minutes to play, and the Irish in their own territory, Ara went for it on fourth and 2. And the final decision to run the ball on the last play of the game was dictated by field position, the MSU five-back defense, and a weakened quarterback—not by an unwillingness to go for the win.

Still time to *remember*. This was the poll bowl, USC and Notre Dame. The Trojans were humiliated, 51-0. O'Brien hit 21 of 31 passes for 255 yards. Seymour caught 11 for 150 yards and two touchdowns. Conjar scored after 17 grinding plays. Schoen ran 44 yards with an intercepted Trojan pass for a score. Azzaro kicked a field goal. O'Brien unleashed a 66-yard drive of passes. Seymour scored from 13. And again from the 39. It was 31-0 at the half. USC fumbled on their second play. Danny Harshman, Eddy's replacement, scored a 23-yard touchdown. Eddy slanted in with a 7-yard score. Linebacker Dave Martin intercepted a pass and went in from 33 yards out.

This national championship team has to be considered for all-time status. It had 11 All-Americans (and five others too young in 1966). Ten of the starting offensive 11 played pro ball, as did eight defenders. They trampled the opposition 362 points to 38. They had six shutouts. The All-American list was Eddy, Lynch, Regner, Page, Duranko, Hardy, Seymour, Seiler, Goeddeke, Schoen, and Conjar.

1966 record: 9-0-1 (.950)

Record to date: 493-136-36 (.768)

1967

The 1967 team was stuck at the outset with the number-one rating. The sophomores of 1966 were maturing and were a real threat on offense. Behind Hanratty, there was a decline in the quality of the backs—Bleier and Harshman were dependable, solid players but lacked game-breaking speed. Jeff Zimmerman, at fullback, was not quite a Conjar. Seymour remained as a deep threat. On defense, Page, Duranko, and Lynch had to be replaced. The defensive line had Hardy and Kuechenberg, with Mike McCoy as a good reserve. Most linebackers returned and all of the secondary, who had enough speed to handle all but the fastest deep threats.

Notre Dame, as a 35-point favorite, beat the University of California 41-8. Hanratty went 15 for 30; Seymour caught six, one a 9-yard touchdown. Bleier caught another Hanratty touchdown pass. O'Brien threw a 14-yard touchdown to Gladieux. Harshman and Azzaro accounted for the rest. Cal's passing was inept—two of 20. Linebacker Dave Martin intercepted as many of their passes as Cal caught.

Great three-sport athlete and consensus All-American Kevin Hardy.

Headaches for the 1967 opposition—Coley O'Brien, Terry Hanratty, and Jim Seymour with Ara.

Purdue's Mike Phipps led an inspired team to a 28-21 upset. Hanratty threw 63 passes, completed 29, for 336 yards and one score, but four were intercepted. Purdue scored on the kickoff and intercepted a Hanratty pass on the return drive at their 19. The Fighting Irish scored, Hanratty tallying on a 1-yard plunge. The second quarter was frustrating for Notre Dame as they had 32 snaps but no score. Purdue's Perry Williams scored and they made a 2-point conversion for a 14-7 lead. Bleier tied it in the third quarter with a 1-yard run on a 94-yard march. Leroy Keyes scored from the 5 to answer. Hanratty threw three passes and a touchdown to Paul Snow from the 27. Purdue drove; a face mask penalty led to a touchdown pass by Phipps from the Notre Dame 31. Keyes defensed Seymour in key situations and took him out of the game.

The Irish rebounded against Iowa, 55-6. Hanratty had a 35-0 first half, hitting nine of 10 passes. The scoring was: a Hanratty rollout touchdown from the 2; Zimmerman from the 2; a 22-yard pass to Bleier; a Schoen interception of an Ed Podolak pass returned 34-yards for a touchdown; Zimmerman for a 14-yard touchdown. The reserves tallied three more times.

USC and O.J. Simpson beat the Irish at home, 24-7. It started out well enough as Notre Dame intercepted three USC passes and held O.J. to 41 yards

Terry Hanratty zips through the snow and the Middies in a 43-14 rout in 1967.

in the first half. Hanratty scored from the 3 in the second period for a 7-0 lead. But the Irish fumbled a kickoff on their 18. McKay used O.J. on six of seven plays for the score . A USC interception led to O.J.'s 36-yard touchdown burst, and a poor punt led to a USC field goal. USC had seven interceptions and put Hanratty out with a concussion. Simpson scored again after a Mike Battle interception. Seymour, with

Dick Swatland, starting RG in 1966 and 1967, All-American in 1967.

Mike McGill, tough LB for the Irish from 1965 to 1967, All-American in 1967.

two dislocated fingers, caught passes good for 170 yards.

The Fighting Irish dumped Illinois 47-7, decimating their running game with minus 4 yards on the day. Azzaro hit two field goals; and Notre Dame scored six touchdowns: a punt return by Schoen led to Zimmerman going up the middle for a 7-yard score; an 18-yard Hanratty to Seymour touchdown; Gladieux on an end run; and a Hanratty to Seymour touchdown pass just before the half. In the second half, Tom

Quinn and Bob Gladieux each scored. The Illini used one of their four interceptions to score. Hanratty was now trying to force the ball to Seymour more than he should have, probably because it worked better than the running game.

MSU, a star-depleted team, was also minus six players suspended for curfew violations. The Fighting Irish won 24-12, due to Duffy's defense of Seymour, who was held to one catch. That opened up Zimmerman, who scored all of the Fighting Irish touchdowns on runs of 7 and 47 yards to go with a 30-yard scoring pass from Hanratty. Azzaro kicked a field goal. Dwight Lee managed two late touchdowns. Zimmerman hammered the Spartans for 135 yards; they in turn ran 91 yards all day.

In the next game, a few snowflakes turned into a blizzard, and Navy scored two touchdowns. But by the time they scored, Notre Dame had wrapped up a 43-14 win with five first-half touchdowns shared among Zimmerman, Bleier, and Hanratty. The Irish ran for 313 yards.

The Fighting Irish shut out Pitt, 38-0. Hanratty scored two first-half touchdowns and Zimmerman another, as Notre Dame built a big early lead. O'Brien led a scoring drive in the second half, and Dave Haley went in from the 1-foot line. O'Brien ran for 2 points as Notre Dame tried to impress the polls. This was done without Seymour, who was home with a leg injury. Schoen set a new interception return record with a 40-yard runback.

Georgia Tech, the 500th victim of Notre Dame, had a 3-0 lead and played well for a quarter until Notre Dame's size and talent wore them out. Hanratty led a 77-yard scoring drive, capped by a 38-yard strike to Gladieux. Bleier's Notre Dame career ended a game early with ligament damage, but he scored two touchdowns before he told anyone about it. Zimmerman scored a first-half touchdown and Gladieux chipped in with one in the second half. A field goal made the final score 36-3.

Bleier was out, and Hardy was hobbled when the Fighting Irish visited Miami. They pulled out a tough 24-22 win over a determined Miami team. Azzaro kicked a 22-yard field goal. Hardy's punts were ineffective and Miami had good field position, leading to a 9-yard touchdown on a pass. Harshman fumbled the kickoff, Miami recovered and scored its second touchdown 18 seconds after its first. Those were the only touchdowns against the Irish all season in the second quarters of games. Smithberger intercepted a Miami pass and Hanratty went to work: a 14-yard pass to Seymour, a 39-yard flare pass to Zimmerman, a keeper for 9, and Ed Ziegler ran in from the 1. Azzaro made a field goal, but Miami answered with its own for a 16-10 halftime score. In the third quarter, Notre Dame scored using 11 runs,

George Kunz, an all-time lineman for the Irish, played some TE in 1967, was a consensus All-American in 1968.

Bob Olson, three-year starter at LB from 1967 to 1969, All-American in 1969.

with Zimmerman for five of them in a row for 36 yards. Azzaro's point after put Notre Dame up 17-16. John Pergine deflected a field goal, and later he intercepted a pass; Gladieux ran twice from their 38 for the final Notre Dame score. Miami scored again; linebacker Bob Olson preserved the win when he broke up their 2-point try.

The Irish overcame a .500 start to come in 5th nationally. The running game matured by mid-season to surpass the 1966 total. The defense, however, allowed 17 touchdowns. Three players were repeat All-Americans: Schoen, Seymour, and Hardy. They were joined by McGill, Pergine, Swatland, and Smithberger.

1967 record: 8-2-0 (.800)
Record to date: 501-138-36 (.768)

1968

Hanratty, Seymour, and Kunz were seniors. The offense was in pretty good shape. However, three linebackers and all of the secondary had to be replaced. Ara switched O'Brien to left halfback; his running mate was Gladieux. Hanratty's backup was Joe Theismann. The defense was anchored by Mike McCoy, one of the most impressive physical specimens (6'5", 270, 56" chest) ever to play under the Dome. Bob Olson was the only returning linebacker. Everyone else behind the line would have to learn their assignments quickly. The offense would be a constant scoring threat. The defense would be able to stop the run and hope that the young secondary could handle the passing game.

Oklahoma had not changed much since 1966, they were still small and quick. The Sooners faced an offensive line that averaged 233 pounds and a defensive line that went 246—and all of them were fast. Oklahoma lost 45-21. Gladieux scored on a 1-yard blast; the Sooners hit Eddie Hinton for a 72-yard touchdown, and Steve Zabel for a 16-yard touchdown pass. The second quarter belonged to Hanratty and Seymour for two more scores. In the second half, Gladieux scored twice, and Zimmerman ate up the clock with many of his 17 runs for the day. Chuck

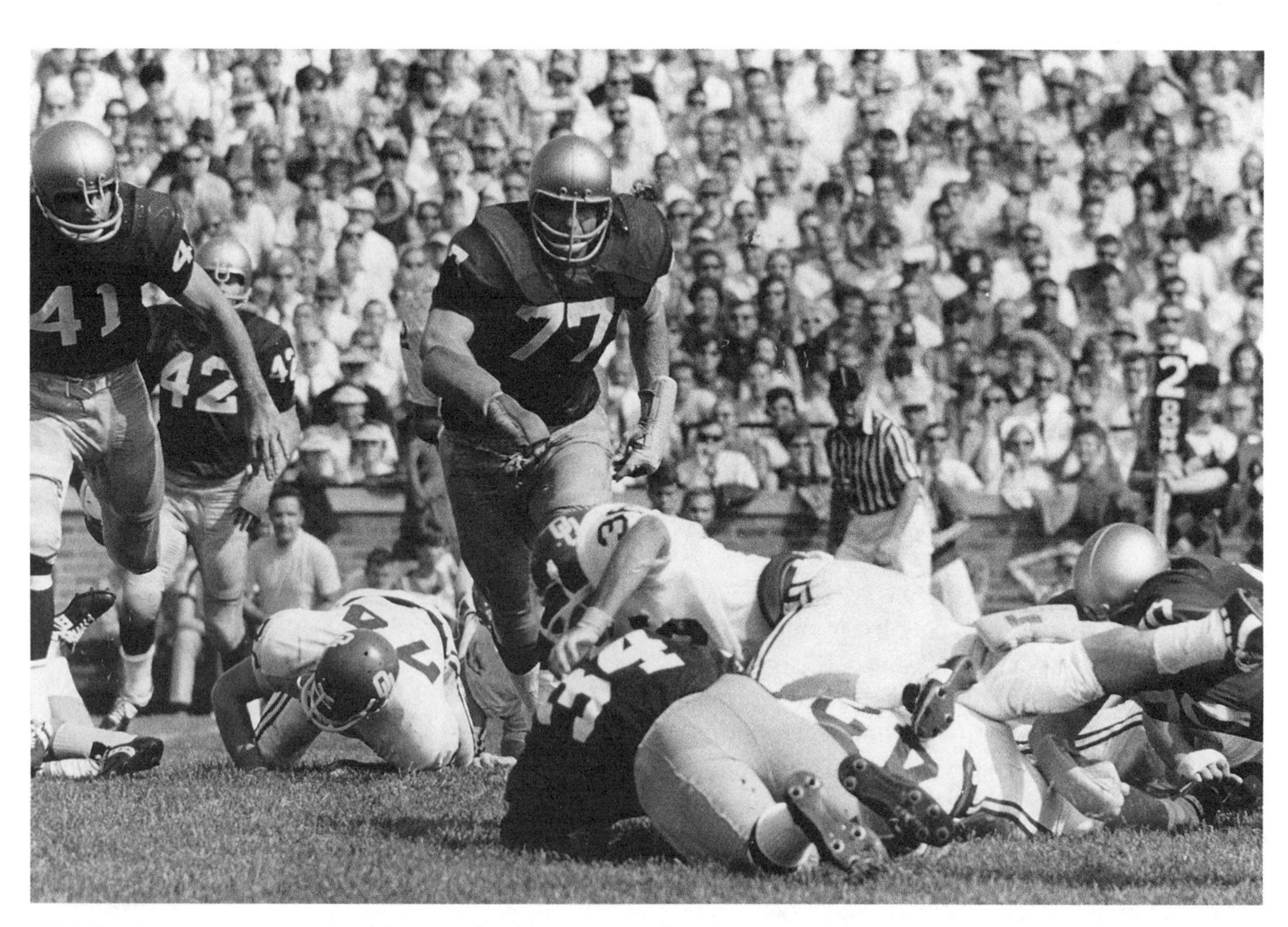

DE Mike Kondrla has just finished off a Sooner runner in the 1968 Irish 45-21 win as McCoy (77), Lavin (41), and Kelly (42) make sure that it's over.

Bob Gladieux, starting RH in 1968, had one of the best seasons on record that year.

Landolfi ran for a 6-yard touchdown. Notre Dame amassed 357 yards in 69 runs.

It was a bad sign that all of Oklahoma's scores came on passes. Phipps knew what to do; Purdue won 37-22. The defenses gave up a combined 55 first downs and 933 yards. Hanratty threw 43 times, completing 23 for 294 yards and two touchdowns, but three were intercepted. Notre Dame started with a patient ground game, scoring on Denny Allan's 5-yard slant outside. Phipps used key passes to move the sticks, and Keyes ran past Irish deep backs for a 16-yard touchdown. The Fighting Irish gave them the game in the next 4 minutes with a Hanratty interception and a Gladieux fumble, both converted to touchdowns. Hanratty threw a 13-yard touchdown to Tom Eaton. Other drives misfired; Gladieux missed a touchdown pass; Notre Dame also missed a field goal. Purdue scored two more touchdowns in the fourth quarter. The Irish kept trying and scored on an 8-yard flip from Hanratty to Denny Allan. Three turnovers turned into Purdue scores; three more killed Irish drives.

Iowa started out with a 38-yard touchdown pass, but Notre Dame answered; Hanratty pushed it over from the 3. After a punt, Gladieux ended a 67-yard march with a touchdown catch. But Iowa tied it with their next possession. Hanratty used the last moments of the first quarter on a 69-yard bomb to Gladieux, and Allan went in over left tackle from the 2. Notre Dame tallied five more touchdowns to Iowa's two for a 51-28 win. Hanratty and O'Brien scored, and subs racked up three more.

Northwestern played tough but submitted 27-7. Hanratty scored on a 7-yard run. In the second half, Gladieux scored twice, and O'Brien caught a touchdown pass. The backs gained 308 yards to the Wildcats' 93.

In a 58-8 win over Illinois, Hanratty surpassed Gipp's career yardage record of 4,110. Notre Dame amassed 673 yards of total offense. Hanratty passed for 212 yards and three touchdowns—to Seymour, Gladieux, and O'Brien. Ron Dushney, O'Brien, and Theismann scored on the ground. The Fighting Irish rushed for 461 yards on 67 plays, 6.8 yards per try.

Duffy Daugherty told reporters he'd open up with an onside kick if he had the chance. He did and Michigan State recovered, winning the game 21-17. They scored on that first drive and it was the difference. Kuechenberg scored on a fumble recovery, Gladieux tallied once, and Hempel kicked a field goal. MSU added two more touchdowns. Hanratty had the team on the MSU 2 with a first-and-goal; three

Terry Hanratty, consensus All-American in 1968.

runs failed; he went to Seymour on fourth down. Seymour was turning to grab the touchdown pass when he was hit by Spartan Al Brenner. No flag—the official who should have called interference had fallen down and missed the play.

The Irish won easily against Navy, 45-14. Hanratty completed 14 of 21 passes for one touchdown, to Seymour, and directed his backs to 337 yards rushing. Gladieux ran 117 yards and scored twice; Hanratty ran for another. Hempel kicked a field goal, and the subs tallied twice. Navy tried running 26 times, gaining only 66 yards.

Hanratty went down for the season with a knee injury in a scrimmage. Theismann, with three days' preparation, led the Fighting Irish against Pitt. Notre Dame obliterated Pitt 56-7. The first drive was 55 yards in four plays, and Gladieux scored. Theismann passed twice to Seymour, for 20 and 29 yards, on the next series before he took it in himself from the 10. The third drive was a clone of the second; Theismann fooled the Panthers with a bootleg play for a tally. Eric Norri scored a safety for 23 points in the first quarter. O'Brien owned the second quarter with two scoring receptions and a touchdown run. The reserves, led by Bob Belden, added the final score when Landolfi scored from the 1. Theismann went seven for 10 for 153 yards and the touchdowns to O'Brien.

Theismann orchestrated a 34-6 Fighting Irish win over Georgia Tech in terrible weather. Gladieux scored two touchdowns, and Ron Dushney ran for 87 yards on 16 carries, while Theismann slithered around in the mud for another 51 yards and a touchdown. Subs scored twice.

USC and O.J. in Los Angeles—the defending national champs and the Heisman winner to be. The Fighting Irish had their great defense and a wounded offense led by a sophomore quarterback. Notre Dame rose to the occasion and held O.J. to 55 yards on 21 carries. Gladieux outpaced the Trojans with 121 yards on 19 runs and one touchdown; Dushney added another while gaining 72 yards. Ara ran a six-man front with two linebackers in tight. USC scored on a pass interception, and Theismann responded with an 86-yard march capped by Dushney's 3-yard touchdown. Gladieux took a pitchout and ran 57 yards for a second touchdown. Theismann scored on a 13-yard pass from O'Brien. USC started passing in the second half and tied it 21-21, the final score. Notre Dame missed two field goals, and USC just missed a touchdown on a dropped ball.

This was the best offensive team Ara had produced—5,044 yards on 3,059 yards running and 1,985 passing. They scored 53 touchdowns and had the fourth-rated rushing defense in the nation, although pass defense was weak all year. Hanratty finished third behind O.J. Simpson in the Heisman race. Kunz, Hanratty, and Seymour, for the third time, were All-Americans.

1968 record: 7-2-1 (.750)
Record to date: 508-140-37 (.768)

1969

Ara had two major concerns for his 1969 team—no returning starters in the backfield (Theismann had been a replacement) and improving the pass defense, which was 81st in the country in 1968. The coaches had confidence in Theismann, but there were no game-breaking backs waiting to move up. The backfield would be rather slow: Ed Ziegler, a two-year sub at fullback, started at left halfback; Denny Allan moved to right halfback. Bill Barz would be the fullback for two seasons. Seymour was gone, but Tom Gatewood was a fine receiver. Two great players toiled in the trenches—tackle Jim Reilly and guard Larry DiNardo. The defensive line featured McCoy and two sophomores, Walt Patulski and Mike Kadish. Three veteran linebackers were on hand, and Clarence

The Northwestern quarterback encounters Mike McCoy in the 1969 game won by ND 35-10.

Larry DiNardo, an all-time player for the Irish, three-year starter at LG, consensus All-American in 1969 and 1970.

Ellis moved into the secondary. For it to work, the backs had to help out Theismann, Gatewood had to mature quickly, and the deep backs had to learn on the job.

For Theismann, the opening moments of the Northwestern game were a nightmare when the Wildcats jumped out to a 10-0 lead on a field goal and an interception. He brought the team back for two first-quarter scores, his own 5-yard run and Ziegler's 18-yard rumble. Northwestern held Notre Dame scoreless for two quarters. Theismann fumbled and had another interception. Irish walk-on Brian Lewallen scored on a 44-yard punt return; Barz broke loose for two touchdowns, of 8 and 2 yards, for the 35-10 Irish win. Theismann's passing was six of 12 for 88 yards, with Gatewood catching only one.

In mid-week, doctors told Zimmerman that he had a kidney ailment that needed treatment. And up next was Mike Phipps and Purdue. Phipps was the first quarterback to go undefeated in three tries against the Fighting Irish; Purdue doubled the Irish score, 28-14. Phipps burned a blitz with a 37-yard touchdown pass in the first quarter, and on a second-quarter drive he made third-down conversions along the way to a 3-yard touchdown by Stan Brown. Theismann led a 79-yard march, ended by a 10-yard pass to Ziegler for Notre Dame's first score. In the third quarter, Notre Dame forced two Purdue punts and then drove to the 26. A bad call, a motion penalty, blunted matters; Theismann was sacked; Phipps scored on a quarterback sneak, and Brown scored a touchdown. Gatewood ended the scoring with a 20-yard touchdown catch. Phipps made 12 of 19 third-down plays; Theismann had an average day, 14 of 26 for 153 yards.

Notre Dame beat a declining Michigan State team, 42-28. Barz bobbled a touchdown catch from their 11. MSU scored after a Fighting Irish quick kick failed to get past a linebacker's chest. Theismann brought the Irish back on an 85-yard drive in 17 plays, with Barz banging in from the 1. MSU's Don Highsmith exploded for a 15-yard touchdown. Theismann directed a go-ahead drive with 2:09 left: from his 29, he went around right end for 13 yards, pitched to Barz for 16, and to Gatewood for 13. From the 29, with MSU in man-to-man formation, he saw Ziegler isolated on a linebacker and Gatewood crossing underneath—he hit Gatewood for the touchdown. Notre Dame controlled the game after that: Theismann on a 7-yard touchdown, a pass to Gatewood for a 23-

Mike McCoy, three-year starter at DT from 1967 to 1969, a consensus All-American in 1969.

yard tally, and Barz for a 1-yard blast. Theismann completed 20 of 33 passes for 294 yards, and the backs rushed for 225 yards.

Army went down 45-0. Hempel started the Notre Dame scoring blitz with a 20-yard field goal. Gatewood ran in a 55-yard touchdown; Theismann scored on a 4-yard run after an interception; and he threw a 7-yard touchdown pass to Gatewood for the 24-0 halftime score. Barz scored from the 1; and then the bench scored—Andy Huff from the 1 and Jim Yoder from the 16. Army's runners gained 47 yards in 29 tries. Notre Dame's backs controlled the game with 365 yards on 80 runs.

The Fighting Irish controlled another great USC runner, Clarence Davis, to earn a 14-14 tie with the number-one Trojans. Davis gained only 75 yards on 30 carries. It was 0-0 at the half; Notre Dame had dodged several scores thanks to Trojan penalties and fumbles. USC had held the Irish offense to 35 yards. In the third quarter, Theismann fired pinpoint passes to move Notre Dame 74 yards in 11 plays; Barz went in from the 1. USC went 75 yards on 10 plays, with a 19-yard touchdown pass; they opened the fourth quarter with an interception, returning the ball to the Notre Dame 15, and scored on pass play. USC punted from their 33. When the ball was snapped, two Trojan linemen were assigned to 274-pound Mike McCoy. Upback Mike Berry was obliterated, and fullback Charlie Evans was removed. The ball was leaving the punter's foot; 9 inches later, McCoy's face mask altered the ball's intended path. Patulski recovered at the 7. A minute later, Denny Allan scored from the 1. On a later drive, Notre Dame got to the 16, but a questionable clipping call moved them back to the 31. Hempel tried a 48-yard field goal. He knew he had hit it dead center, and he had—right into the middle of the crossbar; it bounced back. Ara's decision to move Ellis upfield to CB to cover USC's best receiver may have been the saving decision, allowing tight man-to-man coverage.

Tulane folded 37-0. Ziegler ended a two-drive drought with a touchdown from the 2; then the Irish scored 17 points in the second quarter: a McCoy-caused fumble led to a Huff touchdown from the 4; a 69-yard march and a Huff touchdown from the 1; an Ellis interception set up Hempel's 33-yard field goal. Allan scored from the 1 in the second half to close it

A walk-on who made good—Mike Oriard, starting center for the 1969 squad, an All-American, and a Rhodes scholar nominee.

Jim Reilly, two-year starter at LT, All-American in 1969.

Larry Schumacher, two-year starter at LB in 1968 and 1969.

out. Sub quarterback Bill Etter led all runners with 81 yards on eight carries.

Navy gave up a record 720 yards to the Fighting Irish offense in a 47-0 losing effort; of that 597 yards came on 91 runs. Theismann was held to 123 yards passing on three completions. In the first quarter, Gatewood caught a 35-yard touchdown pass. In the second quarter, Notre Dame scored 26 points: Allan from the 1, Theismann on a rollout for a 46-yard touchdown, Allan recovering a Theismann fumble for a touchdown, and Huff for a 7-yard touchdown. In the second half, Etter made a 79-yard touchdown run and a 15-yarder. He led all runners for the second week in a row with 140 yards on 11 carries.

Notre Dame squashed Pitt 49-7. Theismann completed 9 of 11 passes for 126 yards and three touchdowns to complement 335 yards of rushing. Allan sprinted past left end for a 4-yard touchdown, a 29-yard Theismann touchdown pass to Gatewood concluded a 95-yard march, a 10-yard touchdown pass to Huff, an Allen slant for a 3-yard touchdown, a 3-yard touchdown pass to Gatewood after a botched fake punt by Pitt, an 18-yard touchdown run in the third quarter by Allan, and a 26-yard Etter touchdown dash accounted for the scoring.

Notre Dame pulverized Georgia Tech with 31 opening points. Theismann threw a 16-yard score to Gatewood, and ran 18 yards for another touchdown. Ellis intercepted a Tech pass and charged 70 yards to score. John Gasser did likewise, for a 57-yard runback, resulting in a Hempel field goal of 25 yards. Ralph Stepaniak intercepted a pass and ran it back 51 yards to set the stage for Huff's 1-yard dive. Tech's Bill Ford intercepted a Theismann pass and ran 100 yards for a touchdown. Theismann scored an 8-yarder in the third quarter. Tech kept trying and scored two more touchdowns to make the final score a 38-20 Notre Dame victory.

For the first time in many years, the Irish "had to win" against a service academy opponent—Air Force—when school officials revealed that Notre Dame would go to a bowl *if* they won. Injuries were mounting, and perhaps a little tight over pending prospects, Notre Dame squeaked out a 13-6 win. Allan followed precision blocking for a 39-yard touchdown run. Hempel kicked field goals of 22 and 25 yards. After that, the Fighting Irish held on as Air Force added two field goals in the last quarter. The Falcons only managed 77 yards of total offense.

After a 45-year absence, Notre Dame returned to post-season bowl play—against the number-one Texas Longhorns in the Cotton Bowl. The Fighting Irish opened with an 82-yard drive resulting in Hempel's 26-yard field goal after 6 minutes. Theismann in the second quarter called on Gatewood to delay at the line, then go deep after the secondary had committed themselves—a 54-yard touchdown. The Longhorns' Bertelsen tallied from the 1. The third period was scoreless but the Texas wishbone was working fairly well. In the fourth period, Texas drove again, Worster pounding hard, until Koy scored from the 3. On the return drive, Theismann ran for 14 and 11 yards, threw for 11 yards to Allan, and for a 24-yard touchdown to Jim Yoder. Texas won it on a 75-yard march, making two crucial fourth-down plays, to score from the 1. Their wishbone, good for 331 yards, taught Ara a lesson he would repay in a year. Theismann set a Cotton Bowl record with 279 yards of total offense.

This was a lineman's year for All-American honors: McCoy, Reilly, DiNardo, Olson, and Oriard reaped various awards.

1969 record: 8-2-1 (.772)

Record to date: 516-142-38 (.768)

1970 to 1979

1970

Ara had six starters return to the offense and five starters on defense. There were good replacements at all positions. Theismann would have a season some claim was the best ever by a Notre Dame player. Gatewood's first campaign was almost a carbon copy of Seymour's sophomore year. The offensive line was led by DiNardo, and the defensive line had Patulski and Kadish. Linebackers were solid, and the deep backs were at least adequate. Ellis moved up to the corner from safety. Overall, team speed was better, the defensive line would be a great one, and the offense would be as good as Theismann.

Northwestern lost 35-14. Allan scored from the 6; Gatewood put it there with a 39-yard reception. Theismann ran a bootleg play for a 9-yard touchdown. Fighting Irish errors led to two Northwestern scores—a Barz fumble and a punt runback. Notre Dame struck back—Allan scored from the 3 and Barz with a 17-yard flip from Theismann. In the third quarter, Allan scored his third touchdown on a 1-yard burst.

Notre Dame unloaded on Purdue 48-0, the worst beating in the rivalry to that point. Even though Purdue fielded virtually the same defense as in 1969, Theismann orchestrated 633 total yards to 144 for Purdue. He completed 16 of 24 passes for 276 yards and three Gatewood touchdowns. The Fighting Irish defense grabbed three fumbles and three interceptions. The scores were: a Hempel field goal of 9 yards, Allan on a 4-yard touchdown burst, a screen pass touchdown to Gatewood after a fumble on their 15, a touchdown pass from the 7 to Gatewood, a 20-yard touchdown pass to Gatewood in the third quarter, and a Hempel field goal. Subs Darryll Dewan slammed in from the 4, and Larry Parker sped 63 yards for a touchdown.

No Fighting Irish team had beaten Michigan State at Spartan Stadium since 1949. Theismann's troopers changed that, 29-0, in the 700th football game for Notre Dame. Barz ended a 79-yard drive with a 1-yard touchdown. Theismann ran around for

The 1970 Fighting Irish.

Ara and Joe Theismann ponder a point.

37 yards to set up a Bob Minnix score from the 1. Gatewood caught a Theismann pass for 39 yards, and Gulyas went in from the 2; Theismann made a 2-point conversion. Parker capped it with a 4-yard touchdown sweep with seconds left. Notre Dame's offense netted 513 yards.

Army surrendered 51-10; Notre Dame scored 30 points and gained 345 total yards in the first half. Theismann scored from the 7; he later fired a 40-yard touchdown strike to Minnix; Gulyas scored from the 6 to end the quarter. Patulski got a safety, and Gatewood went in from the 29 with a touchdown pass. In the third quarter, Theismann found tight end Mike Creaney open for a 4-yard touchdown. Subs continued—Dewan cruised for 10, and Pat Steenberge tallied on a 4-yard quarterback keeper. Cadet runners gained 16 yards for the day. DiNardo was injured, and his play was curtailed for the rest of the season.

Missouri fumbled twice and gave away two passes. Hempel put Notre Dame up 3-0, but a bad punt led to a Missouri touchdown by Mel Gray from the 11; the Fighting Irish trailed for the first time all season. Barz caught an 18-yard pass in a third-and-9 situation, and Gatewood regained the lead with a 5-yard touchdown. Missouri attempted an interception; Gulyas caught the pass for a 30-yard touchdown. He also scored on a 1-yard plunge for the 24-7 Irish win.

Navy lost 56-7. Gulyas was hurt; Dewan took his place and ran well on the first drive, carrying six times for 30 yards and a touchdown from the 5. Navy tied it, but Notre Dame's backs scored five more touchdowns with 408 yards of rushing; Gatewood scored twice. Barz scored from the 2 and then the 1, Gatewood tallied on two passes from Theismann,

The 1970 coaching staff.

Allan chipped in with a 3-yard touchdown, and sub John Cieszkowski ran 30 yards for a touchdown and Minnix ran in from the 5.

Pitt played two ball games—one in which they led 14-13, the other in which they disintegrated, losing 46-14. In only the seventh game of the season, Theismann surpassed Hanratty's total yardage mark. Allan scored from the 3, then Barz from the 3 in the second quarter. Pitt used an Irish fumble and an interference call to get its scores on short runs. They tried to intercept a Theismann pass, tipped it twice, but Allan caught it and ran 45 yards for the touchdown. Pitt fumbled two plays after the kickoff and Theismann struck quickly, freezing their safety with a fake before he hit Allan with a 54-yard touchdown pass. He hit Gulyas for a 35-yard touchdown and Mike Creaney for a 78-yard score, one of the longest on record for an Irish tight end. Cieszkowski bulled in twice in the fourth quarter. Notre Dame gained 606 yards on the day.

Perhaps the Irish read too many clippings about their high ratings in the polls, beating Georgia Tech only 10-7. Tech held the Fighting Irish scoreless in the first half. Theismann could not get the team deep into Tech's territory until late in the third quarter, missing 11 third-down conversions. Tech also shut down Gatewood. Tech loaded their linebackers towards the tight end and brought a safety over on Gatewood. Ara countered with the plan of running two tight ends with Gatewood angling across the middle against the flow—*somebody* had to be open. Scott Smith hit a field goal in the third quarter for Notre Dame, then Tech burned Mike Crotty on a 66-yard touchdown pass. Theismann lost a possible touchdown when Tech intercepted at their goal. The Irish held, and Tech was forced into its 11th punt. Starting from the Notre Dame 20, Theismann worked the crossing pattern for a 46-yard pass to Gulyas and Allan ran into the Tech line five times to score the winning touchdown. Ellis stopped their final threat with an interception on his 27. Tech's running game managed only 36 yards all day.

Tom Gatewood,Theismann's favorite target in 1970, All-American in 1970 and 1971.

Clarence Ellis, three-year starter in the defensive backfield, All-American in 1970 and 1971.

The game with LSU was even tighter, with Notre Dame prevailing 3-0. Great defense by both teams was the story of the game. Notre Dame's running was throttled to 78 yards. Only aggressive defense and multiple sacks kept the Fighting Irish in the game. Hempel finally made a 24-yard field goal with 2:54 left in the game for the winning score.

For the second time, USC ruined a perfect season for Ara when it defeated Notre Dame 38-28.

On a sodden field that had suffered many college and pro games in recent weeks, Theismann scored from the 25 in the first quarter. A Hempel field goal missed by inches a bit later. USC scored two quick touchdowns on short spurts by Clarence Davis. The field was now a quagmire. USC's Sam Dickerson scored, literally taking it away from Clarence Ellis. USC hit a field goal, and Cieszkowski intercepted a Theismann pass from the 9 for a touchdown. In the third quarter, Dewan fumbled on his 19. USC scored, but it took one of their tacklers to recover it. Forty-two seconds later, Theismann lost the handle on the wet, slimy ball; USC scored. Theismann fired to Parker, who dashed 46 yards for a touchdown; he then used 17 plays to score again, on a quarterback sneak from the 1. Conditions and bad luck conspired to produce three interceptions. When the splashing was over, Theismann had completed 33 passes in 58 tries for 526 yards. Poor running cost the game; Notre Dame gained a miserable 31 yards. It was the fourth time that USC had foiled Notre Dame in a bid for an undisputed national title.

There was still Texas to play in a rematch of the previous year's Cotton Bowl. The Longhorns were number one; no one had beaten them in 30 games. Parseghian came up with what he called a "mirror defense" against their wishbone. He had a linebacker shadow each Longhorn back and force them to make a decision to go upfield or run into the sidelines. Forcing the wishbone runners to make the decision nullified the wishbone's predication of making the defense commit itself. If they changed to quick-hitting plays, then it wasn't the wishbone anymore and would be handled accordingly.

Ara's plan worked flawlessly. The Longhorns, who ran 333 yards in the 1970 Cotton Bowl, were held to 216. The wishbone is a high-risk offense; Texas mishandled the ball nine times. All of the scoring happened in the first half. Texas kicked a 23-yard field goal after Happy Feller gained 63 yards on an option play. Three minutes later, Notre Dame drove 80 yards in 10 plays, capped by a 26-yard Theismann pass to Gatewood. Texas fumbled the next kickoff and Tom Eaton recovered on their 13. Six plays later, Theismann scored on a keeper. In the second quarter, a 53-yard drive resulted in a 15-yard touchdown run by Theismann. Hempel wrapped up the scoring with a 36-yard field goal. In the second half, Texas was unable to handle the mirror defense. The Fighting Irish won 24-11. The win put Notre Dame second (AP) and fifth (UPI) in the national rankings.

Theismann accounted for 2,801 yards of the total 5,105 yards gained for the year, easily one of the best individual performances in Fighting Irish history—and not done at the expense of the team. DiNardo, Ellis, Theismann, and Gatewood made All-American teams.

1970 record: 10-1-0 (.909)
Record to date: 526-143-38 (.770)

1971

This is the year that might have been. A number of quality players returned, especially on the two lines. The big loss was Theismann. Ara would have to emphasize defense, and hope someone would emerge as the offensive leader. The fact that his teams never lost more than two games in a season is a testament to his coaching and motivational skills. He would need them all in 1971. Bill Etter was slated to start, and did, until an injury in the fourth game ended his career. He was a gifted runner, with the best speed at quarterback since Frank Dancewicz. In 1969, he had led the team in rushing average with 10.7 yards gained per run, but he had missed all of 1970 with an injury. When he went down, Cliff Brown stepped in, another good runner who lacked great passing skills. There were

Cliff Brown, starting QB for most of the 1971 season.

good, not great, backs, so the weak passing game would eventually allow defenses to stack against the run. Gulyas and Minnix ran as halfbacks, and Andy Huff returned from a year's absence to start at fullback. This was a faster backfield than the 1970 unit but lacked the extra dimension Theismann had contributed. The offensive line was solid; Gatewood and Creaney had real potential, but they needed someone to throw to them. The defensive line was awesome, with Patulski and Kadish at 260 each, Greg Marx, almost their equal in skill, and Fred Swendsen. The linebackers were solid, led by Eric Patton and Jim Musuraca. All starting deep backs returned. It was the most experienced defense Ara had fielded.

Northwestern managed only a touchdown while Notre Dame posted 50 points. The Fighting Irish defense scored two touchdowns; Northwestern surrendered two fumbles, seven interceptions, and a blocked punt. Gulyas scored from the 3 after Patulski blocked a punt; Minnix tallied from the 4 in the second quarter; Steenberge passed to Gatewood for an 8-yard touchdown; Bob Thomas kicked a 36-yard field goal; Cieszkowski slammed in from the 4 for a 30-7 halftime score. Stepaniak and Crotty scored with interceptions from 40 and 65 yards, and Greg Hill ran in from the 4. It was Ara's highest-scoring opener.

Mike Kadish, three-year starter on the defensive line from 1969 to 1971, a consensus All-American in 1971.

Walt Patulski, All-American defensive end in the early 1970s when Ara had a dominating defensive line.

The pace shifted radically against Purdue under copious amounts of rain and mud. The Fighting Irish won 8-7 in a comeback. Otis Armstrong scored for Purdue on a 26-yard screen pass from Gary Danielson. The intense rain slowed everyone down, until a low punt snap in Purdue's end zone sent their punter running; just as he tried a desperate kick, he was hit, and Swendsen scored a touchdown. Steenberge passed to Creaney for the 2-point conversion. The defense won the game.

The defense also put in a stellar performance in a 14-2 win over Michigan State. The offense scored early and then disappeared, but the defense rocked the Spartans all day. Minnix scored from the 1 to end an 8-minute, 80-yard drive. He tallied again, from the 5, after Musuraca recovered a fumble at the MSU 17. MSU scored 2 points when Etter wisely fell on his own fumble in his end zone. The second half was composed of lost opportunities. MSU held them to 92 yards passing. Spartan runners gained only 32 yards on the ground.

Miami lost 17-0, but Notre Dame lost Etter in the second quarter (a knee injured in the MSU game finally gave out). Cliff Brown came in and moved the team; Thomas kicked a 38-yard field goal. In the third quarter, Brown moved the team 66 yards, with Huff scoring on a 16-yard run. Brown ran 33 yards, and Dewan scored on a 6-yard touchdown run. Notre

Mike Creaney, three-year starter at TE.

Dame passed for 35 yards, but the defense allowed only 60 yards rushing and 51 yards passing.

Bob Thomas put up three field goals as the first scores in the game against North Carolina. Ellis saved the shutout when he dodged six blockers on a kickoff to tackle the runner; he got an interception on the next play. Kadish deflected a field goal try in the third quarter. Gatewood scored on a 4-yard pass from Brown in the last quarter. Notre Dame still had not hit the century mark in passing. Final score: 16-0.

McKay and USC took it to the defense, winning 28-14. An interception led to a 31-yard touchdown pass. Gary Diminick returned the kickoff 66 yards and Huff piled in from the 1 to tie. USC scored almost immediately: a long kickoff return and a 24-yard touchdown pass. Sam Cunningham scored in the second quarter from the 1. Brown tried to pass the Fighting Irish into contention but USC intercepted him and returned it 53 yards for their last touchdown and a 28-7 halftime lead. Cieszkowski got the only second half score, a 4-yarder.

Larry Parker cuts upfield in the 1971 Irish win over Tulane.

Andy Huff, starter at FB in 1971 and 1972.

The Fighting Irish won a boring game against Navy, 21-0. Gulyas scored from the 1 to end a 78-yard first-quarter drive; Minnix scored twice in the second quarter, from the 1 and the 10. Navy couldn't move, and the Fighting Irish muddled along in the second half.

The offense finally jelled against Pitt, 56-7. The running game exploded for 464 yards and seven touchdowns. Gulyas scored three times from the 1-yard line. Gatewood went in for an 8-yard touchdown, and Larry Parker scored from the 9 and the 6. Willie Townsend tallied from the 12, and Dewan crunched in from the 5. Pitt had only 113 yards of total offense. Patulski hurt a knee and was taken away on a stretcher.

Notre Dame won 21-7 over a mediocre Tulane team. The Green Wave scored first and led through halftime. Brown finally scored from the 1 to tie. Creaney tallied with an 8-yard pass after Gatewood caught an 18-yard pass. Brown scored from the 5 in the fourth quarter to end a 20-play, 75-yard, 9:13-minute drive. The passing yardage went up to 154 yards for the day.

LSU ended the season on a sour note with a 28-8 win, the worst defeat for Ara to that point. Future NFL star Bert Jones threw touchdowns of 36 and 32 yards,and scored from the 5 himself. LSU attacked the defense, ran for 143 of their 299 yards, and set up the passing game well. Notre Dame did not respond except with yardage—323 total yards.

For the season, total yardage fell off 34 percent, from 5,105 yards to 3,329. The passing game dropped a precipitous 60 percent, which led to a 35 percent decline in touchdown production. The team fell out of the top 10 ranking, a first in Ara's era. Patulski, Ellis, Kadish, and Gatewood made All-American teams.

1971 record: 8-2-0 (.800)
Record to date: 534-145-38 (.771)

1972

The Fighting Irish were in a holding pattern in 1972—consolidating, gaining experience, and assessing personnel. Interior linemen were needed, three on each side of the ball—and a quarterback. When the shuffling was done the offensive line was solid; Willie Townsend was an adequate replacement for Gatewood. Tom Clements, a talented sophomore with quick feet, a fair arm, and an excellent football mind, won the quarterback job. The starting backs were Darryll Dewan, Gary Diminick, and Andy Huff.

This was the first year of freshman eligibility; Steve Niehaus of Moeller High in Cincinnati would immediately help the defensive line (although he was out after the fourth game). Greg Marx returned, and reserves moved up. Ara stuck with the 4-4-3, and the linebackers were a good group, especially Musuraca and Drew Mahalic on the outside. The linebackers were quicker, as were the deep backs. There were some fine reserves—especially Eric Penick, Art Best, Wayne Bullock, Mike Fanning, Jim Stock, and Greg Collins.

Northwestern looked tougher than usual, having lost to Michigan only 7-0. The Fighting Irish left Evanston with a 37-0 win. Dewan scored from 30 yards out, and Cieszkowski slammed in from the 2. In the second quarter, Thomas hit field goals of 23 and

The 1972 coaching staff.

Greg Marx, three-year starter on the defensive line in the early 1970s.

26 yards. Jim O'Malley intercepted a Wildcat pass, Townsend ran a reverse for 30 yards, and Huff piled in from the 1. Thomas made it 30-0 in the first half with a 47-yard field goal. The reserves played the rest of the way; Penick gained 87 yards on the day and scored the final touchdown.

A star-studded Purdue team, led by Darryl Stingley and Dave Butz had lost twice already. The Fighting Irish held them off 35-14, gaining 636 yards of total offense. Penick ran 133 yards on 12 carries. Clements completed 17 of 24 passes for 287 yards. At the end of the first half, the Irish had 403 yards to Purdue's 39. Creaney scored on a 39-yard pass from Clements and set up another touchdown with a 30-yard catch before Penick dashed in from the 14. Clements threw a 62-yard touchdown pass to Willie Townsend at the beginning of the second quarter. In the third quarter, Diminick ran 42 yards, and Cieszkowski blasted in from the 1. Huff scored from the 1 after an 84-yard clock-killing drive. Later Purdue scored two touchdowns.

Michigan State was running a primitive wishbone. Their defense, led by Brad Van Pelt, held Notre Dame to two field goals until the last 5 minutes. The Fighting Irish defense held off MSU and picked off enough passes to halt MSU drives. Thomas kicked his third field goal in the fourth quarter, and Huff scored from the 1 after a Ken Schlezes interception for Notre Dame's 16-0 victory.

Notre Dame nailed a seventh straight win over Pitt, 42-16. Huff scored in the first half with bursts from the 1 and the 4; Pitt closed in with a third-quarter touchdown and 2-point conversion. They were threatening again, but Mahalic intercepted a pass and ran 56 yards for a touchdown. Later, Penick scored., and Art Best scored on a 56-yard run, his first carry for Notre Dame.

Missouri upset things with a 30-26 win over the Fighting Irish, even though Nebraska had routed them 62-0 a week earlier. They ran 77 plays to Notre Dame's 63. They scored first after an interception of a Clements pass. Clements directed a 66-yard drive with Huff scoring from the 1. Missouri pounded back, especially up the middle (Niehaus was hurt), and scored again. Cieszkowski tied it from the 1 after an 81-yard return drive. The next Mizzou touchdown was right out of the Charles White method—with the runner over the goal line but the ball suspended in the air about five feet above and behind him. Notre Dame fumbled a punt and a kickoff to let the Tigers score two field goals, then they hit another one. Clements and Huff scored touchdowns for the final 30-26 result.

Ara's teams never lost back-to-back games in the regular season. Texas Christian University lost 21-0. During the week they had denigrated the Fighting Irish defense. So, while Notre Dame amassed 522 yards of offense, TCU managed only 70 on the ground and 62 on passes. Jim Roolf scored first, on an 11-yard pass from Clements, following a Schlezes interception. Irish turnovers stopped further scoring until the third quarter when Best broke loose for a 57-yard touchdown. In the fourth period, Roolf ran an end around for 36 yards, and Penick jetted 11 yards for the last touchdown. On the day, Penick made 158 yards on 16 carries.

Although Navy had its best team in a decade, Notre Dame won easily, 42-23. Diminick ran 84 yards for a touchdown on the opening kickoff. After that, Notre Dame gained 597 more yards of offense. Clements moved the team 85 yards on the next drive and scored from the 18 with a keeper. His 4-yard touchdown in the next quarter made it 21-0. Schlezes ran a punt back 46 yards, and Penick made a 27-yard touchdown. Diminick capped a drive with a 7-yard touchdown run for a 35-0 halftime score. The Middies scored twice, and Al Samuels scored from the 4 with the reserves to end it.

The Fighting Irish grounded Air Force, 21-7. The referees could have been the deciding factor in a closer game when they blew a "play" dead—a Clements fake to Penick into the line—when the real play was a 35-yard pass to Townsend. The Falcons boasted a superior passing game so Ara switched to a 4-3 and held them to eight completions in 25 tries, while intercepting four passes. In the second quarter Diminick scored from the 7, and Townsend caught a 13-yard Clements touchdown pass. Air Force scored on a 51-yard run and played a good game, until they fumbled late in the fourth quarter, allowing Huff's touchdown run of 13 yards.

An Orange Bowl bid depended on a win over Miami, which Notre Dame earned 20-17. It was almost negated when someone threw a snowball during an Irish field goal try that ruined the kick. Miami scored a field goal, but Clements masterminded a 90-yard return march and finished it with a 10-yard touchdown to Townsend. Miami fumbled the kickoff, and Huff scored from the 1 moments later. Clements scored the last Fighting Irish touchdown on a 1-yard sneak in the third quarter, but Miami tallied twice more and then barely missed a field goal try.

This young Fighting Irish team met USC in Los Angeles. Anthony Davis racked up six touchdowns, something never done before to the Irish. Ara used his speediest kickoff coverage people, but they overran Davis who took it all the way. Notre Dame came back for a Thomas field goal. Davis scored again from the 1 after an interference call. Penick fumbled on the 9 and Davis scored after two tries. Clements threw a 5-yard touchdown pass to Townsend. In the third quarter, a USC interception led to another Davis touchdown, so Clements clinched a touchdown with an 11-yard swing pass to Diminick. Mike Townsend intercepted his 10th pass of the season, a record, to lead to a Clements touchdown pass to Creaney, who made a career-best catch, for a 25-23 score, USC up. Davis then ran another kick back 96 yards for a touchdown. Deflated, the Irish watched two more USC scores, another by Davis and one by Cunningham. Final score: USC won 45-23.

After that, Notre Dame had to face Heisman winner Johnny Rodgers and the supporting cast from Nebraska in the Orange Bowl. It was Ara's worst defeat, 40-6. Rodgers scored four touchdowns and threw for another. Pete Demmerle scored Notre Dame's only touchdown on a 5-yard pass from Clements. The Huskers gained 560 yards of total offense to Notre Dame's 207.

As a young team, it had won some games it should have lost, lost when it could have been in the game, and was beaten by its betters. Greg Marx and John Dampeer were the All-American selections.

1972 record: 8-3-0 (.727)
Record to date: 542-148-38 (.770)

1973

The offensive line Ara fielded produced one of the most devastating rushing attacks in Notre Dame history. The line was led by tight end Dave Casper, moved from tackle, Frank Pomarico, and Gerry DiNardo. Clements returned at quarterback, and halfbacks Art Best and Eric Penick were both capable of scoring from any spot on the field. Wayne "The Train" Bullock was fullback. It was probably the best backfield Ara coached at Notre Dame, with the possible exception of 1966. Hanratty was a better passer, but Clements was the better ball handler. The 1966 offensive line was more dominating, and Eddy had an ability to exploit seams that other backs never saw; the 1973 backfield was faster. The 1973 defensive line was awesome, starting with Ross Browner, perhaps the best player in cleats, even as a freshman. Then came Niehaus, Mike Fanning, and Mike Stock, whose

Tom Clements on the loose against USC in 1973.

Four members of a great defensive line in 1973: Willie Fry, Mike Fanning, Steve Niehaus, Ross Browner.

specialty was sheer speed on his pass rush. The linebackers were solid; Collins and Mahalic as outside linebackers had excellent range. The secondary had excellent speed and a fine talent in freshman Luther Bradley. This was a dominating team in almost all areas.

Although Northwestern had already beaten Michigan State, Notre Dame shut them out, 44-0. Browner blocked a punt for a safety. Penick scored on a 16-yard run, and Demmerle caught a 9-yard touchdown pass from Clements. Ron Goodman slashed in for a 9-yard score in the second quarter; 3 minutes later, Clements sneaked in from the 1. He passed for another touchdown to make the halftime score 37-0. Northwestern had -8 yards rushing. The last touchdown was Diminick's, a 21-yard sprint.

Purdue played a good game but lost 20-7. Best set up a Thomas field goal with a 64-yard run; Purdue scored on a 64-yard pass play to Larry Burton. Best scored from the 9 to regain the lead through halftime. In the third quarter, Bullock slammed in from the 1, and the reserves moved well enough for Thomas to hit a 42-yard field goal. Purdue's running was held to 33 yards all day.

Michigan State was in a slow recovery from mediocrity and played well enough to blunt early Fighting Irish drives. Twice in the first quarter, long field goal tries failed. Finally, Notre Dame put together an 80-yard drive, all on runs, with Bullock muscling in from the 1. Later in the second quarter, Clements struck quickly with a four-play, 63-yard drive, started with a 30-yard screen pass to Casper and ended by a 10- yard touchdown pass to Demmerle. In the third period, a fumble led to an MSU field goal; then an interception was run back for a Spartan touchdown. A sequence of fumbles killed time MSU needed, and Rudnick saved the 14-10 Irish win with an interception on the last play.

The Fighting Irish were underwhelmed to play Rice, and played poorly in the early going. A Rice fumble, picked up by Stock, led to a Bullock touchdown blast. Penalties marred the second quarter, but Clements threw a 21-yard touchdown pass to Casper. Good running by Best and Diminick in the third quarter led to Bullock's smash from the 1. The defense held Rice to minus 14 yards for the second half. Cliff Brown ended the scoring with a 38-yard touchdown run for the final 28-0 score.

Army was defeated 62-3. Notre Dame was scoreless in the first quarter, but Penick scored early in the second quarter. After that, the Fighting Irish rolled: Casper on a 34-yard touchdown pass; Best on a 5-yard scoring run; Casper for a 3-yard touchdown pass from Brown; Penick scored from the 6; and Brown to Al Hunter for a touchdown after an interception. Reserves scored the rest; the best play was Tim Simon's 73-yard punt return for a touchdown.

USC was next, only a tie with Oklahoma blemishing their record. Rudnick deflected a punt, and Thomas turned it into a 42-yard field goal. Rather than

Ross Browner, an all-time Irish great, comes up quick to greet Pitt's Tony Dorsett.

risk a Davis touchdown return, the Fighting Irish squibbed the kick. The Trojans scored anyway, Davis going in from the 2. Another bad USC punt led to a Thomas field goal of 43 yards. For the third time, USC had a bad punt, and the Fighting Irish finally moved in for a touchdown, helped by two Demmerle catches and ended by Clements over left guard. Reserve quarterback Frank Allocco had been watching the Trojan coaches as they signalled plays; he thought he had figured out their blitz call. In the third quarter, Notre Dame had the ball on its 15. The Trojans blitzed, and Clements pitched out to Penick in motion to his left, who turned upfield behind blocking by DiNardo and Pomarico, and ran for an 85-yard touchdown. This single play was one of the most electrifying moments in recent Notre Dame football history. USC returned a drive, with Lynn Swann scoring from the 27. Clements fumbled, but it was recovered by Russ Kornman; Thomas kicked a 32-yard field goal. Luther Bradley stopped a late drive with an interception. Great rushing defense won the game; USC made only 66 yards all day, while the Irish ran for 316 yards in their 23-14 victory.

Navy was next, and they played well for most of the first quarter until a good punt return led to Penick scoring from the 11. Al Hunter scored in the second quarter from the 3 after plays by Demmerle, Clements, and Hunter set it up. In the third period, a Greg Collins interception reached the Navy 19. Demmerle made a circus catch at the 1, and Clements tallied. After Potempa recovered a fumble, Al Samuel scored from the 7. Mahalic intercepted a Navy pass on the Notre Dame 34. Subs scored two more touchdowns: a 9-yard touchdown from Brown to Townsend and a Parise run. Stock earned a safety to wrap up the scoring and a 44-7 win. Twelve Irish runners rushed for 447 yards.

Art Best turns the corner against Air Force in the 48 - 15 blowout near the end of the 1973 championship year .

Al Hunter, first Irish player to rush for 1,000 yards.

Pitt's Tony Dorsett had run for 1,139 yards in eight games. He would make a career of running well against the Fighting Irish, starting with 209 yards in 29 runs in a losing effort, 31-10. The Panthers fumbled three times early, and the third led to Bullock hammering three times from the 24 to score. Before the half ended, a deliberate drive ended in a Thomas field goal; Pitt kicked one as well. In the third quarter, Notre Dame's defense started to create situations rather than wait for Pitt errors. Collins intercepted a Pitt pass and returned it to the Notre Dame 42. Bullock took over again, gaining 32 of 58 yards plus the score from the 9. A long Diminick kick return set up Bullock's third touchdown to end it.

Penick led a touchdown parade as Notre Dame swamped Air Force 48-15. He scored on runs from the 4 and the 6 as Notre Dame set off a 21-0 first-quarter avalanche. Air Force was unable to move—they even tried a 62-yard field goal in exasperation.

Notre Dame jumped out to a 24-0 lead over Miami. They scored on a Demmerle touchdown run from the 21 and a 24-yard field goal by Thomas in the first half. Demmerle scored two touchdowns to start

Father Joyce, Ara, and Moose with the MacArthur Bowl in honor of the 1973 championship.

Mike Townsend, consensus All-American at FS in 1973.

the second half, with catches from the 15 and the 7. Cliff Brown led a touchdown drive with the reserves. The Fighting Irish dominated both sides of the ball. Ten Notre Dame runners amassed 477 yards. The 44-0 win gave Notre Dame its first perfect season since the Leahy era.

The Sugar Bowl against Alabama pitted two offensive machines against each other (Notre Dame was ranked 3rd, and Alabama was ranked 1st), as well as a wishbone team against a great Fighting Irish defense. In the first quarter, the defense held the wishbone to 0 yards in 12 plays. Clements used Demmerle on receptions of 19, 26, and 14 yards to lead to Bullock's 6-yard touchdown; the point after was missed. Alabama went ahead 7-6 with a 6-yard touchdown run to end a 52 yard march. They kicked off, and Al Hunter flashed his 9.3 speed on a 93-yard touchdown return. Clements fired a 2-point conversion to Demmerle for a 14-7 lead. Alabama kicked a field goal; the halftime score was 14-10. Alabama took the lead on a 93-yard touchdown drive in the third quarter. Both teams missed field goals. Mahalic grabbed a mid-air Crimson Tide fumble at their 12. Penick scored on a counter play behind a Casper block. Alabama scored when quarterback Richard Todd drifted away from a play to get lost behind the flow and then caught a touchdown pass. They missed the point after but led 23-21. The Irish worked a patient drive; Thomas kicked a field goal for a 24-23 lead. Fans watched breathlessly as a third-and-8 developed deep in Notre Dame's territory; Clements threw from his end zone to tight end Robin Weber and cinched the 24-23 win and the national championship.

This undefeated season was a total team effort—great offense and great defense. Only two players made All-American, Casper and Mike Townsend.

1973 record: 11-0-0 (1.000)
Record to date: 553-148-38 (.774)

1974

It's always difficult to defend a national crown. Casper, Pomarico, Mike Townsend, and Rudnick had to be replaced due to graduation. Four more, however, were lost for the year due to a controversial dorm violation (females were present in their rooms beyond curfew): Browner, Bradley, Hunter, and Fry. Penick, Quehl, and Simon suffered injuries. Still, Notre Dame had plenty of good players returning. Clements and Demmerle, Best at left halfback, Al Samuels at right halfback, and Bullock at fullback all returned. But Best would break his jaw and not fully recover. Others would have to fill in and develop quickly.

Wayne Bullock, 1974 fullback.

Reggie Barnett, three-year standout as a DB from 1972 to 1974.

The defensive line was awesome again, featuring Niehaus, Fanning, and Stock. Mahalic and Collins returned and Tom Eastman started in the middle. Reggie Barnett led a largely untried secondary. The offensive backfield was weakened, and there were enough losses in personnel to cause some worry about depth.

Georgia Tech scored first to open the season, but Notre Dame then scored 31 unanswered points. Bullock tied it with a 14-yard touchdown run after a Tech fumble. The Fighting Irish took the lead in the second quarter on a 22-yard Dave Reeve field goal and a 7-yard touchdown pass from Clements to Demmerle. In the second half, Bullock scored from the 1, and Samuels slashed in from the 8 on a sweep. The national telecast caught a great play when Steve Sylvester blind-sided a pursuing Tech lineman as he chased Clements on a broken play.

Notre Dame dropped four fumbles in the first half, and Northwestern held the Irish to a 14-3 halftime lead. The first Fighting Irish score followed a pass to Demmerle that reached the Northwestern 2; Kornman scored. Bullock scored for the second touchdown after a Northwestern roughing penalty boosted a drive. Ron Goodman ran 62 yards to score on the fourth play of the new half. Clements followed a fumble recovery with a drive and a 14-yard touchdown pass to Weber. Frank Allocco scored a keeper after another fumble. Reserves Mark McLane and Terry Eurick punched over an 11-yard touchdown and a 2-yarder, respectively. Future All-American tight end Ken MacAfee (6-5 and 245 pounds) made his freshman appearance. Notre Dame won 49-3.

Purdue stopped the winning streak at 13 with a 31-20 victory. The Fighting Irish self-destructed with early fumbles and interceptions. Purdue enjoyed a 21-0 lead after only 11 plays. Their scores came on a 1-yard quarterback keeper around end, a 52-yard scoring sprint, and a 21-yard interception return. Notre Dame shanked a punt, and Purdue nailed a 47-yard field goal. Bullock scored early in the second quarter. At the half, the score was 24-7, and Notre Dame had 208 yards to Purdue's 168. Bullock scored on a short run in the third quarter after a busted punt play. Two scoring opportunities were wasted with loss of possession on downs and an ineligible receiver penalty. Purdue intercepted a pass and made a 6-yard follow-up touchdown. Clements hit Demmerle late with a touchdown pass, too late to change the final outcome. The Fighting Irish beat themselves with offensive mistakes, although they outgained Purdue 407 yards to 270.

The Fighting Irish came back against Michigan State, winning 19-14. In the first quarter, Kevin

Jim Stock, starter at DE in 1973, then as a LB in 1974 and 1975, cat-quick specialist in pass rushing.

Nosbusch recovered a fumble caused by Stock and Fanning. Clements almost got a touchdown out of a pass play to Weber; Bullock plowed in for the score. The Spartans fumbled at their 10, and Bullock scored on the next play. Reeve made a field goal from 38 yards after a bad Spartan punt. He added a 32-yarder in the last period. The Spartans drove 99 yards for their first touchdown, scored again, but Randy Payne intercepted a pass to kill their last good chance. Bullock ran the ball against MSU 36 times, a new record.

Pete Demmerle nears the end zone with a Clements pass in the 38-7 rout of Miami in 1974.

Rice, normally a patsy, went down by the surprising score of 10-3. Notre Dame spotted Rice an early field goal and spent the rest of the game searching for their missing offense. In the second quarter, the Fighting Irish were flagged for illegal procedure; a referee claimed that the linemen's posteriors were not on the same horizontal plane, within an inch's variance. Ara protested with all he had, only to add to the penalty. After five futile drives, Reeve kicked a 45-yard field goal. Rice was kept in check for the rest of the game. In the fourth quarter, Notre Dame used 20 plays to execute an 80-yard drive. Bullock scored from the 2 around left end.

Army was again mismatched, 48-0. Bullock scored from the 6 to lead Fighting Irish backs to 525 yards rushing and 30 first downs, a new record. Bullock scored the second touchdown as well. Clements ran a 7-yard keeper before halftime for a touchdown and a 20-0 score. In the third period, Russ Kornman scored twice, from the 7 and the 4, and Al Samuels went 35 yards on a pitchout to score. Tom Bake scored the same way in the fourth quarter, from the 6.

Miami was 4-1 and had stars Rubin Carter, Dennis Harrah, and Mike Archer. The Fighting Irish won 38-7. Demmerle caught a 53-yard touchdown in the first 2 minutes of the game. Miami later fumbled on a 69-yard punt, at their 9; Bullock rammed in to score on the next play. Reeve made an 18-yard field goal after MacAfee set him up with a 24-yard pass play. Randy Harrison intercepted a pass and ran it back 44 yards for a touchdown. Clements scored on a keeper from the Miami 8, and MacAfee made a 4-yard touchdown catch. Clements was 13 of 19 for 154 yards and two touchdowns.

The 14-6 win over Navy was a turning point in Notre Dame football history; on the flight back from Philadelphia, a weary Ara Parseghian decided he would leave football. He had important family con-

Robin Weber, best known as the TE who caught the game-saving pass from Clements in the great 24-23 win over Alabama in the 1974 Orange Bowl.

siderations and constant pressure; the fun was gone. The Fighting Irish probably played down to the Middies. Goodman fumbled a punt early in the game and Navy kicked a field goal. They added another in the second half for a 6-0 lead. The only decent Fighting Irish drive to that point ended in a missed field goal. The defense turned it up, forced a punt, and Goodman took it back to their 28. Surviving a bad snap at the 5, Clements found Demmerle for a touchdown. Randy Harrison made an interception and returned it 40 yards for a touchdown. It was an ugly win, and Clements had his worst day, 5 of 22 with two interceptions.

They would have to play much better against Pitt and Dorsett if they expected to win. Notre Dame looked proficient on the first possession, and Bullock scored from the 7. But then they had to wait until the fourth quarter. In the interim, Pitt kicked a field goal and scored from the 1. Notre Dame had stopped a Pitt scoring attempt after a blocked Irish punt—this proved to be the game saver. With 8 minutes left, and 55 yards away from the goal, Clements used Bullock for 32 yards on line smashes, and hit Demmerle with a 3-yard touchdown pass for the win. Bullock's 25 runs gave him 193 for the year to break Worden's old record. The Irish won 14-10.

Notre Dame handed Air Force its ninth straight loss of the year, 38-0. Kornman, in for an injured Bullock, scored from the 1, but Parise got it there with a 62-yard jaunt. Parise scored in the second quarter from the 11, and Clements scored from the 9. Allocco scored on a keeper from the 1 for the 28-0 halftime score. In the second half, Reeve booted a 33-yard field goal and Allocco hit Kevin Doherty with a 25-yard touchdown pass.

Gerry DiNardo, starting RG from 1972 to 1974, and a consensus All-American pick in 1974.

USC was the final game. The Fighting Irish blew a two-touchdown lead as USC scored 55 points in a strange game. Mahalic intercepted a Haden pass, and Bullock scored from the 2 to end the short drive. Clements threw to Demmerle for a touchdown from the USC 29. Reeve hit a field goal, and McLane scored from the 9 with a draw play. Anthony Davis scored from the 8 with a swing pass, but USC missed the point after. They then hammered Notre Dame for 49 unanswered points in the second half. Davis ran the kickoff back 102 yards for a touchdown, scored from the 6, and then the 4. J.K. McKay caught an 18-yard touchdown pass, and a 44-yarder. The Fighting Irish fumbled, and Diggs caught a 16-yard touchdown pass. A long Clements pass was returned 58 yards for the final touchdown. USC won 55-24.

After that shock, and knowing it was Ara's last game, the Fighting Irish ruined Alabama's national title hopes with a 13-11 Orange Bowl win. A Crimson Tide fumble at their 16 ended in a Bullock score from the 4. Notre Dame rolled on a long drive, mostly running, and McLane scored from the 9 in the second quarter. The point after was missed. An Irish fumble earned Alabama a field goal. The third quarter was scoreless. The Crimson Tide scored on a 48-yard pass play in the fourth quarter and made a 2-point conversion. The wishbone had foundered on the Notre Dame defense, so the Crimson Tide had to pass. It was their undoing. Barnett intercepted a pass and zigzagged all over the Orange Bowl for the win. The wishbone gained 62 yards all evening. The Fighting Irish players carried Ara off the field and into history.

He had done a great coaching job under tremendous personal and team adversity. He had also set a new standard of excellence for both Notre Dame and college football. All Fighting Irish fans must be thankful that Ara Parseghian led their fortunes for 11 seasons. He was 95-17-4 (.836), just behind Leahy's .855. The 1974 All-Americans were Demmerle, Fanning, DiNardo, Clements, Collins, and Niehaus.

1974 record: 10-2-0 (.750)

Record to date: 563-150-38 (.774)

1975

The university had wanted Dan Devine in 1964, and 10 years later they still did. Devine, like every Fighting Irish coach since 1913, was a son of the midwest. He was born in Wisconsin and grew up near Duluth, Minnesota. He played college football at Minnesota-Duluth, coached an unbeaten high school team in Michigan, and was an assistant coach at Michigan State. His first head coaching position was at Arizona State in 1955, where he gave the school its first undefeated season and bowl bid while compiling a 27-3-1 record. In 13 seasons at Missouri, he won 93 games, second best in the school's history. He had done fairly well at Green Bay, but the situation had deteriorated. Whereas Parseghian had struck more than a few Irish players as a "Napoleonic figure," no one could make that claim of Devine. He was low key, although intense competitive fires burned within. This lack of intensity may be why Devine was not going to be fully accepted into or by the Notre Dame family, as had Ara.

He had a well-earned reputation as a top-notch recruiter. He needed it to rebuild the offensive line, since six starters had graduated. Reserves could move up, including Steve Quehl who had survived a nearly fatal work accident. Ernie Hughes moved in as a sophomore at right guard. MacAfee became a fixture at tight end. Most of the interior men were technicians; only Hughes was a dominating player. Rick Slager started in the backfield, beating out a kid named Joe Montana. Hunter, who had returned from the suspension, was a breakaway threat at all times. Mark McLane was at right halfback (Best had transferred to Kent State). Jerome Heavens would get most of the starting time at fullback. There was great speed in this group, but it would need to jell. The defense had outstanding players in Ross Browner and Niehaus, with Jeff Weston and Willie Fry not far behind. Fry and Browner might have been the best pair of defensive ends in Notre Dame history. Jim Stock moved to outside linebacker, paired with Doug Becker, flanking a burly freshman, Bob Golic. The secondary had plenty of speed, especially with Bradley and Mike Banks.

Rick Slager, Irish QB in 1975 and 1976.

The first game under Devine was against Boston College. Fighting Irish authorities had been reluctant to schedule other Catholic schools in recent years, to prevent a parochial, in-bred reputation. Both teams were tight and made little headway in the first quarter. Notre Dame stopped a Boston College threat at their 23 in the second quarter, and McLane ran 41 yards to Boston College's 9, where the drive stalled. Reeve kicked a 30-yard field goal for an early lead. Boston's Fred Steinfort answered with a 45-yarder; the 3-3 tie held through the half. The second half began as a repeat of the first with fumbles and penalties. Notre Dame took advantage first and moved 40 yards for Jim Browner's 10-yard touchdown run. In the fourth quarter, Randy Harrison grabbed a Boston College pass to set up Hunter's 24-yard dash for the last Irish score. With that, Devine had a 17-3 win over a tougher-than-expected team.

The Fighting Irish blanked Purdue 17-0. Reeve scored with a 29-yard field goal. Old-fashioned, tough football dominated play throughout. Notre Dame missed a field goal in the third quarter, and Purdue sped 66 yards in five plays, reaching Notre Dame's 4. The huge Irish line stopped them; Purdue tried a pass back to the quarterback, as Alabama had in the 1973 Sugar Bowl. The pass went for a touchdown once again, but it was Luther Bradley's on a 99-yard interception return, the longest on the books for Notre Dame. A few minutes later, Al Hunter ran in from the 1 to end the scoring.

Devine had won two games in five days due to the voracious demands of television. They faced an undefeated Northwestern team, who fell readily, 31-7. Northwestern scored first, and Notre Dame unloaded: with Slager hurt, Montana led a 46-yard drive with Hunter scoring from the 4; Jim Browner scored from the 10 after Fry blocked a punt; Montana fired his first Fighting Irish touchdown pass to McLane from the Wildcat 14. In the second half, Reeve nailed a three-pointer and Montana rolled right for a 6-yard touchdown.

Michigan State broke the winning string with a 10-3 win. The Fighting Irish offense was baffled most of the day, and a defensive lapse let the MSU fullback loose for 76 yards, which led to their only touchdown. Montana had a pass intercepted in the MSU end zone. Several fumbles also killed drives. The only Irish score came on a 35-yard field goal. Devine lost five players for part or all of the season during the game.

The game against North Carolina began the legend of Montana as "The Comeback Kid" when he overcame earlier team mistakes to overtake a 14-0 Tarheel lead. Slager had taken Notre Dame to the 8, but a fumble ended that threat. With 2 minutes left in the third quarter, Slager moved the offense well enough for Hunter to score from the 2. The 2-point try missed. With 6:04 left in the game, Montana came in and launched a five-play scoring drive. Hunter scored from the 2 and Montana passed for a 2-point conversion to tie. The Tarheels then missed a 42-yard field goal. With 1:15 left, a draw play was called, but Montana audibled when he saw his split end facing only loose coverage. He was supposed to catch it and step out of bounds, but Burgmeier ran for an 80-yard touchdown to win the game. Montana had thrown four passes and completed 3 for 129 yards, one touchdown, a 2-point conversion, and the win.

Steve Niehaus, after two injury-plagued years, had two fantastic seasons in 1974 and 1975, earning consensus All-American honors in 1975.

Great defensive player Jim Stock.

Air Force scored first with a 45-yard field goal and converted a Heavens fumble into a 16-yard touchdown. Slager responded with a drive that earned a field goal; Montana went in and was intercepted. Air Force kicked a field goal for a 13-3 lead. Heavens shook loose for a 54-yard touchdown run in the third period, but Montana had another pass intercepted on the next series. Air Force turned that into a touchdown from the 1 for a 10-point lead. They made it worse with another field goal. Heavens fumbled, and Air Force fired a touchdown pass for a 30-10 lead. Montana scored from the 3 on a bootleg play. Ten and a half minutes remained. The Falcons intercepted a third Montana pass, but they fumbled. Montana hit McLane for 66 yards to the 7, and fired to MacAfee for the score. Five and a half minutes were left. The defense forced a change of possession and Hunter gained 45 yards before Heavens tallied from the 2 and a 31-30 victory. Fighting Irish rushing gained 320 yards to Air Force's 90.

Fighting Irish fans were relieved to see Anthony Davis was gone, but USC always seemed to come up with something—this time it was Ricky Bell. The Irish scored first with an Al Hunter run of 52 yards, but USC went ahead 7-6 on a touchdown pass. Bradley deflected a Trojan punt for Lopienski's touchdown recovery. But a penalty killed the play, so Bradley deflected the next punt, and Lopienski scored again. USC tied it in the third quarter after an interception, with Bell scoring from the 2. Reeve kicked a field goal. USC ran for a touchdown and hit a field goal for a 24-17 win. Bell gained 165 yards on the day. Montana was 3 of 11 for 25 yards.

Next, Navy lost to the Fighting Irish 31-10. A face mask penalty helped the Middies get a field goal in the first quarter. Browner blocked a punt and scored the touchdown with his recovery. Montana fired another interception. Browner recovered a fumble at the Middie 30, and three plays later MacAfee took a Montana pass and a Middie into the end zone for a touchdown. In the third quarter, Slager replaced Montana (who found out he had a broken finger), and Navy closed the gap with a touchdown. The Fighting Irish defense intercepted another pass, but the offense stalled. Defensive tackle Jeff Weston stole a pass and ran 53 yards for a touchdown. Hunter scored after another interception. Nevertheless, Navy had held Notre Dame's runners to 80 yards on 44 runs.

Against Georgia Tech, Heavens made 148 yards on 18 carries for a 24-3 win. Heavens' rushing yardage was greater than Tech's; they also failed to complete a pass. Slager pitched out to Heavens even though he was flipping through the air after a hit. The score came from the Tech 16. A Reeve field goal made it 10-0 at the half. In the third quarter, Heavens broke it open with a 73-yard touchdown. Dan Knott scored for the reserves.

Pitt was next, and Dorsett was having his usual fantastic year. The Fighting Irish didn't stop him; he ran for 303 yards, including a run of 57 yards to set up a Matt Cavanaugh score, 71 yards for a touchdown, and a 49-yard touchdown to go with 71 yards receiving. Notre Dame scored with two Reeve field goals, a Slager sneak from the 1, and a 10-yard touchdown pass from Slager to MacAfee. Pitt won 34-20.

Miami was more adept at fumbling than Notre Dame. They lost five in a 32-9 loss. The teams traded field goals, and Browner grabbed a fumble at their 12. Heavens scored from the 2. Browner crashed into Pitt's punt formation to surprise the punter for a safety, who was intent on passing the football. It was the second of Browner's career. Becker grabbed a Miami miscue, and MacAfee scored two plays later. Hunter scored from the 4 after another Miami bobble, and Restic took a pitchout to throw to MacAfee for a 10-yard touchdown.

The 8-3 record was not seen favorably in all quarters; it was indicative of the inconsistent play through the season. The offense's production dropped 24 percent, the defense gave up 27 percent more yardage, and touchdown production fell 26 percent. Notre Dame was unranked by AP and 17 by UPI. Niehaus, MacAfee, and Bradley were All-Americans.

1975 record: 8-3-0 (.727)
Record to date: 571-153-38 (.774)

1976

Devine had a strong group, even with Montana out for the year with a shoulder injury. The basic backfield personnel were all returning; the line was solid, especially with MacAfee and Hughes. Tackles Woebkenberg and Steve McDaniels were the largest tandem on record at 269 and 279 pounds. At quarterback, Slager would be alternating with Rusty Lisch and Gary Forystek. Hunter and McLane would start

Ross Browner, an all-time great, four-year starter at LE on defense, consensus All-American in 1976 and 1977, Outland Trophy winner in 1976.

1976 Notre Dame Fighting Irish.

as halfbacks, until McLane was suspended for violating team regulations. Heavens shared the fullback position with freshman Vagas Ferguson. This was a sound, solid offense, but not a great one—not yet.

The defense faced serious losses in the line, with Niehaus graduated, and Weston lost with an injury after the first game. Browner and Fry were the two ends. The linebacking corps was led by sophomores Golic and Steve Heimkreiter; who posed serious problems for opponents. Doug Becker also worked at outside linebacker. Bradley switched from right to left corner, and Burgmeier moved from split end to right corner. Jim Browner moved to strong safety. Joe Restic was the free safety and punter. Of this group, the only concern would be for the young, smallish tackles, Mike Calhoun and Ken Dike.

Pitt with Dorsett was the opener. The Panthers (who would be national champions) won, 31-10. The Fighting Irish scored on a 25-yard touchdown from Slager to MacAfee. Dorsett ran 61 yards on Pitt's first play; six plays later he scored from the 5. Pitt intercepted a Slager pass and scored from the Notre Dame 2. They repeated this pattern for their next touchdown, an interception and a 1-yard touchdown run. Reeve kicked a 53-yard field goal for a Notre Dame record. Pitt answered with a field goal and a touchdown following a bad Irish punt. Dorsett had 181 yards on 22 carries and 754 total rushing yards in four games against Notre Dame.

The Fighting Irish wasted two drives, and then Reeve kicked a 39-yard field goal to take the lead against Purdue. After trading mistakes, Slager pitched out to Hunter, who threw a 33-yard touchdown pass to McLane. As the half ended, Randy Harrison was lost with a broken arm. Purdue penalties and fumbles kept the Irish supplied with opportunities, and Slager scored from the 1. Burgmeier stopped a drive with an interception and a run to midfield. Hunter scored for the 23-0 final score.

In the final scheduled game of the series with Northwestern, Notre Dame won 48-0. The scoring, after a slow start, went like this: Hunter for a 16-yard touchdown in the second quarter, Slager to Willard Browner for an 8-yard touchdown, Slager to Tom Domin for a 70-yard score, Hunter for 37 yards and a tally, and Slager to MacAfee for a 7-yard touchdown. In the final quarter, Rusty Lisch scored from the 4, and Bobby Leopold ran 57 yards with a Wildcat pass to score. Slager set a new record with 12 of 14 passes completed for an .857 mark, breaking Bob Williams' 1949 record.

Against Michigan State, Hunter ran 23 yards to set up Reeve's 47-yard field goal and scored a touchdown from the 6, moments later. Slager threw a 20-yard touchdown pass to Terry Eurick. Late in the fourth quarter, Slager threw a 1-yard touchdown pass to MacAfee. MSU kicked two field goals as a stifling Irish defense stopped MSU cold on its way to a 24-6 win.

Oregon gained no rushing yardage as Notre Dame shut them out 41-0. Slager scored on a keeper from the 1, and he threw an 11-yard touchdown pass to McLane. Hunter ran 9 yards for a touchdown. The Ducks fumbled the kickoff and he scored again six plays later from the 6. Oregon's passing game failed in the second half; Notre Dame intercepted three. Hunter ran a 31-yarder in the third quarter and Ferguson bolted over from the 2.

Solid defense aided a slim 13-6 win over South Carolina. The first Fighting Irish drive went 80 yards in 10 plays concluded by a 10-yard touchdown pass to Willard Browner; Reeve later kicked a 37-yard field goal. In the second quarter, he booted a 30-yarder to pass Bob Thomas for career field goals. The Gamecocks kicked a field goal with 2 seconds left in the half with the help of penalties. They kicked a fourth-quarter field goal. Fry sacked their quarterback and Jim Browner intercepted the last drive.

Steve Heimkreiter, Irish LB from 1976 to 1978.

After disappearing from the second half of the South Carolina game, the Notre Dame offense didn't show up for the beginning of the Navy game. Reeve kicked a 47-yard field goal at the end of the first quarter, and the defense kept Navy off the board to set a record of 21 straight scoreless quarters, surpassing the 1946 record of 20. In the second quarter, Navy used an interception to set up a touchdown pass for a 7-3 lead. They passed for another touchdown. Slager threw a 58-yard touchdown pass to Kelleher, the defense halted Navy, and Hunter scored from the 5. After a Middie fumble, Slager threw a 28-yard touchdown pass to Hunter for the 24-14 halftime score. Navy scored from the 1. Reeve hit another field goal, and Dave Waymer stopped a late threat with an interception; Luther Bradley intercepted a pass in the Irish end zone on the last play. Notre Dame won 27-21.

Georgia Tech took advantage of Irish flaws to win 23-14, and then commented that the Notre Dame players were too fat and too slow. Tech took the lead on a second-quarter field goal. Hunter scored from the 2, and he scored again when a Tech punt never got off, thanks to Ross Browner. Tech came back with a 48-yard run and an 8-yard touchdown dash. Two second-half touchdowns, and paralyzing Notre Dame penalties finished the game.

Alabama, vengeance-minded, came to South Bend. Notre Dame won 21-18, in spite of mangling two scoring chances in the first quarter. Slager threw a 56-yard touchdown pass to Kelleher. Alabama was not moving against the Fighting Irish defense; Slager used Ferguson to set up a Hunter score from the 2. Alabama scored on a 1-yard quarterback keeper. Slick passing on the next Irish drive led to Ferguson's 17-yard run around right end to score. The Crimson Tide intercepted and kicked a field goal; Ozzie Newsome tallied with a 30-yard pass in the fourth period. Lisch replaced an injured Slager, used up the clock on two drives, and Jim Browner intercepted an end zone pass. It had probably been Bear's best chance to beat Notre Dame.

Miami fell 40-27. Reeve kicked a 31-yard field goal; Willard Browner threw Notre Dame's third option pass of the year to Kelleher for a 4-yard touchdown. Heimkreiter grabbed a fumble, and Lisch threw a 42-yard touchdown to Kelleher. Lisch tallied from the 7 for a 23-0 lead, as the defense held Miami to 3 yards rushing and three completions. Lisch scored on a keeper in the third quarter, and Miami broke a kickoff return for a touchdown. Lisch passed sparingly, killing time, and Reeve hit a field goal in the fourth quarter. A Miami fumble allowed Hunter to score from the 14. With the win, Notre Dame accepted a Gator Bowl bid to meet Penn State.

Questionable officiating helped USC win. USC scored with a 6-yard pass to Sheldon Diggs, and made it 14-0 with a 63-yard touchdown pass. In the fourth quarter, Lisch found Ferguson for a 17-yard touchdown pass; a bad call on Bradley for interference led to a Trojan field goal. Lisch scored from the 1 to make the final score USC 17, Notre Dame 13.

In the Gator Bowl, Penn State opened with a field goal, but Eurick returned the kickoff to their 35; Hunter converted a fourth down play and then scored from the 1. A Heimkreiter tackle of a Penn State runner led to a fumble and a 23-yard Reeve field goal. Hunter scored again from the 1, and Reeve booted another 23-yard field goal. Penn State scored on a Fusina to Suhey pass for the final score of a solid 20-9 Irish win.

The 1976 Irish passed for 45 percent more yardage than in 1975, and the defense made the running game even tougher for opponents. A solid group of runners developed, and the core of the defense gained valuable experience. Ross Browner won the Outland Trophy and was joined by fellow All-Americans MacAfee, Bradley, and Fry.

1976 record: 9-3-0 (.750)

Record to date: 580-156-38 (.773)

1977

Joe Montana was back after a year's recuperation—buried in the third team. The offensive line was a record 256 pounds per man. MacAfee was back for

The 1977 Notre Dame Fighting Irish.

Dan Devine and staff in 1977.

a third year as an All-American, and Kris Haines provided good speed and great hands as the split end. Lisch started at quarterback; behind him were Ferguson at left halfback and Dave Waymer at right halfback. Heavens was fullback. When Montana was in, this was an outstanding backfield, with great speed, good size, and good hands. On defense, Browner and Fry were back. The tackles and linebackers all returned, as did the entire secondary. This was a strong team with no apparent deficiencies.

Nevertheless, the Fighting Irish did not have a strong showing against a Dorsett-less Pitt, winning 19-9. A Lisch pass was intercepted, and Matt Cavanaugh threw a 25-yard touchdown pass. Cavanaugh, however, never saw the pass being caught because he was hit by Willie Fry just as he threw; the big end and Cavanaugh landed together, and the fall broke Cavanaugh's wrist. A few plays later, punter Joe Restic missed the snap and Pitt earned a safety. Pitt intercepted another Lisch pass, but without Cavanaugh their offense lacked direction. Lisch found MacAfee for a 5-yard touchdown, but the point after was blocked. Although behind 9-6 at the half, Notre Dame, from the point of Cavanaugh's injury, had allowed Pitt a total of 6 yards. Golic grabbed a Pitt fumble on their 16 and Reeve tied it with a field goal. Ross Browner rounded up a bad pitchout and Reeve made his second field goal. Jim Browner picked up a fumble after a pass reception and Eurick scored from the 4.

Mississippi beat the Fighting Irish 20-13. The only score in the first quarter was an Ol' Miss field goal. In the next quarter, Heavens blasted in from the 2, after a Jim Browner interception, for a 7-3 lead. The Rebels fought back, going 75 yards in six plays, scoring on a 9-yard pass play. Jay Case grabbed an Ol' Miss fumble and Reeve kicked a field goal. Another fumble, another Reeve field goal, and a 13-10 lead. But the Irish offense was misfiring badly. A new Rebel quarterback executed a five-play, 80-yard drive, and finished it with a 10-yard touchdown pass. Notre Dame later fumbled and Mississippi kicked a field goal.

Purdue's freshman quarterback, Mark Hermann, directed his team to a touchdown on its first possession. Becker picked off a Hermann pass on their next series. Lisch threw to Eurick for Notre Dame's first score. Purdue scored a field goal and two more touchdowns on Hermann passes, while Notre Dame managed only one more touchdown before the half. The defense took command in the third quarter, and Forystek moved the team well until his collarbone was broken on a rollout. Montana came in, but no miracle—just a field goal. Hermann kept passing. Bradley intercepted, and the Irish were at their 48. Montana fired to Haines and MacAfee, finally scoring with a 13-yard throw to MacAfee. Purdue was shut down on offense; Montana got the ball at his own 30 with 3 minutes to go. Sixty yards and four passes later, the Fighting Irish were on the Purdue 10. Dave Mitchell ran it in from the 5 for a 31-24 win, the third comeback victory in Joe Montana's career.

Devine gave the start to Montana against Michigan State. A fumble and interception stopped two Notre Dame drives, and MSU scored a field goal. Heavens dropped a perfectly thrown pass, but Notre Dame salvaged a field goal. Notre Dame's Mitchell scored a touchdown to make it 10-3 at halftime. Waymer fumbled; Reeve missed a field goal. But the defense was hammering the Spartans. A Golic interception led to a 40-yard Reeve field goal, and a Restic pick netted another field goal. The Spartans later kicked one to end it at 16-6 in favor of the Irish.

Against Army, Heavens became the first modern Fighting Irish runner to gain 200 yards on the ground (John Farley had once run for 464 yards in the 1890s). Penalties, fumbles, and poor passing meant a scoreless first period. A bad Army punt gave Montana the chance he needed; he directed a 47-yard drive in five plays. Heavens picked up 43 of the yards and scored from the 3. In the third quarter, with a scant 7-point lead, Notre Dame kept the ball for 10 minutes. After six straight runs by Heavens, Reeve kicked a 29-yard field goal. Mike Whittington intercepted an Army pass, and Montana moved in for the kill. Eurick ended a 75-yard drive with a 2-yard touchdown burst, and later scored from the 3. The final score was 24-0.

Ken MacAfee, a three-year starter at TE and consensus All-American in 1977, cuts to the middle of the Georgia Tech defense in the 1977 blowout.

For USC, Devine concocted a ploy to add more charge to his players. After their pre-game warmup, they returned to the lockers to find new kelly green jerseys with gold numbers. The locker room went nuts at the sight. Fans went berserk when the team came back out. The Trojans first drive ended with a missed field goal, and Notre Dame's offense did what it was supposed to do—take it right to the other team, control the line of scrimmage, and make no mistakes. Heavens ran well, and Montana looked sharp; Dave Mitchell scored with a 4-yard run. USC missed another field goal, but Eurick fumbled, and USC scored an easy 3-yard touchdown. Charles White coughed up the ball on his 14, and Montana sneaked in from the 1 six plays later. A bobbled point-after snap ended up as a 2-point conversion for the Fighting Irish. Bradley intercepted a USC pass, the 16th in his career. The Irish seemed stopped, but Burgmeier

Joe Montana, one of the most famous Notre Dame graduates.

called a fake field goal and moved the sticks. Montana tossed a 12-yard scoring pass to MacAfee for a 22-7 lead. Golic blocked a punt, and tackle Jay Case scored on a 30-yard runback. In the third quarter, Montana put together a good drive and a 1-yard touchdown lob to MacAfee. The teams traded touchdowns, Montana's on a 1-yard keeper. Lisch threw a 4-yard touchdown pass to Kevin Hart for the 49-19 final score. Years of frustration seemed redeemed by this win.

That victory helped the offense start playing with intensity and competence. Navy went down 43-10. Heavens scored a 49-yard touchdown. Reeve kicked three field goals in the second quarter. Montana scored from the 1 on a sneak and later threw a 7-yard touchdown to Mitchell. Reserves scored the last two touchdowns: Jim Stone on a 58-yard sprint and Leopold with an interception and a 50-yard return.

The next game was a grudge match for Notre Dame's linemen—Georgia Tech, who bragged in 1976 that the Fighting Irish were slow and fat. Georgia Tech lost 69-14. There was no scoring for more than a quarter. Notre Dame then rained touchdowns: Montana from the 1 (followed by a kickoff return for a score), Eurick with an 8-yard touchdown pass, Haines with a 19-yard touchdown pass, Waymer with a 68-yard touchdown pass, Heavens from the 2, Ferguson from the 1 and from 56 yards out, Jim Stone from the 21 and 24, and Speedy Hart with a 31-yard pass from Tim Koegel. The Fighting Irish offense exploded for 667 yards.

Ernie Hughes, starter at RG from 1975 to 1977, ready to unload on a Georgia Tech defender in the 1977 rout.

Vagas Ferguson's quick start against Clemson in 1977.

The Fighting Irish nipped Clemson 21-17. Joe Montana pulled out a win. Heavens scored from the 5, but early in the second quarter Irish drives fizzled. Clemson kicked a field goal, and their quarterback shook loose for a 10-yard touchdown run. In the third quarter, Clemson showed their "twelfth man" play; referee W.R. Cummings "threw" a good brush block to spring their tailback for a 2-yard touchdown. A Clemson fumble at the Notre Dame 16 gave Montana what he needed. Montana scored from the 1 after a drive in which he faced a second-and-31 on penalties. Mike Calhoun recovered his second fumble, and Montana wrapped it up with a quarterback sneak from the 1.

After that narrow escape, Notre Dame beat Air Force 49-0. Ferguson ran for a 56-yard touchdown on the first play. Ferguson scored again from the 9. A 13-yard Falcon punt set up a Heavens score from the 1. In the second quarter, four gains set up Ferguson's touchdown from the 2. Haines capped the first half with a 33-yard touchdown pass from Montana. Reserves finished it: Eurick from the 1 and Steve Schmitz on an 11-yard touchdown pass from Lisch. Notre Dame gained 680 yards to the Falcons' 102. Notre Dame accepted the Cotton Bowl bid to play Texas and Heisman winner Earl Campbell.

Miami was dispensed with 48-10. Fry welcomed their freshman quarterback with two sacks. Golic grabbed a fumble after the first sack, and Ferguson scored from the 11. The second led to Leopold's third career touchdown from the 17. Miami scored its 10 points in the second quarter. Montana fired back with a 23-yard touchdown pass to Haines. In the third quarter, Montana decimated Miami's defense with three long drives. MacAfee caught touchdown passes of 3 and 4 yards. Mitchell scored between those two from the 4. Lisch went in from the 1. Notre Dame gained 404 total yards, while Miami gained only 28 yards on the ground.

Texas was hot, and Campbell reportedly was unstoppable. But he mishandled a pitchout on their fifth play, and Browner recovered the ball. Reeve kicked a field goal. The Longhorns got to the Irish 13 on good runs, but then they started to pass and their quarterback was sacked twice. They kicked a field goal to end the first quarter tied 3-3. Montana led the Fighting Irish back to the 6; Eurick scored on the first play of the second quarter. Moments later, the Texas quarterback dropped the ball and Fry recovered. Eurick ended a short drive with an 8-yard touchdown blast. Texas intercepted a Montana overthrow, but Texas quarterback McEachern threw a pass right to Becker on the 40. He ran to the 17, and three plays later Montana threw a touchdown pass to Ferguson. It had been a disastrous quarter for Texas. Golic and Bradley blocked a field goal, but Texas scored a touchdown with no time on the clock for a 24-10 Longhorn deficit at the half. In the third quarter, Heimkreiter intercepted a pass, and Ferguson ran for a 3-yard touchdown. Ferguson scored from the 26 in the fourth quarter for a 38-10 triumph. Campbell gained 116 yards on 29 carries, which was remarkable since Golic was on him all day. For Notre Dame, Heavens gained 101 yards, and Ferguson 100. The Fighting Irish won the national championship with their convincing win over an undefeated number-one team.

Ross Browner won the Maxwell Award and the Lombardi Award. MacAfee won the Walter Camp Award. Other All-Americans were Bradley, Hughes, Golic, Fry, and Burgmeier. It's a shame that Montana was not similarly recognized, but perhaps it's even worse that he *never* reached that collegiate height.

1977 record: 11-1-0 (.916)
Record to date: 591-157-38 (.776)

Jerome Heavens, Irish FB in 1977 and 1978.

1978

Devine had to replace key personnel—the right side of the offensive line, both defensive ends, and the left corner. Five were All-Americans. There were capable replacements, but it's hard to fill in for All-Americans. The backfield, newly configured with a pro-style flanker, featured Montana, Ferguson, Heavens, and Pete Holohan as the flanker. There was excellent potential for scoring. The defensive linemen were slightly smaller than those on the offense; the premium on defense was placed on quickness and mobility. Weston and Calhoun were experienced tackles, but the ends were new to starting. The linebacking corps was in fine hands with Golic, Heimkreiter, and Leopold. Waymer switched from offense to fill Bradley's shoes. The safeties were Jim Browner and Restic. Overall, the defense probably would be vulnerable to the run.

The defense of the national title started with two losses, a pattern not seen in two decades under the

Jim Browner, starter at FB and at SS, specialized in blitzing for the 1977 and 1978 Irish.

Dome. The first loss was to Missouri, 3-0; Notre Dame had not been shut out since the 0-0 tie with Miami in 1965. Against Mizzou, missed opportunities were the story: a fumbled snap at the Missouri 18; a Montana fourth-down run stopped short at the Missouri 11; failure to convert a recovered fumble on Notre Dame's 17 into points; a personal foul at the 4 moving the ball back to the 19; a muffed field goal snap and a misfired pass to the "hot" player (the player who is supposed to go for the ball). With 13 minutes left in the game, Missouri moved from its 14 to the Notre Dame 16 and scored the game's only field goal. Notre Dame had three more chances: a fourth-down run by Heavens was stopped short at their 28; with 3:31 left, Ferguson fumbled on their 25; and Harrison fumbled a punt with 1:15 left. Devine blamed his coaching for the loss in not taking his chances with the field goal sooner. It was the most embittering loss of his Notre Dame career.

The next loss was to Michigan; the series had been renewed after a 35-year hiatus. The Wolverines defeated Notre Dame 28-14 in South Bend (as had Missouri). A fumble on the kickoff led to a Montana 6-yard touchdown pass to Dennis Grindinger, his tight end, for an early lead. The next two Fighting Irish drives were ended by a penalty and a dropped pass, followed by a missed field goal. The Irish were on Michigan's 33 but lost a pitchout. Michigan put together its own drive, with Rick Leach going in from the 4. The Irish helped out with two offside penalties. Montana brought Notre Dame back, and Ferguson scored from the 4. In the third quarter, a Fighting Irish drive died at the Michigan 24. More adversity—two interceptions—led to two Wolverine touchdowns from Leach to Clayton of 5 and 17 yards. They also scored Michigan's last touchdown, a 40-yarder. Montana was nailed for a safety. The bright spot was Golic's 26 tackles, a new Irish record.

The Fighting Irish nipped Purdue 10-6. The offense was uninspired, but the defense was stifling. Purdue led at the half on two field goals. The Irish offense asserted itself on a short drive of 46 yards; Heavens scored from the 27. Joe Unis kicked a 27-yard field goal halfway into the third quarter. Heimkreiter made 24 tackles and intercepted a Purdue pass at the Notre Dame 21 in the last 2 minutes.

The offense showed more signs of waking up in a 29-25 win over Michigan State. The Spartans scored on a 25-yard Morten Anderson field goal. Heavens scored from the 1, set up by a Montana to Haines pass of 35 yards. MSU passed for a 59-yard gain to set up another field goal. The next Fighting Irish drive, of 78 yards, was the first of the year in which the offense dominated its opponent. Done basically on the ground, Montana ended it with a 1-yard sneak. Greg Knafelc passed to Nick Vehr for a 2-point conversion. The last score of the half came when Jim Browner stripped a receiver of the ball and ran 45 yards for a touchdown. MSU scored in the third quarter, making it 22-13. The Fighting Irish drove 81 yards in 11 running plays. Ferguson scored from the 11. MSU scored twice, but failed with both 2-point conversions.

Pitt went down 26-17. Heavens opened with a 2-yard smash to end a drive begun by Tom Gibbons' interception. That was it for Notre Dame's scoring for more than two quarters. Pitt tied it with a second-quarter drive of 79 yards, capped by a 3-yard touchdown run. They scored a 33-yard field goal after Jim Stone fumbled. Pitt scored a quarterback keeper in the right corner of the end zone. Montana led an 86-yard drive and finished it with an 8-yard touchdown pass to Haines. The 2-point try failed, and Notre Dame was down 17-13. Pitt was stopped after one first down, and Montana was 59 yards from a win. He hit Haines for 29 yards, and Dean Masztak for 22. Eventually, Montana wiggled in from the 1. With 7 minutes left, Pitt fumbled; Case recovered at their 29. Montana flipped a 3-yard pass to Ferguson for the insurance touchdown. Heavens gained 130 yards on 30 carries and surpassed Gipp's all-time running total of 2,341 yards.

Notre Dame was playing well, and beat Air Force, 38-15. Chuck Male kicked a field goal of 42 yards. Restic intercepted an Air Force pass, and Ferguson scored from the 24 for a 10-0 lead. The Falcons scored after Notre Dame botched a reverse, but Montana tallied on bursts of 1 and 4 yards for a 24-7 halftime lead. Haines increased it with a 56-yard touchdown reception, and Grindinger scored with another Montana pass, from the 9. Air Force scored a touchdown and a 2-point conversion.

Notre Dame needed an impressive win against Miami to keep the bowl committees interested. Little happened in the first quarter; then Heimkreiter tackled a tight end, who fumbled. Golic recovered on their 30. Six runs later, Ferguson scored from the 4. Male hit a 47-yard field goal after a Restic fumble recovery in the third quarter. Ferguson added another touchdown with a 3-yard blast, and Waymer intercepted a pass to set up Male's 37-yard field goal. Miami never was able to get Ottis Anderson into scoring territory, as Notre Dame prevailed 20-0.

Navy was number one in total defense and number two in rushing defense; they were undefeated in seven games. Notre Dame won 27-7. Ferguson rushed for 219 yards, the best single game effort in the modern era (to give Notre Dame its top two single game runners in the *same* backfield). Montana flipped a 20-yard touchdown pass to Haines after Weston recovered a Middie fumble. Four plays later, Case picked up a loose ball; Male kicked a 38-yard field goal. Heavens started a drive with a 39-yard sweep and finished it with a 3-yard touchdown run. Navy fumbled, and Ferguson sprinted 80 yards for another touchdown and a 24-0 lead. Three later Fighting Irish drives were stopped at the 1, 2, and 12. Male hit another field goal in the third period and Navy scored with 12 seconds left in the game.

Dave Huffman, Irish starter at center from 1976 to 1978.

Tennessee was defeated 31-14. Male kicked a 24-yard field goal. The Volunteers came back with a 6-yard touchdown on an option play. A bad Tennessee punt in the second quarter led to another Male field goal for a 7-6 halftime score. Freshman Bob Crable blocked a punt at the Tennessee 16, and freshman Pete Buchanan muscled in from the 2 for the touchdown. Montana hit Holohan for a 2-point conversion. Waymer returned a punt 46 yards to their 30; Male kicked his third field goal, another 37-yarder. A good Restic punt put the Volunteers in trouble at their 3; they tried passing, but Calhoun tackled their quarterback, who lost the ball. Hankerd recovered at the 3, and Montana took it in from the 5 moments later. The Volunteers scored on a 73-yard pass when Restic and Waymer eliminated each other on the coverage, but Restic later intercepted and ran back a 30-yard touchdown.

The Irish ended Georgia Tech's seven-game winning streak, 38-21. Ferguson ran 68 yards on the second play from scrimmage to set up Male's 23-yard field goal. Ferguson's running kept Georgia Tech off balance in the second quarter; Montana threw a 20-yard touchdown to Pete Pallas. Ferguson ran for a 20-yard touchdown. Tech scored on a 10-yard pass play for a 17-7 halftime score. In the first half, Ferguson gained 188 yards. Most of the third quarter was a defensive standoff, but Montana moved Notre Dame 52 yards and went over from the 1 to score. He found Haines for a 5-yard touchdown in the fourth quarter. Tech scored on a 64-yard pass play. Jim Stone racked up a score from the 5 with the reserves. Tech got the last score on a 6-yard pass. Ferguson gained 255 yards, a single game record, and Montana hit 10 consecutive passes to tie Bertelli's record. The Fighting Irish accepted a bid to play Houston in the Cotton Bowl.

But USC was first; it was one of the all-time great games, with 949 yards of total offense in a 27-

Ross Browner and Bob Golic do a number on Earl Campbell in the 1978 Cotton Bowl win over Texas that cinched the national title for the Irish.

25 Trojan win. For three quarters, Notre Dame only had two Male field goals and trailed 24-6 going into the last period. USC had scored on a 30-yard pass, a 35-yard pass, a 39-yard field goal, and a 1-yard touchdown by Charles White. A Notre Dame drive died when Montana fumbled at the USC 1; the Trojans killed the clock with a 96-yard drive that ended in a missed field goal. That time was crucial, as it turned out. Montana spotted Haines in a soft spot in the USC coverage and threw a 57-yard touchdown pass. The Trojans drove to the Notre Dame 38 and punted to the Irish 2. Less then 7 minutes were left. Montana passed for 81 yards: four throws to Haines of 7, 18, 19, and 20 yards, one to Masztak to the 17, and his own run of 15 to the 3. Buchanan slammed in over right guard to make it 24-19. After a poor USC punt, the Irish took over at the Trojan 43. With 1:35 left, Montana passed and ran, throwing a 2-yard touchdown to Holohan. Notre Dame led, 25-24. The 2-point try failed. USC "won" the game when a Weston hit and fumble recovery was ruled an incomplete pass, allowing a USC field goal with seconds left. (In the Rose Bowl, White would "score" a touchdown without the ball on another official's error.) Montana amassed 358 yards on 20 of 41 passes. Haines caught nine for 179 yards and one touchdown.

The Cotton Bowl was played under bizarre conditions. There were 39,500 fans imitating empty seats because of bitterly cold temperatures and ice that forced people to stay home. The game itself got off to a Marx Brothers' "Duck Soup" start when both kickoff teams lined up and faced each other—eventually, the Cougars kicked off to Notre Dame. Randy Harrison made a 56-yard return on the ice. After slipping and sliding, Notre Dame scored on a 66-yard drive, with Montana skating to a touchdown in the right corner from the 3. Crable recovered Houston's kickoff fumble, and Buchanan bulled in from the 1 six plays later. Both conversions were missed. Then a referee ruled that a punt had touched Waymer, so the Cougars got the ball on the Notre Dame 12. Houston scored for a 12-7 game. In the next quarter, moving into the unpredictable, bitter wind, a Fighting Irish fumble gave Houston another score. A fluttering Montana pass was intercepted, and Houston kicked a field goal. Another interception gave them another field goal. In the third quarter, with no sign of Montana, the Cougars put together a short drive and scored on a 2-yard quarterback keeper. Houston blocked an Irish punt and scored three plays later for a 34-12 lead.

By this time the soup was beginning to work—given to Montana at halftime for hypothermia. There were only 5 minutes left in the third quarter when Montana arrived. Notre Dame had not moved past its 21 in his absence. His second play was an interception. Montana had the wind to his back in the fourth quarter and went to work on the 22-point deficit. He started with yet another interception, but Houston did not get a first down in the last quarter, and the ball came right back. Tony Belden blocked a Houston punt, and Steve Cichy scored with the deflection after a 33-yard return. Montana made a 2-point conversion; the score was 34-20 with 7:25 left. Houston had to punt again. Good passing and an interference call got Montana to the 2; he scored on a rollout and threw a 2-point conversion to Haines. Waymer broke up a third-down pass moments later, and Houston had to punt. Montana, with 2:25 left, got to the Houston 20, but fumbled. The Irish got the ball back with 28 seconds. Montana threw into the right corner to Haines, but he just missed. He tried it again, and it worked. The score was 34-34. A penalty on the kick made Unis kick again, and it was good—35-34, Notre Dame's 600th victory. This finish might rival the 1935 win over Ohio State.

There was no justice for Joe Montana. After his great personal feats in 1978, he was once again not elected to an All-American team. Golic and Dave Huffman earned the honors, and deserved them.

1978 record: 9-3-0 (.750)
Record to date: 600-160-38 (.775)

1979

All the Irish needed in 1979 was a replacement for "The Comeback Kid." Rusty Lisch, the 1977 early season starter, was on hand, with capable replacements in the wings. Ferguson was back. John Sweeney was at least adequate as fullback. Freshman split end Tony Hunter, provided good speed and great size. The line was solid, with veteran leadership and excellent size. This offense would have a one-dimensional running game and a serious deep threat in Hunter, but lacked the sparkle that Montana provided.

The defensive line came in at 235 pounds per man (as opposed to 255 pounds for the offensive line). The linebackers were also smaller than the previous group, but faster. Crable held down the middle, flanked by Whittington and Leopold. Waymer led a young group of deep backs.

This young team, with no proven leader, went to Ann Arbor for its maiden outing against a loaded Michigan team. They did not score a touchdown and gave up 306 yards to Michigan's offense while they gained only 179 yards, completing five of 12 passes. They also won, 12-10, on Male's four field goals, a defense that kept Michigan penned up in the second half, and Crable's block of a field goal with 6 seconds left in the game. Ferguson carried 35 times (63 percent of the offensive plays and 77 percent of the running plays). Michigan kicked a field goal of 30 yards. Male hit a 40-yarder after Anthony Carter fumbled a punt. In the second quarter, the Wolverines drove 80 yards, scoring from the 1. The Irish kicked a 39-yard field goal for a 10-6 halftime score. In the third quarter, the Fighting Irish drove 65 yards for a Male field goal. Less than 5 minutes later, he kicked a 39-yard field goal and Notre Dame led 12-10. In the fourth quarter, Michigan intercepted a pass to start its final drive, which Crable ruined with his block.

Nineteen Irish players were injured when the game with Michigan was over. Devine called for some trickery at the first opportunity against Purdue—a fake field goal try at the Boilermaker 17. It worked, and Greg Knafelc found Masztak for a touchdown pass. Purdue tied it 12 plays later on a 15-yard pass. Male hit two field goals in the next quarter, the second set up by a fake flanker reverse which turned into a 34-yard pass from Holohan to Hunter. The Fighting Irish moved well in the third quarter on a 62-yard drive ended by a Koegel to Nick Vehr touchdown pass from the 4. Purdue made a long drive and scored from the 1, and then intercepted a pass and converted it into a

The 1979 Tri-captains, Tim Foley, Dave Waymer, Vagas Ferguson, and Coach Devine.

touchdown. The Irish never made another first down, and a fourth-quarter Purdue touchdown won it 28-22. It was Notre Dame's 800th game.

The seventh-ranked Michigan State team opened the home season for Notre Dame, losing 27-3. They could not move the ball well, and two drives spent in their half of the field eventually earned Hunter a 14-yard touchdown pass from Lisch. Two drives later, Male booted a 49-yard field goal. Michigan State punted badly, and Male kicked a 36-yarder. MSU finally booted a 53-yard field goal, equal to any ever kicked in the stadium. A hard hit on their only ambulatory quarterback by Hankerd turned their punter into a quarterback. Ferguson scored on a 24-yard run, they punted, and Ferguson ran 48 yards down the sideline for the last touchdown.

Against Georgia Tech, Dave Duerson, replacing the injured Waymer, intercepted a Georgia Tech pass on their 41 and ran it back to the 8. Ferguson scored from the 3. Tech scored on an 80-yard pass when their quarterback bobbled the snap just long enough for the deep backs to read a running play. A Scott Zettek tackle led to another Duerson fumble recovery; Ferguson gained more yardage, and Ty Barber ran it in from the 4. Tech hit a 41-yard field goal in the second quarter. In the fourth quarter, Tech lost a lateral to Crable, and Ferguson scored on a 17-yard run for the 21-13 Notre Dame win.

Notre Dame bombed Air Force 38-13, with scores on each of the first three possessions: a Ferguson blast from the 5, a 43-yard Male field goal after a Leopold interception, and a Lisch sneak from the 3. The defense was now missing five starters. Air Force scored a touchdown, and the Irish came back, led by a 59-yard pass to Holohan; Vehr gained the last 17 yards on two receptions and scored. The Falcons dropped the ball on the kickoff, Dan Stone recovered, and Ferguson ran it in. The last Fighting Irish touchdown went to Hunter twice—an 80-yarder lost to a penalty and a 75-yarder.

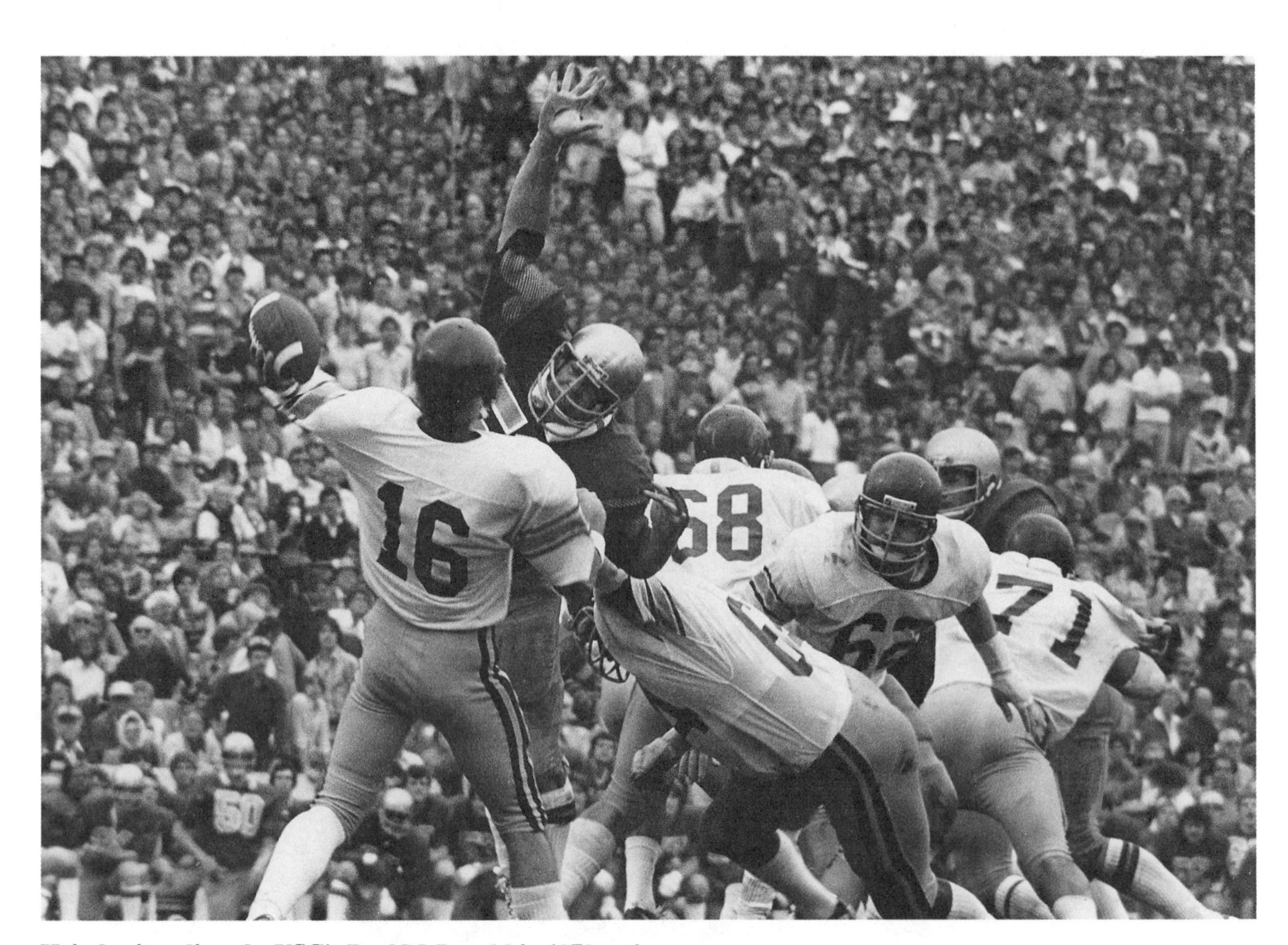

Heimkreiter disturbs USC's Paul McDonald in 1979 action.

Bobby Leopold, speedy Irish LB in 1978 and 1979 scored 2 career TDs with interceptions.

USC won 42-23, as the teams amassed 1,128 yards of offense. Early in the game, Ferguson became the all-time rushing leader on a 79-yard run. Notre Dame failed to score and USC drove 99 yards for a touchdown. Ferguson tied it with a 1-yard slam just before the half. In the third quarter, USC rolled against the Fighting Irish defense; Charles White scored from the 3. Ferguson led the Irish back, but Lisch fumbled. White scored from the 1. Lisch's passing set up a 21-yard touchdown burst by Ferguson, but USC exploited the Irish secondary for a 12-yard touchdown pass. Hunter caught two from Lisch for 66 yards and Stone scored from the 2. USC burned the deep backs again with a 46-yard pass, and White scored from the 1. The Irish answered with a 42-yard field goal. An interception set up White for another 1-yard touchdown run. For the game, White carried 44 times for 261 yards and four touchdowns to Ferguson's 25 runs for 185 yards and two scores. White averaged almost 6 yards per carry, and Ferguson almost 7.5. USC's quarterback, Paul McDonald, passed for 311 yards to Lisch's 286.

Notre Dame beat South Carolina 18-17, winning in the last 42 seconds. Notre Dame kicked a field goal in the first half, and then watched the Gamecocks score 17 points in the third quarter: a 62-yard pass, a 49-yard run, and a 39-yard field goal. Ferguson made a 26-yard touchdown near the end of the quarter. After a 9-minute South Carolina possession, Lisch had 1:36 left, trailing 17-10. He completed three passes and grabbed a deflected pass for a short gain. From their 14, he fired to Masztak for a touchdown and a 17-16 score. Lisch threw to Holohan in the left corner of the end zone; he juggled it but brought it in for the conversion and the 18-17 win. It was Lisch's finest hour as an Irish quarterback.

The Fighting Irish barely beat Navy, 14-0. Lisch led a 73-yard drive and scored from the 1 early in the game, followed by lost opportunities, until Ferguson rammed in a 3-yard touchdown in the fourth quarter to finish a 70-yard, six-run (all his) drive. The Irish defense held Navy in check throughout.

The Irish were in the running for a Sugar Bowl bid, but Tennessee destroyed that with a 40-18 win. Ferguson scored from the 1. The Volunteers went ahead 7-6. Tennessee scored 23 points in the second quarter: their second-string fullback ran for three touchdowns, and Lisch went down for a safety. Ferguson answered with a 2-yard scoring run. In the third, Tennessee scored another 10 points on a fullback touchdown and a field goal. Ferguson scored from the 10 to end it. The Volunteers ran for 352 yards, much of it up the middle.

Clemson nipped the faltering Irish 16-10 in South Bend. Clemson was ranked 14th, but Notre Dame beat themselves with turnovers. Male booted a 42-yard field goal. Freshman Phil Carter made a good showing on a second quarter drive to help divert attention from Ferguson, who scored from the 2. A dropped punt led to a 33-yard field goal by Clemson; they controlled the ball, keeping it for 22 minutes in the second half. A second field goal made it 10-6, but a Ferguson fumble on the Notre Dame 20 gave Clemson an easy touchdown. Hunter tipped a pass at the 3, and Clemson recovered.

A 6-4 Notre Dame team went to Tokyo to play Miami on a marshy field. The Japanese would have liked a better record from the Fighting Irish, but Notre Dame won 40-15 anyway. Ferguson slushed 35 times for 177 yards, and Waymer scored twice on interceptions. Ferguson scored a 2-yard touchdown, and Waymer picked a Jim Kelly pass at the 3 for a touchdown. Miami drove for a touchdown. The Fighting Irish came back all the way to the 1 but did not score. Crable blocked a punt for a safety, and Male hit his 13th field goal of the year, a new record. Ferguson ran twice from the 18 for a touchdown, and scored again from the 1 in the fourth quarter. Waymer's second interception went for 37 yards and his second touchdown before Miami scored with 4 seconds left.

Ferguson ended his year with a record 1,437 yards running, 17 touchdowns, and 3,472 career rushing yards. The second leading 1979 rusher for Notre Dame, Ty Barber, had 172 yards. This was the worst Notre Dame season in 16 years. Ferguson and Tim Foley earned All-American honors.

1979 record: 7-4-0 (.636)

Record to date: 607-164-38 (.773)

1980 to 1989

1980

On a Saturday in fall practice, Devine revealed that this would be his last season at Notre Dame. He was not being pressured by anyone; he enjoyed the support of the administration, there was team unity, and there was no undue alumni pressure. His wife's deteriorating health was the deciding factor. He had agonized over his commitments to players and family. The tri-captains (John Scully, Bob Crable, and Tom Gibbons) spoke to the team alone and emphasized playing for the institution, not the coach.

The team came together and played as they should. Hunter was back as a deep threat; the line had some excellent players, especially Tom Thayer, Tim Huffman, and Dean Masztak, Devine's favorite tight end. Mike Courey started as quarterback for two games, but freshman Blair Kiel would take over. Phil Carter was the wave of the near future—a fast, small back with great leg drive and lateral mobility. Jim Stone was behind him. Sweeney returned at fullback from a broken ankle. Holohan returned as flanker. This was a large, fast offensive outfit.

The defense had three returners on the line and a combination of speed and size. The linebackers were a strong contingent—Crable, Mark Zavagnin, and Joe Rudzinski. The deep backs lost Waymer, but Stacy Toran would hold the job for four years, and Duerson returned. This was a good squad with some heavy hitters in key places.

The first test was against Purdue, and the Fighting Irish passed 31-10. Mike Courey shredded the Purdue secondary with 10 of 13 passes for 151 yards and a touchdown. Carter led the runners with 142 yards on 29 carries. Harry Oliver kicked a 36-yard field goal, and Courey led the team on a return trip of 57 yards, running and passing well; Rob McGarry went in from the 2. Purdue was unable to move for the third time and Masztak caught a 28-yard pass from Courey and Carter slammed in from the 1. Purdue drove 74 yards but stalled at the Irish 9; they booted a field goal. The Fighting Irish fumbled, and Purdue scored a touchdown from the 4. In the third quarter, Courey and Hunter conspired on a drive, highlighting it with a 57-yard play that left the deep backs baffled; Hunter scored from the 9. The Irish defense clamped down, getting minus 54 yards in sacks. Courey closed the scoring with a 14-yard run in the fourth quarter.

After waiting two weeks, Notre Dame met Michigan. The Wolverines drove, but a field goal try missed. In the second quarter, a 16-play drive ended

Dean Masztak, starting TE in 1979 and 1980, in a 18-17 squeaker over the Gamecocks.

when Phil Carter ran in from the 6. Michigan couldn't move and punted. Courey threw a 16-yard pass to Hunter and a 10-yard touchdown pass to Holohan. Michigan scored. Michigan intercepted a pass at midfield to set up the tying touchdown, a 9-yard pass with half a minute to go in the half. In the third quarter, Anthony Carter returned the kickoff 67 yards, and they rammed it in from the 2. The Fighting Irish offense stalled, but John Krimm intercepted a pass and returned it 49 yards for a touchdown. Oliver missed the point after. A Michigan fumble was recovered by Crable. Hunter threw a 31-yard pass off a fake reverse, and Phil Carter ran in from the 4 for the 26-20 lead. Michigan came right back, led by Butch Woolfolk's running, for a touchdown pass from the 1. A 2-point try missed, and they led 27-26. Devine sent in Kiel at quarterback, his first college experience, with the ball on the Notre Dame 20 and 41 seconds left. With fitful passing and a penalty, Kiel coaxed the Irish to the Michigan 34 with 4 seconds left. Oliver came in for a 51-yard field goal try, with Koegel holding, against a 15 mph wind. His longest try had been a 38-yarder in a junior varsity game. Oliver made the kick for a dramatic 29-27 Irish victory. Devine was so choked with emotion afterwards, he was unable to speak to the media.

The Fighting Irish beat Michigan State 26-21. The Spartans took the early lead on a Morten Anderson field goal, and drove 60 yards in 10 plays for a touchdown and a 9-0 lead. Oliver kicked two field goals, 44 and 49 yards, for a 9-6 halftime score. Notre Dame took the lead in the third quarter with a 51-yard march and Carter's 12-yard touchdown run. The defense stopped MSU, and Notre Dame scored another field goal from 27 yards. The Spartans used four plays to score. With the score 16-15, Jim Stone scored from the 1. Oliver booted another field goal. Carter ran the ball 40 times, a new record, for 254 yards, but he was injured, and Stone would take his place.

Miami was led by a quarterback who had been recruited by Penn State as a linebacker, Jim Kelly. Oliver made a field goal early in the second quarter. A

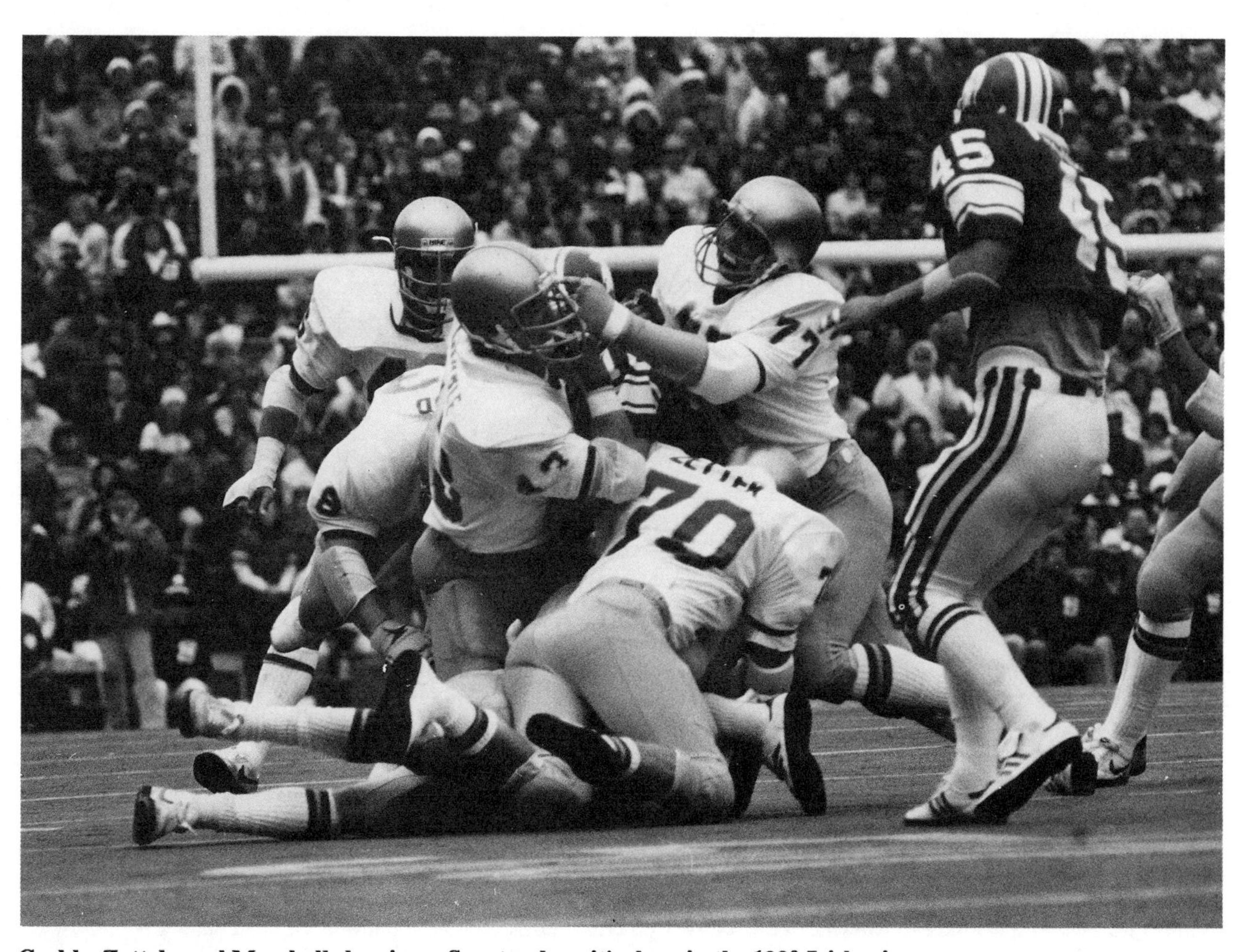

Crable, Zettek, and Marshall showing a Spartan how it's done in the 1980 Irish win.

good punt return by Duerson set Kiel up on their 29, and he scored from the 4 a few plays later. Rick Naylor recovered Miami's fumble of the kickoff and Oliver kicked another three-pointer. In the third quarter, another Oliver field goal followed yet another fumbled kickoff. Kelly hit a touchdown pass early in the fourth quarter. Gibbons intercepted a Kelly pass and ran it in for a 53-yard touchdown. Kelly threw a 37-yard touchdown pass to make it 22-14. Oliver hit another field goal, and Stone ran in a 27-yard touchdown in the final seconds. Stone carried 38 times for 224 yards to lead all runners.

Army lost 30-3. Stone scored from the 4 in the second quarter. Oliver kicked a 49-yard field goal, and Zavagnin recovered a blocked punt in the end zone for a touchdown. Army scored in the third quarter; Kiel scored on a 1-yard keeper. Army tried to play catch up, but Zavagnin intercepted a pass and Ty Barber scored from the 1. Stone again led all runners with 122 yards on 25 carries.

The Irish slipped by Arizona 20-3. Kiel used half of the first quarter to engineer the first score, his own from the 1. Arizona kicked a field goal in the second quarter. Kiel ran on a fake punt—for an 80-yard touchdown. Oliver finished with two field goals. Stone passed the century mark for the third game, with 105 yards on 29 carries.

Navy fell 33-0. Navy backed up Notre Dame to its 8, but Stone broke out for a 73-yard gain. Barber scored from the 9. Navy fumbled the kickoff on their 21, and Tim Marshall recovered. Six plays later, Pete Buchanan slammed in from the 3 for a 12-0 lead. In the second quarter, Stone scored a 13-yard touchdown, and Dave Condeni threw to Vehr for a 2-point conversion. Navy fumbled at their 15. Zavagnin recovered. A disgusted Navy defense played well, and Oliver kicked a field goal for a 23-0 lead. He booted one more, and Notre Dame held a 26-0 halftime lead. In the fourth quarter, with Courey at quarterback, Greg Bell ran for a 27-yard touchdown. Stone set a record with his fourth consecutive 100-yard plus game: 33 runs for 211 yards.

Georgia Tech tied 3-3. Notre Dame was ranked number one, while Georgia Tech had won one game. Tech booted a field goal in the second quarter. Notre Dame lost five fumbles and had to contend with a

Crable and Gramke prepare to interfere with Eddie Lee Ivery's plans in a 3-3 game with Georgia Tech.

An exalted Devine after the 7-0 win over 'Bama in 1980.

tough Tech defense all day. With less than 5 minutes to go in the game, Oliver hit a 47-yard field goal after a Stacy Toran interception. Stone was held to 85 yards.

Alabama promised to be tougher, much tougher. Zettek slammed Alabama's Major Ogilvie hard on the first play for a 2-yard loss (Ogilvie ran for 4 yards all day). In the second quarter, Hankerd recovered a Crimson Tide fumble at their 12, but Kiel muffed a snap and lost it. Zettek recovered another Alabama miscue at their 4. Four tough, crunching plays later, Carter dove for the game's only score. Oliver missed a field goal when he slipped, but Crable stopped an Alabama fourth-down play, and Bear Bryant had lost his fourth and final game to the Irish by a 7-0 margin.

An improved Air Force team played a tough game but lost 24-10. They staked an early lead on a field goal; in the second quarter Oliver kicked one after a fumble. In the third quarter, the Fighting Irish took command, led by Carter's 13 runs on a 14-play drive, gaining 71 yards, and scoring from the 2. Stone scored after the Falcons were stymied again. Air Force threatened in the fourth period with an interception and a follow-up touchdown, but Notre Dame killed the clock with an 80-yard drive. Stone scored a 2-yard touchdown. Carter ran 181 yards on 29 carries; Stone chipped in with 71 yards on 18 runs.

The new head coach was announced before the next game—Moeller High's Gerry Faust. It was a distraction during the days prior to the USC game. The Trojan defense kept Notre Dame from moving the sticks until the last 10 seconds of the first half. An Irish fumble at their 31 led directly to the first USC score, a 6-yard run by their fullback. They followed it with a field goal. Oliver booted a field goal following

Blair Kiel, first four-year starter at QB since Dorais.

Phil Carter goes into a cavernous hole between Sweeney and Foley in the 1980 Sugar Bowl action with Georgia.

a Trojan fumble at their 1-yard line, which Notre Dame could not convert into a touchdown. In the fourth quarter, USC made a 17-yard field goal and scored another touchdown for the 20-3 final score.

The Georgia Bulldogs were number one and had freshman phenomenon Herschel Walker for the Sugar Bowl game with the Irish. To start the game, the kickers did the scoring: Oliver with a 50-yarder and Robinson with a 46-yarder. Their ensuing kickoff was the turning point when Jim Stone called for Barber to take the kick, but Barber didn't hear the call, and the ball bounced around near the goal as Georgia players ran toward it. Stone saw the ball too late and Georgia had it at the 1. Two plays later, Walker bulled in for the touchdown. Another Notre Dame fumble, at their own 22, led to another easy touchdown for Walker. Good Georgia defense kept Notre Dame from scoring until the third quarter, when Carter went in from the 1. A final interception in the fourth quarter wrapped it up for Georgia, 17-10. Notre Dame outgained Georgia 328 yards to 127 and demolished their passing game (1 of 12 for 7 yards). Walker had 36 carries for 150 yards. One more time, too many Irish mistakes cost the game.

The passing game fell off 57 percent from 1979. The running game worked better. The defense improved greatly, but the story of this year was trying to get by with a freshman quarterback. Devine was leaving behind a good team for Faust. Scully, Crable, and Zettek were the All-American choices.

1980 record: 9-2-1 (.791)
Record to date: 616-166-39 (.774)

1981

Gerry Faust brought an incredible record from Moeller High in Cincinnati: 174 wins, 17 losses, and two ties for a .907 winning percentage (70-1 from 1975-1980). He was a demanding coach who preached excellence and commitment. He had an abiding love for Notre Dame, and the admiration was reciprocated. He had sent many players to college ball from Moeller—at one point when Notre Dame met Michigan, a dozen starters for the two teams came from Moeller. He thrived on pressure.

The big question was whether Faust would be able to make the adjustment to the college game. Notre Dame's experience with Brennan in the mid-1950s was potentially analogous, although Brennan was not much older than the seniors he coached. There may be disparities in the skills of players in college, but coaching skills are more widely and uniformly excellent in college than in high school. Great coaches, their chosen systems, and their chosen talent meet in big games. If there are failures over many years in any variable, either the coach changes or departs. It is rare for college coaches to be "outcoached" on a consistent basis. This general concern—the ability to coach at the college level—would be watched carefully by those closest to the program.

Faust inherited a good team, perhaps on the verge of becoming a great one. It had good size and excellent speed. Kiel could throw to Hunter (who was moved three times, ending at tight end) or to freshman

Phil Pozderac, 6' 9" and 270 pounds, started at RT in 1980 and 1981.

Joe Howard. The interior line was the largest on record, 260 pounds, with the right side gargantuan—Mike Shiner at 6-8 and 270 pounds and Phil Pozderac at 6-9 and 270 pounds. Phil Carter was tailback, and Sweeney returned at fullback. The defensive line was all new and tipped the scales at 245 pounds per man. It was vulnerable to the run. The linebackers returned as a unit and the secondary had two fine players in Duerson and Toran. Both units would face some difficulties in making the transition to different coaching and theories, and all would suffer a morale problem as the high promise of the pre-season disintegrated into the first losing season in 18 years.

The first score of the new era followed a Rudzinski hit on the LSU quarterback. He fumbled, Kevin Griffith recovered at the LSU 20, and Kiel hit Moriarty with a 7-yard touchdown. Faust's first Fighting Irish touchdown happened within 3 minutes. About 4 minutes later, the Irish had another touchdown after Greg Bell ran 41 yards down the sideline, and Carter scored from the 1. In the second quarter, Hunter scored from the 1 on a wingback run. Toran intercepted a touchdown pass in his end zone, and Crable smashed a drive with three straight tackles; LSU fumbled on fourth down at the Notre Dame 2. LSU kicked a field goal after a Kiel pass was intercepted. At the end of the third quarter, Koegel fired a 6-yard touchdown pass to Condeni. LSU scored in the final seconds as Notre Dame won 27-9.

Ranked first in the country, the Fighting Irish went to Ann Arbor and lost 25-7. Michigan moved 74 yards on the ground before missing a field goal. The

Greg Bell against LSU in 1981.

Irish drove back to the Michigan 4. Condeni tried a pass from a fake field goal formation, throwing to Hunter, who was tackled at the 4—no field goal, no touchdown. Michigan stormed back with four unanswered touchdowns: a 71-yard bomb to Anthony Carter, a 15-yard strike to Carter, a 1-yard smash by Lawrence Ricks, and a 6-yard quarterback keeper. Koegel found Masztak for an 8-yard touchdown completion, but it was too late. The Wolverines manhandled the defense for 304 yards on the ground, to only 70 for Notre Dame.

The Purdue team did not look as strong. After a scoreless opening quarter, a Fighting Irish drive launched Chris Smith for a 1-yard touchdown, set up by Koegel's passing. In the third quarter, Oliver missed a 51-yard field goal, and Purdue tied. Late in the fourth quarter, Carter scored on a 30-yard run and put Notre Dame ahead. They had used 50 seconds and left Purdue with almost 3 minutes. A badly underthrown pass missed its target, but a nearby Boilermaker made a great diving catch at the Notre Dame 1. The defense pushed them back, but on a fourth-down play they scored with a 7-yard pass and made a 2-point conversion, with 19 seconds left, to win 15-14.

The Irish reached .500 with a 20-7 win over Michigan State. Greg Bell scored after Griffith recovered a Spartan fumble on their first play. Bell scored again from the 30 on a run up the middle. In the second quarter, MSU exploited a lapse in coverage for a 63-yard touchdown pass. The Fighting Irish kicked a 38-yard field goal. The defense played tough the rest of the way. Griffith grabbed another fumble, MSU missed a field goal, and Oliver made one for the 20-7 final score. Bell had 165 yards on 20 carries, but lost a 75-yard touchdown run on a penalty.

Stacy Toran, a defensive key for Faust's teams.

Against Florida State, the first Notre Dame drive ended in an Oliver field goal. The halftime score was 3-3. Zavagnin intercepted a Florida State pass on the first play of the second half, at their 7. Notre Dame kicked a field goal. Florida State ran 53 yards in two plays and scored on a 17-yard pass play. Notre Dame kicked another field goal. The only Irish touchdown came on an 80-yard drive and a 1-yard hurdle by Bell. Florida State intercepted a Kiel pass at the Notre Dame 31 and scored five plays later with a 5-yard pass. Seven minutes remained, but the Fighting Irish were unable to move and lost 19-13. The Notre Dame air game was absent: 38 yards on six completions.

Faust had two weeks to get the Irish ready for USC. Kiel played the whole game for stability; Hunter went to split end to cover for an injury. The Fighting Irish played well: Carter outgained Marcus Allen, 161 yards to 147, and the Trojan passing game was a mere 46 yards. But they lost to USC 14-7. The first half was scoreless, although Notre Dame reached the USC 2 where a field goal try backfired. In the third quarter, USC scored on three runs, with a touchdown from the Notre Dame 14. Four minutes later, Notre Dame scored after an 80-yard drive; Carter went in from the 5. In the fourth quarter, a good USC punt nailed Notre Dame at their 4. This bad field position resulted in a short Trojan drive, capped by a 26-yard counter play for the touchdown. Joe Howard returned the kickoff 56 yards but the drive died, and the final possession ended with a Kiel fumble.

Navy had high hopes, but Notre Dame brushed them aside 38-0. Hunter was at tight end; Howard moved to split end. These changes invigorated the passing game to end up with 249 yards. Kiel scored from the 1 after a 34-yard strike to Howard. Howard scored on a reverse of 13 yards, with the key block made by Kiel. Hunter scored on a 27-yard pass from Kiel, and Kiel found Howard with a pass that he turned into a 52-yard touchdown and a 28-0 halftime score. In the second half, an Oliver field goal followed a Rudzinski fumble recovery, and Koegel threw a touchdown pass to Moriarty. Navy ran for 38 yards on the day.

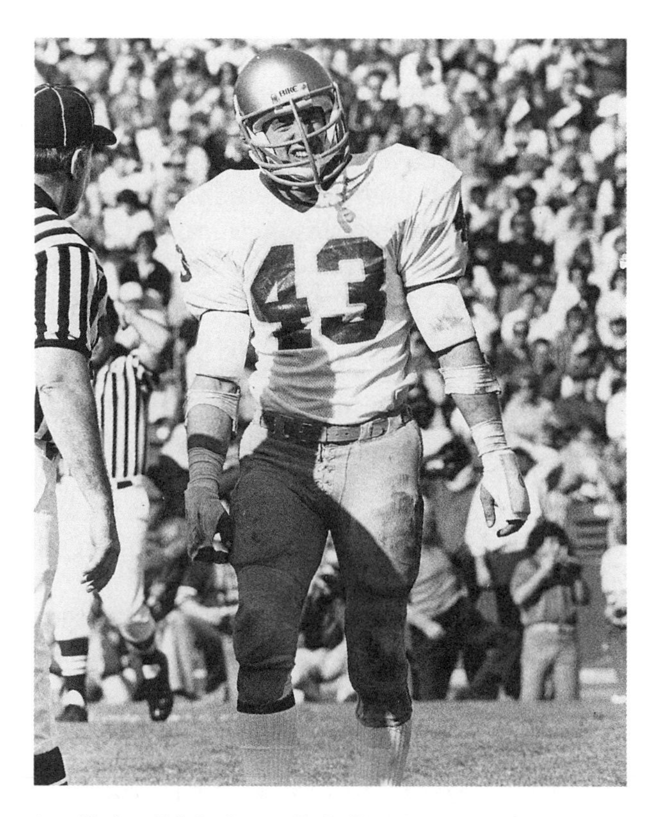

An all-time Irish player: Bob Crable, three-year starter at LB, consensus All-American in 1981.

Notre Dame registered a 35-3 win over Georgia Tech. Tech kicked a field goal to open, and later punted to the Irish 7. After losing yardage, Kiel dropped back into the end zone, found Howard, and threw to him at the 46. Howard completed the longest-ever pass play for Notre Dame, a 96-yard touchdown. Tech held the Fighting Irish for three series, but in the second quarter Kiel threw to Howard for a 58-yard score. In the third quarter, three wingback reverses sparked an 80-yard march and a 20-yard score by John Mosely. To start the last quarter, Crable intercepted a pass and returned it 33 yards to the Tech 26. Koegel passed to Mosely for a 14-yard tally. Duerson intercepted another pass, and Koegel lofted a 10-yard scoring pass to Tim Tripp.

Air Force fell next; Carter led the way with 156 yards on 27 runs and two touchdowns. Kiel ran for 31 yards, and Carter sped in from the 9. In the second quarter, Joe Johnson grabbed an Air Force fumble at their 19. Carter ran five times, scoring from the 2, for the 14-0 halftime lead. No one scored in the third quarter, but Air Force started a drive that ended later with a touchdown run from the 9. Carter gained 41 yards, and Bell ran around right end for a 17-yard

Dave Duerson following the prescribed strength conditioning.

touchdown. With Howard double-teamed, Hunter shook loose for an 18-yard reception to set up Moriarty's 5-yard touchdown. Freshman Mark Brooks scored from the 12 to wrap up the 35-7 win.

For the first time in more than 50 years, Penn State and Notre Dame met in the regular season. Penn State won 24-21, even with injured Curt Warner seeing very limited action. Jon Williams ran for 192 yards. They took the kickoff to mid-field, Williams ran for 39 yards, and for 4 more for the touchdown. Kiel answered with a 40-yard strike to Howard, and Carter scored on a 1-yard dive. Duerson dropped a punt on his 12, and Penn State scored a touchdown seven plays later. The Nittany Lions made a field goal. Kiel threw a 17-yard score to Hunter. In the third period, Crable intercepted a pass at their 32 and ran it to the 5. Kiel found Sweeney for a touchdown from the 4. Penn State intercepted a pass at mid-field, and Blackledge scored after good running by Williams got him to the 1. Notre Dame had the ball twice more but could not score.

Miami beat Notre Dame 37-15 and guaranteed the losing season. Bell scored for Notre Dame when he ran 98 yards with a kickoff return. Oliver hit a field goal, and Duerson ran 88 yards for a score on an interception. The rest was Notre Dame punting and Miami's Jim Kelly passing for touchdowns. Miami racked up 462 yards of offense to Notre Dame's 200. A pattern also emerged of the Fighting Irish defense tiring in the late stages of a game.

The season showed a Notre Dame team that could score fairly well, blow out weak teams, stay close to the stronger teams, and look bad too often. The rushing defense allowed 37 percent more yardage than in 1980, the running game declined too much for consistent ball control, but the passing game increased substantially with a maturing Kiel and the emergence of Howard. With this losing season, a more realistic view of Faust began to prevail. Crable and John Krimm earned All-American status.

1981 record: 5-6-0 (.454)
Record to date: 621-172-39 (.769)

1982

No one was more surprised by the 1981 results than Gerry Faust. Four close losses turned the season into ashes: Purdue, 15-14; FSU 19-14; USC, 14-7; and Penn State, 24-21. One field goal and three touchdowns distributed in these games would have made a 9-2 year. Four losses were to Top 20 teams. So Faust recruited a superb class, tried to delegate matters better, and hunkered down to do the extra work that might pay off.

The offense was talented: Hunter and Howard as receivers, Kiel in his junior campaign, Carter at tailback, and Moriarty at fullback. Allen Pinkett, a freshman, backed up Carter. The receiving corps plus tailbacks would be among the fastest in recent memory. The line was massive, strong, and quick. The defensive line was an improved version, and had some very promising youngsters, such as Mike Gann, and in the wings Eric Dorsey. Bob Crable was gone, but Zavagnin, Rudzinski, and Naylor were back, with Mike Larkin also available (although injuries nagged his career). In the secondary, Toran and Duerson led the list. This appeared to be a marginally better defense than the 1981 group, although Duerson was vulnerable on deep throws.

The first night game at Notre Dame was played against Michigan. Nose guard Jon Autry welcomed them with a fumble recovery at their 12, and Mike Johnston booted a field goal 2:22 into the game. In the

Head Coach Gerry Faust confers with All-American Tony Hunter in 1982 action.

second quarter, Zavagnin picked up a loose ball, and Moriarty scored from the Michigan 24. The rest of the quarter was a punting clinic until the Fighting Irish broke loose on a 65-yard drive, capped by Johnston's 37-yard field goal with 2 seconds left in the half. Anthony Carter scored in the third quarter on a 72-yard punt return, but he was hurt later and taken out. Johnston kicked another field goal of 41 yards. Bell scored a touchdown from the 10. Michigan scored a field goal and a touchdown later for the 23-17 Irish victory. Notre Dame hammered a good Michigan defense for 419 yards of total offense.

Against Purdue, Moriarty scored a touchdown from the 2, helped by his run of 30 yards and catches by Hunter and Howard. The Fighting Irish struck for another score, a 3-yard smash by Moriarty. Purdue marched 80 yards, finishing with a 2-yard touchdown pass, and then tied the game with a 5-yard touchdown pass. Notre Dame scored two more touchdowns to win: Carter from the 6 and the 10. Greg Bell broke a leg. The offense gained 403 total yards. Notre Dame won 28-14.

Irish DT Mike Gann and LB Mark Zavagnin against Michigan State.

Michigan State went down next, 11-3—the first game without a touchdown by either team since 1906. Gann registered a safety in the first quarter when he split the blockers and tackled an escaping Spartan quarterback in his end zone. Johnston scored field goals of 33, 29, and 42 yards. The Notre Dame defense manhandled the Spartan running game, allowing 19 yards for the day, but the Irish offense worked for only 280 total yards.

The Fighting Irish running defense allowed Miami only 67 yards on the ground to help in a 16-14 win. Gann grabbed a loose ball on their 12, and Kiel scored from the 6. Miami ended a 74-yard drive with a 1-yard touchdown pass. Moriarty broke loose on a 21-yard run, and Mike Johnston kicked a 29-yard field goal. Miami took a 14-10 lead with a 79-yard touchdown pass play. Notre Dame booted a field goal, but another drive died at the Miami 6. There were less than 3 minutes left. The defense stopped Miami, and Notre Dame got the ball back on its 30. Kiel used a blend of runs and passes to get to the Miami 15 with 11 seconds remaining; Johnston kicked the winning field goal.

The modest winning streak of four games died with a last-second Arizona field goal in a 16-13 loss. Johnston kicked a 22-yard field goal on the opening drive, and Pinkett made a darting 25-yard touchdown run. Arizona came back in the third quarter with two Max Zendejas field goals, both from turnovers. Mike Golic fell on a loose ball at the Arizona 35, and Johnston converted with his ninth straight field goal. The Arizona return drive chewed up 79 yards and more than 5 minutes. They jammed it in from the 1 to tie, 13-13. The Notre Dame offense couldn't move, punted, and watched as Arizona's Zendejas booted a 49-yard field goal with no time on the clock.

Oregon tied the Fighting Irish, 13-13, holding Notre Dame to 80 rushing yards. Oregon fumbled at its 30; Pinkett ran for 24 yards and then scored from the 6. The Ducks made a field goal in the third quarter. After an interception, Johnston made a 42-yard field goal for a 10-6 lead. The Ducks took the lead with a touchdown plunge from the 1. Kiel used the remaining time in a good passing show to get to the Oregon 18. Three passes missed, and Johnston kicked the tying field goal with 11 seconds left.

The Fighting Irish beat Navy 27-10 on 328 yards of offense. In the first quarter, Johnston missed his first field goal in 14 tries. In the second quarter, Kiel led a drive with six completions in six throws, capped by a 3-yard flip to Chris Smith for the touchdown. Navy was unable to move, and Johnston booted a 40-yard field goal. Jack Shields recovered a Middie fumble, and Johnston kicked another field goal four plays later. In the third quarter, Navy trapped Kiel for a safety. A Zavagnin interception led to an 18-yard scoring pass to Moriarty. Fifteen seconds later, Duerson stole one and took it to their 12; Pinkett scored. Navy scored a touchdown late in the game. Pinkett led the rushers with 129 yards on 27 carries.

Notre Dame beat the number-one team, Pitt, 31-16. The Panthers hit field goals of 48 and 22 yards in the opening quarter, answered in the second quarter by Johnston's 38-yard effort. Pitt was stopped, punted, and Kiel fired a 30-yard pass to Moriarty, who scored later from the 3. Pitt QB, and future NFL star, Dan Marino led a 98-yard scoring drive in the third quarter. Carter threw a 54-yard touchdown pass to Howard. Pitt drove again for a 48-yard field goal. After an exchange of possessions, Pinkett bounced out of three tackles for a 76-yard touchdown run. Pinkett scored again with a 7-yard touchdown for Faust's best victory.

Standing 6-1-1, Notre Dame closed out the season with three losses. Against Penn State, Kiel was out with a shoulder injury. Ken Karcher led a first-quarter touchdown drive, throwing to Chris Smith for the score from the 8. Penn State's Todd Blackledge scored on a quarterback keeper from the 1. A missed pitchout gave Penn State the ball and a field goal at the end of the half. In the third quarter, Pinkett ran 93 yards with a kickoff for a go-ahead touchdown. In the fourth quarter, Penn State's Curt Warner scored with a 48-yard pass. On the kickoff, the Fighting Irish returner's knee touched at the Notre Dame 1, and Pinkett was trapped for a safety. The Irish later missed a field goal, and Penn State made one for the 24-14 final score.

Air Force's 30-17 win was the low point. Their wishbone kept the defense befuddled for 366 yards. A Hunter fumble at the Notre Dame 35 led to a Marty Louthan score from the Notre Dame 2; a Karcher pass was intercepted, and they scored again for a 14-0 lead. Air Force hit a field goal for a 17-0 halftime score. Notre Dame opened the new half with a field goal. Louthan saw the Irish linebackers split wide and took a quick snap for a 55-yard run. The Falcons scored from the 3. Two Falcon field goals in the fourth period kept the score distant. Jim O'Hara threw two late touchdowns for the Irish—a 28-yarder to Moriarty and a 55-yard score to Howard. The Falcons ran for 296 yards against Notre Dame. It was after this game that rumors circulated that Faust could be outcoached—that he was not a good field strategist.

Allen Pinkett exults after a 76-yard TD burst to help beat Pitt in 1982.

Tony Hunter, instant starter for the Irish in 1979, All-American in 1982.

Kiel was back for the USC game and led a 74-yard touchdown drive after USC missed a field goal. Moriarty slammed in from the 2 for the score. In the second quarter, Johnston kicked a 40-yard field goal, answered by a 35-yard Trojan effort. In the middle of the third quarter, Johnston booted a 47-yard field goal for a 13-3 lead, but USC came back in eight plays and a 5-yard touchdown run. A Fighting Irish drive stalled; Karcher threw from a fake field goal play, but the touchdown dribbled off the receiver's fingers. So did the game—USC marched back, and the referees signalled a touchdown although the ball was snugly in Kevin Griffith's hold at the Notre Dame 2. The USC runner dove over the goal without the ball. The score stood as a 17-13 Irish loss.

Only the loss to Air Force was a blowout. Faust's Irish played well against Penn State, could have won the Arizona game, and should have beaten USC. Duerson, Hunter, and Zavagnin made All-American teams.

1982 record: 6-4-1 (.590)
Record to date: 627-176-40 (.767)

1983

After three excellent recruiting years, Faust had more of the best football prospects than any other school in the country. The Fighting Irish were big, fast, physical, and well conditioned. But allegations were mounting, especially from a disgruntled former assistant coach in Colorado, that Faust did not understand how to use the hashmarks in play-calling, and that he underestimated the need for total team speed. The players nitpicked about little things—the presence of Faust's youngest son in team meetings and too much praying by the head coach—revealing an unhappy state of affairs. Faust claimed, rightfully so, that the team had been "that close" (fingers about 1/8-inch apart) to outright success. Bert Metzger had said 50 years earlier that Rockne "coached in inches." If it took inches, they weren't coming under Faust often enough. There seemed to be some lurking, hidden, flaw eating away at the team's potential for success.

The 1983 Fighting Irish squad was loaded with talent. Kiel, threatening to break some long-standing records, was the first four-year starter at quarterback since Dorais (though Steve Beuerlein would get the starting nod later in the season). Pinkett shattered Salmon's 1903 point total and Gladieux's total offense mark. Joe Howard was at split end. Mark Bavaro replaced Tony Hunter. The offensive line was the most massive on record, coming in just under 275 pounds (and with only 12 percent body fat). The defensive line was solid, led by Gann and Mike Golic. Eric Dorsey and Jon Autry shared nose tackle. The linebackers were a quick, young group, but lacked a hammer. The secondary had Toran for only part of the year, and a good hitter in Joe Johnson.

The explosive offense showed in a 52-6 obliteration of Purdue. The offense clicked: a 9-yard touchdown pass, Kiel to Bell; Bell for a 2-yard touchdown; a Johnston field goal of 31 yards after a Golic fumble recovery; a Bell touchdown from the 2 after a Golic-caused interception; and a Tony Furjanic interception led to a Bavaro touchdown catch from the 17. At the half, Purdue's offense had been held to 33 yards. In the third quarter, a 61-yard pass to the Purdue 1 led to a Pinkett touchdown; Bell scored from the 6, after Tim Marshall picked up a fumble; Hiawatha Francisco gained 81 yards on nine carries, and Byron Abraham tallied a 3-yard touchdown. The Irish offense pounded Purdue for 522 yards—339 running and 183 passing.

Unfortunately, the momentum did not carry over to the Michigan State game. The Spartans, not a great team, played a great game to win 28-23. Bavaro scored on a 2-yard pass from Kiel. Three plays later, MSU tied it with an 81-yard scoring pass after two Fighting Irish deep backs knocked each other out of the play. After trading punts, Bell sprinted 50 yards down the sidelines for a touchdown, but MSU intercepted a pass and scored two plays later. Five minutes later, Daryl Turner made a second touchdown catch. Kiel tied it 21-21 at the half with a 13-yard pass to Howard. MSU's defense fended off the Irish for the third quarter; the Spartans used an interception and a 42-yard run to earn a 5-yard touchdown. MSU gave up a safety with 4 seconds left. The Notre Dame offense, good for 446 yards, could not overcome four fumbles and three interceptions.

Miami, the eventual national champions, shut out Notre Dame 20-0. Two turnovers gave Miami easy first-half touchdowns. They kicked two second-half field goals. Three Fighting Irish turnovers were directly involved in the scoring. Notre Dame's offense outgained Miami's 335 yards to 296, but Miami's quick defense held Pinkett to 65 yards on 15 tries. It was bad enough that the players decided to hold a team-only meeting, choosing to have some fun and play for themselves.

Steve Beuerlein, passed for 1,000+ yards as a freshman.

It worked well enough for a 27-3 win over Colorado. With Steve Beuerlein at quarterback, Pinkett scored from the Colorado 10 on the opening drive. Colorado answered with a field goal, and then it was all Irish: a Johnston field goal after a 58-yard Beuerlein-to-Howard pass; a 31-yard Mark Brooks touchdown run; a Chris Smith 29-yard touchdown run; and a fourth-quarter 39-yard field goal by Johnston. Notre Dame gained 494 total yards, 334 of it on the ground.

The Fighting Irish next beat South Carolina 30-6. After a 53-yard Pinkett run, Johnston booted a 49-yard field goal. Beuerlein fired a 29-yard touchdown to Chris Smith. Johnston hit a 27-yard field goal after an interception and a 41-yarder after a fumble recovery. Beuerlein made it 23-0 at the half with a 58-yard scoring pass to Pinkett. The Gamecocks converted a turnover into a touchdown. Pinkett wrapped it up with a 2-yard touchdown near the end.

Army surrendered 42-0. Half of the scoring occurred in the first quarter: Mike Kovaleski intercepted a Cadet pass at their 5, and Pinkett scored; Pinkett gained 45 yards on two runs, and Beuerlein hit Bavaro with a 22-yard scoring strike. After another punt, Pinkett broke three tackles on an 11-yard touchdown run. Army changed its coverages and the passing game slowed down in the second quarter. In the second half, Pinkett ran twice for 29 yards and a touchdown; 235-pound Mark Brooks demolished Cadet tacklers on a 6-yard score. Kiel led some freshmen on a 79-yard march in the fourth quarter and scored when he turned to hand off, saw no one, and ran over some Cadets for the touchdown.

Faust used every motivational trick he could muster for a win over USC (mired in NCAA-rules violations for academic malfeasances): he taped photos on the Irish lockers showing the "winning touchdown" in 1982 (USC runner in the end zone, ball several yards upfield, and referee calling touchdown); he played a Pat O'Brien rendition of a Rockne pep talk; and he reverted to green jerseys. It worked for a 27-6 victory. Pinkett rolled with an option pass to Bavaro that went for 59 yards to the USC 21. Pinkett scored on an 11-yard touchdown run. He struck from the 9 to end a 55-yard drive. Naylor intercepted a Trojan pass, and Johnston made a 30-yard field goal try for the 17-0 halftime score. A wilting USC defense allowed huge chunks of yardage in the third quarter after another Naylor interception. Pinkett ran in from the 11. An interference call set up an easy touchdown for the Trojans. Johnston booted a 39-yard field goal for the final score. Pinkett gained 122 yards on 21 carries, tying Stone's record of four consecutive century games.

Pinkett broke the record the next week against Navy, as the Fighting Irish defense handled Navy star Napoleon McCallum. The first score followed Howard's 30-yard end around; Beuerlein fired a 5-yard pass to Milt Jackson for the touchdown. Howard threw a touchdown to Jackson, a 29-yarder. Navy kicked two field goals in the second and third quarters, while its defense sparred with the Irish. Pinkett broke it open with a 6-yard touchdown run. He fumbled and Navy scored. Pinkett wrapped it up with a touchdown from the Navy 3 for Notre Dame's 28-12 win.

Pittsburgh won a close game, 21-16. To open, Pitt scored two touchdowns, one on a 44-yard pass and the other on a 10-yard run after Pinkett fumbled deep in Notre Dame's territory. The Fighting Irish, on two long drives in the third quarter, settled for Johnston field goals. Pitt scored an 80-yard touchdown in the fourth quarter. Two Pitt interceptions killed Irish drives; too late, Kiel threw a touchdown pass to Pinkett of 9 yards. Pitt gave up a safety to round out the scoring.

Penn State defeated Notre Dame 34-30. The Nittany Lions started the scoring by kicking a first-quarter field goal; Notre Dame hit one to start the second quarter. The Nittany Lions came back with an 80-yard drive, capped by an 11-yard scoring pass. Pinkett turned it on with great outside running to set up his own 17-yard touchdown. Paterno's team went ahead 13-10 with a field goal late in the half. In the third quarter, Beuerlein converted a third-down situation with a pass to Bavaro, and Pinkett tallied from the 16. Penn State scored a 46-yard touchdown on a screen pass to regain the lead. Starting from their 6, the Fighting Irish drove 94 yards; Pinkett scored from the 1. Penn State made a 29-yard scoring pass to go ahead again. Notre Dame marched 77 yards and Pinkett blasted in from the 1. Penn State's quarterback ran for an 8-yard touchdown with 19 seconds left. Faust would be haunted by a quarterback sneak call at the end of the first half, which ended a drive at the Penn State 1. In spite of 526 yards of offense, it was another Irish loss.

Air Force won a 23-22 squeaker. The Irish wasted a first-quarter drive. The Falcons hit a three-pointer in the second quarter, and intercepted a Kiel pass for a quick touchdown. Pinkett ran 41 yards and 7 yards for a touchdown. In the third quarter, his 37-yard run set up Johnston's tying field goal from 37 yards out. Pinkett caught a 46-yard pass from Kiel to set up Milt Jackson's 9-yard touchdown catch. The conversion was blocked. Early in the fourth quarter, Kiel hit Howard for a 67-yard score, but the 2-point conversion misfired. The Fighting Irish muffed an interception, and the Falcons scored on a 48-yard Louthan pass. A clipping penalty negated Alonzo Jefferson's touchdown kickoff return. Stuck at their 5, Notre Dame punted and gave up a touchdown on a long drive. The Falcons missed the point after—but Notre Dame was offside, and Air Force made it on a replay. Kiel got the Irish within field goal range, but the Falcons deflected the ball on the game's last play.

Mike Kovaleski, started as a LB as a freshman in 1983.

Despite its 6-5 record, Notre Dame accepted a bid to meet Boston College in the Liberty Bowl, a family affair in that its director was a Notre Dame grad. Boston College's Flutie threw a 13-yard touchdown pass to end their first drive, but they missed the point after. The Fighting Irish offense showed a new wrinkle—the backs were split farther apart and Smith ran more to confuse Boston's keys on Pinkett. Both men gained 100+ yards as Notre Dame won 19-18. Notre Dame took the lead after Pinkett ended an 87-yard drive with a 1-yard blast. After Gann blocked a Boston College punt, Kiel threw to Alvin Miller for a

13-yard score, but that point after was blocked. Pinkett jammed in from the 3 midway through the second quarter. Doug Flutie got two more scores on passes, but Boston College couldn't convert either 2-point try.

Faust's offense in 1983 was 30 percent more productive (4,713 yards to 3,640 in 1982). Pinkett gained 1,394 yards as a sophomore. The Fighting Irish were still that 1/8-inch away from the pinnacle of college football, but excuses were wearing thin. Pinkett and Larry Williams made All-American teams.

1983 record: 7-5-0 (.583)
Record to date: 634-181-40 (.764)

1984

The key administrators were not giving Faust strong votes of confidence, so the overall mood under the Dome was not the best. Players, fans, and alumni were not not fully supportive of Faust either. Injuries would keynote the season, starting with Pinkett's ankle injury in spring drills. The offensive line on paper was a devastating group, but it did not work together as a unit. The backfield was in good shape: Beuerlein as a mature sophomore, All-American Pinkett, and fullbacks Smith and Brooks. Bavaro was all-world in the opinion of football enthusiasts, and Tim Brown, a freshman, was at flanker. The defensive line featured Gann and Wally Kleine (6-8, 278 pounds), the largest man there since Mike McCoy or Steve Niehaus. Mike Golic was there, too. Injuries hit the linebackers hard. The deep backs were a bit small and green, but they had good speed. Francisco moved over there from the crowded tailback spot.

Purdue started the season (one that would see seven Irish opponents go to bowl games). Tim Brown fumbled the kickoff at the Notre Dame 12, and Purdue converted it to a 31-yard field goal. The Fighting Irish dominated the rest of the quarter with two long drives; Pinkett scored an 11-yard touchdown and Brooks went in from the 3-yard line. Jim Everett closed the gap with a 6-yard touchdown pass in the second quarter. A Purdue interception led to another field goal, Notre Dame led 14-13 at the half. Brooks fumbled on the Purdue 3 to begin the third quarter (one of five for the day). The Boilermakers marched 92 yards and made another field goal. Everett passed for a touchdown in the fourth quarter. Beuerlein hooked up with Milt Jackson on a 26-yard pass on the return drive, and Pinkett scored from the 6. But a Beuerlein pass was picked off, dooming the Irish to a 23-21 opening loss. Everett completed 20 of 28 for 255 yards.

The Fighting Irish trailed Michigan State 17-0 at the end of the first quarter. MSU's first score, a 15-yard run, came through hard work and good passing. After an Irish fumble, the Spartans ran 23 yards for a touchdown; 6 seconds later Notre Dame fumbled again, and MSU kicked a field goal. John Carney made a 42-yard field goal to make it 17-3 at the half. After stopping the Spartans in the third quarter, Beuerlein threw a 40-yard touchdown pass to Pinkett, but MSU hit a field goal for a 20-10 lead. The Fighting Irish scored on an 8-yard pass from Beuerlein to Jackson. Mike Haywood blocked an MSU punt, and Beuerlein pitched to Pinkett for a 5-yard touchdown. Notre Dame won 24-20.

A Colorado team, saddened by the brain injury to their great tight end Ed Reinhardt, lost 55-14. The Fighting Irish exploded for eight unanswered scores in their first 10 possessions. Pinkett scored with runs of 1, 4, and 13 yards; Alonzo Jefferson scored twice from the Buffalos' 3; Milt Jackson caught a 9-yard touchdown pass from Beuerlein; Brooks ran for a 9-yard touchdown; and Notre Dame made two field goals. Gann and Greg Dingens grabbed fumbles, and Haywood intercepted a Colorado pass.

The Fighting Irish beat Missouri 16-14, when the Tigers missed a field goal at the end. The defense stopped Mizzou at the Notre Dame 1 on the first possession, but surrendered 433 yards on the day. The Tigers trapped Pinkett for a safety on Notre Dame's first play from scrimmage, but they fumbled three plays later and Carney kicked a field goal. After a Tiger punt, Beuerlein threw a 74-yard touchdown bomb to Reggie Ward, the longest of the season. Missouri punted, and Carney kicked another field goal. In the third quarter, Missouri drove 76 yards, scoring on a 15-yard pass. Pat Ballage broke up their 2-point try. The final Irish points, a 37-yard Carney field goal, followed a Gann hit and a Kleine fumble recovery. Mizzou intercepted a Beuerlein pass, scored, but failed to make their 2-point try. Their last-minute field goal try just missed.

A disastrous mid-season slump started with a 31-13 loss to Miami and Bernie Kosar. Pinkett's ankle had been sore, and he was starting a slow decline. Notre Dame had a 10-7 halftime lead on a safety, a 4-yard touchdown pass from Beuerlein to Jackson, and Jefferson's 2-point conversion run. Early in the third quarter, John McCabe grabbed a Miami

1984 Fighting Irish.

fumble, and Carney booted a 39-yard field goal. It was all Miami after that, as Alonzo Highsmith creamed the Irish defense for three short touchdowns on two runs and a pass. A field goal wrapped it up.

Beuerlein had bruised a shoulder, and Pinkett was in pain; for the first time in history, Notre Dame lost a third consecutive game to a service academy, when Air Force won 21-7. The Fighting Irish were at least 40 pounds bigger per player, just as fast, and would send at least a dozen men into the NFL, but Air Force's wishbone worked for 371 yards. The Falcons scored on runs of 5, 1, and 5 yards. Notre Dame's score came on a 2-yard pass from Scott Grooms to Milt Jackson. The Falcons held Notre Dame to 90 yards rushing (Pinkett was limited to 76 yards with his ankle) and 117 yards passing. "Oust Faust" bumper stickers were seen around campus.

South Carolina beat Notre Dame in South Bend, 36-32, although it was an exciting game. The Fighting Irish gained 415 yards of offense, and Pinkett reached the 100-yard mark for the first time in the season. Following an Irish fumble, Allan Mitchell scored on a 1-yard plunge. Notre Dame scored 17 points in the second quarter: Pinkett's 6-yard touchdown run to crown an 80-yard drive, Bavaro's 6-yard scoring pass from Beuerlein after a Troy Wilson interception, and Carney's 48-yard field goal. South Carolina scored a 2-yard touchdown as well. In the third quarter, Mike Golic recovered a fumble, and Carney kicked a 47-yard field goal. Gann pulled in a loose ball, and Beuerlein scored with a 6-yard pass from Pinkett. The 2-point try failed. A 10-minute period in the last quarter spelled doom in spite of the 26-14 Irish lead. After an Irish punt, South Carolina drove 76 yards for a touchdown from the 1. They scored another from the Irish 33 on a run. Another Fighting Irish fumble led to a 4-yard score. Pinkett came back with a 1-yard touchdown, but Beuerlein had his last pass intercepted.

This misery at home continued on the road, as the Fighting Irish travelled to play the sixth-ranked LSU Tigers. Dalton Hilliard scored the first touchdown after a Fighting Irish fumble at mid-field. They missed a field goal after an interception, and Notre

Dame made the next four scores: Pinkett rammed in from the 1 to end a 79-yard drive, Carney kicked a 44-yard field goal, Pinkett ran in from the LSU 2 after a 48-yard march, and Carney kicked a 37-yard field goal. LSU intercepted a pass, and Hilliard ran 66 yards for a touchdown; Carney booted another field goal after a 15-play drive. The Fighting Irish defense stopped a fourth-down play at their 28; Brooks pulverized some tacklers as he went in from the 3. LSU scored late in the game for the 30-22 win. Pinkett picked up 166 yards on a record-tying 40 carries—in awful heat.

The usual ho-hum game with Navy turned into a serious scare before Notre Dame won 18-17. Pinkett slashed in from the Navy 1, but Navy used three turnovers for three scores, getting two touchdowns and a field goal to take the lead at 17-7. Pinkett charged back on an 83-yard march, hurtling in from the 1. Howard grabbed a 2-point pass from Beuerlein for a 17-15 deficit. With 1 minute to go, the Fighting Irish had to get Carney into field goal range. After five plays, Carney made a 44-yarder with 14 seconds left.

Notre Dame annihilated Penn State, a team known for its defense, 44-7, staggering Paterno's team with 543 yards of offense. The teams traded touchdowns in the first quarter; Pinkett scored on a 1-yard blast. Then the Fighting Irish attack decimated Penn State in the second quarter with 24 points: Pinkett stepped around right end for a 17-yard score, and ran for a 66-yard tally; Carney nailed a 28-yard field goal after an interception; Pinkett slipped in again from the Penn State 1. Carney kicked two more, and Jefferson went in from the 1 to end it. Pinkett gained 195 yards on 34 runs, and Beuerlein completed 20 of 28 passes for 267 yards.

Mike Golic, 1984 defensive end.

The last time the Fighting Irish beat USC in Los Angeles was in 1966. Notre Dame needed a win to clinch a bowl bid. It was a mudbath. USC committed six turnovers, five of them on lost center snaps. The first quarter was uneventful, except for players adjusting to an absence of footing. USC struck on a 3-yard touchdown lob. Notre Dame marched 76 yards, with Tim Brown catching an 11-yard touchdown pass from Beuerlein. Rick DiBernardo fell on a loose ball at the USC 44 to set up a Pinkett touchdown from the Trojan 3. In the second half, Carney kicked two field goals. The Fighting Irish won 19-7. Faust had his seven wins, as he had predicted in a *Sports Illustrated* article. The bowl bid followed, to meet SMU in the Aloha Bowl.

Notre Dame entered the game ranked 18th against 10th-ranked SMU, the college team with the most wins at that point in the decade. As it turned out, it was the best team money could buy, and their program received the NCAA's death penalty not long after this game. SMU went up 14-0 on an 8-yard run and a 12-yard pass. Brown returned the second kick-off 53 yards, and Notre Dame scored in seven plays. Pinkett ran for a 10-yard gain and scored on a 17-yard pass from Beuerlein. More sharp passing led to Carney's career-best field goal of 51 yards. SMU kicked one as the half ended. In the third quarter, Brooks ran in from 11 yards out. Though injured, SMU's Reggie Dupard twice made fourth-down conversions that kept a drive alive. A quick whistle overturned an Irish fumble recovery, and SMU kicked a field goal. Dupard scored again, and Carney hit a 31-yard field goal. With Pinkett gone due to a shoulder separation, Beuerlein used the passing game; his last one went off Milt Jackson's fingertips, who was open in the end zone. SMU won 27-20.

The running game declined dramatically in 1984 due to injuries, changes in the line, and Pinkett's bad ankle early in the season. Only nine touchdowns were thrown, but 19 interceptions were taken away—a very bad ratio. Three straight home losses in mid-season soured the campaign, and continued mediocrity threatened to end Faust's tenure at Notre Dame. The All-Americans were Bavaro, Larry Williams, Mike Kelley, and Gann.

1984 record: 7-5-0 (.583)
Record to date: 641-186-40 (.762)

1985

This was the last year of Faust's contract. What kind of a season would he need to renew? Most observers put the minimum number of wins at eight, as well as a strong bowl showing. The sharks called for nine or 10 wins. It would be difficult because talent was spread more evenly around the country. Faust's .554 won/loss percentage was more than 200 points below the school's average after nearly 100 years of football. The critics were not in a reasonable mood.

Pinkett and Beuerlein returned on offense, followed closely by Tim Brown. Frank Stams, a 6' 4", 229-pound sophomore, was fullback. Milt Jackson left school due to an illness, so Alvin Miller and Tony Eason filled in at split end. Bavaro went on to pro ball; Tom Rehder, 1984 defensive lineman at 6' 7" and 243 pounds, replaced him. The entire starting offensive line was made up of seniors, and the hope was that they could avoid the crippling injuries suffered in 1984. There were no truly dominating players, but a steady group of linemen. The defensive line lost Mike Griffin early in the year, and Eric Dorsey took over at nose tackle. Wally Kleine was the other known quantity. The linebackers had experience, but there were no dominant players. The same was true of the secondary, although Ballage was a hitter in the mold of Joe Johnson. Problems included getting production from the fullback spot, keeping the defensive line healthy, and avoiding the drive-killing errors of recent years.

The Fighting Irish met Michigan in Ann Arbor and once more scored only field goals, as they had in 1979; Michigan won, 20-12. Carney scored the Irish points on boots of 34, 41, 47, and 25 yards. Pinkett was contained, gaining 89 yards on 22 carries. Notre Dame led 9-3 when Alonzo Jefferson fumbled a

1985 Fighting Irish.

kickoff (and was lost for the year with an injury). Michigan scored with a quarterback draw play, and then they scored just enough to put it out of reach, while fending off Notre Dame. The loss revealed that the team was not sharp, especially in the line play that allowed six sacks.

Faust tried to improve morale by suiting up 117 players for a home game with Michigan State. The first half was a 7-7 affair. MSU's Lorenzo White scored from the Irish 4. The defense held him in check after that, and Tony Eason scored a touchdown on a 17-yard pass from Beuerlein. In the second half, Tim Brown ran 93 yards on a kickoff return through the clutching Spartans for a touchdown. MSU hit a field goal. Brown victimized MSU on a 49-yard pass play and Pinkett made a 2-yard touchdown—his 674th career run, a new record. Stams lurched in for a touchdown from the 5 for a 27-10 win. Pinkett earned 116 yards on 25 carries, the 16th time he had gone over 100 yards.

Before the Purdue game, Athletic Director Gene Corrigan was seen having coffee with an old friend from Virginia, Lou Holtz, who was coach at Minnesota. Notre Dame lost 35-17. Beuerlein completed 7 of 25 passes for 88 yards, but Terry Andrysiak looked sharp in relief. Purdue's Jim Everett had a record 368 yards on 27 of 49 passes and touchdowns of 15, 12, and 32 yards to go with their 1-yard touchdown run and a 30-yard interception return for a tally. Pinkett was targeted by the defense and gained only 45 yards on 21 tries. He scored in the fourth quarter on a 3-yard run, and Hiawatha Francisco scored from the Purdue 1. Carney kicked a 48-yard field goal. With this loss, opponents were averaging nearly 350 yards per game against Notre Dame's defense.

After three straight losses to Air Force, the Fighting Irish allowed a 77-yard touchdown off a blocked field goal try for another loss. Air Force's wishbone gained 412 yards; quarterback Bart Weiss was uncanny in his decisions. Thirteen Irish penalties for 97 yards contributed to the 21-15 loss. Carney hit field goals of 28 and 33 yards, and Weiss completed an 80-yard drive with a 24-yard touchdown pass. Air Force kicked a field goal, and Carney booted his third, a 40-yarder. In a display of poor planning and poise, with 18 seconds on the clock in the second quarter, Carney's field goal team tried to line up without a time out. They lost the race and were behind 10-9. DiBernardo recovered a fumble, and Pinkett scored from the 2, but Joel Williams dropped the 2-point conversion pass. The Falcons made a field goal, and scored on a blocked field goal play in the fourth quarter. They made the 2-point play. Falcon linebacker Terry Maki not only deflected the field goal try but made 19 unassisted tackles and was in on 11 others for a total of 30. The Falcons became only the fourth team this century to defeat the Irish four times straight.

The Fighting Irish beat Army 24-10 in a good showing, lacking fumbles and drive-killing penalties. An early Army fumble led to Pernell Taylor's 4-yard touchdown. On their next possession, Notre Dame scored with a 19-yard pass to Brown from Beuerlein. An Army 37-yard pass play and a lateral for 4 more yards made it 14-7 at the half. A Pinkett run in the second quarter put him atop all Irish runners with 3,472 yards. He iced the game with a leaping, twisting effort from the Army 1, and Carney tacked on a field goal.

This up-down team demolished USC, 37-3. George Streeter put a tremendous hit on the opening kickoff returner and the Fighting Irish took over at the USC 12 after the Trojan left on a stretcher. Pinkett scored from the 2. Beuerlein scored his first Notre Dame touchdown on a keeper from the USC 6. Carney booted a 26-yard field goal in the second period. Andrysiak led the reserves on a 55-yard march, and Stams pounded in from the 5. Carney hit another field goal for a 27-0 halftime lead. Faust had the green jerseys ready for the second half. The teams swapped field goals in the third period, and Andrysiak fired an 8-yard touchdown to Joel Williams in the last quarter. It had been nearly a quarter of a century since Notre Dame had beaten USC three straight times.

The Fighting Irish made Navy and McCallum the next victim. Notre Dame amassed 544 yards of offense in a 41-17 rout. Andrysiak started and went into the record books with five straight completions, for 10 in a row from the previous games. Pinkett scored from the Navy 2 to tie. Pinkett's second tally was sparked by freshman Mark Green's 40-yard dash. Navy hit a field goal, and Pinkett ran 43 yards to set up Stams' 1-yard touchdown. After a McCallum fumble, Andrysiak hit Reggie Ward for 17 yards, and Pinkett scored on a 29-yard run. In the fourth quarter, Tim Brown shredded the deep backs for a 48-yard touchdown pass play from Andrysiak. Francisco later scored on a 15-yard burst and Navy scored. Pinkett had his fourth 100-yard game against Navy—this time 161 yards on 27 runs. The Fighting Irish had never looked this good over a period of time under Faust.

They kept it up against Mississippi with a 37-14 victory. Andrysiak started, but Beuerlein went in after

The crowd looks on as Steve Beuerlein, No. 7, gets ready to rifle one.

three listless possessions. Meanwhile, the Fighting Irish defense was manhandling the Rebels, allowing only five first downs well into the third quarter and no scoring until halfway into the last period. Carney scored a 41-yard field goal in the first quarter. In the next period, Steve Lawrence ignited a drive with an interception, and Pinkett closed it out with a 2-yard touchdown run. Beuerlein followed that up with a 73-yard drive, featuring passes of 16 and 14 yards to Brown, the latter for a touchdown. At the half, Mississippi had minus 5 yards passing. In the third quarter, Lawrence snatched a fumble in midair and ran 79 yards to the Rebels 5. Pinkett ran in from the 2, his 52nd career touchdown. Andrysiak threw a 22-yard touchdown pass to Rehder. Mississippi worked for two touchdowns near the end and Corny Southall scored an 8-yard touchdown for the Irish.

A mudbath contributed to Penn State's 36-6 win, a game in which Notre Dame looked so bad that it had to seal Faust's fate. Penn State intercepted three passes, blocked a punt, and grabbed a fumbled kickoff for 19 points. An early Fighting Irish field goal try was a comedy of errors, and the Nittany Lions came back to score on a 21-yard pass. Their kicker booted three field goals, and they added a 2-yard touchdown to make it 23-0 at the half. In the third quarter, an interception led directly to a quarterback sneak for another Penn State score. Yet another interception and a blocked Irish punt kept their kicker busy with two more field goals. Francisco averted a shutout with a 2-yard touchdown run.

The Fighting Irish looked better against LSU, but the Tigers won 10-7, keeping the Irish from having an unblemished slate of home wins. It was the final nail—Faust resigned on Tuesday, November 26. Fighting Irish errors helped LSU: the Tigers blocked two Carney field goals, tipped another, and killed two Notre Dame drives with interceptions. Pinkett became the first Irish runner to have three consecutive 1,000-yard seasons, and surpassed the 4,000-yard mark by the end of the game. This was offset by LSU's passing game, which decimated the Irish secondary for 294 yards on 31 of 42 passes. Near the end of the game, Eric Dorsey stripped a Tiger runner of the ball, but a Beuerlein pass hit Brown in the chest, and he dropped the ball. Brown scored earlier on an 18-yard end around. LSU scored with a 27-yard field goal, their kicker's first in college. In the fourth quarter, the LSU tailback jammed in a touchdown from the Irish 2.

Faust told the press conference that he wanted the school to have a good chance in the recruiting season, and that he wanted the seniors to have a "chance to go out in style against a real good opponent in Miami." Hiawatha Francisco observed that Faust "needs a rest." Everyone agreed that he was a nice guy and deserved better. Lou Holtz was named head coach on November 27.

A demoralized team lost one of the worst games Notre Dame ever played, 58-7, as Miami ran up the score. The Fighting Irish made every mistake possible. Pinkett asked his younger teammates to remember the humiliation. He scored his last touchdown on a 3-yard play when Notre Dame was behind 20-0. Miami was still throwing long passes in a 21-point fourth quarter.

The Fighting Irish were outscored for the year, 234 to 230, but the two blowout losses made up most of that. They lost three close games. In his five years, Faust's teams lost 15 games by eight points or less, but won only eight such games. Pinkett was an All-

American, and Tim Scannell made second-team All-American. Faust left Notre Dame with a 30-26-1 record, a .535 percentage. He became the head coach at the University of Akron.

1985 record: 5-6-0
Record to date: 646-192-40 (.758)

1986

Lou Holtz had his work cut out for him, but that seemed to be the way he liked things. Perhaps the consummate overachiever, he was a fireman who took over programs on the downside and turned them around. Self deprecating—a trait perhaps necessitated by his physical dimensions beside the football giants—he considered himself not very smart and not very impressive; however, tremendous competitive fires burned within, very much like Rockne. Holtz was a child during Leahy's glory years after the war, and he was impressed by the glamor and mystique of Notre Dame. His high school years were unimpressive, and he went to Kent State for college. He played two years as an undersized linebacker and left playing the game following injuries. But he was a keen student of the game and hung on in coaching circles, including a 1964 stint at South Carolina where Paul Dietzel kept him on the staff although he had to cut his pay to the bone. If not for that gesture of good faith, Holtz would not have gone on to be the head coach at William and Mary, then North Carolina State. He achieved greater distinction at Arkansas and Minnesota, but it was his work at William and Mary that caught Gene Corrigan's attention, then with Virginia in the ACC. Corrigan was impressed with how much Holtz got out of his undermanned squads. What might he be able to do with a program that automatically interested the best players in the country? If he could win 116 games and lose only 65 at places that were relative backwaters, and do it without compromise, then he might be the man to turn the Notre Dame program around.

Holtz liked option football, but the Fighting Irish had never been an option team, and the personnel showed it. The players had been recruited to fit a classic passing attack; he would have to make the best of it. For starters, he had Beuerlein and Tim Brown on offense. Beuerlein had a great arm, but he did not have the quick feet needed to make the option run as designed. The basic problem, however, was in front of Beuerlein: few of the 1985 starting linemen returned; Rehder moved from tight end to left tackle, and Heffern moved to right guard. Some others moved up, and the coaches held their collective breaths.

Freshman linebacker Mike Stonebreaker.

The 1986 Fighting Irish team.

Pinkett was gone, and sophomore Mark Green got the call. Frank Stams, the 1985 fullback, would be hurt and lost for the year; he would later switch to defense. Brown was a constant threat, but Holtz knew he was playing with a hand he had not dealt.

The defense was in slightly better shape. Faust left few down linemen, and Banks was moved to try to rectify that. Wally Kleine provided some stability, but there was no depth behind him. The linebackers were led by Cedric Figaro and Mike Kovaleski (in his fourth year as a starter). The secondary had George Streeter in his sophomore year, a safety who was one of the hardest hitters on record, and Steve Lawrence in his second year as a starter. Stan Smagala and Pat Terrell were in the wings. As a group, this was a fair group of players, but there was not a dominant force.

Hopes were high that Holtz would get the bugs ironed out, but most recognized that this was going to be a jury-rigged endeavor until Holtz had the personnel he preferred to coach.

The maiden outing was against Michigan. The Fighting Irish showed plenty of spunk, and they did a little of everything—from the power I to the wishbone (a trait that Holtz would show in remaining years). Michigan prevailed 24-23, but they knew they had been in a game. Indeed, they lost everything but the score. The Fighting Irish handed it to them with numerous non-scoring drives, two fumbles inside the Michigan 20, an interception in the Michigan end zone, a missed point after, a narrowly missed 45-yard field goal, and tight end Joel Williams's apparent touchdown was ruled out of bounds. Beuerlein passed Theismann's career passing yardage as he hit 21 of 33 passes for 263 yards. Tim Brown scored on a 3-yard run, but the Wolverines drove back for a Jamie Morris touchdown. Mark Green scored in the second quarter with a 1-yard run, and Michigan booted a 23-yard field goal for the 14-10 halftime lead for the Irish. The Wolverines took command in the third period with two Morris touchdown runs, offset by a touchdown pass from Beuerlein to Williams—but Carney missed the point after. In the fourth quarter, Williams lost the touchdown reception on an out-of-bounds call. Carney kicked a 25-yard field goal for the final score. The Fighting Irish gained 455 yards of total offense against the third-ranked team in the country.

Michigan State won 20-15 in East Lansing. Again, Notre Dame prevailed in total offense, but most of the Irish yardage came on passing; only 82 yards were earned on the ground. Lorenzo White blasted Notre Dame for 147 yards on 41 carries. Carney kicked a 27-yard field goal, but the lead lasted about 5 minutes before the Spartans' Todd Krumm intercepted a Beuerlein pass and ran 44 yards for a touchdown. An MSU field goal ended the first half scoring. The Spartans kicked another field goal in the third quarter, and Notre Dame answered with a 38-yard touchdown pass from Beuerlein to Williams. MSU took command in the fourth quarter with a five-play 80-yard drive, capped by a 40-yard touchdown pass. Anthony Johnson ran in from the 5 for the final Irish tally. Beuerlein's two tries for 2-point conversions failed, as did his attempt at a quick-kick, which dribbled 19 yards. Krumm sealed the loss with an interception in the final moments. Although the interceptions looked like the problem, it was really the failure of the running game. Holtz wanted a ball-control offense built around successful running and long drives. If that worked, then the rested defense could dominate when they were on the field. The Irish defense held MSU to 13 points, but they didn't get the help they needed from the offense.

Purdue lost 41-9. The Fighting Irish hammered out five scoring drives before the Boilermakers could respond. The defense held Purdue's running game to 54 yards on 22 carries. It was a vindication of Holtz's plans. Pernell Taylor ran for a 2-yard touchdown, Carney kicked a 42-yard field goal, Johnson went in from the 2, Milt Jackson caught a 35-yard touchdown pass from Beuerlein, Carney kicked a 49-yard field goal, Johnson scored on a 13-yard burst, and Green ran in from the 27. The Irish gained 478 yards of offense and Holtz had his first Notre Dame win.

Alabama stuck the Fighting Irish for a 28-10 loss. After four straight Irish wins, the Irish were going into a heated atmosphere, literally and figuratively. Notre Dame lost three interceptions and two of four fumbles. Beuerlein suffered a concussion when Cornelius Bennett blindsided him. The Irish gained 324 yards to Alabama's 354, but good drives were killed by turnovers. Tim Brown scored with an 8-yard pass from Beuerlein and Carney added a 22-yard field goal. Two Crimson Tide's scores came via long-distance routes—a 66-yard punt return and a 52-yard Mike Shula pass.

More mistakes combined to give Holtz a fourth loss—this time to Pitt, 10-9. Notre Dame almost had it won, but Pitt blocked a punt with less than 3 minutes to go and made a field goal with 1:25 left. The defense had to keep Notre Dame in the game; five sacks almost did the job, too. All Notre Dame scores came on Carney field goals, of 35, 48, and 20 yards. He missed a 38-yarder in the closing seconds. The defense held Pitt's runners to 23 yards on the day. Pitt's passing

Cedric Figaro, three-year starter at LB.

game, however, worked for 310 yards and set up a quarterback sneak for their touchdown. This loss made it the worst Fighting Irish start since the days under Kuharich in 1962, certainly not what Holtz wanted.

The Fighting Irish next faced Air Force and their troublesome wishbone. The Falcons were averaging nearly 30 points a game and amassing impressive yardage, but Notre Dame stopped them, 31-3. The defense disrupted Air Force's offensive flow. After an Air Force field goal, Notre Dame attacked with impunity: Tim Brown for a 95-yard kickoff touchdown return, a 1-yard Beuerlein run, a 27-yard Carney field goal, a 1-yard Taylor smash, and a 1-yard Johnson plunge. The Irish gained 356 yards, with 237 yards on 61 runs.

The Fighting Irish beat Navy, 33-14. Beuerlein's 248 yards passing, on 15 of 22 for two touchdowns, made him the all-time offensive yardage leader for Notre Dame. Cedric Figaro led the defense, which held Navy in the first half to 1 yard rushing; Figaro also recovered his sixth fumble of the year, a new record. The Irish led 28-0 at halftime on a 2-yard touchdown pass from Beuerlein to Williams, a 77-

yard bomb from Beuerlein to Brown, an 11-yard Pernell Taylor touchdown blast, followed by his 1-yard touchdown slam. Carney added a field goal in the third quarter from 19 yards out before Navy scored. The Irish tacked on a safety, and Navy scrapped for another touchdown on a 21-yard pass. Notre Dame had 480 yards of total offense to Navy's 211.

The Fighting Irish obliterated SMU 61-29. Tim Brown gained 235 offensive yards; the Irish used 10 running backs for 322 yards on the ground, scored on 11 of 15 possessions, and gained 615 yards of total offense. Freshman linebacker Mike Stonebreaker led the team with 10 tackles. Brown scored two touchdowns—a 15-yard run and an 84-yard strike from Beuerlein; Carney kicked four field goals—38, 40, 30, and 22 yards. Anthony Johnson, Pernell Taylor, Aaron Robb, and Andrysiak also scored touchdowns.

Against the third-ranked Nittany Lions, the Fighting Irish did everything but win the game. Critical errors nullified an otherwise stellar effort on both sides of the ball: on a first-and-goal play, the second-string tight end failed to get on the field, and Penn State stopped the ensuing play; Tim Brown lost a 97-yard kickoff return for a touchdown on a clipping call. Penn State won 24-19. The Fighting Irish offense gained 418 yards to Penn State's 314. Beuerlein was 24 of 39 throws for 311 yards and two touchdowns; Brown scored both on passes of 14 and 8 yards. Carney hit field goals of 20 and 38 yards. The Irish had a final chance with less than 4 minutes to go. They drove to the Penn State 6-yard line, but Paterno turned loose two blitzes for a loss and a sack; and a touchdown pass glanced off Joel Williams' fingertips. A fourth-down pass was completed short of the goal. Penn State went on to the national title.

Eighth-ranked LSU nipped the Fighting Irish 21-19. This loss guaranteed the first back-to-back losing seasons for Notre Dame since 1888. In the first quarter, LSU gained 178 yards and two touchdowns before the Irish offense got its first snap in the 14th minute of the quarter. Tim Brown sandwiched a 96-yard kickoff return for a touchdown in between the LSU scores. Carney booted a 49-yard field goal, but LSU was whistled offside before the kick. Carney then missed a 44-yarder. In the second half, Carney added field goals in each quarter, and D'Juan Francisco caught a 14-yard touchdown pass from Andrysiak with less than 4 minutes to go in the game. LSU's defense held Notre Dame to 270 yards of total offense.

Notre Dame won its fourth consecutive game against USC on Carney's 19-yard field goal on the game's last play. His kick, set up by Tim Brown's 56-yard punt return, capped a come-from behind win for the Fighting Irish, who went into the fourth quarter trailing 37-20. Carney's kick was his 21st field goal for the season, a new Irish record. Beuerlein ended his career with four touchdown passes and 18 of 27 passes for 285 yards. Mark Green gained 119 yards on 24 carries as the Irish amassed 490 yards of total offense. Beuerlein's touchdowns went to Andy Heck for 5 yards, to Braxston Banks for 22 and 5 yards, and to Milt Jackson for 42 yards. He threw another—to Trojan Lou Brock, who went for a 58-yard touchdown. Carney added field goals of 33 and 32 yards as Notre Dame slipped past USC 38-37.

The last games were a microcosm of the season—occasionally thrilling offense, sometimes suspect defense, costly errors, and the ability to score long-distance touchdowns. Offensive output increased 23 percent, mainly from a passing game that picked up 2,444 yards (53 percent of the total offense). Scoring increased from 230 points to 299, and oppo-

Lou Holtz, the 25th Notre Dame head football coach.

sition scoring fell, as did opposition yardage. The team had one of the worst starts on record, corrected itself in mid-season, and then lost two heart-breaking games to top-ranked teams. Holtz's squad lost five games by a total of 14 points. Tim Brown, Wally Kleine, and Cedric Figaro earned All-American honors.

1986 record: 5-6-0 (.454)
Record to date: (.754)

1987

Would those hopeful glimmers from 1986 become the glowing center of rekindled football proficiency in Holtz's second year, Notre Dame's centennial year for football? The all-time passing yardage and total offense leader, Beuerlein, had graduated. It would be difficult to replace the experience of any 39-game starter, but the problem was magnified when it was the quarterback. Terry Andrysiak was a possibility, and there was an unknown quantity—Tony Rice, who was more in the mold of an option quarterback, but who had not been able to practice his freshman year due to Proposition 48. Tim Brown was the Heisman front-runner. He finished 1986 ranked third nationally for all-purpose yardage production. He had to be more than a well known diversionary figure. Veterans returned for the line, as did most of the backfield.

Tim Brown, Notre Dame's seventh Heisman Trophy winner.

The defense was a different matter. Only one of the top seven tacklers returned; Figaro and Griffin missed spring ball. The kicking game would be with new players, and no one threatened to be confused with Carney. Wes Pritchett led a group of untried linebackers. Stonebreaker was lost for academic reasons. George Streeter and Brandy Wells headlined the secondary; Stan Smagala moved up and added blazing speed on the right corner. Mike Griffin overcame back surgery to lead a light, relatively untried defensive line. In sum, the team had a solid core, but the question marks were major, especially at quarterback and the defense in general. At least the players knew the system better than before.

The Fighting Irish stunned Michigan 26-7 in Ann Arbor, Schembechler's first-ever home opener loss. The Irish were ready, and the Wolverines weren't. Notre Dame recovered three fumbles and made four interceptions. Andrysiak played well, completing 11 of 15 passes for 137 yards and an 11-yard touchdown pass to Brown, who made the catch in between two defenders. Braxston Banks ran in from the 1 to end a 55-yard drive. Freshman Ricky Watters ran 16 yards following an interception by Corny Southall to score. Ted Gradel had opened the scoring with a 44-yard field goal after Figaro's interception, and added a 38-yarder in the fourth quarter.

The Fighting Irish returned home to smash Michigan State 31-8. Tim Brown became the first player in college football history to return consecutive punts for touchdowns, both in the opening quarter, the first from 71 yards and the second from 66. On the opening kickoff, Spartan Blake Ezor took the kick, surveyed what was headed his way, and stepped back into his end zone for a safety. Notre Dame's defense recorded eight sacks, grabbed two fumbles, and made two interceptions. Linebacker Ned Bolcar recovered a fumble and made an interception; freshman Todd Lyght made the other interception. Andrysiak made nine of 17 passes for 105 yards. Anthony Johnson went in from the MSU 3 for a third-quarter touchdown, and Gradel kicked field goals of 27 and 37 yards. Jeff Kunz tackled the Spartan quarterback for a safety to round out the Irish scoring. MSU's Andre Rison caught a 57-yard touchdown pass in the fourth quarter for MSU's lone score.

Purdue went down 44-20. The score is misleading, because the Fighting Irish took an early lead, lost it, and had to roar back. Notre Dame mounted a 10-0 lead in the first quarter on a 25-yard Gradel field goal and a 6-yard Johnson touchdown. In the second quarter, Purdue scored 17 unanswered points with two touchdown passes and an 18-yard field goal. With only 36 seconds left in the half, Johnson scored from the Purdue 1 to make it 17-17. In the third quarter, Purdue kicked another field goal. Notre Dame took control as Johnson scored his third touchdown, from the Purdue 8, and Brown went 49 yards with an Andrysiak pass. In the fourth quarter, Gradel added two field goals of 28 and 44 yards, and Southall intercepted an errant pass and ran 57 yards for a touchdown. Holtz had used the fourth offensive series to showcase the option game with Tony Rice for a 74-yard march that ended in a Mark Green fumble. Notre Dame gained 476 yards of offense to Purdue's 263.

Unbeaten and ranked fourth, the Fighting Irish went to Pitt and lost a tough contest 30-22. Pitt led 27-0 at halftime, and Notre Dame lost their starting quarterback on the last play with a broken collarbone. The Panthers scored on a 31-yard pass, a 260-pound Craig Heyward touchdown from the Notre Dame 1, a quarterback touchdown run from the 2, and another Heyward run from the 1. Tony Rice made his starting debut in the second half, hitting Brown with a 25-yard pass on his first play, and eventually scoring from the 16. In the final quarter, Braxston Banks slammed in from the 1 after Lyght blocked a punt, Pitt hit a 20-yard field goal, and Mark Green scurried in from the 17 before Brown scored a 2-point conversion run. Pitt's defense held Notre Dame to 296 yards, and Heyward ran 42 times for 132 yards and two touchdowns. In addition to losing Andrysiak, Southall also went down with severe ligament damage (he was out for four games and was replaced by Brandy Wells).

The loss of Andrysiak made Holtz turn to the basics. Against Air Force, the Fighting Irish kept the ball on the ground for 69 time-consuming, energy-sapping rushes as Notre Dame gained a season-high 354 yards on the way to a 35-14 victory. The Irish were both bigger and faster than the Falcons. Their quarterback, Dee Dowis, however, turned in a good individual performance. Tony Rice garnered the first two touchdowns for Notre Dame, using his reading abilities to score from the 1 and the 4 in the first quarter. Air Force answered with a 4-yard touchdown in the second quarter. Irish fullbacks took over the third quarter when both Anthony Johnson and Banks slammed in from the 1 for touchdowns. Dowis led a fourth-quarter drive of 78 yards, capped with a 1-yard touchdown run, but Tim Brown returned a 57-yard punt for his third such touchdown of the season. He also lost a 74-yard touchdown reception on a penalty call.

Ranked tenth, the Fighting Irish defeated USC for the fifth straight time, 26-15. The running game was the deciding factor; Irish runners gained 351 yards. USC scored first, and quickly, on a 9-yard Rodney Peete pass. The next five scores were Notre Dame's: a 26-yard Gradel field goal, a Rice option for his own 26-yard touchdown, a 5-yard Tim Brown run, and a 32-yard Gradel field goal with 2 seconds left in the first half. In the second half, Mark Green scored from the USC 11. The Trojans punched over a late touchdown against Irish reserves. Linebacker Ned Bolcar led an aroused Fighting Irish defense with 13 tackles, a fumble recovery, and an interception. With this win, there were no Trojan football players on that squad who had beaten Notre Dame.

Notre Dame beat Navy easily, 56-13. The Fighting Irish trampled the Middies with 630 yards of total offense (406 rushing and 224 passing). The defense played as if they could take the ball away with impunity—and did on several occasions. Holtz went into the fourth teams on both sides of the ball. Among the starters, Anthony Johnson scored four touchdowns on six carries. Mark Green made nine carries for 102 yards and a touchdown, and Tony Brooks ran 82 yards on 12 carries and a touchdown. Tim Brown added to his Heisman-nominee laurels with a 51-yard touchdown catch from Kent Graham.

Boston College played Notre Dame on nearly even terms for much of the next game before the Fighting Irish ground game took command for a tough 32-25 victory. Gradel opened with a 25-yard field goal following a Kent Graham strike to Brown for 58 yards. Boston College fired back with a drive and a 3-yard touchdown pass. Gradel hit a 21-yard field goal in the last minute of the quarter. Boston College took the lead in the second quarter with a 31-yard field goal, and extended it with an 11-yard touchdown after an interception. In the third quarter, Green sprinted 33 yards for a touchdown. Boston College's Darren Flutie caught a 31-yard touchdown pass, and the Eagles made a 2-point conversion for a 25-12 lead. Wes Pritchett recovered a fumble, and eight plays later Anthony Johnson boomed over a 1-yard touchdown. The defense asserted itself the entire fourth quarter and Boston was unable to move the sticks. Banks scored from the 1, and Green made eight

Tim Brown, holder of many Notre Dame records.

consecutive runs, the last a 2-yard touchdown. He led all runners with 152 yards and two touchdowns on 23 carries, as Notre Dame compiled 454 yards of total offense.

The Fighting Irish avenged the 1986 loss to Alabama, 37-6, amassing 465 yards of offense to the Crimson Tide's 185, the 11th-ranked team in the nation. Alabama scored a 34-yard field goal. Gradel kicked a career-best field goal of 49 yards. After an exchange of possessions, Rice ran 12 yards for a touchdown. Heck caught a 3-yard touchdown pass from Rice, and Gradel hit a 21-yard field goal before Alabama scored its second one. Gradel boomed one more in the third quarter, from 22 yards, while the Irish defense kept Alabama from converting a third down the entire quarter. In the fourth quarter, Green and Watters ran 74 and 75 yards down the sideline stripe. Tim Brown gained 225 all-purpose yards and became the all-time career reception yardage leader for Notre Dame with 2,371 yards.

Ranked seventh, and with national championship thoughts, the Fighting Irish met Penn State and lost a thriller 21-20 when a 2-point try fell short with 31 seconds left in the game. The Nittany Lions ran well and played gutsy defense, as did the Irish. Both teams gained 312 net yards, both lost a fumble, and both had an interception—although Penn State's interception killed an Irish scoring threat. Penn State followed up a fumble recovery of a punt for a 10-yard touchdown run. Rice ran 32 yards for a score. In the second quarter Blair Thomas scored on a 1-yard run. Rice matched that with a touchdown from the 11. Penn State used an interference call to keep a drive alive, although it took three runs to go the final 3 yards. Notre Dame used its last possession to get Johnson in close for a touchdown try from the 1—he made it, but a good Penn State defense stopped Rice just short of the victory. It was Penn State's sixth win in the seven most recent games against the Irish and Notre Dame's 200th loss.

Notre Dame went to Miami to play its 900th game, losing 24-0. The offense did not materialize; Miami kept Notre Dame to 169 yards total and sacked Irish quarterbacks six times. Miami's Melvin Bratton scored two short touchdowns, Leonard Conley scored from the 6, and a field goal rounded it out as the 'Canes gained 417 total yards.

With its 8-3 record, Notre Dame met Texas A & M in the Cotton Bowl. Texas A&M had all of its starting linebackers in the decade drafted by NFL teams. The Fighting Irish ground game was held to 74 yards on 36 runs, and 203 yards passing did not make up the difference as the Aggies amassed 407 yards of total offense. Tim Brown scored on a 1-yard pass from Andrysiak, but the defense could not stop A & M after that. Gradel added a 36-yard field goal in the second quarter. The final score was 35-10 in favor of Texas A&M.

Total offense for the year, compared to 1986, fell off marginally, but the passing game was more than 1,000 yards less and 10 fewer touchdowns. The running game carried the team to a more successful season since opponents gave up 2,773 yards, roughly 33 percent more yardage on the ground, a vindication of Holtz's theory of a ground game controlling the clock, keeping the opponent's offense off the field, and resting one's defense. Clearly, the Irish had turned a major corner. Tim Brown became Notre Dame's seventh Heisman Trophy winner and was a consensus All-American. Others earning All-American honors were Chuck Lanza, Ned Bolcar, and Cedric Figaro.

1987 record: 8-4-0 (.666)
Record to date: 659-202-40 (.753)

1988

Although some fine players returned from the 1987 team, two matters were readily apparent: it would be hard to replace a Heisman winner who had been involved in so many phases of the offense, and the entire starting offensive line was gone. The defense was big, strong, fast, and especially talented in the linebacking corps and the secondary. Since 1987 had shown that Notre Dame could run like Holtz wanted (and all top rushers were back), the whole theory could now be applied—the controlling ground game augmented by a dominating defense. It looked good on paper.

Holtz made some personnel adjustments—Heck from tight end to tackle, and Watters to flanker. Only Tim Grunhard had more than 15 minutes of offensive line experience. The others had potential. Rice returned at quarterback, Green at tailback, and Johnson and Banks as fullbacks. Tony Brooks and Rodney Culver looked promising as running backs. Rice, however, did not have a major league arm; he had thrown for only one touchdown in 1987. However, he could move the ball on the ground as an option quarterback; he had a sense of when to keep or pitch and when to cut upfield or swing wide. Many defenders, frozen in indecision, would attest to his skills.

Chris Zorich, 1988 starter at NT.

Quarterback Tony Rice, 1988 Fiesta Bowl MVP.

The defensive line was reworked and had some talented youngsters, especially Chris Zorich at nose tackle. Frank Stams had made the switch successfully to defensive end. The linebackers were among the best ever assembled at Notre Dame: Pritchett and Stonebreaker started, and All-American Bolcar relieved them. Pat Terrell switched to free safety, and veterans Streeter, Smagala, and Lyght teamed with him to make this an impressive and very fast group.

Overall, the defense had to play great football in the early part of the season to give the offensive line time to jell as a unit. Watters had to grow into his new position, and Rice had to develop an improved passing game so that opponents would not be able to load up against the run. Holtz had been recruiting speed, speed, and more speed at virtually every position (no starter slower than 4.8). And in the speed department, the coaching staff took immediate notice of freshman Raghib Ismail, the fastest player ever in pads at Notre Dame.

Part of the plan worked well in the first quarter against Michigan. Watters returned a punt return for an 81-yard touchdown. But Rice came up empty on his first nine passes. The Fighting Irish ground game worked well and the defense stopped a highly-touted Michigan ground game. Notre Dame's new kicker, Reggie Ho booted a 31-yard field goal near the end of the first quarter, and added a 38-yarder in the second quarter before Wolverine Leroy Hoard ran in for a touchdown. Michigan took the lead in the third quarter on another short run. Ho kicked a 26-yard field goal in the fourth quarter, and Michigan booted a 49-yard field goal. With 1:13 left, Ho won the game with a 26-yard three-pointer. The Wolverines drove back, only to miss a field goal on the last play. The stats showed a glaring deficiency—only 40 yards on three completed passes, but the Irish won 19-17.

A similar pattern emerged as Notre Dame defeated Michigan State 20-3 in East Lansing. The Spartans kicked a 39-yard field goal but the Fighting Irish defense allowed only 89 yards on 35 carries. But Rice hit only two of nine throws for 50 yards. The Irish won it with good defense and running, especially in the second half when they dominated MSU with 195 yards on the ground. Mark Green led the runners with 125 yards on 21 carries, but Notre Dame lost both Banks and Johnson to injuries; Brooks took over. Ho kicked field goals of 31 and 22 yards, Rice made an 8-yard touchdown run, and Stonebreaker scored after an interception and 39-yard return.

The Fighting Irish defeated the Boilermakers 52-7. Touchdown passes from Rice to Derek Brown and Ismail showed that Holtz had been trying to improve this phase of the offense and also revealed the tremendous talent just waiting to get on the field. It was 42-0 at the half, as Notre Dame gained 468 yards of total offense. The scoring was: Rice on a 38-yard touchdown run, Rice to Brown for an 8-yard touchdown, Rice to Ismail for a 54-yard strike, Green for a 7-yard touchdown scamper, Watters on a 66-yard punt return, Brooks with a 34-yard touchdown pass from Steve Belles, Billy Hackett for a 44-yard field goal in the third quarter, and Culver for a 36-yard touchdown in the fourth quarter.

Against Stanford, Rice tied a Fighting Irish record for consecutive completions (with the first four coming against Purdue) when he completed his first six of the game. He ended the day with 11 of 14 for 129 yards and one touchdown as the Irish gained 467 total yards for a 42-14 victory. The ground game worked as diagrammed for 332 yards on 61 carries. Rice also ran well and handled the option game with flair; he scored the first touchdown on a 30-yard dash in the first quarter. Mark Green ran in from the 1 in the second quarter. Rice ran for a 2-point conversion to make it 14-0. Tony Brooks made a 5-yard touchdown next. Stanford came back on a 68-yard drive, capped by a 1-yard touchdown. Ismail took the kickoff back 35 yards, and Anthony Johnson later made a touchdown from the 1. In the third quarter, Rice threw a 3-yard touchdown pass to Derek Brown, but Stanford drove for a second touchdown. Rice scored on a 6-yard run in the fourth quarter to wrap it up.

Notre Dame won a tough game 30-21 in Pittsburgh. Pitt took the early lead on a 42-yard touchdown pass. Rice led Notre Dame for a tally four plays later, due in part to Brooks' 52-yard run; Rice scored from the 2. After a Pitt punt, the Fighting Irish drove 86 yards and Johnson scored from the 1. Pitt scored a touchdown on a 33-yard pass. Ho kicked a 37-yard field goal seven plays later to make it 17-14 at halftime. Pitt tied it midway through the third quarter with a 44-yard field goal. Braxston Banks caught a 30-yard pass from Rice, and scored with a 1-yard run. The Panthers booted another field goal, but Mark Green capped a drive with an 8-yard scoring run.

Todd Lyght, starter at CB for 1988 National Champions.

Perhaps the close score of the Pitt game was the result of Notre Dame being preoccupied with thoughts of undefeated Miami. Certainly Frank Stams had terrible recollections of the 58-7 defeat suffered by Notre Dame in his first season. Stams played his heart out in a 31-30 win over Miami. The defense planned to pressure Miami's quarterback Steve Walsh to cut down his reading and reaction time—Stams was the man, rushing Walsh from the outside. He had Walsh on the run much of the day, tipped a pass that went to Terrell for an interception and a 60-yard touchdown, recovered a fumble, and caused a crucial fumble in the fourth quarter. Walsh still managed to pass for 248 yards in the first half and a 21-21 halftime score. Rice scored on a 7-yard run; Miami tied it in the second quarter on an 8-yard pass. On the next Fighting Irish drive, Ismail caught a 57-yard pass from Rice and Banks scored on a 9-yard pass. Stams tipped a Walsh pass, and Terrell ran the interception in for a score. Walsh closed out the half with two touchdown passes. In the third quarter, Miami gambled with a fake punt that Notre Dame stopped, and Pat Eilers scored from the 2 after a short drive. At the end of the third quarter, Jeff Alm intercepted a Walsh pass to lead to a Ho field goal and a 31-21 lead. Miami scored twice after that, but Terrell batted down a Walsh throw for a 2-point conversion with 45 seconds left in the game. In spite of giving up 481 yards of offense to Miami, this all-out defensive effort must be counted among the top two or three in Irish football history.

Notre Dame sustained the intensity against Air Force, 41-13. The Falcons and their wishbone had been running for big yardage with impunity, but they hadn't played anyone like Zorich and Stonebreaker. The defense dismantled their wishbone in the first half, allowing only 39 yards. Air Force made it a game, however, trailing only 20-13 at the half. They scored first with a 22-yard field goal, and Mark Green scored from the 7 after a 71-yard return march. The Falcons hit another field goal, but Notre Dame drove back and Rice made a touchdown from the 4. Johnson tacked on a 4-yard touchdown before Air Force tallied a 3-yard score for the half. Irish speed and passing took over—Brooks scored on a 42-yard strike from Rice; Watters caught a 50-yard option play bomb from Belles for a touchdown, and a 28-yard touchdown pass from Rice.

Notre Dame beat Navy 22-7. The defense held Navy to two first downs and 46 yards of total offense in the first half. In the first quarter, Rice followed up a Navy fumble with a 10-yard touchdown strike to Derek Brown. Culver scored on a 22-yard dash. Ho

"Rocket" Ismail, fastest player in Notre Dame history.

tacked on a 29-yard field goal to end the half. In the third quarter, Mihalko went in from the 1 to end a 67-yard opening drive, and then the offense disappeared for the rest of the day. The Navy quarterback shook loose for a 22-yard touchdown run near the end of the third quarter.

Holtz put the team through some serious self-examination and tough drills after the uninspired game with Navy. Notre Dame then demolished Rice 54-11. The Fighting Irish gained 439 yards of total offense. Holtz used 12 different running backs to generate 294 yards on the ground. The Owls scored first when they took the kickoff back 70 yards in 10 plays and kicked a 23-yard field goal. The next six scores were by Notre Dame: Ismail streaked 87 yards for a touchdown with the kickoff, Mark Green gained 40 yards to set up Johnson's 2-yard touchdown, Johnson scored again from the 2 after Brown set it up with a 41-yard reception, Brooks scored from the 1 and Johnson made the 2-point conversion, and Hackett kicked a 42-yard field goal. In the third quarter, Pritchett grabbed a fumble and Culver launched himself 19 yards for a touchdown. The Rice Owls booted a 45-yard field goal, and Notre Dame scored three more: Ismail returned the kickoff 83 yards for a touchdown, Hackett kicked a 28-yard field goal, and Joe Jarosz ran for a 6-yard touchdown after Steve Roddy recovered a fumble. The point after was blocked and a Rice player ran it back for 2 points, the first time this happened to Notre Dame under the new rules.

The 21-3 blitz of Penn State guaranteed Penn State its first losing season in half a century. The Nittany Lions played a gritty game but still gave up 502 yards of total offense. Rice made a 31-yard run to spark a drive that ended in his own 2-yard touchdown. Green broke loose for a 22-yard touchdown run near the end of the half but Penn State kicked a field goal on the last play of the period after a face mask penalty. In the third quarter, Ismail streaked down the sideline and Rice hit him with a pass for a 67-yard touchdown.

The game between the two top-rated teams in the country, Notre Dame and USC, took a back seat to Holtz's sending Watters and Brooks home for disciplinary reasons—they had been too late for team meetings too often. He'd done it before at Arkansas in a bowl game, and other players picked up the slack for the upset win. Something like that would have to work in this case, because these players were important elements in the total package. The team pulled together, and the offense clicked when it had to. On Notre Dame's first play from scrimmage, from their own 2, Rice went to Ismail for a 55-yard gain that would have been a touchdown had "Rocket" not lost his balance. On their next possession, Rice took an option play outside left and found himself *and* a running back isolated on a single defender. After the shake and bake, Rice streaked to a 65-yard score. Rodney Peete worked a careful drive in the second quarter to garner a 1-yard touchdown by Scott Lockwood. A Fighting Irish possession got nowhere, and Peete fired a pass to his left, but the receiver had fallen down. Smagala intercepted it, and took off down the right sideline, avoiding a USC lineman, to score on a 64-yard return just before the halftime gun. Peete hurt his shoulder attempting a tackle after Stams blindsided him. In essence, the game was over. In the third quarter, USC kicked a 26-yard field goal. In the fourth quarter, Green stepped in for a 1-yard touchdown. Rice ran for 86 yards and passed for 91 more as the Irish won their sixth straight game over USC, 27-10. In an attempt to stir up victory juices, a clip from the 1964 USC upset win was shown on the Coliseum's big screen, but it was not to be.

Undefeated and ranked number one, the Fighting Irish went to Tempe, Arizona, to meet undefeated, third-ranked West Virginia in the Fiesta Bowl. The Mountaineers experienced a clinic in team speed, losing 34-21. Notre Dame had a perfect 12-0 season and an undisputed eighth national championship. The Irish jumped out to a 15-0 lead before a Notre Dame penalty gave West Virginia their initial first down—in the second quarter. Hackett kicked a career-best 45-yard field goal. After a futile possession by West Virginia, a Fighting Irish drive resulted in Johnson's 1-yard touchdown. In the second quarter, Culver made a 5-yard touchdown run before the Mountaineers tallied a 29-yard field goal. Ismail used his speed for a 29-yard pass play and an Irish touchdown. Another West Virginia field goal made it 23-6 at the half. In the third quarter, Ho kicked a 32-yard field goal after a Pat Terrell interception. West Virginia got its first touchdown on a 17-yard pass. In the fourth quarter, Rice threw a 3-yard touchdown pass to Frank Jacobs. The Mountaineers scored at the end. Notre Dame had 455 yards of total offense to the Mountaineers' 282; Rice was named Offensive Player of the Game, and Stams was named as his defensive counterpart.

Mike Stonebreaker, 1988 consensus All-American.

For the year, the Irish averaged 108 more yards per game of total offense than did their opponents (388 to 280) and increased the offensive production in both rushing and passing. The average scoring differential increased from 13.3 in 1987 to 20.3, nearly a three-touchdown differential against the 1988 opponents. The 1988 team ran the ball superbly, passed it competently, and played excellent defense. Overall team speed made this a tough team to play against. It was probably among the top four or five teams ever produced under the Dome. Stams, Heck, and Stonebreaker were consensus All-Americans, while Zorich and Pritchett also earned All-American accolades.

1988 record: 12-0 (1.000)
Record to date: 671-202-40 (.756)

1989

Defending national champs quickly learn that every opponent wants to take its shot at dethroning them. The Fighting Irish also faced the prospect of playing five of their first six games on the road in 1989. Seven starters were gone, including Green and Heck on offense, and Stams, Streeter and Pritchett on defense. The team was in good shape at most spots, but the 1989 team would be unable to sneak up on people. It was an established fact that Holtz was a marvelous coach, had had four great recruiting classes, and that his brand of football worked at Notre Dame. The Fighting Irish under Holtz were no longer an unknown.

On offense, most skill position people returned, although there were several position changes. To get Ismail into the action, he took over at flanker; Watters replaced the departed Green at tailback, and Eilers went to split end. Rice was at quarterback—the first Irish quarterback since Hornung in 1956 to lead the team in rushing (121 carries for 700 yards and nine touchdowns in 1988). He had good runners behind him—Johnson, Culver, Watters, and Ismail. In Derek Brown and Ismail, he had two dominating players as his receivers. Four starting linemen returned to make this offensive unit a potentially more explosive one than the 1988 squad.

The defense was in good hands in important spots, especially among the linebackers and secondary. The flanks on the line would have to be replaced, and filling Stams' shoes would be a tall order. That job fell to Scott Kowalkowski. Zorich and Alm returned, and Donn Grimm and Andre Jones joined Bolcar to make the linebackers a solid group. The deep backs added D'Juan Francisco to Lyght, Smagala, and Terrell for a fast, smart group.

The Fighting Irish and their 12-game winning streak met Virginia and their five-game streak in the Kickoff Classic at the Meadowlands. In the first half, the Irish defense dominated: the Cavaliers rushed for scant yardage and missed nine of 12 passes with two interceptions, while Notre Dame rang up a 33-0 halftime score. Lyght's interception to end Virginia's first series led to a Watters' touchdown of 2 yards. The

Raghib Ismail, 1989 consensus All-American.

Tony Rice, 1989 All-American and tri-captain.

Cavaliers could not move the ball, and Rice led the Irish back for a touchdown by Johnson from the 1-yard line. Thirteen of the first 15 plays had been runs for the Irish. After another futile Cavalier possession, Rice fired to Ismail for a 52-yard advance, and Culver jetted over from the 2 for a 19-0 lead. At that point, the Cavaliers had two first downs. In the second quarter, another long drive, sparked by a Rice-to-Ismail pass for 24 yards, ended with a 1-yard Johnson blast. Rice completed a 30-yard pass to Watters to set up a 3-yard Rice touchdown. The third quarter passed uneventfully as Holtz looked over junior personnel. Virginia's Shawn Moore threw for two touchdowns in the fourth quarter before Hentrich hit a 32-yard field goal near the end of the game for the 36-13 final score. The Irish ran for 300 yards using 11 backs. Their total output for the day came to 477 yards to the Cavaliers' 231.

Notre Dame went to Ann Arbor to face an aroused Wolverine team and nearly 105,000 fans. Holtz played the game conservatively: Rice threw only twice and the Fighting Irish ground game ran 54 times for 213 yards. The Michigan line, as big as the Redskins' famous Hogs, was able to open holes for only 119 yards. Speed was the difference—Rocket Ismail returned two kickoffs for touchdowns, both in the second half, the first for 89 yards and the second for 92. The first Irish score came on the only pass completion for the day, a 6-yarder from Rice to Johnson. Michigan threw a 9-yard touchdown, but the conversion kick failed. Ismail opened up the second half with his 89-yarder, and Hentrich added a 30-yard field goal. In the fourth quarter, Elvis Grbac made his appearance as the Wolverine quarterback. He passed 5- and 4-yard touchdowns to make a game of it. In between, Ismail made his 92-yard touchdown. The 24-19 score was Holtz's third straight win over Schembechler, a first against him.

The Fighting Irish played their third game as the home opener and squeaked out a 21-13 win over Michigan State. Mistakes were the order of the day—two interceptions and a fumble by Rice helped an opportunistic MSU defense led by linebacker Percy Snow. Watters scored on a first-quarter 2-yard run and a second-quarter 53-yarder that started, ironically, when Rice fumbled the snap. A fumble by Culver led to an MSU field goal and an interception let the Spartans have a second field goal for a 14-6 halftime score. The Spartans gained only 75 yards rushing for the day. In the third quarter, their second interception led to a 30-yard touchdown pass. Anthony Johnson made a 1-yard touchdown blast, and the defense took over again. MSU would not kick to Ismail, with the inevitable tradeoff of good field position for Notre Dame.

Purdue turned the ball over eight times in a 40-7 Fighting Irish win. Holtz played the starting offense only into the second quarter, used 12 running backs, and amassed 530 yards. Johnson ran for a 6-yard touchdown shortly after Smagala smothered a Purdue fumble. Rice added a 4-yard touchdown a few minutes later for a 14-0 first-quarter lead. Tackle Jeff Alm intercepted a Purdue pass and used his 270 pounds to chug 16 yards for the third touchdown. Terrell intercepted a Purdue pass in his end zone. Rice found Derek Brown for a 38-yarder, and Johnson slammed in from the 1. Watters wrapped up the first half scoring with another 1-yard run. Hentrich hit two field goals in the fourth quarter, and Purdue finally found the end zone with a touchdown pass.

The Fighting Irish went to the Bay area and beat Stanford 27-17 for their 17th consecutive win—but it wasn't easy. Stanford, from the films, knew what to expect for a run defense. So they threw and kept throwing—Steve Smith heaved the ball 68 times, completing 39, for 282 yards and one touchdown. The Irish picked off three, and two led to scores. Stanford kicked two field goals in the first quarter to take a 6-0 lead, but Rice optioned for a 38-yard gain to set up Johnson's 7-yard touchdown in the second quarter. After exchanging some punts, Francisco intercepted a wayward pass, and Culver tallied a 2-yard touchdown. Stanford scored a third-quarter touchdown on a 2-yard pass and a 2-point conversion run. They kicked to Ismail, who made a 66-yard runback. Johnson pounded in from the 1 to put Notre Dame in front again. Notre Dame booted two field goals to one for Stanford; Terrell's interception set up the second Irish field goal.

The undefeated Fighting Irish met undefeated Air Force. Notre Dame gained 149 yards to Air Force's 11 in the first quarter. It was 21-0 before Air Force moved the sticks. The defense crunched Air Force's wishbone, so Air Force threw for 306 yards and two touchdowns. Johnson scored on a 1-yard blast. Watters scored on a 5-yard run. Ismail sped 56 yards on a punt return for a touchdown. The Falcons fired back with a 61-yard touchdown pass. The Irish bounced back, flashing Ismail out of the tailback spot, and Johnson caught a 27-yard touchdown from Rice. Air Force quarterback Dee Dowis hit a 26-yard touchdown pass, but Ismail closed out the half with a 24-yard touchdown run. Hentrich added two field goals, the second after a Lyght interception, and Air Force scored two fourth-quarter touchdowns on the ground for a 41-27 final score. The teams amassed 929 yards of offense on the day, 455 for Notre Dame and 474 for Air Force. Ismail accounted for 180 yards of all-purpose offense.

USC came to Notre Dame and nearly beat the Irish behind the leadership of Todd Marinovich, their lefty quarterback. The Fighting Irish pulled out the win, 28-24, but found themselves in the hole on two uncharacteristic fumbles by Ismail—one on the opening kickoff and the other on a punt at the end of the first quarter. USC converted both turnovers into touchdowns on Marinovich passes. Ismail returned a kickoff 58 yards to set up Rice's 7-yard touchdown run. The Trojans hit a 28-yard field goal in the second quarter for a 17-7 lead. Rice led a good drive in the

Chris Zorich, 1989 consensus All-American.

third quarter, running 24 yards to set up Watters' 2-yard touchdown. In the fourth quarter, on a third-and-1 play at the USC 35, Johnson got the call for a fullback dive but he broke it for the score. USC drove back on the next series to tally on a 16-yard pass. Rice led a careful 80-yard drive to win the game, capped by his own 15-yard touchdown burst. Marinovich tried a long pass for the win, but it fell incomplete.

Pitt came to Notre Dame undefeated and ranked 7th, but went home sadder and wiser after a 45-7 drubbing. They scored on an 8-yard pass, and then the roof fell in on them. In the first half, Notre Dame scored a safety when Pitt's quarterback slipped in the end zone; an Ismail-led drive ended in a 1-yard Culver touchdown; and Terrell returned an interception for a 54-yard touchdown. In the second half, Watters scored from the 2 after Kowalkowski recovered a fumble; Ismail ran for a 50-yard touchdown; Culver scored from the 1 after a Francisco interception; and Steve Belles ran 13 yards for a touchdown after a Lyght interception. The Irish kept it simple with 57 rushing tries for 310 yards, a 5.4-yard average.

Navy succumbed 41-0 as Holtz kept the Fighting Irish on the ground, this time with 60 runs by 13 ball carriers for 414 yards, an unstoppable 6.9-yard average. The victory tied the Irish record, set under Leahy, of 21 consecutive wins. It was Holtz's 150th career win. Watters led with nine carries for 134 yards, including a 43-yard run on the game's first play from scrimmage and a second-quarter touchdown run of 48 yards. His first long gain set up a Rice touchdown run of 6 yards. Ismail broke loose for a 30-yard gain, but suffered a groin pull and sat out the rest of the game. Culver scored from the 11. Billy Hackett followed Watters' touchdown with a 27-yard field goal to make it 24-0 at the half. He added a 39-yard field goal in the third quarter, and reserves Dorsey Levens and Ted McNamara wrapped up the shutout with touchdown runs of 2 yards and 1 yard, respectively, in the fourth quarter.

SMU, who was trying to rebuild its program after their NCAA death penalty,was not much of a challenge. SMU lost a half yard on each of 13 rushing tries for minus 7 yards for the day. They did complete 30 of 59 passes for 206 yards. Holtz had told his charges to run at will (54 carries for 362 yards) but not to score unnecessarily, so the final was 59-6. The win set a new record for Notre Dame with 22 consecutive victories. The scorers were: Watters for a 35-yard touchdown, Pete Graham on a 1-yard sneak, Andre Jones for 2 points on a blocked point after (SMU had scored on a 5-yard pass), Hackett with a 34-yard field goal, Watters on a 97-yard punt return, Johnson for a 4-yard touchdown burst, a safety when a reserve SMU quarterback stepped out of his end zone, and Walter Boyd for a 14-yard touchdown. In the third quarter, reserve Rusty Setzer added a touchdown from the SMU 2, and Hackett kicked a 32-yard field goal. In the fourth quarter, Rick Mirer threw a 33-yard pass to Mihalko to set up Rod West's 1-yard touchdown. Ismail gained 135 all-purpose yards on 10 attempts.

Penn State fell victim to Notre Dame's ground game, 34-23. The Irish showcased their runners 71 times for 425 yards, a record against Penn State. Rice and Watters both ran for more than 100 yards, and Ismail was just behind them. Penn State's defense simply wilted against the insistent Notre Dame ground game. Blair Thomas scored midway into the first quarter on a 2-yard blast. Rice used up much of the rest of the quarter to lead a drive capped by his 5-yard touchdown burst. Penn State earned a field goal, but Notre Dame took the lead with two touchdown drives, the first completed by Watters with a 12-yard run and the second by Johnson's 1-yard slam. The Irish defense forced a fumble, which Smagala recovered at the Penn State 14; Rice took it in from the 1 moments later. Thomas, who made 133 yards on 26 runs, scored from the Irish 3. Hackett booted two field goals in the last quarter, and Penn State got a 5-yard touchdown pass.

The winning streak ended at 23 games against Miami, 27-10. Miami did not break, not even on a third-and-44 which they converted just moments after they had recovered their own fumble that had passed through the hands of Notre Dame defenseman Devon McDonald. Those two plays turned the tide. Miami scored for a 24-10 lead in the third quarter, and Notre Dame never recovered. They had come back from a 10-0 first-quarter deficit when Hackett kicked a 22-yard field goal, and Bolcar intercepted a Craig Erickson pass and ran 49 yards for a touchdown. But the Irish offense was bottled up all day by an aroused, speedy Miami defense; Miami allowed only 142 yards on 45 carries, about 3 yards per run below the average of previous games. Rice completed seven of 15 for 106 yards, and the kick return game was also held in check.

Notre Dame rebounded to drill top-ranked Colorado 21-6 in the Orange Bowl. Having beaten nine bowl teams and winning 12 games, Holtz staked a claim on the national crown but Notre Dame came in number two when the votes were counted (Miami was number one). The first half was scoreless.

Colorado's star running back, Eric Bieniemy, broke loose from the Irish 35 and threatened to go all the way, but he dropped the ball at the Irish 18. In the third quarter, the Fighting Irish scored in seven plays, with Johnson drilling in from the 2 for the touchdown. Ismail made a 35-yard touchdown on a reverse. Colorado answered with a 39-yard touchdown run by Darian Hagan. In the fourth quarter, Johnson led a long, time-consuming drive and scored from the 7 for the final 21-6 score.

The Irish improved their ground game by nearly 20 percent, and scoring went from 359 points in 1988 to 406. The passing game produced about the same yardage, but the Irish scored primarily on the ground in 1989, a testament to their faith in the offensive line. Lyght and Zorich were consensus All-Americans, and Rice, Ismail, Bolcar, Alm, and Grunhard also won All-American honors.

1989 record: 12-1-0 (.923)
Record to date: 683-203-40 (.759)

1990 to 1991

1990

When Tony Rice graduated, the Fighting Irish lost a quarterback who had directed them to a 28-3 record as a starter. A glance down the chart located two sophomores—Rick Mirer and Jake Kelchner. Kelchner went down with a broken right collarbone in the first quarter of the spring game. Mirer had passed for 3,973 yards and 30 touchdowns in his senior year at Goshen, Indiana. As a reserve behind Rice, he got mop-up duties in eight games in 1989, carrying 12 times for 32 yards and completing 15 of 30 passes for 180 yards and one interception. Holtz tried not to put too much pressure on him, but Mirer had been assigned the number three jersey, Montana's old number. In Mirer, Holtz had a quarterback closer to the classic dropback mold of Montana or Beuerlein rather than the option running dimension Rice had provided.

Two starters returned to the interior offensive line, and the backfield boasted Watters, Tony Brooks (back after a year of working on academics), Culver, Ismail, Mihalko, Dorsey Levens, and Jerome Bettis. The receivers were led by Derek Brown and Ismail. This group had more than enough speed and good size, while the line had fine size and mobility. Mike Heldt, Tim Ryan, and Mirko Jurkovic led the workers in the trenches.

The defense had some returning stalwarts, notably consensus All-Americans Zorich and Lyght. Stonebreaker and George Williams returned from a year away from football. The linebackers also included Kowalkowski and Demetrius Dubose.

The team's strength was in its runners and receivers on offense, and the nose tackle and line-

Rick Mirer, QB starter in 1990-1991.

backer spots on defense. Lyght, in the secondary, was a proven All-American, but the rest of the deep backs were untested. The offensive line had to mature to provide the sophomore quarterback enough time to read the complicated defenses.

Michigan provided the first test, and the Fighting Irish almost flunked. Elvis Grbac was back, assisted by Jon Vaughan as a running back. Vaughan ran 22 times for 201 yards. The Irish won 28-24, their fourth straight win over the Wolverines, when Mirer hit Adrian Jarrell with an 18-yard touchdown pass inside the 2-minute mark of the fourth quarter. The sophomore opened the scoring with a 2-yard run, capping a short drive after Greg Davis recovered a Michigan fumble. The Wolverines kicked a field goal, and Tony Brooks ran for a 2-yard touchdown to end a long answering drive. Future Heisman winner Desmond Howard tallied in the second quarter on a 44-yard pass from Grbac; the score at the half was 14-10. Michigan owned the third quarter; they put together a long drive that ended in a 1-yard touchdown run, and Howard scored on a 25-yard pass from Grbac following a Tony Brooks fumble. Notre Dame won the game in the fourth quarter with two long drives, the first capped by Culver's 1-yard run and the Mirer to Jarrell pass for the second. Howard returned a kickoff to the Wolverine's 41. Reggie Brooks cinched it with an interception of a Grbac pass. The Wolverines both ran and passed for more yardage than did the Irish; the difference was the Irish converted an early fumble into a touchdown and then stopped Michigan's final drive with an interception. In between, there were plenty of scares for the Irish faithful.

Michigan State took Notre Dame all the way, only to lose 20-19; the offense brought Notre Dame back from a 19-7 deficit. Watters dashed in from the 5 late in the first quarter and showed the Spartans to be a very determined group. They played the best quarter of defense to be seen in the whole season and stopped Notre Dame without a first down in the second quarter. Meanwhile, the Spartans scored 12 points on a 43-yard field goal, a safety on a blocked punt, and a touchdown from the 1 seven plays after the free kick. Tico Duckett scored a 1-yard touchdown after the Fighting Irish failed to convert a fourth-down try. The offense struck in the fourth quarter—first on a Ricky Watters touchdown from the 1; Stonebreaker grabbed an interception but the team stalled, and then scored on a Culver smash from the 2. A Mirer pass deflected off the pads of a Spartan, and Adrian Jarrell grabbed it at the MSU 2. The tight score was reflected in the teams' yardage figures—311 for Notre Dame, 313 for MSU.

An assertive Fighting Irish defense, sparked by Kowalkowski (one fumble caused, one recovered, and constant pass rush pressure) led Notre Dame to a 37-11 win over Purdue. The offense sputtered to two Hentrich field goals in the first quarter, answered by a Purdue field goal. In the second quarter, Notre Dame scored 21 unanswered points. Mirer tallied from the 12 on a run to end a five-play, 66-yard drive. After Zorich recovered a fumble caused by Kowalkowski, Ismail ran 64 yards on a reverse for another touchdown—the drive's only play. Then a 15-play drive helped kill the clock, capped by Culver's 2-yard score. In the third quarter, Kowalkowski grabbed a Purdue fumble at their 33; Shawn Davis later scored from the 1. Hentrich added his third field goal as Notre Dame dominated much of the game for the win, allowing a late Purdue touchdown and 2-point conversion. Two passes took up most of that drive, a 58-yarder and a 37-yard scoring throw from Eric Hunter to Curtis McManus. The Irish ground game made 65 carries for 362 yards.

Three disastrous fumbles in the kicking game led to Stanford's 36-31 upset win. Ismail was out of the game with a deep thigh injury and his replacements, Watters and Jarrell, dropped two and one punts, respectively. Stanford scored following two of those turnovers. Although Tommy Vardell scored four Stanford touchdowns, it took a Mirer pass slipping off Derek Brown's fingertips in the end zone on the game's last play to seal Notre Dame's fate. The Fighting Irish had a 24-7 lead in the second quarter on a Mirer touchdown from the 1 in the first quarter, a Hentrich field goal of 29 yards, an 11-yard Tony Smith touchdown reception from Mirer, and another Mirer to Smith touchdown from 15 yards. Good defense set up Smith's scores; Devon McDonald grabbed a fumble to set up the first and Rod Smith blocked a punt to create the second opportunity. Vardell cut into that lead with a 1-yarder for a 24-15 halftime score. He did it again halfway into the third quarter, but Culver answered with a 1-yard bolt. Vardell scored at the end of the third quarter from the 1, and once again in the fourth quarter, for the final 36-31 score. Mirer moved the Irish 47 yards in the last 30 seconds, only to see the touchdown pass fall to the ground as Brown stretched to bring it in. Irish mistakes built Stanford's confidence and tough inside running by Vardell (13 carries for 37 yards but four touchdowns) caused Notre Dame to lose its number-one ranking.

Raghib Ismail vs. Michigan.

Air Force lost 57-27, due in large part to breakdowns in their punting game. Mihalko blocked consecutive punts that led to touchdowns. Their punter, perhaps a bit disoriented, was tackled for a safety as well. The Fighting Irish gained 542 yards of total offense, and Mirer had an excellent passing day, hitting 11 of 15 for 253 yards and two touchdowns. The Irish scores were: a Hentrich field goal of 28 yards, two Dorsey Levens touchdowns of 2 and 5 yards, an Ismail touchdown of 52 yards on a Mirer pass, and a Mirer to Brown touchdown pass of 5 yards for a 31-7 halftime score. Mihalko's punt blocks led to Levens' first touchdown and Brown's touchdown. In the third quarter, Lamar Guillory tackled the punter for a safety and Hentrich added a 26-yard field goal. The Irish added three touchdowns in the fourth quarter to two for Air Force—Watters slammed in from the 4 and the 1, and Jeff Burris scored from the 1. Ismail had six catches for 172 yards.

Now ranked sixth, the Fighting Irish faced Miami, also once beaten and ranked second. When the cheering subsided, Notre Dame had won 29-20. Defense did it with two interceptions, one in the fourth quarter, and two crucial fumbles recovered in the fourth quarter. The first quarter was a 10-10 deadlock: Miami recovered an Irish fumble and drove 25 yards for a touchdown. Hentrich kicked a 25-yard field goal. Miami's Huerta booted a 23-yard field goal, and Ismail zoomed 94 yards with the kickoff for a touchdown. Greg Davis intercepted a pass, and Hentrich boomed a 44-yard field goal. Miami replied with an 80-yard drive and a 1-yard touchdown by quarterback Erickson. Hentrich hit his third field goal with 4 minutes left in the half; Miami led 17-16. In the third quarter, Hentrich entered the record books when he hit two more field goals of 36 and 35 yards. George Williams recovered a Miami fumble to set up the first kick. The defense played inspired football to hold Miami to minus 8 yards rushing for the third quarter. Miami closed the gap to 2 points when Huerta kicked a 25-yard field goal. The Irish dominated the rest of the quarter. Mirer capped it with a pass play, which had literally been invented at the team breakfast that morning, for a 21-yard touchdown to Culver, who dragged a Miami deep back the last 5 yards into the endzone. The 'Canes fumbled at the Irish 23 and Stonebreaker recovered the loose ball with 4:44 remaining.

Emotionally drained, the Irish stumbled to a 31-22 win over Pitt in Pittsburgh; Zorich hurt a leg in the third quarter. Pitt's quarterback, Alex Van Pelt, hit 37 of 51 passes for 384 yards and two touchdowns, but not enough to offset their 84-yard ground game. Devon McDonald recovered a Pitt fumble at their 16; Brooks scored from the 2 four plays later. Lyght made an interception in the Irish end zone; Brooks capped it with a 28-yard touchdown blast. Pitt scored on a 9-yard pass near the end of the first half. In the third quarter, Hentrich kicked a 39-yard field goal. Ismail, early in the fourth quarter, made a 76-yard touchdown run from scrimmage, the longest such run in his career. Pitt's passing game set up a 1-yard touchdown plunge. They tried an onside kick, but Tony Brooks smothered it. Six plays later, aided by an Ismail run of 18 yards, Mirer ran in from the 1. With under a minute to go, Van Pelt threw his second touchdown pass.

Notre Dame tangled with Navy in a surprising 52-31 win, one that saw the teams gain 859 yards of combined offense. The Fighting Irish were taken aback when Navy opened up in a wishbone, having prepared for a wide-open passing attack. Jerome Bettis smashed over from the 1 near the end of the first quarter. Navy tied it, using a 44-yard pass from quarterback Alton Grizzard to set up a 1-yard score. Hentrich kicked a 31-yard field goal to end the next series. Navy tied with 14 seconds left in the half with a 27-yard field goal. Notre Dame scored 42 second-half points: Culver for a 7-yard touchdown on the opening drive, Watters on a 2-yard slam, and Mirer on a 30-yard touchdown sprint. An Irish fumble at their 19 led to Grizzard scoring on a 6-yard run. In the fourth quarter, Mirer hit Ismail for a 21-yard gain, and Brooks ran the last 2 yards to make it 38-17. Navy pulled to within two touchdowns on a 19-yard touchdown pass by Grizzard. Mirer floated a pass to Ismail, who made it a 54-yard touchdown. Grizzard fired a 7-yard touchdown pass. Navy tried an onside kick; Lyght recovered just as two Middies zoomed past him. Looking up and seeing no one, he ran 53 yards for his first touchdown.

Again ranked number one, the Fighting Irish were still not favored to beat Tennessee on the Volunteers' home turf. In the first quarter, Tennessee bracketed an Irish touchdown with field goals. The Notre Dame score came on a 41-yard pass from Mirer to Culver. The second quarter was slow-paced, and Hentrich kicked a 26-yard field goal. Tennessee took the lead in the third quarter on a Carl Pickens circus catch for a 33-yard gain, which set up a 10-yard scoring run. Watters took a handoff and hit the middle, broke an arm tackle and ran past the secondary, all of whom took bad angles to catch him. Tennessee's Andy Kelly threw to Alvin Harper for a 32-yard score, and the Volunteers led 20-17. Hentrich tied it six seconds into the fourth quarter with a 20-yard field goal. Tennessee mounted a 12-play drive that netted

Quarterback Rick Mirer.

a 45-yard field goal. After an exchange of possessions, Mirer floated one to Culver who broke it for a 20-yard gain; Watters scored from the 10. Donn Grimm intercepted a pass, and Ismail rocketed for a touchdown on a 44-yard reverse play. Tennessee came back for a 23-yard touchdown pass from Kelly with less than 2 minutes to play. The Volunteers stopped Notre Dame from running out the clock, but Rod Smith intercepted Kelly to secure the win. The Irish won 34-29, but Kelly had riddled the secondary for 399 passing yards.

Looking at Penn State, Holtz opined the day before the game that no one outcoaches Joe Paterno. Not even when Paterno is down 21-7, the halftime score. Up to that point, Notre Dame made Penn State look miserable. Watters scored a 22-yard touchdown and Brooks a 12-yarder. Penn State's Tony Sacca threw a 32-yard touchdown pass near the end of the quarter. In the second quarter, Penn State had the Irish on their 8-yard line with a good punt. Mirer used 16 plays for 92 yards, scoring himself from the 1. With mere seconds left in the half, Hentrich missed a field goal. The Fighting Irish had pounded Penn State for nearly 300 yards of total offense, but Ismail reinjured his thigh and did not play in the second half—a fact Paterno admitted he did not notice until halfway through the third quarter. Notre Dame did not score again, and Penn State won 24-21 when a Mirer pass was intercepted in the last minute of play. The winning field goal came with only 4 seconds on the clock. Without Ismail—or even the threat he represented—Notre Dame's offense never left its end of the field in the second half.

USC was next. They had beaten Penn State early in the season. Having lost seven in a row to Notre Dame, and under the leadership of Todd Marinovich, USC was primed for the game. Oddsmakers had Notre Dame as the underdog. The defense had, in losing to Penn State, allowed 20 or more points for seven consecutive games for the first time in Notre Dame history. But the defense had the final say this time—a 10-6 win, five sacks of Marinovich, and Notre Dame's eighth straight victory over USC. The Trojans scored two field goals, one in the first quarter and one in the third; the Fighting Irish scored on a 30-yard Hentrich field goal in the second quarter, and a Tony Brooks touchdown of 1 yard on an option pitchout in the third quarter. USC's runners made 29 yards on 28 carries, with Marinovich's sacks chopping off about 50 yards of their total.

In the Orange Bowl against top-ranked Colorado, Notre Dame beat itself with five turnovers and a questionable clipping penalty on what appeared to be Ismail's game-winning kickoff return in the last minute. In the third quarter, the Fighting Irish lost three turnovers in four snaps. Colorado played a good, steady game, refusing to panic when their starting quarterback was lost to a knee injury. In fact, the defense seemed out of synch as they had to adjust to a new quarterback. Colorado scored a 22-yard field goal early in the second quarter. On the next Notre Dame possession, Watters scored a 2-yard touchdown, but Hentrich's point-after kick was blocked. The Irish nursed a 6-3 lead at the half. Hentrich made a 24-yard field goal on the first possession of the second half but an Irish fumble on their own 40 eventually led to a 1-yard touchdown by Bieniemy for Colorado's 10-9 win.

The two regular season losses, to Stanford and Penn State, were by a total of 8 points and came within the combined last 40 seconds of those two games. The common denominator was that Ismail was not able to play. With him out of the lineup, the quick-strike offense became a plodding affair; defenses were less distracted by his scoring threat. The same held true, in a way, in the Orange Bowl loss to Colorado when his touchdown was wiped out by the penalty call.

The 1990 team's rushing game fell off about 37 yards per game, compared with 1989, although the passing game increased about 53 yards per game. The 1989 team allowed opponents only 295 yards of total offense per game, but the 1990 defense allowed opponents 390, which accounts for the average opponent's score of 22.6 points per game in contrast to 15.3 in 1989. Ismail, Lyght, Stonebreaker, and Zorich were consensus All-Americans, and Mike Heldt also earned All-American accolades. Zorich won the Lombardi Trophy and Ismail was named the Walter Camp player of the year.

1990 record: 9-3-0 (.750)
Record to date: 692-206-40 (.759)

1991

Some great players graduated after the 1990 season. Chris Zorich returned to his home from the Orange Bowl game to find that his mother had passed away. Zorich's loss led to Ismail's decision to forego his final season of college ball for a multi-million dollar pro contract in Canada. Like Zorich, Ismail was very close to his widowed mother and decided to make his contribution to her well-being as soon as possible.

Losing four two-time consensus All-Americans, three on defense, and the other the leading candidate for the Heisman in 1991, crimps a coach's plans. With the exception of Ismail's departure, the offense posed no major problems for Holtz. It was on the defense where he would be hard pressed to fill vacancies.

The backfield returned virtually intact—Mirer, Culver, Tony Brooks, and Bettis. For sheer talent among runners, this unit ranked with the very best—excellent speed and size, superb blocking, and good receiving. The flanker's position required a talent search, but Lake Dawson prevailed as a capable deep threat to complement Tony Smith. Derek Brown returned for his fourth year as the starting tight end. The line had good returning personnel in Mirko Jurkovic, Gene McGuire, and Justin Hall.

The entire defensive line had to be replaced. Troy Ridgely returned from a year's absence (academics) to provide some maturity and savvy. Untried youngsters had to learn the ropes quickly. The linebacking corps was in better shape with DuBose and Devon McDonald. Sophomore Pete Bercich had to grow quickly into the middle linebacker spot. Talented, speedy Willie Clark switched again to help at free safety. Jeff Burris, Tom Carter, and Rod Smith rounded out the secondary—short on experience but long on speed. Injuries kept Holtz from starting the same defensive unit in back-to-back games the entire season.

The Fighting Irish opened up at home against Indiana, a team they had not played since 1958. The usual clunkers and jitters plagued the offense on its opening three possessions. Likewise, the defense had its problems throughout the game, in spite of making four interceptions, in allowing a mediocre Hoosier team to make 25 first downs and 418 yards of total offense. Finally, 10 minutes into the first quarter and behind 3-0, Demetrius DuBose intercepted a Hoosier pass and ran 49 yards for a touchdown. Hentrich missed a second-quarter field goal, and Indiana marched 79 yards to score on a 5-yard quarterback run. Culver answered with a 19-yard touchdown run to put Notre Dame ahead 17-10. The Hoosiers gained 60 yards on four throws to grab the lead again. Mirer, with the blocking help of Adrian Jarrell who took out the Hoosier corner, made a 46-yard touchdown to recapture the lead. Indiana tried an on-side kick, but the Irish grabbed it and Tony Brooks scored a 13-yarder. In the third quarter, Indiana booted a 29-yard field goal. Mirer executed a 12-play drive, hitting passes to Lake Dawson and Derek Brown, before running in from the 6. Rod Smith intercepted a Hoosier pass. Reserve tight end Irv Smith got loose in the Hoosier secondary, caught a Mirer pass at the IU 28, and dragged three Hoosiers the rest of the way for a 58-yard touchdown play. In the fourth quarter, the teams traded touchdowns, an Indiana pass and a Mirer 1-yard plunge, for the 49-27 Irish victory. Other than Smith's touchdown, it had not been pretty; the secondary looked vulnerable and the defensive line had not dominated. Rod Smith led the team in tackles with 11.

Michigan's Elvis Grbac had never really had a bad day against the Fighting Irish, even though he had lost both prior games. With the help of a large offensive line and eventual Heisman winner Desmond Howard, the Wolverines ended Notre Dame's regular season four-game winning streak with a well played 24-14 victory. Grbac played a nearly perfect game, completing 20 of 22 passes for 195 yards and the back-breaking 25-yard touchdown throw to Howard, who made a catch fully stretched out in the end zone. An interception led to Michigan's opening score, a field goal in the first quarter. Howard added a 29-yard touchdown on a reverse play in the second quarter. An Irish fumble shortly after that led to a 16-yard touchdown run by Ricky Powers. With 17 seconds left in the half, Mirer hit Bettis with a 3-yard pass. In the third quarter, Mirer fired a strike to Tony Smith for a 35-yard touchdown to make it 17-14. With 9:02 left in the game, Grbac called the touchdown play, pump-faked, and Howard opened up a tiny seam for the touchdown catch and the win. The Wolverines' 428 yards of total offense confirmed Notre Dame's defensive problems. Michigan's Ricky Powers hammered the Irish for 164 yards on 33 carries; Notre Dame's running game was held to 78 yards.

Michigan State had already been beaten by Central Michigan, but the Fighting Irish knew that each game was critical. They came out running—76 carries for 433 yards as they smothered the Spartans 49-10. Seven players scored touchdowns and Mirer fired three touchdown passes. The scorers were: Reggie Brooks for a 2-yard touchdown burst, his first touchdown for the Irish; Tony Smith with a 29-yard touchdown pass from Mirer; Derek Brown for a 55-yard touchdown pass and run from Mirer. MSU made a field goal and a 48-yard touchdown pass to Courtney Hawkins for the 21-10 halftime score. The third quarter belonged to Notre Dame—Irv Smith with a 2-

Jerome Bettis, 1992 Sugar Bowl MVP.

yard touchdown pass from Mirer, Tony Brooks with a 9-yard touchdown blast, and Mirer with a 12-yard scoring run. In the fourth quarter, Willie Clark ran in from the 1-yard line to make the final score 49-10. The Fighting Irish gained 650 total yards.

Purdue lost 45-20 as Bryant Young played a "career game" with two fumble recoveries, three tackles behind the line of scrimmage, and six other tackles. Mirer was nursing bruised ribs, so freshman Paul Failla started; Mirer took over, completing 12 of 14 passes for 139 yards and two touchdowns. Purdue scored on a 1-yard run, but four Irish scores followed: Mirer on a 29-yard run, Bettis on a 6-yard blast after a Young fumble recovery, Derek Brown on a 5-yard touchdown catch after another Young fumble recovery, and Bettis plowing over from the 2. Purdue scored on a 19-yard pass, but two more Irish scores slammed the door on their comeback: Hentrich hit a 33-yard field goal, set up by Tony Brooks' 57-yard run, and Mihalko powered over for a 1-yard touchdown.

The torrid scoring pace of 39 points per outing kept up in a grudge match against Stanford, 42-26, the first time since 1943 that Notre Dame had exploded for four 40-point games in the first five. Lake Dawson scored on a 27-yard touchdown pass from Mirer. Bettis followed up a DuBose fumble recovery with the first of his four touchdowns for the day, this on a 3-yard burst. Early in the second quarter, Bettis ran 28 yards to the 1, and slammed over for the touchdown on the next play. Mirer ended the next drive, sparked by Bettis and Tony Brooks, when he slipped over from the 1. Down 28-0, Stanford scored on a Vardell run of 27 yards for the 28-7 halftime score. Stanford got two more Vardell scores in the second half and a touchdown on a quarterback keeper, but Bettis scored twice, once in the third quarter with a 13-yard touchdown pass from Mirer, and after a Rod Smith interception in the fourth quarter with a 1-yard run. He led all rushers for the day with 179 yards on 24 carries; Tony Brooks added 122 yards on 17 carries.

Against Pitt, the Irish kept up the scoring pace with a 42-7 rout, although Pitt held them to a 0-0 affair in the first period. Early in the second quarter, Irv Smith recovered a fumble after a punt; Bettis slammed over from the 1 seven plays later. Pitt was unable to move, punted, and Reggie Brooks returned it for a 26-yard touchdown. Notre Dame scored twice in both of the remaining quarters: Irv Smith with a 2-yard touchdown pass from Mirer and Mirer with an 8-yard keeper in the third quarter. Pitt's Van Pelt fired a 51-yard touchdown after an interception. Bettis ran for 66 of 80 yards on the next drive, scoring with a bruising 40-yard run. Reserve quarterback Kevin McDougal made a 5-yard touchdown keeper.

Air Force played a good game, losing 28-15. They ran the ball 75 times, gaining 354 yards. Still, Air Force was able to get into the end zone only once. The Fighting Irish picked up 420 total yards to control the outcome. The Falcons scored a field goal but couldn't stop the return march. Bettis powered in from their 7 to make it 7-3. Air Force kicked a field goal in the second quarter, stopped Notre Dame, came back, and missed a field goal. Mirer hit Tony Smith with an 83-yard touchdown bomb on the next play. Troy Ridgley grabbed a fumble on their 36; Bettis ran it in from the 3 to end Notre Dame's first half scoring. The Falcons kicked another field goal on the last play of the half. They tried an onside kick to open the second half, it backfired, and Bettis ran 19 yards for a touchdown moments later. The Falcons scored a touchdown in the fourth quarter to make it 28-15. Two defensive linemen went down with bad ankles—Bryant Young and Eric Jones. Irish players complained that Air Force used illegal cut blocks to do the damage.

Injured and somewhat suspect on defense, the Fighting Irish faced USC. The Trojans were spoiling for a win—and almost got it, though Notre Dame prevailed 24-20. Holtz tinkered with personnel to patch together a defensive line. Bettis surprised the Trojans with his speed and strength on a 53-yard touchdown run to start his day's work of 178 yards on 24 carries. In the second quarter, Bettis ran 23 yards to set up a 14-yard touchdown pass from Mirer to Brooks for a 14-0 halftime cushion. In the third quarter USC's Deon Strothers made a 29-yard touchdown run. Bettis killed a drive with a fumble. Following a DuBose fumble recovery, Bettis ended an 89-yard drive with a 1-yard touchdown blast. The Trojans forced a Mirer fumble on a sack at the Notre Dame 20, and Mazio Royster converted the turnover with a 14-yard touchdown run. Hentrich kicked a 34-yard field goal, and USC scored a touchdown on their next drive. They tried an onside kick and Irv Smith came away with the ball; the Irish killed the clock for the ninth consecutive win over USC.

Winless Navy succumbed 38-0, following a week in which Holtz put the Fighting Irish through their most strenuous workouts of the season to sharpen the team for Tennessee and Penn State. Mirer threw three touchdown passes to earn the single season all-time touchdown passing record with 17. Derek Brown caught a 2-yard touchdown, after a 22-yard strike to Tony Smith. Hentrich booted a 35-yard field goal and Bettis caught a 9-yard scoring pass from Mirer. In the third quarter, Mirer threw a 13-yard score to Smith. Bettis slammed over from the 1 in the fourth quarter and Reggie Brooks made a 65-yard run to set up his 3-yard touchdown. Mirer threw for 303 yards on 17 of 23 attempts. Devon McDonald led a solid defensive effort with one sack and two other tackles for losses.

The high-water mark for the Fighting Irish occurred in the first quarter of the Tennessee game when they held a 21-0 lead. However, the Irish lost the game 35-34 to see their chances for the national crown ended. The Irish stunned Tennessee with three scores in the first quarter: a 12-yard touchdown run by Brooks, a 79-yard touchdown run by Tom Carter with an interception, and a 10-yard run by Mirer. In the second quarter, the Volunteers made a touchdown pass. Hentrich kicked a 24-yard field goal. Bettis made it 31-7 with a 2-yard run. With only 14 seconds in the half, the Volunteers blocked a Hentrich field goal try and took the ball in for an 85-yard score. In the melee, Hentrich went down with a sprained knee. Coach Johnny Majors could see that Notre Dame was having its way on the ground, with 233 yards in one half. He strangled the run in the second half, forced a milder passing game, and Tennessee picked off three Mirer throws. When it was over, Tennessee scored three more times on short drives. Walk-on kicker Rob Leonard saw his 27-yard winning field goal attempt deflected at the line of scrimmage. The Fighting Irish won the stats, but Tennessee won the game.

Defeated, deflated, and nursing some lingering injuries, the Fighting Irish went to Penn State, losing 35-13. In a lackluster performance, they gained only 90 yards on the ground, and gave up 239 yards running and 151 passing. Penn State racked up a 21-0 first-quarter lead. Bettis scored in the second quarter on a 2-yard effort, and William Pollard caught a 38-yard touchdown pass from Mirer in the third quarter. Holtz was so distressed he admitted that he wanted to practice right there, at Penn State, just hours after the loss.

Two weeks later, and about six time zones across the world, the Fighting Irish faced the University of Hawaii and piled up 499 yards of total offense for 48 points—and they still almost lost the game, 48-42. The defense was nearly in total disarray due to innumerable personnel changes on the line. Only Tom Carter's two interceptions and a fumble recovery by Troy Ridgley staved off a strong first-half performance by Hawaii. By that time, Notre Dame led 28-10. Culver made a 3-yard touchdown run to convert Carter's first interception. Ridgley's fumble recovery led to Tony Brooks' 13-yard touchdown run. In the second quarter, Culver ran 52 yards to set up a touchdown run of 11 yards by Mirer. Hawaii scored on a touchdown pass, and Brooks tallied again after a 47-yard screen pass to Culver set it up. Hawaii ended the half with a field goal. Bettis scored twice in the second half, on 4- and 2-yard runs, for a record 16 touchdowns on the ground for the season. Hawaii hammered away at the Irish defense on its way to 473 yards of total offense, and the highest point total against Notre Dame in an Irish win. Bettis missed a 1,000-yard season when he was held to 31 yards on 12 carries.

Notre Dame had redeemed itself some with a strong final game, but critics said the 9-3 record was unworthy of the Sugar Bowl and third-ranked Florida. However, Holtz, given enough time to do a thorough coaching job, would always keep the Fighting Irish in a game. He used his time wisely and retooled the defense so that steady pressure and good containment forced a hobbled Gator quarterback to throw into no fewer than six defensive backs. The odd defense, a 3-2 look with six backs deep, initially looked porous. The Gators opened up a 10-0 first-quarter lead with a 15-yard pass for a score and a 26-yard field goal. They added another field goal in the second quarter before a quick strike of 40 yards from Mirer to Dawson scored. The Gators kicked another field goal at the end of the half. Trailing 16-7, the Fighting Irish closed the gap in the third quarter with a 23-yard field goal by a kicker recruited from the soccer team, Kevin Pendergast; Hentrich had reinjured himself in the first half. Irv Smith filtered into the end zone on a play-action pass to score with a 4-yard pass from Mirer. Florida booted two more field goals in the fourth quarter, but Bettis made three touchdown runs. The first capped a patient drive and gave Notre Dame its first lead. The Gators tried to jam the line of scrimmage, and Bettis scored on runs of 49 and 39 yards on almost identical plays. The Gators scored on a pass, but it was too late. Holtz's "bend but don't break" defense allowed 511 yards, but Bettis led a dominating ground attack and Mirer completed 14 of 19 passes for the 39-28 win.

Notre Dame finished 12th in the nation, even though they had beaten some teams ranked ahead of them. The 1991 Fighting Irish set records with 59 touchdowns scored, 425 points, and 5,466 yards of total offense. The first two records had lasted for nearly eight decades, shattering records set when Rockne was in his junior season, 1912. The defense, however, allowed 1,103 more rushing yards than in 1990, while also allowing opponents to run more total plays and maintain longer ball possession.

Holtz signed a new five-year contract, a relief after earlier rumors that he was headed to the Minnesota Vikings. There were some immediate concerns, not the least being the status of his starting quarterback, Mirer, who was considering turning pro (weeks later, Mirer decided to return for his senior year). And he certainly knew that the defensive line would need a major infusion of talent. Brooks and Culver were gone from the backfield, as was Derek Brown after 4 years as the starting tight end (although Irv Smith looked quite capable).

1991 record: 10-3-0 (.769)

Record to date: 702-209-40 (.759)

THE FUTURE

Sometime in the 1997 season, the Notre Dame football team will play its 1,000th game. If past trends have any merit, the Fighting Irish cumulative record will be approximately 740 wins, 220 losses, and 40 ties. It is likely that Holtz will have completed his second five-year contract and might be starting another. The Fighting Irish will have challenged for one or two more national crowns and may have won one or both. A Notre Dame quarterback or running back or wide receiver will have challenged for or won the Heisman, the eighth such honor for a Notre Dame student-athlete. The same will be true for linemen and linebackers regarding the Outland Trophy, the Lombardi Award, or the Butkus Award.

Despite individual accolades, it will be the excellence of the Notre Dame program that will continue to hold true in the 1,000th game. The Fighting Irish will continue to graduate more than 95 percent of those who come on football scholarships. These fine players will continue to be leaders on the campus and go on to distinguished careers after graduation. The program will be the model for others. If other programs would act in the ethical interests of their athletes, many abuses currently found in collegiate athletics would simply disappear. This is ultimately what distinguishes Notre Dame football from other programs: no one else has yet found the key to such total team success—a condition that goes far beyond the stadium on game day into the lives of all alumni and the mainstream of society.

Chapter 7

The Fighting Irish Player Roster

From 1887 to 1991, Notre Dame played 951 games of football, and 2,250 players represented the university on the gridiron, although many more may have aspired to play. Memories of the vast majority of those who played for Notre Dame are somewhat vague, obscured—or enlarged in some cases—by time and distance. Perhaps the young man labored in the anonymity of the interior line, or played when records were kept haphazardly. As recently as 1950, at the height of the Leahy years, Ed Flynn made the team and appears to have played—but that's all that is known. At one point in the lifetime of this project, I had envisioned listing *all* Fighting Irish players, but that was not feasible. Instead, using no particular guidelines other than an abiding interest in Notre Dame football, a sense of its growth and development, and some notion of "what makes a story," roughly 300 players have been selected for inclusion in the roster that follows.

Most of them were heroes in their careers—but not all. There are some surprises. Most had some golden moments in that autumn light of a late afternoon playing football for Notre Dame. A select few knew only golden moments, even when tinged with the little failures that the game manages to propel into the stream of time at a crucial moment. Some men go beyond enjoying golden careers. These men are in the pantheon of American sports: Red Salmon, Knute Rockne, George Gipp, the Horsemen, Moose Krause, Angelo Bertelli, Johnny Lujack, Leon Hart, Johnny Lattner, Paul Hornung, Joe Theismann, Ross Browner, Joe Montana, Allen Pinkett, Tim Brown, Chris Zorich, and Raghib Ismail. All were stunning actors in the drama, both on the gridiron and in life. The brilliant play happens suddenly, unfolds in 10-12 seconds, and is gone. Film and video cannot revive the total moment—Gipp's frenetic playing against destiny, Shakespeare's winning pass to Millner to beat Ohio State in 1935, Lujack's open-field tackle of Blanchard in 1946, Penick's game-winning touchdown run to start the second half of the 1973 USC game, Montana's winning throw in the 1979 Cotton Bowl, or the team defense that beat Miami in 1988. Film, video, and books cannot fully catch the sounds, the sights, the collective emotion, the tension, the mounting hopes or fears, and the breathlessness. We try to stop the golden moment, suspend it, make it linger. But it leaves us . . .

What follows involves players from all decades of Fighting Irish football and at all positions. Record-keeping today is an impressive effort and players in the last few decades have had their careers recorded in exquisite detail. But when it started in 1887, and for many years after that, football was a fad. Who in 1887 could have foreseen what that mayhem would become? So many of the interesting facts and records of players are long gone. A few players still shine through—take a careful look at John Farley, for instance. Enough said. Here come the Irish . . .

ALLAN, DENNY. 1968-1969-1970; HB; 5-11, 188; Ashtabula, OH. Two-year starter as RHB in 1969 and 1970. Teamed with Theismann for good outside quickness and excellent receiving skills. In 1968, made 33 runs for 105 yards and three TDs, caught seven passes for 93 yards and one TD, and returned seven kickoffs 183 yards. In 1969, had 148 carries for 612 yards and nine TDs, caught 11 passes for 199 yards, and returned 10 kickoffs for 185 yards. In 1970, had 111 carries for 401 yards and seven TDs, and caught 11 passes for 166 yards and one TD. For his career, had 292 runs for 1,118 yards and 19 TDs, caught 29 passes for 458 yards and two TDs, and returned 17 kickoffs 368 yards for a total of 1,944 yards.

ALM, JEFF. 1986-1987-1988-1989; DT; 6-7, 270; Orland, Park, IL. Excellent DT for the first four Holtz teams, a key member of the stifling defense featured by the 1988 national champs. Great pass rusher, excellent pursuer, and tremendous obstacle for QBs. Teamed with Zorich. In 1986, backed up at DT; made four tackles. In 1987, backed up at DT; made five tackles. In 1988, started at DT for the national champs; made 50 tackles, eight for -25 yards, caused two fumbles, recovered one fumble, broke up three passes, and made three interceptions (to tie for the team lead) for eight return yards. In 1989, started at DT; made 74 tackles, one sack for -4 yards and six others for -20 yards, caused one fumble, broke up six passes, and had one interception for 16 return yards. Made All-American. In his career, made 133 tackles, with one sack for -4 yards and 14 others for -45 yards, caused three fumbles, recovered one fumble, broke up nine passes, and made four interceptions for 24 return yards.

ANDERSON, EDDIE. 1918-1919-1920-1921; E; 5-10, 166; Mason City, IA. Four-year starter at right end; teamed with Gipp on undefeated squads of 1919 and 1920. Good receiver and excellent defensive player. In 1919, made an interception and TD runback in win over Purdue. In 1920, caught a 60-yard pass from Gipp in win over Valparaiso. Had a long reception from Gipp in shutout of Purdue. Scored twice with short passes in win over Northwestern. Scored last TD of season recovering a blocked MAC punt. In 1921, caught three passes from Mohardt in loss to Iowa. Helped beat Purdue by blocking a punt for an Irish TD. Caught four Mohardt passes in win over Indiana. Contributed to win over Nebraska by recovering two fumbles and blocking well for game's only TD. In win over Army, recovered a fumble on their 20 and blocked a field goal try. Scored against Rutgers with an 84-yard pass from Mohardt and recovered a fumble. Caught a 45-yard TD pass in win over Marquette to go with two sacks and two other catches. All-America pick.

ANGSMAN, ELMER. 1943-1944-1945; HB, FB; 6-0, 185; Chicago, IL. Tough, speedy runner during relatively lean years with Leahy gone to war; excellent defensive player. In 1944, started at FB and gained 233 yards on 58 carries. Lost 11 teeth in Navy game but continued to play. In 1945, started at RHB and led backs with 616 yards on 87 carries for seven TDs and seven yards per carry.

ARRINGTON, DICK. 1963-1964-1965; T, G; 5-11, 232; Erie, PA. Started at LT in 1963. Started at RG in 1964. Started at RG and DT in 1965. Tremendous upper body strength and superb quickness; excellent blocker and also wrestled. In 1963, blocked a Syracuse PAT in close loss. Made 40 tackles for the year. In 1964, was an important member of the offensive line that helped Huarte win the Heisman and nearly went undefeated. In 1965, was a two-way starter even though two-platoon football was back. Made 36 tackles for the year. Consensus All-American.

ASHBAUGH, PETE. 1941-1942-1946-1947; QB, HB, K; 5-9, 175; Youngstown, OH. Known as a great defensive backfield specialist. Fine speed, great hitter. In 1941, had one interception and a 15-yard runback. In 1942, had a 40-yard punt return to the Illini 1-yard line in 21-14 win. In 1946, in rout of Iowa made a fumble recovery on the ND 8, an interception plus a 38-yard runback to lead to a TD, and a 32-yard kickoff return. Caught one pass for 28 yards. In 1947, played exclusively as a defensive ace; saw 224 minutes of action.

AZZARO, JOE. 1964-1965-1966-1967; K; 5-11, 190; Pittsburgh, PA. Starting kicker on early Parseghian teams. In 1964, booted two PATs and a 30-yard field goal in tough win over Pitt. For the year, made seven PATs and one field goal. In 1966, was an integral part of a great scoring machine. Hit eight straight PATs against Duke. Kicked the field goal that tied MSU 10-10, and missed one by a foot that would have won the game. Made a 38-yard field goal and six of seven PATs in rout of USC. For the year, hit 35 of

38 PATs and four of five field goals for 47 points. In 1967, kicked field goals of 23 and 24 yards in win over Cal. Beat Miami with a 22-yard field goal. For the year, hit 37 of 40 PATs and eight of 10 field goals for 61 points. In his career, kicked 74 PATs, 13 field goals, and scored 113 points.

BACHMAN, CHARLIE. 1914-1915-1916; G, FB; 5-11, 187; Chisholm, MN. Rugged, spirited player for Jesse Harper's powerhouse teams in the early years of Notre Dame's emerging national fame. Started at RG in 1914. Started at fullback in 1915. Against Alma, scored on a short run and set up another with a 60-yard sprint. In win over Haskell, shed six tacklers and scored on a 40-yard punt return. In win over Creighton, ran for 89 yards, scored a TD, returned a kickoff 25 yards, and intercepted two passes. Scored a TD in big win over Texas. Led Irish runners with 120 yards in win over Rice. Started at LG in 1916. Named All-American.

BARNETT, REGGIE. 1972-1973-1974; DB; 5-11, 181; Flint MI. Smart, fast defensive back for Parseghian's last three teams. Key player in 1973 national championship season. Started at RCB in 1972. For the year, made 24 tackles, broke up four passes, recovered one fumble, intercepted two passes for 16 return yards in 274 minutes. Started at LCB in 1973; made 29 tackles, one for -2 yards, broke up six passes, had two fumble recoveries, and one interception. Started at LCB in 1974. Saved a narrow win over Alabama in Orange Bowl with an interception within game's last two minutes. For the year, made 37 tackles, three for -10 yards, led team with nine passes broken up, had one interception. For his career, made 90 tackles, four for -12 yards, broke up 19 passes, recovered three fumbles, and made four interceptions.

BARRY, NORM. 1917-1918-1919-1920; HB; 5-10, 170; Chicago, IL. Steady, heady player with the misfortune of playing behind Gipp for most of his career. Excellent blocker. Competed hard with John Mohardt for playing time, to the detriment of opponents. In 1917, ran more than 50 yards for a TD in win over MAC. In 1918, caught a 22-yard TD pass from Gipp in win over Purdue. In 1919, scored one TD in win over Northwestern. In 1920, started at RHB. Tallied two TDs in win over Kalamazoo. Ran for two TDs and caught a TD pass from Gipp in win over Northwestern—Gipp's last pass before his death three weeks later. Helped sustain a long TD drive with excellent end runs in win over MAC.

BARZ, BILL. 1968-1969-1970; HB, FB; 6-2, 216; Country Club Hills, IL. Theismann's fullback in 1969 and 1970. Excellent blocker, steady runner, and good receiver. In 1969, had 362 yards on 90 carries for five TDs, was second in receiving with 24 catches for 262 yards and two TDs (when it was rare to throw to fullbacks). In 1970, had 88 carries for 352 yards and four TDs and caught 13 passes for 127 yards and one TD. For his career, had 178 carries for 714 yards and nine TDs, and caught 37 passes for 389 yards and three TDs for 1103 all-purpose yards.

BAVARO, MARK. 1981-1982-1983-1984; TE; 6-4, 246; Danvers, MA. Tremendous talent; devastating blocker with good hands, size, and speed. In 1981, played briefly against Navy and Georgia. In 1982, was supposed to back up Tony Hunter. Played briefly in Michigan game and reinjured an old hand problem; lost for the season. In 1983, started at TE. Scored with a 17-yard TD pass from Kiel in win over Purdue. Caught a 2-yard TD pass from Kiel in loss to MSU. Made 22-yard TD in win over Army, on a pass from Beuerlein. Caught a 59-yard option pass from Pinkett in win over USC. For the season, Bavaro caught 23 passes for 376 yards and three TDs. In 1984, saw more action than any other Fighting Irish receiver. Led in receptions with 32 for 395 yards. Caught four against MSU and Missouri and kept Notre Dame close with a 5-yard TD catch in tough loss to South Carolina. Caught two passes in close loss to SMU in Aloha Bowl. For the season, Bavaro caught 32 passes for 395 yards and one TD. In his career caught 55 passes for 771 yards, good for four TDs. Made All-American.

BEACOM, PAT. 1903-1904-1905-1906; G, T; 6-2, 220; Sheldon, IA. One of the Fighting Irish mainstays at the turn of the century; not highly skilled at first, but developed into dominating player. In 1903, started at LG for an undefeated Irish team. In 1904, started at LG. Scored twice on "tackle back" plays against Ohio Medical. Rushed for more than 50 yards to help an ailing Notre Dame team beat DePauw. In loss to Purdue, was an effective runner in only TD drive. Started at LG in 1905. Scored three TDs and ran for more than 60 yards in win over North Division H.S. Wabash held him to 30 yards rushing in their surprising win. Tallied two TDs against American

Medical. Ran for two more TDs in win over DePauw. Kicked PAT in win over Bennett Medical College. Started at LT in 1906. Scored two TDs and kicked one PAT in win over Franklin. Blocked a Hillsdale punt to set up TD on a linebuck; added insurance TD and PAT. Scored three TDS in shutout of Physicians and Surgeons. Lost a TD on a penalty, but Notre Dame won over Purdue 2-0.

BECKER, DOUG. 1974-1975-1976-1977; LB; 6-2, 224; Hamilton, OH. Key player in 1977 national championship season; quick, played with reckless abandon, good tackler. In 1974, made 12 tackles, one for -19 yards, recovered two fumbles, and played 36 minutes. In 1975, started as OLB. Made 72 tackles, four for -8 yards, broke up one pass, and recovered three fumbles in 184 minutes. Grabbed a Miami fumble on their 20 that led to a TD in win. In 1976, started as OLB. Made 89 tackles, four for -27 yards, broke up two passes, and had one interception in 233 minutes. His good hit created a Miami fumble to set up a TD in Irish win. In 1977, started as OLB; teamed with Golic and Heimkreiter. For the season, made 81 tackles, three for -16 yards, broke up one pass, recovered one fumble, and intercepted one pass for 29-yard runback. In Cotton Bowl win over Texas, intercepted a pass and returned it 23 yards to set up third Irish TD. For his career, made 254 tackles, 12 for -70 yards, broke up four passes, recovered six fumbles, and had three interceptions.

BELL, GREG. 1980-1981-1982-1983; TB, WB; 6-0, 205; Columbus, OH. Speedy, powerful runner in Faust years. Effectiveness limited by injuries. In 1980, gained 66 yards on five carries, for 13.2 average, and scored one TD in 3:36 minutes. In 1981, backed up Hunter at WB, probably a misuse of his skills; gained 512 yards on 92 carries for four TDs, caught 11 passes for 135 yards, and led team with 13 kickoff returns for 371 yards, including 98-yard TD run against Miami. In limited action in 1982, carried 24 times for 123 yards, caught three passes for 20 yards, returned three kickoffs for 50 yards, and one punt for 12 yards. In 1983, another limited season, scored four TDs against Purdue in blowout win: on a 2-yard run, a 9-yard pass from Kiel, another 2-yard run, and a 6-yard run. Ran 50 yards for TD in loss to MSU. Ran back punts in Liberty Bowl win over Boston College. In his career, Bell had 158 carries for 870 yards and nine TDs, caught 20 passes for 220 yards and one TD, returned 16 kickoffs for 421 yards and one TD, and one punt 12 yards. He reached 1523 yards for 11 TDs in 195 career attempts.

BERGMAN, ALFRED (DUTCH). 1910-1911-1913-1914; HB, QB; 5-8,160; Peru, IN. Fast, shifty, smart runner and field general. Played with Dorais and Rockne. In 1910, backed up at RHB. In 1911, started at RHB. Had 20-yard TD run, 40-yard kickoff return, and 40-yard punt return in win over Ohio Northern. Led Fighting Irish in rushing and scoring in win over St. Viator; scored on runs of 15, 40, and 40 yards and on pass from Dorais. Scored one TD on a 65-yard punt return in win over Butler. Entered record book with 105-yard kickoff return against Loyola—*without scoring* (the field was longer then), but scored three of 14 TDs for the day. In 1913, backed up at RHB. In 1914, started at QB. Scored two of 15 TDs against Rose Poly. Played well in shutout loss to Yale: had runs of 20 and 15 yards, a 35-yard punt return, and threw two passes for 48 yards. Rushed for 160 yards against South Dakota, scoring on end runs of 50 and 60 yards, passed for another 50 yards, and made one PAT. Against Haskell, scored on a 35-yard run with a lateral and on punt returns of 80 and 85 yards (and lost an 80-yard TD run for stepping out of bounds). Gained more than 245 yards of total offense in win over Carlisle with two kickoff returns of 50 yards each, 50-yard TD runback of a dropped punt, 60 yards on two punt returns, and two pass completions. Closed career with TD against Syracuse.

BERTELLI, ANGELO. 1941-1942-1943; HB, QB; 6-1, 173; West Springfield, MA. The "Springfield Rifle;" first QB of early T-formation teams under Leahy. Great team leader, superb passer, somewhat slow for HB, so moved to QB. First Notre Dame player to win Heisman Trophy. In 1941, started at LHB and hit 70 of 123 passes for 1,027 yards and eight TDs; gained 56 yards with 40 carries; had one interception, a 17-yard kickoff return, and made three of three PATs. Completed six of seven passes in first game, one a 16-yard TD to Bob Dove, and kicked two PATs, in win over Arizona. Fired TD pass to George Murphy and hit four passes in a row on TD drive in shutout of Georgia Tech. In win over Illinois, fired 13-yard TD pass to Juzwik and 40-yard TD pass to Evans. In win over Navy, 42-yard pass to Earley set up first TD; fired 18-yard pass to Juzwik. Beat Northwestern with TD pass to Bolger. Teamed with Dove for brilliant passing in win over USC; made winning score with 18-yard pass to Evans. For the year, had 70 completions in 123 tries for 1,027 yards and eight TDs. In 1942, switched to QB. Got on wrong train as the team took the right train to Madison but made it to game; Irish tied Wisconsin 7-7; had only four completions; new backfield set dropped five fumbles. Had three passes intercepted in loss to Georgia Tech. Made nine straight completions in win over Stanford and hit four TD passes: 36 yards to Dove, 16 yards to Limont, 26 yards to Murphy, and 15 yards to Livingstone for 14 of 20 for 233 yards. Threw 47-yard TD to Livingstone in win over Iowa Pre-Flight. QB sneak for TD was the difference in 21-14 win over Illinois. Scored on short TD run against Navy and had an endzone interception in 9-0 win. Threw 17-yard TD to Murphy in 13-0 win over Army. Had 7-yard TD pass to Dove in loss to Michigan. Helped beat Otto Graham and Northwestern with 31-yard TD pass to Creighton Miller. In win over USC, fired TDs of 48 yards to Miller and nine yards to Livingstone. For the season, completed 74 of 165 throws for 1,044 yards and 11 TDs. In 1943, won Heisman Trophy on six games played before his service call-up. Recovered Pitt fumble and dove two yards for TD in shutout win. To beat Michigan, completed five of eight passes for 172 yards, scored one TD, and threw two TDs, one a 70-yarder to Earley. Led starters to five TDs in 22 plays against Wisconsin in 50-0 blowout. In last home game, completed five of seven in shutout of Illinois, including 47-yard bomb to Julie Rykovich for the first score. Against Navy, threw three TD passes and ran for another. For the year, completed 25 of 36 for 511 yards and 10 TDs. He was in the Marines shortly thereafter. In his career, completed 169 of 324 passes for 2,582 yards and 29 TDs.

BETTIS, JEROME. 1990-1991-; FB; 5-11, 247; Detroit, MI. Awesome force in Fighting Irish running game in sophomore year. Tremendous leg drive, upper body strength, and quick start for size make him one of the most difficult runners to tackle in recent memory. Threatens to surpass some of Pinkett's scoring records. In 1990, backed up at FB. For the year, had 15 carries for 115 yards and one TD. In 1991, started at FB. For the year, had 168 carries for 972 yards and 16 TDs, and caught 17 passes for 190 yards and four TDs for a new single-season records of 20 TDs and 120 total points. In the 39-28 comeback win over Florida in the Sugar Bowl, won MVP by gaining 150 yards on 16 carries and scoring three second-half TDs of 3, 49, and 36 yards, to go with stunning blocking and 5-yard catch. Two-year career shows 183 carries for 1087 yards good for 17 TDs and 17 receptions for 190 yards and four TDs. His two seasons have produced 1277 yards in 200 attempts good for 21 TDs. Barring injury, promises to be a two--time All-American.

BEUERLEIN, STEVE. 1983-1984-1985-1986; QB; 6-3, 201; Fullerton, CA. One of the most impressive QBs for the Fighting Irish in recent years, perhaps the best pure passer since Montana. Excellent arm, good leadership skills, and pinpoint accuracy. Holds virtually all of Notre Dame's passing and total offense records. Had some great offensive weapons to work with in Pinkett and Tim Brown. May not have been fully appreciated since his career spanned some rather dismal years. In 1983, started at QB for eight games. For the year, had 23 carries for -9 yards, and 75 completions in 145 throws for 1,061 yards, four TDs, and six interceptions. In 1984, started at QB. For the year, had 58 carries for -75 yards, completed 140 of 232 throws for 1,920 yards, seven TDs, and 18 interceptions, and caught one pass for six yards and a TD. In 1985, started at QB. In the Aloha Bowl, hit 11 of 23 passes for 144 yards and one TD as SMU won 27-20. For the season, had 43 carries for -19 yards and one TD, and completed 107 of 214 passes for three TDs and 13 interceptions. In 1986, had 53 carries for 35 yards and one TD, completed 151 of 259 passes for 2,211 yards, 13 TDs, and seven interceptions. For his career, had 177 carries for -68 yards and two TDs, completed 473 of 850 passes for 6,527 yards, 27 TDs, and 44 interceptions, and caught one pass for six yards and one TD. He was involved in 6,465 yards of offense for 30 TDs. He holds Notre Dame's career records for most pass attempts, most completions, most passing yards, most interceptions, most total offensive attempts (1,027), and total offense yardage.

BLEIER, ROCKY. 1965-1966-1967; HB; 5-11, 195; Appleton, WI. Steady, dependable runner, blocker, and receiver for Parseghian on 1966 championship team with Hanratty and Seymour; captain in 1967. In 1965, as a reserve RB averaged 5.6 yards per carry on 26 runs for 145 yards and two TDs; caught three passes for 42 yards and made one tackle. In 1966, started at RHB with Hanratty, Eddy, and Conjar in the backfield. Gained 282 yards on 63 carries for four TDs; was second on team with 17 receptions for 209 yards; punted 16 times for a 39.6-yard average; and returned three kickoffs 67 yards. In 1967, started at LHB and gained 357 yards on 77 carries for five

TDs; caught 16 passes for 171 yards and two TDs; punted 23 times for a 33.0-yard average; and returned nine kickoffs for 201 yards. For his career, made 166 runs for 784 yards and 11 TDs, caught 36 passes for 422 yards and two TDs, and returned 12 kickoffs 268 yards for a career total of 1,474 yards.

BOLAND, JOE. 1924-1925-1926; T; 6-0, 221; Philadelphia, PA. One of the all-time greats; assistant coach under Elmer Layden, 1936-40; well known speaker; and the radio "Voice of the Irish" for years. Very quick for a big man; was a good tactician as a key lineman in Rockne's shift offense in the final year of the Four Horsemen as a reserve and the first year with Christy Flanagan. Started at LT in 1925 and 1926, but an injury curtailed his senior year. In 1925, blocked two punts in a close win over Minnesota. In 1926, was headed for another blocked punt against Minnesota, but was kicked in the leg and was lost for the season.

BRACKEN, BOB. 1904-1905-1906; HB, QB; 5-11, 165; Polo, IL. Three-year starter in the backfield. Played good defense and was capable of breaking loose for long gains. In 1904, started at RHB. Playing under Red Salmon, scored three TDs in shutout of American Medical. In 1905, started at LHB. In 58-0 loss to Wisconsin, recovered a Badger fumble for a touchback, ran for short yardage gains, and stopped a probable Badger TD, after a 55-yard gain, with a flying tackle. Scored three TDs on long runs in 142-0 "game" against American Medical and started to give the linemen the ball for fun (they ended up with more TDs than the backs). In 1906, started at QB. In opening win over Franklin, scored on 35-yard run and 40-yard sprint. Scored one TD in 17-0 win over Hillsdale. Returned a punt 105 yards against Physicians and Surgeons, but it was called back for stepping out of bounds. Helped beat MAC 5-0 with runs of 20 and 15 yards on a muddy field. Rushed for important short yardage gains in 2-0 win over Purdue to go with a good punt return and a fumble recovery. Returned punts for 35 yards in loss to Indiana. Named to All-State team. Was an assistant coach in 1907.

BRADLEY, LUTHER. 1973-1975-1976-1977; SS, CB; 6-2, 202; Muncie, IN. Very quick defensive back for Parseghian and Devine; constant scoring threat. Played on two national championship teams (1973 and 1977). In 1973, started at SS and led Notre Dame with six interceptions for 37 return yards; made 27 tackles, one for -2 yards; led the team with 11 passes broken up; and recovered one fumble. Missed 1974 over a parietals infraction. In 1975, started at RCB and made 56 tackles, two for -5 yards; broke up two passes; blocked one punt; and made four interceptions for 135 return yards and one TD in 303 minutes of play. Entered the record book by intercepting a HB option pass intended for the Purdue QB and running 99 yards for a TD. Made All-American. In 1976, started at LCB and made 50 tackles, two for -23 yards; broke up seven passes; recovered one fumble; blocked one kick; and intercepted two passes in 272 minutes of action. Made All-American. In 1977, helped win the national championship with 45 tackles, seven passes broken up, and five interceptions for 46 return yards. Consensus All-American. For his career, made 153 tackles, five for -30 yards; broke up 27 passes; recovered two fumbles; blocked two kicks; and intercepted 17 passes for 218 return yards and one TD.

BRANDY, JOE. 1917-1919-1920; HB, QB; 5-8, 147; Ogdensburg, NY. Slick ball handler and excellent field general. Teamed with Gipp in two undefeated seasons, 1919 and 1920. In 1917, backed up at RHB. Led backs in rushing in tie with Wisconsin. Scored TD in win over South Dakota. Scored Notre Dame's only TD in 7-2 win over Army, a drive started by his interception; also recovered a fumble. In 1919, backed up at QB. Scored TD in rout of Western Normal. In 1920, started at QB. Kicked one PAT in win over Kalamazoo. Directed parade of TDs in rout of Western Normal. Scored winning TD against Indiana. Threw 5-yard TD pass to Eddie Anderson in win over Northwestern. Recovered a fumble in win over MAC.

BRENNAN, TERRY. 1945-1946-1947-1948; HB; 6-0, 170; Milwaukee, WI. Started for three undefeated Leahy teams. Good, quick runner and receiver, and excellent defender. Became Notre Dame's head coach in 1954. In 1945, rushed 57 times for 252 yards and backed up at LHB. In 1946, started at LHB and led the nation's best rushing team with 329 yards on 74 carries, caught 10 passes for 154 yards, returned kickoffs for 111 yards, and scored six TDs. In 1947, gained 404 yards rushing, led team with 11 TDs, led in carries (87), led in receptions (16) and yardage (191), and led in punt returns with 11 for 115 yards—all despite a season-ending knee injury in the eighth game. In 1948, started at LHB and rushed 48 times for 284 yards, a 5.9-yard average, and caught five passes for 102 yards. For his career, made 266 runs for 1,269 yards; caught 31 passes for 447 yards; made 111 yards in kickoff returns and 115 yards in punt returns; and scored 17 TDs as he gained 1,942 all-purpose yards.

BRILL, MARTY. 1929-1930; HB; 5-11, 190; Philadelphia, PA. A transfer to Notre Dame from Penn, much to Rockne's delight. Teamed with Carideo, Savoldi, Elder, and Schwartz to give the Fighting Irish, undefeated in 1929 and 1930, tremendous depth and skill in the backfield. Very fast, powerful, blocker. Never played in a losing game for Notre Dame. In 1929, played great defense to help Notre Dame beat USC. Caught 25-yard pass to set up winning TD against Northwestern. In 1930, used lateral passes to Savoldi, who scored on two of them to beat Navy. Scored first Irish TDs in win over Pitt, from the 23 and 2. Annihilated Penn with three TDs and 125+ yards of rushing—including 65-yard TD run—in 60-20 win. Scored on 3-yard run off a fake pass in win over Drake. In 7-6 win over Army, made a perfect open-field block in the secondary to spring Schwartz for 54-yard TD run. Scored six TDs for the year. Made All-American.

BROOKS, TONY. 1987-1988-1990-1991; TB; 6-2, 223; Tulsa, OK. Powerful, speedy TB for Holtz. Exploded to a quick start, broke tackles, and then accelerated in the open field. In 1987, backed up at TB. Carried three times for 7 yards in 1988 Cotton Bowl against Texas A & M. For the year, carried 54 times for 262 yards and one TD, caught three passes for 38 yards, and returned one kickoff 2 yards. In 1988, backed up at TB for the national champions. Made 11 carries for 35 yards in Fiesta Bowl win over West Virginia. For the season, in spite of a painful foot injury, carried 117 times for 667 yards and two TDs, and caught seven passes for 121 yards and two TDs. Missed 1989 for academic reasons. In 1990, backed up at TB. For the year, made 105 carries for 451 yards and four TDs, caught three passes for 47 yards, and returned four kickoffs 67 yards. In 1991, started four games at TB. For the year, had 147 carries for 894 yards and five TDs, and caught 11 passes for 126 yards and one TD. Gained 68 yards on 13 carries in win over Florida in the 1992 Sugar Bowl. For his career, had 423 carries for 2,274 yards and 12 TDs, caught 24 passes for 332 yards and three TDs, and returned five kickoffs 69 yards. His career offense reached 2,675 yards in 452 attempts and 15 TDs.

BROWN, BOB. 1895-1896; HB; 5-10, 162; Sheldon, IA. Came from same small Iowa town as Pat Beacom a few years later; part of the renewed interest in football at Notre Dame after three-year lapse (1889-1892). Tough, quick player, adept at long runs from scrimmage. In 1895, started at RHB and led Irish runners for yardage in the season even though he did not play all the way. Had 40-yard TD run in shutout of Northwestern Law. Helped beat Illinois Cycling Club with 130 yards rushing and two TDs; made seven runs of more than 13 yards. Rushed for 155 yards and one TD while recovering three fumbles in win over Physicians and Surgeons. In 1896, started at LHB and rushed for 120 yards against South Bend Commercial A.C., with TD runs of 50 and 65 yards to go with a TD plunge. Helped beat Albion with a TD and 50 yards of punt returns. Scored a TD in loss to Purdue. Helped demolish Highland Views 82-0 with three TD runs of 60 yards each.

BROWN, DEREK. 1988-1989-1990-1991; TE; 6-6, 252; Merritt Island, FL. Premier TE in college football, long-distance threat with superb size, good speed, and good hands. Integral part of offense since freshman year. In 1988, started at TE in fifth game for the national champions. For the year, caught 12 passes for 150 yards and three TDs. Caught two passes for 70 yards in Fiesta Bowl win over West Virginia. In 1989, started at TE. For the year, caught 13 passes for 204 yards. Had one reception for 12 yards against Colorado in the Orange Bowl. In 1990, started at TE. For the year, caught 15 passes for 220 yards and one TD. In Orange Bowl loss to Colorado, caught four passes for 56 yards. In 1991, caught 22 passes for 325 yards and four TDs. Caught one pass for 11-yard gain in Irish win over Florida in 1992 Sugar Bowl. For his career, caught 62 passes for 899 yards and eight TDs.

BROWN, TIM. 1984-1985-1986-1987; FL; 6-0, 195; Dallas, TX. Heisman Trophy winner in 1987, Notre Dame's seventh; tremendous deep threat for Faust and Holtz in passing game and on special teams. Had 4.38-speed in the 40-yard dash, superb instinctive moves, sixth sense for avoiding tackles, good hands, and a willingness to catch passes on crossing patterns over the middle. In 1984, backed up at SE. For the year, had one carry for 14 yards, caught 28 passes for 340 yards and one TD, and returned seven kickoffs 121 yards. In 1985, started at FL. For the season, carried four times for 30 yards and one

TD, caught 25 passes for 397 yards and three TDs, returned 14 kickoffs 338 yards for one TD. In 1986, started at FL. For the year, had 59 carries for 254 yards and two TDs, caught 45 passes for 910 yards and 5 TDs, returned 25 kickoffs 698 yards for two TDs and two punts for 75 yards. Made All-American. In 1987, started at FL. For the season, had 34 carries for 144 yards and one TD, caught 39 passes for 846 yards and three TDs, returned 23 kickoffs 456 yards and 34 punts 401 yards for three TDs. Consensus All-American and Heisman Trophy winner. For his career, had 98 carries for 442 yards and four TDs, caught 137 passes for 2,493 yards and 12 TDs, returned 69 kickoffs 1,613 yards for three TDs and 36 punts 476 yards for three TDs. His career yardage was 5,024 yards on 340 attempts for 22 TDs, an average of 42.3 yards for each scoring play. He holds Notre Dame's records for most career receiving yards, most kickoff returns in a season (25 for 698 yards in 1986), most career kick returns, most career kick return yards, and is tied with Ismail for most career kick returns for a score (six).

BROWNER, JIM. 1975-1976-1977-1978; FB, SS; 6-3, 204; Warren, OH. Middle brother of three Browners to play at Notre Dame. Excellent defensive player, especially hard tackler. In 1975, backed up at FB, and was third in rushing with 394 yards on 104 carries for two TDs, caught two passes for 16 yards, and made two tackles in 137 minutes of play. In 1976, started at SS and led DBs with 80 tackles, four for -14 yards; broke up three passes; blocked one kick; and intercepted two passes in 242 minutes. In 1977, started at SS and led DBs again with 73 tackles, nine for -53 yards; broke up five passes; recovered five fumbles; made one interception; and returned eight kickoffs 133 yards in 244 minutes for the national championship team. In 1978, started at SS and led DBs with 75 tackles, five for -38 yards; broke up four passes; recovered three fumbles; and made two interceptions for 64 return yards and one TD. For his career, made 230 tackles, 18 for -105 yards; broke up 12 passes; recovered eight fumbles; and made five interceptions.

BROWNER, ROSS. 1973-1975-1976-1977; DE; 6-3, 248; Warren OH. All-time great Notre Dame player—four-year starter, devastating pass rusher, extremely quick, extraordinary nose for the ball, and a threat to make a big play at any time. Played on two national championship teams (1973 and 1977). In 1973 as freshman, started at DE and was third on team with 68 tackles, led in tackles for losses with 15 for -104 yards, broke up one pass, recovered two fumbles, blocked one kick, and scored a safety. Did not play in 1974 after being suspended, with five others, over infractions of dorm regulations. In 1975, started at DE and made 71 tackles, 16 for -78 yards; broke up two passes; and scored one TD and a safety in 247 minutes. In 1976, started at DE and won the Outland Trophy for 97 tackles, 28 for -203 yards; broke up seven passes; recovered four fumbles; and blocked one kick in 273 minutes. In 1977, started at DE and made 104 tackles, 18 for -130 yards, and recovered two fumbles. In his career, made 340 tackles, 77 for -515 yards; broke up 10 passes; recovered eight fumbles; blocked two kicks; and scored two safeties and one TD. Consensus All-American in 1976 and 1977.

BUDKA, FRANK. 1961-1962-1963; QB; 6-0, 190; Pompano Beach, FL. Part of the QB shuffle in early 1960s; good runner, fair passer, and good defensive skills, who was probably played out of position for much of his career. In 1961, backed up at QB, but led Notre Dame in passing with 646 yards on 40 of 95 passes for three TDs; ran 31 times for 20 yards and one TD; returned one kickoff for 10 yards; made 21 tackles and two interceptions; broke up three passes; and led team with three fumble recoveries in 217 minutes. In 1962, backed up at QB. Hit only two of nine passes for 25 yards, gained 21 yards on 12 carries, returned one kickoff for 20 yards, caught one pass for 19 yards, made 51 tackles to lead DBs, broke up eight passes, and intercepted one pass for a 10-yard runback. Also played FL to help vitalize a moribund Irish offense. In 1963, back at QB and completed 22 of 41 passes for 251 yards and four TDs; ran for 97 yards on 47 carries and scored four TDs; and made four tackles. For his career, hit 64 of 145 passes for 690 yards and seven TDs, rushed 78 times for 117 yards and five TDs, caught one pass for 19 yards, broke up 11 passes, made three interceptions, recovered three fumbles, and made 71 tackles. His career all-purpose yardage was 826 yards in 143 attempts for 12 TDs.

BULLOCK, WAYNE. 1972-1973-1974; FB; 6-1, 223; Newport News, VA. Powerful runner and excellent blocker under Parseghian; key backfield man in the 1973 championship season. Hard to stop in scoring range. In 1972, as a reserve, carried 27 times for 123 yards and caught two passes for 32 yards. In

1973, started at FB, teaming with Clements, Best, and Penick, and led the Fighting Irish with 752 yards on 162 carries for 10 TDs, caught eight passes for 83 yards and one TD, and returned two kickoffs 39 yards. In 1974, started at FB and led runners with 855 yards on 203 carries for 12 TDs, caught 11 passes for 103 yards, and returned one kickoff seven yards. For his career, ran 392 times for 1,730 yards and 22 TDs, caught 21 passes for 218 yards and one TD, and returned three kickoffs 46 yards for a career yardage total of 1,994 yards.

BUONICONTI, NICK. 1959-1960-1961; G, LB; 5-11, 210; Springfield, MA. Gritty, dependable, overachieving lineman and linebacker; excellent tackler; good blocker. Played in a dismal period of Notre Dame football. In 1959, started at LG and was third-leading tackler with 67; broke up one pass. In 1960, backed up at LG but led team with 74 tackles, blocked two kicks, and broke up one pass. In 1961, started at LG and was second on team with 71 tackles; broke up one pass, recovered one fumble, and blocked one kick. For his career, made 212 tackles, blocked three kicks, recovered one fumble, and broke up three passes. All-American in 1961.

BURGMEIER, TED. 1974-1975-1976-1977; SE, S, CB; 5-11, 187; East Dubuque, IL. Speedy, sure-handed DB on 1977 national championship team. Three-year starter, with one spent at SE. In 1974, backed up at FS and made six tackles. In 1975, started at SE, had one carry for 50 yards, caught 10 passes for 185 yards and one TD, returned nine punts 52 yards, and made four tackles, one for -3 yards. In 1976, switched to defense and started at RCB; made 54 tackles, one for -2 yards; broke up three passes; recovered one fumble; intercepted two passes for 42 yards; and handled 20 punts for 138 yards in returns. In 1977, started at RCB; made 54 tackles, one for -9 yards; broke up six passes; ran once for 21 yards; threw one pass for a 2-point conversion; made four interceptions and 100 yards in runbacks; and returned 18 punts 82 yards. For his career, carried twice for 71 yards, caught 10 passes for 185 yards, threw a 2-point conversion pass, made 118 tackles, three for -14 yards, broke up nine passes, recovered one fumble, made six interceptions for 142 return yards, and handled 47 punts for 272 yards for a total of 670 yards.

CALHOUN, MIKE. 1976-1977-1978; DT; 6-5, 250; Austintown, OH. Three-year starter at DT; steady, dependable player, with good quickness; on national championship team in 1977. In 1976, started at DT and made 92 tackles, 12 for -41 yards; broke up eight passes; recovered two fumbles; and blocked one kick. In 1977, started at DT and made 76 tackles, 13 for -63 yards, and recovered three fumbles. In 1978, started at DT and led linemen with 99 tackles, eight for -39 yards, and broke up one pass. For his career, made 267 tackles, 33 for -143 yards; broke up four passes; recovered five fumbles; and blocked one kick.

CALLICRATE, DOM. 1905-1906-1907; E, HB; 5-11, 160; Granger, IN. All-purpose player and three-year starter, with good speed, toughness, and the ability to break a long gainer. Played with Red Miller and Bob Bracken, a good QB of the day. In 1905, started at RE. Scored one TD in 142-0 rout of American Medical. Ran for another TD in rout of DePauw. Used a "fake sideline play" for 12-yard gain in loss to Indiana. In 1906, started at RH. Scored one TD in shutout of Physicians and Surgeons. Lost 60-yard TD play on a penalty in 2-0 win over Purdue. Was only effective Notre Dame runner in loss to Indiana. In 1907, started at RH and scored one TD in opening shutout of Physicians and Surgeons. Shocked Olivet with a 100-yard kickoff return, and scored on 5-yard plunge. Made 75 yards in 0-0 tie with Indiana. Scored one TD in win over St. Vincent's.

CANNON, JACK. 1927-1928-1929; G; 5-11, 193; Columbus, OH. The last Fighting Irish player to play without benefit of a helmet. A very quick, rugged, reckless, determined ball player; good blocker; great tackler. In 1927, backed up at LG. In 1928, backed up at RG. In 1929, started at LG. In the 1929 game with Army, won by Elder's interception and TD return, was involved in half of Notre Dame's tackles. Consensus All-American in 1929.

CARBERRY, GLEN. 1920-1921-1922; E; 6-0, 180; Ames, IA. A tough, speedy player, especially good on defense; good football mind; later coached at Fordham. Played with both Gipp and the Four Horsemen. In 1920 and 1921, backed up at LE. In 1922, started at LE and captained the team.

CAREY, TONY. 1964-1965; DB; 6-0, 190; Chicago, IL. Excellent defensive back for early Parseghian teams—tough, rangy, fast; devastating tackler. Teamed with Longo and Rassas to make formidable secondary unit. In 1964, started at RH and made 46 tackles, broke up 10 passes, recovered one fumble, and led team with eight interceptions for 121 return yards. Made second team All-American. In 1965, started at RH and made 34 tackles, broke up three passes, recovered one fumble, and made three interceptions for nine return yards. In relatively brief career, made 80 tackles, broke up 13 passes, recovered two fumbles, and made 11 interceptions for 130 return yards.

CARIDEO, FRANK. 1928-1929-1930; QB; 5-7, 175; Mt. Vernon, NY. One of Rockne's best QBs: chesty, heady, excellent field general, good runner, blocker, good kicker, and excellent defender. Always found a way to win. Involved as a player in the 1928 win over Army ("Win One for the Gipper"). QB for the first recognized consecutive national championship teams in 1929 and 1930. Led famous backfield players: Marchy Schwartz, Marty Brill, Jack Elder, and Joe Savoldi. In 1928, subbed at QB. Scored TD against Drake on a sneak. Subbing for injured starter, scored only TD in shutout win over Penn State by crawling into the end zone. Returned a punt 50 yards in loss to USC. In 1929, started at QB. In win over Navy, made two PATs, an interception plus runback to the Navy 32 to set up winning TD, and completed pass to Elder while on one knee. Helped beat Georgia Tech with a 75-yard punt return for TD, plus good passing and kicking. Against Northwestern made 85-yard interception return for TD. Made All-American. In 1930, started at QB. Against Northwestern, dropped five punts inside their 5-yard line. With Brill, made block to spring Schwartz on 54-yard TD run in 7-6 win over Army; kicked PAT for the win. Kicked two PATs and caught 19-yard TD pass from Schwartz in win over USC—Rockne's last game. Repeat consensus All-American.

CARNEY, JOHN. 1983-1984-1985-1986; K; 5-10, 170; West Palm Beach, FL. Walk-on player who earned kickoff team start as freshman. Generated tremendous distance on kickoffs. All-time leader in field goals, attempts, and percentage. In 1983, handled kickoff duties. In 1984, handled place kicking duties. For the season, was perfect on 25 PATs and made 17 of 19 field goals for 76 points. In 1985, handled place kicking. For the year, made 21 of 24 PATs and 13 of 22 field goals for 60 points. In 1986, handled place kicking. For the year, made 24 of 26 PATs and 21 of 28 field goals for 87 points. For his career, made 70 of 75 PAT kicks and 51 of 69 field goals for 223 points.

CARROLL, JIM. 1962-1963-1964; G, LB; 6-1, 225; Atlanta, GA. Hard-nosed lineman and linebacker; spiritual leader of Parseghian's first team (1964). In 1962, started at LG; was third on team with 58 tackles, and recovered two fumbles. In 1963, started at RG; made 59 tackles, broke up one pass, and blocked one kick. In 1964, started at ILB, captained the team, and set new record for tackles with 140. Also intercepted one pass and broke up four others. Made second-team All-American. For his career, made 257 tackles, blocked one kick, recovered two fumbles, intercepted one pass, and broke up five passes.

CARTER, PHIL. 1979-1980-1981-1982; HB, TB; 5-10, 197; Tacoma, WA. Short, strong, quick runner; prototype of backs for the next several seasons. In 1979, played in nine games, rushed 27 times for 145 yards to lead team with 5.4-yard average; and caught one pass for four yards. In 1980, started at HB but missed four games. Set new record with 40 carries in one game, against MSU. Was second leading rusher with 186 runs for 822 yards and 6 TDs; also caught five passes for 27 yards. Averaged 117 yards per game, second best for all Irish runners to that point. In 1981, carried 165 times for 727 yards and six TDs, was third in receiving with 14 catches for 57 yards, and was second leading scorer with 36 points. In 1982, ran 179 times for 715 yards and two TDs, caught 12 passes for 85 yards, threw one pass for 54-yard TD, and returned one kickoff 18 yards. For his career, rushed 557 times for 2,409 yards and 14 TDs, caught 32 passes for 173 yards, threw one pass for 54-yard TD, and returned one kickoff 18 yards for 2,600 total yards.

CARTIER, GEORGE. 1887-1889; QB; Ludington, MI. Notre Dame's first QB, from the Iron Country of Northern Michigan, near the home of George Gipp. Cartier Field was named for him, and the Fighting Irish played there until 1930.

CASE, JAY. 1975-1977-1978-1979; DE, DT; 6-3, 239; Cincinnati, OH. Good defensive lineman for 1977 national champions. Part of a defensive line that made it hard for offenses to operate. Three-year starter but injuries ended his senior year early. In 1975, subbed at DT. In 1977, made 36 tackles, three for -16 yards; broke up one pass; recovered one fumble; and scored 30-yard TD on a blocked punt. In 1978, started at DE, replacing Browner; made 72 tackles, leading team in tackles for losses with 12 for -56 yards; broke up two passes; and recovered four fumbles. In 1979, made one tackle before season ended with an injury. For his career, made 109 tackles, 15 for -72 yards; broke up three passes; recovered five fumbles; and scored one TD.

CASEY, DAN. 1894-1895; G; 6-0, 173; Crawfordsville, IN. Part of resurgent interest in football at Notre Dame after it was not played for several years. Good runner, kicker, and defender. In 1894, started at RG. Ran ball several times in Hillsdale game from "guards back" deployment. Rushed for more than 145 yards, scoring TDs from 50 and 25 yards, in shutout win over Wabash. Ran for 35-yard TD in close win over Rush Medical. In 1895, started at RG and captained team. Scored one TD, ran back one kickoff, and made two PATs in shutout of Northwestern Law. Sped for 15-yard TD against Illinois Cycling Club and made all three PATs in win. Scored one TD, made three PATs, and returned two kickoffs 25 yards in shutout of Physicians and Surgeons.

CASPER, DAVE. 1971-1972-1973; T, TE; 6-3, 252; Chilton, WI. A rare starter in the modern era at two line positions. Excellent technician in blocking, with superb lateral quickness for a tackle. As TE on 1973 national championship team, presented formidable problem for defenders. In 1971, backed up at LT and caught one pass for 12 yards. In 1972, played T for most of the year. Caught one pass for six yards and made two tackles for the year. In 1973, started at TE; made 19 receptions for 317 yards and four TDs to go with one tackle. Consensus All-American. For his career, caught 21 passes for 335 yards and four TDs; also made three tackles on special teams.

CASTNER, PAUL. 1920-1921-1922; HB, FB; 6-0, 190; St. Paul, MN. Never played high school football but was developed by Rockne into All-American. Fine athlete in football, hockey, and baseball. As pitcher with the Chicago White Sox, was victimized by Ty Cobb when Cobb stole home from third. Holds Notre Dame's record for career kickoff return average (21 for 767 yards and two TDs, a 36.5-yard average) and single season (11 in 1922 for 490 yards and 2 TDs, a 44.5-yard average). Played both with Gipp and the Four Horsemen. His broken hip in the 1922 Butler game gave Rockne the opportunity to make the moves that brought four gifted sophomores together as starters, and the rest is football history. A powerful, punishing runner, a fine passer, an excellent kicker, and a good defender. In 1920, backed up at FB. Ran for short yardage, kicked one PAT, and intercepted one pass for 35-yard runback in win over Kalamazoo. Made 25-yard TD run in win over Western Michigan. Fired 50-yard TD pass to Chet Grant in win over Purdue. In 1921, backed up at RHB. In close loss to Iowa, kicked 70-yard punt, just missed 50-yard drop-kick field goal, and caught 33-yard pass. Helped beat Purdue with punts of 50, 55, and 45 yards, field goals of 20 and 24 yards, and good short yardage runs. Manhandled Indiana with a fumble recovery, three interceptions, a pass reception for 11-yard TD, and 50-yard TD sprint. In shutout win over Army, made one interception plus 27 yards, and punted 88 yards. Three days later, helped defeat Rutgers with 55-yard TD run, 2-yard TD plunge, 55-yard punt, and field goals of 45 and 43 yards. Ran for three TDs against Haskell, one for 50 yards. Punted well against Marquette, ran for short yardage, and returned two kickoffs 28 yards. In win over MAC, made 65-yard kickoff return, one TD run, and a completed pass. Made second-team All-American as a sub. In 1922, returned a kickoff 95 yards in win over Kalamazoo. Caught TD pass from Stuhldreher in win over Georgia Tech. Personally beat Indiana with a 27-point performance in a 27-0 Irish win: booted two field goals of 43 and 35 yards, ran for TDs of 20 and 22 yards, intercepted a Hoosier pass and ran it back 35 yards for TD, and kicked three PATs. A hip injury against Butler ended it for him.

CHEVIGNY, JACK. 1926-1927-1928; HB; 5-9, 173; Hammond, IN. Good HB for Rockne; a teammate of Christy Flanagan; best known for scoring the first TD after Rockne's halftime pep talk in 1928 Army "Win One for the Gipper" game. When he crossed Army's goal, Chevigny cried out, "That's one for the Gipper!" Later coached briefly at Notre Dame and was head coach at Texas. In 1926, back up at RHB. Scored TD in first varsity game in win over Beloit. Scored against Minnesota on 17-yard run. In 1927, backed up at RHB. His solid running against Georgia Tech helped secure an Irish win. In 1928, started at RHB. Scored Notre Dame's only TD on 3-yard run in loss to Wisconsin. Scored on 10-yard sprint in win over Drake. Scored his TD for the Gipper with 1-yard plunge on fourth down; had to be carried from the field later in the game after recovering a bad snap. Scored his final TD on 51-yard run off a fake reverse in loss to USC.

CLATT, CORNY. 1942-1946-1947; FB; 6-0, 200; East Peoria, IL. Solid performer for Leahy's first T-formation team and the immediate post-war, undefeated teams. In 1942, started at FB. Helped beat Iowa Pre-Flight with an interception and 37-yard TD return. Made 15-yard TD run in win over Illinois. Helped beat Otto Graham and Northwestern with 5-yard TD buck, 1-yard TD dive, 47 yards rushing on TD drive, and an interception to set up a Bertelli TD pass. In 13-13 tie with Great Lakes, scored on 82-yard TD burst. In 1946, backed up at FB and scored the last TD in win over Illinois. Slammed in from the Purdue 2 for TD in Irish rout. For the season, gained 105 yards on 28 carries. In 1947, backed up at FB and scored 4-yard TD in win over Tulane after going 34 yards on three runs to get there. For the year, rushed 11 times for 49 yards and one TD.

CLEMENTS, TOM. 1972-1973-1974; QB; 6-0, 184; McKees Rock, PA. Three-year starter for Parseghian at QB; led offense in 1973 national championship season. Fine field general, excellent ball handler, good passer, and very quick. In 1972, started at QB. For the season, completed 83 of 162 passes for eight TDs and 1,163 yards, and rushed for 341 yards and four TDs on 86 carries. In 1973, led Notre Dame in total offense with 1,242 yards gained on 149 plays for 8.3-yard average. Completed 60 of 113 passes for 882 yards and eight TDs, picked up 360 yards and four TDs on 89 carries, and ran for a 2-point conversion. Saved Sugar Bowl win with daring pass from his end zone to TE Robin Weber. In 1974, started at QB; threw 122 completions in 215 attempts for eight TDs and 1,549 yards, rushed 95 times for 369 yards and two TDs. Helped beat Alabama in 1975 Orange Bowl with 11 runs for 26 yards and four of seven passes for 19 yards. For his career, completed 265 of 490 passes for 3,594 yards and 24 TDs; rushed 270 times for 1,070 yards and 10 TDs and a 2-point conversion for a career total of 4,664 yards and 34 TDs.

COADY, ED. 1888-1889; QB; Pana, IL. Starter at QB for fledgling Irish in four games over two seasons, part of the second wave of participants in the new sport. Was on the field for the first two Irish victories, after starting with three losses. In 9-0 win over Northwestern, faked to a lineman to score an easy TD.

COFALL, STAN. 1914-1915-1916; HB; 5-11, 190; Cleveland, OH. Three-year starter at LHB, the premier position in Harper/Rockne scheme. Fast, elusive; good passer and kicker. In 1914 started at LHB. Scored two TDs and kicked seven PATs in opening win over Alma. Scored four TDs playing only the first half against Rose Poly. In loss to Yale, had 30-yard run and 35-yard pass completion. Played both HB and QB in win over South Dakota and scored on 15-yard run, threw TD pass, returned two punts 65 yards, and booted one PAT. Played great defense and kicked three PATs in win over Haskell. Scored only Irish TD on 1-yard plunge in loss to Army. Against Carlisle, kicked 50-yard field goal, three PATs, and 85-yard punt; completed 20-yard pass; and made TD plunge and assorted short runs. Scored one TD and one PAT in win over Syracuse. In 1915, started at LHB. Against Haskell scored TDs on runs of 20, 15, and 12 yards; added an interception and one PAT. In loss to Nebraska, ran for 50 yards, made two sacks, caught one pass, completed one pass, and scored on 3-yard plunge. Threw 50-yard TD pass that beat Army 7-0. Against Creighton, rushed for 155 yards, scored two TDs and four PATs, completed two passes, and punted 65 yards. Led Notre Dame in 36-7 win over Texas with a TD on a short plunge, 75 yards rushing, one fumble recovery, one interception, 37-yard kick-off return, and three PATs. Two days later, battered Rice with three TDs, including 30-yard run and 90-yard kickoff return, five PATs, 70-yard punt, and 21-yard pass completion. In 1916, started at LHB and captained the team. Scored on 60-yard TD blast in rout of Wabash. Kicked one field goal and one PAT in loss to Army. Scored on two long runs in win over MAC. Made All-American.

COLLINS, GREG. 1972-1973-1974; LB; 6-3, 228; Troy, MI. Teamed with Mahalic and others to give Parseghian a solid linebacking corps in early 1970s. Fast, big, good tackler; good nose for the ball. In 1972, backed up at OLB; made 18 tackles during the season. In 1973, led national champions with 133 tackles, 11 for -58 yards; broke up one pass; recovered two fumbles; and led linebackers with three interceptions and 25 return yards. In 1974, started at OLB and captained team. For the season, led Irish defense with 144 tackles, six for -22 yards, and recovered one fumble. For his career, made 295 tackles, 17 for -80 yards; broke up one pass; recovered three fumbles; and made three interceptions for 25 return yards.

CONJAR, LARRY. 1965-1966; FB; 6-0, 212; Harrisburg, PA. Powerful, quick, with good hands and excellent blocking skills. A rare example for his era of a player dedicated to weightlifting, now a routine aspect of a player's training. In 1965, started at FB. Was second leading rusher on ground-oriented team with 535 yards on 137 carries for seven TDs, caught four passes for 55 yards, had one kickoff return for 10 yards, and made one tackle. In 1966, carried 112 times for 521 yards and seven TDs, caught four passes for 62 yards, returned three kickoffs 39 yards, and ran for 2-point conversion. Made All-American. Scored five career TDs against USC. For his career, carried 249 times for 1,056 yards and 14 TDs, caught eight passes for 117 yards, returned four kickoffs 49 yards, ran for 2-point conversion, made one tackle, and accumulated 1,222 total yards.

CONLEY, TOM. 1928-1929-1930; E; 5-11, 175; Philadelphia, PA. Last team captain under Rockne. Always a deep threat and played solid defense. In 1928, backed up at RE. In 1929, started at RE. Caught Carideo pass for 26 yards to reach Georgia Tech's 2 and set up TD in Irish win. Scored first Irish TD in win over USC with 54-yard pass from Elder to go with several other receptions. In 1930, started at RE and captained the team. Caught 56-yard pass from Schwartz in win over Carnegie Tech. Played brilliant defensive game and blocked superbly in hometown showing against Penn in 60-20 rout. On Schwartz's "perfect play," helped cave in right side of Army's line with block on tackle to help release Schwartz. In big win over USC, Rockne's last before his death, made 37-yard reception from Schwartz. Made second team All-American.

CONNOR, GEORGE. 1946-1947; T; 6-3, 225; East Chicago, IL. Tower of strength on one of Leahy's peerless lines; devastating blocker and fine tackler. In 1946, started at LT and won the Outland Trophy. In 1947, started at LT. Recovered USC fumble and later made the block to spring Sitko on 76-yard TD run.

COUTRE, LARRY. 1946-1947-1948-1949; HB; 5-9, 170; Chicago, IL. Speedy back; had poor eyesight but played great football for undefeated Leahy teams after war. Never played in a losing contest at Notre Dame. Good runner, receiver, and defender. In 1946, as a reserve, ran two times for 11 yards. In 1947, backed at LHB; gained 127 yards on 34 carries for two TDs, caught four passes for 87 yards, and returned three punts 37 yards. In 1948, backed up Sitko at RHB; gained 152 yards on 27 carries, caught two passes for -1 yard, made one interception for 41-yard runback, and recovered one fumble. In 1949, started at RHB for the national champions; was second leading rusher, just behind Sitko, with 645 yards on 102 carries (6.2-yard average), caught 13 passes for 271 yards, and returned four kickoffs 48 yards; led team with all-purpose production of 964 yards. For his career, carried 163 times for 999 yards (6.12-yard average) for nine TDs; caught 19 passes for 357 yards; and returned three punts 37 yards, four kickoffs 48 yards, and one interception 41 yards, for a total of 1,482 yards (7.8 yards gained every time he got the ball), plus one fumble recovery.

CRABLE, BOB. 1978-1979-1980-1981; LB; 6-3, 225; Cincinnati, OH. Fine linebacker for Devine and Faust. High on any list of modern-era Notre Dame stars. Had great range, mobility, reading skills, tackling skills, general toughness, and leadership qualities. In 1978, backed up at OLB; recovered Houston fumble on their 25 to lead to Irish TD in Cotton Bowl comeback win. For the season, made 13 tackles, broke up one pass, blocked one kick, and recovered one fumble. In 1979, started at MLB; won Michigan game with last-second block of a field goal. Made 26 tackles in loss to Clemson. For the season, made almost 20 percent of defense's tackles with 187 (a new record), with 10 for -29 yards; broke up three passes; recovered two fumbles; blocked three kicks; and made one interception—a performance in the range of Ross Browner's Outland Trophy year. Made All-American. In 1980, made 154 tackles, seven for -12 yards; broke up three passes; and recovered two fumbles. Named MVP by teammates; consensus All-American. In 1981, started at MLB. Set record for career tackles during Air Force game. For the year, made 167 tackles, 16 for -54 yards; broke up three passes; recovered two fumbles; and made two interceptions for 60 return yards. Repeat consensus All-American. For his career, made 521 tackles (a new record), 33 for -95 yards; broke up 10 passes; recovered seven fumbles; blocked four kicks; and made three interceptions for 60 return yards.

CREANEY, MIKE. 1970-1971-1972; TE; 6-4, 232; Towson, MD. Big, fast TE for Theismann and Clements; capable of breaking a long one; good blocker; and three-year starter. In 1970, started at TE; caught 18 passes for 418 yards and two TDs (23.2-

yard average). In 1971, started at TE; caught 11 passes for 151 yards and one TD (in a season when the passing game was in disarray). In 1972, started at TE; caught 17 passes for 321 yards and two TDs, and made two tackles. For his career, caught 46 passes for 890 yards and five TDs, and made two tackles.

CROTTY, JIM. 1957-1958-1959; HB, FB; 5-10, 185; Seattle, WA. Good, general-purpose player for Brennan and Kuharich. In 1957, backed up at RHB and contributed to upset win of USC with 57 yards rushing and one TD. For the year, rushed for 69 yards on 14 carries and one TD, returned two kickoffs 91 yards, and broke up three passes. In 1958, started at RHB and was third in rushing with 315 yards on 67 carries; also caught 14 passes for 137 yards and a 2-point conversion; was first on team in kickoff returns with nine for 228 yards; made one interception; returned five punts for 64 yards; recovered one fumble; made 38 tackles, and led team with four passes broken up. In 1959, backed up at FB. For the year, gained 184 yards on 62 carries for three TDs, caught eight passes for 104 yards, made one interception and 6-yard return, and made 29 tackles. For his career, carried 143 times for 568 yards and four TDs, caught 22 passes for 241 yards and one TD conversion, returned five punts 64 yards, returned 11 kickoffs 319 yards, made two interceptions for six return yards, broke up seven passes, recovered one fumble, made 67 tackles, and accumulated 1,134 total yards.

CROTTY, MIKE. 1969-1970-1971; FB, S; 5-9, 180; Seattle, WA. Much like his brother, Jim, an all-purpose player under Parseghian. Originally on offense but switched to defense and stayed there for two years as starter. Had good speed and lateral quickness; good tackler. In 1969, backed up at LHB. For the year, gained 183 yards on 43 carries, caught two passes for eight yards, returned two punts six yards and four kickoffs 111 yards. In 1970, started at S. For the year, led DBs with 77 tackles, two for -8 yards; broke up four passes; recovered two fumbles; led the team with 19 punt returns for 100 yards; and returned three kickoffs 37 yards. In 1971, returned interception 65 yards for TD in win over Northwestern. For the year, led DBs with 65 tackles, made two interceptions for 66 return yards and one TD, and led team with nine passes broken up and 33 punt returns for 297 yards. For his career, gained 807 total yards, carried 43 times for 183 yards, caught two passes for eight yards, made 142 tackles with two for -8 yards, broke up 13 passes, recovered two fumbles, made two interceptions for 66 return yards and one TD, returned 54 punts 403 yards, and returned seven kickoffs 148 yards.

CROWLEY, JIM. 1922-1923-1924; HB; 5-11, 160; Green Bay, WI. Known as Sleepy Jim; the clown of the Four Horsemen. Very fast, but could lull a defense before bursting into action. Played for Curly Lambeau in Green Bay (who played for Rockne in 1918). Later coached at Fordham, where one of his Seven Blocks of Granite was Vincent Lombardi, who completed the cycle when he went to Green Bay and coached Paul Hornung. As one of the Horsemen, had the intangible talent of timing necessary for the dreaded Notre Dame Shift (ends and backfield flexed or shifted in unison just before the snap). The Horsemen operated in the shift before it was legislated into oblivion. In 1922, backed up Layden at LHB. Had 55-yard TD dash in win over DePauw. Led team with 566 yards rushing on 75 carries and in passing with 10 of 21 for 154 yards and one TD; also made two interceptions. In 1923, started at RHB. Ran 68 yards for TD in opening win over Kalamazoo. Intercepted Army pass and returned it 37 yards in 13-0 Irish win. For the season, gained 536 yards on 88 carries, led the team in passing with 13 of 36 for 154 yards and one TD, caught one pass for 44 yards, made four interceptions for 31 return yards, and returned four kickoffs for 89 yards. In 1924, started at RHB. Scored winning TD with 20-yard run in 13-7 Army game. Made 250 yards rushing and one TD in win over Princeton. Caught 65-yard TD strike from Layden to help end Nebraska's winning streak over Notre Dame. Scored on pass from Stuhldreher in win over Carnegie Tech. Made three PATs in win over Stanford in Rose Bowl. For the season, gained 731 yards on 131 carries for six TDs, completed 14 of 26 passes for 236 yards and two TDs, caught 12 passes for 265 yards and three TDs, and returned four kickoffs 52 yards. For his career, gained 1,841 yards on 294 carries for 15 TDs, completed 37 of 83 passes for 544 yards and four TDs, caught 13 passes for 309 yards and three TDs, made six interceptions for 40 return yards, returned four punts 36 yards and eight kickoffs 141 yards. His career totals were 2,911 yards, 18 TDs, and 36 PATs. By any standard, stands as one of the all-time Fighting Irish heroes.

CULLINAN, JOE. 1900-1901-1902-1903; T; 5-10, 177; Notre Dame, IN. Known as Jepers. Teamed with Red Salmon to start to put the Fighting Irish on football map. Was small even then for T; quick, heady player. In 1900 backed up RT. In 1901, backed up LT. In 1902, started at LT. In 1903, started at LT and blocked punt in shutout of Lake Forest; later scored TD. Scored TD against American Medical in 52-0 blowout. Ran for short yardage and returned a kickoff 15 yards in win over Ohio Medical. Was integral part of powerhouse team that shut out nine opponents by combined score of 292 to 0, the only time in Fighting Irish annals for a team with a full slate of games to shut out all opponents.

CULVER, RODNEY. 1988-1989-1990-1991; FB, TB; 5-10, 226; Detroit, MI. Excellent power and speed (4.38 in the 40). Very difficult to tackle, tremendous leg drive, often through a hole and into the clear before the defense could react, and often dragged a pile of tacklers with him. In 1988, backed up at FB for the national champions. For the season, made 30 carries for 195 yards and three TDs, and caught one pass for 10 yards. In 1989, backed up at FB. For the year, made 59 carries for 242 yards and five TDs, and returned three kickoffs 28 yards. In 1990, started at FB. For the year, made 150 carries for 710 yards (to lead team in rushing) and five TDs, caught 13 passes for 155 yards and two TDs, and returned five kickoffs 53 yards. In 1991, started at TB. For the year, made 101 carries for 550 yards and two TDs, caught six passes for 76 yards, and returned three kickoffs 56 yards. Gained 93 yards on 13 carries, returned two kickoffs, and caught one pass for six yards in win over Florida in 1992 Sugar Bowl. For his career, made 340 carries for 1,697 yards and 15 TDs, caught 20 passes for 231 yards and two TDs, and returned 11 kickoffs 137 yards. Total offense was 2,065 yards in 371 attempts for 17 TDs.

CZAROBSKI, ZYGMONT. 1942-1943-1946-1947; T; 6-0, 213; Chicago, IL. Leading orator, raconteur, and jokester of Leahy years, and a professional Irish personality after that. Leahy may have been impossible to take without Ziggy in the wings. Started for three national championship teams. In 1942, backed up at RT. In 1943, started at RT for the national champions. In 1946, started at RT for the national champions. Recovered fumble to lead to TD in win over Illinois. In 1947, started at RT for national champions. Recovered Tulane fumble at the Irish 40 to lead to TD. Made All-American.

DABIERO, ANGELO. 1959-1960-1961; HB; 5-8, 165; Donora, PA. Teamed with George Sefcik as one of "Gold Dust Twins." Fast, shifty runner and receiver; good defensive player. In 1959, backed up at RHB. For the season, made 36 carries for 118 yards, caught six passes for 64 yards, returned four kickoffs 70 yards and four punts 27 yards, and made 13 tackles. In 1960, started at RHB. Led team with 325 yards on 80 carries for two TDs, and in punt returns with eight for 102 yards; caught five passes for 112 yards and one TD; made one interception; returned five kickoffs 114 yards; led team with six passes broken up; and made 37 tackles. In 1961, helped defeat Oklahoma with 176 yards on 11 carries. For the year, led team with 637 yards on 92 carries (for 6.9-yard average) and four TDs; caught 10 passes for 201 yards and one TD; also led in punt returns with 11 for 97 yards; was second in kickoff returns with 203 yards on eight returns; third in tackles with 47; led with five interceptions for 78 return yards; and second with five passes broken up. For his career, rushed 208 times for 1,080 yards and six TDs, caught 21 passes for 377 yards and two TDs, returned 17 kickoffs 387 yards and 23 punts 226 yards, made six interceptions for 78 return yards, broke up 11 passes, and made 97 tackles. His career total was 2,048 yards, done mostly in two seasons.

DAHMAN, BUCKY. 1925-1926-1927; HB; 5-8, 156; Youngstown, OH. Teamed with Christy Flanagan in the years immediately following the Four Horsemen. Speedy, elusive runner; fine receiver; excellent defender; good kicker. Fit Rockne's shift tactics well. In 1925, backed up at RHB. Scored final TD in mismatch win over Baylor with interception and 50-yard runback. Scored in shutout of Lombard. In 1926, backed up at RHB. In opener with Beloit, scored one TD and three PATs in 77-0 win. Ran 65 yards for TD in tough win over Minnesota and Nagurski. Scored TD on 10-yard run in win over Penn State. Scored on 5-yard plunge as Notre Dame beat Georgia Tech. Added two TD runs in shutout of Indiana. In 1927, started at RHB to team with Flanagan. Scored TD to cap 5-play drive in 19-6 win over Indiana. Preserved 7-6 win over USC with 25-yard TD pass from Riley, one PAT kick, and interception on USC's last possession.

DANCEWICZ, FRANK. 1943-1944-1945; QB; 5-10, 180; Lynn, MA. One of fastest players on Leahy's teams, but played in shadows of Bertelli and Lujack. In 1944, started at QB. For the year, rushed 69 times for 230 yards and two TDs, and completed 72 of 153 passes for 999 yards and seven TDs. In 1945, started at QB. For the year, rushed 12 times for 12 yards, and completed 32 of 88 passes for 539 yards and four TDs. For his career, ran 81 times for 242 yards and two TDs, and completed 104 of 241 passes for 1,538 yards and 11 TDs.

DEMMERLE, PETE. 1972-1973-1974; SE; 6-1, 196; New Canaan, CT. Fine receiver for Clements and 1973 national champions. Possession receiver rather than constant deep threat; had great hands and precise moves. In 1972, played only 5:22 minutes but scored Notre Dame's only TD in blowout loss to Nebraska in Orange Bowl. For the season, carried once for 23 yards and caught 5-yard TD pass. In 1973, started at SE. For the year, led Fighting Irish receivers with 26 receptions for 404 yards and five TDs, including three against Miami, the game-winner against MSU, and a 2-point conversion to help beat Alabama in Sugar Bowl. In 1974, started at SE; again led receivers with 43 receptions for 667 yards and six TDs. Consensus All-American and Rhodes Scholar finalist. For his career, caught 70 passes for 1,076 yards and 12 TDs and ran once for 23 yards.

DEVORE, HUGH. 1931-1932-1933; E; 6-0, 179; Newark, NJ. Rockne recruit who played with Moose Krause and for Hunk Anderson. Tough defensive player, tenacious blocker, and good hitter, with fair speed but very strong hands. In 1931, backed up at RE. In 1932, backed up at RE; as a sub in shutout of Army, played with broken hand and caught 45-yard TD pass, made numerous tackles, intercepted a pass, and recovered a fumble. In 1933, started at RE and captained team. Later served two stints as an assistant coach and as interim head coach in 1945 and 1963.

DIMINICK, GARY. 1971-1972-1973; HB; 5-9, 176; Mt. Carmel, PA. Speedy scatback, specialist in returning kicks. In 1971, backed up at LHB. For the season, rushed for 61 yards on 17 carries, caught two passes for 14 yards, and led the Fighting Irish with 199 yards on seven kickoff returns. In 1972, started at RHB. Ran 84 yards with kickoff return for TD in win over Navy. For the season, carried 71 times for 377 yards and two TDs, caught 14 passes for 143 yards and one TD, and led team again with 15 kickoff returns for 331 yards and one TD. In 1973, backed up at LHB for the national champions. For the year, gained 121 yards on 19 carries (for 6.4-yard average) and one TD, caught two passes for 21 yards, and led for the third straight year with eight kickoff returns for 181 yards. For his career, rushed 107 times for 559 yards (5.22 yards per carry) and three TDs, caught 18 passes for 178 yards and one TD, and returned 30 kickoffs 711 yards (23.7 yards per return) for one TD.

DIMMICK, RALPH. 1908-1909-1910; T; 6-0, 225; Hubbard, OR. Bruising, dominant lineman prior to Rockne's arrival as player. Part of team that beat Michigan, and also part of the reason Yost cancelled series over eligibility. Played at Pacific University in Oregon, and apparently at Whitman College before going to Notre Dame. Yost objected to his playing in 1909, along with George Philbrook, also from the Northwest. In 1908, started at RT. Was deployed for short yardage in "tackle back" formation in win over Hillsdale. Ran well for short gains on cross bucks in loss to Michigan, to go with short kickoff return and sack for -5 yards. Made run of 15 yards and recovered fumble in win over Wabash. Scored two TDs in beating Olivet, one on tackle around play. Ran for TD in win over Rose Poly and caught forward pass. In 1909, started at RT. Scored TD on 20-yard run and gained 80+ yards in win over MAC. Played formidable defense in Irish 11-3 "upset" over Michigan. In 1910, started at RT and captained team. Cruised for three TDs in 51-0 win over Akron. Ran for three TDs in win over Rose Poly. Returned to Portland, OR, entered law school, and coached some football. In 1911, accepted invitation to play in Pacific's annual alumni game. During this contest, punctured a lung but kept playing and attended a party later. In tremendous pain and delirious, jumped through a window on upper floor of dormitory, and ran wildly around campus and the streets of Forest Grove with concerned police in hot pursuit. They subdued him and took him to a hospital, where he died 20 minutes later.

DINARDO, GERRY. 1972-1973-1974; G; 6-1, 242; Howard Beach, NY. Brother of Larry, Dominant interior lineman; integral member of the 1973 championship team. Excellent technique; good strength and quickness. In 1972, started at RG and played every minute offense was on the field. In 1973, key member of the line that set running backs free for rushing record of 3,502 yards on 673 carries (about 61 rushing plays per game, or 15 per quarter). In 1974, started at RG and made All-American.

DINARDO, LARRY. 1968-1969-1970; G; 6-1, 243; Queens, NY. Must be counted among all-time greats. Greg Marx, himself an All-American, said that each practice session was clinic in offensive blocking techniques. Instrumental player in success of Theismann-led offense under Parseghian. In 1968, started at LG. In 1969, started at LG and made All-American. In 1970, started at LG and was consensus All-American. Current head coach at Vanderbilt. May be in the picture to coach the Irish in the future.

DOAR, JIM. 1901-1902; HB; 5-11, 185; Cumberland, WI. Played with Red Salmon to give team tremendous striking potential with him on long excursions and Salmon bucking inside. Excellent runner and defender. In 1901, started at LHB. In 1902, started at LHB. Scored two TDs in 12-0 win over MAC, one on 65-yard sprint. Rushed for good short yardage gains and dropped several runners for losses in loss to Michigan. Helped beat Indiana with runs of 50 and 55 yards and kicked one conversion. Scored TD on 85-yard run in 92-0 rout of American Medical, and added 80-yard run later. Helped defeat DePauw with TD run. Shared rushing honors with Salmon in tie with Purdue.

DOLAN, ROSY. 1906-1907-1908-1909; T, G; 5-11, 210; Albany, OR. With Dimmick and Philbrook, part of Northwest connection. Combined with them to give Notre Dame a line not to be lightly regarded. Despite portly appearance, could be counted on for gains of five and six yards when called on. In 1906, started at RT and ran effectively throughout season. Scored a TD the Physicians and Surgeons wipeout. In 1907, had surgery on knee early in season and hoped to play in big games at the end, but the knee did not respond well (one of the first such operations on record at Notre Dame). In 1908, started at RG. Played strong game against Michigan, including a sack. Ran back opening kickoff in win over Indiana. Played every minute of each game. In 1909, started at RG. Rushed for short yardage in win over MAC. Scored two TDs in win over Miami of Ohio. Played every minute for second consecutive year.

DORAIS, GUS. 1910-1911-1912-1913; QB; 5-7, 145; Chippewa Falls, WI. Only four-year starter at QB until Blair Kiel seventy years later. Excellent leader, superb field general, good throwing arm, fine speed, good defender, and very good kicker. Teamed with Rockne to make one of first great passing tandems in modern football. In 1910, started at QB. Made good impression against Akron with fine punt returning and cool demeanor. Kicked three PATs against Rose Poly. In 1911, started at QB. First recorded pass to Rockne was in blowout win over Ohio Northern; directed traffic for six players to score TDs; caught pass from FB Ray Eichenlaub. Helped demolish St. Viator in display of football skills: TD pass to Dutch Bergman, five conversion kicks, 25-yard drop-kicked field goal, and short TD run. Booted five PATs in 80-0 win over Loyola. Narrowly missed field goal against Pitt that would have averted 0-0 tie. Made PAT kick against Wabash in 6-3 win. Missed two field goals in scoreless game with Marquette. In 1912, started at QB and captained team. Kicked three PATs and shared scoring among seven players as they obliterated St. Viator. Kicked eight conversions and had several long kickoff returns against Adrian. Scored one TD and kicked four PATs against Wabash. Kicked 25-yard field goal to beat Pitt 3-0. Led attack in win over Marquette with two TDs—one an 88-yard run during which he shed seven tacklers—to go with six conversion kicks and one field goal. In 1913, started at QB. Scored one TD and kicked seven PATs against Ohio Northern. In first "modern" football game against South Dakota, made two conversion kicks and mixed runs and passes to keep Coyotes befuddled in 20-7 Fighting Irish win. Returned punt 65 yards and kicked 8 PATs in rout of Alma. In win over Army, completed 13 of 17 passes for TDs to Pliska and Rockne, returned punt 30 yards, intercepted a pass in the Notre Dame end zone, and was perfect with five PATs to go with nearly 300 yards of passing. Played brilliantly in win over Penn State: on one drive hit 40-yard pass to Pliska, ran 35 yards, and threw TD strike to Rockne; also made 15-yard kickoff return, two conversions, and 75-yard punt return lost to a sideline call. Beat Christian Brothers with 40-yard TD sprint, a long punt return for a TD, timely passing, and two conversion kicks. Against Texas five days later, scored on 15-yard run after a fake pass, drop-kicked three field goals, and tacked on two PATs. Led Notre Dame to three consecutive undefeated seasons and was instrumental in thrusting the team into the national spotlight.

DOWNS, BILL. 1905; FB; 5-11, 195; Sayre, PA. Fine player for Notre Dame for one season; capable of breaking long gainers for TDs. In 1905, started at FB. Rushed for 75+ yards in win over North Division, including 57-yard TD drive on five carries. Gained 50+ yards on runs in loss to Wabash. Led all scorers in 142-0 rout of American Medical with four TDs on long runs and four conversion kicks; on one TD drive, went 70 yards on two runs. Scored six more TDs one week later against DePauw—10 TDs in a week must be an unofficial Irish record.

DOWNS, MORRIS. 1905; T; 5-10, 185; Sayre, PA. Brother of Bill Downs. In 1905, started at RT. American Medical was just another game for this obscure lineman, except that the runners became fatigued from running for so many TDs and they turned it over to the linemen. Thus, this pudgy T scored two TDs and made four conversion kicks in 142-0 shutout. His scoring spree gave the family 43 points in one game—surely another unofficial record. Ran only for short yardage in losses to Indiana and Purdue.

DUERSON, DAVE. 1979-1980-1981-1982; DB, SS; 6-3, 202; Muncie, IN. Fine defensive back for Devine and Faust; quick, extremely strong; heavy hitter. In 1979, backed up at LCB. For the season, led Fighting Irish with 12 punt returns for 209 yards; made 24 tackles, one for -1 yard; broke up two passes, recovered one fumble; and made two interceptions for 43 return yards. In 1980, started at SS. For the year, made 34 tackles, three for -14 yards; broke up three passes; recovered two fumbles; intercepted one pass for 21-yard return; and returned 25 punts 194 yards. In 1981, started at SS. For the year, made 55 tackles, three for -8 yards; broke up five passes; had two interceptions for 88 return yards and one TD; and returned 32 punts 221 yards. In 1982, started at FS and was tri-captain. For the season, made 63 tackles, one for -2 yards; broke up six passes, and made seven interceptions for 104 return yards; and returned 34 punts 245 yards. Made All-American. For his career, made 176 tackles, eight for -25 yards; broke up 16 passes; recovered three fumbles; had 12 interceptions for 256 return yards and one TD; and returned 103 punts for 869 yards. His total yardage was 1,125 yards.

DURANKO, PETE. 1963-1964-1965-1966; FB, LB, DT; 6-2, 235; Johnstown, PA. Recruited by Kuharich as FB; Parseghian saw lineman. Had tremendous strength and fine quickness as defensive lineman; played crucial role in defensive front for 1966 national champions. In 1963, backed up at FB. For the year, gained 93 yards on 26 carries and made one tackle. In 1964, started at LB; intercepted one pass against Wisconsin but was hurt and missed rest of the year. In 1965, started at LT. Against North Carolina, made 14 tackles. For the season, was second with 95 tackles. In 1966, started at LT. For the year, made 73 tackles, broke up one pass, and recovered one fumble. Made All-American. In his career, rushed 26 times for 93 yards, made 169 tackles, broke up one pass, recovered one fumble, and made one interception.

EDDY, NICK. 1964-1965-1966; HB; 6-0, 195; Lafayette, CA. Fast, elusive, excellent receiver; tremendous ability to find seam and exploit it for long gain. Crucial component of championship efforts in 1964 and 1966. In 1964, started at RHB; gained 480 yards on 98 carries for seven TDs and a 2-point conversion; caught 16 passes for 352 yards and two TDs; and returned seven kickoffs 148 yards. In 1965, started at RHB; led Irish with 582 yards on 115 runs for four TDs; also led in receiving with 13 catches for 233 yards and two TDs; returned three kickoffs 63 yards; and made two tackles. In the championship 1966 season, started at LHB. Consensus All-American. Gained 553 yards on 78 carries (7.1-yard average) for eight TDs; caught 16 passes for 123 yards; returned four kickoffs for 193 yards (48.3-yard average); and made two tackles. For his career, rushed 291 times for 1,615 yards, 17 TDs, and a 2-point conversion; caught 45 passes for 708 yards and four TDs; returned 14 kickoffs 404 yards; and made four tackles. Scored 21 TDs and gained 2,727 total yards for an average gain of 7.8 yards every time he touched the ball.

EGGEMAN, JOHN. 1897-1898-1899; C; 6-5, 256; Fort Wayne, IN. Brawny, tall, heavy, and immensely strong, which was required to do an effective job at center in the rough days of mass plays and wedges. Adept at fending off blockers with one arm and tackling with the other. Somewhat hampered in first two seasons by inexperienced guards, but he habitually pushed the middle of opponents' offensive lines back 5-6 yards at a time. In 1897, started at C. In 1898, started at C. Blocked an Illinois field goal to save game. Recovered MAC fumble and lurched four yards for TD in 53-0 blowout. Michigan triple-teamed him throughout their 23-0 win. In 1899, started at C.

EICHENLAUB, RAY. 1911-1912-1913-1914; FB; 6-0, 210; Columbus, OH. Must be given serious consideration for any all-time Notre Dame team. Started four years at FB; crunching runner with good speed and tremendous strength; fine blocker; good receiver; and adequate passer. Against Army in 1913 his sledge-hammer blows into the line occupied the defense while Dorais and Rockne tuned up the passing game for win. In 1911, started at FB. Scored first TD with 2-yard plunge in win over Ohio Northern, returned kickoff 30 yards, and completed pass to Dorais. Blocked St. Viator kick in easy Irish win. Scored two TDs in win over Butler. Bulled over for TD in win over Loyola. Grabbed Pitt fumble on their 35 in tie game. In 1912, started at FB; scored three TDs in 116-7 opener against St. Viator. Ran for 50-yard TD against Morris Harvey. Scored two TDs in win over Wabash that cinched state title. Had several long runs and one TD in win over St. Louis. Blasted Marquette's defense for four TDs, including 70-yarder in which he carried four defenders with him. In 1913, started at FB; scored four TDs in wipeout of Ohio Northern. Scored two TDs against Alma. Against Army, ran for two TDs and kept the middle of the Cadet line busy with short yardage maneuvers. Finished off Penn State with TD burst. Ran at will and scored one TD against Christian Brothers. Against Texas, made 2-yard TD plunge in Irish win. Made All-American. In 1914, started at FB. Played great game in a losing effort against Yale: a 45-yard kickoff return, then another for 15 yards, 35-yard pass completion, and two runs of 40 yards each to go with assorted shorter runs. Scored on 10-yard run against Carlisle.

ELDER, JACK. 1927-1928-1929; HB; 5-8, 165; Louisville, KY. Olympic sprinter in 100-yard dash; one of the fastest men ever to play for Rockne. Constant threat to break the big one; played especially well on defense. In 1927, backed up at LHB. In 1928, backed up at LHB. Scored TD in win over Loyola with 48-yard run. Showed blinding speed to Carnegie Tech with 65-yard bolt late in a loss. In 1929, started at LHB for undefeated national championship team. Ran 20 and 60 yards for TDs against Indiana; set up TD with a lateral to Mullins that almost broke all the way. Caught Carideo pass for TD in win over Navy. Ran 33 yards from midfield to spark only TD in win over Carnegie Tech. In lackluster game, ran 18-yard TD to help defeat Drake. Threw 54-yard TD pass to Conley in win over USC. In one of the great moments in Irish football history, intercepted a Chris Cagle pass and ran 95 yards up the sidelines for game's only TD in win over Army, thus ensuring consecutive national championships.

ELLIS, CLARENCE. 1969-1970-1971; S, CB; 6-0, 178; Grand Rapids, MI. Fine leader in secondary under Parseghian; had great speed, superb lateral quickness, excellent leaping abiiity, excellent closing instincts, and good tackling skills. In 1969, started at S. For the year, made 31 tackles, led the Fighting Irish with 13 passes broken up, and made three interceptions for 98 return yards and one TD. In 1970, started at LCB. In Cotton Bowl win over Texas, caught 37-yard pass from the split-end position to lead to a field goal. For the season, made 27 tackles, broke up 11 passes, made seven interceptions for 25 return yards, and returned five punts 33 yards. In 1971, started at LCB. Caused Purdue fumble in their end zone that led to TD recovery and win. For the year, made 35 tackles, broke up eight passes, and made three interceptions for 34 return yards. Consensus All-American. For his career, made 93 tackles, broke up a 32 passes, made 13 interceptions for 157 return yards and one TD, returned five punts 33 yards, and caught one pass for 37 yards.

EURICK, TERRY. 1974-1975-1976-1977; HB; 5-11, 196; Saginaw, MI. Good, all-purpose running back with Devine and Montana-led 1977 championship team. In 1974, backed up at RHB; gained 131 yards on 19 carries for one TD, caught one pass for 6 yards, and made one tackle. In 1975, backed up at LHB. For the year, led team in kickoff returns with 13 for 347 yards, gained 154 yards on 36 runs, and caught three passes for 30 yards. In 1976, backed up at LHB. For the year, gained 230 yards on 46 runs, caught five passes for 65 yards and one TD, and returned 10 kickoffs 181 yards. In 1977, backed up at LHB; scored twice in Cotton Bowl win over Texas. For the year, gained 291 yards on 68 carries for four TDs, caught 12 passes for 79 yards and three TDs, was second-highest scorer (behind kicker), returned nine kickoffs 211 yards, and made six tackles. For his career, carried 169 times for 806 yards and five TDs, caught 21 passes for 180 yards and four TDs, returned 32 kickoffs 739 yards, and made seven tackles. Accumulated 1,725 yards of all-purpose offense.

FANNING, MIKE. 1972-1973-1974; DE, DT; 6-6, 255; Tulsa, OK. Big, quick, defensive lineman for Parseghian and a force in the 1973 championship year. Excellent pass rusher, part of defensive line that included Browner, Niehaus, and Stock. In 1972, backed up at DE. Made 13 tackles for the year, two for -10 yards. In 1973, started at DT. For the year, was

Notre Dame's fourth leading tackler with 61, 12 for -76 yards; also recovered one fumble and led defensive linemen with 205 minutes of play. In 1974, started at DT. For the season, made 85 tackles, 12 for -52 yards; broke up one pass; and recovered one fumble. Made All-American. For his career, made 159 tackles, 26 for -138 yards; recovered two fumbles; and broke up one pass.

FARAGHER, JIM. 1900-1901; T; 5-10, 190; Youngstown, OH. Tough, gritty T who could score when needed and who played in spite of having only one eye. In 1900, started at LT and scored three TDs in 64-0 rout of Howard Park. In 1901, started at LT. Blocked punt in 2-0 loss to Northwestern. Scored TD on fumble recovery in win over South Bend Commercial A.C.

FARLEY, JOHN. 1897-1898-1899-1900; E, FB; 5-9, 160; Paterson, NJ. Had extraordinary speed and elusiveness, capable of outflanking almost any defense; good defender; had absolute determination to score. In 1897, started at LE. Against Chicago Dental Surgeons, ran for 184 yards in first half, highlighted by 80-yard TD burst; in the second half, gained 280 more yards for one-game effort of 464 yards on the ground, surely an all-time Irish football feat. In the second half, scored on a short run and made 25-yard TD dash, 50-yard TD sprint, and 85-yard advance with a "backward pass." In 1898, started at LE. Crushed MAC with 220+ yards running, including five runs of 20+ yards, and two TDs on 38- and 45-yard runs. In 1899, started at LE. In 1900, scored on 75-yard run against Englewood High. In win over Howard Park, scored twice and made another 50-yard. Against Rush Medical, had 35-yard run late in the game to save win; also blocked a field goal. Entered the priesthood and stayed at Notre Dame. Eventually lost his legs due to complications from diabetes.

FARRELL, JOE. 1962-1963-1964; HB, FB; 6-0, 205; Chicago, IL. Solid, dependable back who produced well under Parseghian. In 1962, backed up at FB. Carried 70 times for 278 yards and four TDs, caught one pass for 27 yards, returned one kickoff 19 yards, and made six tackles. In 1963, started at LHB. For the season, rushed 33 times for 79 yards, caught three passes for 33 yards, returned one punt 13 yards, made 30 tackles, broke up three passes, recovered one fumble, and intercepted one pass for 14-yard return. In 1964, started at FB for Parseghian. For the year, carried 93 times for 387 yards and four TDs, and caught six passes for 84 yards and one TD. For his career, rushed 196 times for 744 yards and eight TDs, caught 10 passes for 144 yards and one TD, returned one kickoff 19 yards and one punt 13 yards, made 36 tackles, broke up three passes, recovered one fumble, and had one interception plus 14-yard runback. His total career offense was 934 yards.

FEENEY, AL. 1910-1911-1912-1913; C; 5-11, 190; Indianapolis, IN. Teammate of Rockne and Dorais; known for his sharp "passing"—snapping the ball—to *any* back, at various odd angles, and leading them with the ball if they were in motion. Always matched against behemoths that he dispatched. In 1910, backed up at C. In 1911, was tried at G but his talents could not be spared at C. Played good game in narrow win over Wabash. In 1912, started at C and made All-Western (a modified Big 10). In 1913, started at C. Intercepted three passes against Alma, and two Army passes in classic win. Made interception against Penn State that saved win. Named All-Western again. In 1931 Indiana game, prevented Irish back from crashing into a barrier after a long run, and suffered a broken nose for his kindly gesture.

FERGUSON, VAGAS. 1976-1977-1978-1979; FB, HB; 6-1, 194; Richmond, IN. Among the very best who have ever played for Notre Dame. Fine blend of speed, power, finesse, balance, and good hands. Important factor in 1977 championship year as a backfield mate for Montana. In 1976, started at FB. In only eight games, was second leading rusher with 350 yards on 81 carries for two TDs; also caught three passes for 27 yards and one TD, and made two tackles. In 1977, started at LHB. For the year (although missing two games), was second on the team with 80 carries for 493 yards (a 6.2-yard average,) and six TDs, and caught six passes for 96 yards and one TD—in only 90:16 minutes of play. Ran three TDs against Texas in Cotton Bowl win; named outstanding offensive player of the game. In 1978, started at RB and had the best year to date for an Irish running back: gained 1,192 yards on 211 carries for seven TDs, and caught 20 passes for 171 yards and one TD. Caught 2-point conversion pass from Montana in 35-34 comeback win over Houston in Cotton Bowl. In 1979, started at RB and became first Irish runner to go over 1,000 yards twice. For his senior year, gained 1,437 yards on 301 carries for 17 TDs, caught 14 passes for 72 yards, and threw one incomplete pass. His rushing yardage was 71 percent of Notre Dame's ground game in 1979; his carries were 58 percent of all rushes; his 17 TDs were 58 percent of the team's TDs, both rushing and passing. Consensus All-American. For his career, rushed 673 times for 3,472 yards and 32 TDs, caught 43 passes for 366 yards and three TDs, made two tackles, and threw one incomplete pass. His totals were 35 TDs and 3,838 yards.

FIGARO, CEDRIC. 1984-1985-1986-1987; LB; 6-2, 246; Lafayette, LA. Three-year starter at LB for Faust and Holtz. Had good size, excellent strength, fine speed and quickness, and relentless pursuit. Always made things happen around the ball. In 1984, backed up at OLB. For the year, made 30 tackles, one for -7 yards, and broke up one pass. In 1985, started at OLB. For the year, made 62 tackles, two for -5 yards; caused one fumble; and broke up two passes. In 1986, started at OLB. For the year, made 59 tackles, with 3.5 sacks for -31 yards and three others for -11 yards; caused two fumbles; recovered seven fumbles; and broke up four passes. Made All-American. In 1987, started at OLB. For the year, made 53 tackles, three sacks for -28 yards and five others for -15 yards, and broke up two passes. Made All-American. For his career, made 204 tackles, with 6.5 sacks for -59 yards and 11 others for -38 yards; caused three fumbles; recovered seven fumbles; and broke up nine passes.

FISCHER, BILL. 1945-1946-1947-1948; T, G; 6-2, 230; Chicago, IL. Powerful lineman for Leahy's great post-war years. Devastating blocker and tackler. In 1945, backed up at LT. In 1946, started at LG. In 1947, started at LG and led all linemen with 300 minutes of play. In 1948, started at LG. Blocked fourth-down pass to save win over Pitt. Recovered Husky fumble on their 24 to lead to TD in win. Consensus All-American in 1947 and 1948. Won Outland Trophy in 1948.

FLANAGAN, CHRISTY. 1925-1926-1927; HB; 6-0, 170; Port Arthur, TX. Led Irish in ground yardage in each of his varsity seasons to join a select group, including Gipp and Sitko. Flashy, quick runner who fit well in Rockne's scheme whereby LHB did most of the work, including passing. Followed Four Horsemen to give Notre Dame continued offensive threat. In 1925, started at LHB and ran 556 yards on 99 carries for seven TDs and kicked three PATs. In 1926, started at LHB and gained 535 yards on 68 runs (a 7.9-yard average), completed 12 of 29 passes for 207 yards, and returned six kickoffs 183 yards. Made All-American. In 1927, started at LHB. Ran 118 times for 731 yards, caught one pass for 30-yard TD. Made All-American. For his career, ran 285 times for 1,822 yards and 15 TDs.

FOLEY, TIM. 1976-1977-1978-1979; T; 6-5, 265; Cincinnati, OH. Potent force on offensive line for Devine. Strong, with good speed; excellent technician in pass blocking. In 1976, backed up at LT. Played in all games at T and C, and with specialty teams. In 1977, was leader of national championship team. Had an excellent game against Texas in Cotton Bowl—even received MVP votes. In 1978, started at RT. In 1979, started at RT and made All-American.

FORTIN, AL. 1898-1899-1900-1901; T; 5-11, 180; Chicago, IL. Probably youngest man ever to play for the Fighting Irish—played against Illinois in October 1898, when he was 16 years old. In 1898, started at RT. In 1899, backed up at LT. In 1900, a veteran at age 18, was trusted to run with the ball. Scored two TDs against Highland Park. Earned praise for offensive line play in loss to Indiana. In 1901, scored TD in 6-0 win over Ohio Medical. Tallied one TD in win over Lake Forest. Ran for 40+ yards in win over Purdue. Scored one TD in shutout of Chicago Physicians and Surgeons.

FROMHART, WALLY. 1933-1934-1935; QB; 5-11, 183; Moundsville, WV. Solid QB and team leader for Anderson and early Layden teams. Had good speed and was especially adept at broken field running. Also good blocker, fair passer, and good receiver. In 1933, was reserve QB. In 1934, started at QB. Led team with 33 punt returns for 288 yards. In 1934, started at QB. In what has been called the game of the century, caught two key passes on second scoring drive against Ohio State. For the year, led the team with 11 catches for 174 yards and one TD.

FRY, WILLIE. 1973-1975-1976-1977; DE; 6-3, 237; Memphis, TN. Perfect complement to Ross Browner on the opposite side of defensive line, giving Notre Dame two unstoppable ends. Probably best pair of DEs in Irish annals. Was very quick, had good strength, excellent backside pursuit, and a fine nose for the ball. In 1973, backed up Stock at DE. For the year, made 12 tackles, two for -16 yards, and broke up one pass. Missed 1974 due to suspension. In 1975, started at RE. For the season, made 78 tackles, with a team-leading 14 for -100 yards; recovered two fumbles; and blocked one kick. In 1976, started at RE. Made 77 tackles, nine for -65 yards, and broke up one pass. Made All-American. In the 1977 championship season, suffered variety of injuries that reduced his effectiveness but still made 47 tackles, four for -20 yards, and grabbed one fumble. Made All-American. For his career, made 214 tackles, 29 for -201 yards; broke up two passes; recovered three fumbles; and blocked one kick. With Browner, combined for 106 tackles for -716 yards—about the yardage for two complete games against the Irish.

FUNK, ART. 1902-1903-1904-1905; HB, FB, T; 5-8, 175; Lacrosse, WI. Light for a lineman, but was noted for offensive abilities with the ball. In 1902, backed up RHB. In 1903, backed up FB, behind Red Salmon. In 1904, started at LT. Came out late to the team and had to work his way into playing shape. Booted two PATs in tough win over Ohio Medical. Kicked conversion in 6-0 win over Toledo. Ran for important yardage in close win over DePauw. In 1905, started at T. Led Irish runners with 80+ yards in loss to Wabash but could not score; contributed sack for -8 yards. Scored TD on 4-yard plunge in shutout of Bennett Medical.

GANN, MIKE. 1981-1982-1983-1984; DE, DT; 6-5, 256; Lakewood, CO. Fine defensive player for Faust. Relentless pursuer with good quickness and tremendous upper body strength. In 1981, backed up at RE. Saw most playing time of any freshman. For the year, made 12 tackles. In 1982, started at DT. For the year, made 41 tackles, one for -1 yard, and caused one safety. In 1983, started at DT and showed he could dominate in the line. For the year, led the Fighting Irish with six QB sacks for -54 yards, made 52 tackles, caused one fumble, broke up two passes, and had three other hits for -11 yards. In 1984, started at DT. For the year, made 60 tackles, 19 for -127 yards, and broke up two passes. Made All-American. For his career, made 165 tackles, 29 for -193 yards; caused one safety; caused one fumble; and broke up four passes.

GARVEY, ART. 1920-1921; T; 6-1, 215; Holyoke, MA. Played with Gipp and Hunk Anderson. Quick, excellent defender; always around the ball. In 1920, backed up LT. In 1921, started at LT. Had one sack in win over Kalamazoo. In win over Purdue, had a sack for -2 yards and recovered a fumble on their 35-yard line. Returned a kickoff 12 yards in shutout of Indiana. Intercepted a Rutgers pass to set up TD in win. Recovered an Army fumble in 0-0 tie.

GATEWOOD, TOM. 1969-1970-1971; SE; 6-2, 208; Baltimore, MD. Teamed with Theismann to produce potent offensive duo. Had great speed, good size, silky moves, and great hands. In 1969, started at SE. In sophomore year, caught 47 passes from Theismann for 743 yards and eight TDs and ran once for no gain. In 1970, started at SE. Caught 79 passes for 1,166 yards and eight TDs; and gained four yards on one run. Made All-American. In 1971, started at SE but there was no Theismann to throw to him. For the season, caught 33 passes for 417 yards and four TDs, and carried twice for -7 yards. Repeat All-American. For his career, caught 159 passes for 2,326 yards and 20 TDs, and carried four times for -3 yards.

GAY, BILL. 1947-1948-1949-1950; HB; 5-11, 175; Chicago, IL. Good all-purpose back for Leahy. Excellent pass defender; ran the open field with daring and was constant kicking game threat. In 1947, backed up at LHB; ran 12 times for 36 yards and caught two passes for 20 yards. In 1948, backed up at LHB; carried 64 times for 382 yards and four TDs, caught 10 passes for 131 yards and four TDs, and made 12 punt returns for 210 yards. In the championship 1949 season, backed up at LHB but played plenty of defense. Carried 14 times for 47 yards, caught five passes for 60 yards and one TD, and led defenders with four interceptions for 80 return yards. In 1950, backed up at LHB and again played great defense. For the season, carried 21 times for 63 yards, caught seven passes for 57 yards, and returned two kickoffs 42 yards and 14 punts for 96 yards. For his career, carried 111 times for 528 yards, caught 24 passes for 268 yards and three TDs, returned 26 punts 306 yards and two kickoffs 42 yards, and made four interceptions for 80 return yards. Gained 1,224 yards of career offense.

GIPP, GEORGE. 1917-1918-1919-1920; HB; 6-0, 180; Laurium, MI. An immortal. There is perhaps no better player to be found among the 2,000+ who have represented Notre Dame on the gridiron. Averaged 177 yards of offense every time he stepped on a field, and led Notre Dame to consecutive undefeated seasons in 1919 and 1920. Forever wedded in the collective memory to Knute Rockne, but was diametrical opposite. Rockne was not particularly gifted as an athlete but was a diligent worker. Gipp possessed towering array of physical gifts but could have cared less. Painfully shy, yet witty; a gambler—morosely individualistic, diffident, extremely intelligent, and perhaps very insecure; but competitive fires blazed with an intensity unmatched in American sports history.

On the football field, had more than enough speed, good size, enough strength, and an ability to improvise at precisely the right moment to avert a bad situation. This was the key to his prowess on the field, and had little to do with sheer physical gifts. Combination of raw athletic talent with uncanny capacity to do the most unexpected thing—a cutback against the grain, an invented option pass, a field goal try from an unbelievable distance, or some chicanery to upset the opposition. Finally, it is highly unlikely that he ever asked Rockne to "Win One for the Gipper." It's a nice story, and fit Rockne's romanticized notions of football. But Gipp was not a sentimentalist, nor did he talk like that.

In 1917, started at LHB on team depleted by the demands of the war effort. Ran 40 yards (towards 110 for the day, his first game over 100 yards—nine others were to follow) against South Dakota as well as threw for a long gain in 40-0 win. Never scored in 7-2 win over Army, but his running, passing, and defensive play kept the Irish in the game. Suffered a broken leg in Morningside game to end his playing that year. For the year, carried 63 times for 244 yards, completed three of eight passes for 40 yards and one TD, returned eight punts 99 yards, and booted 13 punts 444 yards. In 1918, started at LHB in a non-season, due to the war. Scored twice against Case and made five of 12 passes for 101 yards. Scored two TDs in win over Wabash while rushing for 119 yards. In 7-7 tie with Great Lakes, punted eight times and narrowly missed 40-yard field goal that would have won the game. Hampered by mud against MAC, ran 52 yards, made three of six passes, and punted 10 times before being taken out with a ruptured blood vessel in his face in the third quarter. Dominant force in win over Purdue—two TDs plus 137 yards rushing, including 55-yard run; three of seven passes for 51 yards and one TD; four punts; 25-yard kickoff return; one PAT; and several broken up passes. In scoreless tie with Nebraska, had two long runs towards 76 yards for the day; completed four of nine passes, two for long yardage; punted 12 times; returned kickoff 40 yards; and made one interception. For the season, led Irish with 98 carries for 541 yards and five TDs, led in passing with 19 completions in 45 tries for 293 yards and one TD, and led in scoring with six TDs and seven PATs. In 1919, started at LHB. Gained 148 yards rushing in win over Kalamazoo, but lost TD runs of 80 and 68 yards on penalties. Against Union, scored in three plays from 90 yards out, ending up with 123 yards on 10 runs, two pass completions for 49 yards, and two kickoff returns for 56 yards in 60-7 rout. In win over Nebraska, lateraled to Bergman for 90-yard TD, and hit five of eight passes for 124 yards. Scored twice, gained 85 yards on nine carries, hit two of three passes, and punted twice against Western Michigan in 53-0 win. Gained 82 yards on 18 runs, scored once (with a dislocated shoulder), threw for 57 yards, and drop-kicked 12-yard field goal in win over Indiana. Beat Army with 70 yards on the ground and 115 yards on seven passes. In win over Purdue, hit 11 of 15 passes for 217 yards and two TDs. Helped defeat MAC with 45 yards rushing and 73 yards on five of 10 passes for one TD and two interceptions. In wretched weather, beat Morningside with 94 yards rushing and 66 yards passing, including bomb to Kirk for last TD. For the season, led team with 106 carries for 729 yards and four TDs, completed 41 of 72 passes for 727 yards and three TDs, had 12 punts for 466 yards, led team in scoring, interceptions (three for 32 return yards), and kickoff returns (eight for 166 yards).

The last win closed Rockne's first undefeated season and gave Notre Dame the Western championship. In 1920, started at LHB. In win over Kalamazoo, made two runs of 30 yards, one for a TD, carried 16 times for 183 yards; and completed 28-yard pass to Kiley. In win over Western Normal, scored two TDs, rushed for 123 yards on 14 carries, and kicked two PATs. Beat Nebraska with two passes to Anderson for 60 yards, 25-yarder to Barry, 7-yard TD run towards 70 yards on the day, and one PAT. Against Valparaiso, completed 32- and 38-yard passes, made 10-yard TD run, returned kickoff 15 yards, ran 25 yards to keep a drive alive, scored three PATs, and gained 120 yards rushing and 102 passing. In win over Army, somewhat emaciated due to lingering illness, ran for 150 yards, passed for 123 yards and one TD, amassed 207 yards on kick returns, kicked three PATs, and averaged 43 yards on his punts.

Surveying the wreckage after his 480 yards of offense, the Army coach said, "He's not a football player...he's a runaway sonuvabitch." In crunching Purdue, ran 80 yards from punt formation for TD, passed for 128 yards, and kicked three PATs. In narrow win over Indiana, scored TD on short plunge—with a dislocated shoulder. Closed out career with two TD passes, to Kiley and Barry, in fourth quarter in win over Northwestern. Stayed in Chicago for a few days after the game to help coach friend's football clinic. The bitter weather from the game and the clinic added to growing health problems. In midweek, attended team banquet at the Oliver Hotel in South Bend, but left early and checked into St. Joseph's Hospital. Gipp died three weeks later—and became an instant All-American legend. In his career, handled the ball 594 times and gained 4,781 yards. Many of his offensive records lasted 50+ years.

GLADIEUX, BOB. 1966-1967-1968; HB; 5-11, 185; Louisville, OH. Fine, all-purpose running back for Parseghian. Had deceptive speed, good moves, good hands, and ability to run long distance. In 1966, backed up LHB. Playing for injured Nick Eddy; scored TD on 46-yard pass from O'Brien in 10-10 game with MSU. For the year, made 27 runs for 111 yards and three TDs, caught 12 passes for 208 yards and two TDs, punted 11 times for 35.1-yard average, returned two kickoffs 48 yards, and made one tackle. In 1967, backed up at LHB. For the year, made 84 carries for 384 yards and five TDs, caught 23 passes for 297 yards and two TDs, punted three times for 32.7-yard average, returned one kickoff 19 yards, and made three tackles.

In 1968, started at RHB and had one of the best years on record. Led Fighting Irish with 152 carries for 713 yards and 12 TDs, caught 37 passes for 442 yards and two TDs, returned six punts 91 yards and 11 kickoffs 262 yards to total 1,508 yards. Punted three times for 42.3-yard average; his best was a 61-yarder. In his career, carried 263 times for 1,208 yards and 20 TDs, caught 72 passes for 947 yards and six TDs, returned six punts 91 yards and 14 kickoffs 329 yards, made four tackles, and punted 17 times for a 35.94-yard average. His offensive career total was 2,575 yards and 26 TDs.

GMITTER, DON. 1964-1965-1966; DE, E; 6-2, 215; Mt. Lebanon, PA. Member of the 1964 class of sophomores who challenged for the national crown and won it as seniors (Lynch, Page, Hardy, Regner, Conjar, Goeddeke, and Swatland, among others). Multi-skilled player, part of great defensive front four in 1964, then switched to TE. Excellent quickness and good strength; determined tackler; good blocker on offense. In 1964, started at DE; made 54 tackles for the year, recovered two fumbles, and broke up one pass. In 1965, moved to TE. Playing for a ground-oriented offense, caught six passes for 155 yards and two TDs, made six tackles, and recovered one fumble. In 1966, played much of the year with a bad knee (had surgery after the season) and saw most of passing game go to Seymour. For the year, made four catches for 72 yards and one tackle. In his career, made 61 tackles, recovered three fumbles, and caught 10 passes for 227 yards and two TDs.

GOEDDEKE, GEORGE. 1964-1965-1966; C; 6-3, 228; Detroit, MI. Starting center for Hanratty in 1966 championship year. Excellent blocker with good quickness; often dominating player. In 1964, backed up at C. In 1965, started at C. In 1966, started at C. Was hurt early in tie with MSU, but the injury allowed O'Brien to work with his regular C for the rest of the game. Made All-American.

GOLIC, BOB. 1975-1976-1977-1978; LB; 6-3, 244; Cleveland, OH. Great linebacker for Devine. Had size, speed, quickness, tremendous strength, good reading skills, and excellent tackling. Dominating player on 1977 championship team. In 1975, started at MLB; made 82 tackles, fourth best on the squad as freshman, two for -13 yards. In 1976, started at MLB. Was second leading tackler for the season with 99, six for -25 yards; broke up one pass; and had one interception. In 1977, started at MLB. For the year, made 146 tackles, five for -33 yards; broke up five passes; recovered one fumble; blocked one kick; made three interceptions for 19 return yards; and returned one punt 16 yards. Made All-American. In 1978, started at MLB; set single game record with 26 tackles in loss to Michigan. In his final season, made 152 tackles, five for -23 yards; broke up two passes; recovered one fumble; and had two interceptions for three return yards. Consensus All-American. For his career, made 479 tackles, 18 for -94 yards; broke up eight passes; made six interceptions for 22 return yards; recovered two fumbles; blocked one kick; and returned one punt 16 yards.

GREEN, MARK. 1985-1986-1987-1988; TB; 6-0, 184; Riverside, CA. Three-year starter at TB for Holtz; tri-captain of 1988 national championship team; leading rusher in 1986 and 1987. Superb runner, good receiver, and good blocker. Could play as WR as well as run inside. Had good speed, surprising power and toughness, and very good hands. In 1985, backed up at FL. For the year, carried five times for 64 yards, caught nine passes for 116 yards, and returned two kickoffs 29 yards. In 1986, started at TB for six games. For the year, made 96 carries for 406 yards and two TDs, and caught 25 passes for 242 yards. In 1987, started at TB. For the year, made 146 carries for 861 yards and six TDs, caught 13 passes for 98 yards, and returned one kickoff 17 yards. In 1988, started at TB. For the season, made 135 carries for 646 yards and seven TDs, caught 14 passes for 155 yards, and returned one kickoff 25 yards. For his career, carried 382 times for 1,977 yards and 15 TDs, caught 61 passes for 611 yards, and returned four kickoffs 71 yards. His career total was 2,659 yards and 15 TDs.

GRIFFITH, KEVIN. 1979-1981-1982; DT, DE; 6-3, 242; Kettering, OH. Solid, dependable defensive lineman for Devine and Faust. Very quick in spite of knee problems, good pursuit, and always in the vicinity of the ball. In 1979, started at DT. For the year, made 33 tackles, two for -7 yards; broke up one pass; and recovered three fumbles. Lost the 1980 season with knee problems. In 1981, started at DE. For the season, was third leading tackler with 63 hits, six for -23 yards; broke up five passes; and recovered three fumbles. In 1982, started at DE. For the season, made 65 tackles, six for -38 yards; broke up four passes; and recovered one fumble. For his career, made 161 tackles, 14 for -68 yards; broke up 10 passes; and recovered seven fumbles.

GROOM, JERRY. 1948-1949-1950; C, LB; 6-3, 215; Des Moines, IA. Stellar defensive player for Leahy. Great tackler and inspirational leader. In 1948, backed up at C. Intercepted Nebraska pass deep in their territory to lead to TD in win. Recovered one of fiveWashington miscues to lead to TD in blowout win. In 1949, started at MLB for the national champions. Started rout of Indiana by grabbing Hoosier fumble on their 24. Played decisive part in defeating SMU 27-20 with blocked PAT and an interception to end their final drive. In 1950, started at MLB. Saved win over Tulane with fumble recovery on Notre Dame 10. Blocked Navy punt on their 17 that led to insurance TD in win. Played 465 minutes—86 percent of the total time the Fighting Irish played. Made All-American.

GRUNHARD, TIM. 1986-1987-1988-1989; G; 6-3, 292; Chicago, IL. Excellent offensive lineman for Holtz. Played three different positions (T, C, and G) and handled most of the special teams work as C. Had tremendous speed and quickness, especially seen on punting downs when he would snap to the punter and was often one of the first bearing down on the returner downfield. In 1986, worked mostly as snapper for the punt team. In 1987, backed up at RG. In 1988, started at G for the national champions. In 1989, started at G. Made All-American.

GUGLIELMI, RALPH. 1951-1952-1953-1954; QB; 6-0, 185; Columbus, OH. Leahy's last QB, inspirational leader, fine passer, pretty good runner, and slick pass defender; must be rated near the top of all Irish QBs. In 1951, backed up at QB. Led Irish in upset win over undefeated USC. For the year, completed 27 of 53 passes for 438 yards. In 1952, started at QB. Fired winning TD (16-yarder to Heap) in 27-21 game with Oklahoma. For the year, rushed 48 times for 31 yards and one TD, and completed 61 of 142 passes for 683 yards and four TDs. In 1953, started at QB and teamed with Heisman winner Johnny Lattner for potent backfield combination. Saved tie with Iowa with TD passes to Shannon with two seconds left in the first half and six seconds left in the game. For the year, completed 52 of 113 passes for 792 yards and eight TDs, had 60 carries for 74 yards and six TDs, kicked five PATs, made five interceptions for 47 return yards and one TD, and returned two kickoffs 15 yards in 410 minutes of play. In 1954, started at QB. For the season, completed 68 of 127 throws for 1,160 yards and six TDs, carried 79 times for 95 yards and five TDs, led team with five interceptions for 51 return yards, and made two fumble recoveries in 429 minutes. Consensus All-American. For his career, completed 208 of 435 passes for 3,073 yards and 18 TDs, carried 187 times for 200 yards and 12 TDs, kicked five PATs, made 10 interceptions for 98 yards and one TD, recovered two fumbles, and returned two kickoffs 15 yards. He accounted for 31 TDs and 3,386 total yards.

GULYAS, ED. 1969-1970-1971; DB, HB; 5-11, 190; San Carlos, CA. Dependable back for Parseghian's Theismann-led teams. Tough inside runner; good blocker and pass receiver. In 1969, was reserve DB; gained 20 yards on three carries, returned 14 punts 87 yards to lead team, and returned one kickoff 25 yards. In 1970, started at LHB. Led Irish backs with 558 yards on 127 carries for three TDs, caught nine passes for 189 yards and two TDs, and made one tackle. In 1971, started at LHB. Gained 220 yards on 56 carries for five TDs and caught three passes for 16 yards. For his career, carried 186 times for 798 yards and eight TDs, caught 12 passes for 205 yards and two TDs, returned 14 punts 87 yards and one kickoff 25 yards, and made one tackle. Accumulated 1,115 total yards and 10 TDs in his career.

HAINES, KRIS. 1975-1976-1977-1978; SE; 6-0, 181; Sidney, OH. Speedy wideout for Devine; teamed well with Montana in 1977 national championship season and afterwards. Could go long as well as be possession receiver; had good moves, excellent hands, and good concentration. In 1975, backed up at SE; carried once for 28 yards and returned one punt three yards. In 1976, backed up at SE; caught three passes for 64 yards. In 1977, started at SE. For the year, caught 28 passes for 587 yards and two TDs. In 1978, against Houston in "Frozen Bowl" caught four passes, including an 8-yard TD pass with no time showing to set up winning PAT, and a 2-point conversion. For the year, led Irish receivers with 32 receptions for 699 yards and five TDs and made one tackle. For his career, ran once for 28 yards, caught 63 passes for 1,350 yards and two TDs, returned one punt three yards, and made one tackle.

HAMILTON, DONALD. 1908-1909; QB; 5-10, 175; Columbus, OH. Excellent QB for era; fine punt returner; very adept on end runs for long gains. In 1908 started at QB. First man to throw TD pass for Notre Dame, a 40-yard pass and run bomb to Fay Wood in 64-0 rout of Franklin; also scored TD with 65-yard run, made 45-yard punt return, and returned a kickoff 25 yards in same game. Against Michigan ran for 15 yards, made one conversion kick, and picked up 70 yards on three punt returns to nullify Michigan's punting game (when punts were a first-down weapon to get out of a hole). Against Physicians and Surgeons, scored one TD and kicked three conversions and one field goal. Kicked two conversions against Ohio Northern. Scored all Notre Dame's points with two field goals and added two 50-yard punt returns in 8-4 win over Wabash. Hurt his hip in that game and missed a game, but then replaced another injured QB and led Notre Dame to a 6-0 victory over Marquette. In 1909, started at QB. Returned MAC punt 10 yards in Irish win. Did the same in close win over Pitt. Teamed with Red Miller to beat Michigan for the first time. Kicked three conversions in win over Miami of Ohio. Added five conversions and one 45-yard field goal in win over Wabash.

HANKERD, JOHN. 1977-1978-1979-1980; LB, DE; 6-4, 245; Jackson, MI. Good defensive lineman for Devine—quick, excellent pursuit; good tackler; good nose for the ball. In 1977, for the national champions, backed up MLB. Made 14 tackles and broke up one pass. In 1978, started at DE. For the year, made 55 tackles, nine for -50 yards (second best on the team); broke up one pass; and recovered one fumble. In 1979, started at DE; led linemen with 73 tackles, including a team-leading 14 for -90 yards; broke up one pass; and recovered three fumbles. In 1980, started at DE. Made 35 tackles, five for -11 yards; broke up two passes; recovered one fumble; and blocked one kick. For his career, made 177 tackles, 28 for -151 yards; broke up five passes; recovered five fumbles; and blocked one kick.

HANLEY, DAN. 1930-1933-1934; FB, HB; 6-2, 190; Butte, MT. Played for three head coaches—Rockne, Anderson, and Layden. Was part of elaborate ruse by Rockne to lull USC and the press into complacency prior to 1930 game. Had good speed, but various injuries kept him from going all out. Excellent defensive player. In 1930, backed up at FB for the national champions. In win over Drake, made 34-yard TD dash to go with 25-yard gain. Scored TD in win over Northwestern and made an interception and runback to their 15. Rockne, on train trip to LA, had the speedier Bucky O'Connor wear his uniform and limp in practice. Other fullbacks were gone or hurt, so it looked like the Fighting Irish would meet undefeated USC with a crippled backfield. It worked—O'Connor slashed USC for long TDs. Hanley intercepted a Trojan pass to set up Notre Dame's last TD of Rockne's last win. Injuries cost him both 1931 and 1932. In 1933, after much persistence, backed up HB. In 1934, backed up at RHB. Caught winning TD pass from Pilney to beat Army. Had five carries for 39 yards in win over Carnegie Tech.

HANLEY, FRANK. 1896-1899; T; 5-10, 186; South Bend, IN. Probably qualifies as a "tramp player"—moving from place to place to find a game of football. Was 23 years old when he began at Notre Dame, then played 1897 and 1898 seasons with South Bend Commercial A.C. (but not against Notre Dame). At age 26, finished up with Notre Dame. Was known for his ability to run low with the ball. In 1896, started at RT. Ran 15 yards and scored one TD in shutout of South Bend Commercial A.C. Tallied two TDs in win over Albion. Scored two TDs as the Fighting Irish beat Highland Views. Returned one kickoff, recovered one fumble, and scored one TD in win over Beloit. In 1899, started at RT. Played strong defensive game in win over Englewood H.S.

HANRATTY, TERRY. 1966-1967-1968; QB; 6-1, 200; Butler, PA. Great QB; best remembered for sophomore year (1966) under Parseghian when he teamed with sophomore Jim Seymour for potent passing offense that decimated virtually every team except MSU; he was hurt in that game. Had superb arm; excellent ball handler; great reader of defensive secondary coverages; good runner; and had intangible ability to take a team to new heights. In 1966 started at QB for the national champions. Took team to 8-0 start but a Bubba Smith tackle caused a shoulder injury against MSU. For the year, completed 78 of 147 passes for eight TDs and 1,247 yards; also carried 50 times for 124 yards and five TDs, his longest a 52-yard burst. In 1967, started at QB. For the season, completed 110 of 206 passes for 1,439 yards and nine TDs, carried 75 times for 183 yards and seven TDs, and caught one pass for -2 yards. In 1968, surpassed Gipp's career yardage record against Illinois and hit 116 of 197 passes for 1,466 yards and 10 TDs while running 279 yards on 56 carries for four TDs. Consensus All-American. In his career, completed 304 of 550 passes for 4,152 yards and 27 TDs, carried 181 times for 586 yards and 16 TDs, and caught one pass for -2 yards. His career total was 4,736 yards and 43 TDs.

HARDY, KEVIN. 1964-1965-1966-1967; DE, DT; 6-5, 270; Oakland, CA. Great three-sport athlete—as defensive lineman in football, center/forward in basketball, and right fielder in baseball. Must be considered for any all-time Notre Dame team. Stellar lineman for Parseghian; lined up next to Alan Page on right side in 1966 and to Mike McCoy a year later. Was hard to block, had great quickness, superior strength, and excellent pass rushing skills. O.J. Simpson credited him with the hardest tackle he ever experienced. In 1964, started at DT. For the year, made 38 tackles and blocked two kicks, one going to Page for a TD. In 1965, hurt his back in Purdue game and was lost for the year. In 1966, started at RT for the national champions; made 79 tackles, broke up four passes, recovered one fumble, and punted 10 times for 40.9-yard average. Made All-American. In 1967, was injured on a crackback block in Purdue game. Played with a hurt foot much of the year. For the season, made 33 tackles, broke up two passes, had one interception, and punted 20 times for 32-yard average. Consensus All-American. For his career, made 150 tackles, broke up six passes, recovered one fumble, blocked two kicks, had one interception, and punted 30 times for 35-yard average.

HARRISON, RANDY. 1974-1975-1976-1977-1978; FS; 6-1, 207; Hammond, IN. The only five-time monogram winner in Notre Dame football history. Had good speed and quickness, excellent coverage skills, was a good closer, and generally knew how to be around the ball. In 1974, as a freshman, led secondary with 57 tackles, one for -3 yards; broke up seven passes; recovered one fumble; and made two interceptions for two TDs (44 yards against Miami and 40 yards against Navy). In 1975, started at FS. For the season, made 54 tackles, one for -2 yards; broke up two passes; had one interception and 7-yard runback; and returned two punts for 11 yards. In 1976, started at FS but broke his wrist against Purdue, the season's second game, and missed the rest of the year. Still managed to make 26 tackles and return two punts 17 yards. In 1977, backed up at FS for national champions. For the year, made 18 tackles, broke up one pass, had one interception and 13-yard runback, and returned six punts 36 yards and three kickoffs 46 yards. In 1978, backed up at FS. Started the great comeback of 1979 Cotton Bowl with 56-yard kickoff return. For the season, made 22 tackles, broke up one pass, returned seven punts four yards and five kickoffs 79 yards, and had one interception and 34-yard return. For his career, made 177 tackles, two for -5 yards; recovered one fumble; made five interceptions for 138 return yards and two TDs; returned 17 punts 68 yards and eight kickoffs 125 yards for a total of 331 yards and two TDs.

HART, LEON. 1946-1947-1948-1949; E; 6-4, 245; Turtle Creek, PA.Only lineman ever to win Heisman Trophy. Overpowering force on the lines of Leahy's glory years; instrumental in achieving 39-game winning streak. Never played in a losing contest in four years at Notre Dame. Devastating blocker and tackler; awesome, frightening sight when turned loose on his patented end run or from FB spot. Prototype of today's TE with size, speed, and good hands. In 1946, backed up at RE for the national champions. For the year, caught five passes for 107 yards and one TD. In 1947, started at RE for the national champions. Caught TD pass and recovered two fumbles against Navy and caught winning TD against Northwestern. For the year, caught nine passes for 156 yards and two TDs, recovered three fumbles, and led with 289 minutes of playing time. Named All-American. In 1948, started at RE. For the year, led Fighting Irish with 9.8-yard rushing average on four carries for 39 yards and one TD, caught 16 passes for 231 yards and four TDs, recovered one fumble, and led team with 389 minutes of playing time. Made All-American. In 1949, started at RE for national champions. For the season, rushed 18 times for 73 yards and one TD, caught 19 passes for 257 yards and five TDs, blocked one punt, and recovered three fumbles. Consensus All-American and won Maxwell and Heisman trophies. For his career, carried 22 times for 112 yards and two TDs, caught 49 passes for 751 yards and 12 TDs, blocked one kick, and recovered seven fumbles. His career total of 863 yards averaged 12.1 yards every time he handled the ball. He scored a TD one out of five times he got the ball. Ultimately, the stats are misleading because he changed the whole picture for opponents, both offense and defense; was a complete threat.

HEAP, JOE. 1951-1952-1953-1954; HB; 5-11, 180; Abita Springs, LA. Genuine triple-threat; part of extremely talented quartet of backfield stars under Leahy—teamed with Guglielmi, Lattner, and Worden. One of best small players ever to suit up for the Fighting Irish. Had fine speed and moves, good hands for passing game, and could throw option pass. In 1951, backed up at LHB. For the year, carried 38 times for 166 yards and two TDs, caught two passes for 25 yards, and returned two kickoffs 50 yards. In 1952, started at LHB. For the season, carried 89 times for 383 yards and two TDs, completed seven of 13 passes for 130 yards, caught 29 passes for 407 yards and two TDs, and returned 10 punts 126 yards for one TD and six kickoffs 145 yards for a total of 1,191 yards. In 1953, started at LHB. For the year, rushed 62 times for 314 yards and two TDs, completed four of six passes for 48 yards, caught 22 passes for 336 yards and five TDs, returned seven punts 143 yards (including 99-yard TD return that clinched win over USC), returned four kickoffs 76 yards, made two interceptions, and recovered one fumble. In 1954, started at LHB and became career leader in pass receptions to that point in Irish football. For the season, led team in scoring, carried 110 times for 594 yards and eight TDs, completed all three passes for 32 yards and one TD, caught 18 passes for 369 yards to lead receivers, returned seven kickoffs 143 yards, and made two interceptions and two fumble recoveries. For his career, carried 299 times for 1,457 yards and 14 TDs, completed 14 of 22 passes for 210 yards and one TD, caught 71 passes for 1,137 yards and seven TDs, returned 17 punts for 269 yards and two TDs, returned 17 kickoffs 364 yards, made four interceptions, and recovered four fumbles. His career total was 3,437 yards and 24 TDs; amassed more than 1,000 career yards in both running and pass receiving (a rare feat to that point) and 843 yards on passing and kick returning. (Compare his career statistics with those of Paul Hornung.)

HEAVENS, JEROME. 1975-1976-1977-1978; FB; 6-0, 204; East St. Louis, IL. Solid, dependable player, with fine speed and moves for FB; excellent durability; and fine blocking skills. Teamed with Ferguson and Montana to give defenses serious headaches. In 1975, started at FB. As freshman, led Irish runners with 129 carries for 756 yards and five TDs, caught eight passes for 64 yards, and made one tackle. In 1976, hurt his knee in the third game and was lost for the year. In his shortened season, carried 54 times for 204 yards and caught two passes for 22 yards. In 1977, started at FB for the national champions and lost 1,000-yard season when tackled for a loss on the final play of blowout win over Miami. In win over Texas in Cotton Bowl, carried 32 times for 101 yards. For the season, carried 229 times for a team-leading 994 yards and six TDs and was third in receiving with 12 for 133 yards. In 1978, surpassed Gipp's career rushing record and helped beat Houston in Cotton Bowl comeback win with 16 carries for 71 yards and four receptions for 60 yards. For the year, carried 178 times for 728 yards and four TDs and caught 13 passes for 113 yards. For his career, carried 590 times for 2,682 yards and 15 TDs and caught 35 passes for 332 yards, a total of 3,014 yards of offense.

HEIMKREITER, STEVE. 1975-1976-1977-1978; LB; 6-2, 228; Cincinnati, OH. Three-year starter as LB alongside Golic and for two years with Becker to provide Notre Dame with a fearsome linebacking corps. Had good speed on pass coverage; excellent tackler. In 1975, injuries kept him sidelined most of the year, but still made 22 tackles and recovered one fumble. In 1976, started at OLB and led team with 118 tackles, one for -4 yards, and recovered one fumble. In 1977, started at OLB for the national champions but missed three games with a sprained knee. For the year, made 98 tackles, two for -5 yards; broke up two passes; and recovered one fumble. In 1978, started at OLB. For the year, set new tackling record with 160, three for -4 yards; broke up two passes; and had one interception for a 2-yard runback. For his career, made 398 tackles, six for -13 yards; broke up four passes; made one interception and 2-yard return; and recovered three fumbles.

HEMPEL, SCOTT. 1968-1969-1970; K; 6-0, 235; Copley, OH. Handled most field goal and PAT work for Parseghian's teams led by Hanratty and Theismann. In 1968, kicked 45 of 50 PATs and five of nine field goals for 60 points, made six tackles, and broke up one pass. In 1969, booted 41 of 44 PATs and five of seven field goals for 56 points; also made four tackles. In 1970, led team in scoring with 54 points on 39 of 41 PATs and five of six field goals; made five tackles. For his career, made 125 of 135 PATs, 15 of 19 field goals, scored 171 points, made 15 tackles, and broke up one pass.

HENTRICH, CRAIG. 1989-1990-1991; K; 6-1, 196; Godfrey, IL. Excellent kicker for Holtz; handled both punting and place kicking. Has two best season averages for punting: 44.6 yards in 1989 and 44.88 in 1990. Set single-season mark for PATs in 1991 with 48. Career record holder for punting with 44.2-yard average on 83 punts. In 1989, made eight of 15 field goals and 44 of 45 PATs for 68 points; punted 26 times for 44.6-yard average. Had five punts for 40.1-yard average in win over Colorado in Orange Bowl. In 1990, hit 16 of 20 field goals, all 41 PATs, and averaged 44.9 yards on 34 punts. Made 73 consecutive PATs until one was blocked in loss to Colorado in Orange Bowl. In 1991, did most of the kicking until injured in Tennessee game. Made five of eight field goals, all 48 PATs, and punted 23 times for 42.9-yard average. Kicked one PAT in win over Florida in 1992 Sugar Bowl before re-injuring leg and leaving the game. In three seasons, kicked 29 of 43 field goals and 133 of 134 PATs for 220 points, and punted 83 times for 44.2-yard average.

HERING, FRANK. 1896; QB; 5-9, 154; South Bend, IN. Invented Mother's Day; a number of awards in his name have been offered for excellence in Notre Dame's spring practices. Played E and QB for Chicago in 1893 and 1894; moved to Bucknell for 1895 season and to Notre Dame for final year. Infectious leadership; confident, poised, keen student of the game adept at exploiting an opponent's weaknesses. Both coach and captain in 1896. After 46-0 win over South Bend Commercial A.C., several of their players enrolled at Notre Dame and played in the following years. During 82-0 mangling of Highland Views, shared 15 TDs among nine players, with none for himself. First Notre Dame player to stay and coach full-time.

HOGAN, DON. 1962; HB; 5-11, 185; Chicago, IL. Great speed, moves, good hands during sophomore year. An automobile accident during Christmas vacation killed his sister and crushed his hip. Made valiant effort to recover, but had to leave the game. Wrote farewell letter to his teammates that stands as testament to his courage and determination in the face of terrible odds. In 1962, started at RHB. Led team with 454 yards and three TDs on 90 carries, was second in receiving with 12 catches for 146 yards, second in kickoff returns with nine for 206 yards, and made 2-point conversion and 15 tackles. Of 1,000-yard rushers in the post-war era, his 1962 rookie yardage was second only to Worden's 686 yards.

HOLOHAN, PETE. 1978-1979-1980; FL; 6-5, 228; Liverpool, NY. Excellent wide receiver for Devine. His size made a great target; had good moves and great hands. In 1978, started at FL in Montana's final year. For the season, caught 20 passes for 301 yards and one TD. In 1979, started at FL; caught 22 passes for 386 yards, completed two of three passes for 81 yards, returned one kickoff for no gain, and tallied a 2-point conversion to beat South Carolina. In 1980, started at FL. For the season, caught 21 passes for 296 yards and one TD, and lost 12 yards on his only carry. In his career, caught 63 passes for 983 yards and two TDs, carried once for -12 yards, completed two of three passes for 81 yards, returned one kickoff for no gain, and tallied a 2-point conversion.

HORNUNG, PAUL. 1954-1955-1956; FB, QB; 6-2, 205; Louisville, KY. All-time Notre Dame star. Fine blend of size, speed, moves, passing and kicking skills, and leadership qualities. Unusually good on defense to go with obvious offensive talents. Won Heisman Trophy when Notre Dame won only two games for the year—the fourth Heisman winner in a decade. In 1954, backed up at FB but saw some action as QB. For the season, carried 23 times for 159 yards (6.9-yard average) and two TDs, hit five of 19 passes for 36 yards, averaged 39 yards on six punts, booted six PATs, returned one kickoff 58 yards, had three interceptions for 94 return yards, and recovered one fumble. In 1955, started at QB. Carried 92 times for 472 yards and six TDs, completed 46 of 103 passes for 743 yards and nine TDs, kicked five PATs and two field goals, returned six kickoffs 109 yards, had five interceptions for 59 return yards, recovered two fumbles, and punted 30 times for 33.9-yard average. Made All-American.

In 1956, played with two dislocated thumbs near the end of the season. Carried 94 times for 420 yards and seven TDs and completed 59 of 111 passes for 917 yards and three TDs to be the first Irish player since 1938 to lead the team in both passing and running; returned 16 kickoffs 496 yards for one TD; returned four punts 63 yards; booted 14 PATs; had 55 tackles; and made two interceptions for 59 return yards. Consensus All-American and Heisman Trophy winner. For his career, carried 209 times for 1,051 yards and 15 TDs, completed 110 of 233 passes for 1,696 yards and 12 TDs, booted 25 PATs and two field goals, made 10 interceptions for 212 return yards, recovered three fumbles, returned 23 kickoffs 663 yards for one TD, returned four punts 63 yards, and punted 69 times for 36.1-yard average. His total was 3,622 yards and 28 TDs.

HOWARD, JOE. 1981-1982-1983-1984; SE, FL; 5-9, 170; Clinton, MD. Integral part of offense for Faust. Extremely fast, as shown in record-setting 96-yard TD pass and run against Georgia Tech in 1981 from Blair Kiel. In 1981, broke into starting lineup midway into the season and had most playing time of freshman class, 114:29 minutes. For the year, caught 17 passes for 463 yards, a record 27.2-yard average, and three TDs. In 1982, started at SE; caught at least two passes each game except against Pitt (one, a 54-yard TD play). For the year, made 28 receptions for a team-leading 524 yards and two TDs, ran twice for 28 yards, returned one punt for -2 yards and five kickoffs for 111 yards, and made five tackles. In 1983, started at SE. For the year, led team in yardage on receptions with 464 yards on 27 catches and two TDs, passed for 29-yard TD, carried four times for 61 yards, returned 28 punts 202 yards and one kickoff seven yards. Made one catch for 47 yards in Liberty Bowl win over Boston College. Played basketball as walk-on for Digger Phelps. In 1984, started at SE and became fifth leading receiver even though his stats fell off. Caught 13 passes for 212 yards for the season. In Aloha Bowl, caught two passes for 24 yards and returned four punts 42 yards as Notre Dame lost a close game to SMU. For his career, carried six times for 89 yards, caught 85 passes for 1,472 yards (17.3 yards per catch) and seven TDs, completed one pass for 29-yard TD, returned 29 punts 200 yards and six kickoffs 118 yards, and made five tackles. His total was 1,639 yards and eight TDs.

HUARTE, JOHN. 1962-1963-1964; QB; 6-0, 180; Anaheim, CA. Sixth Heisman Trophy winner for Notre Dame. Almost forgotten man on roster until Parseghian took a look around and told him, "You're my quarterback." The rest is history, but only a short, one-season history. Good ball-handler but had curious throwing delivery—almost sidearm—with great accuracy and soft touch; quiet, forceful leader. His 1964 stats with Jack Snow reveal how his talent had been wasted while the program floundered. His senior year also revealed the kind of passing tandems that Parseghian consistently produced: Hanratty to Seymour, Theismann to Gatewood, Clements to Demmerle. In 1962, backed up at QB. For the season, completed four of eight throws for 38 yards and lost 14 yards on three carries. In 1963 backed up at QB; showed flashes of his ability throughout pitiful season: completed 20 of 42 passes for 243 yards and one TD, also kicked one PAT. In 1964, started at QB. Led the Fighting Irish back to national prominence after five years of misery, making strong claim on the national championship (recognized as such by the MacArthur Bowl award). Completed 114 of 205 passes for 2,062 yards and 16 TDs, carried 37 times for seven yards and three TDs, and caught one pass for 11 yards. For his career, carried 51 times for -60 yards and three TDs, completed 138 of 255 passes for 2,543 yards, 17 TDs, and 11 interceptions. His total was 2,483 yards and 20 TDs. Consensus All-American and Heisman Trophy winner.

HUFF, ANDY. 1969-1971-1972; HB, FB; 5-11, 212; Toledo, OH. Dependable, productive runner for Parseghian's teams led by Theismann and Clements. Especially valuable in short yardage situations; good blocker; and good hands. In 1969, backed up at RHB. For the season, carried 69 times for 265 yards and five TDs, caught four passes for 28 yards and one TD, and returned one kickoff 12 yards. Lost 1970 due to severe shoulder injury during spring practice. In 1971, started at FB. For the year, carried 69 times for 295 yards and two TDs and caught four passes for 39 yards. In 1972, started at FB and had best day against Navy, gaining 121 yards on 16 carries. For the season, carried 115 times for 567 yards and a team-leading 10 TDs, caught nine passes for 102 yards, returned two kickoffs 40 yards, and made one tackle. For his career, carried 253 times for 1,127 yards and 17 TDs, caught 17 passes for 169 yards and one TD, returned three kickoffs 52 yards, and made one tackle. His career total came to 1,348 yards and 18 TDs.

HUFFMAN, DAVE. 1975-1976-1977-1978; T, C; 6-5, 245; Dallas, TX. Known for wearing red elbow pads so his mother could see him in the melee of the line. Dominant player for Devine, especially in 1977 championship season. Very dependable at C; excellent run and pass blocker. In 1975, backed up at T. Often used in double TE sets opposite MacAfee; caught one pass for 16 yards against Miami. In 1976, started at C. Made two tackles in 308 minutes. In 1977, starting C on great offensive line. Helped dominate line of scrimmage in Cotton Bowl win over Texas. Played 308 minutes and made two tackles. Made All-American. In 1978, started at C. Threw devastating block that helped spring Montana for a score on fourth-quarter rallying drive that beat Pitt. Consensus All-American.

HUGHES, ERNIE. 1974-1975-1976-1977; DE, G; 6-4, 253; Boise, ID. Fine offensive lineman for Parseghian and Devine; key member of offensive line on 1977 national championship team. Had good quickness, superior strength, and excellent technique. In 1974, backed up DE and made four tackles in 13 minutes of play. In 1975, started at G and played 322 minutes; made five tackles and recovered one fumble. In 1976, started at G; made two tackles, recovered two fumbles, and played 318 minutes. In 1977, part of a superb offensive line as starting G. For the season, made three tackles and ran one yard with kickoff return. Made All-American. Played super game in Cotton Bowl win over Texas to help Heavens and Ferguson both reach century mark in rushing; manhandled Outland Trophy winner, Brad Shearer, who made only one disappointed, frustrated tackle.

HUNTER, AL. 1973-1975-1976; HB; 6-0, 190; Greenville, NC. Fine back, though moody, who provided superior speed for 1973 national champions. Ran 9.3 in the 100; had good moves and strength. In 1973, backed up RHB. Shocked Alabama by running 93 yards with second half kickoff for a TD in the Sugar Bowl. For the season, carried 32 times for 150 yards and three TDs, caught two passes for 12 yards, and returned three kickoffs 114 yards, including 74-yarder against Navy. In 1974, was suspended. In 1975, started at LHB. For the year, carried 117 times for 558 yards and eight TDs, caught 10 passes for 87 yards, returned five kickoffs 141 yards, and threw 2-point conversion pass to Haines in loss to USC. In 1976, started at LHB to become Notre Dame's first 1,000-yard rusher in a season; against Miami became Notre Dame's all-time leading rusher at that point. For the year, carried 233 times for 1,058 yards and 12 TDs, caught 15 passes for 189 yards and one TD, completed one pass for 33-yard TD, returned 12 kickoffs 241 yards and four punts 1 yard, and made one tackle. Could have played in 1977 but turned pro under acrimonious circumstances. For his career, carried 382 times for 1,766 yards and 23 TDs, caught 27 passes for 288 yards and one TD, completed one pass for 33-yard TD, returned 20 kickoffs 496 yards and four punts 1 yard, threw 2-point conversion, and made one tackle. His offense totalled 2,584 yards and 25 TDs.

HUNTER, ART. 1951-1952-1953; C, E, T; 6-3, 226; Akron, OH. Multi-talented lineman for Leahy. Had good size, speed, quickness, strength, and blocking and tackling skills. Leahy kept moving him around and he did well in all positions. Closest comparable player—Dave Casper. In 1951, started at C. In 1952, started at RE. Caught 16 passes for 246 yards and one TD. In 1953, started at RT; grabbed muffed snap in Georgia Tech's end zone for TD. Recovered three fumbles and led the team with 423 minutes of playing time. Consensus All-American.

HUNTER, TONY. 1979-1980-1981-1982; SE, WB, TE; 6-5, 226; Cincinnati, OH. Great size, speed, hands, moves, and strength. Multi-talented threat; played several positions and could create big gainer from each (but may have never found right position). In 1979, started at SE. Made 690 yards on 27 receptions (25.6-yard average) for two TDs to lead team. In 1980, started at SE. For the year, caught 23 passes for 303 yards and one TD and carried five times for 52 yards. In 1981, moved to WB; also played some TE, probably his natural position. For the year, caught 23 passes for 303 yards and two TDs and carried 27 times for 68 yards and one TD. In 1982, started at TE; caught 42 passes for 507 yards but did not score, and made five tackles. Made All-American. For his career, carried 32 times for 120 yards and one TD, caught 120 passes for 1,897 yards and five TDs, and made five tackles. His total was 2,017 yards and six TDs.

ISMAIL, RAGHIB. 1988-1989-1990; FL; 5-10, 175; Wilkes Barre, PA. Fastest player in Irish history. Timed at 4.12 in the 40 by NFL scouts. Not merely a speedster, could put moves on people and also go into the middle. Averaged 61 yards for TD plays for career. Tremendous ability to be near top speed in one or two strides. Could break tackles with leg drive, and was hard to hit. In 1988, started at SE for the national champions. For the year, made 12 catches for 331 yards and two TDs, and returned 12 kickoffs for 433 yards and two TDs and five punts for 72 yards. In 1989, started at FL. For the season, had 64 carries for 478 yards and two TDs, caught 27 passes for 535 yards, returned 20 kickoffs 502 yards for two TDs, and had seven punt returns for 113 yards and one TD. Consensus All-American. In 1990, started at FL and worked some at TB. For the year, carried 67 times for 537 yards and three TDs, caught 32 passes for 699 yards and two TDs, returned 14 kickoffs 336 yards for one TD, and returned 13 punts 151 yards. Consensus All-American; named Walter Camp Outstanding Player of the Year; was second in Heisman Trophy balloting. Bypassed final season to turn pro. For his career, made 131 carries for 1,015 yards (7.7 yards per carry) for five TDs, caught 71 passes for 1,565 yards (22 yards per catch) for four TDs, returned 46 kickoffs 1,271 yards (27.6 yards per return) for five TDs, and returned 25 punts 336 yards (13.4 yards per return) for one TD. His career totals were 273 attempts for 4,187 yards and 15 TDs—15.3 yards per attempt. In the 1,000-yard club in three different categories: runs, catches, and kickoff returns.

JEWETT, HARRY. 1887-1888; FB, HB; Chicago, IL. At one time reportedly held world's record for 100-yard dash, but his recorded time in a race with Michigan's fastest runner, prior to first Notre Dame football game, ended with him in second in a losing time of 11 seconds. In 1888, scored Notre Dame's first TD in 26-6 loss to Michigan. Grantland Rice wrote, "... Jewett secured the ball, and by a magnificent run made touch-down in Ann Arbor ground . . .[his] play was an elegant one and it caught the fancy of the crowd who were evidently pleased to see the Michigan team's [shutout] record broken."

JOHNSON, ANTHONY. 1986-1987-1988-1989; TB, FB; 6-0, 220; South Bend, IN. Powerful, hard-hitting, tough runner; played integral part on 1988 championship squad. Hard to bring down, seemed impervious to pain, and was pulverizing blocker. Especially tough in scoring territory. In 1986, backed up at TB. For the year, had 80 carries for 349 yards and five TDs, and caught six passes for 53 yards. In 1987, started at FB. Led Irish runners with eight carries for 20 yards against Texas A & M in Cotton Bowl. For the season, had 78 carries for 366 yards and a team-leading 11 TDs, caught four passes for 110 yards, and returned two kickoffs 55 yards. In 1988, started at FB. For the year, carried 69 times for 282 yards and five TDs, caught seven passes for 128 yards, and returned two kickoffs 27 yards. In 1989, started at FB and was a tri-captain. For the year, carried 131 times for 515 yards and 11 TDs, caught eight passes for 85 yards and two TDs, and returned three kickoffs 42 yards. For his career, had 358 carries for 1,512 yards and 32 TDs, caught 25 passes for 376 yards and two TDs, and returned seven kickoffs 127 yards. His career total was 2,015 yards and 34 TDs. He ranks third on all-time rushing TD list and fourth overall.

JOHNSON, JOE. 1981-1982-1983-1984; FS, SS; 6-2, 185; Fostoria, OH. Real hitter; excellent on safety blitzes and run support. In 1981, backed up at FS and played the most of any freshman on defense. Made 22 tackles, broke up two passes, and had one interception for the year. In 1982, started at SS. For the season, made 55 tackles, six for -22 yards; broke up two passes; and had two interceptions for 56 return yards. In 1983, started at SS. For the year, made 50 hits; caused three fumbles; recovered two fumbles; broke up three passes; and had four QB sacks for -47 yards, three other tackles for -23 yards, and one interception for a 6-yard return. In 1984, started at SS and was a tri-captain. For the year, made 60 tackles, broke up two passes, caused two fumbles, and registered one safety. For his career, made 187 tackles, 13 for -92 yards; had four interceptions for 61 return yards; caused five fumbles; recovered two fumbles; and forced one safety.

JOHNSTON, MIKE. 1980-1981-1982-1983; K; 5-11, 184; Rochester, NY. Walked on and did not receive scholarship until 1982. In 1980, handled kickoff duties and had one PAT. In 1981, handled kickoffs again. In 1982, set single-season record with 19 field goals in 22 attempts, including three that were the difference in win over Michigan, and was 19 of 19 on PATs for 76 points. In 1983, made 12 of 21 field goals and 33 of 34 PATs for 69 points. In his career, made 31 of 43 field goals and 53 of 54 PATs.

JUZWIK, STEVE. 1939-1940-1941; HB; 5-9, 185; Chicago, IL. Sturdy, quick HB for Layden and Leahy. Also played strong defense and was good kicker. In 1939, backed up at RHB. Made 32-yard run to set up only Irish TD in win over Northwestern. In 1940, started at RHB. Led team with 71 carries for 407 yards, also had 89 yards on passes, scored seven TDs, made one PAT, led in scoring with 43 points, including 84-yard interception runback for a TD. In 1941, was Bertelli's favorite receiver. For the year, carried 101 times for 386 yards; caught 17 passes for 305 yards; scored eight TDs; kicked 13 of 19 PATs; and had 23 punt returns for 290 yards, one kickoff return for 20 yards, and three interceptions for 39 yards for a total of 1,040 yards.

KADISH, MIKE. 1969-1970-1971; DT; 6-5, 260; Grand Rapids, MI. Dominant defensive lineman for Parseghian. Big, quick, strong; excellent pass rusher and run stopper. Teamed with McCoy, Patulski, and Marx to give Notre Dame a nearly impenetrable defensive line. In 1969, started at DT and made 68 tackles, six for -27 yards; had one interception; and broke up one pass. In 1970, started at DT; made 47 tackles, four for -15 yards, and recovered one fumble. In 1971, started at DT. Led team with 97 tackles (one of the last interior linemen to do so), eight for -40 yards, and broke up six passes. Made All-American. For his career, made 212 tackles, 18 for -82 yards; had one interception; broke up seven passes; and recovered one fumble.

KANTOR, JOE. 1961-1963-1964; FB; 6-1, 212; Cleveland, OH. Solid performer in a period of turmoil in the program; probably under-utilized, but helped give stability and maturity in first year of Parseghian era. Had good size, adequate speed, good blocking skills, and good strength. In 1961, backed up at FB; made five carries for 39 yards, made six tackles, and broke up one pass. Injuries kept him out of action in 1962. In 1963, started at FB. For the year, led team with 88 carries for 330 yards and two TDs, caught two passes for 24 yards, returned one kickoff 11 yards, broke up one pass, and made one tackle. In 1964, backed up at FB. Scored what would have been winning TD in USC game to insure undefeated season, but lost it on a holding call. For the season, carried 47 times for 158 yards and one TD, caught two passes for 43 yards, and returned one kickoff eight yards. For his career, carried 140 times for 527 yards and three TDs, caught four passes for 67 yards, returned two kickoffs 19 yards, broke up two passes, and made seven tackles. For his career, gained 613 yards and scored three TDs.

KEGLER, BILL. 1896-1897; FB; 6-0, 173; Bellevue, IA. Solid, all-around player—good runner, defender, and kicker. In 1896, started at FB and did place kicking and some punting. Part of the decision the only time Notre Dame players quit a game—trailing Physicians and Surgeons 4-0 and after a squabble over a possession matter, the Irish players simply walked off the field with 10 minutes remaining in the game. Made four conversions in 46-0 rout of South Bend Commercial A.C. Punted for 53-yard average against Albion, one for 65 yards, and made two conversion kicks in an Irish shutout. Scored one TD, rushed for 40+ yards, but missed two crucial conversions in 28-22 loss to Purdue. Scored TD in 82-0 win over Highland Views a week later. Helped defeat Beloit with one TD, good short yardage running, and good punting. In 1897, started at FB. In a tie with a much bigger Rush Medical squad, stopped some end runs, made a sack, punted well, and in the fashion of the day, was "pushed (by 256-pound Eggeman) into the line like a battering ram" on several plays. Scored only TD of game in win over DePauw, on 5-yard run. Scored two TDs on long runs in win over MAC.

KELLY, BOB. 1943-1944; HB; 5-10, 182; Chicago, IL. Fine running back for Leahy; had excellent speed for breaking long runs and catching the long pass. In 1943, backed up at RHB. In shutout win over Army, rushed 11 times for 27 yards and intercepted two passes. Caught two Lujack passes for TDs in win over Northwestern. Scored TD in win over Iowa Pre-Flight on 4-yard run. Started at RHB in 1944. For the year, carried 133 times for 676 yards and eight TDs, scored five TDs with pass receptions, and kicked six PATs to lead team with 84 points. Made All-American.

KELLY, JIM. 1961-1962-1963; E; 6-2, 215; Clairton, PA. Fine player who labored for Fighting Irish teams that did not score well nor move the ball well. Had good size, speed, moves, hands, and defensive skills. In 1961, backed up at RE. For the year, caught nine passes for 139 yards and two TDs, made 26 tackles, and recovered one fumble. In 1962, started at RE; had record-setting day against Pitt with 11 catches for 127 yards and three TDs. For the year, set new season totals for receptions and yardage; caught 41 passes for 523 yards and four TDs, made 21 tackles, broke up one pass, and recovered one fumble. Made All-American.In 1963, started at LE. Playing for an inept offense, caught 18 passes for 264 yards and two TDs, made 21 tackles, broke up two passes, intercepted one pass for 10-yard runback, and returned one kickoff nine yards. Repeat All-American. For his career, caught 68 passes for 926 yards and eight TDs, recovered two fumbles, broke up three passes, made one interception for 10-yard runback, returned one kickoff nine yards, and made 68 tackles. His offensive total was 935 yards.

KELLY, LUKE. 1908-1909-1910-1911; T, G; 5-9, 185; Boston, MA. Tough lineman who specialized in quick penetration on defense to mess up plays; also adept at blocking kicks and catching passes. Called best player on 1911 team (which included Rockne, Dorais, Philbrook, Eichenlaub, and Bergman). In 1908, started at LT. Scored TD in 88-0 rout of Physicians and Surgeons. Scored TD in 11-0 win over Indiana by falling on a loose kick in the end zone; also made 15-yard pass reception. Blocked Ohio Northern kick near their end zone and Art Smith recovered and scored. In 1909, backed up at RG. In 1910, backed up at RG. Knifed through Marquette's line and nailed their runner for a fumble, recovered for a TD and a 5-5 tie. In 1911, started at RT; elected captain. Blocked kick to avert a loss in 0-0 tie with Pitt. Caught 5-yard pass in another scoreless game with Marquette. Named to second team All-Western.

KIEL, BLAIR. 1980-1981-1982-1983; QB; 6-1, 206; Columbus, IN. First four-year starter at QB since Dorais 70 years earlier. Very strong for QB, good speed, good throwing arm for both distance and accuracy, and good punter. In 1980, started at QB. Played superbly at QB and as punter in 7-0 win over Alabama; also played well in Sugar Bowl loss to Georgia. For the year, carried 71 times for 148 yards and three TDs, completed 48 of 124 passes for 531 yards and five interceptions, averaged 40.1 yards on 66 punts, and had most playing time of any QB since Dorais—250 minutes. In 1981, started at QB. Led Irish in passing with 67 completions in 151 tries for 936 yards, seven TDs, and 10 interceptions; carried 31 times for 53 yards and one TD; and booted 74 punts for 39.9-yard average. In '82, completed 118 of 219 passes for 1,273 yards, three TDs, 10 interceptions, and .539 completion rate (fourth best in Irish history to that point); carried 44 times for -29 yards; and punted 77 times for 42.4-yard average. In 1983, started at QB. For the year, hit 64 of 115 passes for 910 yards, seven TDs, seven interceptions, and .557 completion rate; crunched 43 punts for 39.6-yard average; and carried 19 times for -8 yards and one TD. For his career, carried 165 times for 164 yards and five TDs; completed 297 passes in 609 throws for 3,650 yards, 17 TDs, and 32 interceptions; and punted 260 times for 40.67-yard average, second-best behind Shakespeare's 40.71 average at that point. His punts traversed 10,534 yards, but the number also signifies plenty of stalled drives. His 609 passes set record for most attempts, and was second only to Hanratty in completions (297 to 304). His career offense was 3,814 yards and 22 TDs.

KILEY, ROGER. 1919-1920-1921; E; 6-0, 180; Chicago, IL. Multi-talented athlete, teamed with Gipp as aerial tandem for undefeated 1920 squad. Had excellent speed, ran precise routes but had to ad lib when Gipp did, and played good defense. In 1919, backed up at LE. In 1920, started at LE. Caught 38-yard pass from Gipp in win over Valparaiso. Caught two passes from Gipp in win over Army, one a 35-yard TD. Caught several passes from Gipp in shutout of Purdue, one for 30 yards. Caught TD pass in win over Northwestern—Gipp's last game. All-American selection. In 1921, started at LE. Scored one TD in win over DePauw. Scored Notre Dame's only TD on 50-yard strike in 10-7 loss to Iowa; also made five other receptions and blocked a punt and returned it to the Iowa 25. Recovered Purdue fumble in Irish win. Caught 11-yard pass in win over Indiana. Scored two TDs on passes of 55 and 18 yards from Mohardt in shutout of Army. Scored against Rutgers three days later with 25-yard pass. All-American; captained basketball team; played second base for baseball team his senior year.

KIZER, NOBLE. 1922-1923-1924; G; 5-8, 165; Plymouth, IN. Originally went to Notre Dame to play basketball, but Rockne snatched him for football. Was perfect example, with Bert Metzger a few years later, of Rockne's "watch charm guard"—small, extremely quick, intelligent, and very tough. Rockne taught how to use leverage, angles, and the opponent's momentum to neutralize his charge, much like modern brush blocking. Fixture at RG for 1923 and 1924 seasons, when Seven Mules led Four Horsemen to fame and the national crown in 1924.

KLEINE, WALLY. 1983-1984-1985-1986; DT; 6-9, 274; Midland, TX. Fine DL whose size and agility posed problems for QBs intent on passing or staying in the pocket. In 1983, backed up at DT. For the season, made five tackles, one sack for -10 yards and one for -3 yards, and caused one fumble. In 1984, started at DT. For the year, made 48 tackles, two sacks for -16 yards and 11 for -25 yards; broke up one pass; caused three fumbles; and recovered three fumbles. In 1985, started at DT but missed four games with a knee injury. For the season, made 36 tackles, five sacks for -21 yards and six for -25 yards, and caused two fumbles. In 1986, started at DT. For the year, made 74 tackles, five sacks for -40 yards and eight for -27 yards, and broke up three passes. Made All-American. For his career, made 163 tackles, 13 sacks for -87 yards and 26 for -80 yards; caused six fumbles; recovered three fumbles; and broke up four passes.

KOKEN, MIKE. 1930-1931-1932; HB; 5-9, 168; Youngstown, OH. Classic triple-threat—excellent speed, good passing arm, and good leg for kicking. In 1930, backed up at LHB for national champions. Scored TD against Pitt with 5-yard run around right end; also made 19-yard run. In 1931, backed up LHB. Led team with three TDs and four PATs in win over Drake. Threw lateral pass to Host for 11-yard TD in win over Pitt. Threw lateral pass to Leahy for 13-yard TD in win over Carnegie Tech. In shutout of Penn, ran 22 yards for TD and passed 11 yard for another to go with one PAT. Threw TD pass to QB in win over Navy. In 1932, started at LHB. Fired 20-yard TD pass to Banas in win over Haskell. Against Carnegie Tech, made 58-yard TD run, gained 116 yards rushing, completed 31-yard pass, and kicked two PATs. Closed Irish scoring in win over Kansas with 3-yard plunge. Against Northwestern, threw 21-yard TD pass and 18-yarder to set up another score. Passed five yards to Melinkovich for TD in win over Army. Gained 375 yards on 105 carries and made four interceptions for 32 return yards in the year.

KOVALESKI, MIKE. 1983-1984-1985-1986; LB; 6-2, 218; New Castle, IN. Speedy, tough four-year starter at LB. Had excellent range; good hitter; had knack for being around the ball. In 1983, started at WLB. For the year, made 62 tackles, one sack for -10 yards and two for -4 yards; caused two fumbles, broke up four passes; and had one interception for five return yards. In 1984, started at WLB. For the year, led team, despite nagging injuries, with 108 tackles, two for -4 yards, and broke up two passes. In 1985, started at WLB. For the year, was second on team with 95 tackles, two for -20 yards; caused two fumbles; and broke up two passes. In 1986, started at ILB and captained team—first solo captain since Bleier in 1967. For the year, made 88 tackles, three for -8 yards, and broke up one pass. For his career, made 353 tackles, one sack for -10 yards and nine for -36 yards; caused four fumbles; broke up nine passes; and had one interception for five return yards.

KRAUSE, ED (MOOSE). 1931-1932-1933; T; 6-3, 220; Chicago, IL. One of greatest both in terms of athletic achievements and service to Notre Dame as coach, athletic director, and general figurehead of Fighting Irish excellence. Recruited by Rockne in response to rule changes that had all but gutted the shift, changes that placed a premium on size rather than sheer speed and quickness. Never played for Rockne, but was involved in fall and some spring practices, as well as Rockne's lectures on the game. Thus, important bridge to the past, having served as AD until the early 1980s. First All-American for Notre Dame in both football and basketball. In football, was dominating lineman. In his words, "I was double- and triple-teamed for my entire career." In 1931, backed up at LT. In a scoreless tie with Northwestern, provided scoring opportunity with recovery of blocked punt, but offense couldn't capitalize. The Irish defense recorded six shutouts in nine games. In 1932, started at LT. Blocked two Drake punts in shutout win, one for a safety and the other for a TD. Recovered Carnegie Tech fumble to set up TD in shutout win. Was the main man in a defense that registered six shutouts. In 1933, started at LT. Made All-American. Hampered by offense that scored only 32 points in nine games. Led team to two shutouts. Blocked punt for a TD in 7-0 win over Northwestern and set up blocked punt to defeat Army 13-12.

KUECHENBERG, BOB. 1966-1967-1968; T, DE; 6-2, 245; Hobart, IN. Excellent lineman during Parseghian's Hanratty years, showing versatility by starting on both sides of line. Had excellent quickness and strength, and very good technique. In 1966 started at RT for national champions; part of offensive line that reached new levels of effectiveness and protection for Hanratty. Made one tackle. In 1967, switched to starting DE. For the season, made 32 tackles, returned one kickoff for no gain, and broke up four passes. In 1968, started at DE. For the year, made 44 tackles, eight for losses; broke up two passes; and recovered two fumbles. Never made All-American. In his career, made 77 tackles, eight for minus yardage; broke up six passes; recovered two fumbles; and fielded a kickoff for no gain.

KUHARICH, JOE. 1935-1936-1937; G; 6-0, 193; South Bend, IN. Excellent lineman for Layden—tough, smart, indomitable. Later had illustrious coaching career, but it didn't work at Notre Dame—his career record from 1959 to 1962 is only losing one in school's history. In 1935, backed up at RG. In 1936, started at RG. In 1937, started at RG.

KUNZ, GEORGE. 1966-1967-1968; T, TE; 6-5, 240; Arcadia, CA. Must be considered among all-time great linemen for Notre Dame. Had excellent size, mobility, and superb technique. Close observers called him most dominant lineman of the last quarter century. In 1966, started at RT for national champions but was injured in Northwestern game and sidelined. In 1967, played both T and TE; caught seven passes for 101 yards. In 1968, started at RT and was co-captain. Consensus All-American.

KURTH, JOE. 1930-1931-1932; T; 6-2, 204; Madison, WI. Fine lineman for Rockne and Anderson. Had excellent quickness, good strength, and good technique. Especially good on defense. In 1930, started at RT for national champions. Helped save opening win over SMU with open-field tackle of back loose on a long run. Key blocker in many long TD runs for the year. In 1931, started at RT. Played strong defensive game against Pitt but ignored a doctor's warning not to play; spent three days in the hospital. Made All-American. In 1932, started at RT. In win over Northwestern, tackled punter for big loss to set up Irish TD drive and later blocked a punt to create another scoring opportunity. Deflected USC quick kick in losing effort. Repeat All-American.

LAMBEAU, CURLY. 1918; FB; 5-10, 188; Green Bay, WI. Flamboyant one-year player for Rockne in shortened season; teammate of Gipp. Excellent blocker and good short-yardage runner. In 1918, started at FB. Scored first TD of season in win over Case. Scored two TDs in slaughter of Wabash. Rushed for effective short yardage in win over Purdue and in tie with Nebraska. Returned to Green Bay. Later coached Jimmy Crowley before he went to Notre Dame.

LAMONICA, DARYLE. 1960-1961-1962; QB; 6-2, 205; Fresno, CA. One of best pure passers for Notre Dame; also could run and kick well. Had excellent arm, showed good leadership, and played defense well in last one-platoon era. Closest recent player with similar skills was Blair Kiel. In 1960, started at QB and showed good maturity as sophomore. For the season, hit 15 of 31 passes for 242 yards, five interceptions, and no TDs; gained 73 yards on 26 carries; punted 23 times for 37.4-yard average; had one interception and 18-yard runback; returned one punt for 10 yards; made 33 tackles; and broke up two passes. In 1961, started at QB. For the year, hit 20 of 52 passes for 300 yards, two TDs, and four interceptions; carried 44 times for 135 yards and three TDs; punted 29 times for 38.4-yard average; made 29 tackles; and had two interceptions for 54 return yards. In 1962, started at QB; completed 64 of 128 throws for 821 yards, six TDs, and seven interceptions; carried 74 times for 145 yards and four TDs; made three tackles; had one interception; broke up one pass; and punted 49 times for 36.5-yard average. For his career, carried 144 times for 353 yards and seven TDs; completed 99 of 211 passes for 1,363 yards, eight TDs, and 16 interceptions; made 65 tackles; made three interceptions for 54 return yards; broke up three passes; and punted 101 times for 37.25-yard average. His career offense totaled 1,770 yards and 15 TDs.

LANDRY, JACK. 1948-1949-1950; HB, FB; 6-1, 180; Rochester, NY. Good, dependable running under Leahy. Wasn't flashy or given to many long gainers, but could be counted on for consistent gains and was hard to bring down near goalline. In 1948, backed up at RHB. For the year, carried 80 times for 309 yards and six TDs, caught one pass for 10 yards, and returned two punts 35 yards. In 1949, backed up at FB for the national champions. For the year, carried 37 times for 147 yards and two TDs. In 1950, started at FB. In the year, carried 109 times for 491 yards and two TDs, led in kickoff returns with 11 for 195 yards, and caught seven passes for 57 yards. For his career, carried 226 times for 947 yards and 10 TDs, caught eight passes for 67 yards, and returned 11 kickoffs 195 yards and two punts 35 yards. His career total was 1,244 yards and 10 TDs.

LARKIN, MIKE. 1981-1982-1984-1985; LB; 6-1, 210; Cincinnati, OH. One of speediest linebackers ever to suit up for Notre Dame; made up in intensity and quickness what he lacked in size. Brother of Cincinnati Reds' Barry Larkin. In 1981 backed up at OLB; made 10 tackles, one sack, and one fumble recovery. In 1982, started at OLB. Made 112 tackles, second best that year; led with eight hits for -23 yards; and broke up three passes. Lost 1983 with a twice-broken arm. In 1984, slated to start at OLB but a knee injury curtailed his action until late in the season. For the year, made 39 tackles, two for -3 yards, and broke up one pass. In 1985, started at ROLB. For the year, made 40 tackles, 11 for -46 yards, including five QB sacks. In his career, made 201 tackles, 21 for -72 yards; made six QB sacks; recovered one fumble; and broke up four passes.

LARSON, FRED (OJAY). 1918-1920-1921; C; 6-1, 190; Calumet, MI. One of toughest men to play for Rockne. Key lineman in blocking scheme for Gipp. In 1918, started at C. In 1920, started at C for undefeated Irish. Played most of second quarter in win over Army with torn muscles and partially dislocated hip. In 1921, backed up at C. Lost his monogram for playing in a semi-pro game.

LATTNER, JOHNNY. 1951-1952-1953; HB; 6-1, 190; Chicago, IL. Needs to be rated near top of all Fighting Irish players even though not outstanding in any particular phase of game. Good at almost everything—a rare commodity even in one-platoon football days. Best compared to George Gipp for dramatic flair to get job done in any of a dozen different ways. Had certain raw-boned appearance, but closer examination showed a whippet in cleats. In 1951, backed up at RHB. For the season, carried 68 times for 341 yards and six TDs, caught eight passes for 157 yards, completed one of two passes for 23 yards, returned 10 punts 91 yards, made five interceptions for 66 return yards and recovered four fumbles to lead team in turnover recoveries, and punted 26 times for 32.4-yard average—all in 401 minutes. In 1952, started at RHB. For the year, carried 148 times for 732 yards and five TDs, caught 17 passes for 252 yards and one TD, completed two of five passes for 33 yards, returned seven punts 113 yards and three kickoffs 45 yards, recovered three fumbles, had four interceptions for 58 return yards, and punted 64 times for 36.6-yard average. Consensus All-American. In 1953, started at RHB. Carried 134 times for 651 yards and six TDs, caught 14 passes for 204 yards and one TD, completed only pass for 55-yard gain, returned eight kickoffs 321 yards for two TDs, returned 10 punts 104 yards, had four interceptions for four return yards, recovered one fumble, and punted 29 times for 35-yard average in 421 minutes of action. Consensus All-American and won Heisman Trophy (Leahy's fourth winner). For his career, carried 350 times for 1,724 yards and 17 TDs, caught 39 passes for 613 yards and eight TDs, completed four of eight passes for 111 yards, returned 27 punts 308 yards, returned eight kickoffs 366 yards for two TDs, made 13 interceptions for 128 return yards, recovered eight fumbles, and punted 121 times for 35.3-yard average. His total offense was 3,250 yards and 22 TDs.

LAW, JOHN. 1926-1927-1928-1929; G; 5-9, 163; Yonkers, NY. Quality in small package; model for Rockne's type of guard—very tough and very quick. In 1926, backed up at RG. In 1927, backed up at RG. In 1928, started at RG. In 1929, started at RG for national champions.

LAYDEN, ELMER. 1922-1923-1924; HB, FB; 6-0, 162; Davenport, IA. The quiet Horseman; went in at FB in 1922 Butler game following Castner's injury to complete quartet—most famous and arguably greatest backfield in Irish history. Had tremendous acceleration; at 162 pounds, was largest of quartet. Great punter, a key skill in those days. In 1922, started at LHB. Intercepted Army pass to preserve 0-0 tie. Caught TD pass from Stuhldreher in win over Carnegie Tech. Threw TD pass to Miller in 14-6 loss to Nebraska. In 1923, started at FB. Broke open tight game with Princeton with interception and 40-yard TD runback in 12-0 win. Kept Purdue bottled up with punts averaging 48 yards in 34-7 win. Scored TD dive in win over Carnegie Tech. Made 2- and 3-yard TDs in win over St. Louis. Made All-American. In 1924, started at FB for national champions. Scored first TD of game against Army that led to Grantland Rice's creation of the Horsemen mystique; also stole pass at midfield to begin drive that would win the game. Scored insurance TD with 17-yard run in win over Princeton. Scored on plunge in win over Georgia Tech. Played great game to avenge two earlier defeats by Nebraska—threw 65-yard TD pass to Crowley and ran for 30-yard TD. Intercepted pass and ran 40 yards for TD in 13-6 win over Northwestern. Scored two TDs in win over Stanford in 1925 Rose Bowl—on 3-yard plunge, 78-yard interception return, and 70-yard interception return with 30 seconds left in the game; also returned punt 90 yards that kept Stanford mired at its end of the field. Consensus All-American. In his career, carried 293 times for 1,296 yards and 10 TDs, completed 13 of 29 passes for 242 yards and two TDs, caught 11 passes for 145 yards and three TDs, snagged seven interceptions for 122 return yards, returned three punts 28 yards, 13 kickoffs 259 yards, and booted 12 PATs. His career total yardage reached 2,092 yards in 356 attempts good for 15 TDs.

LEAHY, FRANK. 1928-1929; T; 5-11, 183; Winner, SD. Very hard, driven worker. Tried to catch on as C but that didn't work out. In 1928, backed up at LT. In 1929, subbed at RT and saw action in most games for national champions, but an arm injury limited effectiveness. In 1930, was ready to start, but in last practice before opener with SMU, tore knee cartilage. Spent part of his recuperation period at Mayo Clinic with Knute Rockne as a roommate, who was there for treatment of phlebitis. Their time together allowed him to imbibe Rockne's wisdom, and a coach was born. A few months later, Rockne was killed. A decade later, Leahy became head coach.

LEHMANN, BOB. 1961-1962-1963; G; 6-0, 215; Louisville, KY. Fine leader for struggling Irish. Had great desire and intensity; overachiever physically and was often overmatched, but willed his way into playing success. Good blocker but excelled on defense. In 1961, backed up at LG. Made 41 tackles in 258 minutes. In 1962, started at RG. Led goalline stand that resulted in 2 yards from Notre Dame 3 before an Oklahoma fumble was recovered and the Fighting Irish won 13-7. For the year, was second with 61 tackles, recovered one fumble, and blocked one kick in 367 minutes. In 1963, started at RG and was captain. Made 20 tackles against Staubach and Navy in losing effort. Made 18 tackles against Pitt in loss. Intercepted Syracuse pass in loss. For the season, was second with 95 tackles, blocked one kick, recovered one fumble, and intercepted one pass. Made All-American. For his career, made 197 tackles, recovered two fumbles, blocked one kick, and had one interception.

LEMEK, RAY. 1953-1954-1955; G, T; 6-1, 205; Sioux City, IA. Solid, consistent lineman for Leahy and Brennan. Excelled on defense with good quickness. In 1953, started at LG. In rout of USC, intercepted pass and returned it to their 43 to set up TD. Intercepted pass to provide opportunity for last Irish TD in win over SMU. Played 347 minutes. In 1954, started at LG. Recovered Texas fumble at the Notre Dame 6 to preserve shutout. Helped tackle for a safety in loss to Purdue and broke up pass in win over Pitt. Set up score with interception of pass on the 37 in lopsided win over Penn. In 1955, started at RT and was captain. Grabbed Miami fumble on their 33 to lead to TD in shutout.

LEWIS, AUBREY. 1955-1956-1957; HB; 6-0, 185; Montclair, NJ. World-class sprinter's speed to complement Hornung in 1955 and 1956. Fastest man to have played for the Irish to that point. Tremendous threat to break long run or pass; played sterling defense. In 1955, backed up at LHB. For the season, carried 56 times for 222 yards and two TDs, caught 32-yard TD pass, returned four kickoffs 91 yards, and intercepted four passes for 38 return yards. In 1956, started at LHB. For the year, carried 59 times for 292 yards, caught 11 passes for 170 yards and one TD, returned six kickoffs 167 yards and five punts 46 yards, had three interceptions for 39 return yards, and recovered one fumble in 286 minutes. In 1957, had some excellent games but the stats fell off sharply: carried 11 times for 20 yards, caught two passes for 96 yards and one TD, returned one kickoff 21 yards and two punts 27 yards, missed two pass attempts, and recovered one fumble. For his career, carried 126 times for 534 yards and two TDs, caught 14 passes for 220 yards and three TDs, returned 11 kickoffs 279 yards and seven punts 73 yards, went 0 for 2 in passing, made seven interceptions for 77 yards, and recovered two fumbles. His career figures totaled 1,183 yards and five TDs.

LIND, MIKE. 1960-1961-1962; FB; 6-1, 200; Chicago, IL. Good FB for Kuharich's teams led by Lamonica. Career was cut short by a plague of injuries. In 1960, started at FB. For the season, carried 53 times for 167 yards and one TD, caught two passes for 10 yards, made 17 tackles, broke up one pass, and recovered one fumble in 147 minutes. In 1961, started at FB. For the campaign, rushed 87 times for 450 yards and four TDs, caught four passes for four yards, made 31 tackles, and broke up four passes in 261 minutes. In 1962, injuries limited him to eight carries for 13 yards and one pass for four yards. For his career, rushed 148 times for 630 yards and five TDs, caught seven passes for 18 yards, made 48 tackles, broke up five passes, and recovered one fumble. His career total was 648 yards and five TDs.

LINS, GEORGE. 1896-1897-1898-1899-1900-1901; C, G, FB, HB, E; 6-0, 185; Wilmington, IL. Set record for varsity career longevity. May have played in 48 games, but records are spotty. Played with John Farley and Red Salmon. All-around player or at least pliable regarding coaches' playing suggestions. Played as many as three different positions in one season; had enough speed to go long distances; and was good blocker. In 1896, backed up at C. In 1897, started at LG but played C too. Was C in shutout win over Rush. Helped in strong defensive effort that shut out DePauw. Played at LG in 62-0 win over Chicago Dental—the game in which Farley ran for more than 400 yards rushing from scrimmage and most TDs came on runs of over 50 yards. Tallied two TDs as RHB in win over MAC, his third starting position. In 1898, started at RHB. Had good short yardage runs in win over Illinois. Scored TD and ran 80+ yards in 52-0 blowout over MAC. In 1899, subbed at RHB. Scored TD with 6-yard run in win over Englewood H.S. Played well in 12-0 win over Northwestern; made one run for 4 yards, then quit team for unknown reasons. In 1900, came back. Started at LE much of the season, but scored on 95-yard run and long end run from FB spot in win over Goshen. Scored on 10-yard burst in win over Howard Park. Strong running near the goal helped earn 5-0 win over Rush. In 1901, started at LE but also played LHB. Scored only TD in win over Beloit. Went back to E in wins over Purdue and Indiana.

LIVINGSTONE, BOB. 1942-1946-1947; HB; 6-0, 175; Hammond, IN. True speed merchant; always threat to break long play either running or receiving. Good kick returner and played well as DB. In 1942, started at LHB in new T-formation. Caught 42-yard TD pass from Bertelli in shutout of Stanford. Helped beat Iowa Pre-Flight with 47-yard TD reception from Bertelli. Scored on 14-yard run in win over Northwestern. Missed three seasons while serving in Army. In 1946, backed up at LHB. For the season, rushed 40 times for 191 yards and two TDs, caught three passes for 38 yards, and gained 146 yards on kickoff returns. In 1947, backed up at LHB for the national champions. For the year, gained 242 yards on 45 runs and scored four TDs, caught four passes for 78 yards, returned four punts 88 yards and two kickoffs 42 yards, and had two interceptions for 45 return yards.

LONERGAN, FRANK. 1901-1902-1903; E, HB; 5-10, 168; Palo, IL. Appreciated for speed, punt coverage, and lead blocking, as E, in blocking for plays coming in his direction. In 1901, started at RE. Made 50-yard TD run, kickoff return of 15 yards, 30-yard run from scrimmage, and fumble recovery in win over Physicians and Surgeons. Helped save narrow victory over Beloit with fumble recovery. Averaged 21 yards for four kickoff returns in win over South Bend Commercial A.C., the longest for 40 yards. In 1902, started at RE. Sprinted for 17-yard gain at crucial moment before Notre Dame took control of MAC in 33-0 win. Helped shutout Lake Forest with long TD run around end. Ran for short yardage against Michigan in loss. Recovered fumbled punt in Ohio Medical game, and ran 45 yards to score. Raced for three TDs against American Medical, two on runs of 85 and 90 yards, in 92-0 rout. In 1903, started at RHB for undefeated and unscored-upon Irish. Returned punt for TD, ran 45 yards from scrimmage, and made three conversions against American Medical in 52-0 win. Scored one TD against Missouri Osteopaths. Made 45-yard TD run against Northwestern, but lost it on a penalty call; game ended 0-0, the only blemish that year. Scored final Irish TD on 15-yard run against Ohio Medical.

LONGO, TOM. 1963-1964-1965; DB; 6-1, 200; Lyndhurst, NJ. Fine DB for first two Parseghian teams. Had good coverage speed, and was a great hitter. In 1963, played in special defensive situations. Made two interceptions for eight return yards. In 1964, started at RCB. Led DBs with 72 tackles, recovered one fumble, broke up 10 passes, and intercepted four passes for 27 return yards. In 1965, led DBs with 73 tackles, broke up two passes, recovered one fumble, and made four interceptions. For his career, made 145 tackles, recovered two fumbles, broke up 12 passes, and made 10 interceptions for 44 return yards.

LUHN, HENRY. 1887; HB. It all started with this man. Coach, captain, and first HB for Notre Dame (the one holding the football in the team photo). Became a physician and lived in Spokane, WA.

LUJACK, JOHNNY. 1943-1946-1947; QB; 6-0, 180; Connellsville, PA. Strong candidate for all-time QB for the Fighting Irish. Tremendous competitor; had charisma that infected teammates with greater drive to win. Poised, with great arm, good quickness, and good running and kicking skills. Equally skilled on defense. In 1943, backed up at QB for the national champions (Leahy thus had two eventual Heisman Trophy winners stacked at one position). Led team in passing with 34 completions in 71 throws for 525 yards and four TDs, and carried 46 times for 191 yards. Served in Navy in 1944 and 1945. In 1946, started at QB. For the season, gained 108 yards on 23 carries, and completed 49 of 100 passes for 778 yards, six TDs, and eight interceptions. Recovered three fumbles to tie for lead. Consensus All-American. In 1947, started at QB for national champions. For the year, carried only 12 times but gained 139 yards for 11.1-yard average; hit 61 of 109 passes for 777 yards, nine TDs, and eight interceptions; and led in takeaway interceptions with three for 44 return yards. Won Heisman Trophy and was consensus All-American. For his career, completed 144 of 280 passes for 2,080 yards, 19 TDs, and 16 interceptions; and made 81 carries for 438 yards and two TDs. His offensive production totaled 2,518 yards and 21 TDs.

LUKATS, NICK. 1930-1932-1933; HB; 6-0, 185; Perth Amboy, NJ. Good reserve HB for Rockne's last year and two-year starter for Anderson. Good passer, consistent runner, and fine blocker; played featured LHB position in football scheme of the day. In 1930, backed up at LHB. Missed 1931 with a broken leg. In 1932, backed up at LHB. Helped beat Haskell with 23-yard TD sprint. Scored one TD and threw 44-yard TD pass in win over Drake. Had great game against Carnegie Tech: hit passes of 21, 25, and 21 yards on long TD drive, made block that took out eight players to spring Jaskwich on TD punt return, and added 15-yard run on another long drive. Losing to Kansas early in the game, dashed 45 yards to tie score and provide impetus to win. Threw crucial 25-yard pass in win over Navy to set up TD chance at Middie 11; also punted once to their 3. For the season, led team in passing with 13 completions in 28 tries for 252 yards and two TDs. In 1933, started at LHB. In 12-2 win over Indiana, had 53-yard TD run, four rushes for 19-yard TD drive, and 70-yard punt. Scored winning TD in 13-12 game with Army. For the year, led team with 339 yards on 109 carries, in passing with 21 of 67 for 329 yards, and in scoring with two TDs; also intercepted two passes.

LYGHT, TODD. 1987-1988-1989-1990; CB; 6-1, 184; Flint, MI. Outstanding DB under Holtz. Came as WR but made switch to defense and had immediate impact—had more starting time in 1987 than any other freshman. Superb speed and excellent coverage skills; at his best with the ball in the air. In 1987, backed up at RCB. For the season, made 29 tackles, caused one fumble, broke up two passes, and had 1 interception. In 1988, started at CB for national champions. Led team with six tackles in Fiesta Bowl win over West Virginia. For the year, made 36 tackles, three for -8 yards, and broke up nine passes. In 1989, started at CB. Made four tackles, one for a loss, in Orange Bowl win over Colorado. For the year, made 47 tackles, one for -1 yard; broke up 6.5 passes; and had eight interceptions for 42 return yards and one TD. Made All-American. In 1990, started at CB. For the year, made 49 tackles, broke up three passes, and had two interceptions for 13 return yards. Made three tackles and one sack in Orange Bowl loss to Colorado. Consensus All-American. For his career, had 161 tackles, four for -9 yards; caused one fumble; broke up 20.5 passes; and had 11 interceptions for 55 return yards and one TD.

LYNCH, DICK. 1955-1956-1957; HB; 6-0, 180; Bound Brook, NJ. As any trivia buff knows, scored to beat Oklahoma in 1957. Prior to that, had not been used on regular basis in two seasons, but had broad range of skills. In 1955, backed up at RHB. For the year, carried 24 times for 124 yards and one TD. In 1956, backed up at RHB. For the season, carried 14 times for 10 yards, caught five passes for 54 yards, and returned two kickoffs 53 yards. In 1957, started at RHB. Scored with 3:50 remaining to give Notre Dame 7-0 win over Oklahoma and end their 40-game winning streak. On that play, QB Williams faked to Pietrosante up the middle and pitched out to Lynch on the right for 3-yard TD run. For the year, was second in rushing with 77 carries for 287 yards and a team-leading five TDs, completed two of five passes for 26 yards, led in receiving with 13 for 128 yards, led in kickoff returns with six for 163 yards and in punt returns with four for 43 yards. In his career, carried 115 times for 421 yards and six TDs, caught 18 passes for 182 yards, completed two of five passes for 26 yards, and returned eight kickoffs 216 yards and four punts 43 yards. His career offense was 888 yards and six TDs.

LYNCH, JIM. 1964-1965-1966; LB; 6-1, 225; Lima, OH. Must be seriously considered for place on any all-time Irish team. Fine competitor; intense but always under control. Had good speed, strength, and mobility, as well as nose for the ball. One of best strategic thinkers fielded by Notre Dame on defense. Saw team go from 2-7 in his freshman year to win it all in 1966. In 1964, started at OLB. Played in six games until injured during Navy game. For the year, made 41 tackles, broke up one pass, and played 117 minutes. In 1965, started at OLB (sixth in total defense nationally). For the year, led team with 108 tackles, broke up three passes, and intercepted one. In

1966, started at ILB and captained national champions. Led defense that put together three straight shutouts, with six for season; held 10 opponents to 38 points. For the year, made 106 tackles, three interceptions for 12 return yards, broke up two passes, and recovered one fumble. Consensus All-American; won Maxwell Award as top college player; Academic All-American. In his career, made 255 tackles, broke up six passes, made four interceptions for 12 return yards, and recovered one fumble.

MacAFEE, KEN. 1974-1975-1976-1977; TE; 6-4, 251; Brockton, MA. One of the best TEs ever to play for Notre Dame. Had perfect dimensions for the modern TE, with enough speed to have played from SE position. Had fine hands and uncanny sense for finding seams in coverages to help Clements and Montana. In 1974, backed up at SE until an injury gave him chance to move to TE. In win over Miami, caught 14 passes for 146 yards and one TD. In 1975, started at TE. For the year, led receivers with 26 catches for 333 yards and five TDs and returned one kickoff for no gain. Made All-American. In 1976, started at TE. For the year, led team with 34 catches for 483 yards and three TDs, returned three kickoffs 34 yards, and made one tackle. Consensus All-American. In 1977, started at TE for national champions. For the year, caught 54 passes for team-leading 797 yards and six TDs to go with two tackles. Consensus All-American and the Walter Camp Player of the Year. For his career, caught 128 passes for 1,759 yards and 15 TDs, returned four kickoffs 34 yards, and made three tackles.

MacDONALD, TOM. 1961-1962-1963; HB, DB; 5-11, 180; Downey, CA. Speedy, crafty defensive specialist, one of best pass defenders in Irish annals. In 1961, backed up at LHB. For the year, carried two times for three yards, returned two punts four yards, had one interception for 23 return yards, made eight tackles, and broke up two passes. In 1962, played as defensive specialist and set new record with nine interceptions in a season. For the year, carried 10 times for 14 yards, caught one pass for no gain, made 29 tackles, had nine interceptions for 81 return yards, returned two kickoffs 30 yards, and broke up five passes. In 1963, played as defensive specialist. For the season, had six carries for 20 yards, caught two passes for 34 yards, returned eight kickoffs 146 yards, made 47 tackles, broke up six passes, had one fumble recovery, and made five interceptions for 63 return yards and one TD. For his career, had 18 carries for 37 yards, caught three passes for 34 yards, broke up 13 passes, made 85 tackles, made 15 interceptions (then a record) for 167 return yards and one TD, recovered one fumble, returned two punts four yards and 10 kickoffs 176 yards. His career total was 418 yards for one TD.

MAHALIC, DREW. 1972-1973-1974; LB; 6-4, 222; Farmington, MI. Converted from QB; fixture as LB and helped win national crown in 1973. Had good range; excellent hitter and good defensive thinker, probably helped by his knowledge of offense as former QB. In 1972, started at LB and made 77 tackles, four for -15 yards; had two interceptions for 59 return yards and one TD; and broke up one pass. In 1973, started at LB. In the Sugar Bowl, intercepted Alabama pass on their 21 and took it to the 12; Penick scored winning TD on next play. For the year, made 59 tackles, one for -1 yard; broke up two passes; recovered one fumble; and made one interception. In 1974, started at LB. For the year, had 117 tackles (second best on team), six for -27 yards; broke up four passes; recovered one fumble; and made one interception. For his career, made 253 tackles, 11 for -43 yards; had four interceptions for 59 return yards and one TD; broke up seven passes; and recovered two fumbles. Played in the last College All-Star game under Parseghian.

MARTIN, JIM. 1946-1947-1948-1949; E, T; 6-2, 204; Cleveland, OH. One of premier linemen during undefeated streak for Leahy. Very strong, cat quick, and tough competitor; had served as marine in WWII. As war hero, kept football in perspective. In 1946, started seven games at LE as freshman. Recovered three fumbles for the year. In 1947, started at LE for national champions. For the year, rushed 10 times for 86 yards and one TD, and caught 13 passes for 170 yards. In 1948, started at LE. Blocked Purdue punt which Panelli carried 70 yards for TD in 1-point win. Caught 13-yard TD pass from Tripucka in blowout of Nebraska. For the year, caught 14 passes for 98 yards and one TD. In 1949, switched to T for national champions. Made All-American. For his career, carried 10 times for 86 yards and one TD, caught 27 passes for 268 yards and one TD, blocked one kick, and recovered three fumbles.

MARX, GREG. 1970-1971-1972; DT; 6-5, 265; Redford, MI. Integral part of impressive front four groups. Had excellent size and strength and very good quickness. Broke an arm in 1969 and missed the year. In 1970, started at LT. For the year, made 82 tackles, six for -25 yards, and broke up two passes. In 1971, started at RT. For the year, was second on team with 85 tackles, with 12 for -44 yards, and broke up three passes. In 1972, started at RT. Was second in stops with 96; led team with six for -36 yards; and broke up one pass. Consensus All-American. For his career, made 263 tackles, 24 for -105 yards, and broke up six passes.

MASZTAK, DEAN. 1978-1979-1980-1981; TE; 6-4, 240; Toledo, OH. Fine TE for the Devine and Faust. Had great size, mobility, hands, and blocking skills. In 1978, backed up at TE. For the year, caught 13 passes for 236 yards, carried twice for three yards, and returned one kickoff for no gain. In 1979, started at TE. For the season, led Irish receivers in playing time, and caught 28 passes for 428 yards and two TDs. In 1980, lost about half of the season with a bad ankle. For the year, caught eight passes for 97 yards. In 1981, missed final five games with another injury, but caught 13 passes for 163 yards and one TD. For his career, carried two times for three yards, caught 62 passes for 836 yards and three TDs, and returned one kickoff for no gain.

MAZUR, JOHN. 1949-1950-1951; QB; 6-2, 198; Plymouth, PA. Good QB for Leahy. Had good arm and leadership skills. In 1949, backed up at QB for national champions. For the year, completed two of five passes for 36 yards, both passes for TDs and carried two times for no gain. In 1950, backed up at QB. For the season, carried two times for -7 yards, and completed 13 of 24 passes for 177 yards, two TDs, and one interception. In 1951, started at QB. For the year, completed 48 of 110 passes for 645 yards, five TDs, and 12 interceptions; and scored three TDs. For his career, carried four times for -7 yards; completed 63 of 139 passes for 858 yards, nine TDs, and 13 interceptions; and scored three TDs.

McAVOY, TOM. 1905; E; 5-10, 160; Corning, NY. one-year starter and then oblivion. Fine year marked by some long gains. In shutout of MAC, his 60-yard run was highlight of the day. Had a fumble recovery, a 20-yard kickoff return, and good short yardage rushing in loss to Wisconsin. In loss to Wabash, returned punt 10 yards and kickoff 10 yards, and made sack for -10 yards. Scored three TDs and two conversions in 142-0 rout of American Medical—his longest score was on 110-yard run. Had longest run from scrimmage, 25 yards, in loss to Indiana. Ran 60 yards with kickoff in shutout of Bennett Medical.

McCOY, MIKE. 1967-1968-1969; DT; 6-5, 274; Erie, PA. Dominating force on defensive line; almost staggering physical dimensions and strength. In 1967, started at DT and teamed with Hardy to present fearsome defensive line. For sophomore year, made 43 tackles, two for losses, and intercepted one pass. In 1968, started at DT. For the season, made 72 stops, eight for -34 yards, and broke up seven passes. In 1969, started at DT. Made 88 tackles, 10 for losses; made one interception; broke up seven passes; and returned one punt 25 yards. Consensus All-American. For his career, made 203 tackles, 20 for losses; intercepted two passes; and returned one punt 25 yards.

McDONALD, PAUL. 1907-1908; FB, HB; 6-0, 180; Columbus, OH. Well-rounded player just before Rockne and Dorais era. Had exceptional speed and could break long gainer either from inside or outside. Also kicked, passed, and played great defense. In 1907, started at FB. Scored two TDs in win over Franklin. Scored two TDs in win over Olivet by recovering a fumble and running 40 yards for one score and then executing cross-buck for 50 yards for the other. Had longest run from scrimmage, 25 yards, in 0-0 tie with Indiana. On an end run, scored on 75-yard run and added 60-yard dash against St. Vincent's to help secure 21-12 win. In 1908, backed up at LH. Made 65-yard TD run and kicked one conversion. Slashed through Franklin's defense for three TDs, one a 65-yard run, and kicked three conversions in a Fighting Irish victory. Scored two TDs and kicked one conversion in win over Physicians and Surgeons. Scored three TDs and one conversion in win over Ohio Northern. In win over Wabash, rushed for short yardage, threw one completed pass, and made the first recorded Irish interception.

McGEE, COY. 1945-1946-1947-1948; HB; 5-9, 155; Longview, TX. Speedy, elusive runner—very hard to contain. Part of talent for post-war Leahy teams. In 1945, backed up at HB. Had three carries for 29 yards. In 1946, backed up at LHB. For the year, averaged 11.9 yards per carry with 250 yards on 21 carries for three TDs. In 1947, backed up at LHB for national champions. For the year, carried 36 times for 158 yards, caught six passes for 92 yards, and returned six punts for a team-leading 162 yards. In 1948, carried only twice for five yards. For his career, carried 62 times for 442 yards and five TDs, caught six passes for 92 yards, and returned six punts 162 yards. His career offense totaled 696 yards and five TDs.

McGLEW, HENRY. 1900-1901-1902-1903; QB, E; 5-8, 170; Chelsea, MA. Teammate of Red Salmon. Especially adept at breaking long gainers and playing excellent defense. Was not prone to making mistakes. In 1900, backed up at QB, but also played elsewhere. Subbed for Salmon at LE in win over Goshen. In 5-0 win over Rush, fell on a loose kick on their 20 to help save win. In 1901, started at QB. In 2-0 loss to Northwestern, recovered blocked punt and prevented TD, stopping a runner on a long gain with a desperation tackle. The Indiana coach called him the best QB in the state after engineering 18-5 win. In 1902, started at QB. Against American Medical, made runs of 80, 65, and 40 yards and scored one TD. In 1903, started at LE for undefeated Irish as they racked up a season of shutouts. Scored one TD and ran all over American Medical in 52-0 rout. Scored one TD in win over Missouri Osteopaths and teamed well with Salmon and his booming punts to execute perfect downfield coverage, often stopping runners before they could take a step. Helped tame Ohio Northern 35-0. Never fumbled, a difficult feat given the conditions and kind of football played.

McKENNA, JIM. 1935; QB; 5-10, 169; St. Paul, MN. The man in the street who found himself directly involved in "the game of the century"—Notre Dame against Ohio State in 1935. A marginal player; was not even on the traveling squad. Layden told him that he could pay his own way to the game and lurk on the sidelines. Was last player available for duty as substitute when Layden needed a replacement for injured Andy Pilney. Went in with the play that won game. After football, earned a Ph. D. in chemical engineering.

MELINKOVICH, GEORGE. 1931-1932-1934; HB, FB; 6-0, 180; Tooele, UT. Recruited by Rockne as all-purpose back; three-year starter for Anderson and Layden. Had good speed, power, and hands. In 1931, switched to FB and started after Lukats broke his leg. Scored two TDs in 63-0 shutout of Drake. Plunged for one TD and caught 17-yard TD pass from Schwartz in win over Pitt. Scored from the Haskell 5 and 6 within moments of each other in win. In 1932, started at FB. Ran 31 yards for TD in shutout win of Drake. Scored one TD on short plunge, caught 25-yard pass, and ran 27 yards to keep another drive alive in win over Carnegie Tech. Made 20-yard TD run in win over Kansas. Against Northwestern, sped 98 yards with kickoff for a TD; also ran for 56 yards on three carries in the fourth quarter to preserve a shutout. Caught 5-yard pass from Koken for first TD in win over Army. Led team for the year in rushing with 88 carries for 536 yards and four TDs and in receiving with seven catches for 106 yards and one TD. Missed 1933 with kidney ailment. In 1934, switched to RHB due to death of Johnny Young and started. Made only Irish score in loss to Texas (coached by Jack Chevigny). Ran 60 yards for TD in win over Purdue and caught 5-yard pass from Layden to set up TD plunge. Workhorse in win over Wisconsin with 25 carries for 86 yards. Led backs with 63 yards on 11 carries in win over Carnegie Tech. For the year, led team with 324 yards on 73 carries and in scoring with six TDs.

MELLO, JIM. 1942-1943-1946; FB; 5-11, 185; West Warwick, RI. Powerful, low-slung FB for Leahy. In 1942, backed up at FB. Scored 3-yard TD in 7-7 tie with Wisconsin. In 1943, started at FB for national champions. For the season, was second among Irish runners with 137 carries for 714 yards and five TDs. Was in Navy in 1944 and 1945. In 1946, started at FB. For the year, carried 61 times for 307 yards and six TDs, and caught two passes for 40 yards. In his two seasons as a starter, carried 198 times for 1,021 yards and 11 TDs.

METZGER, BERT. 1928-1929-1930; G; 5-9, 149; Chicago, IL. Epitome of Rockne's "watch-charm guards." But even Rockne had his doubts and questioned him, to receive the polite reply: "Yes, sir, I'm small but I'm rough." Often outweighed by 80 or 90 pounds, used incredible speed to be halfway into his block before an opponent knew what was happening. Typified Rockne-style of line play. In 1928, backed up at RG. In 1929, backed up at RG for national champions. In 1930, started at RG for national champions. Wreaked havoc in Army secondary, especially on Schwartz's "perfect play" for the 7-6 win. Unanimous All-American selection.

MILLER, CREIGHTON. 1941-1942-1943; FB, HB; 6-0, 185; Wilmington, DE. Son of Red Miller and nephew of Don Miller; last of Miller clan that played for Notre Dame over 35-year span. Could do almost anything on the field, and appears to have done quite a bit off the field, too. Never accepted a scholarship, so he had some leverage with Leahy. Very much in the Gipp mold. His senior year stands among the very best for any Fighting Irish player. In 1941, backed up at FB. Carried 23 times for 183 yards and one TD, caught 40-yard TD pass, and punted four times for 49-yard average. In 1942, started at RHB. In 32-20 loss to Michigan, scored on 3-yard run and on 14-yard run off a Statue of Liberty play. Against a loaded and highly favored Great Lakes team, ran for 68-yard TD in 13-13 tie. In 1943, started at LHB for national champions. In win over Michigan, scored on 66-yard burst and gained 159 yards for the day. For the season, led team with 911 yards on 151 carries (only second time an Irish runner gained more than 900 yards to that point), led in scoring with 13 TDs (the most scored until Gladieux got 14 in 1968), led with seven punt returns for 151 yards, and led in kickoff returns with four for 53 yards.

MILLER, DON. 1922-1923-1924; HB; 5-11, 160; Defiance, OH. Rockne called him the best open-field runner he ever had. Averaged 6.8 yards per carry for his career. Was especially good shaking loose on runs to the outside. In their three years together, led the Horsemen in rushing two of three years, in receiving all three years, and in scoring once. Almost did not go to Notre Dame; Rockne cajoled him into attending. In 1922, started at RHB. Opened with 95-yard kickoff return and TD runs of 30 and 14 yards. Scored 10-yard TD run in win over Carnegie Tech. Scored only Irish TD in loss to Nebraska on pass from Layden. For the year, gained 472 yards on 87 carries for three TDs, caught six passes for 144 yards and one TD, and returned five kickoffs 179 yards. In 1923, started at RHB. Ran for 59-yard TD in 74-0 shutout of Kalamazoo. Caught 35-yard pass from Stuhldreher and scored on 22-yard run in 13-0 win over Army. Made 2-yard TD run in 25-2 win over Princeton. Crunched Georgia Tech with scoring runs of 59 and 23 yards to go with 30-yard reception; also lost 88-yard TD run on penalty. Scored two TDs against Purdue. Made 38-yard TD run in win over Butler. For the year, gained 698 yards on 89 rushes for 7.7-yard average and nine TDs, caught nine passes for 149 yards and one TD, had one interception, and returned four punts 69 yards and one kickoff 15 yards. In 1924, started at RHB for national champions. Scored two TDs in shutout of Lombard. Had key runs of 11 and 35 yards and 35-yard reception to keep drives alive in win over Princeton. Ran 40 yards with Stuhldreher pass for TD in win over Carnegie Tech. For the year, carried 107 times for 763 yards and five TDs, caught 16 passes for 297 yards and two TDs, threw one incomplete pass, had two interceptions for 43 return yards, and returned one kickoff 20 yards. For his career, carried 283 times for 1,933 yards and 17 TDs, had one incomplete pass, caught 31 passes for 590 yards and four TDs, had three interceptions for 43 return yards, returned four punts 66 yards and seven kickoffs 214 yards, and scored 22 TDs. His career offense totaled 2,846 yards in 329 attempts for 22 TDs, an average of 8.65 yards per attempt.

MILLER, RED. 1906-1907-1908-1909; HB; 6-0, 175; Defiance, OH. First of Miller clan to attend Notre Dame; father of Creighton. First truly great back to play for Notre Dame after Salmon; a four-year fixture at LHB. In 1906, started at LHB; returned kickoff the length of the field against MAC in 5-0 win. In 1907, started at LHB. Scored one TD in win over Physicians and Surgeons. Called upon to play C for the rest of the season; scored two TDs against Franklin. In 1908, started at LHB. Scored three TDs and two conversions in win over Physicians and Surgeons. Dashed Indiana's hopes with 175 yards rushing, including runs of 20, 25, 40, 45, and 20 yards, to go with fumble recovery in 11-0 win. In 1909, started at LHB. Scored one TD against Olivet, and ran back a punt 90 yards. Against Rose Poly, scored four TD runs. In close win over Pitt, rushed for 53+ yards and recovered onside kick. Scored two TDs in win over Wabash. Walter Camp saw him play against Michigan and called him one of the best in the land.

MILLNER, WAYNE. 1933-1934-1935; E; 6-0, 184; Salem, MA. Fine E and three-year starter for Anderson and Layden. Excellent blocker and defender, good pass catcher. In 1933, started at LE. Blocked Army punt late in the game, and recovered it for a TD to preserve comeback win. In 1934, started at LE. In 1935, helped beat Kansas with 50-yard TD pass from Shakespeare. In best game of the century, caught game-winning TD pass from Shakespeare to beat Ohio State. Consensus All-American.

MIRER, RICK. 1989-1990-1991-; QB; 6-2, 215; Goshen, IN. Irish QB for beginning of new decade. Excellent dropback passer: strong arm, good delivery, good reader of coverages; runs well enough to operate out of option occasionally. Good leadership skills. Has potential to set new passing records, barring injury. In 1989, backed up at QB. Played in eight games; carried 12 times for 32 yards; and completed 15 of 30 passes for 180 yards, no TDs, and one interception. In 1990, started at QB. In loss to Colorado in Orange Bowl, completed 13 of 31 throws for 141 yards and three interceptions; and carried six times for -2 yards. Had 98 carries for 198 yards and six TDs, to go with 110 of 200 passes for 1,824 yards, eight TDs, and six interceptions. In 1991, started at QB. For the year, carried 75 times for 306 yards and nine TDs; completed 132 of 234 passes for 2,117 yards, 18 TDs, and 10 interceptions. In 39-28 win over Florida in Sugar Bowl, completed 15 of 19 passes for 154 yards, one interception, and two TDs (40 yards and 4 yards). For his career to date, has 185 carries for 536 yards and 15 TDs; and completed 257 of 464 passes for 4,121 yards, 26 TDs, and 17 interceptions. His career offense totals 4,657 yards in 649 plays for 41 TDs.

MOHARDT, JOHNNY. 1918-1919-1920-1921; HB; 5-11, 170; Gary, IN. Man behind Gipp; would have started anywhere else. Had fine speed, good hands, and passing arm needed by LHB in Rockne's offense. In 1918, backed up at RHB. In 1919, backed up at LHB for undefeated Irish. Scored one TD in blowout of Mt. Union. In 1920 backed up at LHB for undefeated team. Scored on short run in win over Western Normal. Subbing at RHB in win over Nebraska, ran 25 yards at a crucial moment and made several short gains to help win 16-7. Scored on 5-yard blast in win over Valparaiso. Scored two TDs, ran well for short yardage, and caught a pass from Gipp in defeat of Army. Threw TD pass to Eddie Anderson and had an interception in win over Northwestern. Started at LHB against MAC as Gipp was on his deathbed; his end sweeps were a key in winning. In 1921, started at LHB. Rushed for 100+ yards, scored on runs of 30 and 40 yards, and completed 35-yard pass to Anderson in win over Kalamazoo. In loss to Iowa, rushed for 75+ yards; passed for 215 yards, including 50-yard TD strike to Kiley; and tackled a Hawkeye after a long interception return. In win over Purdue, carried 18 times for 80 yards and TDs of 5 and 7 yards. In win over Nebraska, ran wild with off tackle plays and scored game's only TD on a short plunge. Against Indiana rushed for 43 yards on 13 carries, and completed six straight passes for 53 yards, one an 11-yard TD. Beat Army with three TD passes, 45-yard kickoff return, and 15-yard TD run as part of 73 yards rushing and 200 yards passing. Against Rutgers three days later, threw TD passes of 25 and 8 yards to go with 51-yarder to Wynne and one pass broken up. Ran twice for 50 yards against Haskell. Against Marquette, gained 96 yards on six carries, including 48-yard TD jaunt to go with 45-yard TD pass to Anderson. Scored once against MAC in shutout. His senior year was one of the best on record: led in rushing with 781 yards on 136 carries, led in passing with 53 of 98 for nine TDs and 995 yards, led in scoring with 12 TDs for 72 points, and personally accounted for 126 of Notre Dame's 375 points to outscore the opponents 126 to 41. Registered nearly 2,000 yards of offense (1,821 yards on the record). Walter Camp put him on the second team All-American squad.

MONAHAN, BILL. 1897-1898-1899; HB, FB; 5-8, 150; Chicago, IL. Probably smallest FB in midwest, variously listed in contemporary accounts at 140-145 pounds. Good runner and packed power unapparent on his frame. Also described as "scientific" player. In 1897, started at RHB. In game in which Farley rushed for 464 yards, gained 106+ yards on 18 carries for one TD, including runs of 30 and 23 yards, had 20-yard kickoff return, and fumble recovery for 7 yards. In 1898, started at FB. In 5-0 win over Illinois, gained 110+ yards; carried 10 straight times up the middle for 60 yards. Scored three TDs against MAC, all on short plunges, in 53-0 win. In 1899, backed up at FB.

MONTANA, JOE. 1975-1977-1978; QB; 6-2, 191; Monongahela, PA. Probably best Irish QB since Lujack; certainly among top three or four for all-time consideration. Known as "The Comeback Kid" for orchestrating unbelievable wins over several seasons. Not QB for any lengthy period until late in career, even in 1977 championship season. Classic QB: good size, fair speed, very quick feet, sharp, snappy release on passes, and fine downfield and peripheral vision. Had many intangibles—charisma, confidence in the clutch, teammates' respect, and general knowledge of the game. In 1975, backed up at QB. Saw action in seven games. For the season, hit 28 of 66 passes for 507 yards, four TDs, and eight interceptions; and had 25 carries for -5 yards but two TDs. Missed 1976 due to a shoulder separation. In 1977, started as third-string QB. For the year, completed 99 of 189 passes for 1,604 yards, 11 TDs, and eight interceptions; and ran 32 times for 5 yards, six TDs, and a 2-point conversion. In 1978, started at QB. For the year, completed 141 of 260 passes for 2,010 yards, 10 TDs, and nine interceptions; and carried 72 times for 104 yards and six TDs. For his career, completed 268 of 515 passes for 4,121 yards, 25 TDs, and 27 interceptions; and carried 129 times for 104 yards and 14 TDs. His career offense totaled 4,225 yards on 397 attempts for 39 TDs.

MORIARTY, LARRY. 1980-1981-1982; FB; 6-2, 223; Santa Barbara, CA. Did not play football for three years after high school due to illness and injury. Rare transfer player at Notre Dame; started at Santa Barbara City College in 1979. Tremendously strong—could bench press 485 pounds. Had good quickness and good blocking skills. In 1980, backed up at FB. Carried three for 78 yards. In 1981, backed up at FB. For the season, carried 20 times for 94 yards and one TD, and caught three passes for 30 yards and two TDs. In 1982, started at FB. For the year, carried 88 times for 520 yards and five TDs, and caught 18 passes for 170 yards and two TDs. For his career, carried 111 times for 692 yards and six TDs, and caught 21 passes for 200 yards and four TDs. His career offense was 892 yards in 132 attempts for 10 TDs.

MORSE, JIM. 1954-1955-1956; HB; 5-11, 175; Muskegon, MI. Fine, all-purpose running back; three-year starter. Had good speed, some fine moves, excellent hands, and ability to make something out of nothing. In 1954, started at RHB. For sophomore season, had 68 carries for 345 yards and two TDs, caught 15 passes for 236 yards and 3 TDs, gained 166 yards on five kickoff returns, and picked up 31 yards on four punt returns. In 1955, moved to LHB and started. For the year, carried 92 times for 404 yards and three TDs, led team with 17 receptions for 424 yards and three TDs, returned five kickoffs 88 yards and six punts 26 yards, and had two interceptions for 26 return yards. In 1956, started at RHB. For the year, rushed 48 times for 148 yards, led team with 20 receptions for 442 yards and 1 TD, completed five of seven passes for 68 yards, and returned four kickoffs 72 yards and one punt 12 yards. For his career, gained 2,443 yards for 12 TD in 292 attemptss.

MULLEN, JACK. 1894-1895-1896-1897-1898-1899; E; 5-8, 155; Iona. MN. Only three-time captain and one of two to play six seasons for the Fighting Irish (George Lins was the other). Absolutely fearless player; "courageous almost to a fault." In 1895, started at RE. In 1896, started at RE. One of those who left the field in protest to end game with Physicians and Surgeons. Rushed for short yardage in loss to Stagg's Chicago team. Made 90-yard TD run and short TD run in win over South Bend Commercial A.C. Scored one TD in 82-0 rout of Highland Views. In 1897, started at RE and captained team. Made fine run for 18 yards around left end in 0-0 game with Rush. His good running set up lone score in 4-0 win over DePauw. In 1898, started at RE and captained team. Played well on defense and made short gains in 5-0 win over Illinois. Scored one TD and rushed for 50+ yards in rout of MAC. In 1899, started at RE and captained team. Ran for 70 yards on 10 carries in win over Englewood H.S. Played well in 23-6 loss to Chicago. Let several different players serve as game captains and in took himself out to allow others to get some experience.

MULLINS, LARRY (MOON). 1927-1928-1929-1930; FB; 6-0, 175; Pasadena, CA. Good FB for Rockne. Had good strength; was excellent blocker, but bad knees kept him from being fast. Was scoring threat close to the goalline. In 1927, backed up at FB. In 1928, backed up at FB. Gained most of the yardage in 80-yard TD drive in win over Drake. Recovered two fumbles and scored only Irish TD in loss to Carnegie Tech. In 1929, started at FB for national champions. Scored winning TD against Navy on 1-yard plunge. Blasted for 2-yard TD in win over Georgia Tech. In win over Drake, ran for 25-yard TD and carried three consecutive times inside the Bulldog 35 to sustain another TD drive. In 1930, competed with Savoldi for starter's job. Had bothersome knee injuries all year. Lost 60-yard TD run in win over SMU due to a penalty. Rammed in from the 1 in win over Pitt. Scored TD plunge in win over Drake. In win over Army, his block caved in Army's right end to let Schwartz loose in the secondary for "the perfect play."

MURPHY, GEORGE. 1940-1941-1942; E; 6-0, 175; South Bend, IN. Dependable, solid E for Leahy's first two teams. In 1940, backed up at RE. In 1941, started at RE. Caught Bertelli pass for first score in win over Georgia Tech and blocked a Tech punt to lead to another score. For the year, caught 13 passes for 130 yards and one TD. In 1942, started at RE and captained team. In shutout of Stanford, scored on 47-

yard pass from Bertelli. In 17-0 win over Army, caught 17-yard TD pass from Bertelli. Long-time assistant coach at Notre Dame.

MUTSCHELLER, JIM. 1949-1950-1951; E; 6-1, 198; Beaver Falls, PA. Part of 1949 national championship team and twilight years of Leahy's era. Picked up slack when Hart graduated by breaking his single season receiving record and Wightkin's yardage figures for ends. In 1949, backed up LE and played mostly defense. Intercepted SMU pass in all-time great game to ensure undefeated season. For the year, caught two passes for 27 yards, recovered one fumble, and made one interception. In 1950, started at RE. For the season, led Irish receivers with 35 catches (breaking Hart's figure of 19) for 426 yards (breaking Wightkin's record of 309), scored seven TDs, and returned one kickoff 12 yards. In 1951, started at RE and captained team. For the year, led team with 20 catches for 305 yards, scored two TDs, and returned one kickoff 13 yards. Made All-American. In his career, caught 57 passes for 458 yards and nine TDs, recovered one fumble, had one interception, and returned two kickoffs 25 yards.

NIEHAUS, STEVE. 1972-1973-1974-1975; DE, DT; 6-5, 270; Cincinnati, OH. Premier defensive lineman. Severe knee injuries during his first two seasons, limited playing time. Had it all—tremendous size, awesome strength, great speed, mobility, and relentless pursuit. Best DL under Parseghian, except possibly for Page. In 1972, started at DT for five games before an injury ended his season. For his partial year, made 47 tackles, two for -14 yards. In 1973 for national champions, played partial season. Had 35 tackles, three for -12 yards. In 1974, started at DT. Made 95 tackles, 13 for -82 yards; broke up two passes; and recovered one fumble. Made All-American. In 1975, started at DT. First modern lineman to lead Fighting Irish with 113 tackles, seven for -20 yards. Consensus All-American. For his career, made 290 tackles, 25 for -128 yards; broke up two passes; and recovered one fumble.

NIEMIEC, JOHN. 1926-1927-1928; HB; 5-8, 170; Bellaire, OH. Played in shadow of Christie Flanagan until 1928. In 1926, backed up at LHB. Scored one TD and kicked two PATs in win over Beloit. Booted two PATs in win over Minnesota. Kicked three PATs in drubbing of Penn State. Caught game-winning TD pass in win over Northwestern. Completed 18-yard pass in win over Georgia Tech. Caught game-winning TD pass against USC. In 1927, backed up at LHB. For the year, led Irish passers with 14 completions in 33 tries for 187 yards. In 1928, started at LHB. In loss to Wisconsin, completed passes of 20 and 16 yards to Colrick in Notre Dame's only scoring drive. Won Navy game with TD pass to Colrick on a slant pattern. In win over Drake, threw 13-yard TD pass to Colrick and kicked two PATs. Made PAT to ice win over Penn State. Before 78,188 people in Yankee Stadium, threw 45-yard desperation pass to Johnny "One-Play" O'Brien for the 12-6 winning margin in "Win One for the Gipper" game with Army.

NOSBUSCH, KEVIN. 1972-1973-1974; DT; 6-4, 265; Milwaukee, WI. Good defensive lineman for Parseghian. Had good size and quickness; impressive hitter. In 1972, started at DT. For the year, made 39 tackles, three for -9 yards. In 1973, backed up DT for national champions. For the season, made 21 tackles, four for -34 yards. In 1974, started at DT and had his best season: made 79 tackles, nine for -40 yards, and recovered one fumble. For his career, made 139 tackles, 16 for -83 yards, and recovered one fumble.

O'BRIEN, COLEY. 1966-1967-1968; QB, HB; 5-11, 180; McLean, VA. Remarkably talented player; "played bigger" than his true dimensions. Had good arm, good speed, fine football mind, and infectious intensity. Helped save 1966 national crown by going into MSU game when Hanratty was knocked out and a week later by leading 51-0 defeat of USC. In 1966, backed up at QB. For the season, rushed 40 times for 135 yards and two TDs, and completed 42 of 82 passes for 562 yards and four TDs. In 1967, carried 34 times for 123 yards and one TD, and completed 16 of 41 passes for 220 yards and one TD. In 1968, started at LHB to provide "two-QB" look. Played in same backfield with both Hanratty and Theismann. For the year, had 64 carries for 314 yards and three TDs, caught 16 passes for 272 yards and four TDs, returned one punt 13 yards and four kickoffs 156 yards, and completed one pass for 13 yards. For his career, accounted for 1,808 yards of offense, ran for six TDs, caught three TD passes, and threw five TD passes.

OLSON, BOB. 1967-1968-1969; LB; 6-0, 230; Superior, WI. Fierce competitor at ILB spot; three-year starter; rugged; physical; tremendous hitter. Led team all three years in tackles made. In 1967, started at ILB. For the year, made 98 tackles with six for losses, broke up five passes, and recovered one fumble. In 1968, started at ILB. Made 128 tackles (the most in five seasons) with eight for losses, and broke up three passes. In 1969, started at ILB. Set new record with 142 tackles with 10 for losses, had one interception for 15 return yards, broke up one pass, and recovered one fumble. Made All-American. For his career, made 368 tackles, 24 for losses; had one interception for 15 return yards; broke up nine passes; and recovered two fumbles.

O'MALLEY, JIM. 1970-1971-1972; LB; 6-2, 221; Youngstown, OH. Good ILB for Parseghian. Had good speed and could unload on ball carriers. In 1970, backed up at MLB. For the year, made 12 tackles. In 1971, started at RILB. For the season, made 72 tackles and broke up one pass. In 1972, started at ILB. Led team for the year with 122 tackles, three for -31 yards; broke up one pass; recovered one fumble; and had one interception. For his career, made 206 tackles, three for -31 yards; broke up two passes; recovered one fumble; and had one interception.

ORIARD, MIKE. 1968-1969; C; 6-3, 221; Spokane, WA. Walk-on who became team captain. Centered for both Hanratty and Theismann. Had good blocking technique and good quickness. In 1968, backed up at C. In 1969, started at C and was co-captain. Later, authored football book, *The End of Autumn.*

PAGE, ALAN. 1964-1965-1966; DE; 6-5, 238; Canton, OH. All-time great. Had almost unstoppable combination of size, speed, quickness, and strength. Part of extremely talented core of defenders for Parseghian. In 1964, started at DE. For the year, made 41 tackles, two fumble recoveries, and scored one TD on 57-yard runback of a blocked punt. In 1965, started at DE. For the season, made 30 tackles, broke up one pass, and recovered two fumbles. In 1966, started at DE for national champions. For his final year, made 63 tackles and broke up one pass. Consensus All-American. For his career, made 134 tackles, recovered four fumbles, broke up two passes, and scored one TD.

PANELLI, JOHN. 1945-1946-1947-1948; FB; 5-11, 185; Morristown, NJ. Fine FB for Leahy's undefeated teams. Had good speed and could break a play wide open; excellent blocker; played good defense. His favorite play was to break a long run off a lateral pass, a play he worked to perfection with Lujack and Tripucka. In 1945, backed up at FB. For the season, carried 18 times for 115 yards and two TDs. In 1946, backed up at FB. For the year, carried 58 times for 265 yards and four TDs. In 1947, started at FB for national champions. For the year, carried 72 times for 254 yards and four TDs, and caught three passes for 38 yards. In 1948, started at FB. For the year, carried 92 times for 692 yards (7.5-yard average) for eight TDs, and returned one punt 70 yards. For his career, carried 240 times for 1,326 yards (5.5-yard average) and 18 TDs, caught three passes for 38 yards, and returned one punt 70 yards. Gained 1,434 yards of offense in his career.

PATULSKI, WALT. 1969-1970-1971; DE; 6-6, 260; Liverpool, NY. One of the very best; instant starter; three-year fixture on left side of some very impressive defensive fronts. Had excellent size, good speed, mobility, lateral quickness, and strength, a model of a DE. Should be ranked near top at this position for all-time consideration. In 1969, started at DE. For the season, made 54 tackles, six for losses; broke up three passes; and recovered two fumbles. In 1970, started at DE. For the year, made 58 tackles, 17 for a team-leading -112 yards; broke up one pass; and recovered two fumbles. In 1971, started at DE and led defense to number-three ranking against the run, and number four for total defense. For the season, made 74 tackles and led team with 17 for -129 yards; broke up six passes; recovered one fumble; and returned a blocked punt 12 yards. Consensus All-American. For his career, made 186 tackles, 40 for -241 yards; broke up 10 passes; recovered five fumbles; and returned one blocked punt 12 yards.

PENICK, ERIC. 1972-1973-1974; HB; 6-1, 209; Cleveland, OH. Fine running back for Parseghian. Had explosive speed, good strength, good moves, and good hands. Best remembered for 85-yard TD run against USC in 1973, a single play that did as much as any other to earn the national championship. In 1972, backed up at RHB; led team with 124 carries for 727 yards and five TDs, caught two passes for nine yards, and returned two kickoffs 20 yards. In 1973, started at RHB. Scored winning TD of Sugar Bowl against

Alabama that cinched 11-0 season. For the year, carried 102 times for 586 yards and seven TDs, and caught two passes for 16 yards. In 1974, a knee injury suffered in spring practice ended his bright promise; played in four games:. Gained 14 yards on 12 carries and caught one pass for two yards. For his career, carried 240 times for 1,327 yards and 12 TDs, caught five passes for 27 yards, and returned two kickoffs 20 yards for a total of 1,374 yards.

PERKOWSKI, JOE. 1959-1960-1961; FB, K; 6-0, 200; Wilkes-Barre, PA. Good all-purpose FB, defensive player, and K. Kicked game-winning field goal against Syracuse in 1961 after time had expired due to a penalty on the previous play when he faced making a 56-yarder. In 1959, backed up at FB. For the season, carried 53 times for 164 yards, caught two passes for 12 yards, made 12 tackles, had one interception, and broke up one pass. In 1960, backed up at FB and handled place kicking. For the year, carried 25 times for 131 yards, caught one pass for 10 yards, returned one kickoff 10 yards, made 10 tackles, and kicked nine PATs and one field goal. In 1961, did the place kicking and led team in scoring with 31 points. For the year, caught one pass for 25 yards, made three tackles, and kicked 16 PATs and five field goals. In his career, carried 78 times for 295 yards, caught four passes for 47 yards, made 25 tackles, had one interception, returned one kickoff 10 yards, broke up one pass, and made 25 PATs and six field goals. His career totals were 352 yards and 43 points.

PETITBON, JOHN. 1949-1950-1951; HB, S; 6-0, 185; New Orleans, LA. Excellent defensive player with exceptional speed. In 1949, played at S. For the year, carried three times for -9 yards, recovered one fumble, and made three interceptions for 62 return yards, including 43-yard TD against USC. In 1950, started at LHB. For the season, carried 65 times for 388 yards and three TDs, caught 18 passes for 269 yards and two TDs, had one interception, returned one punt 14 yards, and returned two kickoffs 69 yards. In 1951, had 48 carries for 227 yards and three TDs, caught eight passes for 105 yards, returned 14 punts 189 yards and three kickoffs 115 yards for one TD, and had two interceptions for three return yards. For his career, carried 116 times for 606 yards and six TDs, caught 26 passes for 373 yards and two TDs, recovered one fumble, had six interceptions for 65 return yards and one TD, and returned 15 punts 203 yards and five kickoffs 184 yards for one TD. Gained total of 1,432 yards of offense and scored 10 TDs.

PHELAN, JIM. 1915-1916-1917; QB; 5-11, 182; Portland, OR. Three-year starter at QB for Harper. Quadruple threat—kicker, passer, runner, and defender. In 1915, playing with reserves against Alma, scored fourth-quarter TD on straight buck over C, and passed to Yeager for TD. Started the next week against Haskell and threw several passes for short gains in shutout win. In loss to Nebraska, returned two punts for 25 yards, made short yardage rushes, returned a kickoff 10 yards, made one interception, and completed a pass to Cofall. Helped win close game with South Dakota on a daring punt return to the Coyotes 20; team scored on next play for game's only TD. Scored two TDs on plunges against Creighton, made an interception and 20-yard runback, completed one pass for 15 yards, kicked one conversion, rushed for 48 yards, and returned a punt 21 yards. Scored TD on plunge in win over Texas to go with an interception and a 12-yard kickoff return. Against Rice two days later, rushed for short yardage, made an interception, and returned a kickoff 12 yards. In 1916, started at QB. Scored one TD in blowout win over Wabash and led team to several annihilations in the season. In 1917, started at QB. Scored first TD of year with a plunge against Kalamazoo; added two more later in the win. Near end of Wisconsin game, tried to drop-kick a 61-yard field goal, but the ball hit the cross bar and fell back on the field to keep it a scoreless tie. Played in only those two games before being sent to Camp Taylor in Louisville, Kentucky, for the war effort.

PHILBROOK, GEORGE. 1908-1909-1910-1911; G, T; 6-3, 225; Olympia, WA. Came with Dimmick from Northwest to become integral part of Notre Dame football. One of Irish greats for first third of this century, and perhaps any period. Excellent blocker; had good speed and great size for his era; could kick and receive passes. Best known for blocking—could make a hole just about where and when he wanted. In 1908, backed up LG; used mainly for punting. In 1909, started at LG. Rushed for one TD in 58-0 win over Olivet. Scored 50-yard TD pass in 60-11 rout of Rose Poly. Recovered MAC fumble and ran for short yardage in win. Scored two TDs in rout of Miami of Ohio. Scored TD against Jesse Harper's Wabash team in shutout. Named to All-Western team. In 1910, started at LT. Against Akron (neé Butchel), started around end on "tackle around" play but fumbled, recovered the ball, composed himself, dusted off three converging tacklers, and went on for a 75-yard run. In 1911, started at LT. The coach decided to use him only against major schools, but there were only two—Pitt and Marquette. Was used primarily as pass receiver because of his height. Caught 20-yard pass in 0-0 tie with Pitt.

PIEPUL, MILT. 1938-1939-1940; FB;6-1, 206; Thompsonville, CT. Powerful FB for Layden. Could also kick and play solid defense. In 1938, backed up at FB. In 1939, started at FB. Scored two TDs in 1-point win over SMU. Scored winning TD on 1-yard plunge against Navy. In close loss to Iowa, slammed for 4-yard TD. Smashed through Northwestern's defense for Notre Dame's only score in 7-0 win. Scored TD on a reverse in loss to USC. For the year, led in rushing with 414 yards on 82 carries and led in scoring with six TDs. Never fumbled in the season and was stopped for losses only three times. Made All-American. In 1940, started at FB. Tallied two TDs in rout of Carnegie Tech. Helped beat Stagg's Pacific team with 17-yard TD run and an interception a minute later to set up another TD. In 10-6 win over USC, booted 25-yard field goal and scored on 3-yard run. Led team with 122 yards on four kickoffs.

PIETROSANTE, NICK. 1956-1957-1958; FB; 6-2, 215; Ansonia, CT. Very powerful FB for Brennan. Punishing runner able to break tackles, could also punt well and play solid defense. In 1956, backed up at FB. For the season, had eight carries for 27 yards. In 1957, started at FB. In busy season, led team with 449 yards on 90 carries for two TDs, caught four passes for 5 yards, had one interception, made 37 tackles, recovered two fumbles, returned one kickoff 18 yards, broke up two passes, and punted 39 times for 39.6-yard average. In 1958, started at FB. For the year, led with 117 carries for 556 yards and four TDs, caught 10 passes for 78 yards, made 44 tackles, returned one kickoff 17 yards, broke up three passes, and punted 26 times for 33.7-yard average. Made All-American. For his career, carried 215 times for 1,032 yards and six TDs, caught 14 passes for 83 yards, had one interception, made 81 tackles, made two fumble recoveries, returned two kickoffs 35 yards, broke up five passes, and punted 65 times for 37.24-yard average. His career total offense was 1,150 yards and six TDs.

PILNEY, ANDY. 1933-1934-1935; HB; 5-11, 175; Chicago, IL. Good, all-purpose back for Anderson and Layden. Never started, but saw plenty of action and always made a contribution, often making the difference. Best remembered for heroics against Ohio State in 1935. In 1933, backed up at LHB. Scored winning TD against Northwestern on 13-yard run. His TD was one of only five scored all season by Notre Dame. Led team in punt returns with nine for 124 yards. In 1934, backed up at LHB. In win over Wisconsin, fired 30-yard completion to Davis to start first scoring drive, and made two runs near the goal to keep the drive moving. Pounded Carnegie Tech with 11 rushes for 46 yards in 13-0 win. In 10-6 loss to Navy, almost turned tide with 32-yard run, 62-yard kickoff return, and 27-yard TD throw to Peters. In 1935, backed up at LHB. Tossed TD pass in win over Wisconsin and ran 40 yards for another. Fired both TD passes to beat Navy 14-0. Against Ohio State, started at LHB in second half with the Irish trailing. Started first Irish TD drive with 47-yard punt return to their 13, then threw to Gaul reaching the Buckeye 1; and Steve Miller scored; with less than three minutes to play, completed pass to Fromhart that reached the Ohio State 24, passed again to Fromhart for 10 yards, and ended with 15-yard TD pass to Layden; on winning TD drive, took busted play from the Irish 45 to the Ohio State 19, but was hurt on the tackle and carried off on a stretcher. From there, saw Shakespeare's pass to Millner for winning TD. Made All-American.

PINKETT, ALAN. 1982-1983-1984-1985; TB; 5-9, 184; Sterling, VA. Supremely gifted runner; among Notre Dame's best running backs. Had tremendous speed, leg drive, overall strength (bench pressed 385 pounds), lateral mobility, darting quickness, good hands, and ability to break any play wide open. In 1982, grew into playing time slowly, but carried 107 times for 532 yards and five TDs, caught nine passes for 94 yards, and returned 14 kickoffs 354 yards for one TD. In 1983, started at TB and had best sophomore year for any Irish running back. Carried 252 times for 1,394 yards and 16 TDs, caught 28 passes (to lead team) for 288 yards and two TDs, threw one pass for 59 yards, and scored a 2-point conversion. Played well in Liberty Bowl win over Boston College with 28 carries for 111 yards and two TDs. Made All-American. In 1984, started at TB. For the year, carried 275 times for 1,105 yards and 17 TDs, and caught 19 passes for 257 yards and one TD. Made honorable mention All-American. In Aloha Bowl against SMU, carried 24 times for 136 yards and one TD; became all-time Irish rushing leader for bowl games. In 1985, started at TB and became first Irish running back to have three consecutive 1,000-yard seasons. For his final year, carried 255 times for 1,100 yards and 11 TDs, and caught 17 passes for 135 yards. Made All-American. For his career, had 889 rushing attempts for 4,131 yards and 48 TDs, caught 73 passes for 774 yards and three TDs, returned 14 kickoffs 354 yards for one TD, completed one pass for 59 yards, and scored a 2-point conversion. Scored 320 points, had 21 games rushing for 100+ yards, gained 5,259 yards, scored 53 TDs, was first Irish back to go over 4,000 yards rushing, and was fourth all-time NCAA TD producer (behind Tony Dorsett, Doc Blanchard, and Steve Owens).

PLISKA, JOE. 1911-1912-1913-1914; HB; 5-10, 170; Chicago, IL. Fine runner and pass receiver for team that launched Notre Dame into the national spotlight. Excellent speed and elusiveness made him a long-distance threat on any play. In 1911, backed up RHB. Scored one TD against Ohio Northern and added 30-yard run. Ran for 1-yard TD in win over St. Viator. Scored TD in rout of Loyola. Against St. Bonaventure, scored three TDs, kicked three conversions, intercepted a double pass, and returned kickoff 10 yards. In 1912, started at RHB. Scored career-high four TDs in win over Adrian. Led team with three TDs against St. Louis in 47-7 victory. Scored in first three minutes in shutout of Marquette. In 1913, started at RHB. Ran for three TDs in win over Ohio Northern. Scored three TDs in win over Alma. Against Army, caught two of Dorais' passes for 70+ yards and scored two TDs. In 1914, started at RHB. Against Alma, had three TD runs up the middle and around the ends of 50 yards or better, a 65-yard punt return, and one conversion kick. Dashed for 35-yard TD in win over South Dakota. Had 110+ yards rushing in win over Carlisle, scoring on runs of 60 and 35 yards. Ended career with TD in win over Syracuse.

POTTIOS, MYRON. 1958-1959-1960; C, G; 6-2, 220; Van Voorhis, PA. Strong lineman under Brennan and Kuharich; played for defense that was burdened by offensive ineptitude. Had excellent skills as LB and was good blocker. In 1958, backed up at C. For the year, made 32 tackles, had one interception, and recovered one fumble. In 1959, started at LG but was injured in fourth game to end his season. In his partial year, made 24 tackles. In 1960, started at LG and LB. Blocked Pitt PAT in close loss. Won game ball for defensive effort in shutout win over USC when Trojans rushed for only 74 yards and lost 17-0. For the season, led Irish with 74 tackles and had one blocked kick. Made All-American. For his career, had 130 tackles, one blocked kick, one interception, and one fumble recovery.

PRUDHOMME, EDWARD. 1887-1888-1889; FB, HB; Bermuda, LA. One of the founders. Hard to judge these players since their game is only vaguely related to what happens today. His play was characterized as "strong." In 1887, started at FB in second game. In 1888, started at FB; on April 20 kicked first-ever conversion for an Irish football team in 26-6 loss to Michigan. Kicked two conversions in Notre Dame's first win, 20-0 against Harvard in December. In 1889, switched to RHB and captained team. After graduation, returned to Louisiana and became state legislator.

PUPLIS, ANDY. 1935-1936-1937; QB; 5-8, 168; Chicago, IL. Typical multi-purpose QB for Layden—good runner, receiver, and kicker. Had capacity to turn small gains into breakaway runs. In 1935, backed up at QB. Had 70-yard punt return against Wisconsin. In 1936, started at QB. For the year, led team in kickoff returns with five for 136 yards (27.2-yard average). In 1937, started at QB. Averaged almost 10 yards per run—18 carries for 177 yards; caught four passes, averaging 19.5 yards per catch. Completed two of four passes and made two interceptions for 31 return yards. Scored three TDs and made six of eight PATs to lead Irish in scoring with 24 points. His yardage for the season came to 569 yards on 46 plays, or 12.4 yards per play.

RASSAS, NICK. 1963-1964-1965; HB, DB; 6-0, 185; Winnetka, IL. Walk-on who became consensus All-American. Had good speed and moves for offense but defending in secondary was natural gift. Covered ground well, had real nose for the ball, and was instant threat to return interceptions and kicks for TDs. In 1963, backed up at HB. Saw spot action; made eight carries for 33 yards, caught one pass for nine yards, and made two tackles. In 1964, started at S but also caught 2-yard TD pass from Huarte in rout of Purdue. For the year, made 37 yards on three carries, caught two passes for 4 yards and one TD, returned four kickoffs 103 yards and 15 punts 153 yards, made 51 tackles, broke up four passes, and had one interception for 23 return yards. In 1965, started at S and had one of the best years for DB on record. Made 53 tackles, broke up three passes, had six interceptions for 197 return yards and one TD, and returned four kickoffs 82 yards and 24 punts 459 yards for three TDs. Consensus All-American. For his career, carried eight times for 33 yards, caught three passes for 13 yards and one TD, made 106 tackles, returned eight kickoffs 185 yards and 39 punts 612 yards for three TDs, had seven passes broken up, and made seven interceptions for 220 yards and one TD. His total reached 1,063 yards, virtually all on runbacks and turnovers, for 5 TDs.

REEVE, DAVE. 1974-1975-1976-1977; K; 6-3, 216; Bloomington, IN. Strong-legged K for Parseghian and Devine; leading scorer for 1977 championship team. In 1974, handled place kicking; made 38 of 40 PATs and seven of ten field goals for 59 points, second on team. In 1975, did the place kicking and made 24 of 26 PATs and 11 of 16 field goals for team-leading 57 points. In 1976, was kicking specialist and set record with 53-yard field goal in losing effort to Pitt. Helped beat Penn State with two PATs and two field goals in Gator Bowl. For the year, made 29 of 33 PATs and nine of 18 field goals for 56 points. In 1977 championship season, helped beat Texas with a field goal and five PATs. For the season, made 39 of 44 PATs and 12 of 20 field goals for 75 points. In his career, kicked 130 of 143 PATs and 39 of 64 field goals for 247 points.

RESTIC, JOE. 1975-1976-1977-1978; P, S; 6-2, 190; Milford, MA. Good punter and DB for Devine. Had great leg for punting and was heady man on secondary coverage, with especially good anticipation. In 1975, handled punting in six games and tossed 10-yard TD to MacAfee in win over Miami. For the year, completed one pass for 10-yard TD and punted 40 times for 43.5-yard average (longest was 61 yards). In 1976, started at FS and punted. For the year, punted 63 times for 41.7-yard average (longest was 63 yards); completed one pass for 4-yard gain; made 54 tackles, three for -10 yards; made four interceptions for 92 return yards; and recovered one fumble. In 1977, punted and started at FS for national champions. For the season, punted 45 times for 38.1-yard average; made 51 tackles, one for -5 yards; led defense with six interceptions for 25 return yards; and carried once for -10 yards. In 1978, punted and started at FS. For the year, had 61 punts for 38.2-yard average (longest was 66 yards); made 51 tackles; broke up eight passes; recovered two fumbles; and had three interceptions for 59 yards. For his career, punted 209 times for 40.24-yard average; carried once for -10 yards; completed two of two passes for 14 yards and one TD; made 156 tackles, four for -15 yards; made 13 interceptions for 176 return yards; broke up eight passes; and recovered three fumbles.

RICE, TONY. 1987-1988-1989; QB; 6-1, 200; Woodruff, SC. Great option QB for Holtz. Had tremendous judgment about run/pitch options, and could throw well enough that it was hard to defend the whole package. At his best when he could break outside around a seal block, with a trailing back, and have two isolate on one defender. Had good speed, tremendous leg drive, and deceptive power. Led team to 28-3 record as starter, including longest winning streak in Irish history—23 games; QB for 1988 national championship season. In 1987, started at QB in fifth game. For the year, made 89 carries for 337 yards and seven TDs; and threw 35 completions in 82 tries for 663 yards, one TD, and four interceptions. In 1988, started at QB. Was Fiesta Bowl MVP with seven of 11 passes for 213 yards and 75 yards rushing. For the year, had 121 carries for 700 yards and nine TDs; and threw 70 completions in 138 attempts for 1,176 yards, eight TDs, and seven interceptions. In 1989, started at QB and was tri-captain. Helped beat Colorado in Orange Bowl with 14 carries for 50 yards and five completions in nine throws for 99 yards. For the season, made 174 carries for 884 yards and seven TDs, and completed 68 of 137 passes for 1,122 yards, two TDs, and nine interceptions. Made All-American. In his career, rushed 384 times for 1,921 yards and 23 TDs; and completed 173 of 357 passes for 2,961 yards, 11 TDs, and 20 interceptions. In his career, was involved in 741 offensive attempts and produced 4,882 yards and 34 TDs.

ROBINSON, JACK. 1932-1934; C; 6-3, 200; Huntington, NY. Gutty C for Anderson and Layden. Played great football in spite of serious eye problems that cost him 1933 season. In 1932, started at C. In 1934, went through five eye operations to be ready to start at C. Saw kickoff that caromed high off shoulder pads of one of the kicking team's linemen and recovered it on a dead run. Had sixth eye operation in mid-season and played the following week. Made All-American.

ROCKNE, KNUTE. 1910-1911-1912-1913; E; 5-8, 165; Chicago, IL. Important as a player, unsurpassed as a coach. Was not supremely gifted as an athlete or player—though did pole vault near world mark. Success came through diligence and sheer determination. Had fair blend of strength and speed, and keen intellectual and psychological approach. Consummate team man; proficient tackler and fierce runner. In 1910, backed up RE and worked some at FB (called himself "the drawback"). In 1911, started at LE. Scored what would have been winning TD against Pitt with 40-yard advance of a fumble, but an inadvertent whistle stopped the play in the 0-0 tie. In 1912, started at LE but suffered from a sprained knee all season. Caught 33-yard pass from Dorais in 3-0 win over Pitt. In 1913, started at LE and captained team. Added long, downfield pass catching to his bag of tricks, but tore rib cartilage in opener with Ohio Northern. Against Army, removed Merrillat, their star E, with a hard tackle and dropped a runner for a loss at Notre Dame's 2 for a safe margin of victory—but is better known for catching 110+ yards of Dorais passes, including 25-yard TD. Caught long TD pass from Dorais in 14-0 win over Penn State. Selected to All-State team for third time, All-Western, and honorable mention All-American by Walter Camp. His .881 winning percentage tops all college and pro coaches.

RUETTIGER, DAN. 1975; DE; 5-7, 200; Joliet, IL. Fine study in persistence and determination; DE with impish dimensions; campus security guard; service veteran; and oldest man on 1975 team at 27. In 1975, backed up at DE (for Browner). In last 28 seconds of 24-3 win over Georgia Tech, sacked QB for 5-yard loss.

RYAN, BILLY. 1907-1908-1909-1910; QB, HB; 5-9, 160; Cleveland, OH. Dependable player during growth spurt before the Irish became a national entity. Good runner and kicker; could be used in variety of ways; and often managed to score. In 1907, started at QB. Ran for one TD and kicked one conversion in shutout of Physicians and Surgeons. Kicked conversion in win over Franklin. Returned two punts for 35 yards in 0-0 tie with Indiana. Helped defeat St. Vincent's with 30-yard field goal. In 1908, backed up RHB. Scored two TDs (one a 10-yard run), made three conversions, and ran for 25 yards in win over Hillsdale. Scored two TDs and booted six conversions in defeat of Franklin. In 1909, backed up at RHB. Kicked three conversions against Olivet. Scored one TD and added three conversions in 60-11 win over Rose Poly. Was leading rusher from scrimmage with 90+ yards in 17-0 win over MAC; also returned punt 10 yards and kicked two conversions. Rushed for short yardage in win over Pitt. Scored clinching TD and kicked one conversion in 11-3 win over Yost's Michigan team—surely most significant win prior to 1913 Army game. Kicked one conversion in 46-0 win over Miami of Ohio. In 1910, backed up at RHB. A bad knee severely curtailed his action for the year.

SALMON, LOUIS (RED). 1900-1901-1902-1903; E, HB, FB; 5-10, 175; Syracuse, NY. Notre Dame's first All-American. Greatest Irish player—at least until Gipp matriculated. In an age when record keeping was inaccurate, some feats are amazing: scored 104 points in 1903 when TDs were five points; led team to 8-0-1 record without a point being scored against it. Absolutely fierce player; unafraid to throw his 175 pounds into any melee; fierce determination to succeed. Excellent punter and defender; had good speed and moves, but was best at bucking into line. In 1900, first known to newspaper readers as "Sammon," started at LE in 55-0 win over Goshen; instrumental in springing several long TDs by Farley and Lins. Stayed at LE for 68-0 shutout of Englewood H. S. Played both LE and FB against Beloit, scoring 2-yard TD and returning one kickoff. Dropped for safety in a 7-0 loss to Michigan. Scored only TD in 5-0 win over Rush Medical. In 1901, started at FB. In 0-0 tie with South Bend Commercial A.C., dashed for 40 and 32 yards and had one punt return. Was tackled for safety in 2-0 loss to Northwestern. Punted for 70 yards in win over Beloit. Scored one TD, made one conversion kick, and had 25-yard kickoff return that featured "clever dodging" in win over Lake Forest. Rushed for 50+ yards, scored one TD, and kicked two conversions in 12-6 win over Purdue. Played C briefly against Physicians and Surgeons to allow John Pick charity TD, but tallied one himself and kicked four conversions. To help the Fighting Irish claim state championship, scored two TDs, kicked three conversions, streaked for 55-yard kickoff return, had 40+ yards from scrimmage, and 65-yard punt return in win over Indiana. In second game against South Bend A.C., an Irish win, blasted 70-yard punt, had 20-yard punt return, recovered a loose kick, and made one conversion kick. In 1902, started at FB. Made one conversion kick and had 15-yard kickoff return in shutout of MAC. In win over Lake Forest, had several punts of 50-60 yards, recovered kick for TD, and ran 15 yards for another TD. Rushed for 90+ yards in 23-0 loss to Yost's Michigan team, including carrying the ball 15 consecutive times on 80-yard drive; also knocked out four times. In 11-5 victory over Indiana, scored two TDs, one a 40-yarder through the assembled Hoosiers; ran 60+ yards from scrimmage; and returned two kickoffs 40 yards each. His punting in 6-5 win over Ohio Medical was the difference; several were bobbled to Notre Dame's advantage. In 12-5 loss to Knox,went ballistic with 85-yard punt, scored a TD, rushed for 40+ yards, and returned one kickoff. In 92-0 defeat of American Medical, scored three of 17 TDs and hit six conversion kicks. Rushed for one TD, kicked two conversions, had 35-yard field goal, and punted for 75 yards on several occasions in 22-0 win over DePauw. His 1-yard TD plunge, the conversion, and a fumble recovery helped tie Purdue 6-6. In 1903, started at FB. Scored three TDs and made three conversions in 28-0 win over Lake Forest. Scored one TD and kicked four conversions in 52-0 win for American Medical. Scored three TDs and three conversions against the Missouri Osteopaths. Rushed for short yardage in tie with Northwestern and made 50-yard punt and a fumble recovery. Coached 1904 team to a 5-3 record.

SCHAEFER, DON. 1953-1954-1955; QB, FB; 5-11, 190; Pittsburgh, PA. Good, all-purpose player for Leahy and Brennan. Made unusual shift from QB to FB. Good runner and kicker; played fine defense. In 1953, backed up at QB. For the season, carried 23 times for 100 yards and two TDs, caught one pass for 42 yards, completed three of eight passes for 39 yards, made one interception for 37 return yards, punted four times for 34.5-yard average, and kicked six PATs. In 1954, started at FB. For the year, led team in rushing with 766 yards on 141 carries and three TDs, caught three passes for 60 yards, returned five kickoffs 82 yards and three punts 60 yards, kicked 22 PATs, and made one interception and one fumble recovery. In 1955, started at FB. Led team with 145 carries and 639 yards and one TD, caught six passes for 36 yards and two TDs, returned two kickoffs 27 yards, completed one pass for 24 yards, made 16 PATs, and had one interception for 21 yards. Made All-American. For his career, carried 309 times for 1,505 yards and six TDs, caught 10 passes for 138 yards and two TDs, returned seven kickoffs 109 yards and three punts 60 yards, completed four of nine passes for 63 yards, made three interceptions for 64 return yards, had one fumble recovery, and kicked 44 PATs and four punts for 34.5-yard average. His career offense totaled 1,939 yards and eight TDs.

SCHILLO, FRED. 1892-1893-1894-1896-1897; T, HB; 5-11, 180; Chicago, IL. Teamed with Lins and Mullen for three seasons to give Notre Dame core of veterans since the three men played a total of 17 years—thanks to liberal eligibility "regulations." By 1896, the student newspaper was viewing him wistfully: "In days gone by, Schillo was looked upon as an extraordinary football player, and this year showed improvement." Had many football skills, but was not a gamebreaker. In 1892, started at LT. In 1893, started at LT. Rushed for 89 yards against Albion, including runs of 20 and 25 yards, in 8-6 win. Ran for 65 yards against DeLaSalle in shutout win, including short TD burst and 20-yarder. Ran for 8-yard gain in 22-10 win over Hillsdale. In 1894, backed up at RT. In 1896, started at LT. Rushed for short yardage and returned kick in 4-0 forfeit loss to Physicians and Surgeons. Picked up at least 12 yards in loss to Stagg's team. Tallied one TD in shutout of Albion. In 28-22 loss to Purdue, scored one TD, rushed for short yardage, returned one kickoff 12 yards, and missed his only conversion attempt. Was instrumental in beating Beloit 8-0 by recovering two fumbles and rushing for 25+ yards. In 1897, started at RT.

SCHOEN, TOM. 1965-1966-1967; QB, S; 5-11, 178; Euclid, OH. Fine secondary player for Parseghian's powerful 1966 team. Started as QB in lean offensive year; shifted to defense. Took his understanding of offense into the secondary. Had good speed and instincts; real ball hawk. In 1965, backed up at QB. For the year, completed 13 of 24 passes for 229 yards, one TD, and one interception; had 35 carries for 81 yards; caught one pass for one yard; and made one tackle. In 1966, started at S for national champions. Made 30 tackles, had seven interceptions for 118 yards and two TDs, and led team in punt returns with 29 for 252 yards and one TD. Made All-American. In 1967, started at S. Led DBs with 52 tackles and 11 passes broken up, had four interceptions for 108 return yards, recovered one fumble, and returned 42 punts for 447 yards and one TD. Consensus All-American. For his career, had 35 carries for 81 yards; caught one pass for one yard; completed 13 of 24 passes for 229 yards, one TD, and one interception; made 83 tackles; broke up 11 passes; had 11 interceptions for 226 return yards and two TDs; recovered one fumble; and returned 71 punts 699 yards for two TDs. His career total was 1,236 yards and five TDs.

SCHWARTZ, MARCHY. 1929-1930-1931; HB; 5-11, 167; Bay St. Louis, MS. Best back to play for Rockne other than Gipp. Could do it all—run, throw, catch, block, and tackle. Dominating player, especially in 1930 and 1931 when led in rushing, passing, and scoring. In his three years, team was 25-2-1, won two consecutive national crowns for first time in college football history, and was twice consensus All-American. Would have won Heisman Trophy—if there had been one when he played. In 1929, backed up at LHB for national champions. Ran 8-yard TD in win over Georgia Tech. Ran 40 yards to set up score in win over Northwestern, and passed 25 yards to Brill to set up his own 10-yard TD run. For the year, carried 65 times for 326 yards and three TDs. In 1930, started at LHB for national champions. Scored TD plunges of 5 and 4 yards and threw 21- and 25-yard passes to Conley and Kosky to ensure narrow victory over SMU. Threw 56- and 13-yard TD passes and dove 2 yards for another in victory over Carnegie Tech. In win over Pitt, gained 109 yards on eight carries, including 60-yard TD run. Scored TD on 26-yard run; picked off fumbled kickoff in midair and ran 79 yards before being tackled in win over Indiana. Against Drake, returned kickoff to their 13, completed two passes to set up TD run from their 13, and made 43-yard TD run. On patented "perfect play," a delayed half-spinner, scored 18-yard unmolested run down the sideline to help beat Northwestern. In win over Army at Soldier Field in Chicago, executed classic "51" play (with LHB going off RT) for 54-yard TD run on a terrible field. Threw 19-yard TD to Carideo, lateral pass to O'Connor for 7-yard TD, and 37-yard strike to Conley to keep another drive going; rushed twice for 65 yards to keep USC in hole for Irish shutout—Rockne's last regular game before his death. For the year, led in rushing with 927 yards on 124 carries for 7.47-yard average, led in passing with 17 of 56 for 319 yards and three TDs, and led in scoring with nine TDs. Consensus All-American. In 1931, started at LHB. Ran 11 yards for TD in win over Indiana. Gained 60 yards on 12 carries on sloppy field in 0-0 tie with Northwestern; averaged 46 yards per punt with five booted from his own end zone. Ran 63 yards on 18 carries and fired two TD passes to help beat Pitt. Amassed 188 yards against Carnegie Tech a week later, with 59-yard TD on a spinner and 16 yards on another similar play. Ran 16 yards for TD and threw 50 yards to Chuck Jaskwhich for TD in shutout of Penn. Tallied TD on 16-yard end run in shutout of Navy. Consensus All-American. Led in rushing with 692 yards on 146 carries for 4.7-yard average, led in passing with nine completions in 51 tries for 174 yards and three TDs, and scored five TDs. For his career, rushed for 1,945 yards in 335 carries and 16 TDs.

SCULLY, JOHN. 1977-1978-1979-1980; T, C; 6-5, 255; Huntington, NY. Fine lineman for Devine. Had good size, excellent strength, and exceptional quickness. Overcame injuries early in his career, and a position move, to become one of best interior linemen in recent decades. Most error-free, consistent lineman of his years. In 1977, backed up at T for national champions. In 1978, backed up at LT; played in six games. In 1979, started at C. In 1980, started at C and was tri-captain. Consensus All-American.

SEFCIK, GEORGE. 1959-1960-1961; HB; 5-8, 170; Cleveland, OH. With Dabiero, comprised "Gold Dust Twins." Like Dabiero, was small back who played much larger. Could do many things well—run, catch, block, tackle, play defense, kick, and return kicks. In 1959, started at LHB. Carried 43 times for 206 yards and one TD, caught 11 passes for 203 yards and two TDs, returned seven kickoffs 140 yards, led in punt returns with 10 for 138 return yards, made 22 tackles, broke up four passes, recovered two fumbles, had three interceptions for 35 return yards, and led in punting with 25 for 37.4-yard average. In 1960, started at LHB. For the season, made 50 carries for 248 yards, caught five passes for 106 yards, returned 12 punts 71 yards and 7 kickoffs 170 yards, made 35 tackles, broke up three passes, had two interceptions for 17 return yards, and recovered one fumble. In 1961, started at LHB. Made 72 carries for 335 yards and two TDs, caught five passes for 58 yards, returned five punts 40 yards and three kickoffs 57 yards, made 41 tackles, had three interceptions for 56 return yards, led team with nine passes broken up, and led in punting with eight for 39.4-yard average. For his career, made 165 carries for 789 yards and three TDs, caught 21 passes for 367 yards and two TDs, returned 17 kickoffs 367 yards and 27 punts 249 yards, made 98 tackles, broke up 16 passes, recovered three fumbles, had eight interceptions for 108 return yards, and punted 33 times for 37.88-yard average. His career offense was 1,880 yards and five TDs.

SEYMOUR, JIM. 1966-1967-1968; E, SE; 6-4, 205; Berkley, MI. three-year starter and three-year All-American. Had fine speed, size, great hands, concentration, and silky moves. Provided deep threat.

Appeared suddenly with Hanratty on national scene in 1966 and became media darling. His statistics for individual games were often greater than season or career totals for other players. In 1966, started at LE for national champions. Caught 48 passes for 862 yards and eight TDs. Made All-American. In 1967, started at SE. For the year, made 37 receptions for 515 yards and four TDs. Made All-American. In 1968, made 53 catches for 736 yards and four TDs and recovered fumble for TD. Made All-American. For his career, had 138 receptions for 2,113 yards and 16 TDs as well as TD via recovered fumble.

SHAKESPEARE, BILL. 1933-1934-1935; HB; 5-11, 179; Staten, Island, NY. Fine player for Anderson and Layden; significant feature of struggle between Ohio State and Notre Dame in 1935. Could do it all—run, pass, kick, catch, block, and tackle. Had excellent leadership qualities. In 1933 backed up at LHB. Caused safety in 12-2 win over Indiana. In 1934, started at LHB. Helped win shutout with Carnegie Tech with 56-yard TD sweep. Fired 70-yard TD pass to Vairo in win over Army; his punting kept Army bottled up all day. Scored TD on a plunge in 20-7 win over Northwestern. Fired 51-yard TD pass in 14-0 triumph over USC. For the year, led in passing with nine of 29 for 230 yards and two TDs, and in kickoff returns with 4 for 60 yards. All-American. In 1935, started at LHB. Threw 41-yard TD pass to Millner in win over Kansas. Made 24-yard TD run in win over Carnegie Tech. Caught TD pass in win over Wisconsin to go with 50 yards on 12 rushes. Blasted 90-yard punt in win over Pitt and scored only Irish TD with 5-yard run. In comeback win over Ohio State, replaced injured Pilney with seconds to go and threw game-winning TD to Millner. Against Army, made runs of 16, 15, and 11 yards to keep drives moving; completed 44-yard pass to Millner to set up Notre Dame's only score in 6-6 tie. Completed two long passes in a row for score—a 45-yarder to Fromhart—and swept 8 yards for the final score in win over USC. For the year, led in rushing with 104 carries for 374 yards, in passing with 19 of 66 for 267 yards and two TDs, in scoring with four TDs, and in kickoff returns with five for 123 yards. Consensus All-American.

SHANNON, DAN. 1951-1952-1953-1954; LB, E; 6-0, 190; Chicago, IL. Four-year starter; known best as devastating tackler. In 1951, started at LB. Helped stop Purdue with interception on the Irish 26. Recovered Navy fumble on Middie 22 and blocked for Barrett on 74-yard TD punt return. For the season, had two interceptions and four recovered fumbles. In 1952, started at LB. Slammed into Texas punt returner causing a fumble; recovered it on their 2, setting up insurance TD in 14-0 win. Against Oklahoma, hit kickoff returner Grigg; flipped him in midair and caused a fumble, which led to winning Irish TD. Intercepted pass to stymie drive in shutout of undefeated USC. Ended year with two interceptions for 19 return yards. In 1953, started at LE with return of one-platoon football. Scored both Irish TDs in 14-14 tie with Iowa, with two seconds left in the first half and six seconds left in the game. Caught Lattner pass for 55-yard advance to the SMU 4 and 31-yard strike from Guglielmi to keep the rout going. For the year, caught seven passes for 138 yards and two TDs. In 1954, started at LE and was co-captain. In shutout of Texas, caught 19-yard TD strike from Guglielmi. Caught 41-yard pass from Guglielmi to set up TD in loss to Purdue. Caused Pitt fumble in shutout win. Caught 16-yard pass from Guglielmi in late drive in win over Navy. Caught two Guglielmi passes for TDs, 22 and 18 yards, in win over Penn. Made All-American. For the year, caught 11 passes for 215 yards and three TDs. For his career, caught 18 passes for 353 yards and five TDs, recovered four fumbles, and made four interceptions for 19 return yards.

SHAUGHNESSY, FRANK. 1901-1902-1903-1904; E; 6-0, 178; Amboy, IL. Fast, shifty, excellent runner, prone to long-distance gains. In 1901, backed up at LE and also reserve QB. Improved on defense as season progressed. In 1902, started at LE. Made 40-yard run in loss to Michigan. Returned punts 20, 35, and 25 yards in 11-5 victory over Indiana. In 1903, started at RE. Made 40-yard TD run in shutout of MAC. Made two long TDs in 52-0 rout of American Medical. Recovered a fumble in tie with Northwestern. Rushed for 140+ yards against Ohio Medical, recovered a fumble, and scored 90-yard TD. In 1904, started at RE. Recovered Wabash fumble and sprinted 80 yards for a TD, made 30-yard run from scrimmage, and returned punt 10 yards in 12-4 win. Gained 200+ yards rushing and scored TDs on runs of 45 and 101 yards in 44-0 rout of American Medical. Against Kansas, made 100-yard TD run from scrimmage for the only Irish score in 24-5 loss. Led Irish runners with 70+ yards in loss to Purdue, including runs of 30 and 25 yards.

SHAW, LAWRENCE (BUCK). 1919-1920-1921; T; 6-0, 185; Stuart, IA. Quiet, efficient lineman who had good kicking leg and uncanny ability to be around loose balls and kicks ready to be blocked. It was said that the end next to him would only be a spectator. Part of great lines that paved way for Gipp. In 1919, backed up at LT. In 1920, blocked punt for safety in win over Nebraska. In shutout of Purdue, recovered Irish fumble for TD. Made two PATs in win over Northwestern. Blocked five punts during the season, the last against MAC, to help clinch an undefeated season and Notre Dame's first national championship. In 1921, started at LT. In win over Kalamazoo, deflected punt out of bounds and kicked seven PATs. Recovered DePauw fumble at midfield in win. Had one PAT in loss to Iowa (only loss of varsity career). Booted two PATs in defeating Purdue. Kicked four PATs and deflected punt in win over Indiana. Kicked four PATs in win over Army. Against Rutgers three days later, booted six PATs in rout. Against Marquette, made three tackles and kicked three PATs. Ended season with 38 PATs in 40 tries. Named All-American.

SHEEHAN, CLARENCE. 1903-1904-1905-1906; C; 6-0, 190; Grand Ridge, IL. Tough, active C who had a knack for blocking kicks, finding loose balls, and scoring. Noted for accurate "passing" (snaps to backfield). In 1903, started at C for undefeated, unscored-upon team led by Red Salmon. In 1904, injuries hampered play; backed up at C. Blocked Toledo kick and recovered fumble to preserve narrow victory. Recovered Purdue fumble on Notre Dame's 20 to stop a drive in Irish loss. In 1905, started at C. Led TD parade against American Medical, scoring on 25-yard run, 50-yard run, and recovered kickoff in the end zone; added 35-yard kickoff return. Blocked Indiana field goal attempt in 22-5 loss and showed excellent downfield coverage. In 1906, started at C. Recovered loose kickoff for TD in shutout of Franklin. Grabbed blocked punt on Hillsdale's 20 in win. Blocked MAC punt attempt from their end zone, leading to TD in 5-0 win. Scored TD but lost it on a penalty in 2-0 win over Purdue.

SILVER, NATE. 1902-1903-1904-1905; QB; 5-8, 150; Chicago, IL. Nifty, slippery, quick QB; important in 1903 undefeated season and its consecutive shutouts. Had very quick feet. In 1902, backed up at QB. Scored one TD against American Medical to accompany runs of 65 and 50 yards. Played strong defensive game in 6-6 tie with Purdue; recorded several sacks. In 1903, started at QB and orchestrated undefeated season. In 1904, started at QB. Ran 35 and 25 yards from scrimmage in 12-4 win over Wabash. Played E against Toledo A.A. due to mounting injuries; helped crippled Irish team win 6-0. In 1905, started at QB. Against North Division H.S., returned kicks of 30 and 20 yards as part of a 44-0 rout. In shutout loss to Wisconsin, returned two punts 60 and 45 yards. Tallied three TDs in 142-0 rout of American Medical: 40-yard run, 80-yard kickoff return, and a more modest run; gained 130+ yards on other kick returns.

SITKO, EMIL. 1946-1947-1948-1949; HB, FB; 5-8, 180; Fort Wayne, IN. Key figure in success of Leahy's post-war teams. Bundle of high-strung muscle; averaged six yards from a set position. Hit high gear almost instantly and was good for certain gain; his only problem was in the open with a long run ahead—his muscled legs would tighten up and was fairly easy to catch, if not tackle. Among very best players. Like Hart, never played in losing game. In 1946, started at RHB; led team with 346 yards on 54 carries for 6.4-yard average, scored three TDs, caught three passes for 55 yards, and made two interceptions for three return yards. In 1947, started at RHB for national champions. Carried 60 times for 426 yards and five TDs (7.1-yard average), caught four passes for 48 yards, and returned two kickoffs 52 yards. In 1948, started at RHB. Led team with 742 yards on 129 carries and nine TDs, caught seven passes for 70 yards, and returned one kickoff 76 yards. Made All-American. In 1949, started at FB for national champions. Led team with 120 carries for 712 yards and nine TDs, caught two passes for 15 yards, and returned four kickoffs 89 yards and one punt 23 yards. Consensus All-American; won Walter Camp Trophy as outstanding college player. For his career, carried 363 times for 2,226 yards and 26 TDs, caught 16 passes for 188 yards, and returned seven kickoffs 217 yards and one punt 23 yards. His career total was 2,654 yards and 26 TDs.

SLAGER, RICK. 1974-1975-1976; QB; 5-11, 190; Columbus, OH. Good QB for Devine. Had fair arm and was good runner. Played hard-nosed brand of football. In 1974, backed up at QB. Carried 12 times for 82 yards and completed three of eight passes for 39 yards. In 1975, started at QB though Montana was in the wings. Had 27 carries for 51 yards and one TD, and completed 66 of 139 passes for 686 yards, two TDs, and three interceptions. In 1976, started at QB. In Gator Bowl win over Penn State, hit 10 of 19 passes for 141 yards. For his senior year, carried 49 times for -78 yards and two TDs; completed 86 of 172 passes for 1,281 yards, 11 TDs, and 12 interceptions; made one tackle; and recovered one fumble. For his career, had 88 carries for 55 yards and three TDs; completed 155 of 319 passes for 2,006 yards, 13 TDs, and 15 interceptions; made one tackle; and recovered one fumble. His career offense was 2,061 yards and 16 TDs.

SNOW, JACK. 1962-1963-1964; HB, E; 6-2, 215; Long Beach, CA. Languished in shadow of mediocrity until Parseghian came. Combined with Huarte to provide preview of other game-breaking tandems. Had excellent speed, smooth moves, good power, and great hands. Also punted well. In 1962, backed up at E. For the year, caught four passes for 46 yards, had one interception for 23 return yards, and caught 2-point conversion pass. In 1963, started at RHB; carried three times for 26 yards, caught six passes for 82 yards, and intercepted one pass for three return yards. In 1964, started at LE. Had spectacular season, setting reception records. For the year, caught 60 passes for 1,114 yards and nine TDs, made one tackle, and punted 29 times for 36.4-yard average. Consensus All-American. For his career, carried three times for 26 yards, caught 70 passes for 1,222 yards and nine TDs, had two interceptions for 26 return yards, made one tackle, caught one 2-point conversion pass, and punted 29 times for 36.4-yard average. His career offense totaled 1,294 yards and nine TDs.

SPANIEL, FRANK. 1947-1948-1949; FB, HB; 5-10, 184; Vandergrift, PA. Fine all-purpose back for Leahy; played on two national championship teams. Could run inside and outside, catch passes for long gains, and return kicks for good yardage. Serious TD threat. In 1947, backed up at RHB for national champions. Carried four times for 13 yards. In 1948, backed up at FB. For the season, made 24 carries for 174 yards and one TD, caught one pass for three yards and one TD, and had two interceptions for 33 return yards. In 1949, started at LHB for national champions. Had 80 carries for 496 yards and four TDs, caught 16 passes for 212 yards and three TDs, returned five kickoffs 70 yards and three punts 32 yards. For his career, carried 108 times for 683 yards and five TDs, caught 17 passes for 215 yards and four TDs, had two interceptions for 33 return yards, and returned five kickoff for 70 yards and three punts for 32 yards. His career offense was 963 yards and nine TDs.

STEVENSON, HARRY. 1937-1938-1939; HB; 6-1, 189; Bloomfield, NJ. One of last good players to fill LHB spot in old Notre Dame box backfield. Had good speed, could throw well, and was proficient punter and place kicker. In 1937, backed up at LHB. In 1938, started at LHB. Fired 30-yard TD pass in 52-0 win over Kansas. His 47-yard TD pass was the difference in 14-7 win over Illinois. In 1939, started at LHB and handled most punting chores. Kicked winning field goal in 17-14 victory over Georgia Tech. Fired 50-yard TD pass to Zontini in win over SMU. Scored on 7-yard sweep against Army—his passing got them there; also kicked two PATs in 14-0 win. For the year, led in kickoff returns with five for 85 yards and in passing with 14 of 50 for 236 yards and one TD.

STICKLES, MONTY. 1957-1958-1959; E; 6-4, 225; Poughkeepsie, NY. Fine E for some weak Irish teams. Had excellent size and strength, good speed, good hands, and very good kicking skills. In 1957, started at RE. For the year, made 11 catches for 183 yards and three TDs; led team in scoring with 11 PATs, one field goal, and three TDs for 32 points; made 27 tackles; and broke up two passes. In 1958, started at LE. For the season, led team with 20 receptions for 328 yards and seven TDs; led scoring with 15 PATs, one field goal, and six TDs for 60 points; made 31 tackles; recovered two fumbles; and broke up two passes. Made All-American. In 1959, started at LE. For the season, caught 11 passes for 235 yards and two TDs, had 16 PATs and three field goals for 37 points, made 52 tackles, recovered one fumble, broke up two passes, and blocked one kick. Consensus All-American. For his career, made 42 receptions for 746 yards and 12 TDs, kicked 42 PATs and five field goals, made 110 tackles, broke up six passes, recovered three fumbles, and blocked one kick.

STOCK, JIM. 1972-1973-1974-1975; DE, LB; 6-3, 217; Barberton, OH. Excellent DE and LB for Parseghian and Devine. Exceptional speed and mobility, especially for pass rushing and coverage duties. Good hitter and had knack for getting to loose balls. In 1972, backed up at LE. Made three tackles and one fumble recovery. In 1973, started at RE for national champions. For the season, made 41 tackles, 11 for -66 yards; led the team with four fumble recoveries; and caused one safety. In 1974, started at RE. For the season, made 76 tackles, led defense with 19 hits for -120 yards, led with three fumble recoveries, and broke up two passes. In 1975, started at OLB and was co-captain. For the season, made 84 tackles, two for -12 yards, and broke up one pass. For his career, made 204 tackles, 32 for -198 yards; broke up three passes, had eight fumble recoveries; and caused one safety.

STONE, JIM. 1977-1978-1979-1980; HB; 6-1, 198; Seattle, WA. Backup HB all four seasons but made contribution as kick returner; replacing injured Phil Carter in his senior year. Had a good blend of size and speed; was at his best in the open field. In 1977, backed up at HB for national champions. For the season, carried 29 times for 193 yards and two TDs, and caught three passes for 30 yards and one TD. In 1978, backed up at RB. For the season, had 28 carries for 109 yards and one TD, caught eight passes for 69 yards, and returned 13 kickoffs 242 yards. In 1979, backed up at RB. For the year, carried 37 times for 156 yards and one TD, caught one pass for 3 yards, and led team with 19 kickoffs for 493 yards (25.9-yard average). In 1980, backed up at RB but saw plenty of playing time, including four games with 100+ yards rushing in each. For the season, led team with 192 carries for 908 yards and seven TDs, caught three passes for 29 yards, and led in kickoff returns with 17 for 344 yards. Joined select group of runners in two different 1,000-yard clubs—from scrimmage and on kick returns; had 286 carries for 1,366 yards and 11 TDs, caught 15 passes for 131 yards, and returned 49 kickoffs 1,079 yards. Involved in 350 offensive plays for 7.3-yard average. His career offense totaled 2,576 yards for 11 TDs.

STUHLDREHER, HARRY. 1922-1923-1924; QB; 5-7, 151; Massillon, OH. One of the great ones. Had everything that Rockne demanded of a QB—fine, analytical football mind, certain chestiness, commanding voice, fine arm, excellent punt returning skills (though not particularly fast), and superb blocking abilities (crucial for Rockne's offense). Probably most feared of the Horsemen. Caught Rockne's eye immediately in his freshman year. In 1922, backed up at QB. Scored TD in 46-0 rout of Kalamazoo. Scored TD in 34-7 win over DePauw. Scored TD in 13-3 win over Georgia Tech and fired TD pass to Castner for the other. Saw Four Horsemen come together as a unit in win over Butler when Castner went down with a hip injury and Layden went in at FB. After that, won 22 games and lost only to Nebraska. For the year, carried 26 times for 49 yards and five TDs, completed eight of 15 passes for 68 yards and three TDs, caught six passes for 95 yards and one TD, and returned 28 punts 199 yards and one kickoff 10 yards. In 1923, started at QB. Returned punt 46 yards in win over Georgia Tech. Threw 20-yard TD pass to Cerney in 14-7 loss to Nebraska. Broke open Butler game with 65-yard TD punt return. Led team for the season with 32 punt returns for 308 yards. For the year, carried 26 times for 50 yards and two TDs, completed 10 of 19 passes for 205 yards and three TDs, caught seven passes for 63 yards, made three interceptions, returned 38 punts 308 yards for three TDs, and tallied one PAT. In 1924, started at QB for national champions. Returned punt 35 yards against Princeton, and threw 20-yard pass to Miller to keep another drive going in 12-0 win. Facing 6-0 deficit in game with Northwestern, fired 80-yard TD pass to Crowley and scored on 2-yard sneak. Passed for three TDs in Carnegie Tech game; completed 12 passes in a row for 15 of 19 and scored on 1-yard sneak. In 1925 Rose Bowl win over Stanford, played much of the game with a broken bone in his ankle. For the year, carried 17 times for 19 yards and three TDs, completed 25 of 33 passes for 471 yards and four TDs, caught five passes for 52 yards, returned 22 punts 194 yards for three TDs and two kickoffs 13 yards, and scored one PAT. For his career, carried 69 times for 118 yards and 10 TDs, completed 43 of 67 passes for 744 yards and 10 TDs, caught 18 passes for 210 yards and one TD, made three interceptions, returned 88 punts 701 yards for 12 TDs and three kickoffs 23 yards, and tallied two PATs. Gained 1,796 yards on 221 attempts (8.12-yard average) for 32 TDs and two PATs.

SZYMANSKI, DICK. 1951-1952-1953-1954; LB, C; 6-2, 215; Toledo, OH. Fine LB for Leahy and Brennan. Good hitter; good on pass coverage; always making things happen. In 1951, started at MLB. Recovered Indiana fumble on their 17 to set up Worden's third TD in wild second quarter that doomed Indiana. Intercepted Pitt pass to lead to final TD of shutout. For the season, made three interceptions for five return yards and two fumble recoveries. In 1952, started at RLB. Made interception in win over Navy. In 1953, one-platoon rules cut down his playing time. Backed up at C. For the year, made one interception for nine return yards. In 1954, started at C for six games but was lost in Penn game with ruptured spleen. For the year, had one interception for two return yards and one fumble recovery. For his career, made six interceptions for 16 return yards and three fumble recoveries.

THAYER, TOM. 1979-1980-1981-1982; DT, T, G; 6-5, 268; Joliet, IL. Versatile, immensely strong, highly polished lineman. Good pass blocker and also devastating as pulling lineman for downfield blocking. In 1979, backed up at DT; made three tackles for the year. In 1980, started at RG for six games and led all guards in playing time. In 1981, started at LT and logged most playing time of any offensive lineman. In 1982, had an interesting season due to injuries elsewhere: started three games at strong G, then four at C, and finished up with four at quick G.

THEISMANN, JOE. 1968-1969-1970; QB; 6-0, 170; South River, NJ. One of top-ranked QBs of all time for Notre Dame. Senior year ranks among top individual performances of any era. Had a great arm, quick feet, superb mobility, fine grasp of reading downfield coverages, quick release, supreme confidence, and toughness that belied his slim build. In 1968, backed up at QB, but started last three games when Hanratty was hurt. For the season, made 59 carries for 259 yards and four TDs, hit 27 of 49 passes for 451 yards and two TDs, caught one pass for 13 yards, and returned 14 punts for 99 yards. In 1969, started at QB. In Cotton Bowl, set records with 231 yards passing and 279 yards of total offense, including TD passes of 54 yards and 24 yards. For the season, had 116 carries for 378 yards and six TDs; and completed 108 of 192 passes for 1,531 yards, 13 TDs, and 16 interceptions. In 1970, started at QB. In Cotton Bowl win over Texas, completed nine of 16 passes for 176 yards and ran for TDs of 3 and 15 yards. For his final season, carried 141 times for 406 yards and six TDs, completed 155 of 268 passes for 2,529 yards and 16 TDs, caught one pass for seven yards, and made a 2-point conversion. Made All-American and was second in Heisman voting. For his career, had 316 carries for 1,043 yards and 16 TDs; completed 290 of 509 passes for 4,411 yards, 31 TDs, and 35 interceptions; caught two passes for 20 yards; and returned 14 punts 99 yards. His total offense was 5,749 yards and 47 TDs. He is in the record book for most passes in a season (268 in 1970), most completions in a game (33 against USC in 1970), most completions in a season (155 in 1970), highest career completion percentage (.570), highest passing efficiency rating for more than 100 career passes (136.1), most passing yards in a game (526 against USC in 1970), most passing yards in a season (2,429 in 1970), most passing yards per game (242.9 in 1970), most TD passes in a career (31), most total offense attempts (391 in 1970), most total offense yards in a game (512 against USC in 1970), most total offense yards for a season (2,813 in 1970), most total offense yards per game (281.3 in 1970), most total offense yards per game in a career (187.3 for 29 games), most games with 200 yards or more total offense (eight in 1970), and most points per game (12.4 in 1970).

THOMAS, BOB. 1971-1972-1973; K; 5-10, 178; Rochester, NY. Fine place kicker for Parseghian. Key figure in 1973 championship season. In 1971, led team in scoring with 21 of 22 PATs and five of nine field goals. In 1972, hit all 34 PATs and seven of 11 field goals for 55 points. In 1973, helped win national crown by scoring 70 points—43 of 45 PATs and nine of 18 field goals, including a carryover streak from 1972 of 62 straight PATs, the second highest for the NCAA at the time.

TONEFF, BOB. 1949-1950-1951; DT, T; 6-2, 230; Barberton, OH. Powerful, dominating lineman on both defense and offense. Good size and strength made him a constant threat to both runners and passers. In 1949, started at RT on defense for the national champions. Slammed into Hoosier punter for a safety in his first game. Also blasted through Washington line to block punt in win. In 1950, started at RT on defense. Recovered fumbled snap on North Carolina 10 to lead to first score of Irish win. In 1951, started at RT on offense. Blocked Iowa PAT to earn a 20-20 tie. Made one pass reception for 21-yard gain on tackle eligible play. Made All-American.

TORAN, STACEY. 1980-1981-1982-1983; DB; 6-4, 206; Indianapolis, IN. One of best DBs in Fighting Irish history. Had great size for covering his territory, fine speed, and tenacity and power to make pass-catching in his zone worrisome for a receiver. In 1980, started at LCB after the first two games. For the season, made 30 tackles, two for -10 yards; broke up six passes, had one interception for 10 return yards; and returned two punts 19 yards. In 1981, started at WCB; made 54 tackles, two for -9 yards; broke up four passes; and had two interceptions for three return yards. In 1982, started at SCB; led DBs with 77 tackles, seven for -20 yards; broke up six passes; and had two interceptions. In 1983, started at SCB but arm injuries limited effectiveness. For the year, made 23 tackles and broke up one pass. For his career, made 184 tackles, 11 for -39 yards; broke up 17 passes; had five interceptions for 13 return yards; and returned two punts 19 yards.

TOWNSEND, MIKE. 1971-1972-1973; DB, S; 6-3, 183; Hamilton, OH. Fine DB for Parseghian. Had good size, excellent speed, great vertical leap, and uncanny ability to intercept passes. In 1971, backed up at S. For the season, made five tackles. In 1972, started at LCB. Set new Irish record with 10 interceptions for the year for 39 return yards, made 34 tackles, and broke up four passes. In 1973, started at FS for the national champions. For the season, had 26 tackles, made three interceptions for 47 return yards, and recovered three fumbles. Consensus All-American.

TRIPUCKA, FRANK. 1945-1946-1947-1948; QB; 6-2, 172; Bloomfield, NJ. Very talented QB for the post-war Leahy teams, but played behind Lujack until senior season. Fine arm, sheer daring, and excellent ball handling skills. In 1945, backed up at QB. For the season, carried twice for eight yards and completed his only pass for 21 yards. In 1946, backed up at QB. For the season, carried once for -6 yards, and completed one of five passes for 19 yards. In 1947, backed up at QB for the national champions. For the season, carried five times for -36 yards and completed 25 of 44 passes for 422 yards, three TDs, and one interception. In 1948, started at QB and carried 16 times for -28 yards, and completed 53 of 91 passes for 660 yards and 11 TDs. In his career, carried 24 times for -62 yards, completed 80 of 141 passes for 1,122 yards, 14 TDs, and one interception. His offense total was 1,060 yards and 14 TDs.

VARRICHIONE, FRANK. 1951-1952-1953-1954; G, T; 6-0, 210; Natick, MA. Good lineman for Leahy's last three teams and Brennan's first. Most famous for fainting tactic at end of first half in 14-14 tie with Iowa. In 1951, backed up at RG. In 1952, started at LT. In 1953, started at LT. In opening win over Oklahoma, blocked quick kick to lead to TD. In close win over Pitt, scored a safety. Achieved immortality against Iowa—Guglielmi threw TD pass to Shannon on the next play to end half (Leahy's tactic was legal in 1953; Iowa's Evashevski had used it earlier in the season). Scored TD on a fumble recovery in 40-14 win over SMU. In 1954, started at RT. Recovered Texas fumble on their 48 to lead to final TD of shutout. For the season, led the Fighting Irish with four fumble recoveries. Made All-American.

VAUGHAN, PETE. 1908-1909; FB; 6-0, 195; Crawfordsville, IN. Some credit him with coining the term "Fighting Irish" when he chastised teammates in 1909 game with Michigan by accusing them of not "fighting like Irishmen." At least 11 of 21 names on the 1909 roster were of Irish ancestry, including Maloney, Lynch, Brennan, Kelly, Collins, Duffy, Ryan, and Moriarty. Also credited with being the first man to break a goalpost for Notre Dame, in the same game, when he hit it with (a) his head, (b) his shoulder, (c) both, or (d) none of the above, since he could not remember. In 1908, started at FB. Rammed for two TDs in Hillsdale game, one a 35-yard center buck play. Scored only Irish TD in 12-6 loss to Michigan with 50-yard run on which he broke 8 tackles. Scored one TD in win over Physicians and Surgeons. Ran for TD against Ohio Northern. Rushed for 50+ yards and intercepted a pass in 8-4 win over Wabash. In 1909, started at FB. Ran for three TDs in opener with Olivet. Repeated with three TDs against Rose Poly a week later. Against MAC (eventually MSU), scored two TDs, rushed for 80+ yards, returned a kickoff 15 yards, and intercepted one pass. Rushed for 50+ yards in game with Pitt to go with two punt returns of 15 yards each and a fumble recovery. Scored one TD and took out the goalpost as the Irish beat Michigan in Ann Arbor—the most important game for Notre Dame to that point. Scored one TD in 46-0 rout of Miami of Ohio.

WALSH, ADAM. 1922-1923-1924; C; 6-0, 187; Hollywood, CA. One of the best in the first 60 years of Notre Dame football; candidate for all-time status. Coined the phrase "The Seven Mules" to gain measure of respect and recognition for players who toiled in the obscurity of the trenches while the Four Horsemen cavorted to fame. Superb blocker, particularly adept at snapping the ball to the backs who each had specific needs and likes in receiving the ball. In 1922, backed up at C. In 1923, started at C. In 1924, started at C for the national champions and captained one of the most famous football teams in collegiate history. Played against Army with two broken hands and intercepted a Cadet pass and returned it 20 yards to help save a 13-7 win. Tied Salmon's record of being knocked out four times in one game. Made All-American.

WATTERS, RICKY. 1987-1988-1989-1990; FL, TB; 6-2, 205; Harrisburg, PA. Multi-talented runner and receiver for Holtz. Had excellent speed, good moves, good power, and very good hands. Started as an elusive runner but added some punch in last seasons. In 1987, backed up at TB. Made one carry for -3 yards in Cotton Bowl loss to Texas A & M. For the year, carried 69 times for 373 yards and three TDs, caught six passes for 70 yards, and returned two punts 23 yards. In 1988, started at FL for the national champions. In Fiesta Bowl win over West Virginia, carried three times for six yards and caught one pass for 57 yards to set up TD. In the season, had 30 carries for 71 yards, caught 15 passes for 286 yards and two TDs, and returned 19 punts 253 yards for two TDs and two kickoffs 42 yards. In 1989, started at TB. In Orange Bowl win over Colorado, carried two times for 3 yards. For the year, had 118 carries for 791 yards and 10 TDs, caught 13 for 196 yards, and returned 15 punts 201 yards for one TD. In 1990, started at TB. For the season, made 108 carries for 579 yards and eight TDs, caught seven passes for 58 yards, and returned three punts 25 yards. For his career, carried 325 times for 1,814 yards and 21 TDs, caught 41 passes for 610 yards and two TDs, and returned 39 punts 502 yards for three TDs and two kickoffs 42 yards. His career total was 2,968 yards for 26 TDs.

WENDELL, MARTY. 1944-1946-1947-1948; FB, C, G; 5-11, 198; Chicago, IL. Won three monograms at three different positions; versatility was obviously his strong suit. In 1944, backed up at FB. For the year, carried 31 times for 82 yards and one TD. In 1945, played for Great Lakes and had a good defensive game against Notre Dame. In 1946, backed up at C. In 1947, started at LG for the national champions.

WILLIAMS, BOB. 1956-1957-1958; QB; 6-2, 190; Wilkes Barre, PA. Played for Brennan's last three teams. Had a good arm, ran well, and played good defense. In 1956, backed up at QB. For the year, carried 22 times for 46 yards and one TD; completed 16 of 31 passes for 197 yards, one TD, and 4 interceptions; and returned three kickoffs 45 yards. In 1957, started at QB. For the season, carried 62 times for 144 yards and four TDs; completed 53 of 106 passes for 559 yards, three TDs, and five interceptions; made three interceptions for 28 return yards; returned six kickoffs 102 yards; and made 19 tackles. In 1959, started at QB (but Izo played nearly as much). For the year, carried 44 times for 140 yards and four TDs; completed 26 of 65 passes for 344 yards, four TDs, and nine interceptions; made 23 tackles; and broke up three passes. For his career, carried 128 times for 330 yards and nine TDs; completed 95 of 202 passes for 1,100 yards, eight TDs, and 18 interceptions; made 42 tackles and three interceptions for 28 return yards; broke up three passes; and returned nine kickoffs 147 yards. His career offense was 1,935 yards and 17 TDs.

WILLIAMS, BOB. 1948-1949-1950; QB; 6-1, 185; Baltimore, MD. Fine field general for some of Leahy's most powerful teams. Had pinpoint passing accuracy, and was a good runner and kicker. In 1948, backed up at QB. For the year, carried six times for 11 yards and two TDs, completed eight of 14 passes for 110 yards and two TDs, and averaged 40 yards for two punts. In 1949, started at QB for the national champions and led one of the greatest aggregations of college football talent ever seen. For the season, carried 34 times for 63 yards and one TD, completed 83 of 147 passes (the best passing efficiency ever for Notre Dame) for 1,374 yards and 16 TDs, and punted 42 times for 38.6-yard average. Consensus All-American. In 1950, started at QB. For the year, carried 40 times for 115 yards and two TDs; completed 99 of 210 passes for 1,035 yards, 10 TDs, and 15 interceptions; punted 42 times for 39.2-yard average; and returned one kickoff 12 yards. Made All-American. For his career, made 80 carries for 189 yards and five TDs, completed 190 of 371 passes for 2,519 yards and 28 TDs, returned one kickoff 12 yards, and punted 86 times for 39.12-yard average. His career offense total was 2,910 yards and 33 TDs.

WOLSKI, BILL. 1963-1964-1965; HB; 5-11, 195; Muskegon, MI. Stellar running back for Parseghian's first two teams—rugged, durable, ran with intensive authority. In 1963, backed up at LHB. For the year, had 70 carries for 320 yards and two TDs, caught three passes for 11 yards, led in kickoff returns with 16 for 379 yards, and added six punt returns for 31 yards. In 1964, started at LHB. For the year, led Fighting Irish runners with 136 carries for 657 yards and 11 TDs, caught eight passes for 130 yards, and returned two kickoff 49 yards. In 1965, started at LHB. Set modern scoring record with five rushing TDs against Pitt in 69-13 blowout. For the season, carried 103 times for 452 yards and eight TDs; led team in scoring with eight TDs and two 2-point conversion for 52 points; caught one pass for 8 yards;

led in kickoff returns with six for 131 yards; and made seven tackles. For his career, gained 1,429 yards on 309 carries for 21 TDs, caught 12 passes for 149 yards, returned 24 kickoffs 559 yards and six punts 31 yards, made seven tackles, and scored two 2-point conversions. His career offense total was 2,168 yards and 21 TDs.

WORDEN, NEIL. 1951-1952-1953; FB; 5-11, 185; Milwaukee, WI. Indomitable runner for Leahy's last three teams; owned FB spot for three seasons. Packed tremendous punch in small package. Shredded Purdue's defense for four TDs in his first game. In 1951, started at FB. In sophomore year, made 181 carries for 676 yards and eight TDs, caught 12 passes for 111 yards, and recovered one fumble. In 1952, started at FB. For the year, had 150 carries for 504 yards and 10 TDs, caught 16 passes for 80 yards, and had five kickoff returns for 75 yards. In 1953, started at FB. For the season, carried 145 times for 859 yards and 11 TDs, caught one pass for eight yards, and returned eight kickoffs 164 yards. For his career, had 476 carries for 2,039 yards and 29 TDs, caught 29 passes for 199 yards, and returned 13 kickoffs 239 yards. His career offense was 2,477 yards and 29 TDs.

WYNNE, CHET. 1918-1919-1920-1921; FB; 6-0, 168; Norton, KS. Like many others of this era, went to Notre Dame for another sport, in his case track. Rockne (track coach, chemistry professor, and football coach) had misgivings about possible damage to his track career, but football beckoned. Had excellent speed and power, could catch passes, and play strong defense. In 1918, backed up at FB. In 1919, backed up at FB for the undefeated Irish. In 1920, started at FB in same backfield with Gipp for another undefeated campaign to give Notre Dame an almost unstoppable running game. Scored one TD in win over Kalamazoo. Played fine game in win over Army, including 20-yard TD run down the sideline. In close win over Indiana, made crucial 32-yard kickoff return. Ran with power in victory over Northwestern with gains of 33 and 28 yards. In 1921, started at FB. Scored two TDs in shutout of Kalamazoo, an 80-yard kickoff return and a 10-yard run; also intercepted a pass and tackled a pass receiver for a loss. Scored two TDs in win over DePauw. Rushed for 40+ yards and broke up one pass in close loss to Iowa. Ran 52 yards from scrimmage in 10 tries, including 7-yard TD run, in win over Indiana. Running from the E position, caught 45-yard TD pass against Army and returned two kickoffs 42 and 15 yards to help with win; his play caught the attention of the eastern press. Helped beat Rutgers three days later with 35-yard TD run, picked off a pass, and caught a 51-yard aerial, none of which hurt his image with the eastern press. Gained 55 yards on 6 carries against Marquette, including a 5-yard TD burst, and threw the decisive block to spring Mohardt on a 48-yard run. Scored one TD in shutout of MAC.

YARR, TOMMY. 1929-1930-1931; C; 5-11, 197; Dabob, WA. Part of line that gave Notre Dame undisputed back-to-back championships in Rockne's last seasons. Like most of his linemen, was on the small side but compensated with incredible quickness, superb blocking technique, and tenacious defensive play. In 1929, backed up at C. In 1930, started at C for the undefeated national champs. Intercepted two SMU passes in closing moments of 20-14 Irish win. Wreaked havoc against Drake's aerial game with interceptions and deflected passes. In 1931, started at C and served as captain. Made All-American.

ZORICH, CHRIS. 1988-1989-1990; NT; 6-1, 266; Chicago, IL. Dominating NT with combination of strength (455-pound bench press), speed (4.68-second 40-yard dash), and lateral quickness. In spite of constant double and triple-teaming efforts against him, often tackled runners and receivers on sideline patterns—rare for interior linemen. Came as LB, but made the move to the line. In 1988, started at NT. For the year, made 70 tackles, four for -8 yards, 3.5 sacks for -17 yards, recovered three fumbles, and broke up three passes. In 1989, started at NT. For the season, made 92 tackles, five for -12 yards, three sacks for -27 yards, caused one fumble, recovered two fumbles, and broke up two passes. Consensus All-American. In 1990, started at NT and was a tri-captain. For year, marred by various injuries, made 57 tackles, 12 for -26 yards, had four sacks for -26 yards, caused two fumbles, recovered one fumble, and broke up one pass. Repeat consensus All-American and won Lombardi Trophy. For his career, had 219 tackles, 21 for -56 yards, 10.5 sacks for -70 yards, caused three fumbles, recovered six fumbles, and broke up six passes.

Chapter 8

Fighting Irish Statistics

NOTRE DAME WINS AND LOSSES FOR EACH GAME OF ALL SEASONS:

	Wins	Losses	Ties	W/L%
Game One	87	11	5	.868
Game Two:	75	21	5	.767
Game Three:	71	23	1	.748
Game Four:	77	21	1	.782
Game Five:	73	22	2	.762
Game Six:	69	19	8	.760
Game Seven:	74	16	3	.811
Game Eight:	68	13	6	.816
Game Nine:	56	19	5	.731
Game Ten:	30	23	3	.562
Game Eleven:	9	10	1	.475
Game Twelve:	1	1	0	.500
Game Thirteen:	1	0	0	1.000
	702	209	40	.759

Opponents who wish to avoid losing to the Irish need not schedule a Notre Dame opener. Try catching them late in the season, after the attrition of a tough schedule sets in. Note also the midseason slump where 40% of all Irish ties are lumped together in games six, seven and eight.

NOTRE DAME UNDER THE LIGHTS

In 40 games under the lights, the Irish have won 31 and lost nine (.775—comparable to their winning percentage for all games). Frank Leahy's 1951 team played the first night game, in Briggs Stadium in Detroit, against the University of Detroit, and won handily, 40-6.

The first home win under Musco lights took place at the start of the 1982 season, when Faust's Irish nipped Michigan 23-17. In general, the Irish coaches' records under the lights are remarkably similar to their career totals. Here are the results of Irish night games for each coach:

Leahy:

Home: 0-0-0

Away: 1-0-0

Total: 1-0-0 (1.000)

Brennan:

Home: 0-0-0

Away: 1-1-0

Total: 1-1-0 (.500)

Kuharich:

Home: 0-0-0

Away: 0-1-0

Total: 0-1-0 (.000)

Parseghian:

Home: 0-0-0

Away: 9-2-1

Total: 9-2-1 (.791)

Devine:

Home: 0-0-0

Away: 5-0-0

Total: 5-0-0 (1.000)

Faust:

Home: 2-1-0

Away: 2-1-0

Total: 4-2-0 (.666)

Holtz:

Home: 4-0-0

Away: 6-3-0

Total: 10-3-0 (.769)

WON/LOSS PERCENTAGE FOR NOTRE DAME'S COACHES:

Coach		Record	W/L %	Years
1.	John L. Marks	13-0-2	.933	1911-12
2.	Thomas Barry	12-1-1	.893	1906-07
3.	Victor M. Place	8-1-0	.889	1908
4.	Knute Rockne	105-12-5	.881	1918-30
5.	Jesse Harper	34-5-1	.863	1913-17
6.	Frank C. Longman	11-1-2	.857	1909-10
7.	Frank Leahy	87-11-9	.855	1941-43; 1946-53
8.	Ara Parseghian	95-17-4	.836	1964-74
9.	James Faragher	14-2-2	.833	1902-03
10.	Ed McKeever	8-2-0	.800	1944
11.	Elmer Layden	47-13-3	.770	1934-40
12.	Lou Holtz	56-17-0	.767	1986-
13.	Dan Devine	53-16-1	.764	1975-80
14.	Patrick O'Dea	14-4-2	.750	1900-01
15.	H. G. Hadden	3-1-0	.750	1895
16.	J. L. Morison	3-1-1	.700	1894
17.	Frank Hering	12-6-1	.658	1896-98
18.	James McWeeney	6-3-1	.650	1899
19.	Terry Brennan	32-18-0	.640	1954-58
20.	Hunk Anderson	16-9-2	.630	1931-33
21.	Louis Salmon	5-3-0	.625	1904
22.	Henry J. McGlew	5-4-0	.556	1905
23.	Gerry Faust	30-26-1	.535	1981-85
24.	Hugh Devore	9-9-1	.500	1945; 1963
25.	Joe Kuharich	17-23-0	.425	1959-62
		702-209-40	.759	

Only the top 13 coaches listed above have career marks better than the Notre Dame career average. The records of such contemporary luminaries such as Devine and Holtz are flirting with falling below the mark.

WINS AT HOME AND AWAY FOR IRISH COACHES:

It is tough to win football games on the road for any coach, but Irish head coaches are also burdened with extraordinary expectations of the team's supporters for wins at home. The following chart shows home and away wins and home and away winning percentages for all Irish coaches:

HOME Ws		AWAY Ws		HOME W %		AWAY W %	
1. Parseghian	49	Rockne	60	Harper	1.000	Leahy	.862
2. Rockne	45	Leahy	50	Faragher	1.000	Rockne	.831
3. Leahy	37	Parseghian	46	Salmon	1.000	Parseghian	.805
4. Holtz	29	Devine	28	Place	1.000	Place	.785
5. Layden	25	Holtz	27	Marks	1.000	Harper	.770
6. Devine	25	Layden	22	Longman	1.000	Hadden	.750
7. Brennan	16	Harper	18	McKeever	1.000	Devine	.750
8. Faust	16	Brennan	16	Rockne	.958	Layden	.712
9. Harper	15	Faust	14	Barry	.954	Holtz	.710
10. O'Dea	12	Anderson	9	O'Dea	.928	Morison	.700
11. Faragher	10	Kuharich	7	Parseghian	.883	McKeever	.666
12. Place	10	Place	5	Leahy	.866	Longman	.666
13. Barry	10	Marks	4	McWeeney	.857	Barry	.666
14. Hering	10	McKeever	4	Layden	.833	Faragher	.642
15. Kuharich	10	Faragher	4	McGlew	.833	Anderson	.633
16. Marks	9	Devore	4	Holtz	.828	Brennan	.615
17. Longman	8	Longman	3	Devine	.781	Faust	.483
18. Anderson	7	Barry	2	Hadden	.750	Devore	.409
19. McWeeney	6	O'Dea	2	Hering	.700	O'Dea	.333
20. McGlew	5	Hering	1	Morison	.700	Hering	.333
21. Devore	5	Salmon	1	Brennan	.666	Salmon	.250
22. McKeever	4	McWeeney	0	Anderson	.625	McWeeney	.166
23. Salmon	4	McGlew	0	Devore	.625	McGlew	.000
24. Hadden	3	Hadden	0	Faust	.592	Morison	—
25. Morison	3	Morison	0	Kuharich	.500	Hadden	—

There are no real surprises here; generally, the coaches who do well in their careers (see previous chart) will do well here. Seven of the 25 Irish head coaches were undefeated at home. Three more won at a .900 clip and six others won at home at an .800 pace or better. On the road, only three coaches prevailed at a rate of .800 or better, although a strong group of seven more won more than 70 percent of their road games.

NOTRE DAME'S UNDEFEATED SEASONS

Twenty Irish teams have completed undefeated seasons. In chronological order, they are:

Year	Record	ND-Opp Total score	Avg. Score
1903	8-0-1	292-0	29.2 to 0
1907	6-0-1	137-20	19.57 to 2.8
1909	7-0-1	236-14	29.5 to 1.75
1911	6-0-2	229-9	28.62 to 1.12
1912	7-0-0	389-27	55.57 to 3.85
1913	7-0-0	268-41	38.28 to 5.85
1919	9-0-0	229-47	25.44 to 5.22
1920	9-0-0	251-44	27.88 to 4.88
1924	10-0-0	285-54	28.5 to 5.4
1929	9-0-0	145-38	16.11 to 4.22
1930	10-0-0	265-74	26.5 to 7.4
1941	8-0-1	189-64	21 to 7.11
1946	8-0-1	271-24	30.11 to 2.66
1947	9-0-0	291-52	32.33 to 5.77
1948	9-0-1	320-93	32 to 9.3
1949	10-0-0	360-86	36 to 8.6
1953	9-0-1	317-139	31.7 to 13.9
1966	9-0-1	362-38	36.2 to 3.8
1973	11-0-0	382-89	34.72 to 8.09
1988	12-0-0	393-156	32.75 to 12.75
	173-0-10	5611-1109	30.66 to 6.06

In these 20 seasons, the Irish played at a .978 clip. In 103 seasons, then, Notre Dame teams stood roughly a one in five chance of ringing up an undefeated campaign. In these 20 seasons, the Irish defeated the opposition by an average of 24.6 points.

Rockne's influence looms large here. He played in three undefeated seasons (1911-1913) and coached five others (1919-20, 1924, 1929-30). It is not stretching the point to note that his own protégé, Frank Leahy, coached another six undefeated seasons (giving his 1949 seniors the privilege of playing four seasons without suffering a loss—36-0-2—compared to Rockne's class of four playing years at 24-1-3). Rockne thus either directly played in, or coached 40 percent of Notre Dame's undefeated seasons. His indirect influence, extended through Leahy, has amazingly touched a full 70 percent of Notre Dame's undefeated seasons.

Of these 20 seasons, two in particular stand out—1912 and 1929. The 1912 season, one of Rockne's as a player, saw the Irish manhandle their opponents by a whopping margin of 51 points per game. The 1929 season, a defensive masterpiece, was an incredible feat because the Irish won all nine games on the road—and often without Rockne on the sidelines, due to phlebitis of the leg caused by a sideline pileup that smashed into the coach during the Indiana game. His doctors kept him off his feet as much as possible and curtailed his coaching activities to intolerable limits as far as Rock was concerned.

In the eight undefeated seasons in which Rockne either played or coached, the Irish played 69 games, won 67 of them, and tied two. In those games, they outscored the opposition by 2,061 points to 334, an average score of 29.85 to 4.84, a winning margin of slightly better than 25 points per game—better than three touchdowns and a field goal. In his five undefeated seasons as the head coach, Rockne won all 47 games, his Irish scoring 1175 points to 257, for an average score of 25 to 5.46, a winning margin of 19.54 points per game. Leahy's Irish, in six undefeated campaigns, won 52 games and tied five. In those seasons, they scored 1,748 points to the opposition's 458, for an average score of 30.66 to eight, a winning differential of 22.66 points. Leahy's juggernauts in those years beat the opposition by three more points than did Rockne's, but those three points, combined with Leahy's relentless approach to the game, did not endear him to American sports fans. Rockne whipped you, and you did not feel too bad about it; his guile and wit made it painless. Leahy crunched you, and it hurt. This is reflected in his national reputation. Ara Parseghian's great teams of 1966 and 1973 actually took it to the opponents worse than most of Leahy's crusades: beating the opposition by a hefty 32.4 points in 1966, and by 26.63 points in 1973.

But for sheer whippings, the 1903 season, with Red Salmon playing in his senior year for Coach James Faragher, wins the prize since the opposition did not score for the whole year. Coach John Marks, a decade later, set the record for overmatching the opposition, especially in the 1912 season when the Irish crunched seven teams 389 to 27, a scoring differential of 51.72 points! His two seasons as head coach, in which he won 13 games and tied two, saw the Irish outscore the opposition by the ridiculous figure of 618 points to 36, for an average score of 41.2 to 2.4, a 38.8 scoring differential—in today's scoring, a margin of five touchdowns and a field goal.

UNDEFEATED SEASONS IN RANK ORDER OF SCORING DIFFERENTIAL

	Year	Point diff.	Coach [Remarks]
1.	1912	+51.72	Marks [Rockne's junior year]
2.	1903	+32.44	Faragher [nine shutouts]
3.	1913	+32.43	Harper [Rockne's senior year]
4.	1966	+32.4	Parseghian [six shutouts]
5.	1909	+27.75	Longman [six shutouts + beat Mich.]
6.	1911	+27.5	Marks [Rockne's sophomore year]
7.	1946	+27.45	Leahy [first post-war machine]
8.	1949	+27.4	Leahy [Hart's Heisman year]
9.	1973	+26.63	Parseghian [ND's first 11-0 year]
10.	1947	+26.56	Leahy [Lujack's Heisman year]
11.	1924	+23.1	Rockne [Four Horsemen]
12.	1920	+23	Rockne [Gipp's senior year]
13.	1948	+22.7	Leahy [mid-39 game streak]
14.	1919	+20.22	Rockne [Gipp's junior year]
15.	1988	+20.36	Holtz [ND's first 12-0 year]
16.	1930	+19.1	Rockne [dedicated new stadium]
17.	1953	+17.8	Leahy [the Master's last year]
18.	1907	+16.77	Barry [four shutouts]
19.	1941	+13.89	Leahy [Leahy's first season]
20.	1929	+11.89	Rockne [all games played away]

NOTRE DAME'S WINNING STREAKS

Over the years, the Irish have been fortunate enough to put together some streaks of very impressive football. In chronological order, here are the seasons when opponents most regretted scheduling the Irish:

Seasons:	Streak	(W-L-T)	Coaches
1902-04	14 games	(12-0-2)	Faragher
1908-10	16 games	(14-0-2)	Place/Longman
1911-14	24 games	(22-0-2)	Marks/Harper
1919-21	20 games	(20-0-0)	Rockne
1923-25	16 games	(16-0-0)	Rockne
1929-31	20 games	(20-0-0)	Rockne/Anderson
1946-50	39 games	(37-0-2)	Leahy
1969-70	18 games	(16-1-1)	Parseghian
1973-74	20 games	(19-1-0)	Parseghian
1988-90*	35 games	(32-3-0)	Holtz

*includes ND's longest pure winning streak of 23 straight wins.

NOTRE'S DAME LOSING STREAKS

Losing streaks are not characteristic of Irish football. The Irish did not lose more than two consecutive games until Hunk Anderson's punchless team of 1933. In nine games that year, the Irish had little fight in them, scoring only 32 points, suffering six shutouts, and losing four straight games in the middle of the campaign.

Following are the few losing streaks that mar the Irish record.

Season	Streak	Total Score	Avg. Score	Coaches
1933	4 losses	0-47	0 to 11.75	Anderson
1956	5 losses	48-174	9.6 to 34.8	Brennan
1960	8 losses	93-181	11.6 to 22.6	Kuharich
1961	3 losses	27-42	9 to 14	Kuharich
1962	4 losses	27-107	6.75 to 26.75	Kuharich
1963	3 losses	15-46	5 to 15.33	Kuharich/Devore
1963	5 losses	49-112	9.8 to 22.4	Devore
1982	3 losses	44-71	14.6 to 23.6	Faust
1983	3 losses	68-78	22.6 to 26	Faust
1984	3 losses	52-88	17.3 to 29.3	Faust
1985-86	5 losses	58-148	11 to 29.6	Faust/Holtz

The only surprise here is Holtz, but his '86 team tacked on two losses to a string inherited from Faust's last three games. Otherwise, coaches who enjoy excellent reputations within Notre Dame history are not found on this list.

Looked at another way, certain coaches simply resisted consecutive losses in the regular season. Of those with more than five or more seasons leading the Irish, they are Harper and Parseghian (who lost a bowl game after a closing loss to USC in 1972—then came back to win the national crown in 1973). All other coaches have been the victims of consecutive losses. That Parseghian dodged this bullet for eleven seasons is a testament to his ability to field talented teams with great preparation, composure, and confidence.

Other coaches came close: in twelve seasons, Rockne had consecutive losses once (1928); in eleven seasons, Leahy lost twice in a row only once (1950); in seven seasons, Layden had consecutive losses twice (1934 and 1940); in five seasons, Brennan had two or more losses in a row twice (1956 and 1957); and in six seasons, Devine suffered consecutive losses twice (1978 and 1979).

In six seasons, Holtz has fallen into consecutive losses, surprisingly, five times (three times in 1986, 1987, and 1991).

SCORING DIFFERENTIALS FOR NOTRE DAME COACHES

Notre Dame football teams have played 951 games since 1887. They have scored 23,287 points to the opposition's 9,637 points. In these 951 games, then, the average score has been 24.48 to 10.13; the scoring differential in Notre Dame's history has thus been 14.35 points, slightly better than two touchdowns per game. The following chart reveals the scoring differential over the careers of Notre Dame's coaches.

Years	Coach	Total Points	Avg. Score	Differential
1894	Morison	80-31	16 to 6.2	+9.8
1895	Hadden	70-20	17.5 to 5	+12.5
1896-98	Hering	502-124	26.42 to 6.52	+19.9
1899	McWeeney	169-55	16.9 to 5.5	+11.4
1900-01	O'Dea	406-92	20.3 to 4.6	+15.7
1902-03	Faragher	495-51	27.5 to 2.83	+24.67
1904	Salmon	94-127	11.75 to 15.87	-4.12
1905	McGlew	312-80	34.66 to 8.88	+25.78
1906-07	Barry	244-32	17.42 to 2.28	+15.14
1908	Place	326-20	36.22 to 2.22	+34
1909-10	Longman	428-34	30.57 to 2.42	+28.15
1911-12	Marks	611-36	40.73 to 2.42	+38.31
1913-17	Harper	1219-170	30.47 to 4.25	+26.22
1918-30	Rockne	2847-828	23.33 to 6.78	+16.55
1931-33	Anderson	502-151	18.59 to 5.59	+13
1934-40	Layden	873-415	13.85 to 6.58	+7.27
1941-43	Leahy	2835-996	26.49 to 9.3	+17.19
1946-53	Leahy			
1944	McKeever	272-118	27.2 to 11.8	+15.4
1954-58	Brennan	1007-825	20.14 to 16.5	+3.64
1959-62	Kuharich	724-901	18.1 to 22.52	-4.42
1945 & 63	Devore	363-281	19.1 to 14.78	+4.32
1964-74	Parseghian	3193-1964	27.52 to 16.93	+10.59
1975-80	Devine	1742-963	24.88 to 13.75	+11.13
1981-85	Faust	1283-984	22.5 to 17.26	+5.24
1986-91	Holtz	2169-1220	32.37 to 18.2	+14.17

Coaches' Scoring Differentials in Rank Order

1.	Marks	+38.31
2.	Place	+34
3.	Longman	+28.15
4.	Harper	+26.22
5.	McGlew	+25.78
6.	Faragher	+24.67
7.	Hering	+19.9
8.	Leahy	+17.19
9.	Rockne	+16.55
10.	O'Dea	+15.7
11.	McKeever	+15.4
12.	Barry	+15.14
13.	Holtz	+14.17 (through 1991)
14.	Anderson	+13
15.	Hadden	+12.5
16.	McWeeney	+11.4
17.	Devine	+11.13
18.	Parseghian	+10.59
19.	Morison	+9.8
20.	Layden	+7.27
21.	Faust	+5.24
22.	Devore	+4.32
23.	Brennan	+3.64
24.	Salmon	-4.12 (had a winning season though)
25.	Kuharich	-4.45 (ND's only coach with a losing career record)

POINTS SCORED PER COACH

1.	Parseghian	3193
2.	Rockne	2847
3.	Leahy	2835
4.	Holtz	2169
5.	Devine	1742
6.	Faust	1283
7.	Harper	1219
8.	Berennan	1007
9.	Layden	873
10.	Kuharich	724
11.	Marks	611
12.	Hering	502
13.	Anderson	502
14.	Faragher	495
15.	Longman	428
16.	O'Dea	406
17.	Devore	363
18.	Place	326
19.	McGlew	312
20	McKeever	272
21.	Barry	244
22.	McWeeney	169
23.	Salmon	94
24.	Morison	80
25	Hadden	70

POINTS ALLOWED PER COACH

1.	Parseghian	1964
2.	Holtz	1220
3.	Leahy	996
4.	Faust	984
5.	Devine	963
6.	Kuharich	901
7.	Rockne	828
8.	Brennan	825
9.	Layden	415
10.	Devore	281
11.	Harper	170
12.	Anderson	151
13.	Salmon	127
14.	Hering	124
15.	McKeever	118
16.	O'Dea	92
17.	McGlew	80
18.	McWeeney	55
19.	Faragher	51
20.	Marks	36
21.	Longman	34
22.	Barry	32
23.	Morison	31
24.	Hadden	20
25.	Place	20

HIGHEST COACHING CAREER AVERAGE IRISH SCORE PER GAME

1.	Marks	40.73	1911-12
2.	Place	36.22	1908
3.	McGlew	34.66	1905
4.	Holtz	32.37	1986-91
5.	Longman	30.57	1909-10
6.	Harper	30.475	1913-17
7.	Parseghian	27.52	1964-74
8.	Faragher	27.5	1902-03
9.	McKeever	27.2	1944
10.	Leahy	26.49	1941-43; 46-53
11.	Hering	26.42	1896-98
12.	Devine	24.88	1976-80
13.	Rockne	23.33	1918-30
14.	Faust	22.5	1981-85
15.	O'Dea	20.3	1900-01
16.	Brennan	20.14	1954-58
17.	Devore	19.1	1945; 63
18.	Anderson	18.59	1931-33
19.	Kuharich	18.1	1959-62
20.	Hadden	17.5	1895
21.	Barry	17.42	1906-07
22.	McWeeney	16.9	1899
23.	Morison	16	1894
24.	Layden	13.85	1934-40
25.	Salmon	11.75	1904

AVERAGE OPPONENTS' POINTS ALLOWED PER GAME

1. Place	2.22	1908	14. Rockne	6.78	1918-30
2. Barry	2.28	1906-07	15. McGlew	8.88	1905
3. Marks	2.42	1911-12	16. Leahy	9.3	1941-43;
4. Longman	2.42	1909-10			46-53
5. Faragher	2.83	1902-03	17. McKeever	11.8	1944
6. Harper	4.25	1913-17	18. Devine	13.75	1975-80
7. O'Dea	4.6	1900-01	19. Devore	14.78	1945; 63
8. Hadden	5	1895	20. Salmon	15.87	1904
9. McWeeney	5.5	1899	21. Brennan	16.5	1954-58
10. Anderson	5.59	1931-33	22. Parseghian	16.93	1964-74
11. Morison	6.2	1894	23. Faust	17.26	1981-85
12. Hering	6.52	1896-98	24. Holtz	18.2	1986-91
13. Layden	6.58	1934-40	25. Kuharich	22.52	1959-62

The foregoing charts reveal that the early coaches at Notre Dame were very stingy chaps, many of them allowing only a field goal or less. Harper, Rockne, and Layden stand out for miserliness over extended periods—for a quarter century of football games these three gave up less than a touchdown per game. Parseghian, with eleven seasons, racked up both the most points and allowed the most, but this was in an era when passing was wildly more successful than fifty years before. The high-scoring coaches from before Harper just played smashmouth against inferior opponents. Leahy's winning machines kept opponents under 10 points per game while pounding out big winning margins. With both Parseghian and Holtz, Irish fans could expect plenty of offense and scoring—but they had to hope the other team did not get hot, as USC did in the early '70s when the Trojans exploded for points against frantic, heroic Irish offensive barrages. Rockne, ever the student of theatrics, kept the games pretty close, even while strangling opponents' offenses.

NOTRE DAME SHUTOUTS OF OPPONENTS PER COACH

In 951 football games the Irish have shutout their opponents 286 times (30 percent). The following chart shows the shutout percentages of all Irish coaches.

Coach	Shutouts	Percentage	Years
1. Barry	10 in 14 games	71%	1906-07
2. Faragher	12 in 18 games	66%	1902-03
3. Place	6 in 9 games	66%	1908
4. Longman	9 in 14 games	64%	1909-10
5. Hering	12 in 19 games	63%	1896-98
6. Harper	25 in 40 games	62.5%	1913-17
7. O'Dea	12 in 20 games	60%	1900-01
8. Marks	9 in 15 games	60%	1911-12
9. McGlew	5 in 9 games	55%	1904
10. Anderson	14 in 27 games	51%	1931-33
11. McWeeney	5 in 10 games	50%	1899
12. McKeever	5 in 10 games	50%	1944
13. Hadden	2 of 4 games	50%	1895
14. Rockne	50 in 122 games	40.9%	1918-30
15. Morison	2 in 5 games	40%	1894
16. Salmon	3 in 8 games	37.5%	1904
17. Layden	20 in 63 games	31.74%	1934-40
18. Leahy	26 in 107 games	24.3%	1941-43; 46-53
19. Parseghian	28 in 116 games	24.13%	1964-74
20. Brennan	11 in 50 games	22%	1954-58
21. Devore	3 in 19 games	15.78%	1945; 63
22. Devine	10 in 70 games	14.28%	1975-80
23. Kuharich	2 in 40 games	5%	1959-62
24. Faust	2 in 57 games	3.5%	1981-85
25. Holtz	2 in 73 games	2.73%	1986-91

MOST SHUTOUTS PER COACH

1. Rockne 50 in 122 games
2. Parseghian 28 in 116 games
3. Leahy 26 in 107 games
4. Harper 25 in 40 games
5. Layden 20 in 63 games
6. Anderson 14 in 27 games
7. Hering 12 in 19 games
8. Faragher 12 in 18 games
9. O'Dea 12 in 20 games
10. Brennan 11 in 50 games
11. Barry 10 in 14 games
12. Devine 10 in 70 games
13. Longman 9 in 14 games
14. Marks 9 in 15 games
15. Place 6 in 9 games
16. McGlew 5 in 9 games
17. McWeeney 5 in 10 games
18. McKeever 5 in 10 game
19. Salmon 3 in 8 games
20. Devore 3 in 19 games
21. Hadden 2 in 4 games
22. Morison 2 in 5 games
23. Kuharich 2 in 40 games
24. Faust 2 in 57 games
25. Holtz 2 in 67 games

NOTRE DAME AS SHUTOUT VICTIMS

In 951 games the Irish have failed to score 65 times—only 6.83 percent of the time, as opposed to their turning the trick 286 times (30 percent). Only five of Notre Dame's opponents through the years have an edge over the Irish in this category: Chicago with two in four games, Indianapolis Artillery with one in its only try, Michigan with five in 23 games, Missouri with one in four meetings, and Yale with one shutout in the only encounter of the two teams. Otherwise, the Irish have racked up more shutouts of all other opponents than they have suffered.

Here is the chronological record of Irish coaches as victims of the shutout:

Coach	Shutouts	Percentage of games
Morison	0 in 5 games	0%
Hadden	1 in 4 games	25%
Hering	3 in 19 games	15.78%
McWeeney	2 in 10 games	20%
O'Dea	5 in 20 games	25%
Faragher	2 in 18 games	11%
Salmon	2 in 8 games	25%
McGlew	3 in 9 games	33%
Barry	2 in 14 games	14.28%
Place	0 in 9 games	0%
Longman	2 in 14 games	14.28%
Marks	2 in 15 games	13.33%
Harper	3 in 40 games	7.5%
Rockne	7 in 122 games	5.73%
Anderson	10 in 27 games	37%
Layden	6 in 63 games	9.52%
Leahy	3 in 107 games	2.8%
McKeever	1 in 10 games	10%
Brennan	1 in 50 games	2%
Kuharich	3 in 40 games	7.5%
Devore	1 in 19 games	5.26%
Parseghian	1 in 116 games	.008%
Devine	1 in 70 games	1.42%
Faust	1 in 57 games	1.75%
Holtz	1 in 73 games	1.36%

SHUTOUT LOSS RANKINGS FOR COACHES

	Shutout Losses		Worst Percentage		Best Percentage	
1.	Anderson	10	Anderson	37%	Place	0%
2.	Rockne	7	McGlew	33%	Morison	0%
3.	Layden	6	Hadden	25%	Parseghian	.008%
4.	O'Dea	5	Salmon	25%	Holtz	1.36%
5.	McGlew	3	O'Dea	25%	Devine	1.42%
6.	Hering	3	McWeeney	20%	Faust	1.75%
7.	Kuharich	3	Hering	15.78%	Brennan	2%
8.	Harper	3	Barry	14.28%	Leahy	2.8%
9.	Leahy	3	Longman	14.28%	Devore	5.26%
10.	Salmon	2	Marks	13.33%	Rockne	5.73%
11.	McWeeney	2	Faragher	11%	Harper	7.5%
12.	Barry	2	McKeever	10%	Kuharich	7.5%
13.	Longman	2	Layden	9.52%	Layden	9.52%
14.	Marks	2	Kuharich	7.5%	McKeever	10%
15.	Faragher	2	Harper	7.5%	Faragher	11%
16.	Hadden	1	Rockne	5.73%	Marks	13.33%
17.	McKeever	1	Devore	5.26%	Longman	14.28%
18.	Devore	1	Leahy	2.8%	Barry	14.28%
19.	Brennan	1	Brennan	2%	Hering	15.78%
20.	Faust	1	Faust	1.75%	McWeeney	20%
21.	Devine	1	Devine	1.42%	O'Dea	25%
22.	Holtz	1	Holtz	1.36%	Salmon	25%
23.	Parseghian	1	Parseghian	.008%	Hadden	25%
24.	Morison	0	Morison	—	McGlew	33%
25.	Place	0	Place	—	Anderson	37%

SHUTOUTS BY AND AGAINST NOTRE DAME

The Irish have played football games against 126 different opponents. Of those, Notre Dame has recorded shutouts over 91 of them, while 26 have returned the favor. The Irish hold shutouts over 70 opponents who have not, in turn, been able to keep them scoreless. Only five opponents have turned the tables entirely on Notre Dame, earning shutouts over the Irish, but never being on the receiving end (and two of those, Indianapolis Artillery and Chicago, are not in the football business anymore). The complete list of teams with shutouts of the Irish follows.

Team	Total games	Shutouts of ND	Shutouts by ND
Army	46	8	20
Carnegie Tech	19	2	10
Chicago	4	2	0
Chi. Phys. & Surgeons	9	2	7
Georgia Tech	30	1	4
Illinois	12	1	5
Indiana	28	3	11
Indiana Artillery	1	1	0
Iowa	24	1	4
Marquette	6	2	4
Miami (Florida)	23	3	5
Michigan	23	5	0
MSU	57	4	14
Missouri	4	1	0
Navy	65	2	19
Nebraska	14	3	4
Northwestern	43	4	15
Oklahoma	8	1	2
Penn State	16	1	3
Pitt	53	5	11
Purdue	63	3	10
Rush Med.	4	1	3
USC	63	4	8
Wabash	11	1	5
Wisconsin	16	4	6
Yale	1	1	0

Other significant opponents in the shutout derby are:

Team	Total games	Shutouts of ND	Shutouts by ND
Alabama	6	0	1
Duke	3	0	3
Kansas	5	0	2
LSU	6	0	6
Minnesota	5	0	1
N. Carolina	16	0	3
Penn	6	0	1
S. Dakota	5	0	4
SMU	13	0	1
Stanford	8	0	1
Syracuse	3	0	1
Tulane	8	0	3

In sum, then, 72 percent of Notre Dame's opponents have been whitewashed by the Irish at least once, whereas only 20 percent of ND's foes have been able to do the same. A mere 4 percent have been able to do it to ND without the favor being returned while 77 percent of Notre Dame's shutout victims have not been able to hold the Irish scoreless in a game.

UPSET LOSSES

Countless Irish fans, and an even greater number of the fans of Irish opponents, have experienced the exuberance or desolation of an upset win or loss. Official Notre Dame records identify 48 such football events. Of those 48 upsets (not mild surprises, but amazing wins or losses), the Irish have been the victims 29 times, and the victors 19 times. Since Notre Dame is more likely to be a favored team on a given Saturday (save those few eras when the team was on the downslide), we should not be surprised that they have been upset more often than they upset another team.

UPSET WINNERS OVER NOTRE DAME

Army	0-12 in 1931
Carnegie Tech	0-19 in 1926, 0-7 in 1933, and 7-9 in 1937
Georgia Tech	6-13 in 1942
Great Lakes	14-19 in 1943
Indiana	7-20 in 1950
Iowa	7-10 in 1921, 6-7 in 1939, and 0-7 in 1940
Michigan State	7-13 in 1918
Mississippi	13-20 in 1977
Missouri	26-30 in 1972
Navy	0-3 in 1936
Nebraska	7-14 in 1923 and 0-17 in 1925
Northwestern	7-14 in 1935
Pitt	19-22 in 1952 and 20-34 in 1975
Purdue	14-28 in 1950, 14-27 in 1954, and 20-31 in 1974
SMU	20-27 in 1951 and 13-19 in 1956
Stanford	14-24 in 1963
USC	0-13 in 1938, 20-42 in 1955, 17-20 in 1964, 28-38 in 1970, and 14-28 in 1971

UPSET WINS BY NOTRE DAME

Alabama	13-11 in 1975
Army	35-13 in 1913, 7-2 in 1917, and 12-6 in 1928
Iowa Pre-Flight	28-0 in 1942
LSU	30-22 in 1984
Michigan	11-3 in 1909
Minnesota	7-6 in 1937
Northwestern	26-6 in 1936
Ohio State	18-13 in 1935
Oklahoma	27-21 in 1952 and 7-0 in 1957
Pitt	31-16 in 1982
Texas	14-3 in 1952
USC	27-0 in 1930, 7-2 in 1952, 16-6 in 1959, 17-0 in 1960, and 17-14 in 1963

The series with Army and USC has ironically produced identical results in terms of upsets—Army has three over the Irish and ND has three over Army; USC has five over the Irish, and ND has enjoyed five over the Trojans.

NOTRE DAME COACHES AND UPSET WINS/LOSSES

Irish coaches, always burdened by the high expectations and national rankings for the team, have shared the highs and lows of the upsets over the years. Here is the record for the coaches:

Coach	Upset Wins	Upset Losses	Percentage of W	&	L
Longman	1	0	8%		—
Harper	2	0	6%		—
Rockne	2	5	2%		41%
Anderson	0	1	—		11%
Layden	3	5	6.3%		38%
Leahy	4	6	4.5%		54%
Brennan	1	3	3.1%		16%
Kuharich	2	0	11.7%		—
Devore	1	1	11%		11%
Parseghian	1	5	1%		29%
Devine	0	2	—		12.5%
Faust	2	0	6.66%		—
Holtz	0	0	—		—

The percentage of upset losses from among all losses for Rockne, Leahy, and Parseghian clearly indicates that when they lost, it was often entirely unexpected.

WINNING STREAKS

The following list shows the longest winning streaks either by or against Notre Dame for those opponents who have won or lost more than three consecutive games.

Notre Dame streaks			Opponents' streaks		
Air Force	11	1964-81	Air Force	4	1982-85
Alabama	4	1973-80	Iowa	3	1921-40 &
Army	10	1965-85	Iowa		1956-58
Cal	4	1959-67	Miami	4	1983-87
Ga. Tech	6	1922-27 &	Michigan	8	1887-1908
Ga. Tech		1967-75	MSU	8	1955-63
Illinois	10	1938-68	Northwestern	4	1959-62
Indiana	14	1908-49	Penn State	3	1981-83 &
Iowa	5	1945-49	Penn State		1985-87
Miami	11	1967-80	Pitt	3	1932-34
Michigan	4	1987-90	Pitt		1958-60
MSU	8	1897-09	Pitt		1983-87
Navy	28	1964-91	Purdue	3	1967-69
Nebraska	3	1919-21	USC	5	1978-82
North Carolina	10	1949-59			
Northwestern	11	1965-76			
Oklahoma	5	1957-68			
Penn St.	3	1926-76			
Pitt	11	1964-74			
Purdue	8	1906-23			
Rice	4	1915-88			
South Carolina	3	1976-83			
SMU	3	1930-49			
SMU		1953-55			
Stanford	3	1964-89			
Tulane	8	1944-71			
USC	9	1983-91			
Wisconsin	4	1929-36			

Assessment of the Trends in Player Size

Generally speaking, the trend has been toward larger and, when possible, faster players. Early versions of football involved mass play, with team speed not a requirement, although some jackrabbits were necessary to break away from the melee. For the Irish, there were some remarkably large men in the early goings, such as John Eggeman at 256 pounds at the turn of the century, then Dimmick and Philbrook a decade later. Still, such specimens were surrounded by considerably smaller players, although the tendency from the middle of the 1890s until 1913 was to field increasingly larger players.

Harper began to shift away from that trend, and Rockne changed the pattern completely by fielding teams with much smaller players at four key positions: left guard, center, right guard, and right tackle. His backfields also reversed the trend toward larger players (although he did field large backs in 1929-30, in response to rules changes). The four interior line positions decreased about 10 pounds per man as Rock placed a premium on speed and mobility in the line to match that of his cat-quick backs. This was very subtle football, begun during the Harper years, in which it was not necessary to overpower an opponent, but just brush block, or interfere long enough for a defensive player to be neutralized rather than demolished. Perfection of execution was the desired end. Rockne's backs over thirteen seasons averaged a mere 165 1/3 pounds, and three of the four backfield positions are the smallest on record.

The rules regarding the backfield's shifting were changing in the 1920s and 1930s, partially as a result of the way in which Rock's approach to the game demolished a good Stanford team in the 1925 Rose Bowl. Pop Warner was the chief antagonist in the debate that led eventually to the end of the Notre Dame shift shortly after Rock's death in 1931. It was felt that the shift, which allowed the backfield and the ends to flex or shift into a new position just prior to the snap, gave the offense an unfair advantage. Rock's theory was that it could get the maximum number of players to the point of attack as fast as possible. He was also enchanted with its aesthetic merits. Within a decade after his death, however, the Notre Dame box formation also went into oblivion, to be replaced by the T formation in Leahy's second year—a move against football tradition that required the approval of the Notre Dame administration. In essence, Anderson and Layden fielded teams that were using an obsolete formation, though it was still good enough to make a run at the national crown in 1938.

Leahy was both a pragmatist and an enormously intense competitor. Although Irish teams began to grow larger again after 1931, he accelerated the trend—increasing the size of his linemen by more than 10 pounds per man and his backs by nearly five pounds per man over Layden's teams. The T also shifted the glamor spot in the backfield from the Notre Dame box's left halfback (the position of Gipp, Christie Flanagan, and Marchy Schwartz), to the T's quarterback—(Bertelli, Lujack, and Tripucka, for instance).

Backfields continued to grow larger, although in incremental ways, except for Faust's huge fullbacks, at 6-3 and 231 pounds, easily the largest set of running backs ever fielded at Notre Dame. A major shift appears early in the Parseghian years with the split end. The first split end, as such, for Notre Dame was the silky Jim Seymour, a very large target at 6-4. After his playing years, pass catchers tended to become much smaller targets, about five inches shorter than Seymour. In general, there are outside limits as to the relationship of a runner's size to his speed and quickness. The monstrous backs envisioned in the late Kuharich years—6-4, 235 pounds—never found a starting niche. Within a few years, the size of the backs reached a plateau, except for Faust's fullbacks—and Holtz's Jerome Bettis who, at 252 pounds, is the largest runner for the Irish in any era (unless you count the few times when an Eggeman was turned loose). By the early 80s, the current pattern was set: offensive linemen averaging about 6-5, 265 pounds leading the way for rather small backs, Allen Pinkett being the perfect example at 5-9, 183 pounds. Irish passers were throwing to receivers of about that same size, except for an excellent run of huge tight ends. In fact, this is a correlation to look for in a team's success—a good quarterback hooked up with an excellent tight end, as seen in the following pairs: Clements and Casper, Montana and MacAfee, Rice and Brown, and Mirer and Brown. Add to such pairs the devastating scoring possibilities of a Pinkett or an Ismail, and you can see how defensive coordinators can be driven to distraction. If you design a defense to limit the threatened damage of an Ismail, then you're probably vulnerable to either the shorter routes of a 6-6 tight end over the middle, or the inside blasts of a Bettis, as Florida found out in the 1992 Sugar Bowl. All of this adds up to tremendous offensive firepower. In fact, Parseghian's great 1966 team, which allowed only 38 points in ten games, may be the last time a Notre Dame team truly shuts down its opponents over a whole season. Modern college football rings up big scores; modern defenses are almost incapable of stopping offenses over the long haul of an eleven game season. So, you try to score as much as possible with your offense and special teams, construct long, time-consuming drives, and keep the other offense walking the sidelines. You give up three TDs and hope to score four. It's wide open football and extremely fast.

Modern Irish defense began with two-platoon football in the late 40s. Leahy was able to use defensive specialists like Jerry Groom and John Petitbon. This faded in the 50s as the NCAA tinkered with the rules, but two-platoon football returned in 1964, just in time for Parseghian's first squad to enjoy the benefits. For a while, as seen in Parseghian's teams, a defensive line was likely to be bigger than an offensive line. Changes in pass blocking rules altered that pattern forever in the late 70s so that a defensive lineman's task was less of a rush through the chest of the offensive player than a battle of quickness and leverage. When pass blocking changed from an "in-your-face" struggle to leverage and finesse, the offensive linemen became taller and heavier, and the defensive linemen became, on average, smaller and quicker. This is a timeless conflict in football—the swing of the pendulum between offensive tactics and defensive reactions. In the modern era, though, both sides of the ball are designed around speed—either getting it loose and in the open if you're on offense, or containing it or catching up to it if on defense.

As with backs, linebackers probably have an optimum size for the maximizing of speed and quickness. They seem to have settled in at about 6-2, 225, although Bob Golic and Wes Pritchett were exceptions. But linebackers have unenviable tasks—they have to be physical enough and big enough to stop the run consistently (modern defenses are designed to "feed" plays into them for finishing off), but they also have to assume certain pass coverage responsibilities, either in man-to-man or zone defenses. So, you have to find an athlete capable of taking on a Jerome Bettis at the point of attack on the line of scrimmage, but also fast enough to cover an Ismail or Tim Brown over portions of pass routes through a linebacker's territory. Of course, the nightmare is to be isolated on one of those receivers beyond one's range, either on a miscalled man-to-man, or a blown zone coverage.

Assuming that doesn't happen, a linebacker will pass off a receiver downfield after he's through his zone, and let a deep back take over. It's been said that pass defenders are fast men who can't catch the ball well; if you are both fast and can catch, then you're a receiver. In any case, the greatest consistency in physical dimensions has been in the secondary, again because there are optimum physical dimensions for the tasks required of players. You can't be 6-5, 235, and expect to cover Ismail on 50-yard long post patterns. The player needs to be about Ismail's size, perhaps a bit larger, and use angles, the sidelines, and speed to keep a receiver from breaking loose. This, of course, does not take into account the equally difficult aspect of pass defense involving the reading of fakes and run support—another unenviable job.

And so college football will continue to evolve in relationship to new rules, new or altered offensive and defensive formations and plays, and the physical attributes of the players. The Irish have fielded their first 300-pound player and their first team in which all the starters could run 4.8 40s or less (the '88 national champs). It is hard to determine the point at which growth trends will level off. We might be in the position today of Rockne in 1925 when it was not conceivable that a 265-pound player could have the speed and lateral quickness of a Chris Zorich. Improved diets and better strength and conditioning programs are allowing players to reach their physical and performance potentials sooner than before. Where we go from here over the long haul is not easily detected. We may be sure, however, that it will always be interesting, challenging, and exciting—and that Notre Dame will be among the leaders.

SERIES SCORES

[Numbers following the season and before the result indicate AP rankings for both teams coming into the game. For example, 4-10 indicates Notre Dame stood 4th and the Irish opponent 10th in the AP poll that week]. See keys to neutral sites, p. 406.

* = home game

ADRIAN
(1-0-0)

*	1912		W	74	7
		Total		74	7
		Avg. Score		74	7
		Diff.		+67	

AIR FORCE
(17-4-0)

	1964	6-	W	34	7
*	1969	8-	W	13	6
	1972	12-	W	21	7
*	1973	5-	W	48	15
*	1974	5-	W	38	0
	1975	15-	W	31	30
*	1977	6-	W	49	0
	1978	20-	W	38	15
	1979	10-	W	38	13
*	1980	2-	W	24	10
	1981		W	35	7
	1982	18-	L	17	30
*	1983		L	22	23
*	1984		L	7	21
	1985	-17	L	15	21
*	1986		W	31	3
	1987	11-	W	35	14
*	1988	2-	W	41	13
	1989	1-17	W	41	27
*	1990	1-	W	57	27
	1991	5-	W	28	15
		Total		663	304
		Avg. score		31.57	14.47
		Diff.		+17.1	

AKRON
(1-0-0)

1910		W	51	0
	Total		51	0
	Avg. score		51	0
	Diff.		+51	

ALABAMA
(5-1-0)

SB	1973	3-1	W	24	23
OB	1974	9-2	W	13	11
*	1976	18-10	W	21	18
BM	1980	6-5	W	7	0
BM	1986	-2	L	10	28
*	1987	7-10	W	37	6
		Total		112	86
		Avg. score		18.66	14.33
		Diff.		+4.33	

ALBION
(3-1-1)

*	1893		W	8	6
*	1894		T	6	6
*	1894		L	12	19
*	1896		W	24	0
	1898		W	60	0
		Total		110	31
		Avg. score		22	6.2
		Diff.		+15.8	

ALMA
(4-0-0)

*	1913		W	62	0
*	1914		W	56	0
*	1915		W	32	0
*	1916		W	46	0
		Total		196	0
		Avg. Score		49	0
		Diff.		+49	

AMERICAN MED. COL.
(5-0-0)

*	1901		W	32	0
*	1902		W	92	0
*	1903		W	52	0
*	1904		W	44	0
*	1905		W	142	0
		Total		362	0
		Avg. score		72.4	0
		Diff.		+72.4	

ARIZONA
(2-1-0)

*	1941		W	38	7
	1980	4-	W	20	3
*	1982	9-	L	13	16
		Total		71	26
		Avg. score		23.66	8.66
		Diff.		+15	

ARMY
(34-8-4)

	1913		W	35	13
	1914		L	7	20
	1915		W	7	0
	1916		L	10	30
	1917		W	7	2
	1919		W	12	9
	1920		W	27	17
	1921		W	28	0
	1922		T	0	0
EF	1923		W	13	0
PG	1924		W	13	7
YS	1925		L	0	27
YS	1926		W	7	0
YS	1927		L	0	18
YS	1928		W	12	6
YS	1929		W	7	0
SF	1930		W	7	6
YS	1931		L	0	12
YS	1932		W	21	0
YS	1933		W	13	12
YS	1934		W	12	6
YS	1935		T	6	6
YS	1936		W	20	6

YS	1937	18-	W	7	0
YS	1938	7-	W	19	7
YS	1939	4-	W	14	O
YS	1940	2-	W	7	0
YS	1941	6-14	T	0	0
YS	1942	4-19	W	13	0
YS	1943	1-3	W	26	0
YS	1944	5-1	L	0	59
YS	1945	2-1	L	0	48
YS	1946	2-1	T	0	0
*	1947	1-9	W	27	7
P	1957	12-10	W	23	21
*	1958	4-3	L	2	14
SS	1965	7-	W	17	0
*	1966	3-	W	35	0
YS	1969	15-	W	45	0
*	1970	3-	W	51	10
	1973	8-	W	62	3
*	1974	7-	W	48	0
GS	1977	11-	W	24	0
*	1980	5-	W	30	3
GS	1983		W	42	0
*	1985	-19	W	24	10
		Total		780	379
		Avg. score		16.95	8.23
		Diff.		+8.72	

BAYLOR
(1-0-0)

*	1925		W	41	0
		Total		41	0
		Avg. score		41	0
		Diff.		+41	

BELOIT
(5-0-1)

*	1896		W	8	0
*	1900		T	6	6
	1901		W	5	0
*	1906		W	29	0
*	1925		W	19	3
*	1926		W	77	0
		Total		144	9
		Avg. score		24	1.5
		Diff.		+22.5	

BENNETT MED. COL.
(1-0-0)

*	1905		W	22	0
		Total		22	0
		Avg. score		22	0
		Diff.		+22	

BOSTON COLLEGE
(3-0-0)

FX	1975	9-	W	17	3
LB	1983	-13	W	19	18
*	1987	9-	W	32	25
		Total		68	46
		Avg. Score		22.66	15.33
		Diff.		+7.33	

BUTLER
(3-0-0)

*	1911		W	27	0
	1922		W	31	3
*	1923		W	34	7
		Total		92	10
		Avg. score		30.66	3.33
		Diff.		+27.33	

CALIFORNIA
(4-0-0)

	1959		W	28	6
*	1960		W	21	7
	1965	3-	W	48	6
*	1967	1-	W	41	8
		Total		138	27
		Avg. score		34.5	6.75
		Diff.		+27.75	

CARLISLE
(1-0-0)

C	1914		W	48	6
		Total		48	6
		Avg. score		48	6
		Diff.		+42	

CARNEGIE TECH
(15-4-0)

	Year				
	1922		W	19	0
	1923		W	26	0
	1924		W	40	19
*	1925		W	26	0
	1926		L	0	19
*	1928		L	7	27
	1929		W	7	0
*	1930		W	21	6
	1931		W	19	0
*	1932		W	42	0
	1933		L	0	7
*	1934		W	13	0
	1935		W	14	3
*	1936		W	21	7
	1937		L	7	9
*	1938	5-13	W	7	0
	1939	2-	W	7	6
*	1940	6-	W	61	0
	1941	8-	W	16	0
		Total		353	103
		Avg. Score		18.57	5.42
		Diff.		+13.15	

CASE TECH
(2-0-0)

	Year				
*	1916		W	48	0
	1918		W	26	6
		Total		74	6
		Avg. score		37	3
		Diff.		+34	

CHICAGO
(0-4-0)

	Year				
	1894		L	0	8
*	1896		L	0	18
	1897		L	5	34
	1899		L	6	23
		Total		11	83
		Avg. score		2.75	20.75
		Diff.		-18	

CHICAGO DENTAL
(1-0-0)

*	1897		W	62	0
		Total		62	0
		Avg. score		62	0
		Diff.		+62	

CHICAGO PHYSICIANS & SURGEONS
(7-2-0)

*	1895		W	32	0
*	1896		L	0	4
*	1899		L	0	5
*	1900		W	5	0
*	1901		W	34	0
*	1903		W	46	0
*	1906		W	28	0
*	1907		W	32	0
*	1908		W	88	0
		Total		265	9
		Avg. score		29.44	1
		Diff.		+29.44	

CHRISTIAN BROTHERS
(ST. LOUIS)
(1-0-0)

1913		W	20	7
	Total		20	7
	Avg. score		20	7
	Diff.		+13	

CINCINNATI
(1-0-0)

*	1900		W	58	0
		Total		58	0
		Avg. Score		58	0
		Diff.		+58	

CLEMSON
(1-1-0)

	1977	5-15	W	21	17
*	1979	-14	L	10	16
		Total		31	33
		Avg. score		15.5	16.5
		Diff.		-1	

COE
(1-0-0)

*	1927		W	28	7
		Total		28	7
		Avg. score		28	7
		Diff.		+21	

COLORADO
(3-1-0)

	1983		W	27	3
*	1984		W	55	14
OB	1989	4-1	W	21	6
OB	1990	5-1	L	9	10
		Total		112	33
		Avg. score		28	8.25
		Diff.		+19.75	

CREIGHTON
(1-0-0)

	1915		W	41	0
		Total		41	0
		Avg. score		41	0
		Diff.		+41	

DARTMOUTH
(2-0-0)

FP	1944	1-	W	64	O
*	1945	3-	W	34	0
		Total		98	0
		Avg. score		49	0
		Diff.		+49	

DE LA SALLE
(1-0-0)

*	1893		W	28	0
		Total		28	0
		Avg. score		28	0
		Diff.		+28	

DE PAUW
(8-0-0)

*	1897		W	4	0
*	1898		W	32	0
*	1902		W	22	0
*	1903		W	56	0
*	1904		W	10	0
*	1905		W	71	0
*	1921		W	57	10
*	1922		W	34	7
		Total		286	17
		Avg. score		35.75	2.12
		Diff.		+33.63	

DETROIT
(2-0-0)

	1927		W	20	0
BS	1951	5-	W	40	6
		Total		60	6
		Avg. score		30	3
		Diff.		+27	

DRAKE
(8-0-0)

*	1926		W	21	0
	1927		W	32	0
*	1928		W	32	6
SF	1929		W	19	7
*	1930		W	28	7
*	1931		W	63	0
*	1932		W	62	0
*	1937		W	21	0
		Total		278	20
		Avg. score		34.75	2.5
		Diff.		+32.25	

DUKE
(2-1-0)

*	1958	12-	W	9	7
	1961		L	13	37
*	1966	1-	W	64	0
		Total		86	44
		Avg. score		28.66	14.66
		Diff.		+14	

ENGLEWOOD H.S.
(CHICAGO)
(2-0-0)

*	1899		W	29	5
*	1900		W	68	0
		Total		97	5
		Avg. score		48.5	2.5
		Diff.		+46	

FLORIDA
(1-0-0)

GB	1992	18-3	W	39	28
		Total		39	28
		Avg. score		39	28
		Diff.		+11	

FLORIDA STATE
(0-1-0)

*	1981	-20	L	13	19
		Total		13	19
		Avg. score		13	19
		Diff.		-6	

FRANKLIN
(3-0-0)

*	1906		W	26	0
*	1907		W	23	0
*	1908		W	64	0
		Total		113	0
		Avg. score		37.66	0
		Diff.		+37.66	

GEORGIA
(0-1-0)

SD	1980	7-1	L	10	17
		Total		10	17
		Avg. score		10	17
		Diff.		-7	

GEORGIA TECH
(25-4-1)

	Year	Rank	Result	ND	Opp
	1922		W	13	3
*	1923		W	35	7
*	1924		W	34	3
	1925		W	13	0
*	1926		W	12	0
*	1927		W	26	7
	1928		L	0	13
	1929		W	26	6
	1938		W	14	6
*	1939		W	17	14
*	1940		W	26	20
	1941		W	20	0
*	1942		L	6	13
*	1943		W	55	13
	1944	18-10	W	21	0
	1945		W	40	7
*	1953	1-4	W	27	14
*	1959	-19	L	10	14
	1967	9-	W	36	3
*	1968	9-	W	34	6
	1969	9-	W	38	20
*	1970	1-	W	10	7
	1974	2-	W	31	7
*	1975	12-	W	24	3
	1976	11-	L	14	23
*	1977	5-	W	69	14
	1978	10-20	W	38	21
*	1979	10-	W	21	13
	1980	1-	T	3	3
*	1981		W	35	3
		Total		748	263
		Avg. score		24.93	8.76
		Diff.		+16.17	

GOSHEN
(1-0-0)

	Year	Rank	Result	ND	Opp
*	1900		W	55	0
		Total		55	0
		Avg. score		55	0
		Diff.		+55	

GREAT LAKES
(1-2-2)

	Year	Rank	Result	ND	Opp
*	1918		T	7	7
SF	1942	6-	T	13	13

	Year		Result		
	1943	1-	L	14	19
*	1944	9-12	W	28	7
	1945	5-	L	7	39
		Total		69	85
		Avg. score		13.8	17
		Diff.		-3.2	

HARVARD PREP (CHICAGO)
(1-0-0)

	Year		Result		
*	1888		W	20	0
		Total		20	0
		Avg. Score		20	0
		Diff.		+20	

HASKELL
(5-0-0)

	Year		Result		
*	1914		W	20	7
*	1915		W	34	0
*	1916		W	26	0
*	1921		W	42	7
*	1932		W	73	0
		Total		195	14
		Avg. Score		39	2.8
		Diff.		+36.2	

HAWAII
(1-0-0)

	Year		Result		
	1991	18-	W	48	42
		Total		48	42
		Avg. score		48	42
		Diff.		+6	

HIGHLAND VIEWS
(1-0-0)

	Year		Result		
*	1896		W	82	0
		Total		82	0
		Avg. score		82	0
		Diff.		+82	

HILLSDALE
(4-0-1)

*	1892		T	10	10
*	1893		W	22	10
*	1894		W	14	0
*	1906		W	17	0
*	1908		W	39	0
		Total		102	20
		Avg. score		20.4	4
		Diff.		+15.6	

HOUSTON
(1-0-0)

CB	1978	10-9	W	35	34
		Total		35	34
		Avg. score		35	34
		Diff.		+1	

ILLINOIS
(11-0-1)

	1898		W	5	0
	1937		T	0	0
*	1938		W	14	6
	1940	2-	W	26	0
*	1941	7-	W	49	14
	1942	8-5	W	21	14
*	1943	1-	W	47	0
	1944	1-14	W	13	7
*	1945		W	7	0
	1946		W	26	6
	1967		W	47	7
*	1968	6-	W	58	8
		Total		313	62
		Avg. score		26.08	5.16
		Diff.		+20.92	

ILLINOIS CYCLING CLUB
(1-0-0)

*	1895		W	18	2
		Total		18	2
		Avg. score		18	2
		Diff.		+16	

INDIANA
(23-5-1)

	Year				
*	1898		L	5	11
*	1899		W	17	0
	1900		L	0	6
*	1901		W	18	5
	1902		W	11	5
	1905		L	5	22
I	1906		L	0	12
*	1907		T	0	0
I	1908		W	11	0
I	1919		W	16	3
I	1920		W	13	10
I	1921		W	28	7
*	1922		W	27	0
*	1926		W	26	0
	1927		W	19	6
	1929		W	14	0
*	1930		W	27	0
	1931		W	25	0
	1933		W	12	2
*	1941		W	19	6
	1948	1-	W	42	6
*	1949		W	49	6
	1950	11-	L	7	20
*	1951	14-	W	48	6
*	1955	4-	W	19	0
*	1956	17-	W	20	6
*	1957	16-	W	26	0
*	1958	5-	W	18	0
*	1991	7-	W	49	27
		Total		571	166
		Avg. score		19.68	5.72
		Diff.		+13.96	

INDIANAPOLIS ARTILLERY
(0-1-0)

	Year				
*	1895		L	0	18
		Total		0	18
		Avg. score		0	18
		Diff.		-18	

IOWA
(13-8-3)

	Year				
	1921		L	7	10
	1939	3-	L	6	7
*	1940	7-	L	0	7

*	1945	2-	W	56	0
	1946	2-17	W	41	6
*	1947	2-	W	21	0
	1948	2-	W	27	12
*	1949	1-	W	28	7
	1950		T	14	14
*	1951		T	20	20
	1952	9-	W	27	0
*	1953	1-20	T	14	14
	1954	4-19	W	34	18
*	1955	4-	W	17	14
	1956	-3	L	8	48
*	1957	9-8	L	13	21
	1958	15-6	L	21	31
	1959	-16	W	20	19
*	1960	-2	L	0	28
	1961		L	21	42
*	1962		W	35	12
*	1964	1-	W	28	0
*	1967	6-	W	56	6
	1968	5-	W	51	28
		Total		565	364
		Avg. score		23.54	15.16
		Diff.		+8.38	

IOWA PRE-FLIGHT
(2-0-0)

*	1942		W	28	0
*	1943	1-2	W	14	13
		Total		42	13
		Avg. score		21	6.5
		Diff.		+14.5	

KALAMAZOO
(7-0-0)

*	1893		W	34	0
*	1917		W	55	0
*	1919		W	14	0
*	1920		W	39	0
*	1921		W	56	0
*	1922		W	46	0
*	1923		W	74	0
		Total		318	0
		Avg. score		45.42	0
		Diff.		+45.42	

KANSAS
(3-1-1)

	Year				
	1904		L	5	24
	1932		W	24	6
*	1933		T	0	0
*	1935		W	28	7
*	1938		W	52	0
		Total		109	37
		Avg. score		21.8	7.4
		Diff.		+14.4	

KNOX
(1-1-0)

	Year				
	1902		L	5	12
*	1907		W	22	4
		Total		27	16
		Avg. score		13.5	8
		Diff.		+5.5	

LAKE FOREST
(4-0-0)

	Year				
*	1899		W	38	0
*	1901		W	16	0
*	1902		W	28	0
*	1903		W	28	0
		Total		110	0
		Avg. score		27.5	0
		Diff.		+27.5	

LOMBARD
(3-0-0)

	Year				
*	1923		W	14	0
*	1924		W	40	0
*	1925		W	69	0
		Total		123	0
		Avg. score		41	0
		Diff.		+41	

LSU
(3-3-0)

*	1970	2-7	W	3	0
	1971	7-14	L	8	28
*	1981	4-	W	27	9
	1984	-6	W	30	22
*	1985	-17	L	7	10
	1986	-8	L	19	21
		Total		94	90
		Avg. score		15.66	15
		Diff.		+.66	

LOYOLA (CHICAGO)
(1-0-0)

*	1911		W	80	0
		Total		80	0
		Avg. score		80	0
		Diff.		+80	

LOYOLA (NEW ORLEANS)
(1-0-0)

	1928		W	12	6
		Total		12	6
		Avg. score		12	6
		Diff.		+6	

MARQUETTE
(3-0-3)

	1908		W	6	0
	1909		T	0	0
	1910		T	5	5
	1911		T	0	0
C	1912		W	69	0
	1921		W	21	7
		Total		101	12
		Avg. score		21.83	2
		Diff.		+19.83	

MIAMI (FLORIDA)
(15-7-1)

	1955	5-15	W	14	0
	1960		L	21	28

	1965	6-	T	0	0
	1967	6-	W	24	22
	1971	7-	W	17	0
*	1972	10-	W	20	17
	1973	5-	W	44	0
*	1974	7-	W	38	7
	1975		W	32	9
*	1976	13-	W	40	27
	1977	5-	W	48	10
*	1978	19-	W	20	0
MB	1979		W	40	15
*	1980	7-13	W	32	14
	1981	-9	L	15	37
*	1982	10-17	W	16	14
	1983	13-	L	0	20
*	1984	17-14	L	13	31
	1985	-4	L	7	58
	1987	10-2	L	0	24
*	1988	4-1	W	31	30
	1989	1-7	L	10	27
*	1990	6-2	W	29	20
		Total		511	410
		Avg. score		22.21	17.82
		Diff.		+4.39	

MIAMI (OHIO)
(1-0-0)

*	1909		W	46	0
		Total		46	0
		Avg. score		46	0
		Diff.		+46	

MICHIGAN
(9-14-0)

*	1887		L	0	8
*	1888		L	6	26
*	1888		L	4	10
	1898		L	0	23
	1899		L	0	12
	1900		L	0	7
T	1902		L	0	23
	1908		L	6	12
	1909		W	11	3
*	1942	4-6	L	20	32
	1943	1-2	W	35	12
*	1978	14-5	L	14	28
	1979	9-6	W	12	10

*	1980	8-14	W	29	27
	1981	1-11	L	7	25
*	1982	20-10	W	23	17
	1985	13-	L	12	20
*	1986	-3	L	23	24
	1987	16-9	W	26	7
*	1988	13-9	W	19	17
	1989	1-2	W	24	19
*	1990	1-4	W	28	24
	1991	7-3	L	14	24
		Total		313	410
		Avg. score		13.6	17.82
		Diff.		-4.22	

MICHIGAN STATE
(38-18-1)

*	1897		W	34	6
*	1898		W	53	0
*	1899		W	40	0
*	1902		W	33	0
*	1903		W	12	0
*	1905		W	28	0
*	1906		W	5	0
*	1909		W	17	0
	1910		L	0	17
	1916		W	14	0
*	1917		W	23	0
	1918		L	7	13
*	1919		W	13	0
	1920		W	25	0
	1921		W	48	0
*	1948	1-	W	26	7
	1949	1-10	W	34	21
*	1950	-15	L	33	36
	1951	11-5	L	0	35
	1952	6-1	L	3	21
*	1954	8-	W	20	19
	1955	4-13	L	7	21
*	1956	-2	L	14	47
	1957	15-4	L	6	34
	1959		L	0	19
*	1960	-14	L	0	21
	1961	6-1	L	7	17
*	1962		L	7	31
	1963	-4	L	7	12
*	1964	1-	W	34	7
*	1965	4-1	L	3	12
	1966	1-2	T	10	10
*	1967		W	24	12

	1968	5-	L	17	21
*	1969	-14	W	42	28
	1970	4-	W	29	0
*	1971	4-	W	14	2
	1972	7-	W	16	0
*	1973	8-	W	14	10
	1974	7-	W	19	14
*	1975	8-	L	3	10
	1976	18-	W	24	6
*	1977	14-	W	16	6
	1978		W	29	25
*	1979	15-7	W	27	3
	1980	7-	W	26	21
*	1981		W	20	7
	1982	11-	W	11	3
*	1983	4-	L	23	28
	1984		W	24	20
*	1985		W	27	10
	1986	20-	L	15	20
*	1987	9-17	W	31	8
	1988	8-	W	20	3
*	1989	1-	W	21	13
	1990	1-24	W	20	19
*	1991	8-	W	49	10
		Total		1124	705
		Avg. score		19.71	12.36
		Diff.		+7.35	

MINNESOTA
(4-0-1)

	1925		W	19	7
	1926		W	20	7
*	1927		T	7	7
	1937	-4	W	7	6
*	1938	2-12	W	9	0
		Total		72	27
		Avg. score		14.4	5.4
		Diff.		+9	

MISSISSIPPI
(1-1-0)

J	1977	3-	L	13	20
*	1985		W	37	14
		Total		50	34
		Avg. score		25	17
		Diff.		+8	

MISSOURI
(2-2-0)

	1970	3-18	W	24	7
*	1972	8-	L	26	30
*	1978	5-	L	0	3
	1984	19-	W	16	14
		Total		66	54
		Avg. score		16.5	13.5
		Diff.		+3	

MISSOURI OSTEOPATHS
(1-0-0)

*	1903		W	28	0
		Total		28	0
		Avg. score		28	0
		Diff.		+28	

MORNINGSIDE
(2-0-0)

	1917		W	13	0
	1919		W	14	6
		Total		27	6
		Avg. score		13.5	3
		Diff.		+10.5	

MORRIS HARVEY
(1-0-0)

*	1912		W	39	0
		Total		39	0
		Avg. score		39	0
		Diff.		+39	

MOUNT UNION
(1-0-0)

*	1919		W	60	7
		Total		60	7
		Avg. score		60	7
		Diff.		+53	

NAVY
(55-9-1)

B	1927		W	19	6
SF	1928		W	7	0
B	1929		W	14	7
*	1930		W	26	2
B	1931		W	20	0
CL	1932		W	12	0
B	1933		L	0	7
CL	1934		L	6	10
B	1935		W	14	0
B	1936	13-	L	0	3
*	1937		W	9	7
B	1938	4-	W	15	0
CL	1939	2-	W	14	7
B	1940	7-	W	13	7
B	1941	7-6	W	20	13
CL	1942	4-	W	9	0
CL	1943	1-3	W	33	6
B	1944	2-6	L	13	32
CL	1945	2-3	T	6	6
B	1946	2-	W	28	0
CL	1947	1-	W	27	0
B	1948	2-	W	41	7
B	1949	1-	W	40	0
CL	1950		W	19	10
B	1951	13-	W	19	0
CL	1952	13-	W	17	6
*	1953	1-20	W	38	7
B	1954	6-15	W	6	0
*	1955	9-4	W	21	7
B	1956		L	7	33
*	1957	5-16	L	6	20
B	1958	-15	W	40	20
*	1959		W	25	22
P	1960	-4	L	7	14
*	1961		L	10	13
P	1962		W	20	12
*	1963	-4	L	14	35
P	1964	2-	W	40	0
*	1965	4-	W	29	3
P	1966	1-	W	31	7
*	1967	10-	W	43	14
P	1968	12-	W	45	14
*	1969	10-	W	47	0
P	1970	3-	W	56	7
*	1971	12-	W	21	0
P	1972	12-	W	42	23
*	1973	5-	W	44	7
P	1974	7-	W	14	6

*	1975	15-	W	31	10
CL	1976	11-	W	27	21
*	1977	5-	W	43	10
CL	1978	15-11	W	27	7
*	1979	13-	W	14	0
GS	1980	3-	W	33	0
*	1981		W	35	0
GS	1982		W	27	10
*	1983	19-	W	28	12
GS	1984		W	18	17
*	1985		W	41	17
B	1986		W	33	14
*	1987	9-	W	56	13
B	1988	2-	W	22	7
*	1989	1-	W	41	0
GS	1990	2-	W	52	31
*	1991	5-	W	38	0
		Total		1616	569
		Avg. score		24.86	8.75
		Diff.		+16.11	

NEBRASKA
(7-6-1)

	1915		L	19	20
	1916		W	20	0
	1917		L	0	7
	1918		T	0	0
	1919		W	14	9
	1920		W	16	7
*	1921		W	7	0
	1922		L	6	14
	1923		L	7	14
*	1924		W	34	6
	1925		L	0	17
*	1947	2-	W	31	0
	1948	2-	W	44	13
OB	1972	12-9	L	6	40
		Total		204	147
		Avg. score		14.57	10.5
		Diff.		+4.07	

NORTH CAROLINA
(15-1-0)

YS	1949	1-	W	42	6
*	1950	1-20	W	14	7
	1951		W	12	7
*	1952	16-	W	34	14

	1953	1-	W	34	14
*	1954	5-	W	42	13
	1955	5-	W	27	7
*	1956		W	21	14
*	1958	-11	W	34	24
*	1959		W	28	8
	1960		L	7	12
*	1962		W	21	7
*	1965	4-	W	17	0
*	1966	2-	W	32	0
*	1971	7-	W	16	0
	1975	15-	W	21	14
		Total		402	147
		Avg. score		25. 12	9.18
		Diff.		+15.94	

NORTH DIVISION H.S.
(1-0-0)

*	1905		W	44	0
		Total		44	0
		Avg. score		44	0
		Diff.		+44	

NORTHWESTERN
(34-7-2)

	1899		W	9	0
*	1899		W	12	0
	1901		L	0	2
	1903		T	0	0
	1920		W	33	7
SF	1924		W	13	6
*	1925		W	13	10
	1926		W	6	0
	1929		W	26	6
	1930		W	14	0
SF	1931		T	0	0
*	1932		W	21	0
	1933		W	7	0
	1934		W	20	7
*	1935		L	7	14
*	1936	11-1	W	26	6
	1937	12-	W	7	0
	1938	1-16	W	9	7
*	1939	9-	W	7	0
	1940	14-10	L	0	20
	1941	5-8	W	7	6
*	1942	8-	W	27	20

	1943	1-8	W	25	6
*	1944	11-	W	21	0
	1945	7-	W	34	7
*	1946	2-	W	27	0
	1947	1-	W	26	19
*	1948	2-8	W	12	7
*	1959	-2	L	24	30
	1960		L	6	7
*	1961	8-	L	10	12
	1962	-3	L	6	35
*	1965	8-	W	38	7
	1966	4-	W	35	7
*	1968	5-	W	27	7
*	1969	11-	W	35	10
	1970	6-	W	35	14
*	1971	2-	W	50	7
	1972	13-	W	37	0
*	1973	8-	W	44	0
	1974	1-	W	49	3
*	1975	7-	W	31	7
	1976		W	48	0
		Total		884	296
		Avg. score		20.55	6.88
		Diff.		+13.67	

NORTHWESTERN LAW SCHOOL
(1-0-0)

*	1895		W	20	0
		Total		20	0
		Avg. score		20	0
		Diff.		+20	

OHIO MEDICAL U.
(4-0-0)

	1901		W	6	0
	1902		W	6	5
	1903		W	35	0
	1904		W	17	5
		Total		64	10
		Avg. score		16	2.5
		Diff.		+13.5	

OHIO NORTHERN
(4-0-0)

*	1908		W	58	4
*	1910		W	47	0

*	1911		W	32	6
*	1913		W	87	0
		Total		224	10
		Avg. score		56	2.5
		Diff.		+53.5	

OHIO STATE
(2-0-0)

	1935		W	18	13
*	1936		W	7	2
		Total		25	15
		Avg. score		12.5	7.5
		Diff.		+5	

OKLAHOMA
(7-1-0)

*	1952	10-4	W	27	21
	1953	1-6	W	28	21
*	1956	-1	L	0	40
	1957	-2	W	7	0
*	1961		W	19	6
	1962		W	13	7
	1966	1-10	W	38	0
*	1968	3-5	W	45	21
		Total		177	116
		Avg. score		22.12	14.5
		Diff.		+7.62	

OLIVET
(3-0-0)

*	1907		W	22	4
	1909		W	58	0
*	1910		W	48	0
		Total		128	4
		Avg. score		42.66	1.33
		Diff.		+41.33	

OREGON
(1-0-1)

*	1976	14-	W	41	0
	1982	15-	T	13	13
		Total		54	13
		Avg. score		27	6.5
		Diff.		+20.5	

PACIFIC
(1-0-0)

*	1940		W	25	7
		Total		25	7
		Avg. score		25	7
		Diff.		+18	

PENN STATE
(7-8-1)

	1913		W	14	7
	1925		T	0	0
*	1926		W	28	0
P	1928		W	9	0
GB	1976	15-20	W	20	9
	1981	-13	L	21	24
*	1982	13-5	L	14	24
	1983		L	30	34
*	1984		W	44	7
	1985	-1	L	6	36
*	1986	-3	L	19	24
	1987	7-	L	20	21
*	1988	1-	W	21	3
	1989	1-17	W	34	23
*	1990	1-18	L	21	24
	1991	12-8	L	13	35
		Total		314	271
		Avg. score		19.62	16.93
		Diff.		+2.69	

PENNSYLVANIA
(5-0-1)

	1930		W	60	20
*	1931		W	49	0
	1952	10-12	T	7	7
	1953	1-15	W	28	20
	1954	5-	W	42	7
	1955	6-	W	46	14
		Total		232	68
		Avg. score		38.66	11.33
		Diff.		+27.33	

PITTSBURGH
(36-16-1)

	1909		W	6	0
	1911		T	0	0
	1912		W	3	0
	1930		W	35	19
*	1931		W	25	12
	1932		L	0	12
*	1933		L	0	14
	1934		L	0	19
*	1935		W	9	6
	1936	7-9	L	0	26
*	1937	12-3	L	6	21
	1943		W	41	0
	1944		W	58	0
	1945	3-	W	39	9
*	1946		W	33	0
	1947		W	40	6
	1948		W	40	0
*	1950		W	18	7
	1951		W	33	0
*	1952	8-	L	19	22
*	1953	1-15	W	23	14
	1954	8-	W	33	0
	1956	-20	L	13	26
*	1957	7-	W	13	7
	1958	14-	L	26	29
	1959		L	13	28
*	1960	-14	W	13	20
	1961		W	26	20
*	1962		W	43	22
*	1963	-8	L	7	27
	1964	1-	W	17	15
	1965	4-	W	69	13
*	1966	1-	W	40	0
	1967	9-	W	38	0
*	1968	12-	W	56	7
	1969	8-	W	49	7
*	1970	2-	W	46	14
	1971	8-	W	56	7
*	1972	7-	W	42	16
	1973	5-20	W	31	10
*	1974	5-17	W	14	10
	1975	9-	L	20	34
*	1976	11-9	L	10	31
	1977	3-7	W	19	9
*	1978	-9	W	26	17
	1982	-1	W	31	16
*	1983	18-	L	16	21
*	1986		L	9	10
	1987	4-	L	22	30

	1988	5-	W	30	20
*	1989	1-7	W	45	7
	1990	3-	W	31	22
*	1991	7-	W	42	7
		Total		1374	689
		Avg. score		25.92	13
		Diff.		+12.92	

PRINCETON
(2-0-0)

	1923		W	25	2
	1924		W	12	0
		Total		37	2
		Avg. score		18.5	1
		Diff.		+17.5	

PURDUE
(40-21-2)

*	1896		L	22	28
	1899		T	10	10
*	1901		W	12	6
	1902		T	6	6
	1904		L	0	36
	1905		L	O	32
	1906		W	2	0
*	1907		W	17	0
	1918		W	26	6
	1919		W	33	13
*	1920		W	28	0
	1921		W	33	0
	1922		W	20	0
*	1923		W	34	7
*	1933		L	0	19
*	1934		W	18	7
*	1939		W	3	0
*	1946	3-	W	49	6
	1947	1-	W	22	7
*	1948		W	28	27
	1949	2-	W	35	12
*	1950	1-	L	14	28
	1951	15-	W	30	9
	1952	-9	W	26	14
	1953	1-	W	37	7
*	1954	1-19	L	14	27
	1955	11-	W	22	7
*	1956	18-	L	14	28
	1957		W	12	0
*	1958	11-15	L	22	29

	Year				
	1959	8-	L	7	28
*	1960	12-	L	19	51
	1961		W	22	20
*	1962		L	6	24
	1963		L	6	7
*	1964	9-	W	34	15
	1965	1-6	L	21	25
*	1966	6-8	W	26	14
	1967	1-10	L	21	28
*	1968	2-1	L	22	37
	1969	9-16	L	14	28
*	1970	6-	W	48	0
	1971	2-	W	8	7
*	1972	10-	W	35	14
	1973	7-	W	20	7
*	1974	2-	L	20	31
	1975	9-	W	17	0
*	1976		W	23	0
	1977	11-	W	31	24
*	1978		W	10	6
	1979	5-17	L	22	28
*	1980	11-9	W	31	10
	1981	13-	L	14	15
*	1982	10-	W	28	14
	1983	5-	W	52	6
HD	1984	8-	L	21	23
	1985		L	17	35
*	1986		W	41	9
	1987	8-	W	44	20
*	1988	8-	W	52	7
	1989	1-	W	40	7
*	1990	1-	W	37	11
	1991	5-	W	45	20
		Total		1446	942
		Avg. score		22.95	14.95
		Diff.		+8	

RICE
(4-0-0)

	Year				
	1915		W	55	2
	1973	9-	W	28	0
*	1974	6-	W	10	3
*	1988	1-	W	54	11
		Total		147	16
		Avg. score		36.75	4
		Diff.		+32.75	

ROSE POLY
(3-0-0)

*	1909		W	60	11
	1910		W	41	3
*	1914		W	103	0
		Total		204	14
		Avg. score		68	4.66
		Diff.		+63.34	

RUSH MEDICAL
(3-0-1)

*	1894		W	18	6
*	1897		T	0	0
*	1899		W	17	0
	1900		W	5	0
		Total		40	6
		Avg. score		10	1.5
		Diff.		+8.5	

RUTGERS
(1-0-0)

PG	1921		W	48	0
		Total		48	0
		Avg. score		48	0
		Diff.		+48	

ST. BONAVENTURE
(1-0-0)

*	1911		W	34	0
		Total		34	0
		Avg. score		34	0
		Diff.		+34	

ST. LOUIS
(3-0-0)

	1912		W	47	7
*	1922		W	26	0
	1923		W	13	0
		Total		86	7
		Avg. score		28.66	2.33
		Diff.		+26.33	

ST. VIATOR
(4-0-0)

*	1897	W	60	0
*	1908	W	46	0
*	1911	W	43	0
*	1912	W	116	7
	Total		265	7
	Avg. score		66.25	1.75
	Diff.		+64.5	

ST. VINCENT'S (CHICAGO)
(1-0-0)

	1907	W	21	12
	Total		21	12
	Avg. score		21	12
	Diff.		+9	

SOUTH BEND A.C.
(1-0-1)

*	1901	T	0	0
*	1901	W	22	6
	Total		22	6
	Avg. score		13	3
	Diff.		+10	

SOUTH BEND COMMERCIAL A.C.
(1-0-0)

*	1896	W	46	0
	Total		46	0
	Avg. score		46	0
	Diff.		+46	

SOUTH BEND H.S.
(1-0-0)

*	1892	W	56	0
	Total		56	0
	Avg. score		56	0
	Diff.		+56	

SOUTH BEND HOWARD PARK
(1-0-0)

*	1900		W	64	0
		Total		64	0
		Avg. score		64	0
		Diff.		+64	

SOUTH CAROLINA
(3-1-0)

	1976	12-19	W	13	6
*	1979	14-	W	18	17
	1983		W	30	6
*	1984	-11	L	32	36
		Total		93	65
		Avg. score		23.25	16.25
		Diff.		+7	

SOUTH DAKOTA
(5-0-0)

*	1913		W	20	7
SFS	1914		W	33	0
*	1915		W	6	0
SFS	1916		W	21	0
*	1917		W	40	0
		Total		120	7
		Avg. score		24	1.75
		Diff.		+22.25	

SMU
(10-3-0)

	1930		W	20	14
*	1939		W	20	19
	1949	1-	W	27	20
*	1951	5-	L	20	27
*	1953	2-	W	40	14
	1954	4-	W	26	14
*	1955	11-	W	17	0
	1956	3-	L	13	19
	1957	10-	W	54	21
	1958	7-17	W	14	6
AS	1984	17-10	L	20	27
*	1986		W	61	29
*	1989	1-	W	59	6
		Total		391	216
		Avg. score		30.07	16.61
		Diff.		+13.46	

STANFORD
(6-2-0)

RB	1924		W	27	10
*	1942		W	27	0
	1963		L	14	24
*	1964	2-	W	28	6
*	1988	5-	W	42	14
	1989	1-	W	27	17
*	1990	1-	L	31	36
	1991	8-	W	42	26
		Total		238	133
		Avg. score		29.75	16.62
		Diff.		+13.13	

SYRACUSE
(2-1-0)

	1914		W	20	0
*	1961	-10	W	17	15
	1963		L	7	14
		Total		44	29
		Avg. score		14.66	9.66
		Diff.		+5	

TENNESSEE
(2-2-0)

*	1978	14-	W	31	14
	1979	13-	L	18	40
	1990	1-9	W	34	29
*	1991	5-13	L	34	35
		Total		117	118
		Avg. Score		29.25	29.5
		Diff.		-.25	

TEXAS
(6-2-0)

	1913		W	30	7
	1915		W	36	7
*	1934		L	6	7
	1952	19-5	W	14	3
*	1954	2-4	W	21	0
CB	1969	9-1	L	17	21
CB	1970	6-1	W	24	11
CB	1977	5-1	W	38	10
		Total		186	66
		Avg. score		23.25	8.25
		Diff.		+15	

TEXAS A & M
(0-1-0)

CB	1987	12-13	L	10	35
		Total		10	35
		Avg. score		10	35
		Diff.		-25	

TEXAS CHRISTIAN
(1-0-0)

*	1972	13-	W	21	0
		Total		21	0
		Avg. score		21	0
		Diff.		+21	

TOLEDO A.A.
(1-0-0)

*	1904		W	6	0
		Total		6	0
		Avg. score		6	0
		Diff.		6	0

TULANE
(8-0-0)

*	1944		W	26	0
	1945	5-	W	32	6
	1946	2-	W	41	0
*	1947	2-	W	59	6
*	1949	1-4	W	46	7
	1950	10-	W	13	9
	1969	12-	W	37	0
*	1971	8-	W	21	7
		Total		275	35
		Avg. score		34.37	4.37
		Diff.		+30	

UCLA
(2-0-0)

*	1963		W	27	12
*	1964	4-	W	24	0
		Total		51	12
		Avg. score		25.5	6
		Diff.		+19.5	

USC
(36-23-4)

	1926		W	13	12
SF	1927		W	7	6
	1928		L	14	27
SF	1929		W	13	12
	1930		W	27	0
*	1931		L	14	16
	1932		L	0	13
*	1933		L	0	19
	1934		W	14	0
*	1935		W	20	13
	1936	9-	T	13	13
*	1937		W	13	6
	1938	1-8	L	0	13
*	1939	7-4	L	12	20
	1940		W	10	6
*	1941	4-	W	20	18
	1942	8-14	W	13	0
*	1946	2-16	W	26	6
	1947	1-3	W	38	7
	1948	2-	T	14	14
*	1949	1-17	W	32	0
	1950		L	7	9
	1951	-20	W	19	12
*	1952	7-2	W	9	0
	1953	2-20	W	48	14
*	1954	4-17	W	23	17
	1955	5-	L	20	42
*	1956	-17	L	20	28
*	1957	12-	W	40	12
	1958	18-	W	20	13
*	1959	-7	W	16	6
	1960		W	17	0
*	1961	8-	W	30	0
	1962	-1	L	0	25
*	1963	-7	W	17	14
	1964	1-	L	17	20
*	1965	7-4	W	28	7
	1966	1-10	W	51	0
*	1967	5-1	L	7	24
	1968	9-2	T	21	21
*	1969	11-3	T	14	14
	1970	4-	L	28	38
*	1971	6-	L	14	28
	1972	10-1	L	23	45
*	1973	8-6	W	23	14
	1974	5-6	L	24	55
*	1975	14-3	L	17	24
	1976	13-3	L	13	17

*	1977	11-5	W	49	19
	1978	8-3	L	25	27
*	1979	9-4	L	23	42
	1980	2-17	L	3	20
*	1981	-5	L	7	14
	1982	-17	L	13	17
*	1983		W	27	6
	1984	-14	W	19	7
*	1985		W	37	3
	1986	-17	W	38	37
*	1987	10-	W	26	15
	1988	1-2	W	27	10
*	1989	1-9	W	28	24
	1990	7-18	W	10	6
*	1991	5	W	39	0
		Total		1,211	967
		Avg. score		19.22	15.34
		Diff.		+3.88	

VALPARAISO
(1-0-0)

*	1920		W	28	3
		Total		28	3
		Avg. score		28	3
		Diff.		+25	

VIRGINIA
(1-0-0)

GS	1989		W	36	13
		Total		36	13
		Avg. score		36	13
		Diff.		+23	

WABASH
(10-1-0)

*	1894		W	30	0
	1903		W	35	0
*	1904		W	12	4
*	1905		L	0	5
	1908		W	8	4
*	1909		W	38	0
	1911		W	6	3
*	1912		W	41	6

	Year			Score	Opp.
*	1916		W	60	0
	1918		W	67	7
*	1924		W	34	0
		Total		331	29
		Avg. score		30.09	2.63
		Diff.		+27.46	

WASHINGTON
(2-0-0)

	Year			Score	Opp.
*	1948	2-	W	46	0
	1949		W	27	7
		Total		73	7
		Avg. score		36.5	3.5
		Diff.		+33	

WASHINGTON & JEFFERSON
(1-0-0)

	Year			Score	Opp.
	1917		W	3	0
		Total		3	0
		Avg. score		3	0
		Diff.		+3	

WASHINGTON (ST. LOUIS)
(1-0-0)

	Year			Score	Opp.
*	1936		W	14	6
		Total		14	6
		Avg. score		14	6
		Diff.		+8	

WESTERN MICHIGAN
(2-0-0)

	Year			Score	Opp.
*	1919		W	53	0
*	1920		W	42	0
		Total		95	0
		Avg. score		47.5	0
		Diff.		+47.5	

WESTERN RESERVE
(1-0-0)

	Year			Score	Opp.
	1916		W	48	0
		Total		48	0
		Avg. score		48	0
		Diff.		+48	

WEST VIRGINIA
(1-0-0)

FB	1988	1-3	W	34	21
		Total		34	21
		Avg. score		34	21
		Diff.		+13	

WISCONSIN
(8-6-2)

	1900		L	0	54
M	1904		L	0	58
M	1905		L	0	21
	1917		T	0	0
*	1924		W	38	3
	1928		L	6	22
SF	1929		W	19	0
*	1934		W	19	0
	1935		W	27	0
*	1936		W	27	0
	1942		T	7	7
	1943	1-	W	50	0
*	1944	1-	W	28	13
	1962		L	8	17
*	1963	-6	L	9	14
	1964		W	31	7
		Total		269	216
		Avg. score		16.81	13.5
		Diff.		+3.31	

YALE
(0-1-0)

1914		L	0	28
	Total		0	28
	Avg. score		0	28
	Diff.		-28	

951 games (W 702-L 209-T 40)

	ND:	OPP:
Cum. scoring:	**23,791**	**9,665**
Cum. avg. score:	**25.01**	**10.16**
Cum. diff.	**+14.85**	

KEYS TO NEUTRAL SITES

		ND W-L-T
AS	Aloha Stadium (Honolulu)	1-1-0
B	Baltimore	10-2-0
BM	Birmingham	1-0-0
BS	Briggs Stadium	1-0-0
C	Chicago	4-0-0
CB	Cotton Bowl	3-3-0
CL	Cleveland	5-1-0
EB	Ebbetts Field	1-0-0
FB	Fiesta Bowl	2-0-0
FP	Fenway Park (Boston)	1-0-0
FX	Schaefer Stadium (Foxboro)	1-0-0
GB	Gator Bowl	1-0-0
GS	Giants Stadium (E. Rutherford, N.J.)	9-1-0
HD	Hoosier Dome (Indianapolis)	0-1-0
I	Indianapolis	4-1-0
J	Jackson (Mississippi)	0-1-0
LB	Liberty Bowl	1-0-0
M	Milwaukee	0-1-0
MB	Mirage Bowl (Tokyo)	1-0-0
OB	Orange Bowl	2-3-0
P	Philadelphia	6-0-0
PG	Polo Grounds	2-0-0
RB	Rose Bowl	1-0-0
SB	Sugar Bowl (Tulane)	2-1-0
SD	Sugar Bowl (Superdome, N. O.)	0-1-0
SF	Soldier Field	7-0-2
SFS	Sioux Falls	2-0-0
SS	Shea Stadium	1-0-0
T	Toledo	1-0-0
YS	Yankee Stadium	5-7-3
		65-24-5 (.718)

AWARDS OF NOTRE DAME COACHES AND PLAYERS

No school matches the Irish for Heisman winners, and few are peers regarding the other major awards for excellence. Here are the winners:

The Heisman (outstanding college football player):

1943: Angelo Bertelli
1947: John Lujack
1949: Leon Hart
1953: John Lattner*
1956: Paul Hornung
1964: John Huarte
1987: Tim Brown

* Lattner's award gave Leahy the unbeatable record of having produced no less than four Heisman winners, three of whom played together (Bertelli and Lujack in '43, Lujack and Hart in '47). Hart is the only lineman to win the Heisman. Leahy, furthermore, recruited Hornung, but did not coach him during his three varsity seasons.

The Lombardi Award (outstanding lineman):

1971: Walt Patulski
1977: Ross Browner
1990: Chris Zorich

The Outland Trophy (outstanding interior lineman):

1946: George Connor
1948: Bill Fischer
1976: Ross Browner

The Walter Camp Award (to the top individual in college football):

1977: Ken MacAfee
1987: Tim Brown
1990: Raghib Ismail

The Maxwell Award (to the top college player):

1949: Leon Hart
1952 & 1953: Johnny Lattner
1966: Jim Lynch
1977: Ross Browner

Coach of the Year:

1941: Frank Leahy (Am. Football Coaches Assoc).
1964: Ara Parsehgian (Football Writers)
1966: Ara Parseghian (Am. Football Coaches Assoc.)
1988: Lou Holtz (Football Writers)

Hall of Fame Coaches:

1951: Knute Rockne
1970: Frank Leahy
1971: Jesse Harper
1980: Ara Parseghian
1985: Dan Devine

Others:

- Thirty-one Notre Dame players in the National Football Foundation Hall of Fame (the most of any school.)
- Eight former Irish players are in the Hall as coaches.
- Thirty-three Notre Dame players have won awards as the top scholar athletes in the country since 1952 (the most chosen from any school).
- Fifteen Notre Dame players have earned NCAA post-grad scholarships since 1964.
- Thirteen Notre Dame players have earned National Football Foundation and Hall of Fame scholarships for post-graduate study (the most chosen from any school).
- Notre Dame has been honored five times for having the highest graduation rate in a year for CFA members: 1982, 1983, 1984, 1988, 1991 (120 of 138, 86.9%).
- Two hundred seventy-seven Notre Dame players have been chosen in the NFL draft from 1936-1991.

NOTRE DAME AND ADVERSE WEATHER CONDITIONS

In their 951 games, the Irish have occasionally played in less than ideal weather. Official records show 64 games played in rain, snow, or a combination of the two. Unofficial game accounts from the previous century include numerous accounts of games played in mudbath conditions, but these are not included here. Officially, though, the Irish are pretty good mudders:

Games played in rain: the Irish are 38-11-3 (.759).

Games played in snow: the Irish are 7-1-2 (.800).

Games played in rain and snow: the Irish are 2-0-0 (1.000).

NOTRE DAME WINS BEFORE CAPACITY CROWDS

In 57 percent of games listing attendance— 742 of the 951 played— the Irish have entertained capacity crowds. Here are the results in chronological order:

Coach	W-L-T	Percentage
Rockne	23-7-1	.758
Anderson	2-1-0	.666
Layden	15-6-1	.704
Leahy	52-7-6	.846
McKeever	1-2-0	.333
Brennan	21-13-0	.617
Kuharich	4-14-0	.222
Devore	3-4-1	.437
Parseghian	77-10-2	.876
Devine	41-11-0	.788
Faust	23-20-0	.534
Holtz	52-15-0	.776

Miscellaneous

Here are the results of Irish games at neutral sites, in upsets, and in adverse weather conditions, by coach:

Harper:

2-0-0 at Sioux Falls
1-0-0 in Chicago
3-0-0

2-0-0 in upsets
wins over: Army (2)

2-0-0 in rain

Rockne:

2-0-0 at the Polo Grounds
2-2-0 at Yankee Stadium
7-0-0 at Soldier Field
2-0-0 in Baltimore
1-0-0 in Anaheim (Rose Bowl)
1-0-0 at Ebbetts Field
15-2-0

3-4-0 in upsets
losses to: MSU, Nebraska (2), Carnegie Tech
wins over: Army (2), USC

8-2-0 in rain
2-0-1 in snow
1-0-0 in rain & snow

Anderson:

0-0-1 at Soldier Field
1-1-0 in Baltimore
2-1-0 at Yankee Stadium
1-0-0 in Cleveland
4-2-1

0-4-0 in upsets:
losses to: USC, Army, Pitt, Carnegie Tech

0-0-1 in rain

Layden:

5-0-0 at Yankee Stadium
3-1-0 in Baltimore
1-1-0 in Cleveland
9-2-0

3-6-0 in upsets:
losses to: Northwestern, Navy, Carnegie Tech, USC, Navy (2)
wins over: Ohio State, Northwestern, Minnesota

6-1-0 in rain

Leahy:

1-0-0 at Briggs Stadium
2-0-1 at Yankee Stadium
2-0-0 in Cleveland
0-0-1 at Soldier Field
5-0-2

3-6-0 in upsets:
losses to: Georgia Tech, Great Lakes, Purdue, Indiana, SMU, Pitt
wins over: Iowa Pre-Flight, Texas, Oklahoma

7-0-1 in rain

McKeever:

1-1-0 in Cleveland
0-1-0 at Yankee Stadium

1-0-0 in rain

Brennan:

2-1-0 in Baltimore
1-0-0 in Philadelphia

1-3-0 in upsets:
losses to: Purdue, USC, SMU
a win over: Oklahoma

3-3-0 in rain

Kuharich:

2-0-0 in upsets:
wins over: USC (2)

3-5-0 in rain

Devore:

0-2-0 at Yankee Stadium

1-1-0 in upsets
loss to: Stanford
win over: USC

Parseghian:

4-0-0 in Philadelphia
1-0-0 at Shea Stadium
1-0-0 at Yankee Stadium
1-1-0 in Dallas (Cotton Bowl)
1-0-0 in New Orleans (Sugar Bowl)
1-1-0 in Miami (Orange Bowl)
9-2-0

0-5-0 in upsets:
losses to: USC (3), Missouri, Purdue

6-3-0 in rain

Devine:

1-0-0 at Foxboro, MA
2-0-0 at Cleveland
1-0-0 at the Gator Bowl
2-0-0 in Giants Stadium
2-0-0 in Dallas (Cotton Bowl)
1-0-0 in Tokyo
0-1-0 in New Orleans (Sugar Bowl)
9-1-0

0-2-0 in upsets:
losses to Pitt, Missouri

3-0-0 in rain

Faust:

3-0-0 at Giants Stadium
1-0-0 in Memphis (Liberty Bowl)
0-1-0 in Indianapolis (Hoosier Dome)
0-1-0 in Honolulu (Aloha Bowl)
4-2-0

2-0-0 in upsets:
wins over: Pitt, LSU

2-2-0 in rain

Holtz:

2-0-0 in Baltimore
0-1-0 in Dallas (Cotton Bowl)
1-0-0 in Tempe (Fiesta Bowl)
2-0-0 at Giants Stadium
1-1-0 in Miami (Orange Bowl)
1-0-0 in Honolulu
1-0-0 in New Orleans (Sugar Bowl)
8-2-0

upset:

loss to: Tennessee

0-1-0 in rain

Chapter 9

Fighting Irish Records

Notre Dame Individual Records

Rushing

Rushing Attempts

Game:	40	Allen Pinkett (162 yards) vs. LSU, 1984; Phil Carter (254 yards) vs. Michigan State, 1980
	39	Vagas Ferguson (177 yards) vs. Georgia Tech, 1979
	38	Jim Stone (224 yards) vs. Miami, 1980
Season:	301	Vagas Ferguson (1437 yards), 1979; also holds per-game record at 27.4 (301 in 11)
	275	Allen Pinkett (1105 yards), 1984
	255	Allen Pinkett (1100 yards), 1984
	252	Allen Pinkett (1394 yards), 1983
Career:	889	Allen Pinkett (4131 yards), 1982-85; also holds per-game record at 20.6 (889 in 43)
	673	Vagas Ferguson (3472 yards), 1976-79
	590	Jerome Heavens (2682 yards), 1975-78
	557	Phil Carter (2409 yards), 1979-82

Consecutive Rushing Attempts by Same Player

Game:	8	Mark Green vs. Boston College, 1987; Phil Carter vs. Air Force, 1980; Larry Conjar vs. Army, 1965; Neil Worden vs. Oklahoma, 1952

Rushing Yards

Game:	255	Vagas Ferguson (30 attempts) vs. Georgia Tech, 1978
Season:	1437	Vagas Ferguson (301 attempts), 1979
Career:	4131	Allen Pinkett (889 attempts), 1982-85

Rushing Yards Per Game

Season:	130.6	Vagas Ferguson (1437 in 11), 1979
	126.7	Allen Pinkett (1394 in 11), 1983
	117.4	Phil Carter (892 in 7), 1980
Career:	96.1	Allen Pinkett (4131 in 43), 1982-85
	86.7	George Gipp (2341 in 27), 1917-20
	84.7	Vagas Ferguson (3474 in 41), 1976-79

Games Rushing for 100 Yards or More

Season:	9	Allen Pinkett, 1983
	7	Vagas Ferguson, 1979
	6	Allen Pinkett, 1985
Career:	21	Allen Pinkett, 1982-85
	13	Vagas Ferguson, 1976-79
	10	Jerome Heavens, 1975-78; George Gipp, 1917-20

Consecutive Games Rushing for 100 Yards or More

Season:	5	Allen Pinkett, 1983 (Colorado, South Carolina, Army, USC, Navy)

Games Rushing for 200 Yards or More

Season:	2	Jim Stone, 1980 (Miami and Navy); Vagas Ferguson, 1978 (Navy and Georgia Tech)

Rushing Yards by a Freshman

Game:	148	Jerome Heavens (18 attempts) vs. Georgia Tech, 1975
Season:	756	Jerome Heavens (129 attempts), 1975

Rushing Yards by a Quarterback

Game:	146	Bill Etter (11 attempts) vs. Navy 1969
Season:	884	Tony Rice (174 attempts), 1989
Career:	1921	Tony Rice (394 attempts), 1987-89; holds career per-game record at 58.2 (1921 in 33), 1987-89

Rushing Yards Per Attempt

Game:	(min. 10 attempts)	17.1	John Petibon (10 for 171) vs. MSU, 1950
Game:	(min. 5 attempts)	24.4	Coy McGee (6 for 146) vs. USC, 1946
Season:	(min. 100 attempts)	8.1	George Gipp (102 for 827), 1920
		7.5	Marchy Schwarz (124 for 927), 1930
Career:	(min. 150 attempts)	6.8	Don Miller (283 for 1933), 1922-1924
		6.4	Christy Flanagan (285 for 1822), 1926-28

Rushing Touchdowns

Game:	7	Art Smith vs. Loyola (Chi.), 1911
	6	Bill Downs vs. De Pauw, 1905
Season:	17	Allen Pinkett, 1984; Vagas Ferguson, 1979
	16	Jerome Bettis, 1991; Allen Pinkett, 1983; Bill Downs, 1905; Ray Eichenlaub holds season per-game record at 1.7 (12 in 7), 1913
Career:	49	Allen Pinkett, 1982-85
	36	Louis (Red) Salmon, 1900-03
	32	Anthony Johnson, 1986-89; Vagas Ferguson, 1976-79
	30	Stan Cofall, 1914-16; also holds career per-game record at 1.2 (30 in 25)

PASSING

Pass Attempts

Game:	63	Terry Hanratty (completed 29) vs. Purdue, 1967
	58	Joe Theismann (completed 33) vs. USC, 1970
Season:	268	Joe Theismann (completed 155), 1970
	260	Joe Montana (completed 141), 1978
	259	Steve Beuerlein (completed 151) 1986
	234	Rick Mirer (completed 132) 1991
	232	Steve Beuerlein (completed 140), 1984
	219	Blair Kiel (completed 118), 1982
Career:	850	Steve Beuerlein (completed 473), 1983-86
	609	Blair Keil (completed 297), 1980-83
	550	Terry Hanratty (completed 304), 1966-68
	515	Joe Montana (completed 268), 1975, 77-78
	509	Joe Theismann (completed 290), 1968-70

Pass Attempts Per Game

Season:	28.1	Terry Hanratty (197 in 7), 1968
Career:	21.2	Terry Hanratty (550 in 26), 1966-68

Pass Completions Per Game

Season:	16.6	Terry Hanratty (116 in 7), 1968
Career:	11.7	Terry Haratty (304 in 26), 1966-68

Consecutive Pass Completions

Game:	10	Joe Montana vs. Georgia Tech, 1978; Angelo Bertelli vs. Stanford, 1942
	9	Steve Beuerlein vs. Colorado, 1984; Blair Kiel vs. Navy, 1982
Season:	10	Tony Rice vs. Purdue (4), Stanford (6), 1988; Terry Andrysiak vs. Purdue (2), USC (30), Navy (5), 1985; Steve Beuerlein vs. Michigan State (1), Colorado (9), 1984; Joe Montana vs. Georgia Tech, 1978; Angelo Bertelli vs. Stanford, 1942

Consecutive Games Completing a Pass

Career:	34	Ralph Guglielmi (last four games of 1951, all 10 of 1952, 1953, 1954)

Completion Percentage

Game: (min. 10 completions)	.909	Steve Beuerlein (10 of 11) vs. Colorado, 1984
	.857	Rick Mirer (12 of 14) vs. Purdue, 1991; Rick Slager (12 for 14) vs. Northwestern, 1976
	.813	Bob Williams (13 of 16) vs. Michigan State, 1949
Season: (min. 100 attempts)	.603	Steve Beuerlein (140 of 232), 1984
	.589	Terry Hanratty (116 of 197), 1968
	.583	Steve Beuerlein (151 of 289), 1986
Career: (min. 150 attempts)	.570	Joe Theismann (290 of 509), 1967-68
	.556	Steve Beuerlein (473 of 850), 1983-86
	.553	Rick Mirer (257 of 464), 1989-91

Passes Had Intercepted

Game:	7	Frank Dancewicz vs. Army, 1944
Season:	18	Steve Beuerlein 1984; John Niemiec, 1928; also holds season per-game record at 1.8 (16 in 9)
Career:	44	Steve Beuerlein 1983-86; Terry Hanratty holds career per-game record at 1.3 (34 in 26), 1966-68

Lowest Interception Percentage

Season: (min. 100 attempts)	.0216	Rick Slager (3 of 139), 1975
	.0270	Steve Beuerlein (7 of 259), 1986
	.0300	Rick Mirer (6 of 200), 1990
	.0346	Joe Montana (9 of 260), 1978
Career: (min. 150 attempts)	.0366	Rick Mirer (17 of 464),1989-91
	.0431,	John Huarte (11 of 255), 1962-64
	.0485,	Joe Montana (25 of 515), 1975, 77-78
	.0518,	Steve Beuerlein (44 of 850), 1983-86

Pass Attempts Without Interception

Game:	39	Steve Beuerlein vs. Penn State, 1986

Consecutive Pass Attempts Without Interception

Career:	119	Steve Beuerlien, fifth game through 10th game of 1986

Passing yards

Game:	536	Joe Theismann (933 of 58) vs. USC, 1970
	366	Terry Hanratty (26 of 63) vs. Purdue, 1967
Season	2429	Joe Theismann (155 of 268), 1970
	2211	Steve Beuerlein (151 of 259), 1986
	2117	Rick Mirer (132 of 234),1991
	2062	John Huarte (114 of 205), 1964
Career:	6527	Steve Beuerlein (473 of 850), 1983-86
	4411	Joe Theismann (290 of 509), 1968-70
	4152	Terry Hanratty (304 of 550), 1966-68
	4121	Rick Mirer (257 of 464), 1989-91; Joe Montana (268 of 515), (1975, 1977-78)

Passing Yards Per Game

Season:	242.9	Joe Theismann (2429 in 10), 1970
	209.4	Terry Hanratty (1466 in 7), 1968
Career:	159.7	Terry Hanratty (4152 in 26), 1966-68
	155.4	Steve Beuerlein (6527 in 42), 1983-86
	152.6	Joe Montana (4121 in 27), 77-78
	152.1	Joe Theismann (4411 in 29), 1968-70

Passing Yards Per Attempt

Game:	(min. 20 attempts)	13.1	Rick Mirer (23 for 303) vs. Navy, 1991
		12.8	George Izo (26 for 332) vs. Pittsburgh, 1958
Season:	(min. 100 attempts)	10.1	John Huarte (205 for 2062), 1964
		9.4	Joe Theismann (268 for 2529), 1970
		9.2	John Huarte (255 for 2343), 1962-63
		9.04	Rick Mirer (234 for 2117) 1991
Career:		8.88	Rick Mirer (464 for 4121), 1989-91
		8.67	Joe Theismann (509 for 4411), 1968-70

Passing Yards Per Completion

Game:	(min. 10 completions)	27.4	John Huarte (10 for 274) vs. Navy, 1964
Season:	(min. 50 completions)	18.1	John Huarte (114 for 2062), 1964
		17.8	George Izo (60 for 1067), 1985
Career:	(min. 75 completions)	17.3	George Izo (121 for 2095), 1957-59
		17.0	John Huarte (138 for 2343), 1962-64

Touchdown Passes

Game:	4	Steve Beuerlein vs. USC, 1986; Daryle Lamonica vs. Pittsburgh, 1962; Angelo Bertelli vs. Stanford, 1942
Season:	16	Joe Theismann, 1970; John Juarte, 1964; Bob Williams, 1949
Career:	31	Joe Theismann, 1968-70
	28	Angelo Bertelli, 1941-43
	27	Steve Beuerlein, 1983-86; Terry Hanratty, 1966-68

Touchdown Passes Per Game

Season:	1.7	Angelo Bertelli (10 in 6), 1943
Career:	1.08	Angelo Bertelli (28 in 26), 1941-43
	1.07	Joe Theismann (31 in 29), 1968-70

Receiving

Pass Receptions

Game:	13	Jim Seymour (276 yards) vs. Purdue, 1966
	12	Tom Gatewood (192 yards) vs. Purdue, 1970
Season:	77	Tom Gatewood (1123 yards), 1970
Career:	157	Tom Gatewood (2283 yards), 1969-71

Pass Receptions Per Game

Season:	7.7	Tom Gatewood (77 in 10), 1970
	6.9	Jim Seymour (48 in 7), 1966
Career:	5.3	Jim Seymour (138 in 26), 1966-68
	5.2	Tom Gatewood (157 in 30), 1969-71

Pass Receptions by a Tight End

Season:	54	Ken MacAfee (797 yards), 1977
Career:	128	Ken MacAfee (1759 yards), 1974-77
	120	Tony Hunter (1897 yards), 1979-82

Pass Reception Yards

Game:	276	Jim Seymour (13 receptions) vs. Purdue, 1966
	217	Jack Snow (9 receptions) vs. Wisconsin, 1964
Season:	1123	Tom Gatewood (77 receptions), 1970
	1114	Jack Snow (60 receptions), 1970
Career:	2493	Tim Brown (137 receptions), 1984-87
	2283	Tom Gatewood (157 receptions), 1969-71
	2113	Jim Seymour (138 receptions), 1966-68

Pass Reception Yards Per Game

Season:	123.1	Jim Seymour (862 in 7), 1966
	112.3	Tom Gatewood (1123 in 10), 1970
Career:	81.3	Jim Seymour (2113 in 26), 1966-68
	76.1	Tom Gatewood (2283 in 30), 1969-71

Pass Reception Yards Per Catch

Game: (min. 5)	41.6	Jim Morse (5 for 208, national record) vs. USC, 1955
	26.3	Tim Brown (7 for 184) vs. Navy, 1986
	26.2	Tony Hunter (5 for 131) vs. USC , 1979
	26.0	Tim Brown (6 for 156) vs. Pittsburgh, 1987
Season: (min. 20)	25.6	Tony Hunter (27 for 690)
	22.1	Jim Morse (20 for 442), 1956
	21.84	Raghib Ismail (32 for 699), 1990
	21.75	Dan Kelleher (24 for 522), 1976
	21.69	Tim Brown (39 for 846), 1987
	20.2	Tim Brown (45 for 910), 1986
Career: (min. 35)	22.0	Raghib Ismail (71 for 1565), 1988-90
	21.5	Kris Haines (63 for 1353), 1975-78
	21.2	Jim Morse (52 for 1102), 1954-56
	19.6	Joe Howard (85 for 1663), 1981-84
	18.2	Tim Brown (137 for 2493), 1984-87

Touchdown Receptions

Game:	3	Tom Gatewood vs. Purdue, 1970; Jim Seymour vs.Purdue, 1966; Jim Kelly vs. Pittsburgh, 1962; Jim Mutscheller vs. Michigan State, 1950; Bill Barrett vs. North Carolina, 1949; Eddie Anderson vs. Northwestern, 1920
Season:	9	Jack Snow, 1964
	8	Jim Seymour, 1966; also holds season per-game record at 1.1 (8 in 7)
Career:	19	Tom Gatewood, 1969-71; also holds career per-game record at 0.6 (19 in 30)
	16	Jim Seymour, 1966-68
	15	Ken MacAfee, 1974-77

Total Offense

Total Offensive Attempts

Game:	75	Terry Hanratty (420 yards) vs. Purdue, 1967
	71	Joe Theismann (512 yards) vs. USC, 1970
Season:	391	Joe Theismann (2813 yards), 1970; also holds season per-game record at 39.1 (391 in 10)
	332	Joe Montanna (2114 yards), 1978
	312	Steve Beuerlein (2246 yards), 1986
	311	Tony Rice (2006 yards), 1989
	310	Tom Clements (1918 yards), 1974
	309	Rick Mirer (2423 yards), 1991
Career:	1027	Steve Beuerlein (6459 yards), 1983-86
	892	Allen Pinkett (4220 yards), 1982-85
	807	Joe Theismann (5432 yards), 1968-70
	774	Blair Kiel (3,814 yards), 1980-83
	760	Tom Clements (4664 yards), 1972-74
	741	Tony Rice (4882 yards), 1987-89
	731	Terry Hanratty (4738 yards), 1966-68; also holds career per-game record at 28.1 (731 in 26)

Total Offense Yards

Game:	512	Joe Theismann (71 attempts) vs. USC, 1970
	420	Terry Hanratty (75 attempts)vs. Purdue, 1967
Season:	2813	Joe Theismann (391 attempts) 1970
Career:	6459	Steve Beuerlein (1027 attempts), 1983-86

Total Offense Yards Per Game

Season:	281.3	Joe Theismann (2813 in 19), 1970
	249.3	Terry Hanratty (1745 in 7), 1968
Career:	187.3	Joe Theismann (5432 in 29), 1968-70
	182.2	Terry Hanratty (4738 in 26), 1966-68

Games Gaining 200 Yards Total Offense or More

Game:	(min. 20 attempts)	13.7	John Huarte (20 for 273) vs. Navy, 1964
Season:	(min. 1000 yards)	19.37	George Gipp (164 for 1536), 1920
		8.55	John Huarte (242 for 2069), 1964
Career:	(min. 2000 yards)	7.46	John Huarte (306 for 2283), 1962-64
		7.39	George Gipp (556 for 4110), 1917-20

Points Responsible For (scored and passed for)

Game:	35	Art Smith (7 TDs, 5 points each) vs. Loyola (Chi.), 1911
Season	126	John Mohardt (scored 12 TDs, passed for 9), 1921
	124	Joe Theismann (scored 26 points, passed for 98), 970
Career:	326	Allen Pinkett (scored 320 points, passed for one TD, 1982-85
	280	Joe Theismann (scored 92 points, passed for 31 TDs and one two-point conversion), 1968-70
	264	Terry Hanratty (scored 92 points, passed for 27 TDs and two two-point conversions), 1966-68

Points Responsible For Per Game

Season:	12.4	Joe Theismann (124 in 10), 1970
	11.8	John Huarte (118 in 10), 1964
Career:	10.2	Terry Hanratty (264 in 26), 1966-68
	9.7	Joe Theismann 9280 in 29), 1968-70

Scoring

Points

Game:	35	Art Smith (7 TDs, 5 points each) vs. Loyola (Chi), 1911
	30	Bill Wolski (5 TDs) vs. Pittsburgh, 1965; Willie Maher (5 TDs) vs. Kalamazoo, 1923; Bill Downs (6 TDs, 5 points each) vs. De Pauw, 1905
Season:	110	Allen Pinkett (18 TDs 1 two-point PAT), 1983
Career:	320	Allen Pinkett (53 TDs, 1 two-point PAT), 1982- 85

Points Per Game

Season:	11.7	Louis (Red) Salmon (105 in 9), 1903
	11.1	Alvin Berger (78 in 7), 1912
Career:	10.3	Stan Cofall (246 in 24), 1914-16
	7.4	Allen Pinkett (320 in 43), 1982-85
	7.1	Gus Dorais (198 in 28), 1910-13

Touchdowns

Game:	7	Art Smith vs. Loyola (Chi.), 1911
	6	Bill Downs vs. De Pauw, 1905
Season:	20	Jerome Bettis, 1991
	18	Allen Pinkett, 1983 and 1984
	17	Vagas Ferguson, 1979
	16	Bill Downs, 1905; also holds season per-game record at 1.8 (16 in 9)
Career:	53	Allen Pinkett, 1982-85; Stan Cofall holds career per-game record at 1.25 (30 in 24), 1914-16
	36	Louis (Red) Salmon, 1900-03
	35	Vagas Ferguson, 1976-79
	34	Anthony Johnson, 1986-89

Field Goals

Field Goals

Game:	5	Craig Hentrich (6 attempts) vs. Miami 1990
Season:	21	John Carney (28 attempts), 1986
Career:	51	John Carney (69 attempts), 1984-86

Field Goal Attempts

Game:	7	Gus Dorais (made 3) vs. Texas, 1913
Season:	28	John Carney (made 21), 1986
Career:	69	John Carney (made 51), 1984-86

Field Goal Percentage

Season:	(min. 10 attempts)	.895	John Carney (17 of 19), 1984
Career:	(min. 15 attempts)	.739	John Carney (51 of 69), 1984-86
		.720	Mike Johnston (31 of 43), 1982-83

Consecutive Field Goals

Season:	13	Mike Johnston, 1982
Career:	13	Mike Johnston, 1982

First Notre Dame Field Goal

Mike Daly vs. Chicago, 1897 (35 yards)

Extra Points

Extra Points (PATs)

Game:	9	by four players; last time Ken Ivan (10 attempts) vs. Pittsburgh, 1965
Season:	48	Craig Hentrich (48 attempts), 1991
	45	Scott Hempel (50 attempts), 1968; also holds season per-game record at 4.5 (45 in 10)
	44	Craig Hentrich (45 attempts), 1989
	43	Bob Thomas (45 attempts), 1973
	41	Craig Hentrich (41 attempts), 1990
Career:	133	Craig Hentrich (134 attempts), 1989-91
	130	Dave Reeve (143 attempts), 1968-70; also holds career per-game record at 4.4 (122 in 28)
	98	Bob Thomas (101 attempts), 1971-73

Extra Points Attempted

Game:	12	Frank Winters (made 9) vs. Englewood H.S., 1900
	10	Ken Ivan (made 9) vs. Pittsburgh, 1965
Season:	52	Steve Oracko (made 38), 1949
	50	Scott Hempel (made 45), 1968
Career:	143	Dave Reeve (made 130), 1974-77
	134	Craig Hentrich (made 133), 1989-91
	132	Scott Hempel (made 122), 1968-70
	105	Gus Dorais (made 96), 1910-13

Extra Point Percentage

Season:	(min. 20 made) 1.000	Craig Hentrich (48 of 48), 1991; Craig Hentrich (41 of 41), 1990; Ted Gradel (33 of 33), 1987; John Carney (25 of 25), 1984; Bob Thomas (34 of 34), 1972
Career:	(min. 50 made) .992	Craig Hentrich (133 of 134), 1989-91

Consecutive Extra Points

Career:	73	Craig Hentrich (from 9-30-89 vs. Purdue to 1-1-91 vs. Colorado, first attempt vs. Colorado blocked)

Points by Kicking (PATs and FGs)

Season:	89	Craig Hentrich (16 FGs, 25 PATs), 1990; also holds season per-game record at 8.1
Career:	247	Dave Reeve (130 PATs, 39 FGs), 1974-77

Two-Point Conversions

Season:	2	Bob Minnix, 1971; Bill Wolski, 1965

Two-Point Conversions by Pass

Season:	2	Steve Beuerlein (attempted 5), 1986; John Huarte (attempted 9), 1964

Two-Point Conversions Attempts

Game:	3	Joe Theismann vs. Pittsburgh, 1970; Terry Hanratty vs. Pittsburgh, 1966; John Huarte vs. Wisconsin and Michigan State, 1964
Season:	9	John Huarte, 1964
Career:	10	John Huarte, 1962-64

Interceptions

Interceptions

Game:	3	by 12 players; last time by Dave Duerson vs. Navy, 1982
Season:	10	Mike Townsend (39 yards), 1972
Career:	17	Luther Bradley (218 yards), 1973, 75-77

Interceptions by a Linebacker

Season:	5	John Pergine (72 yards), 1966
Career:	9	John Pergine (91 yards), 1965-67

Interception Yards

Game:	103	Luther Bradley (2 returns) vs. Purdue, 1975
Season:	197	Nick Rassas (6 returns), 1965; also holds season per-game record at 19.7 (197 in 10)
Career:	256	Dave Duerson (12 returns), 1979-82

Interception Yards Per Return

Game:	(min. 2)	51.5	Luther Bradley (2 for 103) vs. Purdue, 1975
Season:	(min. 4)	33.8	Luther Bradley (4 for 135), 1975
Career:	(min. 6)	31.4	Nick Rassas (7 for 220),1963-65

Interception Returns for Touchdowns

Game:	2	Dave Waymer vs. Miami, 1979
Season:	2	Dave Waymer, 1979; Bobby Leopold, 1977; Randy Harrison, 1974; Tom Schoen, 1966
Career:	3	Bobby Leopold, 1976-78; Tom Schoen, 1965-67

Punt Returns

Punt Returns

Game:	9	Tom Schoen (167 yards) vs. Pittsburgh, 1967
Season:	42	Tom Schoen (447 yards), 1967
Career:	103	Dave Duerson (869 yards), 1979-82

Punt Return Yards

Game:	167	Tom Schoen (9 returns) vs. Pittsburgh, 1967
Season:	459	Nick Rassas (24 returns), 1965
Career:	947	Frank Carideo (92 returns), 1928-30; also holds career per-game record at 33.8 (947 in 28)

Punt Return Yards Per Attempt

Game:	(min. 3)	52.3	Chet Grant (3 for 157) vs. Case Tech, 1916
Game:	(min 5)	22.0	Frank Carideo (5 for 110)vs. Georgia Tech, 1929
Game:	(min. 1.5 per game)	19.1	Nick Rassas (24 for 459), 1965
Career:	(min. 1.5 per game)	15.7	Nick Rassas (39 for 612), 1963-65

Kickoff Returns

Kickoff Returns

Game:	253	Paul Castner (4 returns) vs. Kalamazoo, 1922
Season:	25	Tim Brown (698 yards), 1986
	23	Tim Brown (456 yards), 1987
	20	Raghib Ismail (502 yards), 1989
Career:	69	Tim Brown (1613 yards), 1984-87

Kickoff Return Yards

Game:	253	Paul Castner (4 returns) vs. Kalamazoo, 1922
Season:	698	Tim Brown (25 returns), 1986
	502	Raghib Ismail (20 returns), 1989
	496	Paul Hornung (16 returns), 1956; Paul Castner holds season per-game record at 70.0 (490 in 7), 1922
Career:	1613	Tim Brown (69 returns), 1984-87; also holds career per-game record at 37.5 (1613 in 43)
	1271	Raghib Ismail (46 returns), 1988-90

Kickoff Return Yards Per Attempt

Game:	(min. 2)	85.0	Raghib Ismail (2 for 170) vs. Rice, 1988
Season:	(min. 0.5 per game)	44.5	Paul Castner (11 for 490), 1922
Career:	(min. 0.5 per game)	36.5	Paul Castner (21 for 767), 1920-22

Kickoff Returns for Touchdowns

Game:	2	Raghib Ismail vs. Michigan, 1989; vs. Rice, 1988; Paul Castner vs. Kalamazoo, 1922
Season:	2	Raghib Ismail, 1988, 1989; Tim Brown, 1986; Nick Eddy, 1966; Johnny Lattner, 1953; Willie Maher, 1923; Paul Castner, 1922
Career:	5	Raghib Ismail, 1988-90

Total Kick Returns

(Combined punt and kickoff returns)

Game:	10	George Gipp (2 PR, 8 KR, 207 yards) vs. Army, 1920;
Season:	57	Tim Brown (34 PR, 23 KR, 857 yards)
Career:	105	Tim Brown (36 PR, 69 KR, 2089 yards), 1984-87

Kick Return Yards

Game:	254	Willie Maher (80 PR, 174 KR) vs. Kalamazoo, 1923
Season:	857	Tim Brown (401 PR, 456 KR), 1987;
Career:	2089	Tim Brown (476 PR, 1613 IR), 1984-87; also holds per-game record at 48.6 (2089 in 43)

Kick Return Yards Per Attempt

Game:	(min. 5)	30.6	Tim Brown (5 for 153) vs. USC, 1986
Season:	(min. 1.5 per game)	29.5	Raghib Ismail (17 for 505), 1988
Career:	(min. 1.5 per game)	22.6	Raghib Ismail (71 for 1607), 1988-90

Kick Returns for Touchdowns

Game:	2	Raghib Ismail (KR) vs. Rice, 1988; vs. Michigan, 1989; Tim Brown (PR) vs. Michigan State, 1987; Vince McNally (PR) vs. Beloit, 1926; Paul Castner (KR) vs. Kalamazoo, 1922
Season:	3	Raghib Ismail (1 PR, 2 KR), 1989; Tim Brown (PR), 1987; Nick Rassas (PR), 1965
Career:	6	Tim Brown (3 PR, 3 KR), 1984-87; Raghib Ismail (5 KR, 1 PR), 1988-90
	3	Nick Rassas (PR), 1965

All-Purpose Running

(Yardage from rushing, receiving, and all returns)

All-Purpose Yards

Game:	361	Willie Maher (107 rushing, 80 PR, 174 KR) vs. Kalamazoo, 1923
Season:	1937	Tim Brown (254 rushing, 910 receiving, 75 PR, 698 KR), 1986; also holds season per game record at 176.1 (1937 in 110
Career:	5259	Allen Pinkett (4131 rushing, 774 receiving, 354 KO returns), 1982-85; also holds career per-game record at 122.3 (5259 in 43)

Total Yardage

(Yardage from rushing, passing, receiving, and all returns)

Total Yardage

Game:	519	Joe Theismann (526 passing, 7 receiving, minus 14 rushing) vs. USC, 1970
Season:	2820	Joe Theismann (2429 passing, 384 rushing, 7 receiving) 1970
Career:	6459	Steve Beuerlein (6527 passing, 168 rushing), 1983-86

Punting

Punts

Game:	15	Marchy Schwartz (509 yards) vs. Army, 1931
Season:	77	Blair Kiel (3267 yards), 1982
Career:	259	Blair Kiel (10534 yards), 1980-83

Punts Per Game

Season:	7.4	Fred Evans (67 in 9), 1941
Career:	5.5	Fred Evans (105 in 19), 1940-42

Punting Average

Game:	(min. 5)	51.6	Joe Restic (5 for 258) vs. Air Force, 1975
Game:	(min. 10)	44.8	Paul Castner (12 for 537) vs. Purdue, 1921
Season:	(min. 25)	44.9	Craig Hentrich (34 for 1526), 1990
Career:	(min. 50)	44.22	Craig Hentrich (83 for 3671), 1989-91

Defense

Tackles by a Linebacker (since 1956)

Game:	26	Bob Crable vs. Clemson, Bob Golic vs. Michigan, 1978; 1979
Season:	187	Bob Crable, 1979
Career:	521	Bob Crable, 1978-81

Tackles by a Front Four Lineman (since 1956)

Season:	113	Steve Niehaus, 1975
Career:	340	Ross Browner, 1973, 75-77

Tackles for Minus Yardage (since 1967)

Season:	28	Ross Browner (203 yards), 1976
Career:	77	Ross Browner (515 yards), 1973, 75-77

Passes Broken Up (since 1956)

Season:	13	Clarence Ellis, 1969
Career:	32	Clarence Ellis, 1969-71

Fumbles Recovered (since 1952)

Season:	7	Cedric Figaro, 1986
Career:	12	Ross Browner, 1973, 75-77

TEAM RECORDS

Single Game Offense

Rushing

Rushing Attempts - 91 vs. Navy (597 yards), 1969
Fewest Rushing Attempts - 22 vs. Miami (53 yards), 1981
Rushing Yards - 629 vs. Drake, 1931; MR: 597 vs. Navy, 1969
Fewest Rushing Yards - Minus 12 vs. Michigan State (31 attempts), 1965
Rushing Touchdowns - 27 vs. American Medical, 1905; MR: 10 vs. Dartmouth, 1944

Passing

Pass Attempts - 63 vs. Purdue (completed 29), 1967
Fewest Pass Attempts - 0, many times; MR: 1 vs. Iowa, 1945
Pass Completions - 33 vs. USC (attempted 58), 1970
Fewest Pass Completions - 0, many times; MR: 0 vs. Iowa, 1945
Completion Percentage (min. 20 attempts) - .818 vs. Iowa (18 of 22), 1967
Passing Yards - 526 vs. USC (33 of 58), 1970
Fewest Passing Yards - Minus 7 vs. Iowa, 1948
Passes Had Intercepted - 8 vs. Army, 1944
Touchdown Passes - 5 vs. Pittsburgh, 1944; Georgia Tech, 1977

Total Offense

Total Offense Attempts - 104 vs. Iowa (587 yards), 1968
Fewest Total Offense Attempts - 31 vs. Pittsburgh (87 yards), 1937
Total Offense Yards - 720 vs. Navy (99 attempts), 1969
Fewest Total Offense Yards - 12 vs. Michigan State (42 attempts), 1965

Scoring

Points - 142 vs. American Medical, 1905; MR: 69 vs. Georgia Tech, 1977; Pittsburgh, 1965
Touchdowns - 27 vs. American Medical, 1905; MR: 10 vs. Georgia Tech, 1977; Pittsburgh, 1965; Dartmouth, 1944
Extra Points - 13 vs. Rose Poly, 1914; MR: 9 vs. Georgia Tech, 1977; Pittsburgh, 1965
Two-Point Conversions - 2 vs. USC, 1986; Michigan State, 1964
Two-Point Conversion Attempts - 4 vs. Pittsburgh, 1970; Michigan State, 1964
Field Goals - 5 vs. Miami (6 attempts), 1990
Field Goal Attempts - 7 vs. Texas, 1913; MR: 6 vs. Miami (made 5), 1990

Interceptions

Interceptions - 7 vs. Northwestern (185 yards), 1971; Wisconsin (75 yards), 1943
Interception Yards - 185 vs. Northwestern (7 returns), 1971
Interception Returns for Touchdowns - 2 vs. Miami, 1979; Northwestern, 1971; USC, 1966

Punt Returns

Punt Returns - 13 vs. Wabash, 1924; MR: 12 vs. Iowa, 1939
Punt Return Yards - 225 vs. Beloit, 1926; MR: 168 vs. Pittsburgh (10 returns), 1967
Punt Return Yards Per Attempt (min. 3) - 38.3 vs. California (3 for 115), 1965

Kickoff Returns

Kickoff Returns - 9 vs. Iowa (179 yards), 1956;
Kickoff Return Yards - 354 vs. Kalamazoo, 1922; MR: 192 vs Michigan (3 returns), 1989
Kickoff Return Yards Per Attempt (min. 3) - 64.0 vs. Michigan (3 for 192), 1989

Punting

Punts - 16 vs. Indiana, 1921; MR: 16 vs. Army, 1941
Fewest Punts - 0, several times; last time vs. Navy 1990
Punting Average (min. 5) - 51.6 vs. Air Force (5 for 258), 1975

First Downs

First Downs - 36 vs. Army, 1974
Fewest First Downs - 2 vs. Nebraska, 1917; MR: 3 vs. Pittsburgh, 1937
First Downs by Rushing - 30 vs. Army, 1974
Fewest First Downs by Rushing - 1 vs. Michigan State, 1965; Minnesota, 1938; Pittsburgh, 1937; Nebraska, 1917
First Downs by Passing - 19 vs. USC, 1970
Fewest First Downs by Passing - 0, many times; last time vs. Pittsburgh, 1989
First Downs by Penalty - 5 vs. Michigan State, 1986; Georgia Tech, 1968

Fumbles

Fumbles - 10 vs. Northwestern, 1931; MR: 10 vs. Oklahoma, 1952; Purdue, 1952
Fumbles Lost - 7 vs. Michigan State, 1952

SEASON OFFENSE

Rushing

Rushing Attempts - 684 (3119 yards), 1974
Rushing Attempts Per Game - 67.3 (673 in 10), 1973
Rushing Yards - 3502 (673 attempts), 1973
Rushing Yards Per Attempt - 6.2 (556 for 3430), 1921; MR: 5.4 (567 for 3061), 1946
Rushing Yards Per Game - 350.2 (3502 in 10), 1973
Rushing Touchdowns - 42, 1989

Passing

Pass Attempts - 297 (completed 159), 1977
Pass Attempts Per Game - 67.3 (673 in 10), 1973
Pass Completions - 168 (attempted 291), 1986
Completion Percentage - .583 (147 of 252), 1968
Passes Had Intercepted - 22, 1958
Lowest Pass Interception Percentage - .029 (6 of 204), 1990
Passing Yards - 2527 (162 of 283), 1970
Average Passing Yards Per Attempt (min. 125 attempts) - 9.5 (222 for 2105), 1964
Average Passing Yards Per Completion (min. 75 completions) - 17.5 (120 for 2105), 1964
Touchdown Passes - 18, 1977, 1949

Total Offense

Total Offense Attempts - 924 (5105 yards), 1970
Total Offense Attempts Per Game - 92.4 (924 in 10), 1970 (NCAA record)
Total Offense Yards - 5105 (924 attempts), 1970
Total Offense Yards Per Game - 510.5 (5105 in 10), 1970
Total Offense Yards Per Attempt - 6.72 (671 for 4512), 1921; MR: 6.02 (722 for 4348), 1949

Scoring

Points - 389, 1912; MR: 465 in 1991
Points Per Game - 55.6 (389 in 7), 1912; MR: 37.6 (376 in 10), 1968
Touchdowns - 55, 1912; MR: 53, 1949
Touchdowns Per Game - 7.9 (55 in 7); MR: 5.3 (53 in 10), 1949
Extra Points - 49, 1921; MR: 48, 1991
Extra Point Percentage: - 100.0 (41 of 41) 1990, (36 of 36) 1987,
(34 of 34), 1972
Two-Point Conversions Attempts - 12, 1964
Two-point Conversions - 3, 1971, 1970, 1965, 1958
Field Goals - 21 (28 attempts), 1986
Safeties - 2, 1989, 1987, 1983, 1979, 1973, 1959, 1958, 1954, 1949

Interceptions

Interceptions - 29 (374), 1977
Interception Yards - 497 (26 returns) 1966
Interception Yards Per Return (min. 10 returns) - 17.8 (19 for 338), 1945
Interception Returns for Touchdowns - 4, 1966

Fumbles

Most Opponent Fumbles - 51, 1952
Most Opponent Fumbles Lost - 28, 1952

Punt Returns

Punt Returns - 66, 1921; MR: 58 (617), 1939
Punt Return Yards - 617 (58 returns), 1939
Punt Return Yards Per Game - 68.6 (617 in 9), 1939
Punt Return Yards Per Attempt - 18.7 (25 for 468), 1965
Punt Returns for Touchdowns - 3, 1926; MR: 3, 1987, 1965

Kickoff Returns

Kickoff Returns - 49 (1174 yards), 1956
Kickoff Return Yards - 1174 (49 returns), 1956
Kickoff Return Yards Per Game - 117.4 (1174 in 10), 1956
Kickoff Return Yards Per Attempt - 32.2 (36 for 1160), 1922; MR:27.6 (25 for 689), 1957
Kickoff Returns for Touchdowns - 5, 1922

Punting

Punts - 90, 1934; MR: 85, 1941, 1939
Fewest Punts - 23, 1968
Punting Average - 42.4 (78 for 3309), 1982

First Downs

First Downs - 272, 1968
First Downs Per Game - 29.2 (292 in 10), 1968
First Downs By Rushing - 193, 1989
First Downs By Passing - 110, 1977
First Downs By Penalty - 17, 1986

Penalties

Penalties - 101, 1926; MR: 98 (933 yards), 1952
Fewest Penalties - 29, 1939, 1937
Penalty Yards Per Game - 93.3 (933 in 10), 1952
Fewest Penalty Yards - 225, 1939
Fewest Penalty Yards Per Game - 25.0 (225 in 9), 1937

Fumbles

Fumbles - 57, 1952
Fewest Fumbles - 16, 1964, 1950
Fumbles Lost - 29, 1952
Fewest Fumbles Lost - 6, 1981, 1941

SINGLE GAME DEFENSE

Rushing Defense

Fewest Rushing Attempts - 8 by Kalamazoo, 1923; MR: 15 by Pitt (15 yards), 1968
Fewest Rushing Yards - Minus 51 by Wisconsin (28 attempts), 1964
Most Rushing Yards Lost - 141 by USC (43 attempts), 1961
Fewest Rushing Yards Per Attempt - Minus 1.8 by Wisconsin (28 for -51), 1964

Pass Defense

Fewest Pass Attempts - 0 by Carnegie Tech, 1925; St. Louis, 1922; MR: 1 by Georgia Tech, 1976
Fewest Pass Completions - 0, many times; last time by Georgia Tech in 1976
Fewest Passing Yards - 0, many times; last time by Georgia Tech, 1976

Total Defense

Fewest Total Offense Yards - Minus 17 by St. Louis, 1922; MR: 2 by Carnegie Tech, 1941

First Downs

Fewest First Downs - 0 by Wabash, 1924; Kalamazoo, 1923; St. Louis, 1922; Michigan State, 1921; MR: 1 by USC, 1950; Carnegie Tech, 1941

Fumbles

Most Fumbles - 11 by Purdue, 1952
Most Fumbles Lost - 8 by Purdue, 1952

SEASON DEFENSE

Rushing Defense

Fewest Rushing Attempts Allowed Per Game - 29.2 (263 in 9), 1920; MR: 35.7 (321 in 9), 1946
Fewest Rushing Yards Allowed - 495, 1921; MR: 611 (340 attempts), 1941
Fewest Rushing Yards Allowed Per Game - 45.0 (495 in 11), 1921; MR: 67.9 (611 in 9), 1941
Fewest Rushing Yards Per Attempt - 1.4 (365 for 495), 1921; MR: 1.8 (340 for 611), 1941
Rushing Yards Lost by Opponents - 578, 1949

Pass Defense

Fewest Pass Attempts Allowed Per Game - 6.9 (69 in 10), 1925; MR: 9.7 (87 in 9), 1937
Fewest Pass Completions Allowed Per Game - 1.6 (14 in 9), 1924; MR: 3.0 (27 in 9), 1937
Lowest Completion Percentage - .215 (14 of 65), 1924; MR: .306 (41 of 134), 1938
Fewest Passing Yards Allowed Per Game - 15.6, (140 in 9), 1924; MR: 49.4 (445 in 9), 1938
Fewest Touchdown Passes Allowed - 0, 1931, 1924, 1922, 1921; MR: 1, 1946, 1940

Total Defense

Fewest Total Offense Attempts Allowed Per Game - 37.1, 1924; MR: 46.1, 1937
Fewest Total Offense Yards - 651, 1924; MR, 1275, 1946
Fewest Total Offense Yards Allowed Per Game - 72.3 (651 in 9), 1924; MR: 141.7 (1275 in 9), 1946
Fewest Total Offense Yards Per Attempt - 1.8 (468 for 843), 1921; MR: 2.7 (481 for 1283), 1941

Scoring

Fewest Points Allowed - 0, 1903 (9 games); MR: 24, 1946 (9 games)

Punt Returns

Fewest Punt Returns - 5 (52 yards), 1968
Fewest Punt Return Yards - 47, 1954
Fewest Punt Return Yards Per Attempt - 5.0 (28 for 140), 1951

Punting

Most Opponent Punts - 119, 1921; MR: 98, 1939
Most Opponent Punts Blocked - 7, 1933, 1932; MR: 4, 1949, 1938

First Downs

Fewest First Downs Allowed - 42, 1924; MR: 61, 1937
Fewest First Downs by Rushing Allowed - 27, 1932, 1923; MR: 40, 1946
Fewest First Downs by Passing Allowed - 8, 1924; MR: 14, 1937

Miscellaneous

Won-Lost Record: Home and Away -

	Won	Lost	Tied	Pct.
Home	376	78	12	.819
Away	236	106	21	.679
Neutral Sites	90	25	7	.766
Total	**702**	**209**	**40**	**.759**

Consecutive Wins - 23 (1988-89).

Consecutive Games Without Defeat - 39 (1946-50, 2 ties); (1910-14, 3 ties); 26 (1929-30, 1 tie).

Consecutive Losses - 8 (1960).

Consecutive Wins at Home - 39 from 11-9-07 vs. Knox through 11-17-17 vs. MSU; Great Lakes ended the streak with a 3-3 tie on 11-9-18.

Consecutive Wins in Notre Dame Stadium - 28 (from 11-21-42 vs. Northwestern through 9-30-50 vs. North Carolina; Purdue ended streak with a 28-14 win on 10-7-50).

OPPONENT RECORDS

Individual Records

Rushing

Rushing Attempts - 44, Charles White (261 yards), USC 1979
Rushing Yards - 303, Tony Dorsett (23 attempts), Pitt, 1975
Longest Rush - 88, Dick Panin, MSU, 1951

Passing

Pass attempts - 68, Steve Smith (completed 39), Stanford, 1989
Pass Completions - 39, Steve Smith (attempted 68), Stanford, 1989
Passing Yards - 424, Steve Walsh (31 of 50), Miami, 1988
Touchdown Passes - 4, Steve Walsh, Miami, 1988; Pat Haden, USC, 1974; Len Dawson, Purdue, 1954; Fred Benners, SMU, 1951

Receiving

Pass Receptions - 14, Robert Lavette (50 yards), Georgia Tech, 1981; John Jackson (200 yards), USC, 1989; Jim Price (98 yards), Stanford, 1989

Pass Reception Yards - 200, John Jackson (14 receptions), USC, 1989
Touchdown Receptions - Andy Hamilton, LSU, 1971
Longest Pass - Gene Glick to Lynn Chandnois, MSU, 1949

Total Offense

Total Offense attempts - 69, Steve Smith (289 yards), Stanford, 1989
Total Offense Yards - 420, Steve Walsh (52 attempts), Miami, 1988

Scoring

Points - 36, Anthony Davis (6 TDs), USC, 1972
Touchdowns - 6, Anthony Davis, USC, 1972
Extra Points - 6, Eric Hipp, USC, 1979; Bernie Allen, Purdue, 1960; Bob Prescott, Iowa, 1956
Field Goals - 5, Massimo Manca, Penn State, 1985
Longest Field Goal - 60, Don Shafer, USC, 1986

Returns

Longest Interception - 100, Jeff Ford, Georgia Tech, 1969
Longest Punt Return - 80, Jerry Mauren, Iowa, 1959
Longest Kickoff Return - 100, Anthony Davis, USC, 1974; Frank Rieple, Penn, 1955; Joe Williams, Iowa, 1961
Longest Fumble Return - 94, Leroy Keyes, Purdue, 1966

Punting

Punts - 18, Joe Mihm, Carnegie Tech, 1934; Paul Dobson, Nebraska, 1918
Punting Average (min. 5 punts) - 52.8, Bob Huston (5 for 264), Drake, 1937
Longest Punt - 83 yards, Verl Lillywhite, USC, 1946

Career Records

Rushing

Rushing Attempts - 120, Charles White, (648 yards), USC, 1976-79
Rushing Yards - 754, Tony Dorsett (96 attempts), Pitt, 1973-76

Passing

Pass Attempts - 101, Mark Hermann (completed 53), Purdue, 1977-79
Pass Completions - 53, Mark Hermann (attempted 101), Purdue, 1977-79; Scott Campbell (attempted 89), Purdue, 1980-82
Passing Yards - 702, Scott Campbell (53 of 89), Purdue, 1980-82

Touchdown Passes - 5, Jim Everett, Purdue, 1984-85; Mark Hermann, Purdue, 1977-79; Pat Haden, USC, 1972-74; Len Dawson, Purdue, 1954-56.

Receiving

Pass Receptions - 21, Dave Young (246 yards), Purdue, 1977-80; John Jackson (283 yards), USC, 1987-89
Pass Reception Yards - 301, Gene Washington, (16 receptions), MSU, 1964-66
Touchdown Receptions - 3, Andy Hamilton, LSU, 1971

Total Offense

Total Offense Attempts - 117, Scott Campbell (663 yards), Purdue, 1980-82
Total Offense Yards - 754, Tony Dorsett (96 attempts) Pitt, 1973-76

Scoring

Points - 68, Anthony Davis, (11 TDs, 1 two-point conversion), USC 1972-74
Touchdowns - 11, Anthony Davis, USC, 1972-74
Extra Points - 10, Carson Long, Pitt, 1973-76; Bernie Allen, Purdue, 1958-60
Field Goals - 5, Carlos Huerta, Miami, 1988-90; Massimo Manca, Penn State, 1985; Carson Long, Pitt, 1973-76

Team Records

First Downs - 30, by USC, 1978
First Downs by Rushing - 23, by Purdue, 1956
First Downs by Passing - 23, by Miami, 1988
Rushing Attempts - 76, by Nebraska, 1922
Rushing Yards - 411, by Pitt (50 attempts), 1975; by MSU (60 attempts), 1962
Pass Attempts - 68, by Stanford (completed 39), 1989
Pass Completions - 39, by Stanford (attempted 68), 1989
Passing Yards - 424, by Miami (31 of 50), 1988
Touchdown Passes - 4, by Miami, 1988; USC, 1974; Duke, 1961; Purdue, 1954; SMU, 1951
Total Offense Attempts - 92, by Tennessee (516 yards), 1990
Points - 59, by Army, 1944
Touchdowns - 10, by Wisconsin, 1904

Longest Plays

Rushing

Bob Livingstone vs. USC, 1947	92 yards
Larry Coutre vs. Navy, 1949	91 yards
Joe Heap vs. SMU, 1954	89 yards

Pass Plays

Blair Kiel to Joe Howard vs. Ga. Tech, 1981	96 yards
John Huarte to Nick Eddy vs. Pitt, 1964	91 yards
Steve Beuerlein to Tim Brown vs. SMU, 1986	84 yards

Interceptions

Luther Bradley vs. Purdue, 1975	99 yards
Nick Rassas vs. Northwestern, 1965	92 yards
Jack Elder vs. Army, 1929	90 yards

Kickoff Returns

Alfred Bergman vs. Loyola (Chi.), 1911*	105 yards
Joe Savoldi vs. SMU, 1930	100 yards
Greg Bell vs. Miami, 1981	98 yards

* did not score— field was 110 yards long

Field Goals

Dave Reeve vs. Pitt, 1976	53 yards
John Carney vs. SMU, 1984	51 yards
Harry Oliver vs. Michigan, 1980	51 yards
Dave Reeve vs. MSU, 1977	51 yards
Harry Oliver vs. Navy & Georgia, 1980	50 yards

Punt Returns

Ricky Watters vs. SMU, 1989	97 yards
Red Miller vs. Olivet, 1909	95 yards
Chet Grant vs. Case Tech, 1916	95 yards
Joe Heap vs. USC, 1953	95 yards

Fumble Return

Frank Shaughnessy vs. Kansas, 1904	107 yards

Punts

Bill Shakespeare vs. Pitt, 1935	86 yards
Elmer Layden vs. Stanford, 1924	80 yards
Craig Hentrich vs. Colorado, 1990	77 yards

ALL-TIME LEADERS

Rushing

		Carries	Yards	Avg.	TD
1. Allen Pinkett	1982	107	532	5.0	5
	1983	252	1394	5.5	16
	1984	275	1105	4.0	17
	1985	255	1100	4.3	11
Total		***889**	***4131**	**4.6**	***49**
2. Vagas Ferguson	1976	81	350	4.3	2
	1977	80	493	6.2	6
	1978	211	1192	5.6	7
	1979	301	1437	4.8	17
Total		**673**	**3472**	**5.2**	**32**
3. Jerome Heavens	1975	129	756	5.9	5
	1976	54	204	3.8	0
	1977	229	994	4.3	6
	1978	178	728	4.1	4
Total		**590**	**2682**	**4.5**	**15**

Season

		Carries	Yards	Avg.	TD
1. Vagas Ferguson	1979	*301	*1437	4.8	17
2. Allen Pinkett	1983	252	1394	5.5	16
3. Vagas Ferguson	1978	211	1192	5.6	7
4. Allen Pinkett	1984	275	1105	4.0	17
5. Allen Pinkett	1985	255	1100	4.3	11

Game

		Carries	Yards	Avg.	TD
1. V. Ferguson vs. Ga. Tech	1978	30	*255	8.5	1
2. Phil Carter vs. MSU	1980	*40	254	6.4	1
3. Jim Stone vs. Miami	1980	38	224	5.9	1
4. V. Ferguson vs. Navy	1978	18	219	12.2	1
5. A. Pinkett vs. Penn St.	1983	36	217	6.0	4

Passing

Career

		Att.	Comp.	Int.	%age	Yards	TD
1. Steve Beuerlein	1983	145	75	6	.517	1061	4
	1984	232	140	18	.603	1920	7
	1985	214	107	13	.500	1335	3
	1986	259	151	7	.583	2211	13
Total		***850**	***473**	***44**	**.556**	***6527**	**27**
2. Terry Hanratty	1966	147	78	10	.531	1247	8
	1967	206	110	15	.534	1439	9
	1968	197	116	9	.588	1466	10
Total		**550**	**304**	**34**	**.533**	**4152**	**27**
3. Blair Kiel	1980	124	48	5	.387	531	0
	1981	151	67	10	.444	936	7
	1982	219	118	10	.539	1273	3
	1983	115	64	7	.557	910	7
Total		**609**	**297**	**32**	**.488**	**3650**	**17**

Season

		Att.	Comp.	Int.	%age	Yards	TD
1. Joe Theismann	1970	*268	*155	14	.578	*2429	16
2. Steve Beuerlein	1986	259	151	7	.583	2211	13
3. Joe Montana	1978	260	141	9	.542	2010	10
4. Steve Beuerlein	1984	232	140	18	*.603	1920	7
5. Tom Clements	1974	215	122	11	.567	1549	8

Pass Receiving

		PC	Yards	Avg.	TD
1. Tom Gatewood	1969	47	743	15.8	8
	1970	77	1123	14.6	7
	1971	33	417	12.6	4
Total		***157**	**2283**	**14.5**	***19**
2. Jim Seymour	1966	48	862	17.9	8
	1967	37	515	13.9	4
	1968	53	736	13.9	4
Total		**138**	**2113**	**15.3**	**16**
3. Tim Brown	1984	28	340	12.1	1
	1985	25	397	15.9	3
	1986	45	910	20.2	5
	1987	39	846	21.7	3
Total		**137**	***2493**	**18.2**	**12**

Season

1. Tom Gatewood	1970	*77	*1123	14.6	7
2. Jack Snow	1964	60	1114	18.6	*9
3. Ken MacAfee	1977	54	797	14.8	6
4. Jim Seymour	1968	53	736	13.9	4
5. Jim Seymour	1966	48	862	17.9	8

Total Offense

		Plays	Yards	Avg.
1. Steve Beuerlein	1983	168	1052	6.3
	1984	290	1845	6.4
	1985	257	1316	5.1
	1986	312	2246	7.2
Total		***1027**	***6459**	**6.3**
2. Joe Theismann	1968	118	710	6.0
	1969	308	1909	6.2
	1970	391	2813	7.2
Total		**807**	**5432**	**6.7**
3. Tony Rice	1987	171	1000	5.8
	1988	259	1876	7.2
	1989	311	2006	6.5
Total		**741**	**4882**	**6.6**

Season

1. Joe Theismann	1970	*391	*2813	7.2
2. Rick Mirer	1991	309	2423	7.8
3. Steve Beuerlein	1986	312	2246	7.2
4. Joe Montana	1978	332	2114	6.4
5. John Huarte	1964	242	2069	8.5

Punt Returns

		No.	Yards	Avg.	TD
1. Nick Rassas	1963	0	0	0.0	0
	1964	15	153	10.2	0
	1965	24	459	19.1	3
Total		**39**	**612**	***15.7**	***3**
2. Raghib Ismail	1988	5	72	14.4	0
	1989	7	113	16.1	1
	1990	13	151	11.6	0
Total		**25**	**336**	**13.4**	**1**

3. Ricky Watters	1988	19	253	13.3	2
	1989	15	201	13.4	1
Total		34	454	13.35	3

Season

1. Nick Rassas	1965	24	*459	*19.1	*3
2. Ricky Watters	1989	15	201	13.4	1
3. Andy Puplis	1937	21	281	13.38	0
4. Bill Gay	1949	19	254	13.37	0
5. F. Dancewicz	1945	18	240	13.33	0

Kickoff Returns

Career

		No.	Yds.	Avg.	TD
1. Paul Castner	1920	2	55	27.5	0
	1921	8	222	27.8	0
	1922	11	490	44.5	2
Total		**21**	**767**	***36.5**	**2**
2. Nick Eddy	1964	7	148	21.2	0
	1965	3	63	21.0	0
	1966	4	193	48.3	2
Total		**14**	**404**	**28.9**	**2**
3. Paul Hornung	1954	1	58	58.0	0
	1955	6	109	18.3	0
	1956	16	496	31.0	1
Total		**23**	**663**	**28.8**	**1**

Season (min. 0.5 per game)

1. Paul Castner	1922	11	490	*44.5	*2
2. John Lattner	1953	8	331	41.4	*2
3. Raghib Ismail	1988	12	433	36.1	*2
4. Paul Hornung	1956	16	496	31.0	1
5. C. Flanagan	1926	6	183	30.5	1

Punting

Career (avg. per punt)

		No.	Yards	Avg.
1. Craig Hentrich	1989	26	1159	44.6
	1990	34	1526	44.9
	1991	23	986	42.9
Total		**83**	**3671**	***44.22**

2. Vince Phelan	1987	50	2044	40.9
3. B. Shakespeare	1933	5	266	53.2
	1934	41	1638	40.0
	1935	45	1801	40.0
Total		**91**	**3705**	**40.71**

Season

1. Craig Hentrich	1990	34	1526	*44.9
2. Craig Hentrich	1989	26	1159	44.6
3. Joe Restic	1975	40	1739	43.5
4. Craig Hentrich	1991	23	986	42.9
5. Brian Doherty	1973	39	1664	42.7

Interceptions

Career

		No.	Yards	Avg.	TD
1. Luther Bradley	1973	6	37	6.2	0
	1975	4	135	33.8	1
	1976	2	0	0.0	0
	1977	5	46	9.2	0
Total		***17**	**218**	**12.8**	**1**
2. Tom MacDonald	1961	1	23	23.0	0
	1962	9	81	9.0	0
	1963	5	63	12.6	1
Total		**15**	**167**	**11.1**	**1**
3. R. Stepaniak	1969	4	84	21.0	0
	1970	6	55	9.2	0
	1971	3	40	13.3	1
Total		**13**	**179**	**13.8**	**1**

Season

1. Mike Townsend	1972	*10	39	3.9	0
2. Tom MacDonald	1962	9	81	9.0	0
3. Tony Carey	1964	8	121	15.1	0
Todd Lyght	1989	8	42	5.3	0
Angelo Bertelli	1942	8	41	5.1	0

Scoring

Career

		TD	PAT	FG	Pts.
1. Allen Pinkett	1982	6	0	0	36
	1983	18	2 pt	0	110
	1984	18	0	0	108
	1985	11	0	0	66
Total		***53**	**2 pt**	**0**	***320**
2. Red Salmon	1900	3	0	0	15
	1901	7	13	1	53
	1902	11	17	1	77
	1903	15	30	0	105
Total		**36**	**60**	**2**	**250**
3. Dave Reeve	1974	0	38	7	59
	1975	0	24	11	57
	1976	0	29	9	56
	1977	0	39	12	75
Total		**0**	***130**	**39**	**247**

Season

		TD	PAT	FG	Pts.
1. Jerome Bettis	1991	*20	0	0	*120
2. Allen Pinkett	1983	18	2	0	110
3. Allen Pinkett	1984	18	0	0	108
4. Red Salmon	1903	15	30	0	105
5. Vagas Ferguson	1979	17	0	0	102

Field Goals

Career

		No.	Att.	Long
1. John Carney	1984	17	19	48
	1985	13	22	48
	1986	21	28	49
Total		***51**	***69**	**49**
2. Dave Reeve	1974	7	10	45
	1975	11	16	48
	1976	9	18	*53
	1977	13	20	51
Total		**39**	**64**	**51**

3. Mike Johnston	1982	19	22	48
	1983	12	21	49
Total		**31**	**43**	**49**

Season

1. John Carney	1986	*21	28	49
2. Mike Johnston	1982	19	22	48
3. Harry Oliver	1980	18	23	51
4. John Carney	1984	17	19	44
5. Craig Hentrich	1990	16	20	44

Year-by-Year Leaders

Rushing

Player	Rushes	Yards
1918 George Gipp	98	541
1919 George Gipp	106	729
1920 George Gipp	102	827
1921 John Mohardt	136	781
1922 Jim Crowley	75	566
1923 Don Miller	89	698
1924 Don Miller	107	566
1925 Christy Flanagan	99	556
1926 Christy Flanagan	68	535
1927 Christy Flanagan	118	731
1928 Jack Chevigny	120	539
1929 Joe Savoldi	112	597
1930 Marchy Schwartz	124	927
1931 Marchy Schwartz	146	692
1932 George Melinkovich	73	503
1933 Nick Lukats	107	339
1934 George Melinkovich	73	324
1935 Bill Shakespeare	104	374
1936 Bob Wilke	132	434
1937 Bunny McCormick	91	347
1938 Bob Saggau	60	353
1939 Milt Piepul	82	414
1940 Steve Juzwik	71	407
1941 Fred Evans	141	490
1942 Corwin Clatt	138	698
1943 Creighton Miller	151	911
1944 Bob Kelly	136	681
1945 Elmer Angsman	87	616
1946 Emil Sitko	53	346
1947 Emil Sitko	60	426

1948 Emil Sitko	129	742
1949 Emil Sitko	120	712
1950 Jack Landry	109	491
1951 Neil Worden	181	676
1952 John Lattner	148	732
1953 Neil Worden	145	859
1954 Don Schaefer	141	766
1955 Don Schaefer	145	638
1956 Paul Hornung	94	420
1957 Nick Pietrosante	90	449
1958 Nick Pietrosante	117	549
1959 Gerry Gray	50	256
1960 Angelo Dabiero	80	325
1961 Angelo Dabiero	92	637
1962 Don Hogan	90	454
1963 Joe Kantor	88	330
1964 Bill Wolski	136	657
1965 Nick Eddy	115	582
1966 Nick Eddy	78	553
1967 Jeff Zimmerman	133	591
1968 Bob Gladieux	152	713
1969 Denny Allan	148	612
1970 Ed Gulyas	118	534
1971 Bob Minnix	78	337
1972 Eric Penick	124	726
1973 Wayne Bullock	162	752
1974 Wayne Bullock	203	855
1975 Jerome Heavens	129	994
1976 Al Hunter	233	1058
1977 Jerome Heavens	129	756
1978 Vagas Ferguson	211	1192
1979 Vagas Ferguson	*301	*1437
1980 Jim Stone	192	908
1981 Phil Carter	165	727
1982 Phil Carter	179	715
1983 Allen Pinkett	252	1394
1984 Allen Pinkett	275	1105
1985 Allen Pinkett	255	1100
1986 Mark Green	96	406
1987 Mark Green	146	861
1988 Tony Rice	121	700
1989 Tony Rice	174	884
1990 Rodney Culver	150	710
1991 Jerome Bettis	168	977

Passing

	Att.	Comp.	Yards	TD
1918 George Gipp	45	19	293	1
1919 George Gipp	72	41	727	3
1920 George Gipp	62	30	709	3

1921 John Mohardt	98	53	995	9
1922 Jim Crowley	21	10	154	1
1923 Jim Crowley	36	13	154	1
1924 Harry Stuhldreher	33	25	471	4
1925 Harry O'Boyle	21	7	107	0
1926 Christy Flanagan	29	12	207	0
1927 John Niemiec	33	14	187	0
1928 John Niemiec	108	37	456	3
1929 Jack Elder	25	8	187	1
1930 Marchy Schwartz	56	17	319	3
1931 Marchy Schwartz	51	9	174	3
1932 Nick Lukats	28	13	252	2
1933 Nick Lukats	67	21	329	0
1934 Bill Shakespeare	29	9	230	2
1935 Bill Shakespeare	66	19	267	3
1936 Bob Wilke	52	19	365	2
1937 Jack McCarthy	53	16	225	3
1938 Bob Saggau	28	8	179	3
1939 Harry Stevenson	50	14	236	1
1940 Bob Saggau	60	21	483	4
1941 Angelo Bertelli	123	70	1027	8
1942 Angelo Bertelli	159	72	1039	10
1943 Johnny Lujack	71	43	525	4
1944 Frank Dancewicz	163	68	989	9
1945 Frank Dancewicz	90	30	489	5
1946 Johnny Lujack	100	49	778	6
1947 Johnny Lujack	109	61	791	9
1948 Frank Tripucka	91	53	660	11
1949 Bob Williams	147	83	1347	16
1950 Bob Williams	210	99	1035	10
1951 John Mazur	110	48	645	5
1952 Ralph Guglielmi	143	62	725	4
1953 Ralph Guglielmi	113	52	792	8
1954 Ralph Guglielmi	127	68	1162	6
1955 Paul Hornung	103	46	743	9
1956 Paul Hornung	111	59	917	3
1957 Bob Williams	106	53	565	3
1958 George Izo	118	68	1067	9
1959 George Izo	95	44	661	6
1960 George Haffner	108	30	548	3
1961 Frank Budka	95	40	636	3
1962 Daryle Lamonica	128	64	821	6
1963 Frank Budka	40	21	239	4
1964 John Huarte	205	114	2062	16
1965 Bill Zloch	88	36	558	3
1966 Terry Hanratty	147	78	1247	8
1967 Terry Hanratty	206	110	1439	9
1968 Terry Hanratty	197	108	1466	10
1969 Joe Theismann	192	108	1531	13
1970 Joe Theismann	*268	*155	*2429	16
1971 Cliff Brown	111	56	669	4

1972 Tom Clements	162	83	1163	8
1973 Tom Clements	113	60	882	8
1974 Tom Clements	215	122	1549	8
1975 Rick Slager	139	66	686	2
1976 Rick Slager	172	86	1281	11
1977 Joe Montana	189	99	1604	11
1978 Joe Montana	260	141	2010	10
1979 Rusty Lisch	208	108	1781	4
1980 Blair Kiel	124	48	531	0
1981 Blair Kiel	151	67	936	7
1982 Blair Kiel	219	118	1273	3
1983 Steve Beuerlein	145	75	1061	4
1984 Steve Beuerlein	232	140	1920	7
1985 Steve Beuerlein	214	107	1335	3
1986 Steve Beuerlein	259	151	2211	13
1987 Tony Rice	82	35	663	1
1988 Tony Rice	138	70	1176	8
1989 Tony Rice	137	68	1122	2
1990 Rick Mirer	200	110	1824	8
1991 Rick Mirer	234	132	2117	*18

Receiving

	Recps.	Yards	TD
1918 Bernie Kirk	7	102	1
1919 Bernie Kirk	21	372	2
1920 Eddie Anderson	17	293	3
1921 Eddie Anderson	26	394	2
1922 Don Miller	6	144	1
1923 Don Miller	9	149	1
1924 Don Miller	16	297	2
1925 Gene Edwards	4	28	0
1926 Ike Voedisch	6	95	0
1927 John Colrick	11	126	1
1928 John Colrick	18	199	2
1929 John Colrick	4	90	0
1930 Ed Kosky	4	76	1
1931 Paul Host	6	48	2
1932 George Melinkovich	7	106	1
1933 Steve Banas	6	59	0
1934 Dom Vairo	4	135	2
1935 Wally Fromhart	11	174	1
1936 Joe O'Neill	8	140	1
1937 Andy Puplis	5	86	1
1938 Earl Brown	6	192	4
1939 Bud Kerr	6	129	0
1940 Bob Hargrave	9	98	1
1941 Steve Juzwik	18	307	2
1942 Bob Livingstone	17	272	3
1943 John Yonakor	15	323	4

1944	Bob Kelly	18	283	5
1945	Bob Skoglund	9	100	1
1946	Terry Brennan	10	154	2
1947	Terry Brennan	16	181	4
1948	Leon Hart	16	231	4
1949	Leon Hart	19	257	5
1950	Jim Mutscheller	35	426	7
1951	Jim Mutscheller	20	305	2
1952	Joe Heap	29	437	2
1953	Joe Heap	22	335	5
1954	Joe Heap	18	369	0
1955	Jim Morse	17	424	3
1956	Jim Morse	20	442	1
1957	Dick Lynch	13	128	0
1958	Monty Stickles	20	328	7
1959	Bob Scarpitto	15	297	4
1960	Les Traver	14	225	0
1961	Les Traver	17	349	2
1962	Jim Kelly	41	523	4
1963	Jim Kelly	18	264	2
1964	Jack Snow	60	1114	*9
1965	Nick Eddy	13	233	2
1966	Jim Seymour	48	862	8
1967	Jim Seymour	37	515	4
1968	Jim Seymour	53	736	4
1969	Tom Gatewood	47	743	8
1970	Tom Gatewood	*77	*1123	7
1971	Tom Gatewood	33	417	4
1972	Willie Townsend	25	369	4
1973	Pete Demmerle	26	404	5
1974	Pete Demmerle	43	667	6
1975	Ken MacAfee	26	333	5
1976	Ken MacAfee	34	483	3
1977	Ken MacAfee	54	797	6
1978	Kris Haines	32	699	5
1979	Dean Masztak	28	428	2
1980	Tony Hunter	23	303	1
1981	Tony Hunter	28	387	2
1982	Tony Hunter	42	507	0
1983	Allen Pinkett	28	288	2
1984	Mark Bavaro	32	395	1
1985	Tim Brown	25	397	3
1986	Tim Brown	45	910	3
1987	Tim Brown	39	846	3
1988	Rickey Watters	15	286	2
1989	Raghib Ismail	27	535	0
1990	Raghib Ismail	32	699	2
1991	Tony Smith	42	789	4

Scoring

		TD	XPts	FG	Pts
1918	George Gipp	6	7	0	43
1919	George Gipp	7	4	1	49
1920	George Gipp	8	16	0	64
1921	John Mohardt	12	0	0	72
1922	Paul Castner	8	10	2	64
1923	Don Miller	10	0	0	60
	Red Maher	10	0	0	60
1924	Jim Crowley	9	17	0	71
1925	Christy Flanagan	7	3	0	45
1926	Bucky Dahman	6	5	0	41
1927	John Niemiec	4	7	0	31
1928	Jack Chevigny	3	0	0	18
1929	Jack Elder	7	0	0	42
1930	Marchy Schwartz	9	0	0	54
1931	Marchy Schwartz	5	0	0	30
1932	George Melinkovich	8	0	0	48
1933	Nick Lukats	2	0	0	12
1934	George Melinkovich	6	0	0	36
1935	Bill Shakespeare	4	0	0	24
1936	Bob Wilke	6	0	0	36
1937	Andy Puplis	3	6	0	24
1938	Benny Sheridan	4	0	0	24
	Earl Brown	4	0	0	24
1939	Milt Piepul	6	0	0	36
1940	Steve Juzwik	7	1	0	43
1941	Fred Evans	11	1	0	67
1942	Corwin Clatt	5	0	4	30
	Creighton Miller	5	0	0	30
1943	Creighton Miller	13	0	0	78
1944	Bob Kelly	13	6	0	84
1945	Elmer Angsman	7	0	0	42
1946	Terry Brennan	6	0	0	36
	Jim Mello	6	0	0	36
1947	Terry Brennan	11	0	0	66
1948	Emil Sitko	9	0	0	54
1949	Emil Sitko	9	0	0	54
	Billy Barrett	9	0	0	54
1950	Jim Mutscheller	7	0	0	42
1951	Neil Worden	8	0	0	48
1952	Neil Worden	10	0	0	60
1953	Neil Worden	11	0	0	66
1954	Joe Heap	8	0	0	48
1955	Paul Hornung	6	5	2	47
1956	Paul Hornung	7	14	0	56
1957	Monty Stickles	3	11	1	32
1958	Monty Stickles	7	15	1	60
1959	Bob Scarpitto	8	0	0	48
1960	Bob Scarpitto	5	0	0	30
1961	Joe Perkowski	0	16	5	31

1962	Joe Farrell	4	0	0	24
	Jim Kelly	4	0	0	24
	Daryle Lamonica	4	0	0	24
1963	Frank Budka	4	0	0	24
1964	Bill Wolski	11	0	0	66
1965	Bill Wolski	8	4	0	52
1966	Nick Eddy	10	0	0	60
1967	Joe Azzaro	0	37	8	61
1968	Bob Gladieux	14	0	0	84
1969	Scott Hempel	0	41	5	56
1970	Scott Hempel	0	36	4	48
1971	Bob Thomas	0	43	5	36
1972	Andy Huff	10	0	0	60
1973	Bob Thomas	0	43	9	70
1974	Wayne Bullock	12	0	0	72
1975	Dave Reeve	0	24	11	57
1976	Al Hunter	13	0	0	78
1977	Dave Reeve	0	39	12	75
1978	Vagas Ferguson	8	0	0	48
1979	Vagas Ferguson	17	0	0	102
1980	Harry Oliver	0	19	18	73
1981	Harry Oliver	0	28	6	46
1982	Mike Johnston	0	19	19	76
1983	Allen Pinkett	18	2 pt	0	110
1984	Allen Pinkett	18	0	0	108
1985	Allen Pinkett	11	0	0	66
1986	John Carney	0	24	*21	87
1987	Ted Gradel	0	33	14	75
1988	Reggie Ho	0	32	14	59
1989	Anthony Johnson	13	0	0	78
1990	Craig Hentrich	0	41	16	89
1991	Jerome Bettis	*20	0	0	*120

Tackles

1956	Ed Sullivan	79
1957	Jim Schaaf	88
1958	Al Ecuyer	78
1959	Bob Scholtz	84
1960	Myron Pottios	74
1961	Nick Buoniconti	74
1962	Ed Hoerster	73
1963	Bill Pfeiffer	101
1964	Jim Carroll	140
1965	Jim Lynch	108
1966	Jim Lynch	106
1967	Bob Olson	98
1968	Bob Olson	129
1969	Bob Olson	142

1970	Jim Wright	110
1971	Mike Kadish	97
1972	Jim O'Malley	122
1973	Greg Collins	133
1974	Greg Collins	144
1975	Steve Niehaus	113
1976	Steve Heimkreiter	118
1977	Bob Golic	146
1978	Steve Heimkreiter	160
1979	Bob Crable	*187
1980	Bob Crable	154
1981	Bob Crable	167
1982	Mark Zavagnin	113
1983	Tony Furjanic	142
1984	Mike Kovaleski	108
1985	Tony Furjanic	147
1986	Mike Kovaleski	88
1987	Ned Bolcar	106
1988	Wes Pritchett	112
1989	Ned Bolcar	109
1990	Mike Stonebreaker	95
1991	Demetrius BuBose	76

Punt Return Average

		No.	Yds.	Avg.
1919	Joe Brandy	26	186	7.2
1920	Joe Brandy	27	249	9.2
1921	(None)			
1922	Frank Thomas	21	196	9.3
1923	Harry Stuhldreher	32	308	9.6
1924	Harry Stuhldreher	22	194	8.8
1925	Charlie Riley	7	38	5.4
1926	Vince McNally	8	153	19.1
1927	Charles McKinney	5	36	7.2
1928	Frank Carideo	22	239	10.9
1929	Frank Carideo	33	405	12.3
1930	Frank Carideo	37	303	8.2
1931	Emmett Murphy	10	105	10.5
1932	Chuck Jaskwhich	23	254	11.0
1933	Andy Pilney	9	124	13.8
1934	Wally Fromhart	33	288	8.7
1935	Andy Pilney	13	148	11.4
1936	Bob Wilke	5	73	14.6
1937	Andy Puplis	21	281	13.4
1938	Benny Sheridan	11	194	17.6
1939	Benny Sheridan	8	107	13.4
1940	Bob Hargrave	24	176	7.3
1941	Steve Juzwik	22	280	12.7
1942	Pete Ashbaugh	13	196	15.1

1943	Creighton Miller	7	151	21.6
1944	Bob Kelly	12	129	10.8
1945	Frank Dancewicz	18	240	13.3
1946	Bob Livingstone	7	103	14.7
1947	Coy McGee	6	162	27.0
1948	Lancaster Smith	5	157	31.4
1949	Bill Gay	19	254	13.4
1950	Bill Gay	14	96	6.9
1951	Billy Barrett	5	107	21.4
1952	John Lattner	7	113	16.1
1953	Joe Heap	8	143	17.9
1954	Dean Studer	5	62	12.4
1955	Dean Studer	6	92	15.3
1956	Aubrey Lewis	5	46	9.2
1957	(None)			
1958	Pat Doyle	7	64	9.1
1959	Bob Scarpitto	7	118	16.9
1960	Angelo Dabiero	8	102	12.8
1961	Angelo Dabiero	11	97	8.8
1962	Frank Minik	6	41	6.8
1963	Bill Wolski	6	31	5.2
1964	Nick Rassas	15	153	10.2
1965	Nick Rassas	24	*459	19.1
1966	Tom Schoen	29	253	8.7
1967	Tom Schoen	*42	447	10.6
1968	Bob Gladieux	6	91	15.2
1969	Brian Lewallen	7	75	10.7
1970	Mike Crotty	19	100	5.3
1971	Mike Crotty	33	297	9.0
1972	Ken Schlezes	10	138	13.8
1973	Bob Zanot	19	141	7.4
1974	Ted Burgmeier	6	46	7.7
1975	Ted Burgmeier	9	52	5.8
1976	Steve Schmitz	18	168	9.3
1977	Steve Schmitz	14	127	9.1
1978	Dave Waymer	25	175	7.0
1979	Dave Duerson	12	209	17.4
1980	Dave Duerson	25	194	7.8
1981	Dave Duerson	32	221	6.9
1982	Dave Duerson	34	245	7.2
1983	Joe Howard	28	202	7.2
1984	Troy Wilson	11	84	7.6
1985	Troy Wilson	17	144	8.5
1986	Troy Wilson	26	222	8.5
1987	Tim Brown	34	401	11.8
1988	Ricky Watters	19	253	13.3
1989	Ricky Watters	15	201	13.4
1990	Raghib Ismail	13	151	11.6
1991	Jeff Burris	18	227	12.6

Kickoff Return Average

1919 George Gipp	8	166	20.8
1920 George Gipp	11	208	18.9
1921 Chet Wynne	9	258	28.7
1922 Paul Castner	11	490	*44.5
1923 Wille Maher	4	184	46.0
1924 Elmer Layden	5	111	22.2
1925 Rex Enright	4	86	21.5
1926 Christy Flanagan	6	183	30.5
1927 Jack Chevigny	4	91	22.8
1928 Jack Chevigny	5	115	23.0
1929 Joe Savoldi	4	81	20.3
1930 Joe Savoldi	4	186	46.5
1931 (none)			
1932 George Melinkovich	4	164	41.0
1933 Ray Brancheau	7	109	15.6
1934 Bill Shakespeare	4	60	15.0
1935 Bill Shakespeare	5	123	24.6
1936 Andy Puplis	5	136	27.2
1937 (None)			
1938 (None)			
1939 Harry Stevenson	5	85	17.0
1940 Milt Piepul	4	122	30.5
1941 Fred Evans	9	206	22.9
1942 Bob Livingstone	8	184	23.0
1943 Creighton Miller	4	53	13.3
1944 Bob Kelly	8	213	26.6
1945 Phil Colella	5	105	21.0
1946 (None)			
1947 (None)			
1948 Larry Coutre	4	70	17.5
1949 Emil Sitko	4	89	22.3
1950 Jack Landry	11	195	17.7
1951 Billy Barrett	4	86	21.5
1952 Joe Heap	6	145	24.2
1953 John Lattner	8	331	41.4
1954 Jim Morse	5	166	33.2
1955 Dean Studer	5	115	23.0
1956 Paul Hornung	16	496	31.0
1957 Dick Lynch	5	159	31.8
1958 Jim Crotty	12	297	24.8
1959 Bob Scarpitto	12	247	20.6
1960 George Sefcik	7	167	23.9
1961 Angelo Dabiero	8	193	24.1
1962 Ron Bliey	13	309	23.8
1963 Ron Bliey	5	131	26.2
1964 Nick Rassas	4	103	25.8
1965 Bill Wolski	6	131	21.8
1966 Nick Eddy	4	193	48.3
1967 Dave Haley	5	119	23.8

1968	Coley O'Brien	4	156	39.0
1969	Mike Crotty	4	111	27.8
1970	Darryll Dewan	4	91	22.8
1971	Gary Diminick	7	199	28.4
1972	Gary Diminick	15	331	22.1
1973	Gary Diminick	8	181	22.6
1974	Al Samuel	8	150	18.8
1975	Dan Knott	10	284	28.4
1976	Al Hunter	12	241	20.1
1977	Terry Eurick	9	211	23.4
1978	Jim Stone	13	242	18.6
1979	Jim Stone	19	493	25.9
1980	Jim Stone	17	344	20.2
1981	Greg Bell	13	371	28.5
1982	Allen Pinkett	14	354	25.3
1983	Alonzo Jefferson	10	174	17.4
1984	Hiawatha Francisco	6	178	29.7
1985	Tim Brown	14	338	24.1
1986	Tim Brown	*25	*698	27.9
1987	Tim Brown	23	456	19.8
1988	Raghib Ismail	12	433	36.1
1989	Raghib Ismail	20	502	25.1
1990	Raghib Ismail	14	336	24.0
1991	Clint Johnson	9	217	24.1

Interceptions

(Min. 3)		No.	Yds.
1919	George Gipp	3	32
1920	(None)		
1921	Chet Wynne	4	43
1922	(None)		
1923	Jim Crowley	4	31
1924	(None)		
1925	(None)		
1926	Vince McNally	3	0
1927	(None)		
1928	(None)		
1929	Frank Carideo	5	151
1930	Carl Cronin	3	26
	Marty Brill	3	8
	Tom Conley	3	4
1931	Nordy Hoffmann	3	32
1932	Mike Koken	4	32
1933	Nick Lukats	3	22
	Ray Brancheau	3	10
1934	(None)		
1935	(None)		
1936	Bob Wilke	3	33

1937	Ed Simonich	3	10
1938	(None)		
1939	(None)		
1940	Steve Bagarus	4	26
1941	Bernie Crimmins	4	12
1942	Angelo Bertelli	8	41
1943	Creighton Miller	6	78
1944	Joe Gasparella	4	28
1945	Frank Dancewicz	3	31
1946	Terry Brennan	3	18
1947	Johnny Lujack	3	44
1948	Bill Gay	6	83
1949	Bill Gay	4	80
1950	Dave Flood	4	28
1951	John Lattner	5	66
1952	John Lattner	4	66
	Jack Whelan	4	35
1953	Ralph Guglielmi	5	50
1954	Ralph Guglielmi	5	50
1955	Paul Hornung	5	59
1956	Aubrey Lewis	3	39
1957	Bob Williams	3	28
1958	George Izo	4	11
1959	George Sefcik	3	35
	Don White	3	39
1960	(None)		
1961	Angelo Dabiero	5	78
1962	Tom MacDonald	9	81
1963	Tom MacDonald	5	63
1964	Tony Carey	8	121
1965	Nick Rassas	6	*197
1966	Tom Schoen	7	112
1967	Tom Schoen	4	108
	John Pergine	4	19
1968	Chuck Zloch	5	31
1969	Ralph Stepaniak	4	84
1970	Clarence Ellis	7	25
1971	Ken Schlezes	4	63
1972	Mike Townsend	*10	39
1973	Luther Bradley	6	37
1974	(None)		
1975	Luther Bradley	4	135
	Tom Lopienski	4	79
1976	Joe Restic	4	92
1977	Joe Restic	6	25
1978	Joe Restic	3	59
	Tom Gibbons	3	48
	Dave Waymer	3	10
1979	Dave Waymer	4	77
1980	(None)		
1981	Mark Zavagnin	3	27
1982	Dave Duerson	7	104

1983 Rick Naylor	3	24
1984 Pat Ballage	3	41
1985 Steve Lawrence	3	57
1986 Steve Lawrence	3	28
1987 Corny Southall	3	80
Marve Spence	3	18
1988 George Streeter	3	39
Jeff Alm	3	8
1989 Todd Lyght	3	42
1990 (None)		
1991 Tom Carter	5	79

Notre Dame's NCAA Statistical Leaders

The following Notre Dame players were either first or second in key NCAA football statistics for a given season:

Total Offense

	Year	*Statistic*
2. Paul Hornung	1956	1337
2. Joe Theismann	1970	281.3

Rushing

1. Creighton Miller	1943	911

Receiving

2. Jack Snow	1964	60
2. Tom Gatewood	1970	7.7

Interceptions

2. Tom MacDonald (tie)	1962	9
1. Mike Townsend	1970	10

Punt Returns

1. Nick Rassas	1965	459

Kickoff Returns

2. Paul Hornung	1956	496
1. Raghib Ismail	1988	36.1

Scoring

2. Allen Pinkett	1983	10.0
2. Allen Pinkett	1984	9.8

Individual NCAA Records

- Highest Percentage of Field Goals Made 40 Yards or More: John Carney, 1984, .909 (10 of 11)
- Highest Season Percentage of Field Goals Made 40-49 Yards: John Carney, 1984, 1.000 (10 of 10)
- Most Consecutive Career Field Goals Made 40-49 Yards: John Carney, 1984-85, 12
- Most Single-Game Touchdowns Scored on Punt Returns: Tim Brown, 1987, vs. MSU, 2 (held by many others)
- Most Single-Game Touchdowns Scored on Kickoff Returns: Raghib Ismail, 1988 vs. Rice, 1989 vs. Michigan, 2 (held by 5 others)

Team Records

Annual National Leaders

Total Offense:

1943	418 yards per game
1946	441.3 yards per game
1949	434.8 yards per game

Rushing Offense:

1943	313.7 yards per game
1946	340.1 yards per game

Scoring Offense:

1966	36.2 points per game

Punt Returns:

1958	17.6 yards per return

Kickoff Returns:

1957	27.6 yards per return
1966	29.6 yards per return

Total Defense:

1946	141.7 yards per game
1974	195.2 yards per game

Rushing Defense:

1974	102.8 yards per game

Scoring Defense:

1946	2.7 points per game

Miscellaneous Records

- Single-Game Touchdowns Scored on Kickoff Returns: 2, vs. Rice in 1988 and vs, Michigan in 1989 (held by many teams).

- Season Total Offense—Most Plays Per Game: 92.4, 1970 (924 in 10).

- Season Pass Defense—Lowest Completion Percentage Allowed: (min. of 200 attempts) .333, 1967 (102 of 306).

- Season Punt Return Defense—Fewest Returns Allowed—5, 1968 (for 52 yards).

Weight training at Notre Dame

Irish football players participate in year-long, individually computerized weight training and conditioning programs at the 9,000 square foot Loftus Sports Center. Working in groups of 15-20, the players do their warmups and stretching before hitting the weights for periods of 75 minutes, four days each week.

Weight training is combined with various running workouts prescribed by Jerry Schmidt, Notre Dame's Strength and Conditioning Coach. The primary goal is that all such training must augment an individual's speed. After a game, or during the off season, close analysis of a player's performance or workout chart will reveal very precise areas of the body to focus on—perhaps a lineman's neck, a running back's quadriceps, or a receiver's triceps. Once provided an individualized goal, a player will use some of the 40,000 pounds in free weights and 37 exercise machines with 10 exercises done in sets of three to five. On a Monday, Tuesday, Thursday, Friday workout schedule, a typical routine would find a player working his chest, back, and triceps on Monday, then his legs, shoulders, and biceps on Tuesday. The routine is then repeated on Thursday and Friday.

Keeping in mind that the players face the rigors of practice, playing in games, watching films, and training—all of which must be done while staying on top of academics—puts Notre Dame's excellent graduation rate for football players in a more impressive perspective.

Miscellania

** A squad of up to 100 Irish student managers help prepare the team for home and away games. Freshmen apply the mix of lacquer, lacquer thinner and gold dust on up to 120 Notre Dame helmets on Friday nights before home games and Thursday nights of away games. Sixty gallons of lacquer and five gallons of gold dust base are used in a typical season.

** The 14-floor tower of the magnificent Hesburgh Memorial Library at Notre Dame overlooks Notre Dame stadium. As the TV networks are fond of showing, the library's tower is covered by a mural of "Touchdown Jesus." This mural is 132 feet high, composed of 5,714 individual pieces derived from 81 different types of stone from 16 countries. When the mural was being completed during the fall and winter of 1963-64, the tower was covered by a mammoth sheet of canvas that cracked like rifle fire in the frigid, snappy Indiana winds swirling around the building. Many Notre Dame students from that time speak of the difficulties of getting a good night's sleep with all the racket.

** Notre Dame is only the second college football team to win more than 700 games in its history. Michigan has a record of 722-238-33 (.752), a record achieved while playing nine more seasons of football than have the Irish. Playing an eleven game season, the Irish can only gain about one game per decade on the Wolverines if Notre Dame continues to play at a .759 winning rate. So, the Irish will either have to start having a string of seasons with a good many more wins than the Wolverines, wait about 200 years to catch them, or simply be content with second place.

** Dutch Bergman was Notre Dame's first four-sport athlete. He competed for the Irish in football, basketball, baseball, and track from 1911 to 1915.

** The Irish have enjoyed a string of 100 straight home sellouts (59,075 paying fans) since a win over Air Force on Thanksgiving Day in 1973.

** "Win One for the Gipper"—a nice line in a 1940 Hollywood movie, a great motivational tool for Rockne in his 1928 win over Army. With a small pool of talent, barely scraping over .500 on the season, and faced with some rough customers in weeks ahead, Rockne knew he'd have to pull out all the stops to cop a win against a powerful Army team and avoid a losing season. He told Grantland Rice the night before the game that he might have to use "Gipp's ghost." He had used Gipp on other occasions before over the years, but the results weren't as dramatic. The fact is, Gipp probably did not say this, in so many words, to Rock. Players who knew Gipp say that he never called himself "The Gipper." If, on his deathbed, he said anything at all it is more likely that it was unprintable. It would have been more in character for Gipp to have remained cynical to the bitter end. It is also in character for Rockne to have embellished a story with sentimental, romantic overtones. In any case, it worked when he used it, and it has become one of the most famous lines in American sports history.

** The Notre Dame alumni body totals 91,097 people, but only 20,000 seats in the stadium are reserved for them. A computer lottery system in the ticket office sorts out winners from losers in the annual competition among eligible alumni for those precious seats. Talk has gone on for years about either enlarging the current stadium (apparently difficult to do) or building a new edifice to the north of the campus, close to the Indiana toll road. Don't bet your house on either scenario happening very soon.

** The Notre Dame Stadium contains more than 2,000,000 bricks, 400 tons of steel, and 15,000 cubic yards of concrete. Rockne was the driving force behind its design—one loosely modelled on Michigan's enormous stadium. Unbelievably, knowing of college football's tremendous mass appeal, he envisioned the eventual use of television for college football and made sure that there would be good sight lines from virtually any vantage point. Not surprisingly, the press box received almost loving attention to detail from Rockne. No public figure has ever played to the press better.